# TRANSITIONS
Notes on a Proud Past with Attention to Future Annals

## THE COLLECTION
## OF
## WILLIAM C. FRENETTE

© 1996 William C. Frenette

All rights reserved. *Transitions—The Collection of William C. Frenette* is provided exclusively for the user's personal, non-commercial use. No photographs or maps may be reproduced or distributed in any form without written permission from the publisher.

Printed in the United States of America
Publishing Editor: Pamela Frenette
First Printing 2014

Cover photo: Richard Gile—early settler, boat pilot, guide and the first fire observer on Mt. Morris, Tupper Lake, NY. (photographer unknown)

*La vie sans limite*

Bill returning from a ski trip to Avalanche Lake in the Adirondack High Peaks. It was adventures like this that earned him the nickname "Wild Bill".

# Introduction

Bill Frenette was an interesting character. Among his most endearing traits was an insatiable curiosity and desire for great conversation. As we look back, his famous words, "it's just around the next corner" make us laugh, as it was his way of saying "there is plenty of time left in the day, just imagine what we might miss if we stop now."

Bill developed a special relationship with his Uncle, Louis Simmons. Louie was local historian, editor of the *Tupper Lake Free Press* and author of *Mostly Spruce and Hemlock*. Louie left his research notes to Bill. This gift, and a love for a story, prompted Bill to take on the role of Town Historian for the town and village of Tupper Lake, NY from 1995–2007.

Bill penned a series of articles titled, *Transitions: Notes on a Proud Past with Attention to Future Annals*, that were published in the *Tupper Lake Free Press* over the course of many years. *Transitions* were written with an interesting style–some current event of the day was combined with a little known story of the past and woven into a narrative that was meaningful, interesting and fun to read. It was Bill's style: a good story, as factual as could be, with a healthy dose of editorial license thrown in to give it an edge and make it interesting.

As a salesman for Frenette Bros., calling on customers in the North Country provided Bill opportunities to meet and learn from the many characters of our region. Many an outing was the result of some conversation he had with a logger, a hunter or sports enthusiast. No one knew the backcountry like Bill did–there is barely a stream, mountain or stretch of woods in the Adirondacks that he has not visited and his writings reflect these unique experiences.

We present this collection of Bill's articles in the hopes of providing insight, smiles and inspiration to those who read them.

—*William C. Frenette Family*

# CONTENTS

Acknowledgements ................................................... XVII

A Day of Infamy ......................................................... 1

What's in a Name? ...................................................... 4

Raymond or Raymos? Your Choice ................................. 7

The Hermitage of Noah John Rondeau .............................. 9

The Sweet Sweet Smell of Spring .................................. 14

Tupper Lake's Master Sugarers ..................................... 16

Where Eagles Nest ..................................................... 20

Let's Take a Walk ...................................................... 24

The Sabattis Family ................................................... 28

Taking a Look Around ................................................ 31

All Aboard! .............................................................. 34

Uncle A.B. ............................................................... 37

Our Native Sons ........................................................ 41

All in The Line of Duty ............................................... 44

Behind Every Man ..................................................... 47

So Much to Know ...................................................... 50

As Memories Fade ..................................................... 54

Where Do We Go From Here? ....................................... 60

Knotted Roots of Love and Strength ............................... 64

FORE! .................................................................... 68

Confusion Abounds ................................................... 74

Ballads and Folk Songs ............................................... 78

So Much to Know......................................................................82

The Return of the Loon ............................................................86

The Whitney Acquisition .........................................................89

Eau de Bear .............................................................................93

The Long Long Lake ...............................................................98

The Little Hidden Pond .........................................................101

The Renamed Hull's Pond .....................................................105

An Entrepreneur's Legacy......................................................108

Y2K—A Time for Reflection.................................................112

The Tupper Lake Flow...........................................................116

From Celebration to Concern................................................119

Big Tupper Gets Bigger .........................................................123

Bill's Morning with a Dove....................................................129

Scouting the Raquette............................................................133

Romance, Mystery and Murder in the Adirondacks—Part One..........138

    Part Two .......................................................................141

    Part Three ....................................................................145

It's a Small World After All ...................................................149

Tout est Prêt ..........................................................................154

Small Town on a Long Lake .................................................159

Did You Know? Fun Facts and Trivia ...................................163

A Little History of Snowmobiling.........................................166

A Respectful Walk on Salmon Lake ......................................170

A Course Called Herstory......................................................174

Tom Peacock and The Changing Life of Dawson Pond.................177

One Girl's Story.....................................................................182

If These Walls Could Talk ...................................................185

One of Those Somewheres....................................................188

Dr. Webb—Thwarted, Not Stymied .......................................193

The Old M&M ....................................................................197

The Route to Tupper ............................................................202

Peacock's Winter Route........................................................206

Paradise Park........................................................................210

Barbour's Property on Big Tupper Lake................................217

The End of Big Mill .............................................................222

Nostalgic Wanakena .............................................................226

Abandoned Cannons ............................................................230

Glory....................................................................................237

Adirondack Autumn.............................................................240

The Benders ........................................................................243

An Historical View of Municipal Park..................................247

A Close Vote .......................................................................251

Work....................................................................................254

The New Grandstand—1938 ................................................258

The Buttercup Episode ........................................................262

A Letter From 2 P ................................................................267

Old Timber ..........................................................................273

The Harold P .......................................................................277

Everything You Ever Wanted to Know About the Porcupine ............281

Little Joe Gauthier and the Northland Hotel ............................285

The Stetson Slough Fisherman .................................................291

Upper Saranac Forest Controversy............................................295

The Raquette River Oxbow .......................................................299

Motorboats vs. Canoes ..............................................................303

Tupper Lake Timberland Purchases ..........................................307

Deer Hunting Long Ago.............................................................311

Of Lumberjack Spring ...............................................................316

Skiing Editor Louis Simmons....................................................320

What You Lose On The Banan' You Make Up On The Peanut ............326

All Are Welcome at the Lake.....................................................331

Town Feud Ends in Baxter Lake Murder ..................................336

Pinkerton Detective Clueless.....................................................340

A New Village............................................................................344

Of Raquette Pond.......................................................................348

Tupper's Lake and The Lake Simond Trio ................................353

Loggers Learn Mr. Byram's Vision ...........................................357

A Place of Sanctuary .................................................................361

From Near Disaster to Eaglets in Flight ....................................364

Tent Camps—Too Good to Last ................................................369

Our Beloved Mt. Morris ............................................................373

Litchfield Park ...........................................................................378

Litchfield Wild Game Sanctuary...............................................382

Dr. Thissell and the Holy Tree ............................................. 387

Dr. Thissell and the Water Company ..................................... 390

Historical Wanderings ...................................................... 394

Dr. Thissell and Early Pioneer Life ....................................... 398

Why So Healthy ............................................................. 403

Enough is Enough ........................................................... 407

Duality Resolved ............................................................. 412

The Long Journey to the St. Lawrence ................................... 417

A Place of Refreshment .................................................... 422

The Racket Pond House .................................................... 427

Making the Adirondacks Accessible ....................................... 431

Tahawus—He Splits the Sky ................................................ 436

Fire Towers—A Symbol of the Adirondacks ............................. 440

Mining Across the Adirondacks ........................................... 446

The History of Iron Mountain ............................................. 450

Stillwater Plunge ............................................................ 454

Layout of the Northern Adirondacks ..................................... 458

The Day the Woods Blew Down—A Hunter's Perspective ............. 462

The Big Blow of 1950 ....................................................... 466

1908 Adirondack Forest Fires .............................................. 471

The Origin of Tupper Lake ................................................. 476

Tupper Lake Wildlife ....................................................... 479

The Chairlift—Revolutionary People Mover ............................. 484

A Town of Descriptive Names ............................................. 489

French Village ................................................................. 494

Gunk Holing Little Wolf Lake ........................................... 498

1934 Bridge to Nowhere .................................................. 503

The Rest of the Story ....................................................... 508

Spotlight on O.W.D. ........................................................ 511

The People and Camps of Simonds Pond .......................... 516

Mt. Morris ...................................................................... 521

Read Park—Stewards and Neighbors ................................ 525

Lumber is King ............................................................... 529

Follensby ........................................................................ 533

The Town of Axe and Surroundings .................................. 537

The Moody Boys ............................................................. 542

Colonel Baker—Ballad of Glencoe ................................... 546

Racket—Racquette—Raquette Falls .................................. 551

A (True) Fish Tale ........................................................... 556

Mother Johnson .............................................................. 561

Generations of Sturdy Stock ............................................. 566

Growing Pains in a New Community ................................ 571

The Great Fire ................................................................. 574

A Frantic Bucket Brigade ................................................. 576

Drugstores and Diners ..................................................... 580

Sustainable Water Supply ................................................. 584

We Build a Pipeline ......................................................... 588

1856 Saranac Racquette Journey ...................................... 592

Racquette River Watershed ................................................. 596

This Community's First Murder .......................................... 601

Storied Lumbermen and River Drivers................................... 605

Reminiscences of Early Lumbering Days ............................... 610

The Birth of Our First Real Hospital .................................... 614

The Challenge of a Hospital ................................................ 618

Divine Intervention ........................................................... 622

Skenandowa's Kick-Start ................................................... 626

An Oasis of Healthcare ...................................................... 630

Nostalgia for Two Generations of Care .................................. 633

Important Man Things....................................................... 637

1927 Grand Jury Court Case............................................... 641

The Elliot File .................................................................. 645

People vs. Clayton Elliot.................................................... 650

Moody Flow—Contrast of Old Clashing With New ..................... 654

Setting Pole Dam ............................................................. 658

Sunmount—Federal Hospital No. 96 .................................... 662

WWI Creates Need for Veterans Hospital............................... 666

The Fight for the Veterans Hospital ..................................... 670

Otterbrook—A Historical Gem ............................................ 675

Survivors, Neighbors and Charlie's French Vanilla ..................... 678

The Great Oxbow............................................................. 682

Trouble in Paradise .......................................................... 687

Nuggets From a 1938 Bank Bulletin ..................................... 691

# ACKNOWLEDGEMENTS

This collection of Bill Frenette's notes and stories was made possible in large part by Dan McClelland, publisher of the *Tupper Lake Free Press*, and his staff. We appreciate their cooperation in helping us publish this series.

Many stories and pictures were not preserved and no archive for the *Transitions* columns existed. It was by digging through Bill's files and friends like Kitty Villeneuve, who methodically saved many of Bill's articles from the newspaper and provided them to us, that we were able to assemble the best possible collection.

It is important to note that Bill's style was to access many sources. Of course, given the author's penchant for conversation with scores of people, many of the anecdotes, pictures and theories resulted from him pulling data and filling in the blanks from his perspective. These articles represent Bill's version of the truth, understanding that good story telling involves plenty of filling in the blanks.

We are very appreciative to all who contributed to the development of Bill's articles and to those who helped assemble this collection. Unfortunately, we are not able to publically thank each of you by name, but please know we thank you all.

—*William C. Frenette Family*

# A Day of Infamy

FIFTY YEARS AGO THIS week, five young Boy Scouts and their scout master strode out onto Route 30 from the trail that led to Mt. Morris. The trail in those days was located across from the Waukesha Cabins, now owned by Jim and Mary Radimer. The scouts were returning from an overnight encampment at a rustic log camp somewhat removed from the main trail and close to the Mt. Morris Summit.

The scout master was a wonderful fellow by the name of Jack Alexander. In 1893 Jack's grandfather, Jabez Alexander, had purchased the famous Uncle Mart Moody Hotel known as Redside Camp (after the brook that flows across Route 30 into the lake next to the new home presently being built by Gerald Landry). The Alexanders changed the name to Waukesha and successfully managed it for 56 years before selling it to Donat Richer in 1949, a sale which included 450 feet of lake frontage. The mountain cabin was owned by Percy Alexander, Jack's father, and Jack used a trip to the cabin as part of the motivational technique, i.e. the five scouts in his troop (Lions Club Troop 23) with the best yearly advancement record got to accompany Jack on a three-day trip and the opportunity to overnight at the cabin.

I was one of these Boy Scouts on that day along with Harvey Tebo, Brainard Beausoleil, Howard Elilhorpe and I believe Ted Stiokas. (Both Harvey and Brainard went on to become Eagle Scouts, one of the highest ranks attainable.) That same initiative propelled both to obtain college degrees (not as common in those days) and to become highly successful in their chosen careers.

The point of all this is that as we walked down the road toward the Alexander home, we were met by Jack's mother, Aurore. I remember so well that she was totally distraught and blurted out that Pearl Harbor had been attacked by the Japanese and that most of our naval fleet had been destroyed and many Americans killed and wounded. I remember that we Boy Scouts in our naiveté couldn't comprehend the adults' concern. In fact, I remember clearly Howard Elilhorpe saying, "Pearl Harbor? Where is that? We'll wipe out those Japs in a week!" That week turned into four years. All four scouts would enlist to "fight in this righteous war against an evil enemy" as they turned 17 years of age (Harvey even missed his graduation ceremony having been called up just before his senior academic year ended).

If we weren't aware of the seriousness of Mrs. Alexander's shocking news, several Tupper men were painfully aware of the gravity of the situation. Two, Frank McLear and John Parent, were aboard the USS West Virginia and the USS Pennsylvania sunk in the harbor by successive waves of Jap bombers. Sgt. George Goff was in the Philippines. He fought through the siege of Corrigidor, somehow survived the grim death march from Bataan and spent nearly four years in a Japanese prison camp. Nearly a thousand Tupper Lake men and women were to serve with the armed forces during the four years of World War II. They suffered nearly 10 percent casualties in killed, wounded, missing in action and prisoners of war.

*Shown here is President Roosevelt delivering the famous Infamy Speech to congress on December 8, 1941. The President's description of December 7 as "a date which will live in infamy" was borne out. (FDR library photo collection)*

This next Saturday, December 7, 1996, marks that "Day of Infamy." It is a day that we should give pause and remember the remarkable generation that fought in that war, that defeated the Nazis and Fascists and saved the world for democracy, fueled a postwar economic boom, outlasted Communism and ventured into space. That generation born roughly between 1907 and 1927 is now 69 to 89 years old. They must now be judged as parents, for their offspring have grabbed the reins of the community and the nation and will determine its future direction. However briefly, remember that heroic and historic generation when this Saturday, December 7, appears on your calendar.

*Tupper Lake Free Press Print:* December 04, 1996

# WHAT'S IN A NAME?

THE CALLER INTRODUCED HIMSELF as a new member of the community, recently retired from the Eastman Kodak Company. He had a question: "What was the correct name for the hill west of the village on Route 3? Was it Raymond's Hill or was it Raymo's Hill?" He explained that he had heard both names and was confused.

That question prompted a lively discussion the next morning when it was brought up to the group of regulars at Diane's Park Street Bagel and Deli Shop. I volunteered that I had always called it Raymond's Hill. "Not so," came a heated rejoinder from the other end of the counter, between bites of Diane's famous lemon-filled strudels. "I've lived here as long as you have and it's Raymo's Hill." A third opinion was calmly voiced, suggesting that, "Maybe you are both right. Raymo might be the French pronunciation of Raymond."

That made sense and I might have let the question end there. Instead, the question kept popping up in my head. Who was the family or individual the hill was named after?

This type of connection with our past is worthwhile, interesting and even important. After all, it's pretty well known that Demars Boulevard was named after the grandfather (Leon) of my former classmate Ben Demars. Stetson Road (where the first school was located) was named after early settler Royal Stetson;

Hurd Street (Civic Center) was named after John Hurd, whose railroad and sawmill were actually responsible for the founding of this village; Santa Clara Avenue (Clara was John Hurd's wife) was named after the successful lumber company brought to prominence by the Meigs family.

Most folks would connect Larkin Street, Palmer Avenue or Cheney Avenue, but who was Seymour? Or, for that matter, who was Vachereau? Which McCarthy of that prominent family was McCarthy Street named after, or was it a general recognition? Stay with me and let's do a "Travel in Time" and try to determine who the hill in question was named after.

I discovered almost at once that early census reports, which I had hoped would tell me about the different Raymonds (Raymos), could only add to the confusion. Consider the following: In the middle 1800s, writing instruments were primitive. Heck, we were still using ink wells and stick pens when I started school! As a result, the writing was often illegible. Many words were spelled either incorrectly or phonetically. Furthermore, the practice of Anglicizing names made some hard to trace.

In regards to the spelling problem, let's look at some examples from the 1892 census. Oliver Martineau (antecedents of Betty Sarvis) has his name spelled Martino. My wife, not a native, pronounces it Mar-Teen-O, whereas locally the name has always been pronounced Martin-O. Betty tells me it means "skunk water." Two different spellings, two different pronunciations—same family? Some others Oliver and Fred Besaw (was this Bisson?), Cyrell Coro (Couroux, Carrow?), Gokey (Gauthier?), Antonine Charbono (Charbouneau?).

Then, of course, there are the names that have been Anglicized over the years. When did Jardine (Fr: garden) become Gardener? Fire Tower Observer Adelard Fromage was just as often called Adelard Cheese; LeMieux (LaMere, Fr: best, better) became Betters; LeBlanc (Fr: white) became White; and my favorite, Tupper Lake's first settlers, the Charboneau's (Fr: Charbon, meaning coal), was often Anglicized to Cole.

I did discover two Raymonds (Raymos). One was Antonine and the other was George. In the next column I'll tell you how a chance meeting helped solve for whom Raymond Hill was named.

*Tupper Lake Free Press Print:* January 15, 1997

# Raymond or Raymos? Your Choice

THERE WAS A SPIRITED and interesting response to our last column—the discussion of the name of the large hill west of the village (Raymo or Raymond). Space precludes recounting all of the calls and letters, but I'll mention a few.

Jack Fuller called to say he has always known it as Raymo Hill. He suggested that people might be confusing it with Raymond's Restaurant located at the bottom of the hill (Pine Grove). Jack has a point. I remember as a boy helping to deliver huge wooden barrels of beer to Mrs. Raymond for the restaurant, where the feature was a large mug for five cents. Jack also good humoredly noted that people from uptown couldn't be expected to know the proper name. (The Fuller family produced many outstanding athletes and their supporters and fans never let you forget they were from the Junction.)

A very warm letter from Elizabeth Denis of Piercefield was especially interesting. Mrs. Denis wrote that her 98-year-old aunt, Dorothy Proulx Redinger, often talks about Raymond Hill. "She has told me often times, and again today, that the hill was named after her uncle, George Raymond. Although they refer to her uncle as Raymo, she calls the hill where that family lived Raymond Hill!"

Another pertinent letter from Piercefield resident Dick Buckley was written from his winter home in Florida before the article appeared. He wrote of his interest in the settlement of the paper mill at Piercefield and noted that in 1892, when the Piercefield Paper and Mining Company was formed, there did not seem to be any road to connection to Tupper Lake. Dick went on to write: "My files indicate that November 4, 1894, the Tupper Lake Town Board voted to appropriate $100 to buy a right-of-way four rods wide from the Adirondack Land Corp. for the purpose of building a road to Piercefield. In 1897 the Racquette River was bridged and road connections completed linking Piercefield to Tupper Lake." Wow!

History tells us that the first national census was in 1790, ordered by George Washington for the purpose of taxing his fellow countrymen to pay for the Revolutionary War. Temporary U.S. Marshalls rode hundreds of miles to count heads, not arriving in Tupper Lake until 1860. That federal list contained only 30 names, with no Raymo or Raymond among them.

An informal census taken in 1892 by Will LaFountain, a local surveyor, was more helpful. Among the 1,051 citizens enumerated that year were two Raymos. Antoine Raymo (Raymond as it is now spelled), whose occupation was listed as mason, would be the great-grandfather of outstanding educator and coach John Raymond (always a Tupper Laker who only now lives in Saranac Lake) and Jane Raymond Cole.

The other Raymo in the census was George Raymo, legally spelled Raymond in the property deeds. His occupation was listed as Teamster. George owned the entire hill all the way to the Haymeadow entrance. In 1902, when $100 was a lot of money, George paid Pat Moynehan $2,400 for 80 acres of land, including the hill. It would appear that he kept a portion of that land to build a house, held the balance of the 80 acres until 1903 and sold it to Firman Ouderkirk for $5,000 to almost triple in investment in one year! Firman held the property for six years. A succession of familiar names, including Barney Propp, John D'Avignon and Mary Jardine, owned the land until 1947, when it went to Amos LaBarge.

Raymo or Raymond? Lois Brosseau, who lives on Raymond Hill and to whom I owe thanks for much of the data presented here, sums it up best: "Raymond is English. If you want to call it by the French pronunciation, it is Raymo. Your choice."

*Tupper Lake Free Press Print:* February 05, 1997

# THE HERMITAGE OF NOAH JOHN RONDEAU

I RECENTLY RETURNED HOME from an extended stay in Idaho's Sun Valley to find a basket full of mail. Included among the mix of Cabela's, L.L. Bean and yes, even Victoria's Secret catalogs, was a packet containing a videotape. It was from my former neighbor (now living in Syracuse) and close friend, Dave LaVoie. In addition to being one of the best woodsmen I have known, Dave was also an ardent photographer. He was always hauling his vintage Bell & Howell movie camera on our hiking trips. Dave had spliced several different subject matters into a loop of four minutes and transferred the result to a video tape. The first minute or so of that video was of a snowshoe trip that Dave and I, along with the late Louis Simmons, had taken into Cold River country to visit the Hermitage of Noah John Rondeau, mayor of Cold River City, population one.

Noah was the famous hermit who, from 1912 to 1950, lived alone on a small knoll above the Cold River. He was no longer occupying his former "digs" the day of our visit. On November 24, 1950, he became uneasy over the advance winds of the Big Blowdown, and the next day he headed out for the 19 and one-half mile trip to Coreys. Noah took his usual short cut that day through Ouluska Pass (the Indian meaning of Ouluska is a "place of shadows," a good description for this deep defile that goes between Seymour and Seward Mountains).

He only got as far as Martin's caretaker cottage at Avery Rockerfeller's

Ampersand Park (about nine miles) before the fury of the "Big Blow" reached its peak and prevented further travel. The next day Lucien, with two assistants and group of hunters who had been camped on state land near Ward Brook (with mules), started cutting their way out to Coreys, a task that took them two days before they ran into Tupper Lake forest ranger Delbert McNeil and his Conservation Department crew cutting their way from the opposite direction.

Following this storm, the woods would be closed for three years. Ouluska Pass became impenetrable for easy travel, and Noah, at 67 years of age, would end that phase of his life. He would never return to his hermitage.

Salvage operations to remove the jack straw of downed timber were started almost at once and were ongoing the day we made our trip. Giant white pine logs lay stacked at the landings we passed (the local US Bobbin and Shuttle Co. that year brought in many 40-inch diameter logs, some of which were estimated to be 300 hundred years old).

There is a fine shot in Dave's camera footage that shows Louis emerging from the tiny door of Noah's cabin. Louis has a big grin on his face, and it is hard to decide whether he is laughing at the absurdity of this hovel of a camp which Noah had banged together from scraps of lumber scavenged from Alphonse Beaudett's abandoned Santa Clara Lumber Camp or, because of the tiny size (8'x10'). If nothing else, the cabin was efficient in terms of heating, not to mention the ease in which it allowed Noah to reach the pot of stew, which he kept simmering almost year-round on the stove.

Louis is pictured wearing his favorite outdoor outfit, which I used to call his woodman's woolens. This was the de rigueur outfit of the day before miracle fibers like Gore Tex and Capaliene, and is still favored by knowledgeable out-of-doors people. It consisted of woolen trousers laced at the knee, a heavy jacket of the same material and matching hat with ear flaps, all of which were the same green-black or red-black plaid. Mittens were leather with the same plaid back (good nose wipers) and were usually called

On Mayor's Perch
*Famous Adirondack hermit, Noah John Rondeau, dubbed the mayor of Cold River City, population one, enjoys a quiet smoke in the sunshine in front of his rustic abode in the remote Cold River region near Tupper Lake in this old photo.*

"wood choppers" or "Saranac bucks". And, of course, leather-top rubber boots known as "Malones" or "Ballards" made by the Ballard Mill in Malone, NY of local interest, the Ballard design and patterns were purchased by the well-known Woolrich Woolen Co. of Pennsylvania, and Leslie Noelk of Conifer, a principal officer of that company, was involved in the acquisition.

Shortly after our visit and just before the mud season, Noah's cabin was transferred by skidder and truck to the Adirondack Museum. It seems to me that this was accomplished by a lumberman named Crawfoot, who was from the Old Forge area.

I knew Noah only slightly. My first encounter occurred when I was a youngster. Walking along Main Street, I ran into this wiry little man emerging from the restaurant owned by a Greek family named Tagaras (the restaurant was located in the now vacant lot next to the movie theater). Noah was somewhat unsteady on his feet, wearing deerskin clothing, a huge fur hat and a long beard. That image is burned into my memory bank as with a hot ember, and the event probably occurred during Noah's annual Christmas visit to his friend, Frank Hathaway, caretaker of Bartlett's Carry Camp near Upper Saranac Lake.

Years later, when Noah was no longer a hermit, he stayed for a time in Long Lake with a customer of mine, a colorful character named Roy Lash. Roy, whose ample girth belied his stamina, owned the Village Inn and was a trapper and fur buyer who had become a good friend of Noah's in the early Cold River days. Desmond Louce and Ed Wallace, themselves Long Lake trappers, were also good friends. I often sat during those days and talked with Noah. I found him a gentle man, always neatly dressed, his beard well-trimmed.

He was, at times, slightly reserved, even suspicious, but always polite and, if he liked you, he could be very charming.

In his early recluse days, Noah had a lengthy feud with the fledgling Conservation Department (1910-1920s), especially over game laws and license permits. Those problems are curiously reminiscent of the problems the A.P.A. is having with other Adirondackers today.

The state couldn't bother him about the location of his hermitage, however, since it was located in what is known as a Gore. This was a triangular piece of disputed land (about 2,700 acres in size) formed by the failure of the north/south boundaries of Township 27 to be satisfactorily established. This Gore was pre-empted by the Santa Clara Company, which allowed Noah to live there. The state later laid claim to this "unappropriated" land and sued the company for half a million dollars, but Ferris Meigs was able to prove that its original purchase of Townships 26 and 27 gave it title to these lands (that purchase consisted of 35,000 acres at $4.50 per acre, and for over 30 years, many Tupper Lake residents were involved in its timber removal).

Today, only remnants remain to remind us of Noah's location. The Northville to Lake Placid Trail goes right across the knoll with its wonderful mountain and river views. If you look carefully among the raspberry bushes, you can find the various cultivated flowers that have survived from the days Noah planted them from (according to his log) seed packets purchased in this village.

*Tupper Lake Free Press Print:* March 26, 1997

# THE SWEET SWEET SMELL OF SPRING

THERE IS AN OLD SAYING: "Spring is the reward for those who live through the winter." How do we know that spring has arrived? Let's count the ways: my neighbors, Jackie and Al Smith, are back from Florida looking trim and healthy; Charlcie Delehanty has reported seeing two immature and one mature bald eagles as the river opens near the sorting gap; Jessie's Bait Shop has stored their ice augers and hung out their "Maple Syrup For Sale" sign in front of their newly updated fishing equipment; and geese can be seen feeding happily on Mary Burns' front lawn along the Raquette River, recently freed of ice.

Spring is the harbinger of many good things, one of which is that it is the time sap begins to run in the maple trees and heralds the beginning of the sugaring season. How many readers as youngsters have boiled sap in their kitchen? How many of you have seen the paper peel off the walls as steam from the boiling sap filled the kitchen? (It takes about 40 gallons of sap to make 1 gallon of syrup. The rest goes up in steam.) Sadly, making maple syrup, a sustainable, responsible use of a resource, has almost disappeared locally.

There was a period when it was an honored tradition. There were a number of sugar bushes located nearby, each with its own sugar house. The sugar house, usually with a vented roof, contained the evaporator, which in simplest terms consisted of two flat metal pans sitting over a long firebox known as the arch. These pans were divided into multiple interconnected channels, creating a maze that the sap had to follow as it became hotter and hotter and ever more dense.

Sweet smelling steam would chortle from these shacks, producing an enveloping mist not unlike an early spring cloud-laden rain shower. The only thing that could rival that nostalgic smell might be the delicious aroma that would waft its way from blocks in the vicinity of the Sonny Boy Bakery (if you were downtown) or from the Gold Medal Bakery (if you were uptown).

A tantalizing, overpowering, luscious signature presence that cannot be adequately described. You would have to experience it. Of course, that would mean you would have had to have been there at a time when milk came in glass bottles with a two inch collar of thick cream, and kids could go into the neighboring saloon and get a "growler" of beer for their father, who undoubtedly deserved it after a 12-hour day of intensive labor.

"Rush the growler" (a metal pail with a lid) was an expression of the time. The word "rush" had an entirely different connotation in those days. With its strict discipline, woe unto any youngster who didn't get that growler home with the greatest dispatch and with it's contents intact.

For all of its romances as an ancient tradition, sugaring was (and still is) hard work. It meant washing hundreds of buckets; it meant tapping many, many trees by hand with a brace and a bit; it meant gathering scores of buckets (each weighing at least 30 pounds), which had to be carried to a holding tank, where it was then sledged to the Sugar House. If the sap was running good you stayed up all night boiling it into syrup. Remember, too, that it took roughly a full cord of wood (4'x4'x8') to make five gallons of syrup. Even in a small operation, that could mean as much as 30 full cords that most often had to be "bucked" up with a buck saw or a two-handed cross-cut saw. Small wonder that an old-age sentiment after a bone-wearying season was, "Glad to see it come, glad to see it go."

Next column: Tupper Lake's Master Sugarers.

*Tupper Lake Free Press Print:* April 09, 1997

## TUPPER LAKE'S MASTER SUGARERS

THE MAPLE TREE THAT produces maple syrup, the subject of our last column, is the official state tree. Only the yellow birch is nearly as valuable (at the moment) on a log-for-log basis. In the forest, the maple grows to 80-90 feet with perhaps 30 feet of clear stem. In the open the trees quickly branch out in all directions from a short trunk. That is one of the reasons sugarers love to tap trees along the open roadside, the amount of sap that can be obtained from a tree is in direct ratio to the amount of the live crown. The first white people to realize the value of the maple tree were the Canadians. Early French settlers (Les Habitants) in clearing their land were very careful to preserve at least two-thirds of their woodlot that contained maple trees so they would provide "sirop" and "sucre d'érable". In preserving the sugar trees the French habitants were a century ahead of the British colonists, who would settle to the south. I would be willing to bet that some of those same habitants, who eventually crossed the St. Lawrence River into New York and would become the most daring of the early river drivers and the best of the lumbermen, now have descendants in the village.

The method of making syrup over open fires with a deep kettle holding the sap remained unchanged for hundreds of years. After a time, Yankee ingenuity realized that sap could be evaporated much more quickly from a shallow open pan than from a deep kettle and thus the first evaporator pans were born (1863).

The size of a sugar bush is described by the number of buckets you hang, not by how many trees you tap. By that standard the sugar bushes in this area were modest in size. Barry's Pioneer Farm on Stetson Road tapped trees all the way to the back door of Jacob Steshka's Park Street Restaurant, The Hathaway Farm (now owned by Ginny and Glen Snyder) tapped many fine maple trees on their property, Stuart Wilson (now the De Silva property) on Moody Road had a nice operation with excellent syrup and Litchfield Park tapped some of their own maple trees. The syrup produced in its earliest years was used primarily by the family and as gifts for guests and friends until new tax laws demanding bona fide income resulted in a more expanded effort.

Mary Brooks, whose father, Barney Sovey, worked as a guide and assistant to the caretaker at the Read & Strange property for 57 years, tells me that the syrup produced there, high on the slopes of Mt. Morris, went all over the world as gifts for family and friends. Mary, who wrote a composition on maple syrup when we were in school together (Ms. Jacqueline Shaw was our teacher), noted that the Read family preferred syrup in its amber form (best as topping for French toast or pancakes since it has a more pronounced flavor). Mary also remembered that her father told her that it took 50 gallons of sap to make a gallon of syrup. Since the norm is between 33 and 40 gallons, this statement gave me pause. (I knew better than to argue with Mary. Her memory is sharp as a Swiss army knife and besides, who ever won an argument with a woman?)

Whenever I seek information I don't need to log in on the internet. I simply stop by Diane Helm's Adirondack Bagel & Deli. Diane and her coterie of regulars are always ready and eager to give advice on any subject. (The morning I stopped by, the reintroduction of the wolf to the Adirondacks was the heated topic and the rhetoric would have lifted a hot air balloon.) Anyway, between bites of Diane's latest creation, an inside-out chocolate macaroon, I think I learned the reason Mary was correct in her assertion that it took 50 gallons of sap to make a quart of syrup in her father's sugar house. The average sap contains about two percent sugar, and it must be boiled until it reaches a temperature of 210 degrees, or seven degrees higher than the boiling point of water at sea level. So depending on the altitude (the Read family's sugar bush was at 2,030 feet elevation), the boiling point can change accordingly. Atmospheric pressure can also affect the reading. As an example, Ray Martin's Tupper Lake group, who hunt elk each fall in the vicinity of Telluride, CO (elevation 9,300 feet), observed that it took longer to cook their meals at their tent camp location. They discovered that water boils at 193 degrees at that elevation, and that for every ten degree drop in boiling temperature, cooking time is approximately doubled, a pretty drastic inverse ratio between boiling point and altitude. So, Mr. Sovey at 2,000 feet above sea level had to boil the sap longer. In addition, if the sap was less sweet (the lower the sugar content, the more sap required), it would take more sap to make a quart of syrup. Mary tells me that a little trick her father used was to place a thermometer in a pan of water and bring it to a boil, and then he would take whatever figure the water boiled at and add seven degrees to it. This would tell him the correct temperature at which maple syrup would boil for that particular day, and his candy thermometer would then be in adjustment for that perfect temperature of 219 degrees when sap turns to syrup.

In concluding this week's column, I should point out that the name Read & Strange, where Mr. Sovey was employed for so many years, is no longer correct, even though it will always be referred to as such by local old timers. The Strange family interests in the property ended almost 72 years ago. The forest tract was carved and formed by what must have been especially large and abrasive glaciers. Deep passes with roaring brooks cascade alongside intimidating steep rock faces and a deep crystal-clear lake resembling a Norwegian fjord lies in a protective shadow of Mt. Morris. Shielded by ramparts like Buck Mountain and its distant location have given it a singular remoteness. Add to that carefully planned timber harvesting, and it remains arguably one of the finest privately owned woods in the Adirondacks. It has escaped the synergism of destructive natural forces and human

Old Sugar Buckets Give Way to New Over the Years

*Stuart Wilson (Wilson Coal and Feed) built the model sugar house pictured above. Notice the vent (cupola) which in a good sugaring year, would allow nearly 8,000 gallons of water to go through the opening as steam. Below, galvanized buckets festoon the maple trees presently being tapped by Jackie and Larry Denis. Originally buckets were of bark, then of wood. These are aristocrats of the bucket world: tall and slender with a nice taper from top to bottom. Elegant and practical, easy to stock, and leak proof with covers to keep out contaminants.*

exploitation that has so violated other preserves. The Read and Strange Park (there I go again) is a special place, and special places do not stay special by accident! The benevolent stewardship it has received from successive generations of the Read family continues today. In an era of fast-diminishing woodland tracts, it remains an authentic gem and a valuable neighbor of this community.

*Tupper Lake Free Press Print:* April 16, 1997

# WHERE EAGLES NEST

THE CLIMBER WAS JUST under the nest located on the platform of an overhang 100 feet above the talus slope leading to the forest floor. Sprigs of pine with which eagles sometimes decorated their nests were visible and whitewash was splayed along the platform of the overhang, a clear indication that the nest was potentially active.

The climb had looked so easy. Youthful abandon and the excitement of locating the nest had clouded his judgment and now he was stuck. "Why didn't I wait?" he asked himself. "Why not come back with rope and climbing hardware and partner to provide a proper belay?"

He was nervous, very nervous, and a gulf of nausea coursed through his body. Then his legs began to shake, the dreaded "sewing machine leg" phenomenon often experienced by climbers, drawing on his rapidly depleting energy level.

He was getting cold, and worse yet, he was getting stiff. He had to make a move before his tenuous grip gave way and he ended up a wreck of bones at the base of the cliff.

A piece of advice from a fellow climber passed through his mind: *A difficulty encountered poses a question; the movements to resolve it gives it a reply.* "Easy for him to say," he thought to himself.

A small tree lay just off his left shoulder. Once just a seed deposited by a bird or perhaps by the wind, it had somehow found enough sustenance in the thin duff lying in the cracks along the rock face to survive. It might serve as the answer to get him out of his predicament.

Cautiously, with one hand, the climber removed his belt and made loop around the tree trunk. If the tree held, if the belt didn't break, he could lower himself to a toe-hold just out of reach of his left foot.

Fear is an ugly thing, but boldness is equally ill-starred. This was no place to make a mistake.

Slowly, gingerly, his face and body pressed into the rock face to gain as much friction as possible, he gave himself to the tree, murmuring a silent prayer that it would hold. The move worked! He found a toe-hold, then a crack to jam his hand into. One move linked to the next and before he knew it, he found himself lying safely on the ground.

The throbbing of his heart was the only sound he heard until he dimly became aware of his caretaker friend, who had been waiting anxiously, muttering something about his stupidity. It was also an unwarranted intrusion on the eagles, and he never again repeated that mistake.

The location of that mini-drama was at the Hitchins Park, then owned by the A.A. Low family. The caretaker friend was Alvin Cote, and I'm not going to tell you who the foolish climber was.

Two years later (1973) the Low family would sell the remainder of their original estate to the Suffolk County BSA, the eagles would depart and the waters of many of the park's ponds would become highly acidic and could no longer contain trout. A.A. Low's sugar house in his Maple Valley operation would become a hunting camp. The beautiful stone wine cellar set into the side of the hill would remain, but depleted of its stock of vintages going back to 60 years. The three-story employee boarding house, which had become the Low family's rustic camp, would be contaminated with asbestos, vandalized and completely trashed.

In celebration of the Forest Preserve Centennial in 1985, the state purchased 9,248 acres from the Suffolk County BSA. While this has opened access to a recreation-hungry public, the beautiful grounds and buildings in the once proud headquarters remain in deplorable condition.

A preliminary draft of a Unit Management Plan was released in March of this year that will involve this area (see Larry Reandeau's commentary in the April 15 edition of this paper). Public input will be invited sometime this summer, and we can only hope that in some fashion, the mountain empire created by A.A. Low can be restored to a semblance of its former grandeur. This place is, after all, rich in memories for many local residents. Yes, it is owned by all of the state taxpayers, but it is located in our "back yard" and, as such, should have particular interest to former and present citizens of this community when the hearings are held.

And now—the rest of the story!

In this week's *Transitions* column, mention was made of the golden eagle nest, which was vacated by these rare birds from its location on the cliff face of an unnamed mountain in Hitchins Park. A continuation might be of some interest to our readers.

No sightings of golden eagles were reported in that area for almost a year after the birds disappeared. One theory is that the eagles had relied on food from deer killed by the train (where trackage lay a wingbeat and glide from their nest), and the train had virtually ceased operations.

Joe and Eleanor Pisanchin, then caretakers at the Robert Lehman estates on Bog Lake, called me one evening. Joe was certain that a pair of golden eagles was building a nest in a 90-foot white pine that he could see from his cottage window! I turned this report over to Greenleaf Chase, my mentor, who was an acknowledged golden eagle authority with the D.E.C. "Greenie" was skeptical. Golden eagles normally do not nest in trees. Having assured him that Joe Pisanchin was knowledgeable and reliable, he agreed to check it out. What follows is a summary as contained in the *Atlas of Breeding Birds in New York State*:

"Most of the golden eagle nests in New York were placed on inaccessible cliff ledges overhung by a protective tree or rock. This species also occasionally nests in trees. A New York nest was located 90 feet above ground in a white pine. The nest was made of dead sticks and brush of all kinds as well as boughs of mountain ash, American beech and white and red pine. All former New York eyries were located at elevations between 1,500 and 2,600 feet" (NY D.E.C. files).

It continues with a sad note: "Unfortunately, this magnificent raptor has been extirpated as a breeding species in the state (1978) and now only breeds in Maine, where four active nests were reported in 1985 and two in 1986."

Watching these birds build their nests and feed their young was a thrilling sight for the Pisanchins. In a recent phone conversation with Eleanor, she told me that at times, when fishing on the lake near the lofty pine, she and Joe would simply put their fishing rods down and sit enthralled by the spectacle of the majestic birds.

As Paul Harvey would say, "Now you know the rest of the story." Birding chronicles should note the Pisanchins as the original observers; without their concern and courtesy it is possible this sighting located at such a private and remote location quite possibly could have gone unrecorded. This was the only known tree nest of these species in the eastern United States at the time (*Birds of the New York State*, John Bull).

*Tupper Lake Free Press Print:* April 30, 1997

# Let's Take a Walk

TO EVEN THE MOST CASUAL OBSERVER, the year 1996-1997 marks the emergence of a new lifestyle here in Tupper Lake. This is certainly the year of the walker. Demars Boulevard and Stetson Road are just two of the routes where walkers, not unlike lemmings headed for the sea, can be seen at almost any hour of the day or night.

There have always been people living in this community who enjoy walking, of course, but the recent explosion of people walking reflects a quantum leap in the numbers that are enjoying this great, healthy and rewarding pastime.

Here is a suggestion to add some variety to your walk, at only a light extra cost in time, while offering a glimpse of an area that has been historically significant as early as 1892.

Start your walk by first driving out past Bog River Falls, then to Horseshoe Lake, where you make a sharp left over the railroad tracks. Follow this road .3 of a mile after crossing the tracks and park your car near the first gated road on your left. This road was once a railroad spur that went to the station at Horseshoe and was part of the 15 miles of trackage laid out by A.A. Low for his Horseshoe Forestry Company operations.

This operation was a marvel even to Mr. Low's close associates, who were aware of his inventiveness and great energy. He built a huge dam on the Bog River to generate electricity, and when he need more power, he built a second one.

*Pictured above is the dynamic A.A. Low riding on the flat car of his own railroad that connected with the Adirondack Division at Horseshoe Station. (from the collection of the St. Lawrence County Historical Society)*

He harvested timber from his 40,000-acre tract, bottled spring water from large flowing springs on his property and won awards for the quality of his maple syrup. (One year he tapped 10,000 trees!) He even made wine and preserves from native berries on his cutover land. He built a beautiful home on Lake Marion (named after his wife and now part of Otterbrook Park), and when he didn't like the station the railroad built at Horseshoe, he built a handsome depot patterned after one in Garden City, Long Island and sold it to the M&M railroad for $1.

It is hard to imagine as you walk this spur that there was once rolling stock that consisted of two locomotives, a crane, a shovel, a log loader (all powered by steam, of course) and several flat cars designed to ship his products to the city markets by rail.

Walk around the gate, which is only to prevent motor vehicle access, and start your walk, which will take you in only 2.5 miles to what is known as the upper dam and the headquarters of the former Low operations. The trail or road is quite flat, and you will walk alongside a large black spruce swamp or peatlands for almost a mile and a Scotch pine plantation at 1.6 miles. At 2.5 miles, you will be at the dam.

If you have extra time, by all means scurry up Hitchins Mountain. It is only .2 of a mile, mostly across open rock ledges barren of soil due to the fiercely hot flames of the same fire that on September 26, 1908 destroyed the entire village of Sabattis (two miles distant) and was so intense that it warped the rails of the railroad bed as a relief train sent from Tupper rescued the residents and

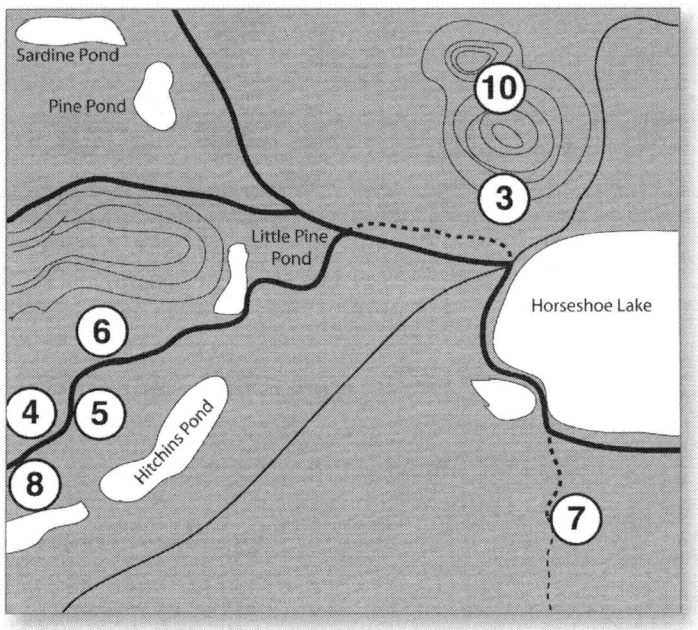

*The Bog River Basin scene of A.A. Low's empire (numerals include the sites of principal activities)*
Item
3. *Horseshoe*
4. *Second dam*
5. *Virgin Forest Springs*
6. *Evaporator*
7. *First dam*
8. *Second dam*
10. *Gold mine*

rolled out between a wall of fire that scorched and blistered cars and caught the caboose on fire.

The reward for this short climb (which starts out as a path to the rear of the two-story building to your right before you approach the dam) is a striking scenic panorama of the wilderness that is the Bog River drainage.

The late Armand Vaillancourt of this village, caretaker and manager of the Low estate for more than 40 years, carried the cremated ashes of A.A. Low to the summit (watched carefully with binoculars by a redoubtable Mrs. Low from her front porch at the base of the mountain), and if you follow the open ridge to its highest point, you will find an iron bolt and plaque in the rock to commemorate him.

A.A. Low was one of the most dynamic entrepreneurs in the history of this region and has left a treasured heritage now available to the public.

Afterward

As a result of that 1908 fire, locomotives would be required to burn oil with no wood or coal allowed except at night. The railroads would have to keep their rights of way cleared and remove all combustible material—a definite hardship that didn't please the railroads.

A "tree lapping" law was established that required tops to be cut up so the branches rested close to the damp earth. The state built 61 fire towers (Mt. Morris had the distinction of being one of the first—July 1908—Richard Gile was the observer), and the fire would become a contributing cause to the liquidation of the Horseshoe Forestry Company.

*Tupper Lake Free Press Print:* May 21, 1997

# THE SABATTIS FAMILY

AS TOWN AND VILLAGE historian, I get a lot of inquiries from people tracing their ancestors. An interesting question was posed to me last week: A woman from Buffalo was tracing her Indian ancestry and has been told she was related to a Sabattis family. Was the settlement mentioned in the recent *Transitions* column named after a person named Sabattis? If so, could I tell her more about that individual and also more about the fire that consumed the settlement?

Sabattis had originally been named Long Lake West. It was the station for the railroad that operated there until as recently as April 1965. It was renamed Sabattis in 1923 when a post office was established there. It was indeed named after Mitchell Sabattis, who lived in Long Lake and was an outstanding woodsman and guide. He became a pillar of the Long Lake community and was a highly religious man. He often preached in the Wesleyan Methodist Church and was given credit for raising most of the funds to build that structure.

I found it interesting that the caller pronounced Sabattis as SAW BAH TEASE. I politely suggested to her that locally it was pronounced SA BAT IS. She replied that SAW BAH TEASE was the way the genealogy authority at the library pronounced it. Almost the very next day I ran into Jim Meehan, manager of the historic photography collection (over 65,000 images) at the Adirondack Museum. Jim told me the following: "Sabattis is the common corruption of Jean (John) Baptiste, as Jean appears as an S (San) in most of the Northern Algonquin." That also explains why I once couldn't locate Saint Germain Pond near Lake Clear until a local aid said, "Oh! You mean SAN GER MAW Pond!" Another such corruption is Santanoni Mountain, which was originally named Saint Anthony.

Mitchell Sabattis was the son of Peter Sabattis, a full-blooded Indian of the Huron Tribe. His Indian name was Pierjon. This fine woodsman lived to be 106 years old and kept a record of his later years on a notched stick that he always carried with him. Captain Peter (he had fought in the Revolutionary War) always claimed that he never slept in a white man's bed. He would accept all other hospitality, but when night came, if the weather was mild he would sleep out of doors. In the cold he would lie down in front of the kitchen stove with a log of wood for a pillow.

Captain Peter was no stranger to Tupper Lake and its surrounding forests and rivers. There is a huge rock or monolith located just downstream of Underwood Bridge known as Captain

*Pictured above is the magnificent Nehasane Lodge that belonged to Dr. William Seward Webb and was located on the shores of Lake Lila. Threatened by the same fire that destroyed Sabattis, it was saved by a shift of the wind. (Bill Frenette collection)*

Peter's rock. It is said he kept his traps hidden there. Three miles below Piercefield on our same Racquette River is an island over a mile wide known as Sols Island, named after Solomon, another of Peter's sons, who was reputed to have been born there.

Historians have concluded that Mitchell Sabattis (descendants still live in Long Lake) was "exceptional both in traits of character as well as exceptional gifts of woodcraft." It has been further noted that "these woods will never look upon his like again." The woman from Buffalo tracing her ancestry can be very proud of Captain Pierjon and his son, Indian chief Mitchell Sabattis.

The fire that totally destroyed the hamlet of Sabattis occurred on September 26, 1908. It had been a dry summer and the worst of the drought occurred after the leaves had fallen. A fall drought poses the most danger for fire as both soil and fallen leaves can be dry as tinder. The inevitable happened when a passing wood-burning train threw out sparks that produced an inferno, quickly spread by strong winds. Sabattis was in the path of this terrifying, uncontrollable blaze. The settlement contained a dozen dwellings, railroad station, a large hotel, a store and storehouses, a new electric light plant, a livery with 200 horses and a large lumber yard. Every structure was consumed. The horses had been turned loose, finding safety in flight before the flames reached the village. The residents escaped on a train sent from Tupper Lake to rescue them. Soon after the train had left, its caboose caught on fire, with 1,500 pounds of dynamite used for blasting catching fire and detonating. The explosion was distinctly heard at Nehasane, eight miles to the south. Today only a battered state memorial sign remains where there was once a thriving settlement.

*Tupper Lake Free Press Print:* June 11, 1997

## TAKING A LOOK AROUND

THERE IS A WALK RICH in scenery and historical significance that readers might enjoy. Drive down Underwood Road, go past the Usher's Farm Greenhouses and nursery yard (great prices and hardy plant material developed especially for this climate—long, harsh winters and short, cool summers).

Park your car at the end of this road near Doug and Sarah Bencze Big Boulder Deer Farm, home of free-range, organic-raised fallow deer. Hey! The trip is already worthwhile and you haven't started your walk.

You will find a foot path here that in a quarter mile will take you to the Adirondack railroad tracks of the New York Central. Before you start (south) up the tracks, notice the fine stand of white birch trees. A spur of the railroad went out from here to a peninsula on the Raquette Pond. Raquette Pond at one time was a receiving and sorting pool for upriver log drives, and a jackworks (escalator) was located at the end of the peninsula, which would load the logs from the pond onto rail cars for shipment. The spur destroyed much of the soil's organic matter, and light seeded catastrophic species such as these paper birch were blown in on the wind to fill the opening.

One individual who used this jackworks was John McDonald, one of the most successful lumbermen in the Adirondacks.

In 1934 he was contracted to lumber Whitney Park, and a way had to be found to get the lumber out. McDonald solved that problem by building a large dam (still there) on Round Pond.

    This enabled him to boom softwood pulp across the flooded pond, down its outlet (Round Pond Stream), past the Luther Owen camp on Bear Brook (now Kavanaugh), into the Bog River, into Big Tupper Lake and thence to the jackworks, where it was loaded on rail for shipment to the St. Regis Co. at Deferiet.

    When the O.W.D. wanted the first-growth hardwood on that property, the resourceful McDonald built a railroad spur (1935) and brought railroad equipment from his Bay Pond (Rockefeller) operation. The spur ran from Rock Pond on Whitney to Brandeth station on the New York Central. Nine miles of this 13-mile spur was on Brandeth land, and the owners were paid a use fee (ten cents per cord of wood transported).

    Today, 62 years later, another successful lumberman, Jeannel Lizotte of this village, has utilized some of this original route for a main haul road, only now 18-wheel trucks do the hauling.

    Continue down the tracks for another quarter mile to the bridge that opens the Raquette Pond for its 90-mile course to the confluence with the St. Lawrence River on Indian reservation lands.

    Surprised at the carpeting laid across the railroad ties as you walk elegantly across the bridge? These were place here by enterprising snowmobilers to facilitate the bridge crossing.

    Look right (downstream) and you will see Captain Peter's rock. Look to the right across Raquette Pond to the village. Author Paul Jamieson in his canoe guide *North Flow* describes this view as "one of the most splendid mountain panoramas in the Adirondack Park that opens across a broad expanse of water. Most prominent are Stony Creek and Ampersand Mountains and the Seward, Sawteeth and Santanoni ranges."

    At the far side of the bridge to your left you'll notice the brick walls of a crumbling building choked and almost hidden by alders and other scrub undergrowth. This was a pulp crossing mill (1889-1899) owned by Champlain Realty, a subsidiary of International Paper Co. It may be hard to believe, but a thriving community known as Underwood existed there. It was named after George F. Underwood, vice president of the International Paper Co. The village contained homes for the mill workers' families, a large boarding house, post office and a school whose first teacher was Etta Eldred (wife of Frank Eldred, at one time the timekeeper for the Santa Clara Co., who lived for many years as my neighbor on Lake Simond Road, now the Doreen Sutliffe residence).

Like Derrick, Brandon and others, this little settlement only lasted about 10 years before the mill closed and Underwood became another "ghost town."

Usher Farms on Underwood Road derived its name from the original Usher Farm, which was located on what is now known as the Nomis Hunting Club lands (Conifer/Massawepie area).

In 1951 the soil on the farm began to lose its fertility and the fields were planted with Scotch pine. Today, the old farm is a sizable plantation of growing timber.

Formerly part of the Emporium Forestry Company holdings, this tract is now owned by the John Hancock Insurance Co. The massive logs that make up the main house of the Underwood Usher Farm were cut, peeled and transported from the original farm by the owner of the Underwood Farm, who was employed as caretaker for a time at the Nomis Club. He also single-handedly built from native stone the impressive fireplace that dominates the main room of the house.

It may be of further interest that the lands surrounding the original farm now enjoy partial public recreational rights due to a conservation easement with New York State (closed to the public from the "opening of the big game season until January 1 and all public use and access will be suspended annually during that time").

This easement will expire in the year 2004 after which full public recreational use will accrue.

*Tupper Lake Free Press Print:* June 25, 1997

# All Aboard!

HERE IS THE PROBLEM: You have a railroad car that weights 50 tons, it is sitting on the rails of a dead end spur (no further train connections) and you want to move it to a location 30 miles away.

Oh, by the way, along the route you must cross two highway bridges, each having weight and height limits that the parlor car may exceed.

That was the dilemma the good folks at the Adirondack Museum found themselves in after having acquired a parlor car that once belonged to financial genius August Belmont.

The museum has put together a historically powerful video presentation of how they solved that particular problem.

Their solution? They hired the local firm of W.C. Johnson & Sons.

That assignment, of course, made a lot of sense. The Johnson firm had, after all, constructed many of the buildings in the museum's outstanding complex, and they enjoyed a reputation of solving the improbable and the difficult.

The museum's story-boarded presentation, based on hundreds of photographs by famed Adirondack photographer Ed Fynmore, depicts wonderfully the ingenuity and the resourcefulness the local firm employed to successfully complete the assignment, so I'm not going to dwell on it here, only urge you to visit the museum and see first-hand how deep go the talents in our little community go (see also Newton Greiner's excellent article in the

*Shown above is the New York Central Railroad station at the Tupper Lake Junction. Shown far right is the Armour meat packing plant, a busy and prosperous operation that enjoyed great local support against its chief competitor, the Saranac Lake firm of Swift & Co. The Armour plant was managed by the late Nedd Sparks from 1899 until his retirement in 1938 at which time he was succeeded by his son, Joseph. (photo courtesy of Adirondack Museum)*

February 1997 issue of this newspaper).

Railroad parlor cars such as the one acquired by the museum were a manifestation of those heady times when the very wealthy thought it would be "droit" to have their own private car and private train to take them wherever they wanted to go.

The cars were magnificent with beautiful interiors of rare woods and sumptuous furnishings, a signature testimonial to great wealth, vision, a sense of exploration and perhaps a bit of "show boating" thrown in.

One of the earliest proponents of this mode of travel was a neighbor of this village, Dr. Seward Webb who owned Nehasane Park, the 40,000-acre estate with which so many Tupper Lake residents have had close connections over the years. He is the same Dr. Webb whose executive ability and drive constructed a railroad against the impossible odds through the unbroken north woods from Remsen via Tupper Lake to Malone and thence into Montreal.

According to Henry Harter in the authoritative study of the Mohawk and Malone railroad entitled *Fairy Tale Railroad*, one such journey taken by Dr. Webb was deemed the most costly and luxurious trip that ever crossed the continent. It was composed of Dr. Webb's private car ELLSMERE, the private car IDLER, the new observation car NA-HA-SA-NE, the private compartment car DAPHNE, a private diner car and a combination car to carry the help and baggage.

The tour departed from Grand Central Station in New York on March 29, 1893 and arrived back in Nehasane in June before the party went on to Dr. Webb's Shelburne Farms in Vermont. Along the 13,000-mile trip they visited California, then north to Vancouver and east to the World's Fair in Chicago.

Among many other trips, Dr. Webb also used his private car to take over 100 guests on what was an annual expedition for hunting in Jackson Hole, WY.

Dr. Webb had set the style and it became widely copied; the August Belmont parlor car named the ORIENTAL, which is now exhibited at the Adirondack Museum, being one such example. These certainly were the great days of railroad travel.

Sadly, it was not destined to last. The railway steadily lost passengers to the automobile, improved roads and airlines. The line that once knew private cars and prestigious sleepers was reduced to carrying four or five riders a day. Finally, on April 24, 1965, a petition to discontinue passenger service on its Adirondack Division was granted to the New York Central by the Public Service Commission.

Looking back, due to the shortages of gasoline, rubber for tires and the increased military traffic, one of the finest and one of the busiest times for the railroad took place during the second World War.

Many servicemen and women of that time, some of them returning home after several years of absence, will remember clearly and fondly the conductor's cry of "Station is Nehasane!"—a clarion call that quickened the pulse with anticipatory excitement and the realization that in only minutes they would be approaching Tupper Lake Junction. There, as the dawn was lighting the sky, they would be greeted by loved ones and be home at last.

*Tupper Lake Free Press Print:* July 23, 1997

## UNCLE A.B.

HELEN FLANDERS FARMER AND her husband, Bob, now call Erie, PA their home. Helen and Bob were early residents of this village and maintain a summer home here and, in case you haven't already met these charming octogenarians, I would like to briefly introduce you to them and at the same time relate a little bit about Helen's favorite uncle, who old timers (like me) knew as A.B. Flanders.

After having moved to Pennsylvania to pursue their respective careers, the Farmers found their family grown and themselves in retirement. They became world travelers—Europe, Asia, South America, etc.—their favorite visit being Ireland, where Helen, pursuing her Irish roots, got to kiss the famous Blarney Stone.

They never forgot, however, the memories of Tupper Lake, where they were born, grew up, graduated from high school and were married.

As the Farmers visited many of the old-world countries, the rivulets of history and tradition they encountered coalesced into a configuration and a pattern emerged. The pattern was the pride that those countries had in their past. Helen and Bob soon found themselves students of history, and with that came the realization that their own home town also contained a rich history, and they became anxious that it would be noted and preserved.

The Farmer family were early settlers in this community and were involved with the growth of railroading. The Flanders family were also pioneers. Helen's father, Bill, owned a grocery store (burned in the 1899 fire). Dan Flanders, an uncle, owned the Prince Albert Hotel and another uncle, Allen, was known as the "dean" of building contractors and at one time owned 556 building properties in Tupper Lake, according to Leo Dayhaw, his former bookkeeper.

Lumbering and railroading, two of the very real reasons that this village was established, survived and prospered. With that realization came also what Helen describes as the verity of impermanence.

As she told me one day recently: "We have both seen so many changes in our lives, traditions lost, scenic places destroyed, a home no longer there, and a lack of interest on the part of the young people in their community's past. We are also well aware that we are nearing the end of our lives. After all, we are both in our late 80s and in our own small way we hoped before we died that some token of recognition might be given to the lumber finishing mill and the important railroad spur that serviced the mill and provided access to uptown.

"With that idea in mind," she continued, "we approached the village board with the request that we be allowed to erect a simple historical monument designed by Mike Richer to be placed on an existing large stone in what is now a mini-park where the uptown train station existed (until 1932, when it was destroyed by a fire and never rebuilt) and near my Uncle Allen Flanders' finishing mill. We also requested and were given generous approval for a small park bench and a flag pole. The marker will bear an inscription noting that this is a historical site, and we feel strongly that it will be an enhancement with significance for residents and visitors alike."

This writer agrees. History, after all, adds to the knowledge of our past and allows the present a better perspective. As a travel in time, history provides a connection and markers such as the one the Farmers wish to endow, and while it is only a punctuation to the real text, it shows that the community has pride in its past. Most residents, I'm sure, will welcome this effort.

Allen Flanders, in whose memory the historical marker is dedicated, arrived in Tupper Lake in 1899, lured no doubt by the prospect of the opportunities available here at the time.

What had been only a cow pasture and clearing belonging to old Bill McLaughlin, the pioneer settlement was growing overnight into a boom town with the result of being a terminus for Hurds Railroad; the town's growth could also be attributed to the enormous railroad and lumber mill that Hurd had erected where the ball diamond is now located.

In a memoir written in July 1981 by the late Tom Fortune who knew A.B. (as he was called) described him this way: "When I came to Tupper Lake in 1917 as a young man 22 years of age to work, I became acquainted with Allen Flanders, who was then in the building business on the lakeshore of Tupper Lake. He had an office (Dave Johnson's law firm building, Lake Street), a bookkeeper, building supply and lumber and everything. I was told at the time Allen had only a team of horses and a wagon when he came to Tupper Lake. He built more houses, I dare say, than any other firm and continued all his life building and selling houses. I would not attempt or guess how many he built during his life. I do know he had 125 houses when he died. Allen was always ready for a deal when a purchaser was short on cash for a down payment. Allen would accept a horse or a cow or model T Ford car to close the deal. He was a man full of business until the day he passed away."

Editor and historian Louis Simmons also noted that, "A $400 loan to a Tupper Lake man, who subsequently 'went broke' in the logging game and settled his debt with a carload of building material, started Mr. Flanders off in the construction business here." Flanders erected some of the first buildings on Whitney Park, and among other constructions jobs were the Kildare Club and Read and Strange Park. Later, in association with Octove Frechette, he built the US Bobbin Mill and the Lake Colby School in Saranac Lake.

A capable and hard-working businessman, he was a sound judge of character, and it is said of him that he extended a helping hand to many a Tupper Lake resident by giving him the opportunity to purchase his own home in the form of rent without a down payment.

The village should be commended for their cooperation and response to a loving niece who sought recognition for a significant individual who was an important part of this town's history.

*Tupper Lake Free Press Print:* August 20, 1997

## OUR NATIVE SONS

I FIRST MET JOHN Courtney in what can only be described as tragic circumstances. Here is how it happened.

A young Air Force pilot, who had only recently graduated from St. Lawrence University, was on a training flight from the Rome Air Force Base. For reasons not fully explained, he lost control of his fighter plane and was jettisoned from his cockpit. The plane crashed into John's sawmill located in the remote Joe Indian Pond area, some 16 air miles north of this village.

A huge search effort was launched to find the young pilot. The flight pattern was pretty well defined, large amounts of radar chaff were discovered near the summit of Mt. Matumbla, and the search effort was centered in that location.

Many local people were involved and the military sent a search group of cold-weather specialists who bivouacked for many days in the cold and snow very near where the proposed prison is to be built. In spite of the efforts, which involved hundreds of man hours, and with all hopes of finding the pilot alive extinguished, the Air Force reluctantly called the search officially closed.

Some people, however, continued the search on their own. I seem to especially remember Bob O'Neil, Louis Henke (now Gnann), and my kid brother, Jim. Thus it was that I found myself skiing generally northwest along the summit ridge and flanks of Mt. Matumbla. Darkness came early that snowy day and I headed for the access road that leads to the Kildare Estate. As I skied along the road heading for the gate house, a pickup truck came rumbling along at high speed heading in the opposite direction. Perhaps surprised at someone skiing under a headlamp in this remote spot, the truck ground to a stop. It was driven by John Courtney, and he was accompanied by a full colonel who was a friend of the missing pilot.

John hurriedly explained that a member of the Sanford family (Kildare caretakers at that time) had been walking along an abandoned log road near the Jordan River, which courses through Kildare property, and had discovered the hapless pilot still strapped into his cockpit seat.

Space and other constraints preclude me detailing the somber evacuation that lasted well after midnight that fateful day, but I do feel compelled to mention the wonderful hospitality extended by the Sanfords. They not only opened their warm house through the late hours but Eloise set a wonderful table of food and even insisted on putting our soaked outer clothing into her dryer. Those caring considerations have always remained in my memory.

As the years went by since that epic night, John of course became a highly regarded community leader and my close neighbor. I often watched him begin his herculean work schedule each day, his pickup crunching the gravel as he turned off Byram Road in the half light of the early morning, and then the clang of his mailbox (everyone else had long ago picked up their mail on the wooden span that holds the neighborhood mailboxes) long after sundown—a very long day indeed.

The point of all this is that an important non-fiction best seller published this summer devotes almost two chapters to a portrayal of John and his son as part of the curve of human occupation in the Adirondack Park.

The title of the book is, *The Adirondacks: A History of America's First Wilderness*. Written by Paul Schneider and published by Henry Holt Co., it is billed as a history book but the author, who has written articles for publications like *Audubon* magazine and *Esquire*, makes it into a narrative which is interesting and entertaining to read.

Schneider writes at one point that "our Adirondacks are bigger than Yellowstone, Grand Canyon and Yosemite combined." But it isn't the size of the Adirondacks that makes our history so hard to encompass. It's the fact that unlike so many other parks, it has human occupation and *that's us folks*, trying to make a living still stay in harmony with the environment.

It is a large conflict and the author doesn't try to evade it. He has, in fact, interspersed this history with vignettes that use present activities and people to illustrate the struggle between the economy and the environment so salient here.

The vignette that takes us into John's everyday world is powerful and I found it fascinating. John's unfortunate death robbed us of his rapier wit and his sometimes controversial counsel. This history book gives us a lasting record that you will want to read.

Incidentally, the editor of this paper will print in next week's edition the chapters that tell us about John and his son, John III. Chapter 20 is entitled *Death and Taxes* and chapter 17 is called *Feller Buncher*.

*Tupper Lake Free Press Print:* September 10, 1997

# ALL IN THE LINE OF DUTY

LAST WINTER THIS COLUMN made mention that on October 15, 1941 the community had a "grim reminder that was a deadly business when a bomber plane of the Royal Canadian Air Force, en route from Halifax, Nova Scotia to Toronto, Ontario, carried three young Canadian flyers to their death here. The big bomber circled over this village obviously seeking a landing area for more than an hour during a driving snowstorm, which cut visibility to a minimum. Its desperate crew tried to land it in the marsh at the foot of Big Tupper Lake, the plane disintegrating in the crash and killing all three instantly."

After describing how two local men, Henry and Wilmer LaVoy, successfully salvaged the motors of that bomber following the failed effort of Canadian military salvage crews, we noted there was some speculation that the bomber may not have been a Lockheed Hudson as reported but rather a British Bristol Beaufort.

Fast forward now to a fascinating letter that I just received from former resident Ed Brusig, who now lives in Washington State. The Brusig family lived directly across from the high school, a section of town known as Sears Hill. The family had settled in Tupper to be near their father, who was an early patient of Federal Hospital No. 96, as Sunmount was originally termed. (Sunmount at that time was a hospital devoted to the care of disabled veterans of America's Armed Forces.)

Ed and his brother, Adolph (Buba), both graduated from

Tupper Lake High School in the mid 1940s, where they were popular and active members of the student body. Following graduation, the Brusig brothers fought in World War II, and this summer both brothers returned for the Moaner Reunion. Buba, from California, and Eddie, from Washington State, where they now live, had successful careers in industry and aviation.

Segments of Eddie's recent letter to me follow. He describes the wonderful time he had at the reunion and adds:

"My sister gave me a year's worth of old copies of the *Free Press* and I've been going through them one by one. The one of Wednesday, February 11, 1998 caught my eye since it described an incident which I was familiar with. The plane that crashed in the marsh was a Lockheed Hudson of the RCAF as Louie Simmons stated. The date I don't remember, but if Louie says it was October 25, 1941, then that's close enough.

"I remember hearing the noise of the twin engines, running outside our house opposite the high school and seeing the Lockheed Hudson (which had twin engines and rudders) fly real low in a light snowstorm.

"If Herb Trimm (I knew him in school) says it was a British Bristol Beaufort, I think he was wrong.

"I knew my planes very well back in 1941, thank you. I made scores of model airplanes then as 14-year-old.

"Back in those days in school we used to have to perform in skits for auditorium. Tableaus, I think, they called them. You remember the time I had one big tableau scene? I was a young kid holding a Lockheed P-38 up with one hand gazing up into the wild blue yonder. Talk about memories! I never forgot my memories of Tupper Lake But to dream of Lockheed and then to actually work for them 19 years later—for 27 years—is really mind boggling. Before Lockheed I worked as a designer for General Electric, American Locomotive Co., and Link Aviation. Then I worked as a Senior Design Engineer for Convair San Diego for five years.

"While employed by Lockheed, we spent five years in Scotland, from 1975 to 1978 and from 1985 to 1987. In our last tour, '85 to '87, I had a good Scottish friend with whom I hiked the Bens and

Moors of Scotland. He told me of a plane wreckage up in Ben Lui at about the 3,000-foot level. One day we made a hike (in 1986) of about four miles to reach the spot, and wouldn't you know it, it was a Lockheed Hudson! I took the numbers down from the tail section and took a lot of pictures, which I have here at home.

"Anyhow, my friend Alan gave me the details as he knew them. The plane crashed in 1946 after the war, and no one was injured as they bailed out.

"Well, I wrote to the British Aircraft Museum at Hendon, England, where they keep records, and asked them for the details of that numbered aircraft. A couple weeks later we had the answer. The plane was only a couple months old when delivered to Scotland. A crew of seven (I think) were flying training flights around Scotland to get acquainted with the Bendix Radio Directional Finder, which was a new piece of equipment. The time was October 1941 (not 1946), and when it slammed into Ben Lui, all the crew died. So, my friend Alan now had a different perspective of what happened 45 years before. He said, 'It had to take an American to come over here to set things right.' I could write a book about my experiences in Scotland but I have been going on too much now in this letter.

"Recollecting the crash in Tupper Lake in 1941, I also put on my boots the next day and tramped out to the wreckage. I think I pried off a bit myself.

"When we found the wreckage on Ben Lui in Scotland, I picked up a piece and stuck it in my pack. Upon investigation I deduced that it was the Radio Directional Finder antenna. The part that caused the crash, according to the letter from the British Aircraft Museum, due to the unfamiliarity of the crew with the R.D.F. I have it now out in the garage.

Your friend,

Ed Brusig

"P.S. While I was watching the Lockheed Hudson go to its doom in Tupper Lake in October 1941, a similar crash was happening at the same time on Ben Lui in Scotland. Weird, wasn't it?"

*Tupper Lake Free Press Print:* October 29, 1997

# BEHIND EVERY MAN

LEWIS AND CLARK—do you remember those names from elementary school history books?

Tonight, on public television, a documentary film (the second part of two-hour segments) entitled *Lewis and Clark: The Journey of the Corps of Discovery*, will be shown. If this second segment is anything like the first segment, which aired last evening, you won't want to miss it. It is not only a valuable historical travelogue, but there are spectacular shots of landscapes of the Great Plains, the awesome Rockies, and the Pacific Northwest.

Equally fascinating is the local connection in the documentary as we meet the Shoshone Indian girl Sacajawea, who is shown leading the expedition through the unexplored, trackless country where she was raised as a child before being kidnapped by a hostile neighboring tribe.

Sacajawea, you may remember, was married to Touissant Charbonneau, uncle to Michael Charbonneau, Tupper Lake's first settler.

In May 1804, Meriweather Lewis, his friend William Clark and four dozen other men set off on an expedition that would take them almost two-and-a-half years to complete. Their mission was to study the unexplored lands along the Missouri River and to find a water passage to the Pacific. They traveled upstream the entire length of the Missouri, a distance of 2,700 miles. It was an inconceivably arduous undertaking and one can only imagine their shock and despair when they got their first look at the Rockies

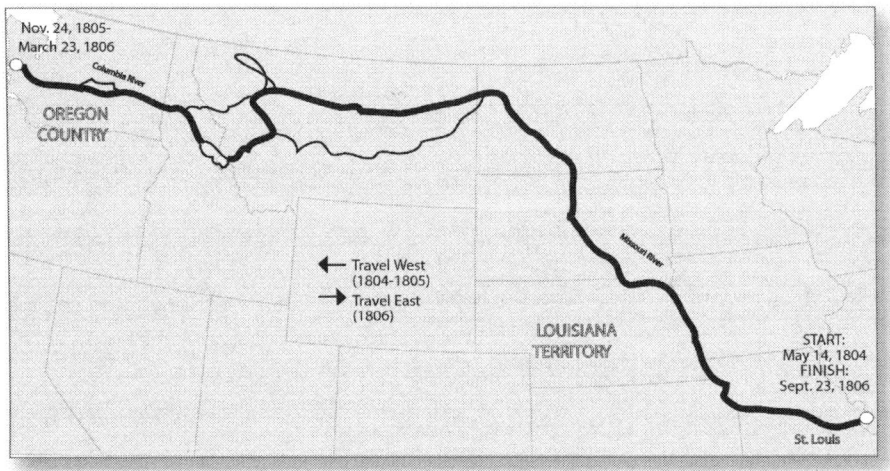

(which they expected to be only foothills), an endless fortress of forbidding snow-capped peaks that stretched to the horizon.

This was one of the most momentous and coveted expeditions in American history. How did Touissant Charbonneau join this expedition whose size was purposefully kept small so they would not alarm Indians to the point of active war and whose members were so carefully selected?

We learn something about it from Clark's notes, in which he writes that "a French man by name Chabonoh visit us, he wish to hire and informed us his 2 squars were Snake Indions."

This uncle of Tupper Lake's first settler was a trader who first started working for the North West Trading Co. (competitor to Hudson Bay Trading Co.). At the time he was living among the Hidatsas Indians as an independent trader. His squaws, or "wives", were Shoshones, or Snakes, from a band that lived in the Rocky Mountains at the headwaters of the Missouri. They were teenagers who had been captured by a Hidatsas raiding party. Charbonneau had won them in a bet with the warriors who had captured them.

The historian Stephen Ambrose relates that "Lewis and Clark eagerly accepted Charbonneau's offer to sign on as an interpreter, not so much for his own sake but because his wives could speak the language of a mountain tribe. So on the spot they signed up Charbonneau and one of his wives. He chose Sacajawea, who was about 15 years old and six months pregnant."

History records that this was a wise move. Sacajawea proved invaluable not only as an interpreter, but also in her memory and ability to guide them through the unexplored wilds of the upper Missouri.

Lewis and Clark both, it may be worth noting, have been criticized for not employing her expertise even more, a failure, it has been suggested, because of the chauvinistic attitude so prevalent at the time.

Touissant is not treated as kindly. For one thing, he was a poor boatsman and afraid of the water, and his inept boat handling several times caused great concern to Lewis (many valuable supplies were in his boat). He was also quite argumentative, often quarreling over trifling matters with Jessuame, the expedition's mulatto who had to interpret Charbonneau's French since he spoke no English. Nevertheless, despite these disapprobations (and his moral values), he must have been a resourceful and rugged individual. Certainly his nephew Michael must have been of that ilk. In 1840, at a time when there were no other settlers anywhere near, he cleared a patch of ground where the present day Racquette River Drive makes a bend in the road near the river (near Mary Alice Burns' residence) and built a cabin. That same summer he made a trip back through the wilderness to the Champlain Valley, stopping along the way to cut and stack wild hay. When the lakes were frozen the next winter he brought back some cattle, driving them through the woods and stopping to feed them on the "catches" of hay.

Charbonneau's wife and children sustained themselves for months in a trackless wilderness until his return. The Tupper Lake Charbonneau name was later Anglicized to Cole (Charbon is French for coal).

One of the Charbonneau's (Cole) daughters had the distinction of being the first bride here. In 1850 she was married on an island in Big Tupper Lake just over the Franklin St. Lawrence County line, known locally as Sally's Rock, located ironically enough near the site in Grindstone Bay where a million-dollar plus "camp" is presently being built for the Klingenstein and Simkins families.

*Tupper Lake Free Press Print:* **November 05, 1997**

## SO MUCH TO KNOW

SEVERAL WEEKS AGO, while skiing at Big Tupper, I found myself sharing one of the double chairs on lift #1 with an attractive young lady who I guessed to be in her early forties. I clanged shut the restraining bar and, as the cable hummed its way across the pulleys and lifted us up the mountain, a conversation ensued that ran something like this:

Me: "The ski area management has done an incredible job in improving the trails, don't you think?"

Her (with a slight accent): "Oh yes! They have most certainly!"

Me (thinking she was a Canadian visitor with French her first language): "Où demeurez vouz au Canada?" ("Where do you live in Canada?")

Her: "Je parle Français, un peu, mais mal, je crois. Je demeure à Poland." (I speak French a little, but poorly, I believe. I live in Poland.)

Me (embarrassed): "Oh, I'm sorry! I thought you might be from Canada."

As the lift continued up the mountain, I learned that my fellow passenger was now living in Philadelphia. In addition to skiing, she loved to sail and play tennis.

Two summers ago, she had discovered the Pine Terrace Resort with its tennis courts and lakeside location and had returned often in all seasons. She added that she had become good friends with Donna and Jerzy Maliszewski, the owners, and agreed that the skiing at Big Tupper had never been any better. The mountains here, she remarked, reminded her of the mountains near her native village in Poland. She had studied world history in school and was fascinated by the American Indian, who she knew had greeted Columbus when he landed on our New England shores.

She asked, "Did Indians inhabit this region?"

My reply to this question (as most readers will readily know) was that the two hostile tribes who claimed the area only visited it from time to time for hunting and trapping. They had their trodden trails such as Indian Pass in the High Peaks, for example, and their favorite camping places such as Indian Point (I.P. Sorting Gap lean-to on Tupper Lake) or Indian Carry (located near Upper Saranac Lake at Coreys), but no permanent settlement has ever been found. The chief claimants to the region were the Mohawks, called Iroquois by the French, and the Algonquins, a Canadian tribe.

I continued that the Iroquois had established good farms in the more suitable terrain of Central New York, where they raised corn and other food. For meat and furs, the Adirondacks was their hunting ground. They were fierce and warlike and greatly feared. Occasionally the Iroquois would meet the Algonquins on the lakes and in the forest and a great battle would result in which the Algonquins were usually the losers.

I was also able to tell her that when we reached the top of the mountain I would point out the MacIntyre Mountain Range only a few air miles away and rising loftily in the view from the ski lift's terminal station. This range is made up of five different peaks and extends for about eight miles running NE and SW. It is considered by many the noblest group of mountains in the Adirondacks.

Three of the peaks have names based on the supposition that the ancient boundary line between the Algonquin nation on the north and the Iroquois on the south ran across what is now known as Boundary Peak. Thus, this peak lies between the two peaks now called Algonquin and Iroquois and is at the present on the boundary between the towns of Newcomb and North Elba (Marshall Mountain and Wright Mountain are the two other peaks in this range).

Digression: On a clear day, 135 lakes may be seen from Algonquin's summit, which at 5,114 feet is the second-highest mountain in the High Peaks.

Indian Pass was called He-no-do-as-da, "The path of the thunderer," by the Indians who used it to bisect the High Peaks. It remains today as wild and dramatic as it was in those ancient times. One passes through a stupendous gorge whose NW wall rises 1,000 feet on Wallface Mountain. For those wishing to visit this place, it is 10.5 miles from Tahawus through the pass to Adk Loj outside of Lake Placid.

The visiting skier also asked about the vicious habit of the Indians scalping their victims. Indian folklore contains a little known story that I told her would best explain that practice. It goes something like this:

"In ancient times a great Algonquin warrior and hunter was surrounded by the dreaded Iroquois while hunting in his favorite place, known by all as Leap of the Foaming Panther (Piercefield Falls). This warrior had killed much game there for the skins and had always left the remains for the birds of prey, who had become his friends.

"As he tried to flee, the body of a great tree lay across the path. He came to it just as a heavy blow felled him. Upon recovering, he found, strangely enough, that he could as easily pass through as over the obstruction. When he reached home, his friends would not talk to him; indeed, they seemed quite unaware of his presence.

"It now occurred to him that he had been killed and was present in spirit only, human eyes not seeing him. He returned to where he had been surrounded and there, sure enough, lay his mortal body quite dead and his scalp was gone.

"A sparrow hawk flying by recognized the disembodied hunter and gratefully offered to restore his scalp. Stretching away in flight, the bird caught up with the Iroquois and plucked the scalp from a bloody pole. The other birds had, in the meantime, prepared a medicine that soon united the scalp to the head. The hunter got well and lived for many years on the shores of a lake

(Tupper Lake) the Indians called Paskungameh, which translated means, "going out from the river." Here he could look out in contentment across to Faraway See Hill (Mt. Morris). Evidently there was a belief that when a person lost his scalp he was dead, and that by taking his scalp along as a trophy, one prevented, as we might say, "a new lease on life."

*Tupper Lake Free Press Print:* January 21, 1998

# AS MEMORIES FADE

MEMORY CAN BE A CURIOUS PHENOMENON. We like to think of it as a simple record, imperfect perhaps, but reasonably immutable and accurate. We even base some aspects of history on it, if not on our own memory than that of someone else's memory.

As you age, through, and hopefully gain experience, you recognize that time edits, as writer Colin Fletcher has noted, it "edits in two ways. It removes insignificant material and it tidies up."

This is where you have to be careful. Memory tends to eliminate almost immediately routine matters of no importance. (Can you remember which sock you put on first this morning?) But it tends to retain events that cause great pain or pleasure.

If you are old enough, you can probably still remember what you were doing when you learned of John Kennedy's assassination. On the other hand, you may encyst rather than "repress" profoundly traumatic events. The images are there vividly recorded but in self-protection you tend to avoid bringing them up into awareness. I can think of a nasty divorce or early retirement compelled by circumstances beyond your control as fitting that category. Most adults acknowledge that kind of elasticity in our memories. We find it less easy to accept that memory, our sole subjective source of history, our personal librarian, can be less than trustworthy.

A decade ago psychologist Elizabeth Loftus wrote, "Our

memories are continually being altered, transformed and distorted." Recently in a technical paper she quoted the case of Jack Hamilton, California Angels pitcher, who on August 18, 1967 in Boston's Fenway Park, effectively ended the potentially brilliant career of 23-year-old Tony Conigliaro when he "crushed the outfielder's face with a first-pitch fast ball."

More than 20 years later, Hamilton (now over 50) can't forget: "I've had to live with it; I think about it a lot. . . . It was like the sixth inning when it happened. I think the score was 2-1 and he was the eighth hitter in their batting order. With the pitcher up next, I had no reason to throw at him!"

In actual fact, it was the fourth inning, no score, two out, nobody on. Tony was batting sixth . . . Hamilton remembered it was a day game because he recalled trying to see Tony in the hospital later that afternoon. The truth is different: The game took place at night.

That such errors commonly occur in what one might expect to be vivid "flashbulb" memories is confirmed by Ulric Neisser, an Emory University psychologist.

The morning after the space shuttle *Challenger* in 1986, he asked his students to fill out a questionnaire: Where were they when they first heard the news? What were they doing at the time? Who were they with? And who first told them the news? Almost three years later, when the students were seniors, he got them to answer the same questionnaire—with one extra question: How sure were they of their answers?

Dr. Neisser's technical paper on the experiment reports that of 44 students who completed both questionnaires "none of the enduring memories was entirely correct. Only three subjects (7 percent) remembered the details correctly but with minor discrepancies . . . 11 subjects (25 percent) were wrong about everything." What's more, the students who got everything wrong were just as likely as the others to be confident of the accuracy of their recall, and no amount of prodding would convince any of them that the "phantom" memories were false—even after they'd seen the original questionnaire in their own handwriting.

In other words, our brains can play tricks on us. Despite scientific research, however, and for all its weight, I am willing to bet that most readers will agree that many times certain vivid personal experiences totally engrave themselves on our memories, and even make you wonder how you can recall so much detail, especially if the experience was many years ago. The following indelible echoes from my own memory is a case in point. The year was 1941, Europe had been embroiled in a bloody war since 1939, and its prospects of escaping Hitler's cold-blooded conquest was in serious doubt. This village was still recovering from the worst depression in history that choked the economy and took a bitter toll as well as created unprecedented unemployment and low wages. Nevertheless, it was a happy, harmonious community, a wonderful place in which to live, and LIFE WAS GOOD!

One of the big "moments" for local youngsters in those days was a Saturday matinee at the local theater just for kids. Remember, there was no television in those days, and money was hard to come by, so you didn't often go to the movies, but if you did your chores (and were awarded your allowance), or found enough soda bottles to turn in for the two-cent deposit, kids could usually come up with the fifteen cents needed for admission and it was a "big deal" and certainly something that was looked forward to eagerly.

The particular day I am talking about was in late October, a dull, chilly, wet day with spitting snow and heavy clouds. My friend, Floyd Hutchins, and I stood in a long line with the other kids in town, a line that stretched past the Holland House (bar, restaurant, and hotel), formerly the Futterman building, to the A&P Store (now Guido's Pizzeria), waiting impatiently for Mr. Olivey, the manager, to open the theater.

As we stood there, we could hear an airplane, its engines throbbing heavily, circling the main street. On one of those numerous circuits it suddenly broke through the cloud cover, and looming above us was the largest airplane that I am almost certain any of us had ever seen (it was rare enough to see even a small plane in those days). The plane was only scant feet above the Martin Bros. grocery store across the street from the theater (now Nice Twice) and an astonished wave of oohs, aahs, and wows resonated up and down the gaggle of kids waiting in line (I can hear today's kids saying, "Awesome!" or "Cool!").

It continued flying over the village like this, trying several times unsuccessfully (I was later told) to land on the golf course fairways.

Finally the theater doors opened and we disappeared into the world of fantasy, little realizing the drama that was being played out in the doomed aircraft above was the real world. Nor could we have known that all too soon many of the youngsters in that movie theater audience would face similar drama where bravery, fear, and anxiety would become all too common a thread in the tapestry of their lives. America, in less than two months' time, would itself be plunged into global war.

As we spilled out of the theater later that afternoon, the darkened street was alive with people, some almost in shock and disbelief as the word spread like wildfire that "the plane had crashed in the marsh near Moody." (Actually to the rear and south of the glacial erratic which my generation knew as Green Island. This island is located in the marsh some distance in back of the present-day bowling alley and today is rapidly being clothed in a mantle of white birch trees, which somehow have found a foothold in the interstices of that great hunk of anorthosite.)

The following is what Louie Simmons was to relate in later years in his book, *Mostly Spruce and Hemlock*:

"Tupper Lake had a grim reminder that war is a deadly business on October 25, 1941, when a Lockheed-Hudson bomber of the Royal Canadian Airforce, en route from Halifax, Nova Scotia, to Toronto, Canada, carried three young Canadian flyers to their deaths here. The big bomber circled over this village, obviously seeking a landing area, for more than an hour during a driving snowstorm, which cut visibility to a minimum. Its desperate crew tried to land it in the marsh at the foot of Big Tupper Lake, the plane disintegrating in the crash and killing all three instantly. The tragedy saddened the community, but a lighter note was when a Canadian military salvage crew, especially trained for the work, spent weeks trying to retrieve the two big motors of the bomber, rigging powerful pumps to sluice away the mud heavy lifting tack and even bringing in a diver to set underwater explosive charges. The eleven-man party gave up after nearly a month's work and returned to Canada.

"Shortly after their departure, two Tupper men, Henry and Wilmer LaVoy, were given the green light to try their hand at the salvage job. Between hunting trips they retrieved both motors, devoting a total of five hours to the project."

Item: Herb Trimm, who grew up in Tupper Lake and returned to retire on Racquette River Drive, remembers that day, crossing from his Stetson Road home to the family barn to do the milking. He watched in fascination as the low-flying bomber made its final approach turn over his father's pasture (now Becky Avenue) in its attempt to land in the marsh, which must have appeared as a field.

Herb, an Air Force veteran, and later associated with the aircraft industry, feels that the plane was more likely a British Bristol Beaufort reconnaissance bomber and not an American Lockheed Hudson as indicated.

Item: A part of Henry's Success in retrieving the motors was the ability to remove his crane from the back of his 2 1/2-ton Mack truck and place it aboard a huge scow belonging to the Villeneuve Lumber Co. He then towed the scow into the marsh directly to the crash site. Once he had located and hooked on to an engine (easier said than done), Henry would operate the crane, reeling in cable until the scow would heel over almost upending itself against the resistance tugging against the crane's boom. At this point, Henry would scramble off the crane and row away in his guideboat (now part of the Adirondack Museum boat collection). He would return periodically, and during his absence some of the muck and suction would have released enough to allow the scow to return to level (and raise the engine that distance).

This was a delicate and dangerous technique and demanded great skill. Henry had to know the critical moment to cease working his crane and scramble down to his boat. He also had to have the patience not rush nature's elemental assistance.

A self-taught mechanical genius who could intuitively employ many of Archimedes' principles without ever having read his works, he was able to complete many complex projects in his lifetime when often more lettered experts had failed.

*Shown is a bomber of the type that crashed Moody marsh. Of the men like the crew of this plane, Winston Churchill would later say in the Commons "Never in the field of human conflict much owed by so many to so few." A tribute valour and stamina that forced Hitler to indefinitely "Operation Sea Lion," the planned invasion of Britian.*

*Tupper Lake Free Press Print:* February 11, 1998

# Where Do We Go From Here?

HE TOLD ME THAT IF I MENTIONED his name, he would break my arm in three places. Having seen this individual open a beer bottle with his teeth, it didn't take me long to readily agree. It seems that H.T. (as I'll refer to him) had just recently been on a drive to Sabattis and had gotten out of his car to sit on the bridge that spans the outlet of Little Tupper Lake. As he sat there looking across to the new building being erected at Camp on the Point, an otter popped its head out of a hole in the ice, carrying a fish in its mouth. As H.T. watched, the otter slithered onto the ice and ate the fish as we would eat an ear of corn.

"I could hear him chewing, 'crunch, munch, munch,'" he told me excitedly. "I must have sat there for half an hour or more, and each time that otter would dive down into that hole I'd time him. The longest period he disappeared was just over two minutes and each time he reappeared he had a fish and would sit there crunching and munching. Anyway, all of a sudden I see this shadow on the snow and I looked up to see a beautiful bald eagle doing a 180-degree turn, probably attracted by the otter or the remains of the fish on the ice.

"Bill, when that eagle lowered that big white fan tail to put the brakes on, so help me, it looked like a beacon light at LaGuardia. It was quite a sight, I'm here to tell you!

"Now the reason I stopped you is because I got to wondering what's going to happen to that great place when it gets sold?

*In 1898-1906 and again in 1934, softwood cut on Whitney park went to Tupper Lake's Santa Clara mill via waterways. Little Tupper outlet was dammed to create a round pond. When the water was released, the logs were flushed downstream into Big Tupper Lake by Tupper Lake river drivers. "The best crisly river drivers in the north woods, they could run those long logs down the whitewater like driving cows to pasture."*

You're a tree hugger," he said with a smile. "Do you know what's going on?

"Hey, my mother was a cook at Brickey's Lumber Camp on Bear Brook and my old man was guiding C.V. when he got that monstrous buck on Pilgram Mountain. A lot of people in town are worried it's going to go to hell," he continued.

"Shucks, they'll fish out those spring holes in Charley Pond outlet in a month's time. Why don't you write something in that column of yours and help us locals keep posted?"

This wasn't coffee shop rhetoric I was hearing. No, there was genuine concern being expressed here, and he had a good point.

The problem is that until the Whitney interests sign the contract selling this portion of their Adirondack land to New York State, few people really know what is going on. I did observe on a recent ski tour near the proposed acquisition that new survey work is being done (Brandeth/Whitney common boundary), but all other work is apparently stalled until a closing takes place.

That conversation with H.T., however, caused me to consider

that people new to this community and perhaps even a generation of young people may not realize that there has been a close association between the folks at Whitney Park and this village almost since the turn of the century. The connections are varied but run the gamut from having been an employee, guest, or, perhaps, a member of a lease arrangement that allowed access and other privileges, or one of the many lumbermen who harvested timber on that large landholding (up until as late as the 1980s, as high as eleven logging crews at one time).

Some historical background may be of interest. Whitney Park was originally formed when, between 1896 and 1898, William C. Whitney and a lumberman named Patrick Moynehan put together many small purchases for a total of 68,000 acres.

Little is known about Moynehan. He did have a reputation, however, for persistently trespassing and cutting timber rights (on state land) to the I.P. Co.

The purchases were made under an agreement in which Whitney furnished most of the financial backing. The two shared the expenses and profits of the first lumbering, and Whitney was to succeed as sole owner in 1914 after the lumbering was completed. At that time, there was a saying around this village that at the onset, Moynehan had the experience, Whitney had the money. At the end, Whitney had the experience and Moynehan had the money. That story may have been anecdotal, but if it were true, today William Whitney's fourth-generation heirs have had the last laugh.

Consider: $13.9 million for 14,700 acres, plus $3.2 million for headquarters (80 acres) and a $3.2 million deal with Adirondack land trust for 36,000 acres not be developed. I'll do the math for you—$20.1 million and counting. Sorry, Mr. Moynehan.

In summary then, a large number of local people have an extra special interest. Yes, even a proprietary interest as planners begin a management plan. We can hope that they follow a sensible direction.

The *Mot du Jour* for this will be vision. It will require combining the present realities (a land ravaged by tornado damage, etc.,

etc.) with the realization that nature has marvelous healing powers and that there are many generations to follow that will exult in this heritage that was protected by us for them to marvel at and to enjoy as a recreational source. However, that doesn't mean inappropriate restrictions or allowing unbalanced input from the environmental lobby. For example, the classification of the neighboring Lake Lila tract as primitive is, in my opinion, flawed and overdue for revision under the mandatory five-year rule. By the way, don't hold your breath waiting for interim plans. This will no doubt be a lengthy bureaucratic and troublesome process with many crochets and quirks certain to surface. Consider, if you will, some of the following that only scratches the surface of the many decisions that will have to be deliberated: Will there be a permit system? Catch-and-release fishing? How about disabled access? Mandatory porta-potties? Snowmobile travel? Fresh-faced assistant rangers with new shoulder patches invading your campsite to give a lecture on wilderness ethics? Removal of bridges like the one over Salmon Lake Outlet: Off limits to mountain bikes?

You get the picture! Stay tuned, stay informed.

*Tupper Lake Free Press Print:* March 04, 1998

# KNOTTED ROOTS OF LOVE AND STRENGTH

AT AN EARLY PERIOD OF OUR HISTORY, Upper Saranac Lake originally drained into the Racquette River. Its waters at that time would have ended up in the St. Lawrence River rather than Lake Champlain.

Today, a low divide of glacial drift created during the Ice Age provides a land barrier that prevents that from happening and separates the two systems. You now cross that barrier on your way to Saranac Lake one-quarter mile after descending Panther Mountain hill.

This means that canoeists traveling from the Saranacs to the Racquette—or vice versa—have to "carry" their boats between the two watersheds. The earliest travelers to do this were the Native Americans, and this very old traditional route came to be known as Indian Carry.

There is strong evidence that the Indians had a summer encampment or, perhaps, even a hunting headquarters on the lake side of the carry. These were the Saranac Indians, and they called the trail they used the Eaglenest Trail.

They claimed as their exclusive hunting grounds not only the Eaglenest Forests, but also those of the Wampum Waters (Stony Creek Ponds), the Stream of the Snake (Stony Creek), the Sounding River (Racquette River), from the Lake of the Blue Mountain to Wild Mountain (Matumbla) at the Leap of the Foaming Panther (Piercefield Falls).

There was a row of tall pines that stood on or near the carry many years ago. These trees showed strange knotty protuberances in their trunks seven or eight feet from the ground. Many people noticed them but no one could explain them until some passing Indians, who claimed to be descendants of earlier dwellers on the spot, gave a solution to the mystery. They said that when these tall pines were saplings, the young warriors of the tribe would show their strength by twisting and tying the slim trees into knots that were never untied.

I'd known of this story, so imagine my astonishment when, at a place where a stream called Bear Brook empties into the Racquette River, I discovered several Tamarack trees that had been tied into knots similar to those from the tall pines. I don't think those knots were Nature's doing—such as trees twisting themselves to seek sunlight beyond the canopy of surrounding mature trees.

My guess is that they were tied in this fashion by a stalwart lumberjack, probably from this community, who was testing or exhibiting his strength. Was he aware that young Native Americans did the same? Or is there some other explanation that, in my naiveté, I have overlooked?

Perhaps the following legend that involves members of the Saranac tribe, Tupper Lake, and Indian Carry may be of interest:

It was during the years when the Saranacs were divided that Howling Wind, one of the young men of Indian Carry, saw and fell in love with a girl from a family on Tupper Lake. He quickly found a way to tell his liking, and the couple met often in the woods and on the shore. He made bold to row her around the quieter bays, and one moonlit evening, he took her to Devil's Rock, or Devil's Pulpit (located on the east shore of Tupper Lake opposite the southwest tip of County Line Island), where he told her the story of the place. This was to the effect that the fiend had paddled on timbers, by means of his tail, to that rock and had assembled fish and game about him in large numbers by telling them that he was going to preach to them. Instead, he pounced upon them and ate all within his grasp.

*Were the Tamarack trees shown here tied into a knot as an exhibit of strength by an unknown lumberjack much as the early Indian braves did as a test of their strength?*

As so often happens in Indian history, the return of these lovers was seen by a disappointed rival who had hurried back to camp and secured the aid of half a dozen men to arrest the favored one as soon as he should land. The capture was made after a struggle, and Howling Wind was dragged to the chief's tent for sentencing. That sentence was death, and with a refinement of cruelty that was rare even among the Indians, the girl was ordered to execute him. She begged and wept to no avail. An axe was put into her hands and she was ordered to dispatch the prisoner. She took the weapon, her face grew stern, and tears dried on her cheeks. Her lover, bound to a tree, gazed at her in amazement. His rival watched, almost in glee. Slowly, the girl crossed the open space to her lover. She raised the tomahawk, and with one blow severed the thongs that held him. Then, like a flash, she leapt upon his rival, who had sprung forward to interfere. She clove his skull with a single stroke. The lovers fled as only those can fly who run for life. Happily for them, they met a party from the "Carry" coming to rescue Howling Wind from the danger that his courtship had exposed him to, and it was even said that this party entered the village, and by presenting knives and arrows at the breast of the chief, obtained superfluous consent to the union of the fugitives. The pair reached the "Carry" in safety and lived long and happy lives together.

It most certainly was my imagination, but one night last summer during a full moon, I was sitting along the river near my house when a birch bark canoe glided noiselessly past me.

A young Indian brave with a single feather in his hair that ran to his shoulders was paddling with a strong, steady stroke. He never removed his paddle from the water in what modern canoeists now call the "Indian Return" stroke.

In the bow was a lovely Indian girl with a delightful smile on her face. In the center of the canoe, tied to the thwarts, was a sling filled with sweet grass in which lay a child singing in a soft voice.

*Tupper Lake Free Press Print:* March 18, 1998

# FORE!

I WAS TALKING WITH Ed LeBlanc this past week, and he was telling me how he had rediscovered the game of golf. "I've been playing now for two years," he noted, "and I can't stress strongly enough how it's added to the quality of my life!"

If you know Ed, you will not be surprised to learn that he attacked playing golf like some of the other passions in his life. Whether it was his teaching career, his ice-fishing exploits, his famous pike burgers, or his equally famous canoe carts based on a Chet Johnson design that he modified and improved and is now part of the Adirondack Museum collection, Ed has had one rule: "Damn the torpedoes and full speed ahead." To Ed, age is just a number. He is a person of tremendous verve and energy.

This winter, for example, while wintering in Florida, he would hit more than 300 golf balls every day at the driving range near his complex at Plaid Pants Village.

Ed plays the Tupper course every day and when he is not part of a foursome, he told me that he practices using three different golf balls, hitting each in turn as he negotiates the eighteen-hole course.

That disclosure made me laugh, and I had to tell him that when I was a caddy, there was a certain physical education teacher from Saranac Lake who was a fitness fanatic and he would appear at the Tupper course and play twenty-seven holes using only a putter and, after each shot, would run to the next. He was actually a good golfer and I often saw him "tater" out 200-yard drives with his hickory-shafted putter. It was only when he would sprint down the fairway to his next approach shot that the other golfers would wonder if "that fellow wasn't a bubble off true."

Strangely enough, I recently read about a "new sport" called speed golf, a.k.a extreme golf. It may sound like the funniest athletic oxymoron since Utah Jazz, but it is catching on.

All USGA rules apply with one exception: flagsticks need not be removed for putting. To calculate your score, add total number of strokes to the minutes you spent running around the course.

The record is 75 in thirty-nine minutes (a phenomenal 114). The day before that same golfer shot a round of 76 in four and a half hours.

Fast play actually helped his game. (It seems that the more problems your swing has, the more they are exacerbated by just standing there thinking about them.)

Imagine the look on your spouse's face when you say: "Bye, Honey. I'm going out to play golf. Be back in forty-five minutes."

Our physical education teacher may have been ahead of his time!

Ed graduated from Holy Ghost Academy in 1938 and is part of the age group (sixty-five plus) the *New York Times* recently referred to as the elderly (thanks a lot), and he remembers that when he was growing up, there was only one golf course in the community and that was a private nine-hole course owned by the Big Wolf Club.

It was located on what had been the Wilson and Robillard farms along the present Haymeadow development. In fact, the Jeannel Lizotte home sits very near a former fairway of that course.

As the late Louis Simmons noted in his book, *Mostly Spruce and Hemlock*, "Golf in those days was about as foreign to the area as boomerang throwing." That was to change, however, when in 1932, W.C. Hull, president of the Oval Wood Dish company, proposed building an eighteen-hole course, impressing on local businessmen that they needed to emphasize tourism as the era of big lumbering was about to decline.

Paul Martin, Lou Quinn and Ellen Shaw's father, was mayor at the time and he agreed with Mr. Hull and, together with four other trustees, set out to raise the necessary funds. As Louis further notes, "Times were hard and money scarce," but in less than a month $15,000 had been pledged toward the $18,000 needed for the first nine holes. That same amount probably wouldn't cover one hole today.

Jack and Laura Nepton owned the old landmark resort, The Prince Albert Hotel, and they donated fifty acres of land on the slopes above the hotel, most of it already cleared from past farm operations. The Oval Wood Dish corporation offered fifty to seventy-five acres as needed and on September 12, 1932 the late Tom Creighton, woods superintendent for O.W.D., had more than fifty men on the site. They used ten teams of O.W.D. horses that pulled scrapers and hauled away stumps and rocks. The job involved cutting twenty acres of timber, and more than $2,200 of the slender golf course "kitty" went into removal of stone, including about $1,000 for dynamite.

Before the onset of winter halted operations, the first nine holes had been almost completed, and the location for the clubhouse cleared of trees and the site staked out. Logs for the building were cut that winter from the slopes of nearby Sugarbush Mountain.

On August, 15, 1933, the following summer, the course was open for play.

The clubhouse and the second nine-hole development were several more years in coming. They were finally made possible by federal financial aid, the property having been turned over to the town to make such aid possible.

Under the direction of foreman James King (who also happens to be restaurant owner Bill King's grandfather), workmen erected the log clubhouse, which was completed in 1937. A macadam road linking the highway at Moody with the clubhouse, a parking area, and the second nine holes were all built with W.P.A. aid.

With the addition, the new section became the first nine holes for play purposes. The new addition opened in August 1941.

I should mention that alongside and part of what is now the Pro Shop was what was known as the Caddy Shack.

This resembled a baseball dugout, and caddies assembled here awaiting assignment by the caddy master according to their status.

The caddies worked under a merit system in which you had to work your way up based on the old-fashioned way—you had to earn it. You did this by: 1) showing up each day, 2) being on time, 3) staying late and carrying double if requested, 4) knowing your

*Teamsters like Joachim Chartrand shown here help guide the ten teams of horses belonging to the O.W.D. that helped clear the stumps and stones from twenty acres of forest to clear ground for the Tupper Lake Golf Course.*

craft and your player's abilities, and 5) being the best you could be and KEEPING YOUR EYES ON THE BALL.

Space precludes telling more about the redeeming values of being a caddy (monetary and otherwise), but I must tell about the annual caddy tournaments.

Originally, the contest was between the Tupper Lake Golf Course caddies and the Big Wolf caddies.

With the closing of the Big Wolf course in the early 1940s, the tournament became one between the Tupper caddies and was a very serious, hotly contested event.

Incidentally, the Big Wolf caddies, most of whom were from the junction, won most of the tournaments, powered by the Keelers, the Fullers, the Bashants, the Forkeys, and the Rae brothers.

Indeed, caddy Patsy Rae often beat the course pro, and Puffer Fuller would go on to become the club champion.

Floyd Bashant, who caddied on both courses, modestly told me that the junction boys held two advantages. First, they had more experience having been playing before the Tupper course came into being and, second, as Floyd puts it, "The Big Wolf course had exceptionally small greens and you had to be very accurate to make them, and that refined our strokes and improved our abilities."

There were actually two other golf courses near this community prior to the building of the Tupper course. Like the Big Wolf course, they were also private, built for their owners and guests.

Route 30 bisects what was once a fairway, and if you look closely, you will discover the remnants of a golf house in the pines located between that route and the road that leads to Coreys. This course was built just prior to 1920 after the venerable Rustic Lodge was razed to provide room.

The second course was located just off the road to Sabattis on property called Sabattis Park, owned by Charles M. Daniels and his wife, Florence Goodyear Daniels. Here they built a fabulous camp they named Tarnedge from the Scottish words meaning "beside the lake." The golf course was built with wheelbarrows and hand equipment alone. It was small (2,600 yards) but it entertained some notable players.

There is a story about that course concerning an achievement by the owner, a noted athlete and Olympic swimmer that deserves telling. Louis Simmons records it as follows:

"On the morning of June 29, 1916, after a 3 a.m. rising and light breakfast, Mr. Daniels teed off at 4 a.m. and played continuously until after 9 p.m. that night. He had carded a total of 228 holes—said to be a world record for a day's play. His total score of 970 figured out to be just over 38 for each nine-hole round—near par figures. By straight away yardage figures, he had covered about 41 miles, and it was estimated 'as the golfer goes,' he actually covered more than 50."

In the end, you see, golf is about tradition: the Green Jacket, the Tupper Open, St. Andrews, Nan and Gordon Peters, the Ryder Cup. They serve as reminders of those before us who helped shape and give history to the game.

*Tupper Lake Free Press Print:* May 16, 1998

## CONFUSION ABOUNDS

WHAT'S IN A NAME? Nothing that couldn't be changed, judging by the changing names of Tupper area lakes, streams, and mountains over the years. Little Wolf was once Lake Pomeroy; Tupper Lake on some early maps was Mort Lake, or its rough English equivalent, "Dead Lake." Eagle Crag and Mount Arab Lake located near Conifer were, until 1916, known as Long Lake and Pleasant Lake respectively.

It did come as a surprise, however, to see area newspapers refer to Cooney Mountain in their account of last week's forest fire off Route 30 near Lumberjack Springs.

As most readers of this column will readily know, they were referring, of course, to Coney (Cone) Mountain. Since future historians may well wonder where "Cooney" (sic) Mountain is, we will try to set the record straight.

First, there was indeed a fire. The nightmare that had been troubling the sleep of local rangers Joe Kennedy and Clyde Black was now a reality. Weeks of above normal, record-breaking temperatures had made the forest floor a tinder box, and with Memorial Day weekend bringing to the woods scores of hikers and campers, their worst fears were realized, and a forest fire was raging on the mountain. Where and when it would move was anyone's guess.

There is no question that, given the conditions, it could have easily been a disaster, and even the century-old Litchfield Chateau was at peril.

A forest fire is a scary ordeal. You are fighting a natural force that is insensitive and often goes beyond any human control.

Fortunately, human intellect can provide a control that exceeds that abstract insensitivity provided by the fire.

It starts with a plan, and the D.E.C. has proven to be very professional in that respect. The site plan chief, Lt. Barstow of Region Six, had several positive things going for him. First, he got full local cooperation.

Gregg Spangler, for instance, who runs Long Lake's Adirondack Air Service and who had spotted the fire at about 1 p.m. that day while conducting a scenic flight, called Shawn Wright, Long Lake fire chief, and gave him the combination to the locked gate into Sperry Pond at the base of the mountain which proved an invaluable source of water for the helicopter and the foot crews.

Most important to the plan, though, were the neighboring volunteer fire departments who had the manpower, the determination and the stamina that allowed them to hoist 70-pound Indian pumps on their backs and labor up the steep side of Coney Mountain, sometimes crawling and heaving themselves forward to reach the fire's location. It also involved finding a helicopter. In this case, the Lifeflight helicopter came to the rescue from its helipad site across from Lumberjack Springs on Route 30 and was instrumental in ferrying water and supplies to the mountain during the seven-hour ordeal.

This successfully controlled fire was a test of individuals was of a plan well executed. It was also a test of how well our local and surrounding fire departments could and would work together. They can all be proud of a job well done.

That said, let's straighten out the misnomer Cooney Mountain.

As you travel up Route 30 near the intersection that leads to Bog River Falls (Route 421 formerly a nineteenth-century wagon road), you will notice two conical-shaped peaks with partially bald tops. Each is in a block of state land surrounded by privately owned property (Litchfield and International Paper Company). One is called Litchfield Hill, or as I prefer, Goodman Hill, named after the Goodman family, who owned a fine stone camp on Big

Tupper Lake for years. You may recall that Andy Goodman, son of the elder Mr. Goodman, gave up the pleasures of summer life at the family camp to help in the integration effort in the South and was brutally murdered by white supremacists and callously buried in the wet cement of a dam that was under construction (see "Mississippi Burning").

The other peak is Coney Mountain with an elevation of about 2,227 feet. If you look closely, you will see a large wooden cross erected by a couple of devout Tupper Lake residents to symbolize their faith in Jesus Christ, and who, perhaps, were influenced by the mountain's similarity to Golgotha (Calvary), where Jesus was nailed to a similar cross.

It was on Coney Mountain that in 1772 one Archibald Campbell and a group of Indians ended their survey of the northern boundary of the Tatten and Crossfield Purchase. They had bushwhacked east from the northwest corner, chopping blazes to establish the boundary of the first major land purchase in the central and western Adirondacks. By the time they reached Coney, they were tired, but they had another more sufficient reason for ending the ground survey here, content with a line of sight eastward. "The rum gave out" was the clinching explanation in Campbell's field notes.

In the fall of 1972, two centuries later, the late Bill Verner of Long Lake and the curator of the Blue Mountain Lake Museum, with some staff members, climbed Coney to commemorate the anniversary of Campbell's aborted survey. After lolling about under the September sun, they descended and drove into Tupper to the nearest bar to share a celebratory shot of rum. As Paul Jamison has noted, "Things are too easy today."

It may be of some interest that Lumberjack Springs was discovered by Louis Osier (Oshier) in 1910. Today it is routinely tested by the New York State Department of Health and continues to run cold and pure.

In 1937 three enterprising Tupper Lakers, who described themselves as Camp Cove (Goodman's Shelter Cove Camp) lumberjacks, erected the splendid spring house that still stands.

We can thank Ed Sabourin, Emil Sabourin, and Pat Arsenault for their talented and thoughtful workmanship.

Puzzler: Was the name Coney originally Cone (i.e. conical in shape) as some sources indicate? Was Goodman Hill also referred to as Cone Mountain (it is also conical in shape), thus making Cone the plural Coney to describe the Coneys? Or was Coney an individual and was Coney Beach (Little Wolf) named after him as well? If so, who was Coney?

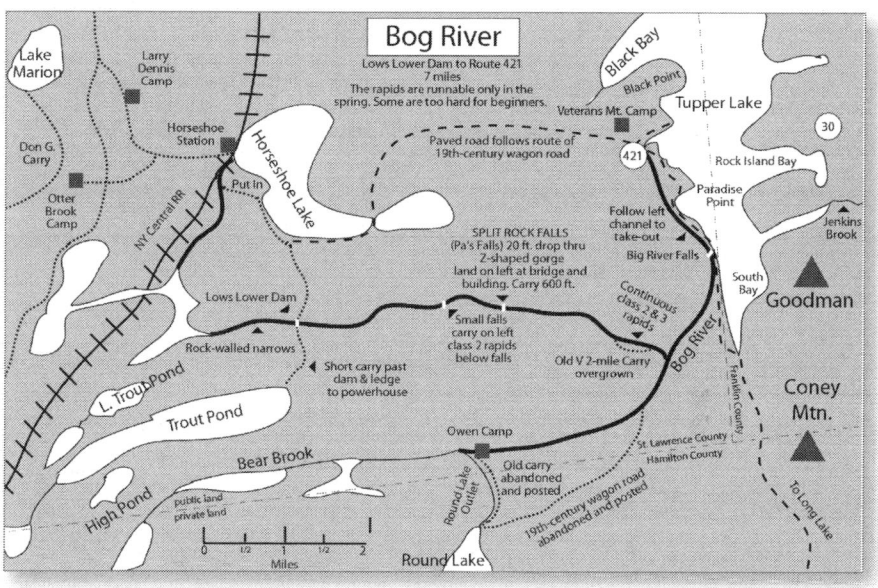

*Climb Goodman (2,160 ft) by going up abandoned blacktop road along Lumberjack Spring and then turn left on a clear day, you can see the tower of Litchfield Chateau. To climb Coney (2,270 ft) follow Franklin-Hamilton County Line off Route 30 marked by blazes. Both are easy climbs.*

*Tupper Lake Free Press Print:* June 10, 1998

# Ballads and Folk Songs

SEVERAL WEEKS AGO I found myself on the Jordan River several miles upstream from where that beautiful remote stream drops suddenly in a series of magnificent cascades into the Raquette River above Crary Dam at a place called Tebo Falls.

The falls were named in the memory of Joe Thibault (Tebo) who drowned there. An old publication by the A. Sherman Lumber Co. of Potsdam (the Box Mark, March, 1926) tells the story this way: "There was a set of falls up there on the Jordan River, maybe a half a mile above the Raquette River, where there was a bridge. They called it a gate dam. They'd flood it and put the logs in there, and then they'd open the gate and drive the logs on down through into the Raquette. Well, they was having a two o'clock lunch when this fella by the name of Joe Thibault jumped up and clapped his heels together a couple of times. And he said, 'The water never ran deep enough in the Jordan to drown a man.' Two hours later there was a drowned man who

*The indomitable Eddie Ashlaw is shown at his home in Parishville in 1971. (photo by Robert Bethke)*

*This modern lumber truck bridge now spans the Jordan River where a century ago the A. Sherman Lumber Co. once had a gate dam. Thousands of logs were held in place by a boom, a series of logs linked by chains just above the dam. On the day of the drive, the gates were removed from the dam and the massed logs would pour out and be driven downstream by the torrent of water released. Joe Thibault drowned just below this location (Tebo Falls). (Bill Frenette photo)*

lay on the bank of the river seventy-five or eighty years ago."

That event inspired a ballad called Tebo, which was often one of the folk songs sung in North Country lumber camps and bar rooms. It should be noted that Tupper Lake bar rooms were favorites among the loggers who enjoyed these traditional folk songs. Stewart Holbrook, "*Yankee Loggers: A Recollection of Woodsmen Cooks and River Drivers*," (NY International Paper Co. 1961) notes that, "The American House, the Canadian Hotel (Joe Gokey's place), the Iroquois, the Altamont and the Holland House, the Faust Hotel, and the Grand Union Hotel at the junction presented unlimited possibilities for entertainment." (It is sobering—no pun intended—to realize that of Holbrook's list, only the Grand Union Hotel, a landmark since 1892, remains today, still going strong under the astute management of Sally Trudeau.)

One of the most popular folk singers at that time, many readers will remember, was the legendary Eddie Ashlaw. Eddie and his wife, Hazel, were among the favorite customers on my beverage sales rounds in the junction when they owned the Grand Union Hotel. Eddie wore many hats: innkeeper, lumber jobber, folk singer, raconteur. He was known as an individual with great generosity who owned considerable real estate and who had the ability to make a fortune, only to lose it through declining market prices or a rainy winter (1951), when he couldn't get his logs out of the woods, or through ill-advised loans to others less fortunate. He would make it all back and then lose it again. There a was a saying in the junction "that fella Ashlaw, take and strip his pockets, bury him naked in a pile of stones, and he'll crawl out with a new suit and pockets full of money."

The last time I saw Eddie was at the Hamm's Inn below Sevey's. He was feeling mellow and nostalgic and he grinned that unforgettable grin and said for all to hear: "I've had my fling and I flung it. I spent it while I had it, and I don't have any regrets." Eddie only sang when he felt like it, and no amount of coaxing could get him to sing otherwise, but this was one of those times and he broke into a song he called "The Roving Ashlaw Man." Robert D. Bethke, author of numerous articles on regional folklore, has recorded the words to that song, which he notes is based in the "Roving Journeyman" family of songs and may have been derived from the Canadian loggers' "Ye Mardens of Ontario." Eddie's rendition is as follows:

> *The Roving Ashlaw Man*
> *I am that roving Ashlaw man, and*
> *I've roamed from town to town,*
> *If liquor don't give you the answer, boys, come on here,*
> *won't you sit down?*
> *With tackle on my shoulder and my peavey in my hand,*
> *When I reach St. Regis Falls, I'll*
> *be a health young Ashlaw man.*
>
> *Well, when I first came to Tupper*

> *Lake, the girls all jumped with joy,*
> *Said one unto the other, "Here comes that Ashlaw boy!"*
> *One treats me to a bottle, while the other to a dram,*
> *And the toast went round the table,*
> *"Here's to that healthy Eddie Ashlaw man."*
>
> *For I hadn't been in Tupper Lake*
> *for a day not only three,*
> *When Papin's lovely daughter, she*
> *fell in love with me.*
> *She said she wanted to marry me,*
> *and takes me by the hand,*
> *And she went home and told her*
> *mother that she loved that Ashlaw man.*

In the next *Transitions* we will continue our account of the Jordan River and the complexity of terms like Park and Preserve, Village and Township.

*Tupper Lake Free Press Print:* July 08, 1998

## SO MUCH TO KNOW

THE JORDAN RIVER, which was mentioned in our last column (the ballad of Tebo falls), has a humble beginning.

It is born only a few miles north of this village in a tiny eyedrop of water known locally as Marsh Pond, or by its more poetic name, Sunset Pond, quite near the Pitchfork Pond Road.

It begins its voyage to the sea via the Raquette River as a narrow, crooked, alder-choked stream. All access here is private (Township 19 Hunting Club), not that it matters because even the most fanatical canoeist would require a machete or chain saw to navigate its convoluted passage that persists for several miles downstream. Perhaps there is a grand design to this initial impenetrability, a kind of cordon that keeps the river solitary, remote, and protected from overuse.

In the Jordan's middle, however, almost as though it didn't want to join its cousin, the Raquette, it widens out from a puny and shallow stream and wanders between towering conifers; white pines over 200 feet tall, virgin aristocrats whose ancestors were sought after by the King's servants, English and French in their turn, as ship masts, for only in a few places did the pine grow tall and straight. For long stretches the river courses through marshland, where numerous whitetail have taken refuge from flies and where they feed in a true aquatic garden, a specimen treasure of what the real north woods is all about.

Just as the upstream portion of the river is private, so is its mouth, and a steep series of rapids and falls over a mile in length discourages upstream travel.

You have already paddled half way down the seven-mile long Carry Dam reservoir from the Parmenter site below Seveys to reach the Jordan's entrance into the Raquette, so continue north another three-fourths of a mile where blocks of state land allow you to carry your canoe a mile or so along a woods road to the stillwater above Tebo Falls.

Most people deplore dams and reservoirs, but Carry Falls Reservoir is worth a visit. It is only a short drive from this village, and Niagara Mohawk has provided a launch site, picnic grounds, places to swim and a campground.

You will find lots of sandy beaches along wooded shorelines, attractive islands, and at three miles wide and seven mile long, you won't feel crowded. If you do visit this man-made lake, you may want to reflect that under the hull of your boat, now covered by up to 70 feet of water, not very long ago (1951) there was an entire settlement that was once known as "Hollywood."

Yep! Hollywood, and it was so named in 1886, *the year before the California movie capitol was also named Hollywood!*

As a boy I used to ride along on my father's soda truck when he would make deliveries to the renowned Hollywood Inn located there. Oh boy, such memories.

Orange Crush in the "crinkly brown bottle," birch beer, sasparilla. Steel tubs of Frenette's Ice Cream, safely ensconced in bulky kapok-insulated containers, surrounded by ice from Dolph Trudeau's ice house to prevent melting.

The Hollywood Inn, which had become one of our valued customers, was built in 1889 by Jerry Reynolds, who recognized the need for a halfway tavern between Potsdam and this village. Remember, it was then a two-day trip by stagecoach drawn by four horses over a poor sand and corduroy road. The following year Reynolds became postmaster at Hollywood as well as innkeeper.

Later the inn was operated by the Day family and in the 1930s by Al and Marion Luchs as a resort hotel and dude ranch.

Little did I realize while riding in that old, hard rubber-tired

*The "cut off" from Raquette River to Simond Pond as it appeared at the turn of the century. The unregulated Setting Pole Dam flooded and killed surrounding timber. In 1934 a new dam effectively controlled and regulated area water levels and stopped indiscriminate flooding. (Stoddard photo)*

Reo truck that during the fall months of 1951, while driving frequently between Canton and Tupper, I would experience the eerie scene of 1,000 flaming stumps touched with fuel oil. Below the inn, all across what was known as the Great Bog (a wide bottom land between hills with the river running through it), not a tree was left standing. The burning stumps looked like the campfires of a large Iroquois war party on some stern mission against the Hurons of Canada. When the proposal to flood the Hollywood settlement surfaced, the owners of the property there put up a strong battle, but they lost the war.

As a county supervisor said to one of the settlement homeowners after his testimony at the courthouse in Canton, "I cannot help but admire your grit in this fight, but for the common people, trying to fight big business for their seeming-just and collective rights is usually like bucking a stone wall." It took six years to complete the project, and in 1957 the dam towered 70 feet above the natural bed of the river, a reservoir of water seven miles long with a shoreline of about twenty-five miles.

Admittedly, the lake created is, yes, I've got to say, beautiful. However, penstocks, dried up sections of river, power plant buildings, tailraces, concrete dams (six in all) have changed the character of the second-largest river in the state.

Today, only a few short sections have retained the vitality and beauty of this once vigorous mountain torrent that rises in a small pond near Blue Mountain Lake and flows northward to swell the St. Lawrence. One such example: One recent summer my wife and I paddled the river from its source to where it enters the St. Lawrence at the St. Regis Indian Reservation. On that trip the river below Hannawa Falls disappeared completely and we had to portage our canoe alongside a huge pipe that towered above us (and held the river) until finally it was disgorged through a turbine and we regained the river bed near Potsdam and were allowed once more to return for a time to the ancient and true passage.

The drowning of the settlement called Hollywood is just another entry, like Brandon, Derrick, Underwood, and Kildare, in the legacy of short-lived Adirondack community settlements. The Raquette will not be as easily vanquished. It will one day return to its natural free-flowing form. Methods of providing power will (and are) changing. The dams will outlive their usefulness or choke on their own unflushed situation in a hundred years or so. A mere blip in geologic time.

*Tupper Lake Free Press Print:* July 29, 1998

# THE RETURN OF THE LOON

PAUL PROVOST STOOD ON THE DECK of friend Greg Gachowski's Raquette River Drive home, his hands clasped as though in prayer.

Paul was indeed making a supplication, but not one of prayer.

Placing joined hands to his pursed lips, he blew hard, and the result was a mournful wail—the signature call of the common loon!

From across the river in a bay of Lake Simond came an answering wail. A wail so like the one created by Paul that it could have been an echo. It was not an echo, however. It was one of a pair of loons that in the past two years has adopted Lake Simond as their territory.

The haunting cry of the loon, the very epitome of wilderness, to be heard so close to the village almost daily, and especially early in the morning or late at night, has to be termed extraordinary.

It is extraordinary because, for one thing, loons return each spring to an increasingly hostile environment.

Along with many other man-made threats to their survival—including harassment by boaters, loss of nest sites by high water, mercury poisoning on their wintering grounds, and the increasing acidification on so many of our local ponds—the loons' chances have become severely threatened. My neighbor and former school chum, Herb Trimm, who has returned here in retirement, sums it up best: "I love to hear the loons across the pond. It reminds me so of the remote ponds I visited as a youngster growing up in this God's country. The best part is that it could indicate that Lake

*The loon shown above is "dancing" on a lake to draw attention from its nearby nest. (photo reprinted from the Adirondack Daily Enterprise)*

Simond has retained its clean water, its sizable fish population and its uncluttered surroundings. We are so lucky to live here!"

Paul Provost agrees with Herb and adds that loons mate for life and return to the same lake year after year. The very fact that for the second year in a row the residents of Lake Simond have watched two chicks hitching a ride on their parents' backs, which is a striking example of breeding success, insures in part that the loons have found a safe haven and will return (if they have a safe migration) next year.

It should be pointed out that Paul only calls loons in August. There are several reasons for this:

First, early in the spring, loons are very territorial and could possibly be upset by Paul's rendition of another loon. Secondly, he doesn't want to disturb them while they are nesting, or later, when the chicks are not capable of swimming or diving. Only when the chicks reach the juvenile stage at this time of year does he call to them.

Despite the loons' threatened existence elsewhere, local observers like Joyce Thomas, Inge Sapp, Dawn Andrews, Greg Smith, Charlcie Delehanty, and Cindy Lewis, to mention a few, report a healthy population and high rate of breeding success in this area. Mrs. Delehanty notes that loons can't fly until they are eleven weeks old. This means that they are confined to the lakes where they are born for that period, and this increases the accuracy and the ease in assessing breeding success. Only one pair of loons in the ten traditional areas surveyed by local observers failed to raise young (Eagle Crag/Sapp). One hatchling was lost to predation (Hitchins Pond/Andrews), and one nesting pair only incubated a single egg (Lows Lake/Andrews).

Sometime next month, the young loons will migrate separately without their parents to the Atlantic Ocean. They will remain there for two or more years until they reach sexual maturity. How do they find their way the first time? How do returning loons time their arrival to coincide precisely with ice out? Science doesn't have these answers. We can only hope that this area will continue to be a safe refuge.

### Loon Vocalizations

The loons vocalizations that Paul Provost can masterfully imitate are listed here with their meanings:

Wail—The signature call. Long, drawn out. Mostly at night or evening to locate other loons or to tell mate it's time to change places on the nest.

Tremolo—Known as the laugh of the insane, a quavering call that is a sign of disturbance.

Yodel—Only the male makes this call. A slow, rising note followed by a series of repeated phrases the more it is agitated. Used when defending or establishing territory.

Hoot—Calm, soft, one-note call given by loons swimming near each other when fishing or when trying to keep chicks nearby.

Combination—This call is sometimes combined with wail. Always tremolo comes first. It may mean loons want to interact (wail) but for some reason feel threatened (tremolo).

*Tupper Lake Free Press Print:* August 12, 1998

# THE WHITNEY ACQUISITION

ONE OF THE FOCAL POINTS in the newly acquired William C. Whitney area located only 14 miles from this village is a section known as the Burn Road. Although this road is relatively new, the fact that it was built and used intensively by local residents and that it follows in places the former road bed of a long ago railroad line built and utilized by the Oval Wood Dish Corp., makes it historically interesting.

Under the present interim custody plan, Burn Road has been designated as a hiking trail. Only the International Paper Co., which has a short-term easement, Whitney Industries, which has access to Frenchman's Mine (sand and gravel), and D.E.C. administrative vehicles will be allowed motorized access. Bicycles are also forbidden until a final classification is completed.

The Tupper Lake and Long Lake town boards have passed resolutions that this classification should be "Wild Forest," which will allow a broader range of recreational use. In the meantime, if you are not fussy about what constitutes a hiking trail, you can walk along this wide gravel road to Rock Pond—distance eight miles, or to Lily Pad Pond—distance 8.2 miles. You can also walk to Camp Bliss, located on the Little Tupper shore, but hurry because the buildings there are scheduled for removal this month—distance 5.7 miles.

It is worth noting that the Whitney acquisition has 11 ponds lying in two major watersheds. Four of these ponds, which lie in the Raquette River watershed (Little Tupper, Rock Pond, Burn Pond and Louie Pond), as well as four which lie in the Black River watershed (Hardigan Pond, Frank Pond, Little Salmon Pond and Lily Pad Pond), are accessible by hiking the Burn Road. Despite the hype, even if you know the spring holes, most of these ponds have low density trout populations. The destruction of traditional fish barriers, such as existed at Touhey Falls and Nehasane Lake, have allowed undesirable migrants such as perch-bass to infiltrate these formerly trout-only waters (Adirondack Lake Survey Corp., 1985). Gill lice have been found to be present on trout in both Little Tupper and Rock Lake, where netting surveys also revealed low or fair abundance and only "limited significance as a fish lake" (Beatty–1950, D.E.C. Trapnetting–1991).

Shingle Shanty Brook, which as late as 1985 was a marvelous trout stream, is now dominated by small mouth bass (Potter Family, Brandeth). These are drastic fish community changes which many who knew these waters at an earlier time will find hard to believe. It is expected the D.E.C. will initiate reclamations and fish barrier efforts.

As the name implies, Burn Road got its name because it passes through large areas of burned-over land. You'll find fields of tall grasses, the regenerative powers in the soil that could produce trees having been lost to the searing heat of fire. Also seen will be exposed rock summits on low hills, its once accumulated mat of organic matter burned away and revegetation only slowly returning. Many fires have occurred here, and Mr. Whitney put observation towers on Salmon Pond Mountain and on Buck Mountain. These towers are still standing but are unmanned due to more effective aerial surveillance.

One such fire in 1913 started near DuMoulin's Banking Grounds in the ruins of an old lumber camp on Brandeth Park just southwest of the Burn Road. The old camp buildings and other debris provided perfect tinder for a conflagration that, aided by strong winds, devastated the surrounding forest for miles. It was thought that carelessness on the part of a nomadic lumberjack, who had slept in one of the buildings overnight, or, perhaps, the sun's rays through broken glass, were responsible for the resulting fire.

As Pauline Brandeth (pen name, Paul Brandeth) has written in *Memories of Albany Mountain (The Enchanted Stream)*: "This graveyard of a forest, once beautiful and gracious, lay about us and the sickly odor of charred woods only served to intensify the realization of irreparable loss."

Ms. Brandeth went on to say that "thanks to the faithful work of the hundreds of lumberjacks who had been toiling without permission for 24 hours, acres of forest were saved from going up in smoke."

Many of these lumberjacks were members of this community, working in camps run at the time by local jobbers Bill McCarthy, George Bushey and Alec Decheine. The boarding house at one of the camps was run by Paul LaPorte and wife. Incidentally, those lumbering operations were a great financial success. A reported price of $750,000 was paid for the softwood stumpage (in nine years they took out 350,000 cords of pulpwood) and prices rose during WWI from $5 to as much as $30 a cord.

If you walk along the sections of this Burn Road today, keep your eyes peeled for railroad spikes and old ties and rails. When local jobbers built this road (North, Giroud, Lizotte) they followed in some places the old railroad grade built and used by the Oval Wood Dish in 1935 to transport the first-growth hardwood they cut in the vicinity of Rock Pond.

Here again local jobbers were in charge of this operation, two of the contractors being Cornelius Buckley and Bert Franks.

The O.W.D. paid $3 per MBF for the hardwood stumpage which they high-graded, taking only 16-foot logs. The manager of Whitney Park at the time was Fred A. Potter, grandson of Dr. Benjamin Brandeth.

I have found that the people that I have spoken with in town are very well informed and hold strong opinions concerning the William C. Whitney area. They are aware that the area is flush with potential, but they also know its blemishes and its shortcomings. "It's been hammered," one knowledgeable lumberman told me. It would seem the majority of local opinion is that there needs to be more honesty in what determines a wilderness classification. Many people point out that Lake Lila, which is classified "primitive/wilderness," has been "beyond capacity" a number of times this summer. "It has become a miniature Rollins Pond," one fellow told me. "It is hardly a wilderness!"

Little Tupper, with its proposal for 80 waterfront campsites on what is effectively a 3.5-mile lake, will not be far behind in joining this characterization.

Note: It is 4.5 miles from headquarters launch to the head of the lake. It is not eight or ten miles as the spin doctors would have the public believe.

Since there are specific restrictions that campsites cannot be built within the unobstructed naked-eye view of the private inholdings (Camp Francis and Camp on the Point), you have—ergo—approximately 3.5 miles.

Little Tupper could become something of a petri dish in the ongoing experiment that has become known as the Adirondack Conflict. Let's hope it doesn't self-destruct.

*Tupper Lake Free Press Print:* September 02, 1998

## EAU DE BEAR

IT WAS THE STENCH THAT AWAKENED ME. A smell like a road kill that had lain in the hot sun for two days after being flattened by a car tire.

A stinking, disgusting odor so overpowering it causes you to gag and forces you to put your hand over your nose so you can breathe.

I struggled to open my eyes, crusted shut in what had been deep sleep, and fumbled for my headlamp. Oh, S--t! There in the light's beam was the ugly snout of a bear forcing its way through the netting of my solo tent door.

Two beady eyes, pumpkin orange in color, reflected in the light, glaring back at me, making the scene even more nightmarish and bizarre.

Some year ago, while hiking in Montana's Glacier Park, my daughter, Aimee, who was a Forest Service park ranger at the time and my companion and guide, had given me a pressurized vial of a substance called capsaicin. It was early spring, the grizzlies had only recently emerged from their dens, and huge tracks crisscrossed every snow field that we crossed. Backcountry rangers like Aimee routinely carried this mace-like cayenne pepper derivative as a last resort weapon in the event of a grizzly attack. That vial was in my personal kit, which lay somewhere alongside my sleeping pad, but I simply could not will my hand to search for it. I'd like to think that such immobility was because I was still groggy from sleep. The truth is, however, I was struck with fear, and the

*Ed Martin with his rogue bear. He could throw a can in the air and put two holes in it before it hit the ground.*

*Hungry or curious bear can be destructive. The camp shown is located in an old lumber camp clearing alongside Sucker Brook in the shadow of Rampart Mountain.*

only reaction I could muster was a scream. A scream so loud and so primal that the bear bowled over in a backward somersault. The bear was then lost to my flashlight beam until suddenly I heard a tremendous splash as the bear floundered across the stream in front of my tent site, and then a great thrashing and crashing as the bear ran headlong through the darkened woods and, as far as I know, is still running.

With adrenaline pumping furiously through my very core, I managed to slither feet-first out of the nylon womb that was my tent.

A fire was quickly coaxed into a violent blaze, the crackling and popping of the resinous softwood providing a certain comfort zone. Now fully awake, I chuckled to myself at the absurdity of having to share my sleeping bag with a stinking hulk of a bear in a tent that barely held room for me.

"Hey, Bill! How do keep a bear from charging?" Answer: "You take away his credit card."

If there is any merit in this encounter with the bear, it might be that bears are unpredictable. I was in a remote, seldom visited place. It was unlikely that the bear was what is known as "habituated"—a bear that has become conditioned to people and thus lost fear of humans.

I had cooked my supper yards away, downwind from my campsite. My provisions, mostly military M.R.E.s (meals ready to eat) in hermetically sealed pouches, were suspended 20 feet above the ground.

Perhaps the answer was just plain curiosity on the bear's part, or it was because I had inadvertently chosen a tent site that was on the bear's turf—his travel corridor?

A different situation exists in established campgrounds like Lows Lake, where designated campsites are within smelling distance of a Boy Scout mess hall. On the equally populated Lake Lila, where dozens of campers fill the air with aromatic scents of steaks and hot dogs as they prepare supper, these bear, unlike bear in wild places, have lost their innate fear. Their ransacking visits have become not only a nuisance but, in some cases, frightening, when the marauding bear refuses to leave. As noted, bear observers call these bears "habituated." Such bears often form a simple association—"people" followed by "food." A bear with this expectation is referred to as food conditioned. The combination of a bear that is both habituated and food conditioned results in the intimidating bear problems that we have heard about this summer.

There was a particular lean-to at Lake Colden where you could almost be assured of a nightly bear visit no matter how cleverly you "bear proofed" the site—that bear finally had to be live-trapped and removed—a technique consisting of a large steel culvert with a spring-loaded door and baited with a side of beef cooked with a blow torch to produce bear-loving odors. The problem with this maneuver is that often even releasing the bear hundreds of miles away, there is no guarantee (as has often happened) that the bear won't make a bee line back home. You are also giving a problem bear to others, and some feel that the whole stressful situation of being trapped, tranquilized, etc. makes the bear even more aggressive. Quite frankly, most rogue bears are now simply dispatched, which is just a euphemism for a dose of lead poisoning.

One resourceful (so they thought) couple who were camping on Hitchins Pond tried a different technique; they put their food supplies in their canoe and anchored it offshore. You guessed it! The bear swam out, swamped the canoe and really created a mess.

There is reported to be a relatively stable population of 4,600 to 5,000 bear in the Adirondacks. With the exception of those garbage or habituated bears, they are mostly timid and especially adept at keeping themselves well hidden.

Even local deer hunters, many of whom spend numerous days in the field, often with sophisticated scent concealment suits with activated charcoal impregnated in the fabric to absorb odor, and utilizing camo paint and tree stands, seldom, if ever, encounter a bear.

That is not to say that even wild, non-habituated bear don't visit the many camps in our area and become destructive. These invasions usually occur in the spring when the bear are ravenous from their long winter sleep (they are not technically true hibernators), or in the fall, especially if there is a poor berry or beechnut crop when they must accumulate fat stores before they den up.

A visit to some of these camps in the unoccupied offseason is a study in inventiveness (and frustration) as the camp owners seek to protect their camp. Bed springs nailed across windows, sharpened cross-cut blades laid along window sills, thick wooden shutters, moth balls suspended in netting and nailed to a building corners—you name it.

At one camp at a Follensby Park lease, broken glass shards were impregnated along window sills. Yes, the bear busted down the front door! He then turned over a large cooking range, tore the door off the propane fridge, and tipped over tables and bunks. To add insult to injury, he got his claws caught in a gallon of paint we used to mark trails and, in his gyrations to rid himself of the can, the lid came off and splashed paint all over the camp. Imprinted in the paint on the floor were his footprints that led to a hole in the side of the camp where he exited.

Two days later, Ed Martin, the camp's best hunter ("walk one, stop two"), who could throw a can in the air and put two holes in it before it hit the ground, caught up to a bear with paint-splattered fur and evened the score.

I once asked the late Dave Short, superintendent of Whitney Park, what he did to protect the dozen of outlying camps under his supervision. Dave told me that the single best deterrent to protect against bear vandalism was an electric fence such as used by farmers to keep their cattle from wandering. When Whitney youngsters were around those fences, he could disconnect the circuit, and the clicking of the battery-operated device alone was ordinarily enough to keep the bears away.

*Tupper Lake Free Press Print:* September 30, 1998

# THE LONG LONG LAKE

THIS PAST SUMMER JANE and Mike Arsenault of Long Lake turned their dream of owning their own business, being their own boss, and being in charge of their own destiny into a reality. Yes, they bought a store just outside the Long Lake village and named it Kickerville Mobil. The store they purchased is what is known in the food industry as a "C" store. C stands for convenience as opposed to super market and other descriptive categories.

As "C" stores go, the Arsenault store is A+. It is modern, clean, well-lighted, has excellent displays and a well-designed layout. An entire wall is devoted to floor-to-ceiling "visi" coolers containing an eclectic mix of beverages, some of which are not found other than in metro stores. The day that I visited the store the staff were bright, friendly and knowledgeable. It was a pleasure to stop there and I left the store not only impressed, but with the certainty that Long Lake's newest entrepreneurs knew what they were doing and would be successful in a very competitive endeavor.

Long Lake has a rich history which its residents are very aware of and cherish. The talented women's war canoe team, for example, named their beautiful vintage wood-canvas canoe the IN CA PAH CO. This was the Indian name for the lake because of the predominance of basswood (linden or popple) along its shores. Roughly translated into English, the name becomes Lindermere and for a time Lindermere was an early and poetic name for the lake. At one time it was also called Wide River, describing a

*Shown here is the former Sagamore Hotel on Long Lake. Built in 1889-1890, it was at that time one of the largest and most modern hotels in the Adirondacks. Your writer delivered many cases of Canada Dry ginger ale and soda water to its bustling beach casino. Note the double-ended guideboat in the foreground. This improved modification from the original square stern was influenced by Caleb Chase of Newcomb and Long Lake craftsmen. (photo from Bill Frenette collection)*

widened channel of the Racquette River, over 14 miles long and nearly a mile wide at its broadest point. This broadening has created one of the most beautiful lakes in the region. Its many islands, long sandy beaches and wonderful views of the Seward and Santanoni Range as you approach where the splendid Cold River joins the Racquette, mark it as unforgettable.

The name Kickerville Mobil, suggesting not only a sense of humor but of history. I couldn't help wonder, however, how many people would relate to this curious name. I quickly learned that people were interested in the whys and wherefores of the name and, if nothing else, it would certainly provide an interesting piece of historical lore.

Long Lake, you see, had grown up on both sides of a narrow of the lake (now spanned by the Route 30 bridge). An itinerant peddler visiting the west shore settlement, so the story goes, was not very well received and promptly named the place Kickerville. When he called the east shore settlement and found his reception was not any better, he gave that settlement the unflattering name of Gougeville! If the story were not largely anecdotal, that peddler certainly must have been a misfit, a real grouch, or both. I have never met a more wonderful, caring, honest, down-to-earth group of people than the residents of the village of Long Lake.

Recently, while hiking into Dog Pond to take in the last weekend of the extended trout season, I ran into a bow hunter. He was a native Long Laker and I was able to test my question on how many people would relate to Kickerville. His response was that the present Walker Road is still referred to by some old-timers as the Kickerville Road, and yes, his parents had often talked about Kickerville but he never heard of Gougeville.

He also told me that the west shore and the east shore settlements were first connected by a cable-operated ferry which was replaced in 1870 by a floating bridge (his mother had pictures of this bridge). Later a suspension bridge was built which was reputed, he had heard, as the longest single span in the state. During the Depression and later in the early 1940s, fill was added to create a causeway which eliminated Pine Island's status as a true island (today's Island Snack Bar) and allowed the present day shorter steel bridge that accommodates Route 30.

*Tupper Lake Free Press Print:* October 15, 1998

# THE LITTLE HIDDEN POND

IF YOU LOOK CLOSELY, the next time you travel to the junction you will spot a tiny pond almost hidden by the beautiful stand of pine that rings its shoreline (just beyond the Racquette Pond overview cleared by Mike Trivieri and before you reach the Aaron Maddox Hall).

The origin of that pond is perhaps less glamorous than other similar ponds which themselves emerged from under the grinding burden of glacier movement some 12,000-14,000 years ago, creating hollows where runoff waters could accumulate.

In fact, less than 100 years ago where the Demars Boulevard pond is now located was a rather large knoll or gravel bank. The road to uptown from downtown Demars Boulevard, which passed in front of that knoll, was only a gravel lane under water much of the time, and residents, rather than walk it, would rent a railroad handcar and pump their way over the railroad's track to the uptown railroad station (located in back of the present day library off Cliff Avenue).

So how did a gravel knoll turn into a lovely pond where a generation of youngsters would fish bullhead in the summer? Where in winter they would clear the snow from its frozen surface to play hotly contested hockey games? Or follow secret trails along the pond's wooded shores to Little Wolf Outlet where mountainous piles of sawdust could be climbed and the remains of the Santa Clara pulp rossing mill (1898-1913) could be explored?

Okay! You guessed it. When the Oval Wood Dish (O.W.D.) Corporation was locating its huge warehouse to accompany their production facilities, which, incidentally, was the largest plant ever erected in Franklin County (1916), they needed to fill in that swampy location alongside Demars Boulevard. This was the only location where fill was needed in the entire project, but early photos of the warehouse construction indicate that the fill around the foundation piers was almost eight feet deep.

The knoll behind the houses of 173-175 Demars Boulevard became the source for this fill! In 1967 the late Gerald P. Hull, who was closely identified with the Tupper Lake operation of O.W.D. from the outset, gave Louie Simmons historical notes of the O.W.D. operation, which included a description of how that fill was obtained and transported. Excerpts from those notes follow:

"The only piece of equipment which could be called even relatively modern by today's standard was a Raymond gasoline combined log loader and shovel which was mounted on some very crude caterpillars. The Raymond log loader, utilizing a drag line, loaded this into bottom dumping wagons.

"The machine kept about 10 teams of horses busy hauling gravel from the knoll to the warehouse site!"

The huge depression that resulted from the removal of the gravel subsequently filled with water and, supplemented by inflow from Racquette Pond, resulted in the ponds thus created.

Fifty-eight years ago, when I knew the pond best (my grandmother Simmons' home where I played and visited regularly was located next to the Presbyterian Church), the pond was much larger than it is today. Floating vegetation has encroached further and further until what was once one body of water is now several smaller containments. The large flower gardens with long rows of roses lovingly tended to by Mrs. W.C. Hull and her gardening staff are no more. The secret wooded paths are now fields cut regularly for their hay. A stark, impersonal modern sewage treatment plant has replaced the pioneer sawmill tailings and the easy access to the Racquette Pond shoreline and its sandy swimming spot. Only the pines along the shore remain. These pines weren't present during the fill removal in 1916. Perhaps that explains why they all appear to be the same height and age. Such stands start during a single season when conditions are just right for large numbers of seedlings to become established in a place free from overhead shade. The sandy soil that made such good fill has kept out the more rampant hardwoods. Thus, today you can walk through an uncluttered understory towered over by 100-foot pines. Here and there are stone steps leading down to crumbling fireplaces. A stone bench marks a place of meditation and spirituality which Mrs. W.C. Hull would walk to from her lovely home on Water Street.

Those ponds, so close to busy Demars Boulevard, are an anomaly and, like most anomalies, are transient. A few eons will see their end. In the meantime, enjoy them when you drive past.

Here in the spring as the first life of the awakened year appears, the Golden Eyes still land as one of the earliest ducks to return.

*Horse drawn dump wagons hauled gravel to the low lying area bordering the road. The till came from a gravel knoll in back of the Presbyterian Church. Back right is the church where services were held from 1901 to 1920. It later the parsonage and is now a private residence.*

In the fall, look for the geese that seek rest there on their long migration flight. You may want to reflect, too, of a proud past when over 600 hardy workers, earning $1.75 for a 10-hour day and employing only the crudest equipment, erected the sprawling Oval Wood Dish factory in an amazing two years.

A financially successful operation, the O.W.D. (named for an early product, an oval wooden dish) was to become the largest lumbering firm in the region. It was to also provide the biggest industrial impetus since the arrival of the railroads and sawmills.

In 1940, a peak year in the demand for the company's product line (clothes, pins, hardwood flooring, an innovative bowl-shaped wooden spoon called Ritespoon, etc.), employment reached almost 600 people and the valuation of plant and equipment was set at $2,500,000. They owned over 80,000 acres of forest land.

History will record that the Oval Wood Dish Corporation provided this village with a new lease to its survival at a time when its population was already beginning to go downhill. Indeed, it may well have been the main reason this community didn't share the fate of other sawmill towns like Brandon and Derrick.

It would be a nice gesture and be historically significant if the Demars Boulevard ponds could be named after the Hull family. It was, after all, their genius and entrepreneurial energies that sparked an operation that can only be described as remarkable.

*Tupper Lake Free Press Print:* November 18, 1998

# THE RENAMED HULL'S POND

IN OUR LAST COLUMN we made mention of the tiny pond just off Demars Boulevard and noted that it was created when fill was removed in 1916. Two things have occurred since that column appeared.

One, the Tupper Lake Preservation Society has framed a resolution to formally name the pond Hull's Pond in recognition of the family who own the pond and who were prominent members of this community. Applications will be made to the National Board of Geographic names in Washington D.C. and to local officials.

Secondly, I have received a wonderful letter from Catherine Grose, who now lives in Albany but grew up near "Hull's Pond." Cathy notes that her memories of the pond represent another generation (ouch!) who were endeared to that place as were the youngsters of my generation.

Cathy has graciously allowed me to share her letter with readers of this column. The "Water Street Gang" and other memories of which she writes represent a slice of our local history and I'm delighted to record it. It follows in its entirety:

*Dear Mr. Frenette,*

"Your wonderful article on 'Hull's Pond,' as we know it, prompted me to write to you. As you know, I grew up on Water

Street, adjacent to the then Gerald and Dorothy Hull home. Vivid and happy memories came flooding to mind when I read your column. I thought it would be nice to share some of these memories with you and let you know that at least one other generation enjoys a close affinity to this special place.

"The Hull property was beautifully maintained in those days. Dorothy Hull took much enjoyment in her gardens. I can still picture the magnificent rows of tulips eagerly viewed from our dining room bay window. The tall hedge row of trees separating the flower garden from the back field and earlier vegetable gardens held particular fascination for me. Beyond the back field one could enjoy a clear view of the ski slope, beautiful in any season. I might add that many a baseball game was played in that back field with the whole Water Street gang, consisting of the Tebo, LaVigne, Demars, Martin, Kiklevich, Beauchamp, Maroun and Grose kids, to name but a few.

"'Hull's Pond' itself was a particular source of enjoyment and wonder. Mrs. Hull would not only let us but would often join us kids in roasting marshmallows in the stone fireplace or enjoy our picnic lunch at the picnic table set there as well. I also clearly remember the stone steps leading down to the fireplace/picnic area. Some of the more hearty souls camped out by the pond in summer months. I must admit I was too afraid of the bears to venture camping out anywhere other than my own backyard in those days!

"As we got a little older, we began exploring the pond in earnest. Fishing, tadpoling and gathering cattails were of prime interest. In the winter we, too, would clear off the snow and enjoy our makeshift skating rink, bumpy as it was!

"I think the most magical and mysterious memory I have of 'Hull's Pond' is the stand of pine trees you mentioned in your article. For some reason this quiet place always stirred a wide range of emotions in me. The bed of pine needles was so thick and beautiful that it had a surreal quality to it. I clearly remember standing alone among those pines with no sound but the wind in the branches and feeling such a sense of spirituality. One of those special moments when you feel the power of nature in every fiber of your being.

"Last but not least, I want to thank you for your very informative and thought-provoking article. It truly brought back wonderful childhood memories! My best to you, Mrs. Frenette and family."

*Sincerely,*
*Cathy Grose*

*Tupper Lake Free Press Print:* December 09, 1998

# AN ENTREPRENEUR'S LEGACY

THE CURTAIN RANG DOWN with a thud of finality and to no ovation this week on a significant piece of Tupper Lake history. The last remaining buildings (over ten in all) of the A.A. Low Horseshoe Forestry Co. are no longer.

Vandalized, neglected, in total disrepair, their removal this week by an operations crew of the D.E.C. was long overdue.

Not only had the buildings in their deteriorating condition become an eyesore, their presence in the vocabulary of officialdom was considered "non-conforming."

Still, as one stands in the midst of the remaining stone walls left as a historical footprint by the wrecking crew, echoes from the past resonate throughout this beautiful spot. The fire-scarred cliffs of Hitchins Mountain still loom above as a giant protective rampart, and the Bog River continues to tumble by on its way to refresh and replenish the waters of Tupper Lake. Thousands of recreationists now and in the future will pass through those former "headquarters" grounds, many insensitive to or not aware of the remarkable activities that took place here. To a great many Tupper Lake residents, however, there are very strong connections, and those memories, even as ghostly echoes, will remain loud and clear. So let me say on behalf of all those with such memories: "Welcome canoeists and hikers to this special place, but please try to understand that our local connections may make us somewhat possessive. This is part of our community's historic past, so treat it wisely and lightly." Sadly, because there is no proper place to store or display memorabilia, many of the important artifacts concerning the A.A. Low operations have been lost to this community. A small collection (mailbags, photos, letters, labels, etc.) can be found in the annex of the St. Lawrence Historical Society in Canton. The Adirondack Museum in Blue Mountain has an especially fine collection that is displayed from time to time, and Piercefield museum is the recent recipient of the Jim Peck collection.

For those readers not familiar with the Horseshoe Forestry Co. or the Bog River Power Co. or Hitchins Corp., as it was also known, the following is an all-too brief summary of that enterprise, with thanks to Paul Jamieson, Ricky Vaillancourt, Howard Reandeau and especially Alvin Cote of this village.

A.A. Low became wealthy as a partner in his father's shipping and importing business. He fell in love with the area around this town and built a summer home near Robinwood on Bog Lake (many residents now have camps on this property under lease from the I.P. Co.). He continued to buy more land (40,000 acres) and built a permanent home on Silver Lake, which he renamed Lake Marion after his wife and daughter (Doug Crary is the present caretaker of this property, called Otterbrook, which is owned by Bishop Moore of New York City).

Mr. Low was an entrepreneur with great energy and talent and held many patents on his numerous inventions. He built a handsome railroad station at Horseshoe, floated logs down the Bog to his sawmill at Hitchins Pond, and later built his own railroad line. He built a three-story boarding house at Hitchins for his employees. Still visible today are the marble catchments over the springs, where he obtained and then bottled quantities of "Virgin Forest Spring" water for city markets. One year he produced more maple syrup than the entire production total of Vermont state.

A Chicago exposition blue ribbon for maple syrup quality hung for many years in the employees' building. He used the berries and other fruit from his cutover land to market preserves. He built a dam on the Bog to generate electricity, and when he needed more power, he built a second one. The lights were never turned off at Headquarters with the excess of electricity thus generated at a time when much of New York was still using generators.

In 1908 a devastating forest fire left his lands in ruins. At the same time the state won a lawsuit charging him with flooding state lands. That combination of events so burdened and depressed Mr. Low that he closed the operations of his empire and four years later he died. (Years later the lawsuit was reversed on appeal and his heirs were repaid the substantial fine plus accumulated interest!)

Somewhere around 1910 the Emporium Lumber Co. bought the sawmill equipment from the Horseshoe Mill and added it to its Conifer operation. The railroad line consisting of three spurs to the New York Central Main Line at Horseshoe ceased operating in 1911 (that rail bed now is a fine hiking and ski-touring access to Hitchins Headquarters, or Upper Dam as it is also known). The property was subsequently split up among other private owners (John Knox at Long Pond, Bishop Moore at Otterbrook, Robert Lehman at Robinwood, and the Hiawatha and Suffolk counties' Boy Scouts of America, etc.). The carry around the upper dam remained in private hands, and access by and large remained as it had been for almost a century, closed to the public. Then in 1985 the state purchased (in celebration of the Forest Preserve Centennial) 9,248 acres of Bog River Flow, which included the carry and the former headquarters (as it is known locally) and opened up most of the headwaters for the public to enjoy. It has become a widely acclaimed and popular canoe route and destination. Granted, its popularity may be troublesome at times, but on balance it has added to the ever-increasing reputation of Tupper Lake being the canoeing center of the Adirondacks. It also remains an important, colorful, and fascinating part of our local history. It is important, I think you will agree, that this aspect not be neglected or forgotten.

To its credit, region six of D.E.C. has shown understanding and wisdom in allowing some of the exceptional stone work to remain. Much of that masterful masonry was done by A. Duffy of Saranac Lake. Another mason was Jim Trombley of this village. In one of the cabins located at the north end of the Hitchins Pond Esker he constructed a foundation wall, a fireplace, and a chimney.

Mr. Trombley employed hundreds upon hundreds of river stones. Each stone is the same baseball size and of a beautiful hue and smoothness caused by millions of years of abrasive action by the Bog River's sand and flowing water.

Like a piece of fine sculpture or other great work of art, shame on us if we allow it to disappear.

"Human history" and "natural history" do not need to be in conflict as the future stewardship for this area goes under scrutiny before receiving its bureaucratic statutory imprimaturs (i.e. wilderness, primitive, or wild forest?).

*Tupper Lake Free Press Print:* January 06, 1999

# Y2K—A Time for Reflection

MILLENNIUM, MILLENNIUM, MILLENNIUM. The word is so ubiquitous lately that I've become slightly impatient hearing and reading about it. Incidentally, I'm not alone in this feeling. I detect the same "turn off" by members of the geriatric club (as they good-naturedly call themselves) during sometimes heated but always fascinating and good-humored discussions around coffee mugs almost each day at Stewart's and McDonald's.

What's the deal here?

With so many people already planning huge celebrations to welcome Y2K, why the lack of enthusiasm among some people? Is it a "grumpy old men" syndrome? I don't think so. Rather, it could be because many of these people are an average age of seventy years. They have lived through three-quarters of the century, whose end people are planning to celebrate.

There is a touch of sadness and nostalgia here, not unlike saying good-bye to an old friend.

This group represents a generation who came of age during the Great Depression and World War II and went on to build modern America. For most of the time, it has been a fun ride, an exciting, rewarding time of epochal transformations in world history and enormous advances in science and technology. Is it any wonder there might be more sadness than joy as the curtain closes on the 20th Century?

I will hasten to add that this feeling has a flip side. The third millennium also means that we celebrate the passing of a thousand years, and we can only hope the new millennium fulfills the promise of a "period of great justice and happiness on earth," as noted in the "Book of Revelation," so there will be celebration among us old timers for this significant event. Yes, there is also an awareness that 1,000 people of that generation die each day. We have reached the twilight of our lives, and if we are still here next January 1, 2000, then that alone might be cause for celebration. Hey! Only 327 days left!

I am compelled to add one more paragraph concerning that generation. Tom Brokaw, in his new best-selling book entitled *The Greatest Generation* tells it best:

"At a time in their lives when their days should have been filled with innocent adventure, love, and the lessons of the workday world, they were fighting in the most primitive conditions possible across the bloodied landscape of France, Belgium, Italy, Austria, and the coral islands of the Pacific. They answered the call to save the world from the two most powerful and ruthless military machines ever assembled, instruments of conquest in the hands of fascist maniacs. They faced great odds and a late start, but they did not protest. They succeeded on every front. They won the war; they saved the world. They came home to joyous and short-lived celebrations and immediately began the task of rebuilding their lives and the world they wanted. They married in record numbers and gave birth to another distinctive generation, the Baby Boomers. A grateful nation made it possible for more of them to attend college than any society had ever educated, anywhere. They gave the world new science, literature, art, industry, and economic strength unparalleled in the long curve of history."

By the way, have you been wondering whether the millennium starts a year from now or two years from now?

Some people say the 21st Century and the new millennium do not begin until January 1, 2001. Those people provide this analogy: "If the scale of our grocer's weighing machine began at one instead of zero, would you be happy when he claims he sold you six ounces of hamburger instead of the five you ordered? It is exactly the same thing with time. We will have had only ninety-nine years of this century by January 1, 2000. We will have to wait until December 31, 2000 for the full hundred."

That fact has not deterred people, however, and celebrations are planned around the world for January 1, 2000.

The Hotel Saranac, for example, recently announced that reservations are fully booked for its Y2K New Year's celebration. Over $50,000 in total prepaid reservations have secured the hotel's 92 rooms a full year in advance.

Our Lake Placid neighbors have plans for a celebration to last the whole calendar year. The year 2000 will be the 200th anniversary of the first Lake Place settlers, the 150th commemoration of the Town of North Elba and the twentieth anniversary of the 1980 Winter Olympic Games held in Lake Placid.

The following is a short list of some notable events that took place in this community during the past that might deserve commemorating:

- 1840—The Michael Charboneau family (aka Cole) became the first settlers. Population, 7.

- 1860—The first census. Population, 30.

- 1890—Tupper Lake leaves the Town of Waverly and establishes the Town of Altamont, becoming one of the youngest towns in the state. Population, 1,000+.

- 1890-1892—The largest sawmill in New York State and Hurd's Northern Adirondack Railroad combine to provide employment and Tupper becomes a "boom town." Webbs Adirondack and St. Lawrence Railroad arrives two years later and makes Tupper the most important junction point between Utica and Malone. Employment opportunities and the population soar.

- 1897-1900—A hundred years ago the first immigrants from the mountain town of Batuta in Lebanon arrive in Tupper. From an original seventeen in number, they and their more than two hundred descendants have become an important part of Tupper's history and are heavily involved in its future.

- 1899-1900—A hundred years ago optimism and confidence

replace despair as the village rebuilds itself after one of the most devastating fires in northern New York destroyed between seventy and one hundred buildings and left the business district in ruins.

- 1900—A hundred years ago, on January 20, 1900, Hose Co. #1 of the new Tupper Lake Fire Department of the Town of Altamont is founded.

—Downtown Tupper experiences an industrial boom as the Santa Clara Co. (Ferris Meigs) moves its substantial operations to the outlet of Little Wolf Pond on the shores of Racquette Pond off Water Street.

—Mt. Arab Lodge No. 847 Free & Accepted Masons become Tupper's oldest fraternal group.

—Tupper becomes the first Adirondack community to establish its own electrical system.

—Beth Joseph becomes the first synagogue in Franklin County.

—O.W.D. (1916) and Sunmount (1920) arrive and save us from becoming a "sawdust town" etc., etc., etc.

*Tupper Lake Free Press Print:* January 27, 1999

# THE TUPPER LAKE FLOW

SCOTT CHARTIER has a routine.

Even before breakfast each morning he sits before a telescope that is focused on what is known as "Moody Flow."

Scott's home, which he and his wife, Mary, have tastefully and skillfully renovated with subtle Adirondack Great Camp influences, is located on a rise close to one of the earliest settlements here, known as the Hathaway Farm.

Here, the Raquette River flows by Scott's front door just before it enters Tupper Lake. The river doesn't linger long here, but makes an abrupt turn as though repelled by the lake's more static waters.

Early writers called this section a delta after the fourth letter of the Greek alphabet which it resembled in shape. In the next mile or so it flows through what is known as the Sorting Gap, where once huge booms secured by stone cribs (several still visible today) contained the river-driven logs.

Local lumbermen working all day and through the night by the aid of torches sorted the logs according to the various lumber companies' brand previously placed on each log by a branding hammer. International Paper, for example, had the brand P, while the Sherman Company was a simple S. This short section of the river usually remains open in all but the most severe temperatures and is a magnet for all manner of wildlife.

That area and the marsh it flows through is the main focus of Scott's observations. The log book that sits alongside his telescope, in which he faithfully records his daily observations, reveals that he is seldom disappointed in locating some interesting aspect of nature's happenings. The "flow" is a dynamic place of interaction between plant and wildlife.

Indeed, his log book is replete with entries that include everything from a group of seven bald eagles feeding on muskrat carcasses to the fascinating encounter and standoff between a white tail deer and two coyotes. Otter, red fox, osprey, numerous types of hawks (including the rare hawk owl) hunting for muskrat and field mice have found in the rich plant life in the flow a Garden of Eden. Some "accidentals" that have been noted include pelicans, western grebe, cattle egrets, Virginia rails and, of course, all manner of waterfowl, including various sea ducks blown off course by heavy winds.

Mrs. Jack Delehanty Sr., who is a well-known birding authority and, like Scott, daily observes the activities in the flow, has recorded 83 different species of birds over the years, which she dutifully reports to the NY State Bird Foundation, noting that it is a "critical habitat in a world where such protection and sustenance is rapidly disappearing."

Such observations are important. For one thing, they play a vital role as a beacon to changes. They can detect early flaws happening to our ecosystem. Why, for instance, were there no cranberries found in the marsh this fall? Climactic changes? Is the quality of the water being degraded?

Why is Mrs. Delehanty suddenly observing so many ravens? Does this increase in her sightings mean an increase in our coyote population? Does it document interactions between species? Consider this interpretation: Ravens can't penetrate the carcass of dead deer for food. Coyote kills, which break the skin, make the meat available, thus more coyotes equal more ravens.

Finally, it proves what an important and valuable asset we have so close to our town. It is much more than a swamp. It is, in fact, a rich and diverse ecosystem niche defined there by animals and the plants they use for a marvelous, complex web of life, each strand being dependent on many others.

This system lesson, where the whole is seen as more than just a sum of its parts, is just now beginning to sink in. Scientists have just barely begun to trace the intricate crossing and anchor points of such a place. Most biologists will quickly tell you how important the "flow" is in terms of the plant life, many with valuable medical applications (some yet undiscovered), and that destruction of such wetlands by draining or filling may severely deplete ground water supplies, for the Moody Flow acts as a giant living biological sponge that collects water and slowly releases it into this area's network of ponds and streams. Beyond all that, and I don't wish to diminish those facts, isn't it also just kind of nice to know that the flow and its wonderful grass-filled, unique, lush appearance is part of this town's everyday scene? In a world of diminishing resources it does make you feel a little proud of where you live.

From a historical point of view, it may be of interest to note that the flow was once covered by a stand of fine timber. An early visitor (1849) named Hammond, who was the editor of the *Albany State Register*, described it this way: "Where the river enters, the land is high and bluff, here the eye falls upon a wide, green natural meadow upon which are thick foliated trees and, as you look upon it, you cannot persuade yourself that you do not see a broad and beautiful farm with extensive orchard and brave old elms left standing as shade trees when the woods were cleared away . . . but it is all wilderness, just as it has been for thousands of years."

Hammond camped on the shore that night. He also killed a panther the next morning, which he shot from a limb 30 feet above the shore of Raquette Pond.

That scene was to last until 1870, at which time the trees were cut for lumber and Potsdam lumber interests built a reservoir dam where the present Setting Pole Dam is now located. The dam was huge, over 10 feet above still water, 300 feet in length with 10 gates and 38,000 feet of cubic stone in its construction. The result was the flooding of lands for nearly 30 miles. All of the fine timber lining the shores were killed, transforming a beautiful section into a dead forest indescribably desolate in appearance.

*Tupper Lake Free Press Print*: March 24, 1999

## From Celebration to Concern

THE YEAR IS 1909 and Titus Meigs is sitting on the veranda of his summer home overlooking Follensby Pond. Mr. Meigs, of course, is the successful entrepreneur who in 1888 helped form the Santa Clara Lumber Company. He is also the great grandfather of Donald Clifford of Big Wolf, the president of the board of trustees for the fledgling Natural History Museum of the Adirondacks.

We can imagine that the day was a Sunday and, in what was probably a somewhat rare time in the normally busy enclave ringing with the shouts of grandchildren and visitors, Mr. Meigs found himself alone. Jim Trombley, his guide, and Angus, the chore boy, were out on the pond, well into Osprey Bay, baiting the lake trout buoy with a mixture of rice and perch chunks.

Mrs. Meigs and the household staff had earlier that morning walked to Teal Pond, a tiny kettle of impounded water where once a large, detached segment of ice became buried during the breakup of a glacier. When the broken ice finally melted out, the enclosing earth caved in over the spot, leaving a hollow that then filled with water. It was a boggy spot and Mrs. Meigs was there to collect cattails (Typha Latafolia).

In just two days the Meigs would celebrate their 48th wedding anniversary and a great party had been planned. The cattails would be soaked overnight in lantern oil and when ignited would be used as torches to add a festive air to the grounds and to guide the guests from the boat landing to the main house called the Birches.

One of the guests expected would be Dr. Ed Emerson, whose father was one of a group of notable intellectuals who had in 1858 spent the summer at the pond in a bark lean-to they called Camp Maple. Their guides have called this learned group the "Philosophers," and their colloquial designation was the one that lasted. Historians now refer to that celebrated spot as the "Philosophers' Camp."

As so often happens when alone and surrounded by the natural beauty of a place like Follensby Pond, Mr. Meigs found himself in a reflective mood. He thought of how well the Santa Clara Company was doing. His son, Titus, had joined the company direct from graduation at Yale and had proven himself an excellent leader and hard worker. Yes, he could be assured that the company would be in capable hands. The operation itself was blessed with exceptional employees. There was Joe Gauthier (Gokey), mill foreman; James Jacobs, who had only recently graduated from Annapolis and was a fiscal whiz; and Gene Bruce, forester and river drive foreman without a peer. In fact, Stewart Edward White, the famous author, had based his hero character in "Riverman" on the Santa Clara foreman. Also outstanding was Fred LeBoeuf, who succeeded Bruce when he went on to national stature in his field with the U.S. Forest Service. Pete LeBoeuf, Fred's son, and Alphonse Beaudette, his son-in-law, were also superior foremen on the various logging operations that contributed to the company's success.

This writer often "shared a pint" with Mr. Beaudette when in his later years he would visit the Grand Union Hotel bar. In his wonderful French-Canadian patois, he would tell me story after story of the Cold River operations. Mr. Beaudette was extremely laudable in his opinion of the father-in-law, whom he termed "the best woodsman ever." He once told me that the engineer Barringer might have been given credit for developing the Barringer Brake (a friction drum with cable to aid the horses in hauling logs down the steep slopes of Seward Mountain), but it was actually Fred LeBoeuf, unlettered but with innate engineering ability, who worked out the inadequacies of this braking system and developed it so it was functional.

As Mr. Meigs continued his reflections, he noted that the company had recently closed some excellent land sales that prompted him to smile. William Rockefeller had recently purchased 85,000 acres in Brandon. Cornell University, seeking to establish a College of Forestry, had purchased 30,000 acres of surplus land, with Axe-Town (Axton) as its center, for the princely sum of $165,000. In addition, the company had successfully defended the lawsuit in which the state had sued them for $550,000 claiming trespass of 2.270 acres in an area known as "The Gore" in Cold River country. (The state tried to claim it as unappropriated lands.)

Yet Mr. Meigs was troubled this early morning. The day before, John Hinkson, the guide and mailman from Tupper Lake, had detoured from his regular mail route and rowed his guideboat two and a half miles upstream from Tromblee's Landing on the Raquette to the Follensby outlet and then up the outlet to the middle of the pond to deliver a specially marked envelope.

Note: As a young man, John Hinkson had worked as a chore boy for Uncle "Mart" Moody at his Redside Camp Hotel (later the Waukesha). Uncle "Mart," through his friendship with U.S. President Chester Arthur, whom he had guided, had at Mart's request agreed to establish the first post office here on April 30, 1884. The President also appointed Mart as the first postmaster.

One of Hinkson's chores was to deliver the outgoing mail to Saranac Lake and to pick up the incoming mail from that community. He would row up the Raquette from this village to Tromblee's Landing, where, for $1, a wagon would transport him and his boat to Upper Saranac Lake (near the present Wawbeek Inn). He would then row down that lake to Bartlett's Carry, where, for fifty cents, a wagon took him to the middle and lower Saranacs, then to the Saranac Lake village, where for seventy-five cents he stayed overnight before returning with the incoming mail—a distance of some fifty-two miles! (In 1885, daily scheduled trips by the steam yachts "Altamount" and "Forester" to

Tromblee's would shorten this trip considerably.) John Hinkson would live to the ripe old age of 85 after a varied career such as crewman for state surveyor Verplank Colvin, lugging surveying gear to the top of Mt. Morris, and as a guide and accomplished boat builder. He died here in 1949.

Mr. Meigs' letter contained a confidential note from an Albany source warning that a proposal was in the planning stage for creating a dam with the Tupper Lake area as the focal point. The lake created by the dam would contain 180 miles of shoreline and would be the largest lake in the Adirondacks. It would submerge Follensby Pond, not to mention Ampersand Lake, Tromblee's, Axton, Litchfield lake holdings on Tupper Lake, and the Barbour Estate (American Legion Mountain Camp). Mr. Meigs' Albany source, history would reveal, was well informed and there was certainly cause for concern. In fact, four stadia parties from this village would begin testing surveys that very summer. I'll provide details of that project in the next column.

*Tupper Lake Free Press Print:* April 14, 1999

# BIG TUPPER GETS BIGGER

IN LAST WEEK'S COLUMN we made note of a proposal made in 1909 to create a dam and a reservoir that could store 10,300,000,000 cubic feet of water and produce 150,000 horsepower near Tupper Lake.

The late Louis Simmons, editor emeritus of the *Tupper Lake Free Press and Herald* and local historian for almost fifty years, felt that from a historical point of view the details of that project rated rekindling. What follows is from Louie's notes as contained in an article he submitted to the *Franklin Historical Review*, Volume 26, 1989. In his typical good humor, he entitled it, "Not Worth a Dam?":

"It was advanced by the New York State Water Supply Commission, and outlined at considerable length in its Fourth Annual Report to the legislature, published in 1909. The Tupper Lake area was the focal point in the proposal, which involved the water storage and power development potential of the Raquette River. Had it been carried to completion as planned in its early stages, it would have made downtown Tupper Lake a cross between Atlantis and Venice—largely under water—and inundated camps along the shores of Big Tupper Lake and other area waters, as well as homes in low-lying sections of the uptown village.

"The project 'died a 'borning,' and its details have been largely forgotten, but from the historian's point of view, they rate resurrections.

"The engineers envisioned a reservoir area in that stretch with a storage capacity of some 10 billion cubic feet by raising the present level of Tupper Lake area waters about 28 feet. That could be accomplished, they found, by adding 15 to 20 feet to the height of the existing dam at Piercefield, or 10-12 feet to the height of what was left of the old reservoir dam at Setting Pole Rapids below Raquette Pond.

"Either stop would have involved some serious problems, they found. 'If either of these dams was to be built it would submerge the little town of Faust (post office designation then for downtown Tupper Lake) and inundate the New York and Ottawa Railroad for a distance of about four miles. Also it would flood the present site of four large sawmills, with their lumber yards and trackage facilities, and inflict considerable damage on the lower margins of Tupper Lake village.' The report prudently added that while these injuries could be repaired by moving the structures to higher ground, "the cost involved is obviously so large as to render it a very serious obstacle."

"We appear to be driven to selection of the narrowest part of the strait, which connects Big Tupper Lake with Raquette Pond," they reported. Their reservations regarding that site are understandable. What had once been a timbered flat, mostly above water, had been turned into a 'stump-covered morass' by flooding when the reservoir dam was built at Setting Pole Rapids, where test borings to a depth of 90 to 100 feet failed to reach rock bottom. Terming it "altogether a forbidding place for a dam site," they could find no better alternative and added that, considering it offered greater water storage potential than all the others combined, it 'seemed to justify extreme measures.'

"Their plans for the dam indicate there were no ribbon clerks among the survey party, whose engineers conceived a monumental project, even by today's standards. They chose for its site the narrowest point of the strait, extending from near the lower section of the present Rock Ridge housing development in uptown Tupper Lake across to the promontory on the west shore. The design called for digging a trench in the mud and silt of the river bottom, from the middle of which sheet piling in three tiers,

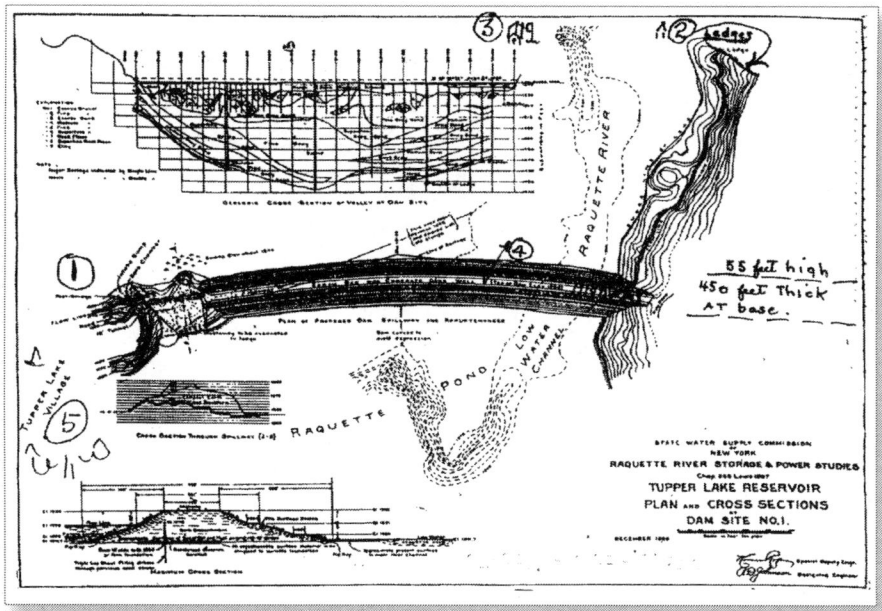

1) Chalmers Point (Rock Ridge Development)
2) Bluffs near Morlows Point
3) MacDonalds Boat Livery
4) Highway across top of dam
5) Tupper Lake village
The dam is 55 feet high and 450 feet thick at the base.

bolted together, would form a water-tight bulkhead driven into the sand. The trench would then be filled with an impervious and tightly packed soil, further strengthened by a curtain wall of reinforced concrete rising to the top of the dam and extending throughout its entire length. On that foundation and with a concrete core, the earth embankment was to be constructed, making a dam 55 feet high, 450 feet thick at the lowest point of the base, 220 feet thick at the water line and 100 feet thick at the top. A masonry spillway would be built on a solid rock foundation at the easterly end of the dam, and provision was made for the necessary gates and a log run to accommodate the spring log drives down the Raquette River, still in progress here in 1908 and for many years thereafter.

*Beavers were the first dam builders. Incredibly at the turn of the century there were less than 15 beavers in the Adirondacks. The efforts of people like Edward H. Litchfield who in 1901 liberated a dozen beavers on his private park help save Castor Canadensis from extinction. (Most of Mr. Litchfield's beavers escaped to the Raquette River system where their numbers steadily increased. They became know as the Litchfield beavers.)*

"The engineers reported that timber in the area to be flooded had already been mostly removed by lumbering or rendered worthless by the great forest fires of 1903 and 1908. The reservoir lake the dam would create was to cover some 15,800 acres—about four times as large as the present Big Tupper Lake and 15 times the size of Raquette Pond. It would have been the largest lake in the Adirondacks, with some 180 miles of shoreline, and have substantially increased the navigable mileage open to the few shallow-draft steamboats that operated on Tupper waters 80 years ago.

"The magnitude of the project is pointed up in the 1909 report. Construction of the dam would have necessitated rebuilding nearly 17 miles of road between Tupper Lake village and Wawbeek, Axton, Ampersand Lake, Tromblee's and Follensby Pond, which would have been submerged. It would have required moving, or rebuilding on higher ground, 172 buildings, including one church, one school, three hotels, 68 dwellings, 14 barns, 57 outbuildings and 28 boathouses. A map prepared by the State Water Commission of the Moody area at the foot of Big Tupper

Lake showed the home locations of many Tupper pioneer settlers which would have been flooded out, including Martin Moody, Jabez Alexander, Colonel William Barbour, Pliny Robbins, Fred Moody, Jim Minogue, Richard S. Gile, J.T. Johnson, C.E. Hathaway and George McBride.

"In addition, the camps and summer homes of many would have to be moved to higher ground, including, on the Big Tupper Lake, the Barbour estate (later the American Legion Mountain Camp), and the Levey, Sprague and Stern camp developments, among others; the lakefront holdings of the Edward H. Litchfield private preserve; the Titus B. Meigs estate and others on Follensby Pond, and a tract of 1,333 acres bordering and surrounding Raquette Falls. The report also noted that some 4,400 acres of state land would also be flooded if the dam became a reality.

"Conceding that 'some inconvenience would doubtless be caused' by the proposed dam, the report said 'the strength of the opposition which is bound to come from some quarters, also the amounts which will be appraised for damages, will depend on the importance which these matters will assume in the public mind. How far the creation of a magnificent lake, which will be larger than any other of the Adirondack plateau and at the same time will be unique among all the beautiful lakes of that region for the notable irregularity of its shore line and the number of its islands, the increased scope of navigation by pleasure craft, and improved transportation will go toward reconciling the permanent and temporary dwellers of that section to the annoyance and moving back their homes and rebuilding their boat landings, and to the minor inconveniences due to periodic variations of water level cannot be foretold at this time.'

"The best laid plans of mice and men, including state engineers, 'gang aft a-glee'… it's interesting to speculate on why a plan which promised major benefits—flood control, development of cheap and dependable hydroelectric power, improvement of navigation and replacement of swamp areas by attractive lakes—never got off the ground. The engineers did an impressive job, starting in the early spring of 1908 with a survey of the Raquette River from

Norwood to the river's source. It was nearly August before the corps of three stadia parties of seven men each, a smaller party of four or five men for the special work, borings, triangulations, etc., was in the field. Nearly all the topographical work was in the woods, where experienced woodsmen had to cut and clear lines for the surveyors and tote in subsistence supplies.

"The great forest fires of 1908 seriously interfered with the work, a dense pall of smoke bringing all operations to a standstill at times in September and October. The entire survey was completed on November 5th, and by December 23rd all notes had been reduced and plotted at the field headquarters in Tupper Lake Village, the corps was disbanded and engineer Erwin E. Haslam and his assistants returned to Albany to complete mapping and put the work in shape for permanent record.

"What killed the reservoir dam project? Probably a combination of factors. Apparently it was a little ahead of its time. Electric power demands had not yet progressed to the point where they would warrant construction of a network of dams. The 'forever wild' concept for the Adirondack Park may have stirred opposition, and the owners of those 172 buildings, which would have had to be moved to higher ground or rebuilt above the flood level, as well as others whose property would have been affected by periodic variations of water level, didn't agree with the survey notion which spoke of these as 'annoyances' and 'minor inconveniences.'

"We wrote the New York State Division of Water Resources in Albany while preparing these notes, but received no answer to our inquiry as to what the deciding factor was in abandoning the project. It is interesting to speculate on what effect the availability of abundant and cheap hydroelectric power would have had on the development of this region if the dreams of the engineers 80 years ago had been a reality. If nothing more, it would have spared homeowners and business interests the 'adjustment factor' tacked on to electric bills in recent years to pay for the costly nuclear power which has virtually doubled those bills."

*Tupper Lake Free Press Print:* April 21, 1999

## BILL'S MORNING WITH A DOVE

IT WAS SOMEWHERE AROUND the year 1966 when I first heard it. It was a sound that always started at the first blush of dawn. That wasn't the only reason it was disturbing, it also was a non-relenting, continuous ooah-cooo-cooo-cooo-cooo, a remorseful kind of call. It was no sound to greet the new day and I found it extremely irritating, quite aside from the fact that it was waking me up so early each morning.

    Finally one morning I could stand it no longer. I would track down this nuisance. Should I take binoculars or my shotgun? I didn't have to travel far from my house before I located the source of the plaintive call. There sitting on a telephone wire was, of all things, a PIGEON!

    Now, pigeons were fairly common around the village in those days.

    The cavernous, high-ceiling, steel-girded buildings of the then abandoned Oval Wood Dish factory, with their broken windows, were home to hundreds of pigeons. Also, dozens of pigeons daily collected under the marquee of Billy Donovan's Park Street movie theater, feasting on the popcorn spilled or discarded by movie goers. This pigeon, however, was different. It resembled pictures that I had seen of a bird called a passenger pigeon, but as far as anyone knew, the very last passenger pigeon died in a Cincinnati zoo in 1916. At one time, I learned, it had been the most abundant bird in the world. Nearly eighteen inches long, handsome in pastel shades of blue,

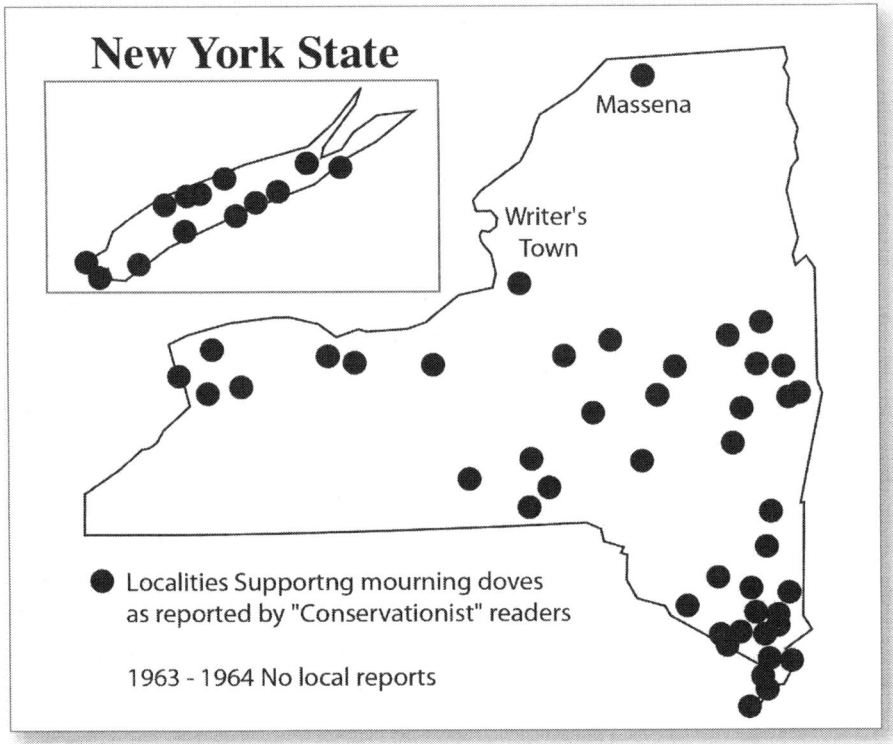

gray, rose and brown, it swept across the sky in immense flocks that sometimes contained billions of birds literally blotting out the sun for hours, almost as if an eclipse had occurred during their passage.

It has been reported that when they gathered to roost for the night, they broke great limbs from forest trees with the sheer weight of their numbers, and the sound of their wings and the noise of their settling could be heard for miles.

Could this be a passenger pigeon?

How could a bird that numbered in the billions upon billions disappear without a trace? Could a few survivors have found refuge in the Adirondacks?

A phone call to Mrs. Jack Delehanty, Sr., arguably the community's leading bird authority, provided the answer. Mrs. Delehanty informed me that I was probably seeing (and hearing) a mourning dove. Also variously known as a "turtle dove," a "wild dove," or a "rain crow."

She also told me that it does resemble the altogether extinct passenger pigeon, and it is often mistaken for that bird, so often, it seems, that ornithologists take little interest in announcements that such a pigeon has been seen. Mrs. Delehanty further informed me that seeing a mourning dove this far north (1965) was most uncommon. Please note that the mourning dove is now (1999) very common in this locality. As an untrained observer, I'm not sure why this is so, except that we now have more open areas (clear cuts, storm damage, etc.) interspersed with trees and woody shrubs that are essential habitat for a sizable mourning dove population. What I do know is that their sudden appearance is significant from a historical as well as an ornithological perspective.

So, while I still personally find its continued call at the first light of day to be annoying and to sound like hopeless sorrow and remorse (unlike, I'll admit, some folks who find it to sound like tenderest love and devotion), isn't it nice to know that this area has provided a sanctuary that allows the bird to hold its own in what was a declining population?

Remember, only a few years ago E.H. Easton, in his two-volume edition of *Birds of New York State*, outlined the doves' distribution, thus "the mourning dove is fairly well established in all parts of New York State excepting the northern portion above 1,000 feet in elevation, where it is rather uncommon. It is occasionally found about the borders of the north woods as at Lake George, Old Forge, Ausable Forks, but is more characteristic of the . . . warmer portions . . . than the cooler districts."

In 1965 no reported observations were made in this locality.

So—welcome, mourning dove. Now you know why we humans find this such a great place to live! You will recognize this dove by its call (ooah-cooo-cooo-cooo). It looks like a pigeon but is slimmer, smaller in size, and has a long, pointed tail. Oh yes, that whistling sound heard so often lately at dusk . . . that's the doves' wings making a whistle that can be heard for up to 200 yards or more. The call, by the way, is performed primarily by unmated males to attract females and establish a pair bond. Once paired, they will remain together throughout the breeding season and perhaps for life.

Fifteen years ago, I ran into a deer hunter who told me that the only game he had seen that day was a wild turkey. When I stopped laughing, he told me that he was from Pennsylvania, and "by gosh, I know a turkey when I see one."

Today local residents are feeding and observing wild turkeys on their front lawns. Local wildlife specialist Jon Kopp and his colleagues at D.E.C. don't bother (unless it has a collar) to record moose sightings any longer because they are so plentiful.

Turkey vultures, a bird that not long ago was uncommon, if not rare, in this locality, now contend with numerous bald eagles over the road-killed deer carcasses put out as food and attraction. Canadian geese have become so plentiful (and prolific) that they have become a problem nuisance on lawns and docks.

Some wildlife like the blue bird has made a comeback because we have stopped poisoning it with D.D.T. and other toxins (thanks to Racheal Carson), but the sudden appearance of other wildlife to our region represents dramatic wildlife changes. What the implications are, I'll leave to the experts.

*Tupper Lake Free Press Print:* May 26, 1999

## SCOUTING THE RAQUETTE

TWENTY-FOUR YEARS AGO, twenty-three Boy Scouts, five adult leaders and ten aluminum canoes embarked on the well-known canoe route on the Raquette River that would take them from Long Lake to this village.

One important purpose of the trip was to enable the boys of Troop 75 from Delmar, NY to earn 50 miler awards. The BSA 50 miler award is given to a scout who completes a 50-mile trip by his own locomotion: on foot, by canoe, etc.

The Long Lake-Raquette River Tupper Canoe route, along with side trips and one portage, provides ample mileage to fulfill the requirements, especially if you include an ascent of Kempshall Mountain, located on the eastern shore of Long Lake about five miles southeast of the village.

What follows are excerpts of that trip as written by scout leader Norbert J. Kirk, which appeared in the May-June 1976 edition of the *Conservationist*. Hopefully, it will be of special interest to readers of this column, particularly the fine reception Troop 75 received from the friendly people of our village. . .

"Anyone who plans on taking the Long Lake to Tupper Lake canoe trip should consider camping at least one night at the northeast tip of Long Lake, just a few hundred feet from the Raquette River entry. There, he will find an exquisite campsite shaded by tall pines, bottomed by a perfectly laid pine needle floor, and fronted by a sandy beach. There are also several good bets for productive nature walks, including an easterly trail that goes straightaway along a land finger pointed toward the river. Gradually, the finger narrows to a peninsula bordered on two sides, respectively, by Long Lake and river backwater area, with the river itself straight ahead. It was in the river backwater area that we saw several deer feeding along the edge just before dusk—and not far away, a heron standing almost elbow deep in the water. A good score for such a short walk.

"The Raquette River is perfect for a beginner to learn canoeing. In the beginning, its greenish waters move lazily northward, giving ample time to instruct young scouts on the fine points of various paddle strokes. Then, after about a mile, all heads perked up at the beginnings of a stronger current. Instead of the greenish water, we were gliding into deep black holes or trying to dodge pebbly, sun-dappled shallows. It wasn't whitewater canoeing, but it was active, strategic canoeing—for about three-quarters of a mile.

"Farther down the river, as we approached our next camp, the river banks began to get higher, the background on both sides began to rise with hills and small mountains, and the pines began to reappear.

"It was at that river campsite that most of us learned about duff fires for the first time. The dictionary defines duff as a thick flour pudding boiled in a cloth bag. In the woods, however, duff refers to masses of pine needles, loose dirt, and tree roots, both living and dead, that form soft, spongy pine needle floors frequently found along rivers. Since duff does not hold very much moisture for very long, it presents a fire hazard.

"Our object lesson in duff fires involved one patrol's cook fire set up near the river bank where a larger pine leaned out over the river. One of the scoutmasters called everyone around the fire and pointed to smoke coming out of the ground in three or four places anywhere from six inches to a foot from the fire perimeter. He then went on to explain what duff was, pointing out that a fire can burn downward into the duff as well as up into the air. Someone asked, 'What would happen?' One thing was that the duff fire could burn and kill the roots of the nearby pine, eventually send-

*Boy Scouts and their leaders at the upstream side of Raquette Falls. A carry of a mile and one quarter around the falls lies ahead. (photo courtesy of Mark Dempf)*

ing it crashing into the river. Under very dry conditions, another possibility was that it could erupt into a surface fire. By the way, it takes gallons of water to really knock out a duff fire.

"The only portage on our trip was around the Raquette Falls area. The over-land distance was about one and a quarter miles. We had planned for two hours at the most, especially since we had eaten considerably into the weight of our gear and were now mostly into dehydrated foods. The fact is, the portage took an entire afternoon, with everyone making three trips. In our miscalculation of time and effort, we learned a number of things, including:

*Aluminum canoes are heavy, and an unladen 15 or 17 footer should be carried by older boys or younger adults with other gear.

*Haversacks with community supplies are likely to be too heavy to be carried by anyone but adults.

*Smaller boys cannot (and should not) carry very much at all, although they can easily make the same number of trips as everyone else.

"The saving factor was that the older scouts were able to motivate the younger ones to keep pace in good spirits. It was one of many good examples of peer leadership on the trip.

"On the last leg of the river, nine of our canoes got lost in the Oxbow area, an involuted combination of tiny islands, inlets, cross channels, and at least one endless circle of wide river—in short, a maze. Our mistake was to permit canoes to paddle out of sight of each other, especially since the last canoe had the only map. Some canoes accidentally made the correct turn and reached the entrance of Simond Pond, the gateway to Tupper Lake, not knowing whether they were in the right place. The last canoe (with the map) didn't know where anybody was. Eventually, everyone got together, and the adult leaders vowed we would not separate again. The scouts weren't worried a bit.

"The Oxbow maze presented us with some unexpected rewards. It is a birdwatcher's paradise, and probably a fisherman's paradise, too, although no one sampled that. Among other things, we saw a heron in flight, a heron wading near the shore, and numerous smaller waterfowl that we could not identify. At one point, we had a water snake keeping up with our canoe for a time. And finally, the blooming water lilies added an ultimate touch of beauty and serenity.

"The mile across Simond Pond was the toughest paddling we encountered. We had to head directly into a stiff wind and make progress on water laced with whitecaps. When we reached the highway bridge at the other end of the pond, the wilderness spell was broken. We suddenly saw cars, trucks, buses, and even buildings of Tupper Lake Village.

"Although we didn't know what the alternatives were, a few of us walked the two miles into Tupper Lake Village. At the suggestion of a resident we asked permission from the Tupper Lake police to camp in the town park. They said we could and, as a result, Troop 75 of Delmar had a bash of a Friday night. First, a short and easy paddle through the shoals of Raquette Pond to the town beach. Then, a quick swim and setting up a camp in a designated area of the park. Meanwhile, a small delegation was sent to the supermarket for fresh meat, fruit, milk, bread, and plenty of candy and soda. After supper, there was a town softball game to watch, and there were stores in town where the scouts could spend their water-logged money on ice cream and more candy. At the time, Tupper Lake Village was the greatest place on earth.

"And so was home when we arrived there the next day."

Note: The Raquette River canoe route continues to grow in popularity. Phil Johnstone, operations chief of Region Five D.E.C., Raybrook provided this column with the following statistics for the year 1998:

Number of people who signed the register—6,300. Ben Woodward, interior ranger at the Falls, estimated five percent of that number were hikers and another five percent probably represented people who arrived via the horse trail on horseback. Given a factor of 50 percent for those who didn't sign in, the estimated number of canoeists passing through Raquette Falls carry would be close to 10,000 for the 1998 season!

*Tupper Lake Free Press Print:* May 19, 1999

# ROMANCE, MYSTERY AND MURDER IN THE ADIRONDACKS—PART ONE

AT THE TURN OF the century, before drug therapy replaced older regimens, the village of Saranac Lake was known as the "Town of Second Choice." That second choice was given to people with tuberculosis when it was discovered that the Adirondack air, purified by pines and other conifers whose aroma it was thought destroyed organic matter, and which was also notably dry, when combined with institutional rest offered a cure to what at that time was considered an incurable disease. Indeed, as Saranac Lake's reputation as a place where many "hopeless" cases found their disease arrested, a large sanatoria industry took place and grew. (In 1920 there were over 150 cure cottages run exclusively for the sick. These cottages cared for the 2,000 patients who were in the village.)

In 1922 a fateful decision for the future of Saranac Lake was made by some doctors, who were the most powerful men in the village. William Chapman White, in his regional study called *Adirondack Country*, put it this way: "The Veterans Administration proposed building a 500-bed hospital just outside of the village. For various reasons, some logical and many fearful, the influential doctors prevailed on the Veterans Administration to build that sanatorium elsewhere. It was built eighteen miles down the road at Tupper Lake, where Sunmount Hospital has been an important factor in the economic life of that town. For that decision many of the townspeople never forgave the doctors, no matter how well-reasoned their arguments."

Thus the opening of Sunmount and the depression of 1929 started a downward trend in the future of the cure-cottage industry in Saranac Lake. Up until that time, of course, a high percentage of those thousands of patients who came to Saranac Lake got well and saw their disease arrested. A number of those people stayed on as residents, many of them famous and wealthy, and Saranac Lake became a "cosmopolitan center in miniature." Readers of this column who are old enough may well remember that there was a certain "snooty" feeling by some Saranac Lake residents toward the French-Canadian lumberjack town of Tupper Lake in those days. To its credit, by virtue of its various and many accomplishments, Tupper Lake finally escaped that ill-founded attitude, but not before it persisted for a number of years.

That having been noted, point out that many patients stayed only long enough to get well and moved on. Among those patients was an individual named Myron Newman, also known as Meyer or Myer Neuman. Newman or Neuman, who was from New York City, left Saranac Lake in 1902 and migrated to this village. He had lived here for four years when he bought a rambling three-story hotel on Park Street, which had been built in 1890 and at that time was called The Globe. The name was changed to Alta Cliff Cottage (this was apparently a very fancy name designed to attract customers. In reality, it was a run-down hotel. The top story was later removed and it was converted into, and has since served as, a two-apartment building. Having escaped the 1899 fire, which destroyed so much of downtown, it must be one of the oldest buildings in the village).

If you drive past the former Alta Cliff Cottage today, the road goes sharply up to the Rock Ridge development. In earlier times an access road contoured left around that "Rock Ridge" and led to a quarry owned by the Town of Altamont. (In 1916 the quarry was given gratis to the O.W.D., which mined it for two years during construction of their plant here.)

Mr. Neuman and his "hotel," like so many others, would most likely have faded into obscurity if it were not for a fateful and tragic turn of events.

It began on a rainy July day when Neuman and his waitress, Clara Greenwood, returning from a shopping trip in the village discovered a young couple sitting on the hotel veranda.

The young man was well groomed, slightly handsome, and well spoken. He introduced himself as Charles George and wife and asked for a room.

He explained that they had just arrived on the six o'clock train from New York and had taken a stagecoach driven by Dan MacDonald from the Junction Station.

Myron Neuman was reluctant, even suspicious, but when the young man claimed (this was a lie) that he had written ahead for accommodations, Neuman finally agreed to take the couple in for the night. That night turned out to be the last night the attractive young "wife" would spend on this earth. Her real name was Grace Brown, pregnant and unmarried, who thought she was on a wedding trip. Her "husband" was not Charles George but Chester Gillette, the preppy, social-climbing nephew of the owner of a shirt factory in Cortland, New York, where he had met Grace when both worked there. Chester Gillette was planning murder, not matrimony, when they visited this community. A murder that would horrify and fascinate millions of people (even today) and would become Upstate New York's most famous murder case. It would later become the basis for Theodore Dresiser's classic novel, "An American Tragedy" as well as the movie "A Place in the Sun" with Montgomery Cliff and Elizabeth Taylor.

Meyer Neuman, his waitress Clara Greenwood, and Daniel J. MacDonald, the local livery owner, would become star witnesses in the murder trial held in Herkimer, New York. The national press would carry sixteen-page supplements that contained their testimony, and Tupper Lake and the Alta Cliff Cottage soon became famous. A fame that might well have led to the kidnapping and the disappearance (despite ransom paid) of Meyer Neuman later in his life. We will follow that testimony given in the Herkimer County Courthouse as it relates to this village in our next column.

*Tupper Lake Free Press Print:* June 23, 1999

# ROMANCE, MYSTERY AND MURDER IN THE ADIRONDACKS—PART TWO

IN OUR LAST COLUMN, we wrote of an attractive, well-groomed young couple who were sitting on the veranda of the former Alta Cliff Hotel, located at the west end of Park Street in this village. They had just arrived on the northbound train from Utica and were seeking accommodations, waiting for owner Myron Newman to return from shopping in the village.

Mr. Newman, you may remember, was from New York, where his family ran a highly successful jewelry business. He had moved to Tupper Lake from Saranac Lake, where he had been seeking a cure for an asthma condition. He had apparently hoped to turn what had been called the Globe Hotel, a rambling three-story building owned by Barney Seigel, into a cure cottage. Mr. Newman had changed the name to the more fanciful Alta Cliff Cottage. Today, the third story has been removed and it survives as an apartment building. Mr. Newman would later be quoted as saying that "he had been schooled in the ancient Chinese art of feng shui" (pronounced fung shway).

He immediately sensed that something was amiss with this couple. The vibrancy, the joie de vie that in classical fen shui terms (I am told) should have been sending a yang (male) yin (female) balance just was not present. Reluctant and suspicious, he nonetheless allowed them to stay.

The young couple, it would turn out, were Chester Gillette and

Grace Brown (Chester had given false identities). They were star-crossed lovers whose fateful story of romance and murder would soon be front-page news throughout the nation and the world.

The story begins in Cortland, New York. The year is 1908. There, Chester was learning the shirt business in this uncle's plant. On the side, he had also managed to become "intimate" with one of "the help," a slender, dark-haired beauty called by her friends "Billie" Brown. Their romance, torrid at first, had soured and become complicated. Chester, the handsome, preppy social climber, had tired of the relationship. Grace had become a burden to his lifestyle and career. Grace, for her part, fiercely loved Chester and, worse yet, she discovered she was pregnant.

You don't often hear the expression today, but at that time and for years to come, a girl who was unwed and pregnant was said "to be in trouble."

It was a monstrous problem and it was, indeed, a big-time trouble. From a historical perspective, it is perhaps difficult today to appreciate fully the predicament in which Grace was trapped. Should her problem have become public knowledge, she would be treated as a social outcast.

With the threat of stigma hanging over her, she could confide in no one—not her parents, who would feel outraged and hurt; nor her companions at the factory, who were too casual with secrets; nor a counselor, for in that day there were none. There was of course the clergy, but whether Grace dared to share her secret with a minister is doubtful and, in any event, he could offer as solutions only prayer and marriage.

Grace may well have resorted to prayer, but marriage was more elusive. It appears there was no way Chester was going to marry this girl he had "got in trouble." That gave him several alternatives: run away to some new place, refuse to marry her and accept the consequences, or deny the relationship and blame the pregnancy on someone else. All of those options only invited scandal and threatened his lifestyle and social standing. The final option that could have occurred to Chester was to get Grace out of the picture permanently.

Grace, at this July date, was now beginning to show signs of her pregnancy. Chester was dating other girls and acting like nothing was wrong. Grace was desperate and constantly in tears. She pleaded with Chester to go on a holiday to someplace remote, like the Adirondacks, where they wouldn't be recognized, where they would have time together to resolve the problem, and where she could hopefully convince Chester to do the proper thing and marry her. Chester agreed, but while Grace was thinking marriage, Chester was planning murder when they randomly picked out Tupper Lake on a railroad timetable as their destination.

The train ride from Utica to Tupper Lake was considered one of the most beautiful in the state, passing through largely unbroken wilderness. Many of the stations along the way were really only platforms where gravel roads bordered the tracks, and horse-drawn buggies arrived to greet each train and take passengers to nearby camps and large hotels that were splendidly isolated on the shores of beautiful lakes.

If Chester had thought that Tupper Lake was to be an isolated platform station like Horseshoe or Sabattis, he was in for a surprise. In 1906, Tupper was a rough and tumble lumbering center with a growing population of around 3,600 people. "A frontier town where murder was committed in the stable to save cleaning the barroom floor," as noted in an article in the New York State magazine, the *Conservationist*.

After talking his way into accommodations, Chester and Grace had dinner and then went for a walk "into the main part of the village and up onto a hill from which they could see the lake." Whether it was because there were too many people for Chester to carry out his murder plans or because they didn't like the view and the surroundings, they decided to leave the next morning.

The hill that the couple climbed that evening is now the location of the Judy Churco home (Tallman Hill). Today it commands an astonishing view. Attractive Racquette Pond lies below, and the long ridge of Matumbla Mountain dominates the landscape beyond.

What Chester and Grace saw that evening, however, was a

Racquette Pond full of stumps, deadheads, and downed timber. The smoke from the seven boilers of Hurd's "Big Mill" would have diminished any view. Small wonder she was disappointed!

In retrospect, it was obvious that the relationship between the couple was reaching a crisis. Clara Greenwood, the young local girl working as a waitress at the Alta Cliff, would later testify in court that the next morning, as they were getting ready to catch the southbound train back to more remote Big Moose, Grace went to Clara and "threw her arms around her and burst into tears."

Once outside, they waited on the sidewalk for Dan McDonald's livery carriage to take them to the Junction Station.

Across the street, young 11-year-old Eddie Timmons* and his mother watched Grace follow behind Chester, crying bitterly. Yes, things were not going well at all!

Conclusion of this article follow in the next *Transitions* column.

*Interview by Dr. Joseph Brownell, professor of geography at the State University of Cortland, with Police Chief J. Edward Timmons, September 4, 1977.

The primary source for this article is "Adirondack Tragedy—The Gillette Murder Case of 1906" by Professor Brownell and Patricia Waurzaszek, 1986, Heart of Lake Publishing.

*Tupper Lake Free Press Print:* August 04, 1999

# ROMANCE, MYSTERY AND MURDER IN THE ADIRONDACKS—PART THREE

IMAGINE, IF YOU WILL, the following scene: A somewhat frail, but a very attractive and oh, so, so very young girl is standing on the curb outside of Myron Newman's Alta Cliff Cottage, located at the west end of Park Street in this village. It is July 1906. The girl is crying uncontrollably, quite near hysteria, the tears pouring across her face as though the heavens had opened, releasing a torrent of rain drops. Did she have a presentiment that this was to be her last day on this earth? What had transpired the night before when she had shared a bed with her lover for what would be the very last time? Had the lad refused to do the gentlemanly thing and marry her, as she so fervently wished? For was she not with his child, unwed and frightened and beginning to show signs of her pregnancy in an unforgiving society that marked the mores of that time?

We will never know the answers to those perplexing questions because no written record exists that could help us. We can only speculate. It would seem, however, that the girl's elusive hope for marriage, which had flared briefly like a nova, was now dark.

Let's quickly note that the original intent of this three-part article was a modest attempt to show what it was like in this community in 1906 through the eyes of two visitors on vacation. The residents worked diligently to recover from the disastrous fire that only a few years before had virtually leveled their town.

That episode must perforce, go to the back burner. It suddenly becomes more compelling to follow the tragic paths of Grace Brown and Chester Gillette, the two visitors, as they board the southbound train at the junction to travel to remote Big Moose Lake, forty-four miles away, by rail.

Briefly, then, it is known that upon arriving in Big Moose, the couple rented a boat described as a St. Lawrence skiff. This is a boat not unlike a guideboat. It is a bit heavier with a wider beam and more stable and, like the guideboat, is propelled by oars.

Big Moose was (and remains) a beautiful lake about a mile wide and four miles long. Cottagers along the lake remember seeing Chester and Grace in several different locations about the lake that fateful day. They were last seen entering Punkey Bay; no other boats were in the bay at that time, about six o'clock in the evening.

Exactly what happened in that bay will probably remain a mystery forever!

The facts that are known for certain are that Grace ended up at the bottom of the lake with a gash across her forehead (and, according to some reports, a loose tooth). Chester ran away into the woods without telling anyone what happened. The boat was found floating upside down with Grace's black jacket on the keel. When all the evidence that was known then and is known now is taken into account, it is very difficult to believe that Chester was not somehow responsible for Grace's death. This, according to Craig Brandon, who has meticulously researched this tragedy in his non-fiction book entitled "Murder in the Adirondacks." Gillette certainly had a sufficient motive and had much to gain by Grace's death. Brandon states: "Whether he verbally abused her to the point that she jumped out of the boat or actually struck her or just threw her out of the boat and let her drown makes little difference morally. He was responsible for the death, no matter how it occurred. But legally, the difference between letting her die and planning her death in detail was the difference between life in prison and the electric chair."

During the last ninety-three years, dozens of people have tried to find once and for all how Grace died that day but so far the proof has eluded them. There is proof that Chester swam to shore and then walked six miles to the Eagle Bay community along the present-day Big Moose highway. He then went to the public dock there and boarded the steamboat "Uncas." Chester was only on the steamboat a short time before getting off at the next stop, the Arrowhead Hotel at Inlet at the end of Fourth Lake.

At this point in the story, we can only ask ourselves, "If he was innocent, why didn't he tell someone about the drowning?" Instead, he registered at the Arrowhead and used it as a vacation base. Twice he climbed Black Bear Mountain. Once he canoed to Seventh Lake and visited Cortland girlfriends he knew were in the area, and he dined at Seventh Lake House.

Meanwhile, when the rented boat didn't return to the livery the next day, the steamboat "Zilpha" lit off its boilers and started a search of the lake. It circled the lake, periodically blowing its whistle, a standard procedure to guide persons lost in the woods back to the lake.

When the overturned skiff was discovered in South Bay, the steamboat secured and began to search the water. "The thirteen-year-old purser of the tiny forty-foot steamer was Roy Higby. Peering over the side, Higby spotted a white blob in the dark waters of the bay. Men in row boats grappled for the sunken form and hauled on board the steamer the body of the dead girl. It was Grace Brown." The crew searched the rest of the day, but, of course, there was no sign of Chester, his suitcase, his tennis racket, or his umbrella. After receiving the coroner's report about the bruises to Grace's head and a tentative conclusion by the coroner of "foul play," a land search was started to find Chester. It didn't take long. Two days after the drowning, using good detective skills and by some lucky breaks, when Chester stepped out of the dining room of the Arrowhead Hotel, Herkimer County undersheriff Austin B. Klock stepped up and arrested Chester Gillette, aka Carl Graham, for the murder of Grace Brown. (Sheriff Klock had accompanied district attorney George W. Ward from Herkimer. George Ward was a lawyer of considerable courtroom skill and a healthy political ambition, with his eye on the post of county judge. There was much to be gained from the publicity surrounding the prosecution of what he sensed could be a sensational murder case. He was to be 100 percent correct in that assumption. The trial was soon front-page news throughout the nation and the world.)

Chester spent the next four weeks in a Herkimer jail cell. Next came a three-week sensational trial.

"He struck her over the head with a tennis racket and tipped over the boat," argued the prosecution.

"Saying she was going to end it all, she jumped into the lake," contended the defense.

"Gillette got scared and fled."

"Guilty as charged," said the jury.

The sentence: Chester was to be taken to Auburn prison and put to death by electrocution.

On March 30, 1909, the signal was given and the electrician at Auburn Prison closed the switch. Chester was jolted by 1,800 volts at seven amperes. After one minute, he was declared dead.

Postscript

1) Meyer Neuman (Alta Cliff owner), Clara Greenwood (waitress), and Dan McDonald (livery owner) all of this village, were called to Herkimer as witnesses in the sensational trial held there at the Herkimer County Courthouse.

2) Meyer Neuman later moved to New York City, engaged in the family owned jewelry business, and disappeared, apparently killed in a kidnapping after the family tried unsuccessfully to deliver the $10,000 ransom demanded.

3) George Ward won the county judge position. Later, he went into private practice and was a prestigious member of the Herkimer community.

The primary source for this article is "Adirondack Tragedy: the Gillette Case of 1906" by Joseph Brownell, Patricia A. Wawrzasezek, 1986, Heart of Lakes Publishing.

*Tupper Lake Free Press Print:* August 18, 1999

# It's a Small World After All

TWO WEEKS AGO MY daughter Mimi and her husband, Cliff, both from Durango, Colorado, and this writer pulled our canoes from the Salmon River at a tiny settlement called Shoup in Idaho's Frank Church River of No Return Wilderness.

We had just completed a nine-day river trip down the Salmon's middle branch. One of the original eight rivers designated Wild and Scenic (1968), the middle branch flows 106 miles northeast through one of the deepest gorges in North America. It's a route of continuous rapids (over 100 in all), many of which are downright intimidating. Fortunately, I had Mimi, a nationally ranked paddler, in the bow of the our white-water canoe and Cliff, a former Utah river guide, helping to pick the proper course in the more difficult sections that required thorough study and scouting to avoid the holes and cataracts that have flipped eighteen-man rafts end over end. Rapids with names like Powerhouse, Pistol Creek, Haystack, and Redside to name a few. The kind of rapids that make you nervously bite your lip, give you a sick feeling in your stomach, and push your heart rate beyond the max. The kind that makes you wonder if you perhaps shouldn't have gone to church more often. The kind where you hope God doesn't think you are a hypocrite as you mutter a silent prayer before you enter the maelstrom, asking that He lets you make it through safely. Moments of anxiety aside, and ignoring a discussion of what causes us to express some deep-seated need to take risk and to

*Thermal springs found hidden above the river corridor provides blissful therapy to tired muscles. (Bill Frenette collection)*

*Deep in the unchartered West, Touissant Charbonneau leads his captive wife, Sacajawea, and infant son, Jean Baptiste, across the Mandan Indian country. (Bill Frenette collection)*

participate in activities close to the metaphorical edge where danger, skill, and fear combine to give us a sense of pushing our personal boundaries, the river we ran is beautiful.

The water is an emerald green and so clear you can see the bottom in twenty feet of water. Honed by wind and water over thousands of years, the canyon walls rise high and bold from the river's edge. The river itself rushes like a run-away train through the Big Horn Crags among the most rugged and wild mountain ranges in the nation.

If that were not enough, it also has numerous, narrow sand beaches for camping, many with hidden hot springs of warm mineral waters to soothe aching muscles and revitalize clammy and cold feet soaked for too long in the frigid river water that had splashed into our open canoes.

All too soon, it seemed we found ourselves entering the main Salmon, and at a take-out called Cache Bar we unloaded our gear and tied our canoes on Mimi's station wagon, which had been left there by a shuttle service.

We were reluctant to leave the river, having achieved, we felt, just the kind of alchemy that such trips, whether we know it or not, often are designed to engender.

Our first stop after leaving the river was a traditional one for Salmon River paddlers. A small general store just upstream from the take-out which advertises itself as making "the thickest milk shakes available anywhere."

The owner turned out to be an attractive girl in her late thirties. She could have been straight out of a Louis L'Amour western novel. Lanky but graceful in her movement, she was wearing a wrist bracelet of stunning turquoise gem stones, and a wide belt fastened with a large buckle on which was welded a caliber 45 silver bullet that held up a pair of loose-fitting carpenter jeans with deep pockets and a hammer loop. The jeans were tucked into a pair of well-worn, hand-tooled cowboy boots. Hanging from her belt was a mini mag flashlight in a holster, a sheathed leatherman tool, and a pager.

She appeared the quintessential rugged individual who holds our imagination as a symbol of the wild west.

I soon learned that the modern gadgets on her belt were due to her being not only the owner of the Shoup Store, Cafe and Cabins, but she was also an outfitter and the resident paramedic in Shoup, Idaho, population 60.

As you might suspect, business in the cafe was not like McDonald's during lunch time, and between spoonfuls of milk shake, I was able to engage her in conversation: "The backboard and the stokes litter behind the counter?" She was also the river medic, she informed me. "Had she lived here long?"

"Yep!" came the reply. "All my life, born here. Family came to these parts around 1880." Seems a fellow named Bill McKay discovered lead in the dump of a badger hole on which he had sat down to rest while hunting stage horses. The result was a mining boom that created the Viola Mine and attracted her great grandfather. It became one of the richest lead mines in the world, but when the mine ran out, so did most of the 3,000 inhabitants who had been lured by the discovery. But her ancestors had stayed. "No regrets, Mister. I love it here. Clean air, clean water, unsurpassed mountains, great fishing and hunting. This is the last frontier." Sensing my interest, she pulled up a chair, straddling it backwards like she was riding one of her horses, which filled the corral in the rear of the store. Looking me straight in the eye, she threw out a question, half query, half informative: Did I know that the first white men to come to these parts were members of the Lewis and Clark Expedition? She explained that the explorers were seeking a contact with the native Shoshoni Indians in order to obtain horses to enable the expedition to cross the mountains as they sought out a route to the unmapped Pacific Ocean.

"It was a well-known fact," she continued, "that the Shoshoni Indians had taken horses from the Spaniards in earlier times." During their winter stay at Fort Mandan in 1804, the explorers discovered a young Shoshoni squaw who had been captured when about eleven years of age and sold as a slave to an enemy tribe. At fifteen years of age, she had become the wife of a French Canadian trapper named Charbonneau. In order to secure her services as an interpreter, Lewis and Clark induced Charbonneau to join the expedition.

# It's a Small World After All / 153

When the explorers finally found the Shoshonis, the Indian girl who came to be known as Sacajawea joyfully recognized the place of her birth and her own people. (Unable to speak English, Sacajawea suddenly began sucking her fingers and dancing with joy among these people who had suckled her as a baby.) When she was called to the council to interpret, she recognized the Shoshoni chief as her brother, afterward called Cameahwart. This remarkable coincidence together with the promise of future trade for the white man's goods were what induced the Indians to supply horses for the journey over the mountains and the eventual success of the expedition.

At this point, our new friend paused to take a sip of black coffee flavored with a splash of Jim Beam. My own hometown pride refused to be stilled and I interjected that I was fascinated by her stories and to be informed that I was sitting near the birth place of Sacajawea was not only exciting but slightly incredible, particularly because there was a connection: Touissant Charbonneau was the uncle of Michael Charbonneau, also originally from Eastern Canada and Tupper Lake's first settler! I went on to explain that I also lived in a special place where some of the rivers still ran free and wild and the mountains, while more gentle than her Bitterroot Range, were also spectacular in their own way. I wanted to tell her more about the Charbonneaus, but just then Mimi gave me a gentle kick under the table with the suggestion that "Dad, we have a ten-hour drive to Boise and if you want to catch your flight to Chicago, we had better hustle along." Reluctantly, I agreed, and we made our goodbyes and thank yous for what had been a pleasant and informative half hour with a very interesting and charming young lady from Shoup, Idaho, birthplace of Sacajawea, the bird woman, captive wife of Touissant Charbonneau.

Next column: Sacajawea is chosen as the main image of the new silver dollar due out in a couple of months.

*Tupper Lake Free Press Print:* September 08, 1999

## Tout est Prêt

"TOUT EST PRÊT," thus did Pierre Cruzatte indicate that "all is ready" as he prepared to run the boiling rapids of the unmapped river. Pierre, as you probably know, was a member of the Corps of Discovery, the expedition charged with finding a route across the continent to the Pacific Ocean.

The Indians living along the river had told the expedition's leader, Capt. Meriwether Lewis, that is was impassable, but Pierre, undaunted by this warning, was willing to try. Would you agree that he probably said something like, "Tabernac, am I not the best boatman, the most fearless and skilled river man of all the expedition members?"

A trait, it should be noted, that would characterize other French Canadians, like those who immigrated to our region and became renowned for their daring ability to run logs flushed through the white water of local rivers. Men with wonderful names like Gerard Arsenault, Alphonse Beaudette, Napoleon (Nap) La Bonadventure, Jean Boudreau, and let's not forget Mr. Hache (Zeno) drove rivers near here right up to the last major drive in the spring of 1950, when Finch Pruyn ran pulp down the upper Hudson.

By the way, as a part of our local history, it may be interesting to note that the transporting of logs by rivers had its origins here in the Adirondacks. Two lumbermen, the Fox brothers, drove the Schroon River on the current of spring freshets in 1813. An experiment that proved successful for many years, right up until the time that trucks like those beautiful machines in Jeannel Lizotte's outstanding fleet and improved highways would supersede the rivers as arteries of transportation and make such a method obsolete.

Perhaps in a later time with improved craft like jam boats or the high-sided, double-ended dory type that Zeno Hache would have been familiar with, the expedition would have made it down the river.

However, despite their best efforts, they found the passage impassable, especially in their hand-hewn dugout canoes.

Capt. Clark named the river The Lewis. Today it is called the Salmon, also known as The River of No Return. (Not in the sense of finality, but only because once you go down, it is difficult to return upstream.)

Clark's journal tells of their dilemma: "The water runs with great violence from one rock to another on each side, foaming and roaring through rocks in every direction so as to render the passage of anything impassable."

They would have to go on horseback. There could be no turning back. President Jefferson had picked them personally for this mission, and they were determined to fulfill that directive. Remember, in that time the United States ended on the eastern backs of the Mississippi River. The West remained an immense blank. To add urgency to their commission was the fact that President Jefferson had just made a surprising deal with Napoleon Bonaparte, who was preparing for another war with England. He had purchased the entire Louisiana Territory, 820,000 square miles, for three cents per acre. With a single stroke on his pen, the President had doubled the size of his country. Lewis and Clark had to find out just what it was Thomas Jefferson and our tax dollars had purchased.

Yes, it was an exploration for the sake of scientific knowledge, but it was also one of imperialism, according to some historians. The President wanted unchallenged possession of the new and huge country he had just purchased from France. The Indians were soon aware of that fact, and while some were friendly

*Pierre Cruzatte boatman in the Lewis and Clark Expedition is shown in the stern with Captain Clark in the bow of their dug-out canoe. (Bill Frenette collection)*

(thanks, in part, to Sacajawea), many tribes were hostile.

Peter Lourie, who is a seasonal resident here, followed the trail of the expedition this summer with his family (Melissa and children Walker and Suzanna). They went by foot, by car, by horseback, and by boat in what had to be a special and rewarding family adventure. While in Kamiah, Idaho, where the corps had been met with "generosity and courtesy" by the Nez Pierce tribe, Peter talked with Allen Slickpoo, who still follows the traditional ways of his ancestors. Peter noted that "Slickpoo was not bitter but the message was strong—Lewis and Clark brought death to the Nez

Pierce way of life. They had opened the way for the missionaries that came a few years later and took away much of their culture."

"It is like a beautiful plant or berry," Slickpoo told Peter, "and you are starving. That fruit looks nice and plump, but then you eat it and it turns out to be poison."

As readers of this column know, the explorers would make it to the Pacific and return safely. They faced bitter cold, sickness and hunger, a nightmarish trip across the Rockies, where they nearly perished, hostile confrontation with Teton Sioux Indians, desperate fights to the death with the Blackfeet, the unknown vastness of the plains and the raw power of raging rivers. It would take them two and one-half years to travel the 4,200 miles from the mouth of the Missouri across unmapped mysterious lands to the Pacific Ocean. These deeds of the men of the Corps of Discovery would stand forever. Their exploits would become an American legend, a part of our history. Others would follow. But they were the first, and never again would the West be the same.

Expedition member and translator Toussaint Charbonneau was originally from eastern Canada and uncle to Michael Charbonneau, who was this community's first settler in 1840.

Toussaint stayed among the Indians of the upper Missouri the rest of his life. He interpreted for government officials, explorers and artists well into his seventies. Sacajawea, his wife, remained with him. In 1809 they traveled down the Missouri to St. Louis, where they entrusted their son, Baptiste, and his education, to Capt. Clark before heading back upriver.

Sacajawea
In 1812 at Fort Manuel, a fur trading post in what is now South Dakota, Sacajawea gave birth to a daughter, Lisette. But that winter she grew ill with fever and died. More about Sacajawea in our next column.

Baptiste Charbonneau
After being educated by Clark as promised, Baptiste, who was born during the exploration and was carried on his mother's back,

never settled down. He traveled to Europe with a German prince for five years, learning several languages. When he returned, Baptiste became a mountain man, not unlike his father and cousin Michael. A guide for the United States troops in the war with Mexico, a magistrate of San Luis Key mission in California. In 1866, at age sixty-one, he heard of gold discoveries in Montana and set on with a wagon train, but died of pneumonia on his way.

Cameahwait, chief of the Shoshones and Sacajawea's brother, was killed in a battle with the Hidatsas, which may have been the same tribe that earlier had taken his sister captive.

*Tupper Lake Free Press Print:* October 06, 1999

## SMALL TOWN ON A LONG LAKE

IN THE EARLIEST OF TIMES it was called Lindermere. A rough translation from the Indian word In-ca-pah-co. It was called that because of the prominence of basswood or American linden on its shores.

Perhaps you remember the elegant thirty-five-foot war canoe with In-ca-pah-co neatly lettered along its hull and paddled by the talented women's team of, yes, Long Lake, as Lindermere is known today.

The same vigor and dedication that characterized the women seated in that canoe continues today among Long Lake residents. As is well-known, the community has gained the admiration and, indeed, the envy of all who are aware of its many successes in building a very pleasant and busy village. It can boast an excellent school system (they pay their teachers well) with an incredibly low student-to-teacher ratio and a high rate of success among its graduates. It has a first-rate medical facility (it attracts young, vigorous, outdoor-loving MDs) and an excellent fire department and rescue squad all located in a vibrant community with honest, sincere, wonderful people. There are approximately 800 year-round residents in that enterprising community, but the town itself consists of an area covering 448 square miles, making it the second-largest town area-wise in New York State. For a time, the closing (temporarily it is hoped) of the nearby National Lead Company's titanium operation in Newcomb due to cheaper

## A Friend To All Who Were Friendly

*Long Lakers were especially welcome to the mayor of Cold Rivers Hermitage. A young Ed Wallace, left, and J.A. Emery were rare visitors in this early 1934 photo. On November 7, 1950 the Helms Aero Service flew Rondeau to Plumbleys, at the head of Long Lake, where he hiked the remaining eleven miles for the last time to his baliwick on Cold River. (Vincent Engels photo)*

## Bridging The Gap
*In 1870 a bridge replaced a cable operated ferry to link Long Lake's narrows. Later a suspension bridge was built (then the longest single span in the state). Fill to the present Island Snack Bar and a short modern bridge gave todays improved approach. Also shown Mrs. Kellogs lake' house (now Hotel Adirondack). (E. Bierstadt photo)*

extraction costs by competitors abroad, impacted local employment opportunities. There was also a sense of personal loss to those who had been employed there as loyal and productive employees for many years. Fortunately, however, other employment opportunities were available. The Adirondack Museum, a ten-minute commute, employs thirty to eighty people (over half of those numbers are, of course, seasonal). Twenty minutes away, Sunmount Rehabilitation Center in Tupper Lake employs over 700 people, and in the same town the O.W.D. has a payroll of over 250 people. Four correctional facilities with a forty-five minute commute also offers employment opportunities. That's just a glimpse of what's available. The point is, it is possible to live in a small town and still find stable (and improving) compensation that will allow you to stay.

Long Lake was one of the earliest settlements in this region. The first settler being Joel Plumley around 1830.

In 1841, there were already eight or nine families (most of whom were from New England) who had found their way to the shores of that beautiful lake and established the beginnings of a settlement.

The names of those early settlers are of great interest, if only because most are familiar today, 158 years later. Names that belong to prominent residents who are direct descendants of those adventuresome pioneers. Those eight or nine families below:

Joel Plumley
David Keller
James and Robert Sergeant
William Kellog
Zenos Parker
William Austin
Isaac Robinson
Lyman Mix
Burton Burlingame

For many years, hampered by its isolation from easy access, the prospects of growth in Long Lake were grim. Until around 1918, the only way to get there was by water. That ruled out even light industry. There was precious little horizontal land, so farming was not a real option. What it did have were beautiful mountains, restful, gorgeous lakes, and secluded ponds.

Thus, if "progress" seemed to be passing them by, it turned out that the very "lack of progress" became of enormous attraction as the "quality of life" revolution started in the 1970s.

The community saw scores of newly retired people and parents not wishing to raise their children in hostile surroundings of the ever-sprawling cities. Increased leisure time on the part of people now only hours away on the Northway from the population centers where they lived also created an influx. And, yes, C.E.O.s from the corporate world who with their Sony Vaio laptops could now conduct their business from modernized gazebos or tea houses transformed into virtual offices equipped with video conferencing and e-mail capabilities. No longer did Father have to reluctantly leave the lake and family on Sunday so he could catch the next day's 5:40 a.m. out of Westchester.

Long Lake has become for many an "oasis from insanity," as one recent transplant termed it. The discovery that many people had known for years (and were not all happy to share) was out!

Howard Frank Mosier, the fine regional novelist writing about Vermont's Northeast Kingdom in his most recent book, *The Fall of the Year*, has one of his characters, Mr. Moriarity Mental, saying: "There's one thing we have to give those small towns. The wonderment ain't all been leached out of them." And in Long Lake there is still all kinds of wonderment.

*Tupper Lake Free Press Print:* December 15, 1999

## DID YOU KNOW? FUN FACTS AND TRIVIA

READERS OF THIS COLUMN are, no doubt, aware of this writer's weakness for trivia. Hopefully, after the chaff was weeded from the wheat, so to speak, a snippet or two were of interest and contained at least a modicum of history.

Fortunately, the editor allows me a certain carte blanche, and so in this last column of the year 1999, I'm going to avail myself of the opportunity to expand my penchant for trivia. To those who have read this far, my best wishes for a Merry Christmas and a prosperous and, even more importantly, a healthful New Year as we enter a new century. I also hope you are trivia fans.

Did you know . . .
- The first couple to be shown in bed together on prime-time television were Fred and Wilma Flintstone.
- Coca-Cola was originally green.
- Every day more money is printed for Monopoly than the U.S. Treasury.
- The Hawaiian alphabet has twelve letters.
- Men can read smaller print than women; women can hear better.
- The city with the most Rolls Royce's per capita: Hong Kong.
- The state with the highest percentage of people who walk to work: Alaska.
- The cost of raising a medium-size dog to the age of eleven: $6,400.
- Intelligent people have more zinc and copper in their hair.

- The world's youngest parents were eight and nine and lived in China in 1910.
- The youngest Pope was eleven years old.
- The first novel ever written on a typewriter: "Tom Sawyer."
- Each king in a deck of playing cards represents a great king from history. Spades, King David; Clubs, Alexander the Great; Hearts, Charlemagne; and Diamonds, Julius Caesar.
- Hershey's Kisses are called that because the machine that makes them looks like it's kissing the conveyor belt.
- The Eisenhower interstate system requires that one mile every five must be straight. These straight sections are usable as airstrips in times of war or other emergencies.
- The name Jeep came from the abbreviation used in the army for the "General Purpose" vehicle, or GP.
- No NFL team that plays its home games in a domed stadium has ever won a Superbowl.

How About This…

The nursery rhyme "Ring Around the Rosey" is a rhyme about the plague. Infected people with the plague would get red circular sores ("ring around the rosey"). These sores would smell very badly, so common folks would put flowers on their bodies somewhere (inconspicuously) to cover the smell of sores ("a pocket full of posies"). People who died from the plague would be burned so as to reduce the possible spread of the disease ("ashes, ashes, we all fall down").

Facts…
- What occurs more often in December than any other month? Conception.
- What separates "60 Minutes" on CBS from every other TV show? No theme song.
- Half of all Americans live within 50 miles of what? Their birthplace.
- What do bullet-proof vests, fire escapes, windshield wipers, and laser printers all have in common? All were invented by women.

- What is the only food that doesn't spoil? Honey.
- What day has more collect calls than any other day of the year? Father's Day.
- What trivia fact about Mel Blanc (voice of Bugs Bunny) is the most ironic? He was allergic to carrots.

*Tupper Lake Free Press Print:* December 22, 1999

# A Little History of Snowmobiling

ONE EVENING LATE THIS FALL I was sitting with some fellow hunters in the main room of an especially fine hunting camp. The large wood stove, consisting of two 55-gallon drums, one placed above the other, was throwing out a wonderful hot white warmth. The stove was burning ash, which is plentiful on this property, having been cut, split, piled and allowed to dry for two years. Above the stove one of the members had placed a hand-lettered sign that read:

> *Beech and Maple, if dry and old*
> *Keep away the winter cold*
> *But ash wood wet and ash wood dry*
> *a king shall warm his slippers by.*
>         *—Anon.*

We had just finished a wonderful dinner prepared by bear slayer and master chef Andy DeVirgeles and, as you might expect, outrageous stories of the day's hunt were flying across the room. At some point during this ritual of swapping tall tales, which is such a traditional part of the hunting camp experience, the discourse turned to snowmobiling.

One of the out-of-town guests in camp that weekend asked if anyone knew the names Sabin or St. Onge.

He went on to explain that he had raced sleds in Michigan's

Upper Peninsula and that at that time those individuals were known to be among the best racers in the National Racing circuit.

The conversation made me realize that snowmobiling was at its absolute peak in this community during the 1970s when Vern Sabin and the father-son team Herve and Oscar St. Onge were burning up the track as consistent winners and respected competitors.

For reasons which are better left to a sociologist or some other analyst to explore, the popularity of snowmobiling in later years flattened out. In the early 1990s it was almost lonely on the trails, even the most ardent snowmobiler of earlier years no longer owned a sled or if they did, it sat unused in storage.

That situation has now again changed and there is presently an explosive resurgence and not only locally but on a national level it has become one of the fastest-growing winter activities. To even the most casual observer, the snowmobiling story, especially if you live in snow country, has to be fascinating.

I'll agree that snowmobiles are something that you either love or hate (sometimes simultaneously). Whatever your feelings as we stand on the brink of the millennium, this machine deserves at least a nod from historians as they evaluate this century's pantheon of human achievements. Now, I'm not suggesting (if you are at least 40 years old) that having been witness to this evolution, from a clumsy box-like affair with cleated wooden tracks to today's sleek chartreuse machines such as exhibited at Eric's new shop, is as momentous as the birth and development of let's say the airplane, nor has it altered our lives in the pervasive way in which technology has transformed the world in the past forty years. The point is we weren't at Kitty Hawk when Orville and Wilber bumped down that pasture trying to get airborne, nor were we living at Silicon Valley.

So who built the first snowmobile? Actually, no one knows despite many people who claim to be the first inventor. No doubt like the Adirondack guideboat, it was the brain-child of many people, each one experimenting with various methods to develop a contrivance that would enable them to travel (in this case) over snow, until a final form evolved.

Many of the early machines were actually an automobile equipped for over-the-snow capability. The Ford Motor Co. built a kind of snowmobile that Admiral Byrd used on his polar expedition in 1928. Ford later decided it had no other commercial value and discontinued production!

In the late 1920s a man named Carl Eliason patented a motor toboggan that had ski-like front runners and a rear-drive track. An improved version of the "motor toboggan" is the first two-man snow machine that I personally remember appearing in this village. It was owned by Cy Malbouf, who at the time was the proprietor of the Evergreen Hotel (now Wheel Inn).

The winter sports club at the time (1955?) hired Cy to bring the ponderous tow rope to the top of Sugar Loaf (new ski slope). When the snows came before the newly ordered tow rope arrived, it took him four days, creating a path 20 feet at a time, which is an indication how primitive those first machines were.

The army developed a troop-carrying treaded vehicle during World War II (1943) called the "Weasel." Leon Lafave of this village, whose military assignment included training sled dogs to be used in winter warfare, once told me in the post-war years, when I would visit with him in his restaurant (now CJ's) that his experience with them while stationed in Montana at Fort Harrison (1st Special Service Force Kiska Operation Italian Campaign) was limited but that his dog teams would mush right by them as they would become mired in the deep high-elevation snows.

Perhaps not the first, but certainly recognition should go to Joseph Armand Bombardier, who developed the snowmobile into the *first saleable product*. Bombardier had founded a small company in the late 1930s and had built large troop-carrying snow vehicles (like the Weasel) for the Canadian government. Then in 1959-1960 two things happened to cause a major breakthrough in developing a small two-person machine.

First was the development of a light-weight engine. The second and prime motivation for Armand was when one of his sons died of appendicitis because the roads of rural Quebec where he lived were blocked by waist-high snow and inaccessible to medical help.

Immediately Armand and his son Germain sought a way to adapt cleated tractor tires used on large vehicles to small machines. Germain developed and patented an all-rubber track with interior steel rods for lateral strength and the machine, nicknamed the "Ski-Doo", was born. In 1962 Elliot W. Hutchins of Malone became the Northeast distributor and sold thousands of the bright yellow machines, which were priced at around $700.

The industry then mushroomed with dozens upon dozens of manufacturers attempting to get in the action (1965-1975).

Many of these companies were short-lived and in the shakeout that followed a company called Polaris emerged as the U.S. leader (Bombardier was Canadian).

*Carl Eliason stands proudly by his prototype "snow toboggan" in this 1933 picture. The first snowmobile to appear in this village around 1955 was an improved version and called the Eliason. (photo courtesy Evinrude Co.)*

*Tupper Lake Free Press Print:* January 06, 2000

# A Respectful Walk on Salmon Lake

I WAS HUNTING WITH MY BROTHER, Jim, toward the end of this year's deer season. We were walking along what had been a main-haul road during recent lumbering operations. We were heading for a piece of cover that somehow had escaped both the big fires and the wind storms that once raged through the area and had only been high-graded when timbered.

We had a respectful walk ahead of us and, as sometimes happens when the tedium of a long walk weighs on you, we found ourselves talking non-stop.

We pretty much solved most of the world's problems, including profound topics such as who would be the NBA's next MVP and what name should be given to the next decade (zero, Ohs, double ohs, aughts? etc., etc.).

We also discussed the mule tracks we had been observing. The tracks had been frozen into semi permanence on the gravel road surface, almost as if they had been cast in plaster.

The interim classification for the newly acquired state land we were on was wilderness. No bicycles, no motorized vehicles, no horses, etc., etc. Mules, it seems got an OK when the hunting party using them (in their words) "threw a curve at the D.E.C." "Mules," they argued, "are not horses." We wondered, that if I used my uni-cycle that I could argue it was not a bicycle. I'm not certain we came to any general agreement on that question, but I think (?) we agreed that mules (and bicycles) were certainly appropriate in that particular location. We might have even agreed that the classification system is flawed.

By this time, we had reached a sturdy, well-built plank bridge over the outlet of Little Salmon Lake just before it empties its waters into Lily Pad Pond. Many years ago, my wife and I had carried our canoe upstream alongside the rapids that exist at this point. We were trying to find traces of the Mac and Mac railroad the O.W.D. had used to carry its logs from Rock Lake on Whitney to the Brandeth Station on the main New York Central Line. It was used only for three years, 1936-1939, before the tracks were pulled, but the ties were left in place and provided a marvelous artery through a very remote and seldom-visited place. Where the swift water ended on that portage we encountered a massive stone wall that was effectively a dam. The rocks making up the wall were enormous, and we both marveled at how they could have been put in place long before the days of mechanized equipment. Some time later I ran into Bernie Dunham, who was employed at Whitney, and he told me that his father, Sanford Dunham, had been involved in building that wall, possibly as a fish barrier. "How did they procure and move and place those huge rocks?" I asked. "They used oxen," he replied, providing the answer to our puzzle.

As we carried our canoe around the rock dam that day, I stumbled upon a hidden cache of at least 20 well-oiled beaver traps in good condition. I never knew for certain, but I always suspected they belonged to some Tupper Lake trappers, Howard LeBlanc, Jack Dewyea, and Percy Trombley.

This trio of first-rate trappers had been given privileges to trap the Salmon Lake watershed by the folks at Whitney Park. This was about the same time I happened upon the traps (mid-1950s).

At that time Tom Fortune owned a J-1 Piper Cub, which he had equipped with skis, and he would fly the trappers and their gear in and out of Salmon Lake, landing on the frozen surface. Tom did this as a good-neighbor gesture. It also provided him with an interesting and adventuresome break from his duties at the hardware store.

As it turned out, it was almost too great an adventure.

Late one March day at the end of the trapping season, Tom landed on the lake and prepared to fly out the group, including their fur and gear. His plan was to take the gear out on the first flight and on subsequent trips fly the trappers out.

Tom tells the story best: "I loaded everything I could on that little plane. What I couldn't stuff in the cockpit, I strapped to the wings. I knew it was a heavy load," he told me at the time, "but it's a big lake with plenty of room to get up speed for the take-off. I taxied to the far end, but as I powered back up the lake, I ran into a large patch of shell ice, which gave way and dropped me down to the main ice sheet. I still had fair forward speed, but the drop lowered the plane, and the prop was dangerously close to hitting the surface ahead of me. It was a frightening moment, and I immediately cut the engine. I jumped out of that plane and, to be truthful, I was plenty scared, and the adrenalin was pumping through me like a race horse approaching the finish line. Meanwhile, the guys on shore, sensing my predicament, started running out to me. By the time they arrived, I had that gear unloaded and sitting on the ice. I was cussing my stupidity at being overloaded and worrying about my beautiful plane being marooned on that isolated lake with the threat of ice-out only days away. I had two of the trappers rock first one wing and then the other, while the third guy and I pushed. I had the cockpit door open with throttle slightly advanced, and when we got the plane up on solid surface, I jumped in and took off. *That was it for me!* I felt sorry for those guys left on the lake. They had a very long walk out with a lot of gear. I didn't worry about them because they were tough, seasoned woodsmen and I knew they could handle it. As for me, I had pushed the envelope far enough, thank you. I never went back."

Incredibly, it had been over forty years since Ginny and I had portaged past this spot, where Jim and I now sat eating our lunch. It was not the same place! Only the rock wall remained the same. Not only had the hand of man had morphed this dynamic change. Nature was the greater villain. In the 1980s a highly localized tornado, which came down in a narrow, nasty swirl of destructive power, flattened thousands of trees. In July of 1995 a straight-line storm called a Derecho totaled what the circular winds of the tornado had left standing. Jim noted my dejection at the havoc that surrounded us. Far more philosophical (and wiser) than I, he offered this counsel: "Bill, it is a natural process, just a blip in time. The forest will actually renew and thrive, become more diverse in the wake of these disturbances. Have faith, brother."

*Tupper Lake Free Press Print:* January 12, 2000

# A COURSE CALLED HERSTORY

LORI GRIFFIN IS AN ELEMENTARY school teacher in a nearby St. Lawrence Co. community.

This past year she instituted a course she calls "herstory." Initially I laughed at that title because it reminded me of a group of women who were upset at words like mandate or manhole cover or the expression "to a man" that means unanimously.

My reaction to those objections was: "Hey, chill out ladies. Isn't that carrying this femme thing a little far?" I soon discovered, however, that Ms. Griffin's course was designed to study the influence of women in American history.

Students will earn a half credit upon completion of the course that meets every other day for a year and is open to boys and girls in grades nine through twelve. Ms. Griffin hoped that by year's end her pupils will gain a better understanding of women's contributions and potentials. "It is not really a feminist course," said Ms. Griffin, who also teaches English along with drama and journalism electives. "It's more of a research of self-identity. It's a celebration of women."

In a recent interview with Jeff Horseman, *Watertown Times* staff writer, this creative teacher explained that a huge part of the course depends on students being able to develop and share their research. "I don't do a lot of lecturing," she explained. "I just show students examples of what I expect and they go out and do it." I'm willing to bet that most readers of this column will agree that this is an interesting way to learn a part of American history. Younger people, in particular, are probably not fully aware of the struggle to obtain political, social, and economic equality for women.

Those of us who can remember when only children wore denim have had the opportunity to observe the dynamic progress of gender equality and civil rights. Younger people, however, are not as likely to be aware of the struggle that was involved. The struggle of people like Susan Anthony, who, with others, worked so hard at the turn of the century for the right for women to vote. It would take over fifty years (1920) until the 19th Amendment to the United States Constitution was finally ratified, guaranteeing that no state could deny the right to vote on the basis of sex.

Or the courage of Rosa Parks, who refused to give up her bus seat to a white person. That refusal challenged the constitutionality of a Montgomery, Alabama, segregation law.

By having the guts to say no, Rosa triggered a boycott of the city's bus system by black commuters. It was one of the most dramatic demonstrations of nonviolent protest in the history of American race relations. Or Sally Ride, who through her considerable abilities became the United States' first female astronaut.

It wasn't too long ago that women were not allowed to participate in certain running marathons. Maybe you remember when the race director of the Boston Marathon was horrified to discover a girl running in that event. (She had used her first initial instead of her full first name to register and covered her curls with a baseball cap.) The director was so incensed that he rushed in among the runners and attempted to forcefully eject her from the pack. (He didn't reckon that her brawny, six-foot, four-inch boyfriend was running alongside her.) In part, because of the publicity resulting from that occurrence, women today make up a large percentage of marathon entries and are even lowering the winning time gaps established by their fellow male runners.

Flashback to the time (remember?) when high school girls had to wear those silly bloomer-like gym suits? When the Physical Education program for girls was typically a lecture on health and some moderate calisthenics? Contrast that to today and high school sophomore Audrey Svoboda doing an outstanding job fending off hockey pucks fired at bullet speed as she holds down the goalie position of the boys' hockey team.

What an excellent opportunity for a college scholarship! Or to move on to the U.S. Women's Team, which is presently such an international power house. Let's admit it, only fierce determination on the part of women has given us the enabling legislation to Title IX, which forced the male-dominated athletic directors almost everywhere to give equal gender weight in budgeting their athletic programs. We can count the success of that mandate in a hundred different ways.

Call me a compassionate liberal but, in my opinion, educator Ms. Griffin has struck a chord of "herstory" that is valuable and, while it may be only a hiccup, it is a start. A start of an awareness of how far women's rights have advanced. It can also provide a focus on women's accomplishments like those of 56-year-old Tara Holonen, who just this week became the first woman president in Finland's history.

*Tupper Lake Free Press Print:* February 16, 2000

# Tom Peacock and The Changing Life of Dawson Pond

IN THE LAST *TRANSITIONS* column, we printed excerpts from an interview with Tom Peacock, an 89-year-old Saranac Lake guide.

The interview was conducted by the *Ausable Forks Record Post* in a column entitled *The Adirondacker* in the October 1941 issue of that paper. We continue this week with further excerpts from that column:

"As we talked on about this and that, we got onto one of Mr. Peacock's favorite topics, trout fishing. He recalled a trip to Racquette Falls along about 1881 or 1882, on the 9th or 10th day of May. There were four in the party, the famous Dr. Ely being one of them. They arrived at Mother Johnson's, near the Falls, about three or four in the afternoon. The water was high, and the ice had not long been out. The guides would put their patrons on the rocks near the foot of the Falls. Then they would hover below in boats. The fishermen would cast their flies in the white foam above. As the trout were hooked, the guides would pull up in boats and net the fish. About an hour of this would tire them all out."

## Mother Johnson's Pancakes

"Supper at Mother Johnson's consisted chiefly of her famous Injun wheat pancakes. (Adirondack Murray raved about them.) These were made with sour dough, were darker than buckwheat and a little bitter. Mother Johnson had two large cabins and two or three smaller ones, a couple of cows and an ox team to draw boats over the carry. There was more fishing that evening and in the next morning. When they started back, they had a bushel of one to three pound speckled trout.

"Dawson Pond is nearby, it is very cold and used to be alive with little trout. You could get three at almost every cast. Tom remembers catching a pack-basket full in a very short time. He says there was nothing in the Adirondacks like it."

## Pike Killed Off Trout

"The apparently capricious act of two men, an old guide at Long Lake, Lysan Hall, and a fellow who was sort of lay minister, killed the trout fishing in the Long Lake, Racquette River system. They went over around Tahawus and brought back eight live pickerel or northern pike. They put these in a brook at Long Lake village. Some people heard about it and caught four, but the others got down into the lake. Presently the pike were so numerous, they seemed to almost fill the river. Then they were thinned out by a horrible disease, a kind of small pox, which attacked the base of the scales. The consequent rotten stench made travel on the river pretty mean for a while.

"Some fifteen to twenty years afterward old John Duckett and John Hanmer put a wash boiler full of pike into Upper Saranac and that cleaned out the trout from all the Saranacs, including the 33 ponds and streams which fed into them. This was a pure spite act. Jesse Corey was running Rustic Lodge at Indian Carry. Corey called Duckett's place on Stony Creek or Spectacle Pond, 'The Pickerel House.' Duckett got mad with tragic results."

Note: The Dawson Pond referred to by Mr. Peacock remained a wonderful place to fish for many years after the old guides' visit. The easiest access was across a private section of land at the northern end of the Racquette Falls Carry, known as "The Clearing." You crossed the clearing through the courtesy of the owners. A courtesy that was always cheerfully extended. (Dawson Pond itself was located on state land.) For many years, getting to the clearing

*At the lower Racquette Falls, "the river drives powerfully through a depression in the volcanic dike that would halt its flow. Crashing with a roar amid clouds of foam and spray into the dark circular pool below." Chas Bryant, 1964.*
*(Bill Frenette photo)*

from Tupper entailed a boat trip of 20 miles more or less, depending where you launched your boat—or a five-mile hike along an abandoned woods road from Stony Pond outlet near Coreys. In addition, you had a mile-long carry to the pond from the clearing at Racquette Falls. There were a good many ponds near here with good trout fishing in those days, and Dawson, understandably, didn't get a lot of fishing pressure. Following the 1950 blowdown, the Cold River area was officially closed to the public. As you can well imagine, the fishing in the ponds located here, and that included Dawson Pond, improved beyond belief.

One of the fishing parties to visit Dawson when the ban lifted in 1955 (actually the same day the woods were reopened) consisted of Bob Gillis, Jim Frenette and cousin of Bob's wife, Maggi, who was visiting from New York City.

The clearing at that time was part of an 89.2-acre parcel owned by Mr. and Mrs. Chas Bryant from Chicago. Mr. Bryant was the former president of Pullman Standard Car Co. The old Racquette

*Shown here is the interior ranger station at Racquette Falls Clearing. It replaced the lodge, which was destroyed by fire in 1970, three years after the state acquired the 89.2-acre parcel owned by Mrs. Mary Bryant. (Bill Frenette photo)*

Falls Lodge built by George Morgan until his death in 1944 had become the Bryant's summer home.

Only the cook was in residence that early morning as the Tupper Trio crossed the clearing. The cook had twice that week been frightened out of her wits by a marauding bear that had tried to beak through the screened porch. You guessed it! When Bob politely rapped on the kitchen window to say hello, the cook became hysterical and let out a scream that could have been heard in Long Lake. After a good laugh by all concerned, the fishermen continued their carry and returned that afternoon with a number of two-pound trout and no fish under a pound in their respective creels.

The fishing would remain excellent until the late 1960s, when several factors combined that led to a steady decline in the pond's productivity. First, the private owner of the property across the river from the clearing began to lease his land. Newly built camps and roads provided easy access adding to the numbers of people fishing the pond. The increased fishing pressure for the following years was overpowering. Secondly, beavers from older colonies to the east took over the pond and dammed its outlet. This raised the water volume and diluted the effect of the cold feeder streams. The pond's shoreline was flooded and the pond warmed to unacceptable temperatures, spoiling the trout fishing. All efforts to legally remove the dam proved futile. On one visit to the pond, I met Gene Freeman returning from the dam. Gene, as Mr. Bryant's caretaker, had tried culverts through the dam, which the beavers plugged at its upstream end. Next, he put a wire fence in front of the culvert, but the beavers plastered it, making a perfect cofferdam that only raised the water level. On the day I met him, the beaver had used his axe and shovel (left at the dam the day before) as reinforcing members in the dam structure.

"That's it!" Gene informed me. "I give up!"

Mr. Bryant, who died in 1966, would be overjoyed.

*Tupper Lake Free Press Print:* June 07, 2000

## ONE GIRL'S STORY

ALONG WITH MORE THAN 5,000 other celebrants, this writer attended the opening ceremonies of the first-ever Winter Goodwill Games. Debuting in 1986, the Goodwill Games were created by Turner Broadcasting to unite the world's best athletes in an atmosphere free from political rivalries and to promote global understanding.

The theme of the opening ceremonies was the Power of Sports.

The idea was to recognize in various choreographed ways that sports play a valuable role in society and that healthy competition is an important element in character development.

One of the presentations on the playbill was the awarding of the ten winners of an essay contest sponsored by the Goodwill Games and the New York State Lottery.

The program was targeted to the impressionable group of sixth, seventh, and eighth graders across New York state and was called the Winter Achievers Writing Contest.

The children were asked to describe how sports have had a positive influence in their lives. Each winner received a computer and laptop. The winners' schools also received a $1,000 credit for computer equipment.

One of these winners was 15-year-old Vickie Cook of South Kortright, NY. Her essay is representative of the other entries and personifies the spirit of the Goodwill Games.

That essay is presented below in this week's column in the hope that readers young (especially) and old will find it both inspirational and interesting.

Vickie wrote:

"Use the talents you possess, for the woods would be very silent if no birds sang except the best." A lot of my classmates, when encouraged to join sports, say something like, "I'm not good enough at this sport; I'll make a total fool out of myself." That's when this quote seems to make good sense. It also reminds me when I've had a particularly bad game to say to myself that it's just a game, and that I'll make up for it by trying even harder the next game.

"Playing sports over the years has affected me in so many different ways. When I was younger I used to play for the fun of it, for something to do. Now it's gotten more serious. It's a whole team effort. If someone doesn't show up for a practice, she lets the whole team down. Being on a team makes everyone feel important, like they're actually making a difference.

"I've played basketball all my life. When I was in third grade, there was a program for third through sixth graders to play every Saturday at school. It was really good for us to get out and do something healthy. It also gave us experience that would help us later on in our sports career. The coaches were all volunteers; no one was getting paid to help us out. We learned the basic skills: dribbling, shooting, pivoting, etc. I played this for all three years that I was eligible to do so. I got a sense of how the game was played.

"Ever since Junior High started, I've played basketball, soccer, and softball, the three main sports our school participates in.

"Soccer has had a huge effect on my life. Soccer requires responsibility, consistency, teamwork, and extreme fitness. During my soccer career, while I was in seventh grade, I had a huge setback. I was diagnosed with exercise-induced asthma. For the rest of the season I couldn't participate in any exercise whatsoever.

"Softball was a true adventure for me in seventh grade. I never had played before, never worn a glove, or thrown a ball. The whole team was new, even our coach. We had to start from the very beginning of how to throw a ball, how to catch a ball, what part of the glove to catch the ball in, etc. She started out in a unique way: playing kick ball. She said that the two had basically the same rules, and since we knew how to play kick ball, this would help us out a lot and it sure did. We had only one game, but we played hard and we learned a lot. We learned how to be a team. That was our goal and we reached it.

"By the end of the season we were probably more than ten times better than when we started out. It was evident that this season had changed every one of us in so many ways. I learned more about everyone on the team. I became a best friend of one of the teammates. We all learned responsibility and discipline. My grades went up. I had more of a positive outlook on life itself. When my social life wasn't going good, I looked forward to the softball practice that afternoon. I took my anger out during that time. That anger would work with me and help me throw the ball harder, run like I was in a race, and be so much more determined.

"I came to a particularly hard time in my life during this season. With a personal problem, I didn't know where to turn. I felt comfortable with my coach and so I went to her. She was there for me and we talked and she made me laugh and by the end of the day I was feeling a lot better. What a great relationship to have between a coach and player. When everyone works together the success is unimaginable.

"Has sports changed my life? Of course, it has. I work harder now, have goals that I set for myself, and I accomplish them. I cooperate better with other people, I set up strategies that work. I have great accomplishments along with the setbacks. I manage my work better. I learned that academics come before sports, but also that sports help with academics. In short, sports shape a person's life. I would be so much different without sports in my life.

"As Robert Frost said, 'The road diverted into two different paths and I chose the one less traveled and it's made all the difference.'"

*Tupper Lake Free Press Print:* February 23, 2000

# IF THESE WALLS COULD TALK

AS MOST READERS KNOW, this community in 1899 was the scene of one of the most devastating fires in Northern New York history. Old photographs show a flatbed of smoking embers extending from High to Lake streets and from Wawbeek Avenue to where Luke's Mobil now stands. Only two buildings remained on what today we call Park Street. One of those was the building which today houses the village offices.

A plaque atop this building's brick front carries the date 1903. That date merely marks the year that the building was "dolled up" with brick exterior. It was actually constructed in the early 1890s, according to Louis Simmons, former Tupper Lake historian. Most old timers of my generation will remember that when we were growing up it was a funeral parlor and a furniture store, a combination I don't remember being regarded out of the ordinary.

The building was owned by a man named A.J. DeShaw (Dish-Shaw).

Mr. DeShaw had a funeral parlor in the rear of the store and furniture store in the front of the store. Large plate-glass windows in the front allowed A.J., as he was known, to prominently display the latest furniture.

Let me tell you a little about A.J.: He was physically a big man of heavy girth. He was always neatly dressed in a great coat and tie and bore a commanding presence. He was a member of the village board for many years. In 1937 he made a bid for mayor as the Republican nominee against Democrat Frank. J. McCarthy.

That contest ended in a dead heat—98.6 votes for each candidate. Somewhat reminiscent of the recent Supervisor's race here, legal opinion was sought and, on legal advice by attorney Howard Main of Malone, two ballots, one marked with the name of each candidate, were placed in a box. The ballot drawn from the box bore the name Frank McCarthy, giving Tupper two more years of Democratic rule. Now accuse me of wandering, if you wish, but I must tell you something also about Frank McCarthy. I found the following entirely be accident as I was looking through the Tupper Lake High School senior year book of 1919, located in the *Free Press* collection a few weeks ago. According to the year book, in a Tri-Lake track meet Francis McCarthy as captain of the Tupper Lake team scored more points than any other man entered in the meet. In what events did he score those points? Get this! The quarter mile, first place, no time given. The half mile, first place, 2 minutes 26 1/2 seconds. The mile, first place, 5 minutes 53 seconds. How about that! Incidentally, in the same race Larry Cherverette, who was a sophomore, won the 100-yard dash. Time: 10.4!

The DeShaw building was erected by a man named Dick Donovan, an early Justice of the Peace, as a theater or Op'ry House. Stock companies filled week-long engagements there, putting on a different show each night. That stage, where thespians displayed their talents, was the last I knew still standing in place at the rear of the building. It has been awhile since I appeared there, but I think the police justice desk sat on that platform and with its extra height it gave the judge a somewhat intimidating position.

The village bought the building in 1954 and paid $18,000 for it, plus the remodeling costs which were subject to a permissive referendum. Today the building is now the subject of a concern that more space is needed to conduct the growing business of running the village.

Whatever the outcome of that concern, the building remains

as one of the few architectural links with village's earliest days.

Take a second look when you go by. There is a powerful lot of history in that old timer, and what stories it could tell, if only it could talk!

*Tupper Lake Free Press Print:* March 01, 2000

## ONE OF THOSE SOMEWHERES

IF YOU REMEMBER WHEN MILK was delivered to your doorstep in glass bottles with three inches of heavy cream suspended on top of the milk, perhaps you will remember the magic of a ride aboard the New York Central's Adirondack Division Railroad. For some the magic was simply hearing the whistle of the morning train as it crossed Demars Boulevard, signaling its moves, speaking a language only railroaders understood. Or perhaps it was the awe of the black smoke billowing from a stack, a vaporous suggestion of the coal-fired engine's power, enough to haul the 150-ton engine and as many as twenty coaches and passengers up the infamous 2,000-foot Big Moose Hill that railroaders called Purgatory Hill.

That magic of the train rides might also have been the memorable sensation of the gentle side sway and rhythmic clicking and clacking of wheel against rail as the train puffed its way along the scenic wonders of places like the Beaver River corridor with its sparkling lakes and streams and fascinating bog lands. Or was it simply the throbbing of those powerful engines as the idling train took on water from the tower that was located near what is now Bill and Sherry's Main Street Restaurant parking lot? (And which, of course, backed up traffic in both directions on the Junction's main street.)

Sometimes that magic was strained, however, such as when the train couldn't make the before-mentioned Big Moose Hill. The train would then have to back down, uncouple the cars and take the "head end" into Otter Lake and put it on the siding. It would then have to back down again and pick up the rest of the train and haul it over the hill back to Otter Lake.

I was on the train one January night when the temperature was hovering around the minus 20 mark. As soon as the train was uncoupled (I was in the rear one half), the passenger car, with its source of heat cut off, almost at once became colder than the cold-storage locker in Bill Spark's Armour plant. I was dressed only in "city clothes," and it was only determined pacing up and down in that car for what seemed like hours that kept me and the other passengers from freezing. As I recall, several passengers did have to be treated for superficial frostbite to their extremities, especially their feet. Perhaps that's why even today I don't venture out without a pair of Sorel pack boots in the trunk of my car, along with extra mittens and a fur hat to my passengers' amusement.

Accompanying this week's column is a map that shows in great detail the railroad lines of those Adirondack and Ottawa Divisions. It might be of special interest, especially to the younger residents and also to our newer residents.

It shows, for example, John Hurd's Northern Adirondack railroad, the first line to reach here when it was established in 1889-1890 and was later (1900) called the New York and Ottawa when construction of the line was completed to Canada's capital city. It also shows the route of Dr. Seward Webb's Malone and Mohawk railroad, which went to Montreal. Dr. Webb's rail line was the first to traverse the Adirondacks, and crossed the Hurd line here in 1891. This "junction" with its roundhouse, shops, and large railroad yard developed into the most important rail junction point between Utica and Malone. It also gave rise to the name "the junction," which even today is considered by many to be a separate section of the village. Actually the last time that name could be accurately applied to our "downtown" was at 6:04 on the morning of May 6, 1937, when train number 62 pulled out of town on its last run to Ottawa. Citing "lack of patronage," the New York Central the very next morning pulled ties and rails on

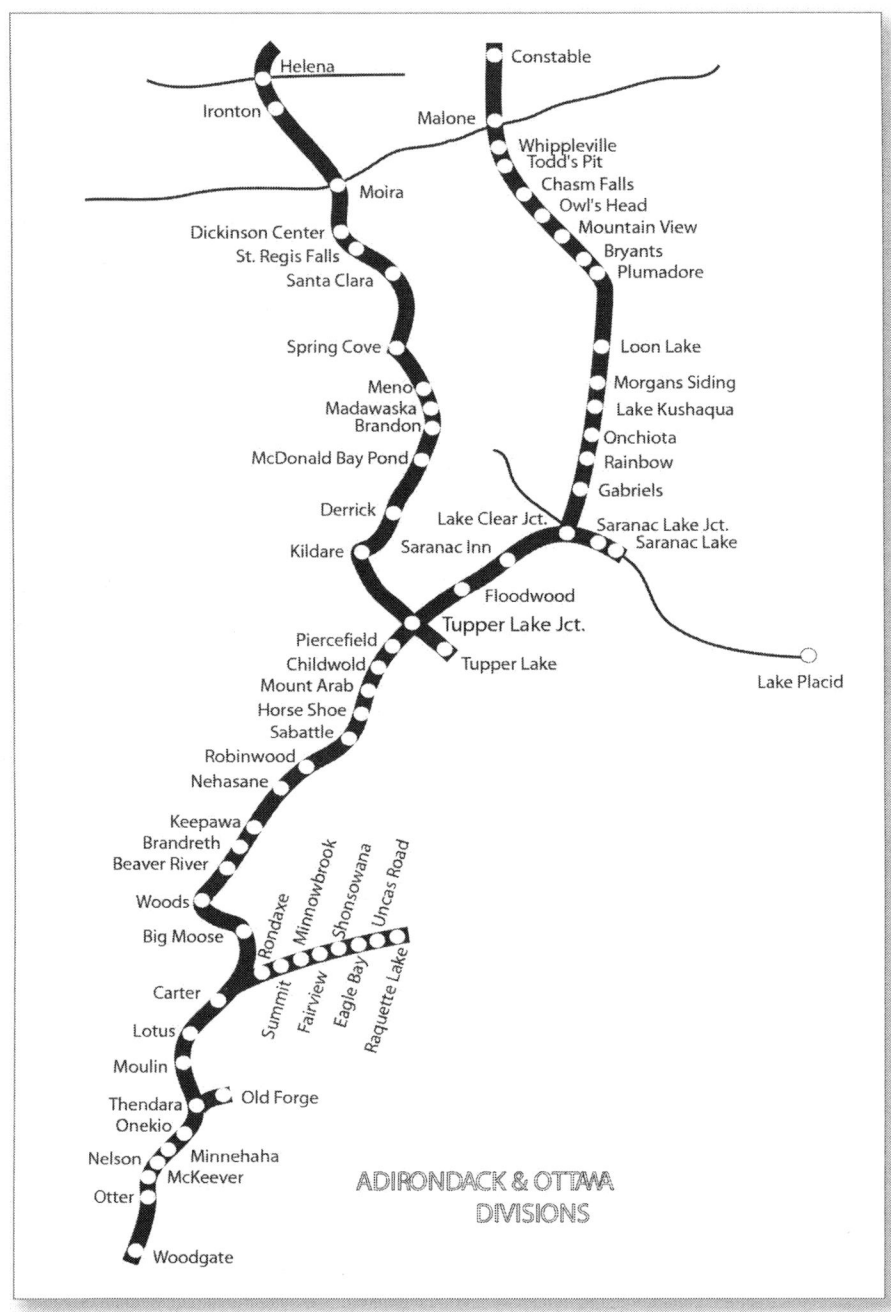

*Map showing in great detail the railroad lines of Adirondack and Ottawa Divisions.*

the 32-mile stretch between here and Santa Clara (named after Hurd's wife Clara, who he considered a saint). Seven miles of track along what we now call the Pitchfork Pond Road were allowed to remain for a few months so the Oval Wood Dish Corp. could remove the harvested timber from its Kildare operations.

There was no more railroad junction since only the Montreal line remained. It was a sad ending for "Uncle John's" railroad, which he built by gradually extending it "nowhere in particular and then creating a semblance of somewhere." One of those somewheres.

One of those sudden somewheres was this village. When it became the terminus of his railway, there was nothing but a cow pasture and clearing belonging to old Bill McLaughlin, a pioneer settler. Hurd built an enormous mill and Tupper Lake began to grow. According to the historian Donaldson: "It grew with surprising rapidity. Its structures were crude and ugly and its inhabitants were tough and lawless. It was like a western frontier town. Then, on July 30, 1899, it was almost completely wiped out by fire. This proved really a blessing in disguise, for on the site of the old village there soon rose a far more sightly, more cleanly, more orderly, and more prosperous one.

If you will again look at the map, you will notice that from the junction almost to the Canadian border the two lines parallel each other. Why didn't Dr. Webb, whose railroad came along after Hurd's Ottawa line, use the existing trackage at least to Moria before turning to Montreal? Not only would he have saved the immense cost of laying a new line, but he would have avoided the very real problem of having to cross state lands. Interestingly, Dr. Webb's line would not have gone through Tupper, as originally planned, but the State refused him right-of-way on his route south of this village. Webb then had to buy 115,000 acres of private land for an alternative route. That brought Webb's line to this village. If he could have used Hurd's connector, it would have solved his problem of crossing State lands, which lay north of this village. Webb, of course, was well aware of those facts, but he was negotiating to buy Hurd's line. Hurd allegedly sold it out from under him. This infuriated Dr. Webb and he vowed he would parallel Hurd's line within a year, and he kept his promise.

We know "Uncle John," who more than any other individual was responsible for the founding of this village, was a reckless speculator in lumber lands. A lover of "the deal," he often took extreme gambles that threatened him financially.

He was also, like many other magnets, as aggressively religious on Sundays as he was aggressively worldly on business days. Why did he apparently play the wrong card in this game with Dr. Webb? And how did Dr. Webb overcome his need to cross constitutionally protected land with his projected route? We will try to answer these questions in next week's column. Stay tuned . . .

*Tupper Lake Free Press Print:* April 12, 2000

# DR. WEBB—THWARTED, NOT STYMIED

IN THE LAST *TRANSITIONS* column it was noted that the original route of Dr. Seward Webb's Mohawk-Malone railroad (later the New York Central) was thwarted when the state refused to allow the line to cross state land. Dr. Webb may have been thwarted but he was not to be stymied. He immediately bought 115,000 acres of private land for an alternative route. That maneuver brought Webb's line to Tupper Lake! There was more state land to cross north of here, but that problem would have been solved if Dr. Webb could use Hurd's existing Northern Adirondack Railroad line as a northern connector. It is not likely that Dr. Webb anticipated a problem here. He was aware that Hurd needed money and Dr. Webb had plenty of that commodity. He had "married well." His bride, Lila Osgood Vanderbilt (for whom he renamed Smiths Lake to Lake Lila at his Nehasane estate), got a $1,250,000 (in 1880 dollars) Fifth Avenue mansion as a wedding gift from Dad. In addition, it wasn't long after that he left the medical profession (not highly regarded in the social pecking order in those days) and surfaced as president of the Wagner Sleeping Car Co., the firm that spawned today's Pullman Car Company.

In other words, as we would say today, "He had deep pockets."

He offered Hurd $600,000 for his Northern Adirondack line. That offer was attractive enough, given Hurd's money problems, that Hurd went to New York and met with Dr. Webb. Apparently a deal was made and the papers were to be signed the next day. That didn't happen. Hurd, instead of signing the papers, simply called the next day to say that the deal was off. Charles H. Burnett, in his privately printed book, *Conquering the Wilderness*, explains how that transaction reportedly went sour:

"That night, Mr. Paine, of the Pope-Paine Lumber Company, saw Hurd at his hotel and offered to raise his price fifty thousand dollars if he would grant an option on the road for a short time. Hurd agreed. The next morning, instead of signing the paper, he merely called to say that the deal was off. There was no angrier man that day than Dr. Webb. Later Paine came in and tried to sell his option at an advance in price. That did not improve the Doctor's temper. He told them both that he would parallel the Hurd Road within a year, and he kept his word."

At this point Webb decided to take his line north to Malone instead of Moira. As mentioned, this meant crossing state land protected by the Constitutional amendment that reads: "Land of the forest preserve shall be forever kept as wild forest lands. They shall not be sold, nor shall they be leased or taken by any person or corporation public or private." Once again thwarted but not stymied, an undaunted Dr. Webb found a solution. He discovered that a Dr. Samuel B. Ward had just recently acquired title to a 30,000-acre tract north of this community. He had gained possession by successfully challenging the state's acquisition of the land by tax sale. Dr. Ward sold a strip through this tract to Webb for the railroad. What was this challenge that defeated the state? Ward's argument, while perfectly legal but which would have been severely questioned by today's environmental watch dog groups, was that the tax sale should be overturned because the original assessment was placed on the entire township, not individual lots, which he said involved both resident and non-resident owners. The comptroller agreed (an acceptance that would also spark debate today) and the tax sale was overturned.

It is ironic that the scrutiny lacking in that decision is today being focused on Dr. Webb's former private station in Nehasane. The D.E.C. is presently trying to decide whether or not the old station has sufficient historic importance to be preserved or if it is non-conforming under the reclassification of Lake Lila. Observers will be watching closely to see if it will be moved a short distance inside the rail corridor—or will the rail corridor be bulged to accommodate the building where it now stands? Or will it be removed? How will this decision affect the buildings at the Santanoni Preserve, which some believe are non-conforming and should be removed?

Anyway, let's continue. As you can imagine, the construction of the line was a major headache with swarms of blood-thirsty black flies, rain, mud, rock ledges that had to be drilled by hand and blasted with black powder, and stumps that had to be dynamited. Intense cold froze the ground to be graded and caused intense suffering among the African-American laborers brought in by contractors from Tennessee, none of whom were properly clothed and were often barefoot when they arrived. There was also the problem of private owners along the route who refused a right-of-way.

One determined private owner, so the story goes, put out armed border guards as the track layers approached. Undaunted, Webb's crew are supposed to have put their stretch through on a dark, stormy night, leaving details to be ironed out by the attorneys the next morning. (And some people considered Hurd a scoundrel.)

The late Louis Simmons, former Tupper Lake Historian, tells of one ingenious "bonus device used to accelerate the construction."

According to Louie, W.N. Roberts took charge of the construction work on the north end and his son, Hershel Roberts, took charge of the southern portion. A friendly rivalry developed between the Roberts father and son to see who could get the most track laid in one day. African-American trackmen made up the gang of Roberts senior, while his son had a crew of sixty St. Regis Native Americans. The number of feet laid by each was posted in the camps nightly. Hershel Roberts devised a scheme to step up completed trackage that worked.

Every morning a keg of beer was carried and set on the grade a good, optimistic distance ahead and the crew was told it could knock off and enjoy the beer when they reached it. With that stimulus the gap was soon cleared at the rate of a mile a day.

Note: There were 3,000 ties to the mile, according to a *New York Herald* reporter, who got the energetic Dr. Webb to slow down for an interview. The reporter wrote that the rails were extra-heavy steel and the road was to have the finest rolling stock ever made. The reporter concluded his article by stating, "There will not be enough traffic to pay for the oil on the wheels. The natives are dazzled."

That reporter should have been standing at the Junction Station here a few years later when traffic hit its peak during the 1932 Olympics. The railroad not only drew in most of the spectators but also a lot of the snow to snow-starved Lake Placid. At the same time, section after section of sleepers sped through the Adirondack night 15 minutes apart. That reporter was the one who would have been "dazzled."

*Tupper Lake Free Press Print:* April 19, 2000

## THE OLD M&M

ON A COLD, LATE October day in the year 1892, workers laying track from the north for the new Mohawk and Malone railroad met track layers coming from the south. They were at a place half a mile north of the Twitchell Creek bridge, not far from Big Moose Lake.

A young assistant engineer drove the last spike—or tried to—the first ten or twelve blows missed, much to the amusement of the railroad workers watching, any one of whom could have hit the spike on the first try. Local snowmobilers on their way to Old Forge and beyond cross that spot on their winter excursions. Work trains on their way to Saranac Lake to improve the prospective scenic corridor to Lake Placid will also cross that historic spot. It marks, of course, the first—and to this day the only—railroad to cross the Adirondacks. Dr. Seward Webb had done what few expected he could. He succeeded with unmatched genius and vigor to complete a railroad line from Herkimer to Malone in only eighteen months after the original survey was taken. At one time over 4,000 men were employed in its construction.

It is still today regarded as an achievement that is a milestone in American railroading.

My grandfather, William Simmons, whose family came to Syracuse, New York, by way of Dusseldorf in the Rhine River Valley in Germany in 1860, was an early engineer on that railroad.

198 / Transitions

The Adirondack Division, right where Dr. Webb put it, curves and all. (photo by David Beetie)

When his work in 1900 began taking him over runs on the Adirondack Division he moved to this community in 1907. My grandmother, Mary Jane Flanagan, who came to this country as a young girl from County Mayo, Ireland, in 1884, often recalled how terrified she was during the first summer they moved here in 1908, when forest fires that destroyed 368,000 acres of Adirondack forest encircled Tupper Lake in a pall of smoke for weeks on end. The neighboring village of Long Lake West (Sabattis) about 14 miles south of Tupper Lake by rail was totally destroyed by a raging forest fire that fall. The estimated 100 town residents lost literally everything. Louis Simmons, my uncle, had noted that while Father never kept any documentation, it was known that he was the engineer of the rescue train that brought the residents out that fateful day. The road to Long Lake was completely cut off by the fire and adding to the danger was 85 cases (1,500 pounds) of dynamite owned by Moyenhan & Sons stored in a small building near the hotel. Also on the siding was a car of kerosene. "Fire was on both sides of the tracks, and the ties were burning, the smoke was suffocating, and the heat was unbearable," according to Katherine Hammer, former Long Lake resident, describing her own escape in the train. (She had been working for the Brandeth & McAlpin families at Brandeth and had stayed over at the Wilderness Inn when located at Long Lake West before heading home to Long Lake.) The train, with its caboose starting to burn, was backed out by "Big Bill" down the track to Horseshoe. They had barely left when the dynamite exploded. The concussion was felt at Horseshoe (four miles away) and at Little Tupper (10 miles away).

On January 24, 1927, Bill Simmons was fatally injured while attempting to thaw out frozen pipes from a catwalk running along the boiler of a locomotive. According to Louie, "He could have just taken the train out of Tupper on a run to Utica, and the accident occurred in bitter, 40-below-zero cold near Childwold, seven miles south of this village. He sustained compound fractures of both legs and internal injuries and died a month later at Faxton Hospital in Utica."

The railroad was to last for 73 years. Improved roads, modern automobiles, and fast-moving tractor trailers to carry freight all contributed to a steady decline as well as did the process of attrition, which continued for many years before the Public Service Commission gave the New York Central permission to end all service over the 142-mile Adirondack Division between Utica and Lake Placid. (In 1964 the railroad had lost its mail contract, which added $100,000 to its annual losses.) The 1964 report estimated its loss at $149,325 plus $41,200 in station costs. Thus, except for a brief time during the 1980 Olympics, the last passenger train on "Webbs Road" was in April 1965. The last freight train hauling five box cars to Saranac Lake and a couple of coal hoppers to Ray Brook passed over the tracks in August 1982. On that last freight run a washout prevented a return trip and the cars had to be ignobly hauled on flatbed trucks to Potsdam, where they were put back into service. In a March 11, 1989 issue, the *Watertown Daily Times* notes that "the private company that had run the 1980 recreational train continued to offer excursions into the Adirondacks but by August 1980 it had experienced its fifth derailment in two months, leading state officials to question seriously the safety of the line. Limited operations between Tupper Lake and Lake Placid resumed in September 1980, but the last run on the line was made in November 1980." The *Times* article concluded that "eventually poor rail conditions contributed to the collapse in bankruptcy of the private company operating the Adirondack Railroad."

This past week, I stopped to examine the huge diesel locomotive and its two vintage Canadian-made dump cars parked on a siding off the Junction's main street, where the rail line crossed the outlet of Little Wolf Creek before it empties into Raquette Pond. I climbed (feebly) down to the large cement ledge that projects from the wall of the well-made bridge that supports the rails and ties. Dozens of large suckers (called Carpe Blanche by early settlers who would put one fish in each hill of potatoes they planted—they were not considered a food fish) covered the stream bottom. They were in spawning posture, the males at this time of year displaying a faint rosy stripe along the middle of their sides, noses pointed upstream against the current, which at this time of year was in flood stage.

I wondered if suckers were under that bridge when in 1892 as many as 27 work trains of 30 cars each rumbled over on the way to where 500 workers were working furiously in the section near the Saranac Inn fish hatchery, working toward the section crews coming north from Tupper, ballasting the track, filling trestles, widening banks, and laying ties. Of course that was at a time when you could catch scores of 2-pound trout in the outlet rapids between Big Wolf and Little Wolf.

Today those trout are gone just as the gigantic 100,000-gallon water tower, the two huge bunker oil towers that fueled the steam engine, and the beautiful railroad station are gone. The vibrancy that marked that place is also gone. I would like to think suckers were spawning at that spot at that time as proof that not everything has changed even as I agree that change is inevitable and often necessary.

That same morning I ran into Gerald Black, who lives in Piercefield. Early that morning he had heard the train whistle coming across the Raquette River flow near his home. "Boy, was that a great sound," he told me. "I hope the D.O.T. and that other outfit can get the line restored so that trains will move trough here once more." A lot of people agree with Gerald.

I like what railroad buff and author Henry Harter had to say in his book, *Fairy Tail Railroad*: "So we can say for the M&M and the St. Lawrence and Adirondack Railway, together the Adirondack Division on the New York Central they came, they struggled, and they stayed to help develop, for all people, the use of the Forest Preserve. When the time comes, they receded into the wilderness to be born again if and when needed."

Let's hope Gerald can again hear that whistle each morning. A clarion call to remind us of a proud past when this village was the brightest star in the constellation of stations that made up the old M&M.

*Tupper Lake Free Press Print*: April 26, 2000

# THE ROUTE TO TUPPER

IN THE LAST SEVERAL columns we discussed the first railroad lines into this community. Prior to that time, which would have been before 1890, travel and obtaining supplies here was largely limited to primitive woods roads and waterways.

If you lived in Boston or Albany, as an example, and wished to come to Tupper you would need to travel first by train to Whitehall, then by steamboat up Lake Champlain to Plattsburgh, where a train would take you to Ausable Forks or Keeseville. From either one of these communities you would need to board a stage coach hauled, as a rule, by six horses. Your route would be over the shoulder of Whiteface Mountain to Bloomingdale by way of Franklin Falls to Saranac Lake. A jolting, often crowded, uncomfortable, tiring ride of some eight hours. The stage coach would take you directly to Martins Landing located on Ampersand Bay at the N/E end of Lower Saranac Lake.

You could then obtain a boat, a guide, and provisions, for the lakes, streams and rivers would become your highway. Rowing up the length of the Lower Lake usually in a Saranac, as the guideboats of that region were called, you would then enter the Saranac River, then cross the Middle Lake or Round Pond, as it is sometimes called, and arrive at Bartletts Carry. Here, where Verge Bartlett had built a hotel (now Bartlett Carry Club), the Saranac breaks through a ledge of anorthosite in a narrow gorge, and a short carry would be necessary. Your guide would then wish his boat was one of Will

Allen Martin's "eggshells," the name given to the extra-light guideboat innovated and built by Martin, who together with Ed Krumholz (first owner of Wawbeek Hotel), had a boat-building business on Saranac Lake. (It may be worth noting that originally the local guides greeted Willie Allen's boat with skepticism, considering it too fragile. They underestimated the superb craftsmanship that allowed the reduction in weight (70 pounds compared to the typical 80-120 pounds for other guideboats of the time). It soon became the most sought-after boat in the area.)

*Guides and clients at Martins Landing September 24 1876. Note that the improved double-end guideboat had appeared by this date. The first two boats from right are older square-stern models, a vestige of early origin. Note also the long thin-edged blade on the single paddle shown. This design allowed a noiseless sculling stroke by stern person. Woe to the person who "dinged" that thin edge on a rock, an imperfection that could render the paddle less quiet.*

Having completed the quarter-mile carry (now one-half mile due to recent re-routing), your guide would row you from the outlet of Upper Saranac Lake directly across that lake to where in 1830 Jesse Corey had a home, now the Wawbeek Hotel location, at a place called Sweeneys Carry. It would be necessary to "carry" overland three miles to the Raquette River, where you would find Tromblee's (Trombley) Landing. Tupper Lake would then be only 9.89 miles down river to the first hotel, which will be Uncle Mart Moody's Mt. Morris house, where it is possible you might run into President Grover Cleaveland or President Chester Arthur (who commissioned Uncle Mart, our first postmaster). Both presidents were fond of Uncle Mart and Aunt Minerva and the wonderful trout fishing then available in Tupper Lake. The Mt. Morris House, later the Prince Albert Hotel, was located on the present Peter Day property, where the turn to the Country Club leaves Route 30 at Moody.

A further word about the famous Sweeney Carry may be of interest: First, it should be pointed out that in later years you could rent a horse and a wagon designed to carry multiple boats that could expedite that carry.

Before that time, some of the guides would let their passengers off at the head of the carry and row alone two miles down the lake.

Here they would use the original and shorter Indian Carry at Coreys to Stony Ponds and access the Raquette at the Stony Creek outlet. After 1870, when the Setting Pole Dam flooded the river almost as far as Raquette Falls, today's twisting Stony Creek would be a straight shot from the last Stony Pond to the river. The solo guide would then row 6.35 miles downstream and rejoin his party at Tromblee's. Extra rowing, to be sure, but probably easier, especially to a guide accustomed to daily 40-mile rowing trips. Permit me to digress a bit further concerning Sweeneys Carry. In 1878 a famous fight for possession took place at that historic spot. Captain James H. Pierce of Bloomingdale claimed the land and so did C.F. Norton, the lumber king. In those days and in this case, possession was nine points of the law. Norton hired O.A. Coville, a well-known guide, to settle on the lake end of the carry and Tupper Lake's Oliver Tromblee to settle on the other. This decisive move ended the fight. Coville and wife saw there was a good chance for business on the carry and decided to stay there. They bought 40 acres from Norton and built a halfway house that became very popular with summer visitors. It is, of course, even more so today under the astute managership of Norm and Nancy Howard as the renowned hotel called the Wawbeek. Tromblee also took a fancy to his end of the carry and stayed on. Mr. and Mrs. Trombley raised their family there, and if you walk down a portion of the "old carry" from the "Y" (Route3/Route 30) you can still find foundation remains of their homestead between the two lean-tos now located there. The maps still show that location as Tromblee's. With the lakes icebound and many times too treacherous for travel, the settlers here were often isolated for weeks at a time in the winter months. How did these early settlers get their winter supplies? We will attempt to answer that question in the next *Transitions*.

*Tupper Lake Free Press Print:* May 17, 2000

# PEACOCK'S WINTER ROUTE

IN THE PREVIOUS *TRANSITION* COLUMN, we wrote of the waterway route via the Saranac's and the Racquette River that was followed by early travelers to access Tupper Lake. It will be recalled that due to only very primitive wood roads, most traffic in and out of this region moved by boat during the wilderness years.

In the winter months, with the waterway's ice locked and often treacherous—particularly in the early spring and late fall, the few settlers here were isolated for weeks at a time. In a 1941 interview with the Ausable Forks Record Post, Tom Peacock, who was, at the time, an 89-year-old Saranac Lake guide, told how as a youngster he would accompany his father, who had a contract to supply food and supplies to lumber camps at Big and Little Wolf Ponds. These camps were probably run by a Maine lumberman named Pomeroy, whose company was the first on record (1850) to begin logging the virgin pine in this area. Pomeroy had a small sawmill located on the outlet of Big Wolf Lake, then known as Lake Kitteridge (Little Wolf was then known as Lake Pomeroy). The mill was of an ancient English upright pattern, and it was not far from the present Bob Tebo house at the dead end of South Little Wolf Road.

Excerpts from that interview follow:

"They would load hay onto lumber sleds in the evening. Next morning, rising hours before daybreak in the dead of winter, they would put 25 to 30 bushels of potatoes and two or three quarts of

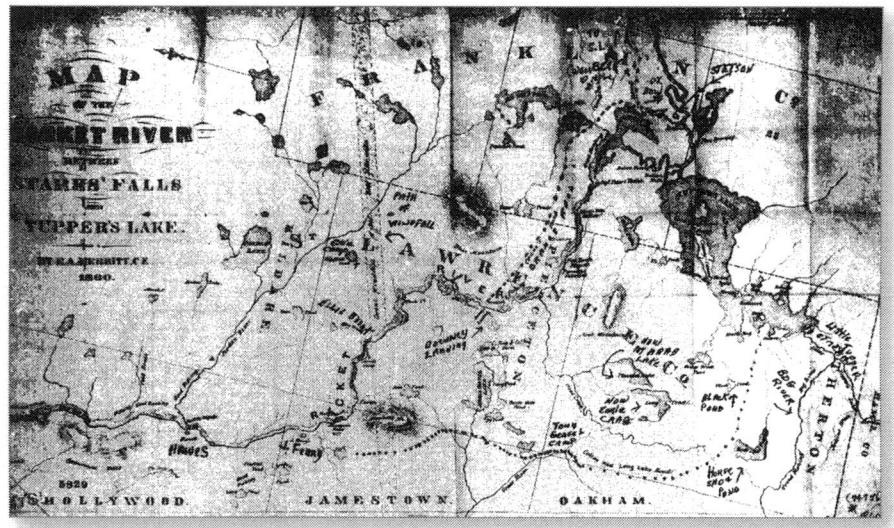

beef on the hay. The start was made about half past 2 or 3, but Tom can remember them still driving through Saranac Lake as early as 3 a.m. They planned to get onto the Lower Lake by daylight. Here were two sleds so the teams could double up if they struck heavy going.

"The route was through the Lower Lake with the turn off to right up the side of the river and then out onto Middle Saranac or Round Lake, as it was called locally. Crossing the ice on this lake, they took to the woods to the left of the river. Crossing the bridge at Bartlett's, they came out on the upper lake above the dam, where, according to Tom, the ice was sometimes poor. Out on Upper Saranac, they went straight across past Deer Island and into the woods at Johnson's Clearing. The country was now level, and for a stretch the crude winter road was in sight of Racquette River. The sleds would usually arrive in camp about 9 a.m. to be greeted by lumberjacks with great enthusiasm. They not only carried food for man and beast, but also brought the mail. Mr. Peacock remarked that in those days, mail was carried through the woods by Tom, Dick and Harry."

Accompanying this week's article is a rare map that shows some of the route Tom Peacock's father no doubt followed. The map was drawn by Edwin Merritt, well known in the Potsdam area at that time as a surveyor and civil engineer.

"These maps," Merritt wrote in a foreword, dated May 1, 1860, East Pierpont, St. Lawrence County, NY, "have been constructed from materials obtained from the most reliable sources. I have visited personally nearly every portion of the territory they cover and made actual surveys of most of the country in the vicinity of Racket River, north of Tupper Lake."

Merritt laid out his map in an unusual basis. North, instead of being at the top, as is customary, is toward the left-hand corner, as the cartographer's arrow near the word "MAP" indicates. This was apparently done to get as much of the river as possible onto the map. Part of the terrain mapped at lower left now lies beneath the water of Carry Lake. Homes of the pioneers along the river are indicated on the map at McEwen's, Hawes' and John Ferry. (Jane Anabella Hawes married this writer's great grandfather, Ezra Frenette, in 1859. Funding for a snowmobile bridge has been confirmed, which will cross the "Racket" near the former Hawes property. Ferry and McEwen family members still live prominently not far from their ancestors' original settlements.)

Landmarks for the boaters were Jamestown Falls, Moosehead still water near Seveys and Downey's Landing, where a road spanned the river in later years, extending from the vicinity of Pitchfork Pond to the old Childwold Park Hotel (Massaweppie).

Downey's Landing, went east to the outlet of Little Wolf Lake and swung south past "Pomeroy's Farm." The lone building marked on the shore of Racquette Pond was the only structure within what is now the village limits of Tupper Lake when Merritt mapped the area in 1860. Crane's Road apparently ended at Stetson's on the Racquette River. Notice that just before the road ends at Stetson's, an interesting road near Pomeroy's Farm leads east to Saranac Lake along the river. Doesn't it seem likely that this would have been part of the route that Peacock used in supplying the lumber camps?

This road apparently led to Wawbeek and followed along the river. Signs of an old road still lie above the boat launch on Route 30 (Crusher) where Cross Clearing Brooks enters the river. Since

Mr. Peacock said that they intersected the woods past Deer Island, it is possible many skiers and hikers use that same route that starts at Bull Point, Route 30, and intersects the Deer Pond trail, coming out at Cross Clearing brook, Route 30, below the Y.

Colton Long Lake road runs between Black Pond and north of Horseshoe Pond. Route 421 now parallels this old road but lies south of Horseshoe Pond. As part of the Adopt-a-Natural Resource Program, this writer maintains the trail to Black Pond from Route 421, but no trace of the old Colton Long Lake road as been discovered.

The road crossed Dead Creek to about where Tony Gensel's Center Pond Camp is located on No-Miss Club lands (headwaters Grasse River). It crossed the Grasse River and thence to the Racquette, which paralleled Colton.

*Tupper Lake Free Press Print:* May 31, 2000

# Paradise Park

I RECENTLY RAN ACROSS a tiny booklet that was apparently a real estate prospectus for property described as Paradise Park. There is no title page, only a black and white photo of a white-tailed deer graces the front cover. On the inside of the back cover we find in large letters:

> Sale Agents—
> William B. May & Company
> 717 Fifth Avenue
> New York City,
> Telephone, Plaza 270
> Other Brokers Protected

Each page in the booklet of twenty pages contains an excellent black and white photograph of various scenes found on and around the property.

Surrounding the pictures are descriptions of the property in flowery prose of that time (not unlike sales pitches of some present-day realtors).

The booklet must have been quite expensive to produce. I soon discovered that "Paradise Park" was the lands on and near Big Tupper Lake that were owned by the Colonel William Barbour family. No date is given anywhere in the booklet. However, in the introduction, reference is made to the late Colonel Barbour. Since

*There was no bridge across Bog River Falls when this photograph was taken sometime around 1918. The only access beyond was by boat or by woods near the Railroad at Horseshoe. (Bill Frenette photo)*

the Colonel died in 1917, the booklet is no earlier than that date. Also, since we know that the state in 1918 purchased some of the property described as being for sale, we can assume somewhat safely that the date for the booklet was that year. This gives us a time frame for the interesting and historically significant descriptions in the booklet. The state, which certainly acted with more dispatch that we see today with its bureaucratic lawyers, purchased in April of that year 190 acres of Colonel Barbour's estate for $150,000. Excluded from the sale were the various buildings and the farm.

These became in 1922 the nucleus of what was known as the American Legion Mountain Camp of the American Legion Department of the State of New York. It included 18 buildings, a road right-of-way to the railroad at Horseshoe Lake (today's Route 421), and a few lots on that lake. The purchase price was $85,000. The local chamber of commerce helped bring the Legion to this area by sparking a fund-raising drive that contributed $10,000 to the project.

This was a truly amazing contribution in those money-tight years. What is even more amazing, however, is that later that same year, this community then raised an additional $20,000 hard-earned dollars this time to buy the 160-acre Hosley Farm, and offered it to the government for $1 as an inducement to locate a proposed new hospital for ailing veterans here. An offer was accepted on June 26, 1922 and became the Sunmount we know today, which has meant so much to the growth and economic stability of our Tip-Top Town.

For younger readers, let me put the amount of money raised by this community into perspective. The average wage for laborers in 1921 was $4 per hour. A carpenter earned $4.25 per hour. $20,000 dollars was a very large sum of money. Indeed, it would be close to $150,000 in today's dollars.

To continue the "Legion Camp" story, it may be worth mentioning that at that time the only access to the "camp" was by boat from the village or by a five-mile dirt road from the Horseshoe railroad station. Subsequently, the state of New York, by a special act of the legislature, built a two-mile macadam road from the Tupper Long Lake highway to the camp, with a graceful stone bridge arching above Bog River Falls.

Many people in this community have strong and lasting ties evoking warm, happy thoughts of the property described in that handsome prospectus.

They have hiked, camped, fished, and yes, "partied" on what is today state land that has become a wonderful resource for the public. In addition, with the establishment of the American Legion Mountain Camp, hundreds of Tupper Lake youngsters of several generations worked there as staff members. Here they learned to row a boat, to swim, to fall in love, to bowl, to hike, and to meet new and interesting people at all levels of the social strata.

Here many of them earned their first wages and developed proper work ethics under the stern tutelage of administrators like Joe Burns and other fair but demanding employers who followed him.

The booklet, then, provides those who care to look back to what this writer feels is an incumbency to convey some understanding

*A.A. Low didn't like the appearance of the Rail Road Station at Horseshoe, so he built a new one. A "stick for stick, pillar for pillar rendition" of the beautiful station located in Garden City, Long Island. He then sold it to the New York central for a dollar. (Photo courtesy of R. Vaillancourt)*

of what early life on *our* lake was like for grandchildren, relatives, and newcomers who will stand in our shoes.

I hope you enjoy the passages quoted from that rare booklet that follow:

"The Sporting Estate of the late Colonel William Barbour, which has been in the family for about sixty years, having been originally established as a Sporting Club, and finally taken over by Colonel Barbour at least 25 years ago, since which time it has been his personal hobby, and having been carefully protected and preserved, is today unquestionably the finest Fishing and Hunting Estate in the Mountains. It has an almost unique possession of virgin forest, the only timber ever having been cut, being softwood, excepting on a small portion of low-land purchased within the last three years from the estate of Augustus A. Low, the object of this purchase being to connect the estate itself directly with the

New York Central Railroad tracks, making available a private station at Horseshoe, which gives easy access to the property.

"Big Tupper Lake, being situated directly in the heart of the Mountains, is preserved from the public by the fact that the entire upper portion is owned by Mr. Edward H. Litchfield, and 'Paradise Park.' The Hamlet of Moody is on the lower end of the lake, eight miles distant, about which there are several smaller camps. The effect of this is that the Deer and other shooting is unsurpassed. Beaver abound and are more abundant than they have been for fifty years. Excellent examples of their interesting work in damming the brooks and streams may be seen about Bridge Brook Pond—fifteen and twenty being frequently seen at that same time. Bear are still more abundant here than in any other part of the Woods and German Wild Boar introduced but a few years ago seem to be becoming numerous. Fox, rabbit, hare, otter, and other small game are fairly abundant. There are also a large number of partridge and other game such as one might expect to find in so highly preserved an estate. The fishing is more than excellent. In the lake itself are bass and pike, while in the deeper waters lake trout and white fish are abundant, the latter affording wonderful sport. On the property are numerous trout streams and two lakes: one, Bridge Brook, a natural trout pond, has been stocked not only with additional brook trout but with steel head trout as well. Horseshoe Pond is famous throughout the Adirondacks for the size of the brook trout taken there, frequently running from three to four and a half pounds. The trout streams include Bear Pond Brook, which is an affluent of the Little Tupper Lake Stream, and was purchased separately from the rest of the property for protection. From all the lakes are also trout streams which provide excellent sport for spring fishing.

"One of the most remarkable features is the fact that the Railroad connection from New York and Boston permits one to breakfast at the camp after one night's traveling from either point and yet the estate is so isolated that after leaving the railroad the entire trip to camp is through the preserve. Arriving there and looking out over the great expanse of lake not a house is to be seen.

"Big Tupper Lake is 1,590 feet above sea level, other portions of the preserve, however, are much higher. The scenic views are absolutely unsurpassed and from the main camp Mount Morris, one of the higher peaks in the entire mountains, looms up across the lake and, covered as it is with hardwood forest, is a magnificent sight in September and October.

"Outside of a road built from Foxhall Pond to Black Pond and also one from Horseshoe to the camp, the entire estate has been saved from the spoliation of roads, etc., the trails being the only means of communication throughout the wilderness.

"The site for the main camp was chosen sixty years ago on account of the peculiar conformation of the shore at this point giving direct views not only down the lake but also to the Bog River Falls, one of the greatest torrents in the Woods. The stand of virgin pines surrounding the buildings is unique and only possible because of the sandy soil at this particular point and the long care which as been taken of it. It is perhaps interesting to note that these pines are reproducing themselves and smaller trees are ready to replace the old ones should they die out.

"The buildings are attractive on account of their simplicity, being of the same construction and character throughout the entire preserve, all covered with Florida hand-hewn cypress shingles which wear to a charming silver gray tint. They consist of three main camps and the farm buildings. The principal camp is on Paradise Point and has a series of detached and semi-detached buildings. There are more or less 20 in all—a large main dining-room with big open fireplace, the walls covered with trophies taken from the preserve. Attached to the dining-room are adequate servants' quarters, etc., all being so thoroughly well arranged and so complete that no difficulty has ever been experienced in keeping City servants. A covered veranda connects the dining-room with the living-room which is probably 30x60 and from which open window in all directions. In this room there is another of the great fireplaces built by the guides, of rocks blasted nearby, which is a feature of almost every room in the entire camp. There are connected with this room masters' bedrooms and baths, also two guests' room above and two detached guests' houses with baths. In addition to these, are guides' houses, guides' dining-room, kitchen, etc., and two large icehouses.

"At the foot of the dining-room steps is the celebrated Coleman Spring which has been mentioned in every book dealing with the Adirondacks since the discovery of the lake and which is the most famous spring in the woods. It flows steadily year round without varying in temperature and runs as a small stream through the front lawn to the lake. This stream has been widened at three points to make attractive trout ponds, each being about 20 x 20. These were made expressly to keep alive the trout which are only slightly hooked during the summer's fishing and here at any time fresh fish can be had at a moment's notice to welcome the unexpected guest. The fish are constantly jumping and playing during the warm weather, thus affording infinite pleasure."

*Tupper Lake Free Press Print:* July 12, 2000

# Barbour's Property on Big Tupper Lake

LAST WEEK'S COLUMN CONTAINED a description of the Colonel William Barbour property on Big Tupper Lake as it appeared in 1920. As we now know, the property was subdivided, 13,190 acres having been sold to New York State and the remaining 1,260 acres sold to the American Legion for a recuperative site for disabled veterans of World War I. The special emphasis of the Legion purchase was to be on the care of veterans convalescing from tuberculosis and the horrible effects of mustard gas poisoning. Until it was outlawed, this deadly form of warfare was sent off from tanks when the wind would blow toward the Allied Forces. Unless the soldiers were equipped with gas masks, there was no way for them to avoid breathing the poisonous fumes that filled the hollows and trenches. I speak of this in part because, along with many other American soldiers, my Uncle Frank Frenette, a member of this community, had his life drastically shortened by the after-effects of this insidious and barbaric form of warfare.

Let's return to the descriptive pages of the now rare sales booklet prepared by the realtors who were offering the Barbour property for sale . . .

"For recreation during the evening, there is an excellently well-equipped bowling alley, at a distance of perhaps 200 yards from the main camp reached by a gravel walk; one of the features to make the alleys more attractive to non-players being a gallery with an enormous fireplace. The Tennis Court is on the road to the farm.

*An unsmiling President Calvin Coolidge shown in the 1926 photo was only one of the many prominent national figures who visited the Legion Camp over the years.*

In the clearing a very fine golf course can be laid out if desired.

"Foxhall Farm is one-half mile from the main camp and is reached through a charming wooded path which passes between the enclosed Deer Parks. The buildings are all modern and up to date. The farmer's house is very unique and picturesque and is so designed that it is intended for use during the period when the main camp is not in occupancy. This building was especially planned so that the farmer can have his quarters under the same roof and yet separated from the rooms which have always been maintained for use by the family for winter sports, snow-shoeing, tobogganing, etc. These master's quarters, properly heated, include accommodations with baths for four or five people.

"In the farm proper there are about 75 acres which have been cleared and provide paddocks, kitchen and flower gardens supplying fresh vegetables and flowers in abundance for the camp.

"There is a very celebrated herd of Kerry cattle (probably about 20 head) which were personally imported from Ireland by Colonel Barbour as being particularly adapted to the rather rigorous winter climatic conditions of the Adirondacks. These have thriven beyond expectation and are an extremely attractive feature of the place. There is also a flock of horned Dorset Sheep. A large flock of wild geese, which during the summer have the freedom of the upper end of the lake, and add to its picturesque beauty.

"About a half mile from the farm are a series of large clearings made by a Shaker Community nearly 100 years ago. These are about 300 acres in extent and affordable land where sufficient grain is raised to maintain the cattle during the winter. Barns capable of storing under cover the entire crops. A macadam road which is used throughout the year connects the farm.

"At Warren Point about three-quarters of a mile north of the farm is another excellently equipped modern camp of about four buildings. The main building is about 140 feet long with a piazza running the full length and situated on the top of a ledge of rocks 40 feet above the level of the water. It overlooks the lake and is designed with a large central living room and a series of guests' apartments opening from the masters' rooms beyond. Upstairs is a solid zinc-lined store-room, proof against vermin, mice, etc. The bathrooms and running water are adequately provided for. The kitchen, servants' quarters, guides' houses, tool houses and boat house are separate from the main building.

"Distant three miles north from Warren Point is still another camp consisting of some ten buildings with adequate dining-rooms, living-rooms, bedrooms, boat-houses, etc., equipped with modern plumbing. This latter camp could be easily separated from the main estate giving adequate shore frontage on Big Tupper Lake—5,000 acres might be apportioned for this, or less if desired.

"Between the main camp and the farm are two deer parks, entirely enclosed by steel wire fences eight feet high, woven in place and which are only separated by the path leading to the farm. These parks have been stocked with Fallow Deer from England as well as the native White-tail. The extent of the parks, however, is so large that it is impossible to estimate the number of deer now in the enclosure. The shelter house for the deer was built upon suggestions given by Mr. Hornaday of the Bronx Zoo and is entirely adequate for their winter protection.

"There are six launches varying from service launches for the farmers' use to the large luxuriously equipped 45-foot Bridge Brook speed launch that is very fast and which is used for communicating with the Post Office at Moody about eight miles distant, where there is a dock adequate for any of the launches.

"The estate proper contains about 27 square miles or between 19,000 and 20,000 acres with over 15 miles of lake frontage.

"The four most important Estates in the Adirondacks, are 'Paradise Park,' The Whitney, the E.H. Litchfield, and the A.A. Lowe. These four preserves grouped, as they are, form a total area of about 120,000 acres representing the largest tract of absolutely protected game preserves that can be found anywhere in the East, with the additional advantage of easy access to civilization.

"The camp may be reached in three ways. During the summer, the Horseshoe route is most agreeable. The train reaches the private station (Horseshoe) on the Adirondack division of the New York Central Railway at about 7 a.m. Grouped at the station are several buildings for game wardens, guides, etc.; also a boat house. After crossing the lake, a team from the farm is waiting at the outlet of the pond (where there is another small boat-house). A beautiful drive through the woods of about one and a quarter hours brings the traveler to the farm, whence camp may be reached by the path or by launch. Still another way is motor up from Saratoga by the new State Highway which crosses Rock Island Bay on the opposite side of the lake, where there is a dock for launches, the distance then from camp being about three miles. The third method is to take the New York Central train past Horseshoe to Tupper Lake Junction and motor from there six miles to Moody (foot of the lake). In winter it is very attractive, completing the trip by driving or skating from this point over the ice.

"The camps are fully furnished and all furnishing, launches, stock, farm implements, etc., will be included in any sale, so that a purchaser can have the enjoyment of immediate possession.

"There are experienced men now employed upon the place who have been in the service of the family for many years and who know the hunting and fishing thoroughly.

"Price $350,000."

The rise and fall of the American Legion Mountain Camp and its property as just described is beyond the scope of this column. Suffice to say, however, that this writer was present in the late 1970s, when auctioneer Chas Vasburgh put property, cottages and their antique furnishings on his auctioneering block. It was a deeply sentimental, disturbing day to see that famous and historic institution go down so cheaply and so ignobly under his auction gavel.

It is useless to look back and speculate now on the failure of the Legion Camp to prosper as a successful operation. Perhaps the nursery rhyme "All the kings horses and the king's men couldn't put Humpty Dumpty together again" is appropriate here.

Those readers familiar with the Mountain Camp may agree with respected historian David Ackerman, who, when speaking of a similar situation, had this to say: "In some respects, the story is not unlike a business school study where developments are examined sequentially to determine whether lessons can be learned having the student look at the ifs and buts as the story unfolds!

"Surely the (Legion Camp) would have made a great case study for a resort management course."

*Tupper Lake Free Press Print:* July 26, 2000

## THE END OF BIG MILL

MANY READERS OF THIS column will no doubt remember the large structure that stood like some sculpture's masterpiece near the present grandstand site at Municipal Park along Demars Boulevard. It was all that remained of the "Big Mill," which was once located there and was a magnet that attracted the kids of my generation. The big challenge was to scale the 15-foot cement foundation wall to the platform where the massive band-saw machinery was once in place. Memories of that time and place came flooding back this week as I watched Tinker Hollingsworth deftly maneuver his large bulldozer, reducing multiple piles of earth into a sub base for a new board walk, a part of the revitalization project for the wonderful asset that is our municipal park.

Of historical interest is the fact that the "Big Mill" was started by John Hurd in 1890 to take advantage of his Northern Adirondack Railroad, which was to reach this town that year. The sawmill was said to be the biggest in the state, producing the chips for pulp and bark for tanneries as well as sawn lumber. The world's record for a single day's sawing was twice broken here.

It may be hard to believe, but an aerial tramway from that mill was built across Demars Boulevard to a series of charcoal kilns that were situated along the north side of Pleasant Avenue. The tramway was nearly an eighth of a mile long. Its purpose was to carry wood chips and other waste from the mill to the kilns where charcoal was made. A railroad siding, which ran along the rear of

*This overview shows the splendid progress being made at the Municipal Park shoreline project. In the foreground town board member Rick Dattola discusses matters with Kris Iregoe of the Flacco and Riley contracting firm. (Bill Frenette photo)*

*Shown here is the Raquette Pond shoreline as it appeared in this pre-1930 photo. The triple-tiered log booms contravened the spring log drive in high water.*

today's McDonald's restaurant, served the kilns to haul away the charcoal, which had a high value in those days.

Accompanying this week's column is an item contained in the September 23, 1937, edition of this newspaper. It may be of general interest as the project to revitalize our park progresses.

### RAZING OF ELLIOTT MILL WILL REMOVE LAST TRACE OF LUMBER LANDMARKS FROM THE PARK SITE
*Machinery Walls Stripped From Abandoned Demars Blvd. Plant Workers Start on Roof Today—Ship Salvage to Potsdam Mill*

"Another mute reminder of Tupper Lake's one-time status as the Adirondack lumber capital is rapidly being effaced.

"Employees of the C.H. Elliot Hardwood Lumber Company are engaged in tearing down the Elliott mill on Demars Blvd. Already the walls have been stripped away, except for a spidery tracery of joists and cross-pieces. This morning they started to rip off the roof. The job will take at least two weeks longer, they estimate, after which nothing will remain to mark the spot on the shore of Raquette Pond which was the scene of four decades of lumbering activity.

"With the exception of the band saw, all machinery has already been removed- snaked by crane from the interior of the building—and shipped to Potsdam, where the lumber from the structure is also going. The crew, pausing to reminisce a moment before tackling their job of destruction this morning, recalled that this same machinery once figured in a world's record of cut lumber. It was hooked up in Hurd's "Big Mill" at the time, the mill, which was owned successfully by the Norwood Manufacturing Company and the Santa Clara Lumber Co. Carriage; band-saw edgers and other machinery used in that record cut are still in good condition, and may see service again soon at the Potsdam Elliott plant. Mr. Elliott bought the old mill and machinery from J. Ferris Meiggs.

"Back in 1923 C.H. Elliott erected a rambling, red mill on the site of the plant now being torn down. It burned down about

*Station is Brandon . . . Bob Eteman negotiates his canoe under the trestle of the former NY & Ottawa Railroad. Bob is on Quebec Brook near the Madawaska Bog. It is part of the controversial 150,000-acre addition to the state's recreational land, acquired in 1998 by easement and purchase from Champion International. How to get there—Madawaska Bog/Flow canoe route via Quebec Brook, six miles to Old New York and Ottawa Railroad Line from the junction of Routes 30 and 86 at Paul Smith's College—take Keeses Mill/Blue Mountain Road west 12 miles to state launch site. Meno Map. (Bill Frenette photo)*

three years later. In 1927 he put up the present plant and engaged in the manufacture of mangle rollers and lumber. 1931 and the depression era saw the mill shut down, never to reopen. In October, 1932, the Village of Tupper Lake purchased for $5,000 a strip of land flanking Raquette Pond from Cliff Avenue to the O.W.D. line, for municipal park's purposes. The Elliott mill lies midway in that tract, and is being torn down to make way for the park development. Sand and top-soil have been trucked in to the tract for the past two years, and the filled in and graded section of the park now reaches close to the Elliott plant. The greenery of an attractive park will cover the old Santa Clara and Elliott mill sites in the near future, leaving nothing but a concrete bandsaw foundation on the site of the "Big Mill" to mark those once-busy spots.

"William Collett, foreman, and Vincent Kavanagh and Fred Brunette are pushing the razing of the Elliott Mill."

*Tupper Lake Free Press Print:* August 02, 2000

# NOSTALGIC WANAKENA

SEVERAL WEEKS AGO, this writer joined a local group of hikers on one of their scheduled weekly trips. The goal this day was a climb up Cat Mountain, located in the Five Ponds Wilderness area near Wanakena and south of Cranberry Lake.

Lumber was king in this area in the early 1900s, and the railroad spurs ran like the spokes of a wheel, reaching out to prime timber areas, formerly too far for the primitive transportation then available to be cost effective. Many of those railroad beds have become a part of today's trail system in the Five Ponds area, and the route chosen by trip leader John Sayles was of special historical interest.

Natural history abounds here, also in the form of the 1995 windstorm called a Derecho (a straight line storm). This storm is considered the largest natural disturbance to affect the Adirondacks. In the Five Ponds, over 60 percent of the trees were blown over. Here is an opportunity to gain your own perspective on whether the downed timber should have been salvaged. Was it a valuable resource that should have been harvested and not left to rot? Or was it just a disturbance that should be left alone since forest communities evolve with such disturbances, and not only survive, but thrive in the wake of such occurrences?

The route the Tupper Lake group followed this day started on the South Shore Road in the hamlet of Wanakena. It follows what had been the road bed of one of the former logging railroads of the

Rich and Andrews Lumber Company. As you might expect, the grades were easy, and a firm treadway provided good walking. The railroad grade ends at a bay of Cranberry Lake called Dead Creek Flow. A red-marked trail with a moderate climb through mature hardwoods and a slight scramble takes you to the summit of Cat Mountain.

It may be of interest that Wanakena, located where the Oswegatchie River flows into Cranberry Lake, didn't exist until 1903. It was a region of primitive forests of spruce and hardwoods, with many great pines towering above the spruce. That changed almost overnight when the Rich and Andrews Lumber Co., which had exhausted its lumber supply in Pennsylvania, acquired 16,000 acres south of Wanakena.

Within a year, that company had built 15 miles of railroad tracks and a large sawmill. They also laid out a planned village

*In 1909, one of the first fire towers in the state was built on Cat Mountain. The original wooden tower was later replaced by one made of steel. Of seven such towers erected in St. Lawrence County, only the tower on Mt. Arab remains.*

with electricity and water hookups. In no time, over 700 people moved in and Wanakena was born. The railroad that the company

*The New York State Ranger School, located in Wanakena, is shown here. It has existed since 1912 and is the oldest institution of its kind in the United States.*

built made it possible to cut one of the last stands of giant pine trees in the park. They cut mostly softwood, and if those trees were impressive, so was the dimension lumber that was sawn from them. Most of the logs were cut to a standard of 20 feet to protect the butt ends. The railroad, with its many spurs, permitted the clearing of 2,300 acres a year, and in seven years, the tract was stripped of its virgin timber, causing the sawmill to close.

At about that same time, the Emporium Forestry Co. opened a mill in Conifer (1911) and built the Grasse River Railroad to Cranberry Lake. This brought about a shift in lumber operations and camps from Wanakena to the Cranberry and Conifer areas. Many Wanakena residents moved to the new locations or to camps run by Tupper Lake operators such as John D'Avignon, George Bushey and Oliver Proulx. Mr. Proulx had a large camp near Dog Pond, where the late Leon LaFave once told me he spent many happy hours as a youngster when his mother was a cook at that camp.

A beautiful meadow, now called Proulx's Clearing, obscures the many remnants of that large camp, but the view down the valley that carries Dog Pond's outlet waters to Cranberry Lake remains impressive. Mr. Proulx certainly picked a beautiful location for his camp site.

The blush was off the rose for Wanakena as a bustling community, but the dew remained, and Wanakena today is a lovely hamlet with large shade trees bordering well-kept homes along quiet streets on both sides of the Oswegatchie River, which still runs vibrant and clear under the connecting bridge. Gone is the large company store where, as a pre-teenage helper on my father's beverage truck, I delivered many cases of Orange Crush in its distinctive "Crinkly Brown" sun-protected bottles. Gone too is the large hotel at the "top of the hill," but not before it became a rip-roaring dance hall and bar when the Benson Mines operation and the Newton Falls Paper Mill provided hundreds of thirsty, fun-loving patrons. What has remained is the Ranger School, the oldest institution of its kind in the United States.

When the Rich Lumber Co. closed in 1912 after its short seven-year interval, some of its land was given to build this remarkable school.

Since that time, associated with the State University College of Forestry at Syracuse University, it has trained thousands of students to become professional foresters, fitted for such positions as forest rangers, estate managers, timber cruisers, scalers and surveyors.

The school is noted for its intensive, no-nonsense curriculum with a heavy emphasis on algebra and geometry, day-long field work and classroom instruction.

You will experience a certain time warp if you visit Wanakena today, but it's a visit you will find rewarding, nostalgic and, yes, historical.

*Tupper Lake Free Press Print:* August 23, 2000

# ABANDONED CANNONS

TWO HUNDRED AND TWENTY-FOUR years ago a party of some 300 Tories and Indians, led by the notorious Sir John Johnson, fighting their way through almost impenetrable virgin wilderness, passed within two miles of the upper end of Big Tupper Lake, in the vicinity of the present American Legion Mountain Camp property. They were fleeing from Johnstown, hotbed of Tory activities, to Canada, and they were in very much of a hurry. They had every reason to believe that a force of Colonists was pursuing them. Because the two huge cannons that they had dragged up through the Adirondack's wilds were impending their flight, they abandoned them. Nearly 40 years ago those same cannons were found, rusting away in the deep woods on the Barbour estate near the head of Big Tupper. The following interesting account of how they came to be there and what became of them this summer was turned over to the *Free Press* by John McCoy of this village. It is from the September 21 issue of a Johnstown, NY, newspaper.

"Through the enterprise of J. Yates Van Antwerp, well known business man, and the cooperation of a number of men familiar with Adirondack trails, two old cannon barrels, which are believed to be the ones abandoned by Sir John Johnson and his followers in their flight to Canada in 1776, have been brought back to this city.

"Mr. Van Antwerp, who is intensely interested in the history of this region, succeeded in securing the cannon as a representative

*During the War of 1812 the state legislature authorized a road to be built from Broadalbin near Albany to an arsenal at Russell near Canton. It followed the likely escape route of Sir John Johnson and was an overgrown hunters' trail when this photo was taken over 40 years ago. All traces have now disappeared. The road crossed the Racquette River on a log bridge near the Anthony Ponds Clearing, crossed near Albany Lake (so named because of the road it became Nehasane Lake) when Dr. Seward Webb purchased it in 1890. The road then came near today's Benson Mines where the roads surveyors made the original iron ore discovery.*

of the Johnstown Historical Society after spending a great deal of time in research and in contacting guides and others who had spent their lives in the section in which the field pieces were found. All of the data he has obtained has been checked and rechecked as to authenticity."

By consulting topographical maps of the Adirondacks and making a thorough study of possible routes to Canada, Mr. Van Antwerp came to the conclusion that the trail pointed out by historians was not entirely correct. As a result of talking to guides and old Adirondack residents, Mr. Van Antwerp discovered that the trail was in a different location than that given in history books.

"The cannons were finally located at the summer home of John

Edward Barbour of Paterson, NJ, of the Barbour Thread Company. His summer home is located at Follensby Pond, six miles from Tupper Lake.

### Barbour Donates the Cannons

"Mr. Barbour graciously donated the cannons to the Johnstown Historical Society when proper details had been furnished him concerning their origin and history.

"After consulting with Mr. Barbour at his summer home, Mr. Van Antwerp mailed him a report showing why he believed these cannons to be the ones Sir John took with him in his flight to Canada.

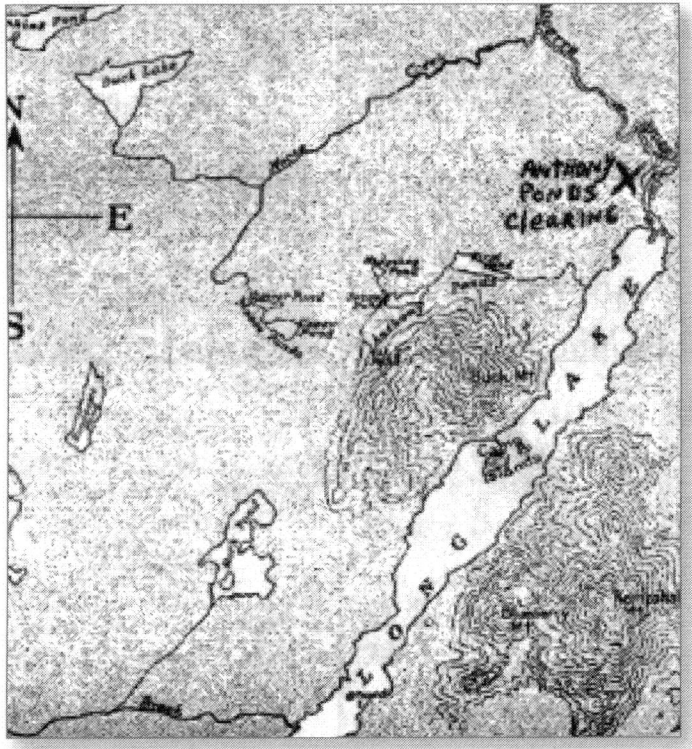

*The map shown here indicates with an X a location known as Anthony Ponds clearing. Sir John Johnson in 1775 is thought to have turned N/W from here then passed the south end of Tupper Lake on his flight to the St. Laurence River, where he was met by Aughnawaga Indians, who took him to Canada and safety.*

*Pictured here in 1917 is the former Barbour Camp on Warren Point, Big Tupper Lake. Two cannons of English make, one of which was found on the Barbour property in 1897, were for many years mounted on the camp's front lawn.*

"In the letter, Mr. Van Antwerp gave a brief resumé of events leading up to Sir John's hasty departure from Johnstown. He explained that Sir John Johnson, an over-zealous Royalist, at the outbreak of the Revolution was placed on parole but meantime was secretly drilling troops and hoarding ammunition in Johnstown.

"Colonial Dayton, in the early spring 1776, was directed to proceed to Johnstown from Albany with a large number of troops to arrest Sir John and to confiscate all war supplies in his possession. Johnson, being warned beforehand of Dayton's approach, broke his parole and hurriedly left Johnstown. He took with him 300 Tories, a number of Indian guides and two pieces of light artillery.

"The trail Johnson followed was from Johnstown to the Sacandaga River, thence to Lake Pleasant, thence to Raquette Lake, by way of Raquette River to Long Lake. From the extreme end of Long Lake, now known as Anthony Pond clearing, Johnson and his followers marched in a north-westerly direction.

"This route passed within two miles south of Big Tupper Lake and continued to the Grass River. They followed the course of this river to the St. Lawrence. Then by means of boats they reached their destination, Montreal, nineteen days after leaving Johnstown.

"Records of that time indicated that the party discarded their snowshoes at Raquette Lake on account of spring thaw and for the same reason disposed of their cannons between Long Lake and Tupper Lake."

Note: Raquette is the French name for snowshoe. That translation and an Indian name meaning noise (racket) have been offered as possible alternative sources of the name for both lake and river. It is also spelled Racquette, a somewhat more stylish form and more French-appearing. There is also some feeling that the snowshoes were abandoned on an island of the river as it flows through Potsdam village and not Raquette Lake (Pilcher).

One historian (Leete) claims that as Scotsmen, Johnson and his followers would never have left perfectly good snowshoes, plus the date of his escape was in May. This historian finds the stories "forced." He further added, "Have you heard the story of the Scotsman who left his change on the bar after buying a drink? You never will." His conclusion was that "the only name that has a clear logical origin is the Indian name translated Racket."

Mr. Van Antwerp concluded his findings in his report to Mr. Barbour with the following summary: "The cannons are of English make and design, built previous to the American Revolution; they were discovered in the approximate location that the Johnson party disposed of them; history records no other expedition into the Adirondacks where cannons of their type were being transported; both cannons were spiked and abandoned, indicating that the Johnson party expected to be pursued, the guns being made useless against the probability of the Colonists recovering them.

"John T. Morrison, president of the Johnstown Historical Society, wrote to Mr. Barbour informing him that Mr. Antwerp had been delegated by the local historical group to ascertain if it were possible to secure the return of the old cannons.

"Mr. Barbour, in his reply to Mr. Morrison's letter said in part:

"Mrs. Barbour and I will be very glad to give these to your society, believing they and their history will be much better preserved in Johnstown than here at our camp.

"When we received these cannons from my cousin William Barbour's sons about fifteen years ago, they were both spiked, but through rust and corrosion the spikes were comparatively loose and have since fallen out and been lost.

"Mrs. Barbour and I appreciate your courtesy in giving us credit for our gift, and if such card is inscribed would also appreciate a copy of same.'

"The gratitude of the historical society to Mr. Barbour for his donation of the cannons was expressed by President Morrison, who promised the donor that the cannons would be properly placed and a copy of the inscriptions sent to him"

Sabbattis Checks Trail

"At Long Lake Mr. Van Antwerp checked with Joe Sabbattis on the trail he believed that Johnson took and found that the trail did exist. His father, Mitchell Sabbattis, a full-blooded Indian, who is referred to in Donaldson's *History of the Adirondacks* as 'the last of the Mohicans,' had seen one of the cannons.

"Other Long Lake guides, Joseph Gokey, Alfred Lappel and James Derwood, men who have guided and trapped in that region all their lives, vouched for the truth of the statements made by Sabbattis.

"Mr. Van Antwerp received valuable information at Tupper Lake from Charles Goodman, a civil engineer, who has a summer home there. Ed Sabourin, who is a guide at Tupper Lake, notified the local historian that the guns had been discovered on the Barbour property and moved to their summer home at Paradise Point (now property Lowe and Rider families—stone house, south bay of Big Tupper Lake).

"Painstakingly following every lead, Mr. Van Antwerp learned from Joseph Burns, superintendent of the American Legion Camp, that the cannons had been removed to Barbour's present summer home at Follensby Lake (now McCormick property).

"In talking to Mr. Sabourin, it was brought out that the cannons were found approximately five miles apart, one in a swamp and the other on a slight knoll. The gun carriages were all rotted away and one could just see the marks of them.

"One of the cannons wheels had fallen off and a beech tree had grown up within the circle of the wheel. In 1900 this tree measured more than two feet in diameter and, at that time, according to forestry experts, was more than 100 years old. In view of the fact that the wheel could not have fallen from the gun carriage until decay had set in and, the fact that the tree was more than 100 years old in 1900, it is reasonable to believe that these cannons were abandoned about the same time of the flight of Sir John Johnson.

"In corroboration of this, it is a well-established fact that two cannons identical with those found stood in front of Johnson Hall at the outbreak of the Revolution and disappeared at the time of Johnson's flight.

"When found the cannons' barrels were sunk deeply into the ground so just the top part was showing. They are made of cast iron, one gun weighing about 1,300 pounds and the other about 700 pounds. One is 54 inches in length and the other about five feet. They fired a fourteen-pound cannons ball.

"Mr. Van Antwerp and an assistant loaded the barrels on a truck yesterday morning (October 6, 1937) and brought them to Johnstown. They were taken to the blockhouse at Johnson Hall that same night. The society plans to restore the cannons to their original position at the Hall."

*Tupper Lake Free Press Print:* September 06, 2000

# GLORY

IT IS PROBABLY SAFE TO ASSUME that during the summer months, local residents cut back on the amount of time they watch television. Even Oprah and Jeopardy take a back seat to pursuits like long evening walks, golfing, fishing and sunset rides in the boat, not to mention camping, gardening and keeping the lawn mowed.

That lack of viewing may have changed this past week due to several historic "firsts" available on our television sets.

One of those opportunities was the wonderful coverage of the high school football games played at night under state-of-the-art lighting at the magnificent Rotary Athletic Field. The Adelphia Cable football network, channels 2 and 22, does a first-rate job in providing this coverage with great camera work and exciting replays all in "living color."

Then, of course, there are the Olympic Games being held in Sydney, Australia. Spectacle and, excitement aside, we were privileged to welcome the very first Olympic games of our new century. If that were not historically enough, how about watching Aboriginal Cathy Freeman, a favorite in the 400-meter run, crossing a pond of water to light the Olympic Flame, symbolically bridging a racial divide that has for years tormented and tainted Australia? Or seeing the teams of North and South Korea, once bitter enemies, entering the stadium as one during the parade of athletes?

The triathlon event became a first also as the Olympics' newest sport. As an early host for this type of event long before it became so wildly popular, members of this community must have been ecstatic to view its Olympic debut. As I sat glued to my television watching those splendid athletes emerge from the swim portion of the race, shedding swim gear as they raced to the transition area to begin their bike leg, I could envision local organizers Ted Merrihew and Jim Frenette carefully monitoring the Australian setup, mentally taking notes to see if the procedure was as smooth as our well-organized local effort.

As a point of history, it may be of interest that the original ancient Greek Olympics were a tribute to the Gods, a show of humanity's capacity for grace, speed and strength.

Our modern Olympic movement was founded in 1896, when a Parisian aristocrat named Baron Pierre de Caubertin became determined to rekindle the ancient ethic.

The Olympics have suffered some abuses over the years, but at least one of De Caubertin's ideals has been realized—that of uniting the world's countries—if only briefly.

I stayed up until the early hours of the morning last week watching the women's mountain bike race. The course was laid out over a working farm just outside of Sydney, a torturous course with gut-wrenching uphills and frightening obstacle-laden downhills, a highly technical course almost three hours long, requiring great daring, stamina and the utmost skill and strategy.

I watched in complete awe as the Swiss woman struggled to keep the lead she had heroically built up while being relentlessly pursued by the best bicyclists in the world. And then, after more than two hours of leading the field, she was suddenly passed in a daring downhill move by the reigning world champion from Italy, who put the hammer down in a mad sprint to the finish. The Swiss woman finished second with the Spanish entry tight by her rear wheel.

Here is where the cynicism about the games vaporizes. Why? Because this was what the Olympics were meant to be. Speed, daring, skill, stamina, determination. Here was a glimpse at the transcendent. The quest to excel. You see these athletes in their glory and cheer, you cry, you smile. Little kids smile. De Caubertin smiles. The Gods themselves smile.

*Tupper Lake Free Press Print:* September 27, 2000

## ADIRONDACK AUTUMN

A NUMBER OF YEARS AGO, in late fall, I spent almost a month boating the Colorado River and hiking the side canyons and the desert terrain of the Grand Canyon. I was part of a small group on a commercial trip put together by my daughter and some of her river-running friends, who had "lucked out" in obtaining a hard-to-get private permit (a cancellation by another party who had waited for two years to get a permit provided that opportunity). Most of the group were former river guides on this river and thus knew the best side of the canyon hikes. They knew also the trails to the oasis villages, where Indians still dwell as they have for centuries. They knew the location of closely guarded secret hot springs and, best of all, they were equal to the river's many formidable challenges—a help to this writer's big water abilities.

From our put-in at Lee's Ferry on the Utah/Arizona border to our take-out at Mile 225 at the Hualapai Indian Reservation, 15 miles from upstream Lake Mead, it was a wonderful and memorable trip; the desert, the canyon and the river were truly beautiful. The strange thing was, that for all its beauty and excitement, as the days wore on, I had a nagging concern: I was going to miss the wonders of our Adirondack autumn! Here is the time when the whole Tupper Lake area explodes in color when for a tantalizing short while, two weeks or so, the Adirondacks are arguably one of the loveliest places on earth, and hey,

I wasn't going to be there.

My partner in our dory was originally from New Hampshire, and he admitted to the same concern, even as he would not admit that the fall display in the Adirondacks was at least equal to that of his New England countryside.

We did agree that the Northeastern landscape provides a setting that no other area of North America can rival. There is a variety in its trees that few other areas achieve. A contrast of beech, maple, sumacs, and poplar that dazzle the senses. Every hillside splashed with sharp shades of all sorts of color, flaming scarlet, lustrous gold, throbbing vermillion, fiery orange.

Younger readers may raise their eyebrows at my concern in missing a single season of fall foliage. The reality is that, as you get older, each such season becomes more important. Call it a milestone, if you will. Older folks treasure such milestones perhaps because they realize that there may not be that many left.

The thing is, we don't get to invert the hourglass that contains the sands of our time on earth. Each grain, as it falls through the glass clicking away the time we have spent in this world and the time remaining, is an inflexible finality that no one escapes. Is it no wonder that people by the bus loads (largely senior citizens, affectionately called "leaf peepers" by us locals) travel hundreds of miles to view the unique wonder of our autumn season.

We are blessed here in the Adirondacks with a perfect balance when our climate in the fall, with its crisp, chilly nights and warm sunny days as experienced this week, bring all the deciduous trees to a coordinated climax.

As Bill Bryson, author of *I'm a Stranger Here Myself*, puts it, "What is all the more remarkable about this is that no one knows quite why this all happens."

He explains that, "in autumn, trees prepare for their long winter's slumber by ceasing to manufacture chlorophyll, the chemical that makes the leaves green. The absence of chlorophyll allows other pigments called cartenoids and xanthophyll, which have been present in the leaves all along, to show off a bit. These pigments are what account for the yellow and gold of birches and beech trees, among others. No one knows why the trees do so when they get nothing evident in return."

"Well, Bill, the trees may not get anything in return, but we most certainly do." It is my hope that everyone reading this column is allowed to view many, many more autumn seasons. A time when the summer bursts into a million glowing tints, heralding yet another milestone and reaffirming that Tupper Lake is a wonderful place in which to live and grow.

*Tupper Lake Free Press Print:* October 04, 2000

## THE BENDERS

MERRIAM WEBSTER'S collegiate dictionary defines the word "bender" as a spree or "an unrestrained indulgence in or outburst of activity esp: binge, carousel." Thus, we might say, "Wow, Joe went on a heck of a bender that lasted all week."

To many people in this community, however, the word has a different and far more nostalgic meaning.

A "bender" to those folks was the innovative machine located in the woodenware division of the Oval Wood Dish (O.W.D.) in a department known as the "Benders."

Developed in 1939, after almost five years of costly experimentation, the machine, with its dies and plugs, produced a wooden spoon that, unlike other flat wooden spoons on the market, had a deep, graceful bowl shape. The finished product was labeled the "Rite Spoon" and soon captured a large market share of the far-reaching wooden spoon business.

The chief designer of the "bender," as I recall, was a man named Arthur Hopkins. Mr. Hopkins was a well-liked, highly regarded figure who became well-known here during his frequent visits to the "Dish" and this community.

Most people called him "Hoppe," and it was widely rumored that he was also the developer of a product called Hoppes, a gun-cleaning solvent that could be found on the shelves of most gun owners in this country. This was at a time when ammunition contained potassium chlorate primers, which turns to potassium chloride when fired, a substance not unlike table salt and highly corrosive to gun barrels.

It should be mentioned that the invention and development of the "bender" was most timely for the O.W.D.

Like most industries in this country, the company was caught up in the desperate days of the 1930s economic depression and was in a struggle for survival.

Year 1940, however, saw an escalated demand for wood products due to the outbreak of World War II in Europe and resulted in its manufacturing and woods operations with employment reaching a high of 539 people. The following year, however, saw this nation drawn into the nightmare of global conflict with the sneak attack by Japan on Pearl Harbor. It was, of course, a singular moment in modern American history, a penetration of our borders by a hostile force. Almost a thousand men and women from this community joined the armed forces to fight the enemy. This severely depleted the available work force, and local women quickly rose to the challenge and became the backbone of production at the O.W.D. No one realized it at the time, but they would become a microcosm of the nation at large in which the old rules of gender and expectation changed radically. It would be the beginning of women in traditionally men's jobs, a liberation that continues strong today and, as the parent of seven daughters, this writer can only highly applaud that change.

High school students also helped fill the worker shortage and, with the cooperation of schools authorities, any student willing to work was allowed to be released from classes in early afternoon to work an abbreviated four-hour shift. Along with many of my classmates, I worked in almost every department of that vast plant (the largest plant ever erected in Franklin County).

From driving the "mercuries," towing dozens of trailers laden with packaged products through the corridors that linked the production facilities to the giant warehouse, which could hold two railroad cars standing at floor level to permit direct loading (a typical thoughtful design among many other found throughout the plant by designer John Graham). To the lumber yards where

I piled lumber alongside an incredibly strong Al Becker (on my first day of work Al secretly nailed my lunch box to the bench in the warming house located mid-way on the tramway, much to the delight of fellow workers as I tried in vain to pick it up at the sound of the company whistle signaling the end of that day's shift).

My favorite place to work was probably the "benders." It was a busy, cheerful place geared to high rates of production. The doctrine of the "scientific management," the system of which work is disassembled into its component parts and the tasks studied for maximum efficiency, was entering the industrial scene at this time. The theory was that there had to be "one best way" to execute any job. I remember being fascinated watching an officer of the company, stopwatch in hand, timing the ladies on the assembly belt where the spoon "culls" were removed and the final product packaged in a quest to make their motions less tiring, easier, and more efficient (a skeptic once told me: "Hell, you don't need a damn stopwatch. Just watch the laziest person on the line").

Overhead, above the "bender" room, were the "rattlers," a large cage-like apparatus that made rattling noises as it tossed the spoons contained inside back and forth and every which way, effectively polishing them to a high luster. From the rattlers the spoons, which had a rich woodsy birch smell, dropped into bins where they then were loaded manually (my job) into hoppers that fed the assembly belt. My foreman in that department was a lovely lady named Mrs. Beulah Delair, whose great smile and gentle manner (if you did your job) made the "benders" one of the more pleasant departments in the O.W.D. factory. Many of those high school students employed at the "Dish" would enter the military before the war's end in 1945. They would return to a prosperous nation and begin to rebuild their lives. Some would go back to work, others would attend college (the G.I. Bill allowed one month's free tuition for every month served plus a modest stipend. I think $50 per month, which, if you didn't try to keep up with the "preppies," was almost adequate). That bill would become part of the greatest investments in higher education that any society ever made and was a brilliant, enduring commitment to the nation's future. For their part, the women who kept the O.W.D. wheels turning during the war's labor shortage now found their gender at new heights. Dual incomes are now the norm and provide an increased standard of living in this community. An evolution still in progress, but given our choices in this year's presidential election, it many not be long before a woman will be our next President.

You go, girl!

<ins>O.W.D. History</ins>

The O.W.D. was founded in Michigan in 1883 by Henry S. Hull. It became the largest single industry in a community known as Traverse City, not far from the famous Upper Peninsula in that state. The corporate name came from its main product in that operation—a thin, shallow, round wooden bowl that constituted the disposable package of its time. It was used in grocery stores and meat markets across the nation for dispensing butter, lard, and ground meat.

During its 24 years of operation in Michigan, the O.W.D. cut 21 million board feet of hardwood timber and shipped a yearly average of 1,000 railroad cars filled with its products all over this country and abroad.

In 1916, the hardwood timber ran out and O.W.D. moved to Tupper Lake.

From *Queen City of the North*, Larry Wakefield author, 1988.

*Tupper Lake Free Press Print:* November 01, 2000

# An Historical View of Municipal Park

A RECENT SURVEY ASKING for input from residents on the future of the Municipal Park elicited an overwhelming response. The information and recommendations contained in the survey's answers will be used as a tool for village and town officials to generate further development of that wonderful community asset.

It is beyond this column to expand on that survey's data, other than to note that it has opened the door for the community at large to voice their opinions, which they did with great fervor.

It should also be noted that the survey, framed by village trustee Mike Demar's study committee on the park's future, had a high rate of response, far in excess of the 10 to 15 percent, is the average for mailed surveys. Given such a high rate of concern, perhaps it would be of general interest to offer a series of brief articles that will give a historical overview of how the park was first acquired by the community, the cost, the former use, etc. After all, not every community is fortunate enough to own such valuable shoreline and extended property.

Let's begin by observing that Racquette Pond is NOT a result of a backwater created by Setting Pole Dam. This popular misconception, which is contained in Seavers' History of Franklin County, can be disproved by the fact that early travelers such as S.H. Hammond, the literary editor of the Albany State Register, described in glowing terms its existence on an 1849 trip to this region. Since no dam was built at Setting Pole or anywhere else

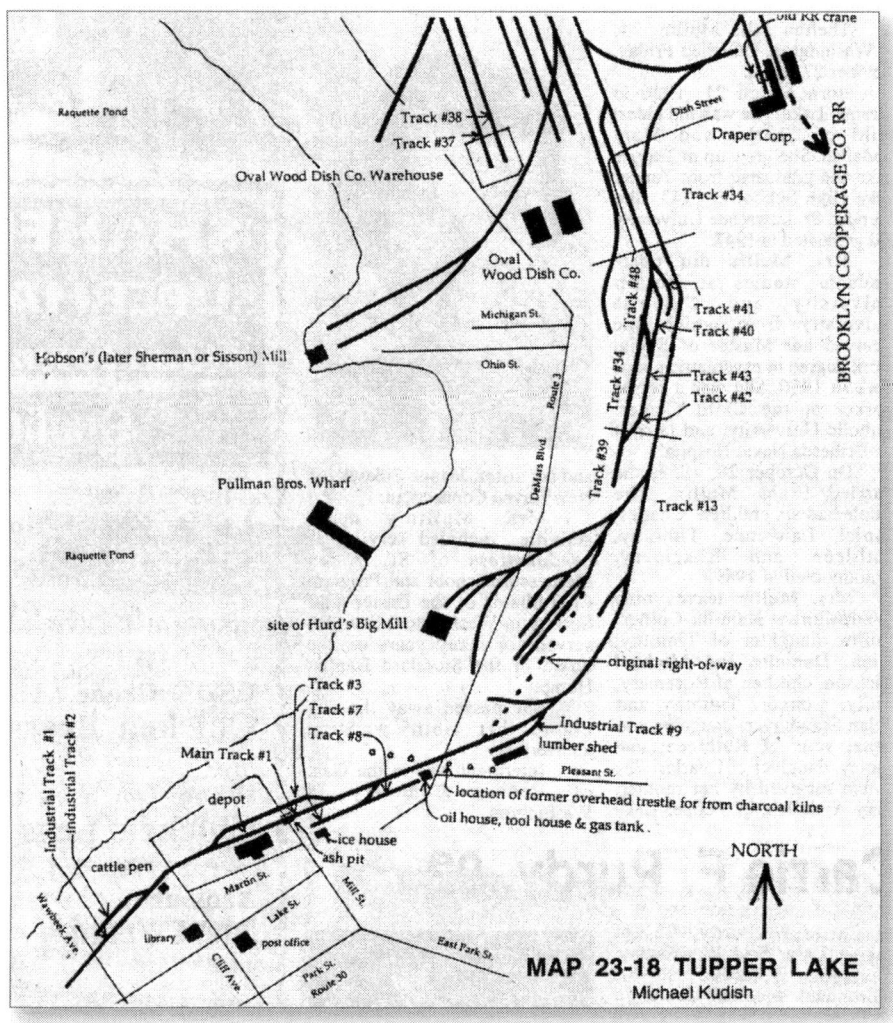

*This map shows some of the early development along the shore of Racquette Pond, now the location of this community's shoreline walk project.*

in the area at this time, historian Seavers was apparently in error. (Setting Pole Dam was built in the 1850s.)

The following description was excerpted from unpublished early notes found in the *Free Press* and written by former editor and historian Louis Simmons:

"Raquette Pond has borne at least three other names over the years, including Whitney Pond, after an early surveyor, Cyrus P. Whitney, who helped survey the area; The Lothrop Stretch, after a member of the Lothrop family of Saranac Lake who lived for awhile on its shores, and Lough Neagh, after a beautiful lake in Ireland, a name given it in nostalgic memory of the Ould Sod by one of the early Irish landowners of the nearly four-million-acre Macomb Purchase. 'Lough Neagh' was promptly corrupted into 'Long Neck' by area Adirondackers, who finally settled for Raquette Pond instead.

"The earliest logging operations in the Tupper area centered around the east shore of Raquette Pond, where the clearing that was left after the virgin pine was cut off in the 1850s by the Pomeroy Lumber Co. became the site some 40 years later for Tupper Lake village.

"Probably no other body of water in the Adirondacks was the setting for more intensive or extensive lumbering operations. Starting around Civil War times and continuing down through the 1920s, spring river drives brought logs cut throughout the Raquette River watershed. Cold River, Bog River and numerous smaller tributary streams down to the sawmill clustered around Raquette Pond shores. A good idea of the size of the annual timber cut is offered in the annual report of the New York State Forest, Fish and Game Commission for 1900, which shows that the A. Sherman Lumber Co., which operated a mill opposite the site now occupied by the O.W.D., Inc., sawed more than 17 million board feet of softwood lumber that year, while the Norwood Manufacturing Co., then operating the 'Big Mill' on Raquette Pond, had a total cut of nearly 22 million feet.

"Lesser cuts were handled at other mills then operating around Raquette Pond, including the pulp mill operated by Champlain Realty near the outlet, where a little separate village, Underwood, complete with school district, flourished from 1899 until the mill shut down in 1910. The foundations of the homes and roofless brick walls of the plant, largely concealed by second growths, are all that remain to mark the site. Gone, also, is almost all trace of a pulp mill operated by the Santa Clara Lumber Co. near where little Wolf Creek empties into the pond.

"Raquette Pond was a headache for boaters in the heyday of logging, the network of log booms, anchored by rock cribs and piles driven deep into the bottom, making navigation a hazardous business. At the point where the Racquette River, swinging north after crossing the foot of both Lake Simond and Big Tupper, begins its roundabout course through Raquette Pond, the 'Sorting Gap' was a key link in the logging operations of the past.

"Here, logs in the thousands converged after the long river drive. Over the years, many major lumbering firms harvested timber along the Raquette River watershed, and to distinguish their own cut, stamped the end of each log with marking hammers, which imprinted the owner's mark in the wood. Log marks, registered with the state, included many familiar to Tupper old timers, among them the marks of G.W. Sisson, Augustus Sherman, Burnham, Loveless Co., Norwood Mfg. Co., Export Lumber Co. and others.

"Keen-eyed lumberjacks manned the floating catwalks of the Sorting Gap around the clock during the closing days of the spring drive, spotting company marks and shunting the logs into the owner's holding booms, from which they were herded, in an Adirondack version of the western roundup, to the firm's mill on the pond shore, or on down the 70 or so miles of river to the mills at Potsdam. International Paper Company's 'Sorting Gap' leanto, open to public use, stands on the shore nearby today as a memorial to a colorful operation of an earlier era.

"Indians made the leanto location one of their favorite hunting, fishing and trapping goals. Old timers here referred to it as Indian Park. Merrit's map of 1858 shows the Indian encampments, where arrowheads and bits of pottery have been found. However, there was never a year-round Indian settlement in the Tupper sector."

Next column: the community originally votes NO to the shoreline purchase.

*Tupper Lake Free Press Print*: November 08, 2000

# A Close Vote

WINTER WAS SLOW TO release its icy grip on this community in March of 1932. Racquette Pond was still completely ice-locked except for a crater-like opening 200 yards off shore from Demars Blvd. near today's pumping station. Here, raw sewage flowing through a pipe before being discharged out into the lake had melted the ice, not unlike some volcanic thermal hot spot. The shark-like dorsal fins of large fish (well fed?) cleaved the water's surface as the fish cruised endlessly back and forth indulging themselves in this warmer, highly oxygenated environment.

The earlier months of that winter had been exceptionally mild, and conditions had been disastrous to the local lumbering and woods operations. This had idled many residents already hit by the desperate economic times of what would be called the Great Depression (1929–1941). The dejection prevailing in the community at this time was lessened somewhat by the prospects of an exciting village election.

For the first time in 15 years, the Democratic party of the village would be represented on the ballot with the names of candidates for the two village positions that were "up for grabs." The positions were those of village trustees, with Albert Deshaw and Henry Rule—incumbents nominated by the Republicans, and Frank Woods, local laundry owner, and Napoleon Grenier, Faust grocer—the Democratic opponents. Adding interest to this election, and central to this column's intent to provide historical background on our municipal park, was the proposition to purchase a site called the Santa Clara tract for the development of a public park. That proposition, as it appeared on the ballot, read as follows:

"Shall the Village of Tupper Lake raise by tax upon the taxable inhabitants and property of the Village of Tupper Lake in the county of Franklin and State of New York the sum of five thousand dollars ($5,000) for the purpose of purchasing a parcel of land in the Village of Tupper Lake?"

Details of the parcel are sketchy but it would appear, from what I can find out, that the parcel consisted of land extending from the "Big Mill" (present day Grandstand) along Lake Street and the waterfront to a point at the junction of Cliff and present day Martin Street. Also note that in consideration of the purchase of this more desirable tract, the remainder of the Santa Clara tract bounded by Demars Blvd. and the pond to the O.W.D. property line would be deeded to the village by the Santa Clara Co.

*Before controls were put into place, Setting Pole Dam was responsible for drowned lands and unsightly shorelines. Photograph was taken near the location of present day I.P. Sorting Gap leanto.*

The records do tell us that the proposition was defeated by the small plurality of 20 votes of a total of 556 votes cast as follows: yes—251, no—271, spoiled—12, blank—22.

Oh yes, the Republicans swept through to victory with substantial majorities in that same balloting. It would be the largest total vote in a municipal election since the incorporation of the village with 1,071 voters going to the polls. So what happened that caused the proposed park purchase to be defeated? Ellen Shaw's father, Mr. Paul Martin, was the mayor at that time, and it was his opinion that misunderstanding as to the location of the proposed section to be developed had clouded the issue. Mayor Martin also felt that objections were raised because of the seller's demand to reserve a 140-foot strip of land along Demars Blvd. and also because of a clause in regard to water rights was not deemed acceptable to the voters (Mr. Martin, who lived in a handsome home on the corner of Mill and Lake streets, was the owner with his brothers Irnie and Henry of Martin Bros., a modern, upscale grocery store and meat market located on Park St. He would become Town of Altamont Supervisor for 14 years until his retirement in 1948).

The following September 15, 1932, the village acquired a new six-month option. The new option would stipulate that "the cement foundations and gang saw now standing (1932) on the site where the Santa Clara Company's 'Big Mill' functioned for many years shall remain as a perpetual monument to the early founders of the village. Storing, driving or sorting logs, pulpwood, etc. will not be permitted on that portion of Racquette Pond conveyed under the proposed transaction."

The new option would also withdraw the reservations objected to in the original purchase offer and more clearly define the location boundaries and uses of the purchase.

Next column: A special election offers the voters a second opportunity to purchase the Santa Clara tract.

*Tupper Lake Free Press Print:* November 15, 2000

# Work

IN TRACING THE HISTORY of the Municipal Park, we learned in an earlier column that the initial proposition to acquire the tract of land for the park's development failed by 20 votes to gain voters' approval. Village officials remained undaunted by this failure and believed that a general misconception figured heavily in the defeat of the project in the balloting, which took place in the spring election of 1932. As a result of this optimism, the village secured a new option on the land that bordered Racquette Pond between Cliff Ave. and the O.W.D. property line. The new option would withdraw the seller's reservations that were objected to in the former option (certain water rights and the exception from purchase of a 140-foot strip). The new proposition would also more clearly define the boundaries of that portion of the tract that was to be developed (below Lake St. and extending from Cliff Ave. approximately to the W.D. Wilson Co., now Major Day car wash and NAPA Auto Parts). With "all their ducks in a row," village officials offered a second opportunity for voters to decide for or against the land purchase through a special election scheduled for that fall. Why were the village officials so concerned that the voters approve this purchase?

The Santa Clara tract was hardly a real estate prize. Racquette Pond was littered with hundreds of half-sunken logs (40 years later, Frank Morrison and his Rod and Gun Club crew were still diligently working to make the pond navigable by removing those hazardous "deadheads").

*This rare 1938 photograph shows the cement foundation and gang saw on the site were the Santa Clara Company's "Big Mill" was located. To the left of the almost completed grandstand is the former Santa Clara office building, later to become John and Edna Salamy's restaurant called the Boulevard. To the right are the former Tessier Lumber Company buildings.*

*In its heyday, the mill cut 250,000 feet per day of pine, pine were larger in size. (photo courtesy of J. Frenette Sr.)*

Also, due to the fluctuating, uncontrolled levels of the Setting Pole Dam, the shoreline was a mess of drowned trees, and the tract was often flooded. Travel to the Junction during these times required going down McLaughlin St., also known as the "back road." In addition, to reach hardpan for construction purposes such as piers, it would be necessary to go down 12-14 feet—about five feet below the level of the Racquette Pond. Five feet of spongy layers of bark and decayed wood laid down years ago when Hurd's historic "Big Mill" operated on the site would have to be removed, etc.

Note: The term "deadhead" comes from the fact that as one end of the floating log becomes "dead" (waterlogged), it will sink. This leaves the "live" end floating at an angle poised like Prince Valliant's lance to spear an unsuspecting boater.

Yes, it would take an immense amount of WORK to create the proposed park. But let's give those village officials and the community voters high marks for vision. We certainly have a beautiful park today, partly as a result of their having acquired the land.

Would you agree, however, that there may have been a second

more compelling reason in the minds or our village officials? A simple equation might explain: Project plus government money equals JOBS!

Remember, this was a time of great despair in this community as elsewhere in the country. Unemployment had reached new highs, as much as 80 percent in some localities. It is hard to imagine in today's economy the sense of ruin that existed. Contemplate long soup lines, respectable men knocking on doors asking if they could do odd jobs in return for a piece of bread, over 400 families in this community on the welfare rolls, seeking fuel, food, clothing and other relief items. Enter at this time a new president—a 50-year-old aristocrat and former NY state governor, Franklin D. Roosevelt, who would become the most important president of the 19th Century. Over the course of his legendary "first hundred days," the government established 15 new legislative initiatives, one of which was to provide work and relief for the jobless under a program known as the Work Progress Administration (W.P.A.).

The necessary first step for work relief was to have a project—ergo—acquire, the Santa Clara tract and provide a project that would meet government guidelines for W.P.A. approval.

The voters got the message and this paper, in its October 27, 1932, edition, would report:

"Tupper Lake took another long stride as a modern mountain resort when voters carried the municipal park proposition, which will give to the village a public recreation center on the shore of Racquette Pond by the overwhelming majority of 173. Out of a total of 492 votes cast, 315 were recorded in favor of the project, 153 against, and the remaining 15 ballots were spoiled.

"Mayor Paul E. Martin has announced that a large force of men will be employed at once in clearing and preparing the large area of the park site, a task which will provide employment for many of the village's jobless."

Note: The W.P.A. would later that year approve a $77,000 grant for filling and grading the park site. The village had won its gamble for federal dollars.

Three years later, October 1937, with the swampy lakeshore still not filled, the funds for truck hire ran out and the project stalled to a standstill. Frank McCarthy was then the village mayor and together with the village clerk, Ned Sparks, they conferred with W.P.A. officials in Albany, who granted a supplementary grant of $59,000. This made a total of $136,000, a huge amount of money in those years! The village had been drawing sand from a pit at Little Wolf, purchased from Eugene Briere. With the new grant, they immediately put 28 men back to work at 40 cents an hour for a 40-hour week. John Hayes, project foreman, marshaled eight trucks and a power shovel (it had been hand-loaded previously) and began drawing 450 to 500 yards of fill daily. Once the fill was completed, work would begin on the new grandstand under the supervision of James King, foreman of that W.P.A. project.

Next: Jim King and crew run into problems erecting the grandstand.

*Tupper Lake Free Press Print:* November 29, 2000

# THE NEW GRANDSTAND—1938

IN SEVERAL OF THE RECENT *Transitions* columns, an attempt was made to trace the historical background of this community's Municipal Park.

It was noted that voters of the community at a special reelection (it failed approval the first time) agreed to purchase the Santa Clara tract, which extended from below the foot of Cliff Ave. to the O.W.D. Corporation line between Racquette Pond and Demars Blvd. The purchase price was $5,000. Work began immediately to fill the low-lying ground and clear out the underbrush in the grove of trees below Mill St. and establishing the shoreline with log and stone ramparts. The total cost approached $136,000, with the town contributing $19,000 and the balance financed by a federal work program known as the W.P.A. Even at depression prices (1932) and wages (40 cents an hour for a 40-hour work week), this was a huge expenditure.

Project foreman for the park was John Hayes, and his crew of 30 men rushed to complete the necessary work. Public pressure was mounting to complete another phase of the project—a huge grandstand and baseball diamond.

The pressure stemmed from the fact that the start of the baseball season was only months away, and it was anticipated that this community would join the Northern New York—Vermont Baseball League.

Baseball fans had no need to worry. W.P.A. construction foreman,

*Construction of the Municipal Park grandstand was well underway when this picture was taken in 1937. To the left of center is the former New Brunswick Hotel (now Rite Aid Pharmacy). To the right is the Tessier Lumber Co. office building.*

Jimmie King, had an impressive batting record (to borrow a baseball term) in completing other local W.P.A. projects.

The year before in 1936, with a crew of 32 men using carefully selected spruce and hemlock logs, Mr. King and crew had built the Rod and Gun Clubhouse. It was finished in June 1936 and remains to this day a highly attractive, well-constructed, one-of-a-kind activity center for the present-day's energetic Rod and Gun Club.

The chinking between logs was barely in place on that building when in June of that year (1936), the W.P.A. approved still another project—a large clubhouse to accompany the Tupper Lake golf course, which had been built privately in 1933. (Note: Since the clubhouse was to be built with federal monies, for eligibility purposes it was necessary to turn the golf course property over to the town.) This arrangement has continued and has been attended with harmony and significant accomplishment as partners with the Tupper Lake Country Club.

The log clubhouse, built with logs cut from the O.W.D.'s nearby Sugar Loaf Mountain, was started in 1936 and finished in the fall of 1937, and was unique among golf course facilities found elsewhere. It was destroyed by fire in 1956.

Construction on the grandstand followed immediately. Construction headquarters were set up at the Tessier Lumber Co. railroad siding (now Ray's Liquor Store and the White Birch Café), where Mr. King had been prudently stockpiling materials throughout the summer in advance of actual construction. It proved to be a difficult project.

Working through the winter, some 131 foundation piers were set, often during extreme weather conditions. Compressed air-driven spades were used to cut through the top layer of soil. At a depth of four to five feet, a spongy layer of bark and decayed wood was encountered. This had to be removed. Nine to ten feet down, workmen encountered heavy logs still in a fair state of preservation, although from their depth having been there for centuries.

*Shown in later years is the completed grandstand. A capacity crowd at the opening ceremonies of the Woodsmen Field Day event makes full use of this extra special facility.*

These had to be cut through to reach a solid foundation base for piers. Readers familiar with the bitter cold winds of Racquette Pond can well appreciate the difficulties and discomfort involved. Despite those odds, the grandstand, baseball diamond, and $1,200 worth of chain link-fence (1,450 foot long and seven feet in height) all were in place for the opening of the 1938 baseball season.

To a community weary from a long, bone-chilling, brutal winter, a stagnant economy that refused to recover, the struggle to keep food on the table and nerves jangled by the rumblings of war around the globe, the new grandstand must have seemed an apparition.

Rising Phoenix-like from the former mud flats of sawdust and bark chips, with its tier upon tier of seating escalating to 40-ft. vantage points, its water fountains, modern showers and locker rooms, underground dugouts, and the baseball diamond itself outlined with lime markings, there was nothing quite like it in the north country.

It was a time known as the "Threadbare Thirties," with few recreational opportunities to escape even for a while the realities of a desperate time in our country's history. Baseball provided one diversion, one pastime that everyone could afford and could enjoy, and Tupper Lake embraced it with great fervor.

Tupper would welcome the first appearance of its home team called The Rangers. They would tangle with manager Hank Hodge's redoubtable Malone Stars. Both teams were made up largely of college baseball stars, and a high level of play was expected.

Following a large parade with bands playing and flags waving, which circled the field, a brief ceremony was held, and Mayor Frank McCarthy threw out the first ball to Mayor Ralph Cardinal of Malone, and the new baseball grandstand and the 1938 baseball season were officially opened and dedicated in high style.

*Tupper Lake Free Press Print:* January 17, 2001

# THE BUTTERCUP EPISODE

I RECEIVED A LETTER THIS WEEK from my former neighbor and good friend Dave LaVoie. Readers will remember Dave as a long-time, popular manager of the A&P grocery store here before he took a career change to become an auditor for a large grocery store chain in the Syracuse area. He presently lives in that area in blissful retirement with his wife, Laura (Snooky Tarbox).

Dave grew up on the shore of Racquette Pond and raised his own family in the house where he was born, a stone's-throw from the pond's waters. Few people knew the surrounding waters as well as Dave. I remember that each spring the D.E.C. would enlist his help in placing the buoys to mark the perplexing route of the "channel" where the river entered the Racquette Pond. A mention of high water annually flooding Demars Blvd. in this column prompted Dave to write that almost every year, high water accompanied by west winds would wipe out the municipal dock located at the end of Wawbeek Ave. next to his house. When the waters finally receded, the town would simply rebuild the dock, which they did for many years. In later years, the Setting Pole Dam level was mandated, according to Dave, at 1,544 feet, and they no longer had to rebuild the dock every spring.

Dave noted in his letter that "veterans (with their sputum cups) from the V.A. hospital liked to sit on the dock in the summertime. There were wonderful sunsets and a good view of the Pond; many

*Somewhere is the steam yacht "Altamont," which operated daily in the 1880s and 1890s between Trombley's Landing and the Tupper Lake House. The boat also made daily trips between Owen's Dock and Bog River Falls. No roads existed beyond Moody at this time, and few sticks of hardwood provided the necessary fuel, a fact noteworthy in today's high fuel costs.*

local people would visit the dock also, and I especially remember that the nuns from Holy Ghost Academy's convent (now Smith's apartment building) would walk most evenings and sit there for a short time as a break in their disciplined lives."

Dave remembered "that the dock was lighted at night by exquisite hurricane-type lamps at each corner, and had an opening where there was no railing in the middle for getting in and out of the boats. It also had a slip on the side, where camp owners could tie up while they did their grocery shopping in the village."

Dave concluded his letter by suggesting that the dock and the boat traffic that utilized it might be of historical interest. He is right about that because even before Dave's childhood memories of the dock, which was known as the Owen Dock in the earliest writings about this area, was a busy place. Roads were few and unimproved in those days, and people traveled largely by boat to an extent that must be incomprehensible in today's fast-paced transportation mode.

Large steam yachts capable of holding as many as 30 passengers made daily trips from Owen's to Bog River Falls and to Sweeney's Carry (Oliver Trombley's Landing) on the Racquette River.

One of the most active steamship operators was a gent named Pliny Robbins. For many years before, it was owned by William Whitney and lumberman Patrick C. Moynehan (1896–1898) and, later after the first lumbering was completed, owned solely by Whitney (1914). Pliny and his wife, Anne, ran the Hamilton House on Little Tupper Lake. Patrons entering Little Tupper from Round Pond would row a mile or more up the lake to Pliny's—nearby today's private inholding called Camp Francis (a parcel excerpted from the state's acquisition of Little Tupper).

We are told that Pliny was a nickname, his real name being Prince Albert. In 1889, he purchased Mart Moody's Mount Morris House at the foot of Big Tupper Lake (Peter Day property), enlarged it to accommodate 50 guests and renamed it the Prince Albert Hotel.

Those passenger launches must have been "the best thing since sliced bread" to the many travelers visiting this region. Not only did they provide cushioned comfort to bodies wracked by stagecoach rides over unforgiving pock-filled carriage roads and hours cramped in the unforgiving seats of a guideboat, but also they would have drastically cut the time necessary to reach various destinations. Certainly to local guides like John Hinkson, one of whose assignments while employed by Uncle Mart Moody was to carry the outgoing mail to Saranac Lake and bring back the incoming mail—a 54-mile row in his guideboat, the introduction of those beautiful steamers must have been providential.

Indeed, in later years Mr. Hinkson himself operated the 42-ft "Little Forester," which "Lish" McCure ran on schedule to carry guests from Trombley's landing to his hotel at the head of Big Tupper Lake (Tupper Lake House, where the former women's infirmary at the American Legion Camp now stands).

It should be pointed out that not all of the guides were pleased with the passenger launches.

Rowing patrons between the various carrys and to the hotel on the lakes represented a large part of their livelihood, and they were threatened by the success of the fast and comfortable steam boats. The guides at Long Lake were especially vexed (they didn't call that community Kickerville and Gougeville without good reason) because the steamer named Buttercup, working in connection with steamers like the Killoquah from Racquette and another on Forked Lakes, and stagecoaches from Blue Mountain Lake, was heavily impacting their businesses. The Buttercup's scheduled run was from Deerland all the way to Racquette Falls. A dam had been built just before the falls on the river to allow navigation, and this was another source on consternation because the dam not only allowed the Buttercup access to the river, but it also flooded the shoreline and the beaches along the lake.

Anyway, one night in 1882 in a series of moves that would make today's eco-terrorists proud, the Buttercup disappeared, and despite being guarded day and night, the dam was blown up (a bullet drilled into the guard's campfire as he sat on watch gave fair warning). As that worthy guard headed for the clearing where the D.E.C. interior station is now located at the end of the carry, the surroundings were rocked by a tremendous explosion and the dam disappeared into history.

It would be 10 years before another passenger launch would appear on Long Lake's waters.

Note: Many years later, the New York State Water Supply Commission, while studying the Racquette River at the outlet of Long Lake for power development, noted "the ruins of an old dam, with crest of elevation at 1,630 feet, are still in evidence, but the lake is not controlled in any way."

It proposed a dam not far from the old dam, which would include the entire basin at Cold River (120 square miles) in the watershed tributary. It further noted that the villages of Long Lake and Grove (?), being mostly situated 50 to 60 feet above present (1,630 feet) lake level, would be beyond possibility of damage by any reasonable reservoir proposition. The dam would have raised the water level five feet, and the land to be flooded would have been "largely controlled by private owners and houses and camps, singly and in small groups which are of frequent occurrence on the shores of the lake." Apparently the project was a little ahead of its time and "died a borning."

Mrs. Howard Seaman, former Long Lake historian, has written a wonderful account of the Buttercup episode, including its eventual recovery in 18 feet of water with a hole in its superstructure (found by scuba divers George Boudreau and Franklin McIntyre in September of 1959) 77 years after it was sabotaged.

*Tupper Lake Free Press Print:* January 24, 2001

# A Letter From 2 P

HER NICKNAME WAS 2 P. I remember her when she was just a squirt of a girl growing up in Moody, brown as a beech nut husk from constantly being out of doors. She was like a fish in the water and despite being the youngest she was clearly the best swimmer among the Moody summer colony kids who frequented the beach next to her house.

2 P wrote to this column recently, a mention of steamboats in a previous column having sparked some strong memories of her youthful days growing up on the lake. Her letter was signed 2 P, which sparked some memories of my own. (I was one of the kids who often swam on that stretch of beach alongside her house.) A glance at the return address disclosed that 2 P is now Mrs. Adele Molinski, living in Hudson, New York. Her letter follows:

"Last week you ran the article about the steam yachts in early traffic on T.L., and under the photo—it stated 'somewhere is the steam yacht 'Altamont,' and memories came flooding back when I used to go to Ketcham's camp (across from our old house) where Daddy Ken Lamoy was caretaker. We used to go over on weekends and help get ready for the summer. On these occasions I did a lot of walking in the woods, fishing, etc. Looking at the shore from Moody Rd.—the second bay over from Mrs. K's—to the left I found the remains of this huge boat and was so excited I took photos—enclosed copies for you. You'd think I found the "Titanic!" This was about spring of '51. I don't know if the remains are still there. Thought this might be of interest to you.

"Tupper will always be my 'heart.' I'll never leave my love memories of Moody esp."

(Signed) 2 P

Note: The Ketcham camp referred to in 2 P's letter was one of the earliest camps on Tupper Lake. Mr. Ketcham, from Yonkers, was a highly successful gentleman, who through his generosity and outgoing personality, was highly regarded in this community. The Ketcham summer home was known as Camp Ashanty, a large complex that included thirteen out buildings. Mr. Ketcham accompanied Uncle Mart Moody to Washington when that famous guide accepted President Grover Cleveland's invitation to visit him at the White House. Mrs. Ketcham was a girlhood friend of Mrs. Cleveland. (The president had been enthralled by Uncle Mart, whom he had met while on a sporting visit to this region during which time he stayed at Moody's Camp Redside Hotel, later the Waukesha cabins.) It is said that Mr. Ketcham took great relish in telling how the old woodsman charmed the president and his friends with his inimitable style of telling his inexhaustible repertoire of "tall, tall stories." After Mr. Ketcham's death, Mrs. Ketcham continued regularly to visit Camp Ashanty for many, many years until 1964. The property is now owned by Robert Abplanalp, successful inventor and businessman, close friend and frequent host to the later former President Richard Nixon at the Tupper Lake camp, now known as Adirondack Fisheries Inc. Mr. Abplanalp worked for many years with his Swiss-born father in a tiny workshop before perfecting the aerosol device that is so ubiquitous today on containers that hold everything from paint to shaving cream. His firm is known worldwide as the Precision Valve Co. Mr. Abplanalp is highly regarded by all who know him in this community as a "regular guy, unassuming and considerate."

It should also be noted that Ken Lamoy, mentioned in 2 P's letter, was not only a caretaker of the Ketcham Camp Ashanty, but also one of only four postmasters following Mart Moody and his wife, "Aunt Minerva" of the Moody P.O. established in 1884 by U.S. President Chester Arthur, a friend of Uncle Mart. He not only named Mart as first postmaster, but also gave him the honor of having the P.O. bear his name. Ken was appointed in 1929 and served until 1954.

So what is the story behind 2 P's "Titanic" discovery on one of her forest ramblings? Any attempt to identify that great old boat, whose final voyage ended in that tiny slip, the shoreline across from Watch Island becoming her gravesite, would necessarily be highly speculative at this late date. There are a few clues, however, and the readers can decide for themselves if such clues permit a possible identification.

*"Each morning the 'Bridgebrook,' its curtains drawn in stormy weather, would come down the lake to get Mrs. Dunn, Colonel Barbour's beautiful secretary, and then bring her back at night to the Robbins Cottage where she stayed (presently Mr. and Mrs. John Hamilton's beautiful home). An impressive gal in her impressive boat." (Aurore Alexander)*

First, however, it is necessary to understand that in the early years of the 1900s and right up to the 1920s when roads and the vehicles to travel them improved, boat transportation was essential, not only to get from one location to another, but also essential in getting supplies to camps and hotels on the various lakes. Equally important was the use of "steamers" to move the huge rafts of logs held together by booms that required towing down the lake to the "Sorting Gap," where the lake's outlet joined the Racquette River. As a result of these needs, there were many large steamboats plying Tupper Lake waters. Some were built locally by master boat builders like Luther Owen, who had apprenticed under Rushton, the renowned Canton craftsman. Others arrived via flat bed on the new M & M railroad from talented builders in Lake George and the river towns along the St. Lawrence River, where steamboats were common as early as the mid-1800s. In my files are some notes written by Aurore Alexander that tell of some of her memories during a lifetime spent in this community and includes a description of some "of the beautiful boats that were so prominent on Tupper Lake."

Mrs. Alexander née Henault and her husband, Percy, in 1910 took over operation from Percy's father, Jabez, of the Waukesha Hotel, one of the first resort hotels in the area which was purchased in 1893 from Mart Moody, who had named it Camp Redside after the brook running alongside (now Radimer, Landry property). The Alexanders built the original Waukesha Grill in 1932 before selling to the late Charles Girard. Several generations will no doubt recall with great nostalgia of the sweet sounds from the saxophone of the incomparable Ray Bourdage as he played "Good Night Sweetheart" at that famous grill's closing time each Saturday night.

In her notes, Mrs. Alexander tells of not wanting to trust her own memory, so she wrote to Hod Bellows, then retired in Florida. Mr. Bellows was one of the lake's premier boat men and a few of the boats (due to space restrictions) that he described in his prompt reply to Aurore to follow. Such a list has important historical value. The number of boats, their types, and where they were built can be regarded as reflections of the social and economic systems within which they were constructed, utilized and discarded. It can also satisfy a simple curiosity about the past and of things not known or easily forgotten.

### The Lillian T

This was a steamboat brought from Lake George by Pliny Robbins, beautifully designed with a galley in back and pilot house in front. It carried up to twenty passengers. Sold to Moynihan (lumberman) to tow logs from Bog River Falls to Pages Bluff. When the Moynihans were finished here, it was drawn out at the Prince Albert dock and dismantled.

### The Ben Harrison

Built for John Hurd, about 1891. Used to tow his logs down the lake. Sixty-five feet in length of heavy timbers. This steamboat was designed with shallow draft, a side wheeler, and it had a snubbing post for towing. It was built locally by a man named VonDell on ways set up between the tenement building and the Owens home on lower Wawbeek Avenue.

### The Fox Hall

The first gasoline launch on Tupper Lake. Built by Luther Owen for Hod Bellows, licensed to carry thirty passengers. Hod would leave Tupper at 8 o'clock every morning, stopping at all the camps to deliver mail and groceries as well as passengers.

### The Uncle Mart, The Paradise Point, The Bridgebrook

All steamboats owned by Colonel Barbour. Remember no bridge to cross Bog River to Barbour's until 1916. When the American Legion bought the Barbour property, they changed the name of the Bridgebrook to Legionnaire. It was used to take patients from the infirmary for rides, especially at sunset. Capacity about thirty passengers.

### The Harold P

Closer to being a tug boat, owned by Moynihan to tow logs. Hod Bellows, engineer. He had a pilot and three deck hands. When towing was finished, the Harold P was drawn out across the lake from Moody.

Was the "Harold P" 2 P's "Titanic?" In her letter, 2 P enclosed several photos that may provide other clues. One shows a circular hole toward the stern that could have held a snubbing post. Another photo shows the boiler, so it was a steamboat. A third photo shows the planking in side view that 2 P indicates ran eight feet from keel to top rail. The planking is laid up in what boat builders call a carvel hull, each of the planks being laid alongside the next one. This is a more economical method than lapstrake or clinker-built hull in which each plank overlaps the one below it like a clapboard house and would be the method of choice for a boat with short-life specialized use like the "Harold P." Such construction also requires constant painting to keep the boat waterproof, which may account for its good condition. After so many years, I'd like to think 2 P's mystery boat was the "Harold P."

What is your opinion?

*Tupper Lake Free Press Print:* March 28, 2001

# OLD TIMBER

WHEN THE ICE AGE ENDED some 12,000 (plus or minus) years ago, the face of the Adirondacks had undergone major changes. The mountains were lower and rounded now, worn down by ice a mile thick. More than 2,000 lakes had been formed in the remolded landscape. The glacier had also formed two major drainage basins for the more than 100,000 miles of flowing waterways. To the east, west, and north, rivers would lead to the St. Lawrence, while the Hudson River carried offwaters to the south. You will agree with me, then, that it was not surprising that when the timber barons began eyeing the forests of this region for its merchantable lumber, the proximity of rivers was an important consideration in evaluating what land they should buy. In short, the waterways offered a solution to the problem of transporting the timbers to downstream mills and was vital to the success of any lumber operation at the time (1860) when no other suitable transportation means were available.

The lumbermen also needed land that contained dense stands of spruce and pine, both of which held the highest market value. These species had several advantages. Not only did they plane well, but both had good strength and a close, straight grain. Another advantage was that they would float and could thus be transported long distances to the mill. (Hardwood does not float and it would be years before it was discovered that it made splendid paper, etc.) Many local streams provided this transportation

Under the Hemlocks
*At the time of this photograph in 1897, the improvement of the cross-cut saw with the addition of a raker tooth to clean out the sawdust, was just beginning to supplement the axe.*

link. Jenkins Brook, the Bog River, Bear Brook, Round Pond Stream, Grindstone Brook, Cold River, Moose Creek, Calkins Creek, and the Racquette River are some of the tributaries that allowed logs to be driven (floated) to the lake to be rafted and towed to the Sorting Gap on the river, where the logs were sorted as to owner and as to their ultimate destination, either further downstream or to the mills on Racquette Pond.

One of the earliest river drives locally was on Round Pond stream, or Little Tupper outlet, as it is also known. As many readers know, this vibrant and beautiful stream joins the Bog River at a location locally called "The Forks" before spilling over Bog River Falls into Tupper Lake. Here the logs would be towed by boats down the lake as far as Pages Bluff. (Note: A boom consisted of large logs, some thirty feet long, firmly fastened end to end by chains attached to ropes passed through holes bored by an auger. The boom would confine the saw logs or pulp into a raft.)

The logs on that first river drive were cut on lands owned by former Secretary of the Navy William C. Whitney and his partner, a crafty Glens Falls lumberman named Patrick Moynihan. Their holdings, later known as Whitney Park, were accomplished by buying many small parcels a little at a time at an average cost of under $4 per acre. When the first cut was initiated in 1896, they had acquired 68,000 acres (which would eventually grow to almost 100,000 acres). An agreement was in place in which the two men would share expenses and profits in this first lumbering, and Whitney would succeed as sole owner after the lumbering was completed. William died in 1904 and the partnership was continued by his son, Harry Payne Whitney, until its dissolution in 1912.

About this time, other regions that had been lumbered earlier had begun to see a decline in the accessible timber resources. The pine was mostly gone, and the spruce was not growing back at a rate faster than that being harvested, due to a failure to cut selectively to insure a new crop in a reasonable amount of time. Also, new state laws of 1885 and 1894 locked up many acres of timber in the Forest Preserve, adding to the exhaustion of this valuable resource. Wealthy landowners, aware of these shortcomings and having vision that went well beyond their lifetimes, began to explore and become among the first to utilize scientific management of their operations.

Seward Webb, at Nehasane in 1893, employed European-trained foresters Gifford Pinchot (*The Adirondack Spruce*) and his protégé, Henry Graves (*Practical Forestry in the Adirondacks*) to "cut as much timber as possible without injuring the productive power of the forest." Whitney and Moynihan followed the lead of their neighbor, Webb, and hired Graves to prepare a plan for the first cut on this largely virgin tract. While it didn't contain the 43 percent proportion of spruce found on Nehasane, it had, nevertheless, dense stands of both pine and spruce that had never seen the woodsman's axe (some of the spruce had been destroyed by bark borers in 1860—"*He lives on pitch, the son of a bitch*"). We will look at Graves' plan in a future article noting, meanwhile, that the death of a million forest patriarchs, some over 200 feet tall with a diameter of six and a half feet, was close at hand.

Timber is, of course, a renewable resource, a necessary product to fill the many and varied needs of a growing nation. Nevertheless, it must have been a sublimely sobering and impressive experience, even to the most hardened woodsman, as one of these giants that had survived the dramatic forces of nature for hundreds of years would, with a quiver, a shudder, and a quaking, surrender with a final groan to the forces of man.

*Tupper Lake Free Press Print:* April 04, 2001

# THE HAROLD P

IN A RECENT COLUMN, mention was made of a steamboat that was discovered abandoned on Tupper Lake's west shore. Based on notes in the files and some photos, this column hazards a guess that the steamboat's identity might be a boat that was known as the Harold P.

This week, we received a wonderful letter from a gentleman named Frederick Culley, which gave that guess some credibility. Mr. Cully's letter follows:

"Mrs. Ethel Delaney of New Hartford, NY, sent me a recent clipping titled '*Transitions*,' and I would like to add some comments and observations which may be of interest to you and your readers.

"Having lived in Tupper Lake and Moody from 1919 to 1929, and graduating from Tupper Lake High School in 1928, I was well acquainted with Kenneth Lamoy, his brother Brainard and father Levi. Kenneth succeeded Mrs. Helen I. Culley as postmaster, who in turn succeeded Fred C. Knapp.

"Martin Moody was the first postmaster from 1884 until 1910.

"W.P. Ketcham, a Wall Street broker who owned Camp Ashanty directly across Tupper Lake from Moody, also had his own private dock at Moody between Knapp's store and Murcheson's boat livery. Directly across the state road from the livery was the new Moody post office and store owned by the Culleys. This was destroyed by fire in 1929.

"While living in Moody, I hunted in the area across the lake between Page's Bluff and the Veteran's Mountain Camp. While doing so, I happened upon the remains of the tugboat, "Harold P." The name was still visible on the transom and was about 75 feet from the shoreline into the woods. The boat was surrounded by second-growth trees the size of which indicated it had been there a number of years. The boat had been stripped of its trappings and only the hull and part of the cabin remained. This tugboat had been operated by my grandfather, Richard S. Gile, hauling rafts of logs from Bog River Falls to the Racquette River on the north end of the lake. He also carried the mail from Tupper Lake to Moody by horse and buggy, sometimes by flat-bottomed boat when the road was impassable due to high water, and later by automobile until 1922. Another reference can be found on page 44 in Louis Simmon's book, *Mostly Spruce and Hemlock*, under Steamboat Days, by Almon T. Clarke, Jr., a reporter for the Utica Dispatch and former Tupper Lake postmaster.

"It is hoped that this bit of information may be of help in establishing the identity of one of Tupper Lake's past historical artifacts."

As Mr. Culley suggests in his letter, the discovery of this great tugboat and the substantial evidence pointing to its identity has strong historical implications. The "Harold P" represents a short, but vital, time in our local history when millions upon millions of saw logs were towed by large, powerful steamboats down the length of Tupper Lake. It represents the days of the river drives when spring freshets released roaring torrents of power that flushed logs down the many tributaries feeding the lake. It was a time when the population of the community rose from a census of 30 residents to 4,000 residents almost overnight, and Tupper Lake had become the lumbering capital of New York State. A humble town of hard-working men engaged in lumbering that suddenly found itself on the threshold of a new era of development. All at once, it would seem, the appearance of railroads and the improvement of the motor vehicle provided the swan song, the ultimate end to the exciting days of steamer tugs like the

*Shown here is Richard Gile, early settler, boat pilot, guide and the first fire observer on Mr. Morris.*

"Harold P" and the "Lillian T" Tupper Lake's deep waters would become the graveyard for countless formerly proud boats, now obsolete and unwanted. A mere punctuation, perhaps, in the text of this town's very rich history, but nonetheless important, romantic and highly unique.

This was also a time of giants like the Moynihan brothers, Pat and Dennis, whose business acumen on land sales and timbering operations made them super rich; of foresters like Gene Bruce and Pete LeBoeuf; river drivers like Alex Reandeau, who drove Bear Brook for the I. P. Co.; and jobbing contractors like Gaspar LaPorte and Albert Brooks, to name a few. Lusty men all, daring, risk-taking, but competent.

Note: Mr. Culley's grandfather, Richard Gile (that he writes of in his letter), was a civil war veteran and one of the early settlers in Moody.

A 1909 map in my possession shows that the Gile home was located near the present Mr. and Mrs. Glenford Snyder home (Hathaway farm). Next-door neighbors at that time were the J.T. Johnson family and the William J. Slater family. The map shows 11 families living in Moody at that time. Mr. Gile, in addition to being mail carrier, boat pilot and guide, was also the first fire observer when Mt. Morris became the site of the first steel fire tower in the Adirondacks in July of 1909.

Mr. Harrington would become the gatekeeper and warden at the Whitney Estate. The family lived in a gatehouse near the 10-mile mark on Little Tupper's east shore (intersection routes 10 and 10A). Many readers will remember the Harrington's sons, George and John, who became prominent citizens of Long Lake. Indeed, the finest pickup truck I ever owned, a beefed-up three-quarter ton Dodge, was purchased from George's Dodge Agency, which was located next to Freeman's General Store, now Hoss's Country Corner.

*Tupper Lake Free Press Print:* April 18, 2001

# Everything You Ever Wanted to Know About the Porcupine

SOONER OR LATER, if you visit the woods often enough, you will encounter one of the laziest animals in the forest. I'm speaking, of course, of the porcupine, whose common name comes from the Latin porcus, meaning pig, and spina, meaning thorns, which refer to its 30,000 barbed quills, its chief defense against predators, allowing it to become slow and lazy. And, yes, it comes with an attitude that seems to say, "No way. Go ahead and make my day!" Or, "Don't even THINK about it!"

My faithful lab, who was intelligent enough to react to hand and whistle signals given from a duck blind in the marsh while recovering downed ducks, and who, no matter how often he got slapped with that thrashing tail resulting in a snout full of barbs, never learned NOT to go after "Porky!"

Actually, those quills are not really barbs. Instead, they have fish-like scales pointing backwards. This quality causes the quills to work forward in a victim's flesh, making the quills both

*This porcupine is celebrating the arrival of spring. The newly swollen spring buds of a sugar maple are favorite foods.*

*Naturalists, school children and visitors will have the opportunity to view and study wildlife on the grounds of the future Natural History Museum. Shown here is a tree on the museum's trail network that has provided lunch for a porcupine. (Bill Frenette photo)*

painful and difficult to remove. By the way, there is no truth to the story that cutting the end of a quill will cause it to deflate and allow it to be removed more easily. I tried this only once. It was difficult to do, the attempt being painful to the dog, and it only shortened the quill, making it harder to grasp with the pliers. I have since learned that a quill, while hollow, isn't filled with air like a balloon but, rather, contains a spongy substance, so this procedure had no merit.

In my early Boy Scout days, we were taught never to kill a porcupine. The wisdom of that day being if a woods traveler was lost and starving, that the slow porcupine could easily be killed by a blow to the nose, providing a survival meal. It wasn't too many years later, however, that such a piece of woods lore became questionable. With no other effective predator except the fisher, whose numbers were decreasing due to habitat loss and unregulated over-trapping, the porcupine multiplied in such numbers that it became a destructive nuisance. There was not only a recurring problem of overpopulation, but also one's dog was more often subject to painful misadventures, resulting in aborted hiking trips and extensive quill removal sessions, sometimes so involved that costly out-of-town trips to obtain the expertise of the vet (usually involving sedation) were required.

Doug Crary, who kept a boat hidden on Center Pond, would put his oars in lengths of stove pipe suspended from trees. Axe handles, outhouse seats, boots radiator hoses, brake linings, and canoe paddles were all vulnerable to being chewed if left unprotected. Also, and to some land owners especially, the most harmful problem was the Porky's appetite for the inner bark of trees, which would cause severe injury to the tree. Or if the chewing completely girdled the trunk, it could actually kill the tree (see photo).

As the porcupine's numbers and damage increased to tolerable levels, various methods of controlling them were devised. Bounties were tried—50 cents to a dollar for a porcupine ear. As with most bounties, this effort to control overpopulation was a failure. In the early 1960s, some foresters experimented with lacing apples with sodium arsenite and rolling them into porcupine dens, where other species couldn't get them. This proved more effective than bounties, but it was costly in terms of manpower. Nature finally provided the solution: the fisher suddenly made a dramatic comeback, and in a short time had reduced the Porky's numbers to a more tolerable level. Today, the porcupine is in balance with its habitat and is far less the destructive terror it once was when it was common to shoot the S.O.B. on sight.

Porcupines mate in the fall (carefully, it is said in jest). The female gives birth to one baby. It is born with its eyes open and is fully furred and quilled. The quills harden in about an hour, whereas little Porky, called a porcupette, is fully armed and dangerous.

In cold weather and deep snow, porcupines den up, but usually only for a few days. If you are in an area where there are a lot of Porkies, the den may be communal. As many as 15 in one den have been reported. In areas of low population, one porcupine may occupy a den. These are usually in a hollow tree, beneath the roots of a tree or in caves among jumbled rocks. The dens are easy to locate in winter because of their easily recognized ditch, or trough, where they leave their wide body trail through the snow. The dens are usually filthy and deeply littered with scat droppings, a disgusting situation if you think about it. I once found a den in hunting season and climbed up on the rocks forming the den, figuring the smell from droppings would mask my human scent. In no time, the stench was so overwhelmingly nauseating that I had to leave.

One hunting season, I returned to my wall tent after several days' absence to find a Porky on my cot. He had been chewing on a supply box made of plywood, and the tent floor and cot were covered with fibrous-like droppings, which this time, fortunately, had a pungent, woody, resinous smell—not at all unpleasant and easy to sweep up.

I don't know about you, but I've had too many problems with this overgrown rodent to like him. He is slow, clumsy, dimwitted, ugly and destructive. Still I would miss his tracks in the snow or seeing him 30 feet up in a tree, munching his woody diet on a branch hardly thick enough to hold a sparrow. You have to admit that, despite all odds, he has been a survivor in the evolutionary scheme of things.

*Tupper Lake Free Press Print:* April 25, 2001

# LITTLE JOE GAUTHIER AND THE NORTHLAND HOTEL

DURING LAST THE LAST week or so, this column has had a number of inquiries concerning the Hotel Northland.

Out-of-town readers will be interested to know that the exceptional snow load from this winter's record-breaking snow levels overwhelmed the structural integrity of the venerable hotel's second-story porch floor. This past week, the entire porch/balcony that wrapped around the building has been removed, giving the hotel a completely different appearance.

Questions have ranged from, "When was the hotel built?" to, "Who built it?" and, "Is it being torn down?"

Researching the history of this impressive hotel became easy when I discovered a clipping by Amon Clarke Jr. in the *Free Press* files. Mr. Clark recorded his memories of early Tupper Lake personages and events in a column entitled *Old Timers Column*. In addition to being postmaster here from 1918 to 1925, Mr. Clark also helped found (and was master of) Mt. Arab Lodge F & A.M. in 1904. His column concerning the Hotel Northland follows (week of January 3, 1935):

"Do you remember 48 years ago when Joseph Gauthier first came to the sector now included in Tupper Lake village?

"The sale on January 1 of this year of one of the oldest landmark hostelries in town recalls many incidents in connection with pioneer days, which will be of interest to older settlers.

"The sale referred to is that of the Northlands Hotel at the juncture of Front Street, Broad Street and Wawbeek Avenue in Lakeview—more commonly known as 'French Village.'

"The ostensible disposers of the property were Mr. and Mrs. Joseph Gauthier and the purchaser is Charles Abdallah, business man of Sears Hill district for several years.

"It is alleged that the transaction approximates $32,000. Possession is to be given the new owner on April 2, next.

"Joseph Gauthier came into this section of the Adirondacks 48 years ago as a young man of 21. At that time there was no village here, no railroads, no post office, only a small 4th class affair at Moody-on-Big Tupper Lake conducted by the late 'Uncle Mart' Moody with but two mails a week up the torturous Racket River valley from Potsdam.

"'Little Joe' Gauthier, as he was always known to his friends, began work in the lumber woods for the late 'John Doe' Anderson, famous pioneer jobber of the early days.

"That year's cut of pulp and soft wood timber was made in the Jenkins Pond sector on what is now part of the Litchfield Park estate of the late Edward H. Litchfield, noted New York City attorney and millionaire real estate dealer.

"The Norwood Manufacturing Co. had the timber rights and the huge annual cut of millions of feet of coniferous logs that floated through Big Tupper Lake and down the Racket River through Potsdam to the company's mills at Norwood.

"Mr. Gauthier worked in the woods winters and each spring aided in the great log drives which were not completed until well into summer months. He recounts many incidents in connection with the old time, but now almost obsolete, log drives—of the dangers and hardships to the hard men who toiled from day break till dark seven days a week—sometimes wet to the skin—sometimes suffering from cold when sudden spring snowstorms and sub-freezing weather would overtake them.

"But the great mass of logs had to be kept moving, and the men always got hot tea or coffee and four meals a day. A majority of the men were French-Canadians with a fairly good number of

*The Hotel Northland was the successor to one of the early hostelries within the village. Shown here is the Canadian Hotel built in 1898, which flourished until 1926 when it was destroyed by fire. (photo courtesy of Goff-Nelson Library)*

sturdy North Country Irishmen.

"Mr. Gauthier tells of one Canadian who came in one spring and applied for a job on the drive. The foreman asked him if he knew how to drive logs. The applicant said, 'What you call dat 4-leg bird dat runs up a tree an' round an 'round de trunk wit his long bush tail over his back?'

"The foreman replied that he must mean a squirrel.

"The man replied, 'Squirrel, dats heem; well dat's me on a log.'

"The man was hired at once.

"When Mr. Gauthier first came into this country he lived for a few years with William McLaughlin (Uncle Mac, as he was known) who had a small farm-house on what later was named Moody Road and owned practically all the virgin woodlands where now stands Tupper Lake village.

"In 1890 the town of Altamont was established when it was set off from the town of Waverly. The Northern Adirondack railway was completed from Moira to Tupper Lake, and in 1892 the Webb railroad was pushed through the woods from Herkimer, via Prospect and Hinckley, to Malone.

"The John Hurd 'Big Mill' was built and a small saw mill was erected a half-mile farther down the shores of Racket Pond by H.H. Hobson, who, in 1891, became the first supervisor of the newly erected town of Altamont.

"Forty-two years ago Mr. Gauthier purchased from Wallace McLaughlin, son of the pioneer William McLaughlin, the large parcel of land in Wawbeek avenue where he built a small frame dwelling with lumber purchased from Hobson.

"Forty years ago, he united in marriage with Miss Mary Provost of Redford. They lived for two years in their modest home, then built the Canadian Hotel on the corner in 1898. It was moderate in size but large in hospitality and soon became the home of large numbers of French-Canadian lumberjacks and log drivers, who crowded the hotel to capacity while waiting for lumbering to start or spring freshets to open the streams for the annual log drive.

"During the early years of the present century the erstwhile hamlet of 300 souls had grown into the thriving Tip Top Town of the Adirondacks and had become a real business center, which has steadily advanced until today, with its 6,000 population, it stands second to Malone, the county seat.

"All those years, the Canadian Hotel was prosperous. Improvements and additions were made and everything seemed bright until fire destroyed the old landmark.

"Nothing was saved. The family and guests barely escaping with their lives. The fire records placed the total loss at $35,000, which included a large stock of supplies, all furniture, bedding, clothing and personal effects.

"The blow was heart-rending, as the owner carried only $2,500 insurance, which was nearly all used up in clearing the mass of debris from the basement and repairing the foundation.

"Mr. Gauthier, with two of his sons, aged 14 and 16 years, respectively, began the task of rebuilding the hotel, which was planned to be a 24-room structure of brick and concrete fireproof construction, to be named the Northlands Hotel.

"In December, 1926, eight months after the destructive fire, occurred the death of Noah Provost who had resided for many years with his sister, Mrs. Gauthier, to whom he left $15,000, practically all of which was expended for material and skilled labor in erecting the new and imposing three-story hotel.

"It was nearly two years before the building was completed, as the owner and his two young sons did all work possible without hiring men.

"Mr. Gauthier states that he plans to erect and occupy a small residence on his farm which is located near the New York and Ottawa railway, one mile below Faust and a short distance from Piercefield road.

"The property, which is owned by Mrs. Gauthier, includes a large area of fertile and tillable land and valuable woodlot.

"A farmhouse formerly stood on the property, but it was totally destroyed by fire several years ago.

"Mr. Gauthier, still plucky despite his 69 years, states that he may also enter the business world again if a suitable opportunity arises before April."

Correction

In a recent *Transitions* article, which featured a photograph of early settler Richard S. Gile, I incorrectly stated that Mr. Gile was a Civil War veteran (1861–1865). Mr. Gile's grandson, Frederick Culley, has kindly set the record straight, noting that Mr. Gile was born in 1850 and enlisted in the U.S. Army at Plattsburgh barracks on June 18, 1870. He was stationed at Fort Meade, Dakota Territory, served as a recruiting officer at Philadelphia, PA, and was discharged from the service in 1883 with a monthly pension of $8. Mr. Culley also noted that Mr. Gile and his wife, Lenora, worked at Litchfield Park—he as gatekeeper and she as housekeeper. The correction is appreciated and I regret the error.

P.S: Mr. Culley, now 90 years of age, recently celebrated his 65th wedding anniversary with is wife, Bertha, and their four children. He is currently writing his autobiography.

*Tupper Lake Free Press Print:* May 02, 2001

# THE STETSON SLOUGH FISHERMAN

THE FISHERMAN HAD BEEN THERE for the past several days, always at the same time in late afternoon and always at the same location. He was fishing in a place called Stetson Slough, where Racquette River Drive turns to follow the bend of that river until the river itself turns toward Moody Bridge to continue its 1,3888 ft. tumble to the St. Lawrence, 96 miles to the north. He was wearing heavy wool pants, seemingly overkill. Later, standing in the evening chill, I realized how practical they were.

Older readers will recognize that his woolens were known as "Malone" or "Ballard" pants, once made at the Ballard Mill in Malone. That fabric design is now the property of the Woolrich Co.

In true Adirondack tradition, he had "stagged," or shortened, the cuff line. This, together with the use of suspenders, allowed for a loose fitting waist, thus creating a "chimney effect" that in turn allowed a layer of insulating air to circulate, reducing moisture to help control heat loss. Early river drivers also stagged their woolen trousers to avoid catching the calks or spikes in their shoes and tripping. Incidentally, the best of these calked shoes was made in Croghan, NY, and river drivers referred to them as "Croghans." They were handmade and would hold the steel calks under conditions much better than other competitive footwear.

It was near this very spot, now called Stetson Slough, that the Charbonneau family from Vermont erected a humble shelter in 1840 and became the first settlers in this community. The name

*An opening was cut into the bank of the river, diverting some of its flow. This allowed logs to be floated across land (known as Stetson Landing) owned by Rueben Royal Stetson.*

Stetson Slough derived from the fact that many years later a small shingle mill was erected on lands originally owned by R.R. Stetson, for whom Stetson Road was also named.

In order to float logs to the mill site, the mill owners dug an opening in the river bank where the river made a wide curve upstream and diverted some of the river's flow, the pirated water then finding its way across the slough and past the mill until it returned to the river just beyond the mill site near the Kirk and Julia Gagnier property. This allowed logs to be floated to the mill for shingle production and is today a wonderful haven for all manner of wildlife, particularly waterfowl.

If that isn't enough history, there is more. This was the location of a movie colony call the YUESS Movie Company. It was a stock company, and many prominent businessmen in town invested more or less heavily in the concern. A number of movies were produced at the "bend 'o the road," as it was called. But the venture folded within a year. Unlike the KANT RIP Garter Co. established in Tupper a few years before, which cleaned out local financiers to the tune of about $50,000, the YUESS Moving Picture Corporation, aka U.S. Moving Picture Corporation, paid back practically all sums prescribed by the stockholders through its treasurer, Nathan Propp (then owner of Propp's Clothing Store, located where the Stewart convenience store now stands). These obligations were liquidated largely through the sale of the 145-acre tract and all cabins, cottages and studios that had been erected to Isaac Badeau of New York City in 1918 and who later sold it in 1924 to Otto Moody of the Bronx, the son of Alric Moody (noted guideboat builder here). The property then became part of the Moody Estate. No trace, not even a foundation, remains today of the ill-starred movie company's presence.

So it was that last week, despite a cold front that had produced temps of 40 degrees, the fisherman was at his usual spot. I was determined to get acquainted. I quickly learned that he had been fishing this river for 46 years. His grandfather, Wilfred LaBrie, had run a farm adjacent to the river and, indeed, his log cabin still remains as the summer cottage of the Mauer family from Rochester, NY, (opposite the Bruce Smith residence on Racquette River Drive). He was fishing so diligently, he said, because he had been delegated to provide enough bullhead for a bullhead feed at the V.F.W. Club. He had also volunteered to do the cooking at the event. To date he had over 60 fish, cleaned and prepared for cooking.

Hey, this operation required a closer look. Observation: the fisherman had cleared off some of the small bushes and created a landing pad, so to speak. Just above the pad, he had placed a comfortable beach chair, to the left of which and within and arm's length was a small beverage cooler and his worms (he had picked 200 night crawlers the night before). To the right was a large bucket to hold his catch. A forked stick, which held his fishing pole, was stuck in the ground in front of his chair. His line was rigged with a sinker at the end, and foot above the sinker a loop line held his baited hook. Okay, you are saying, a pretty straight-forward technique used by most good bullhead fishermen, but wait—the hook he was using was huge—three times the size of a normal bullhead hook. He had filed off the barb, which meant that in landing a fish he had to keep a high pole level and constant tension to prevent the fish from spitting out the hook. Here is the "catch" (pun intended): he simply landed the fish, held it over the pail, and with a slight jerking motion of his pole, the fish came free of the barbless hook and landed in the pail. No injured fish and no swallowed hook requiring cutting the line or using pliers, all the while risking impalement from the "horns" that are characteristic of the horned pout—or bullhead or catfish, as they are called.

Note: Logophiles and other history buffs may be interested that the word "stagged" probably came from the French word "stagga," meaning to castrate a young animal after maturity. River drivers would place their woolen trousers on a splitting block and use an ax to shorten the leg length.

Next column: We learn more about the fisherman and his views on the motorboat ban on our river.

*Tupper Lake Free Press Print:* June 06, 2001

# Upper Saranac Forest Controversy

IN THE SUMMER OF 1901, Eric Swenson sat on the porch of his camp on Upper Saranac Lake contemplatively sipping his morning coffee. The camp, which he had named Camp Arokortu (a rock or two), was filled to overflowing with his family and guests, and the sounds of laughter resonated throughout the lake's Bungalow Bay.

The night before, Mr. Swenson's main guide, A. Parsons, together with several assistant guides and their boats, had rowed a party of 13 across the lake to the Bartlett Carry, which connects Upper Saranac with Middle Saranac by a short overland pathway where they could then walk to the Saranac Club (later Bartlett's) for dinner. Parsons, with the other guides, would use the camp's treasured church boats, also called family boats or sometimes freight boats, according to use. They were larger, heavier and carried more passengers, built along guide-boat lines but not considered "guide" boats.

Edward Pearse, who had formerly managed "Hough's," (Saranac Inn), was their host and provided a fine meal of lake trout, spring lamb (venison) and, from the wine cellar, some wonderful Bass Ale from Canada. There were many guests in the club's dining room that evening, and the Swenson party shared a table with a half dozen other pleasant, entertaining diners. There was J.M. Sparks from the "frontier" town, Tupper Lake, where he managed the cold-storage plant of the Adirondacks Supply

Company (later, Armour & Co.) with his two guests from Chicago, a Mr. Brown and a Mr. Cooper (Armour executives?).

Also at the dinner table were Miss Helen Roosevelt from Hyde Park; Tom Cantwell and Mrs. Cantwell from Malone; W.K. Cavil, who was running a halfway house on the Sweeney Carry (Wawbeek Hotel); Frederick Potter and Orlando Potter, from Sing Sing, NY, who had rowed their guideboat from the Brandeth Camp near Racquette/Long Lakes area; and A.J. Ginsberg (Muriel Ginsberg's uncle, Mr. G's younger brother, skilled amateur photographer, later to become a physician) from Tupper Lake, who was staying overnight and joined them for dinner. It had been a fine evening of good food and newfound friends, with a memorable guideboat row across the Upper Lake under a moonlit sky and calm waters, the beauty enhanced by the soulful cries of the many resident loons.

Yet, this early morning, Mr. Swenson was troubled. A pall of heavy smoke lay over the lake, smoke so thick that it obscured any view of the water. The smoke was coming from a tract of land near Wawbeek Corners (intersection of Routes 3 and 30), where a pioneer forestry experiment was being conducted by the New York State College of Forestry under the auspices of Cornell University and Dr. B.E. Fernow, the appointed director of the college. Dr. Fernow, originally from Prussia, trained at the Forest Academy of Prussia as an early scientific forester.

Dr. Fernow espoused the European ideal of forestry and emphasized economic return over silvaculture (caring for the forest). His plan was to cut all hardwood on the tract down to 14 inches on the butt, and all softwood down to eight inches, on the theory that light and air would thus reach the trees left standing, the growth of which would then be more rapid. It was part of the scheme to fill in vacant places with young pine.

Unfortunately, when about 6,000 acres had been cut over, a wind upturned or snapped off nearly all the trees that had not been felled, whereupon the school cleared the lands so that they were practically bare, and then undertook to reforest with seedlings.

It was the smoke from the fires used to burn the tops and clear the land that was upsetting to the Upper Saranac property owners

*Note: The Paul Smith Society of American Foresters (SAF) presently maintains a one-mile interpretive loop trail with 15 stops called the "Wawbeek Plantation" (.8 mile from the "Y" on Route 30, Wawbeek Corners). Here, 68 acres of hardwood were cleared and white pine planted in their stead along with Norway spruce as part of Fernow's pioneering experiment. It is a worthwhile visit.*

and so concerned Mr. Swenson that summer morning at Camp Arokortu. In addition, the Cross Clearing tract was totally denuded (only 440 acres were replanted) and was visually horrifying even if you believed in the experiment, which most observers did not. Equally disturbing was the rumor that a subsidiary of the American Sugar Refining Co. (Brooklyn Cooperage Co.) was planning to put in a seven-mile logging railroad spur from Upper Saranac Lake shores (good gracious!). This would involve the further destruction of all the trees to a width of 25 yards along the line of the tracks.

Mr. Swenson was a man of action and influence and, as president of the Association of Residents on Upper Saranac Lake, he had as many members of equally influential and concerned allies. The experiment by this German fellow was unacceptable. Thus that same summer of 1901, the association made application to the attorney general "to have the purchase of 30,000 acres of land in Franklin County by Cornell University declared unconstitutional and void and to have the title to said land vested in the People of the State of New York."

This lawsuit would go on for 10 years before it was finally won by Mr. Swenson and friends (1910). In the meantime, when the annual appropriation for the college appeared in the Appropriation Bill of 1903, owing to the hue and cry that had been raised against the college, it was vetoed by Gov. Odell. The consequence of this action deprived the university of state support. It closed its College of Forestry in June of 1903 and dismissed Director Fernow (several years later, Syracuse University would win the Forestry College prize). It did, however, due to a contract with Brooklyn Cooperage entered into by the university in May 1900, continue to cut wood on the college tract under an appropriation for cleaning up and replanting. We will discuss this operation and the Brooklyn Cooperage Co., which was located on Chemical Street near Walt Kennedy's garage (110 ft. smokestack still there) in a later column.

It should be noted that Dr. Fernow's futuristic theories, however sound, had few supporters. The visual horror of the necessary clear-cutting and the burning of the tops to make way for growing the more marketable and valuable softwoods on hardwood sites was too great a disadvantage. While his critics didn't approve his methods, he was never accused of any dishonesty of purpose.

*Tupper Lake Free Press Print:* June 20, 2001

# THE RAQUETTE RIVER OXBOW

SINCE THE EARLIEST OF TIMES, a section of the Racquette River located near this community has been known as the "Oxbow." It has gradually grown to denote a location as well as a particular configuration of the river's course. For example, one might say, "I saw an eagle near the Oxbow," or, "I caught a huge pike near the Oxbow."

The Oxbow name, as is well known, derives from the fact that at this location, the river's course originally made a large bend that resembled the shaped frame forming a collar about an ox's neck, which supported the yoke and was called an oxbow. It has become a term used throughout the world to describe such a bend in a river.

The Tupper Lake Oxbow is a well-known feature of our river and is especially notorious to those boaters who often became confused in its twisted maze (this to the wonderment of locals familiar with the river). Rather than making a left downstream and turn through a break in the bank (dug out before 1865 to expedite log drives), they continue around the "bow" in the river's original course and soon found themselves heading back upstream, passing once again Walt Zurawski's River Road home, signaling their mistake.

Increased prominence has been given to the Oxbow recently as planners involved in the proposed Natural History Museum of the Adirondacks, soon to be built on lands overlooking the river, have quickly recognized that the wetlands surrounding the "bow" are a living ecosystem.

One researcher has called it a classroom without walls, and it has become one of the focal points that will further enhance the learning experience and enjoyment of those visiting the museum. What they will see as they look out over the river from the museum grounds is this very unique wetland framed by the Seward Range and neighboring Santanoni (French corruption of St. Anthony) with its spectacular defining rock slide car cleaved into its flank (rendered from the sword of the mythical god Thor?).

The wetland is an exhilarating landscape of green, dotted with the reds of the high-bush cranberries—cattails standing sentry-like, fluffy brown puffs resembling the whitetail's ear, reminds us that our ancestors used this plant, not only for its nourishing food value, but also as torches to light their darkness. Other plant species include pickeral weed, sundew and water lilies, all emerging in an explosion of varied and dramatic beauty.

*Log jams were a common and often dangerous problem for river drivers as sawed logs were floated down the Racquette River. Here the oarsman, his "jam boat" placed in an eddy formed by the rock holding the logs, helps the crew dislodge the jam with the help of their peaveys. (photo courtesy of Jim Lanthier)*

You may remember from your science classes that the character of a wetland is determined in large part by the amount and quality of water moving through it. My neighbor, Dan Spada, a wetland specialist, tells me "the most fundamental difference between a marsh and bog or a swamp (all wetland types) has to do with groundwater movement. Bogs have almost no groundwater circulation and thus are nutrient-poor and highly acidic so that relatively few plant species live there and not much animal life as a result. The wetland at the Oxbow, on the other hand, is seasonally flooded and so we have a marsh and a forested swamp very rich in nutrients that is much more productive than other wetland types, and it supports plant growth and teems with wildlife—mammals, birds, amphibians, fish."

What a superb classroom for the many students from all over the north country and beyond who will one day visit the Tupper Lake museum!

The Racquette River, so rich in Adirondack history, flows 68 miles before it makes its twisting turn at the Oxbow (from its traditionally acknowledged lake source, the Eckford Chain: Blue Mountain Lake, Eagle Lake and Utowana Lake). It still has 104 miles to go before joining the St. Lawrence River, making it the second-largest river in the state.

As early as 1860, New York State appropriated large sums of money for the improvement of the river for lumber purposes, and as one river traveler put it, "We occasionally see where rocks that interfered with the floating of the logs have been blasted out of the stream and booms and piers constructed to turn the logs in the right direction where otherwise they might run off into ponds or slews." It was about this time, probably in 1860, that the bank of land was cut at the Oxbow to eliminate floating logs having to curve around the bow as evidenced in The Journeyings of James Wood, September, 1865, private printing: "We ran the rapids with good success (note: Dugal Road location), Henry and John walking the rocks, but Harry and Jim running successfully in their boats, a light shower sprinkled us as we put through the 'Dutch' Gap Canal a narrow cut of 30 feet in length and 10 feet deep across the 'Big Oxbow' saving a distance of a mile and a quarter."

By the 1900s, steam boats such as the Altamont, the Forester and the Adirondack, to name a few, were making scheduled runs on the river between Trombley's Landing (Sweeney Carry) and the hotels on Tupper Lake. Unregulated water releases at Setting Pole Dam raised havoc with the river, however, and by 1930, a project was initiated to clear the approximate 16 miles of river from Moody Bridge upstream to the Oxbow. This section of the river was too shallow and full of debris to be used even by guideboats except in high water periods.

The work was done by a crew of C.C.C. (Civilian Conservation Corps.) recruits from Camp 15 at Cross Clearing, working under the supervision of foreman Paul Delaire. An item in the *Tupper Lake Free Press*, November 2, 1933, noted, "1,550 deadheads and logs were removed from the river in the 16-mile stretch covered, which constituted a serious menace to boating." The article concluded with the statement that the project "required a total of 125 man-days of labor."

A note of interest: The large island formed by the river's circular course at the Oxbow was at one time used by the McCarthy farm (later, Pisanchin farm) to harbor large numbers of pigs destined for the slaughter house, located to the rear of the St. Alphonsus cemetery above the river.

*Tupper Lake Free Press Print:* September 19, 2001

# Motorboats vs. Canoes

IN A RECENT COLUMN, this writer described his encounter with an individual who was identified to readers only as "The Fisherman." At that time, he was a daily visitor to a section of the Racquette River known as "Stetson Slough," where Racquette River Drive makes a sharp bend in the road and parallels the river before rejoining Route 3 on Moody Flow.

His daily fishing visits were because he needed to catch enough bullhead for the annual bullhead feed at the V.F.W. Club. We described his unusual technique and the resulting success he was enjoying in procuring enough fish (over 100 bullhead needed for the feed) and the fact that he had been fishing the river for almost 46 years.

I soon recognized him as one of the river's most fervent boatmen. Indeed only hours after the last ice flow had floated downstream and given the river life and movement towards a waiting springtime, I observed him heading up river in his boat. I was to learn that the preceding fall, during the last days of the deer-hunting season, he had been caught by a sudden cold front on a night with no wind, which had ice-locked the bay or slough on the river where his hunting camp was located. This meant laboriously chopping his way through the ice to the river and the necessity of leaving much of his gear behind. The next day, the river itself was locked in icy bondage, and the early spring trip was to retrieve that gear and check the status of his camp.

*Since early times, motorboats and canoes have coexisted on Tupper waters. Shown above: President Howard Taft, with local guides Henry Smith and Del DeLosh, during the President's 1910 visit to the Marshall Sheppy camp.*

On the spring trip upriver, he told me he had spotted five deer and three bald eagles. He noted that given the white head and tail, two of the eagles were mature birds and that the third one had displayed only small amounts of white feathering, which led him to believe it was a younger bird, not yet five years old, at which time his head and tail would display more white. That comment indicated to me that he was a knowledgeable observer and, indeed, I was to learn that he is considered one of the most enthusiastic outdoorsmen in the community.

We talked at that time about the proposal by some groups to ban motorboats on the river. He told me that he failed to understand the logic that would allow one group of legitimate users to have preference over another group of legitimate users. He admitted some motor-boaters go too fast around the tight corners of the river and often don't slow down in passing people's docks, which results in damage to boats tied there, but that awareness of the problem and, perhaps, increased enforcement could correct those objections.

On the other hand, the fisherman continued, he has seen flotillas of canoes, 20 at a time, coming down the river, often eight or more side by side, taking up the complete river's width so the paddlers could talk.

This writer is a canoeist (who also loves his outboard), and I found truth in the fisherman's observations. You will have to admit, the sheer number of canoeists have become overwhelming. Our area now rivals Minnesota's Boundary Waters as a prime waterway destination. This has created problems such as loss of remoteness and quiet, among others. Problems that cannot be laid solely on the doorstep of motorboating. I decided to ask the fisherman one more question: Would you agree that certain waters like the St. Regis Chain of Lakes should be motor-free?

He began to reel in another fish as he answered: "Absolutel,y there is no question that certain ponds and lakes are best left motor-free. Heck, that's a slam-dunk. But not the Racquette River, for cripes sakes!"

I personally enjoyed listening to the fisherman's experienced outlook on things. Lately, I've noticed an increased polarization existing between recreation groups that is disturbing. Such

*You're looking at some of the railroad section gang working out of Tupper Lake Junction about 1924. From left to right are Dominick Lori, Jim Demasie, Jim Buckley, Dan Donovan, Leonard LaCorey, Tupper Lake Supply founder Phil Dattola, George Clark, Jim Seaka and John Amoriell. Two railroad men we missed in our account of the "Next Stop! Tupper Lake" railroad station benefit last week were Mr. Dattola and engine house worker William C. Walsh.*

factions are arbitrary distinctions at best, and ignore the links that exist between different outdoor enthusiasts. After all, many motorboat owners are also fervent canoeists and the same can be said for cross-country skiers who may also be passionate snowmobilers. Or the much maligned hunter to whom the quest for game might well be secondary to just being in the woods and enjoying nature's wonders.

Noted author Alex Shoumatoff in his essay, "The Real Adirondacks", puts it this way: "No one lived full-time in the Adirondacks until the white man came. It was a zone of peace, and even after the white man came, people were basically supportive of each other because they never knew when they might need each other's help. My theory is that the harsh environment, when the temperature can swing 80 degrees in 24 hours, has had an equalizing and harmonizing effect on the people, and this is where the live-and-let-live attitude that is the essence of the local culture comes from."

In conclusion then, there are traditional ways of life here (such as hunting camps and being able to run up the river in a motorboat) that are not really understood by some. An outspoken friend of mine told me recently, with a trace of a smile, "Bill, these critics are good people, no doubt about that. The thing is, they just don't have a clue."

*Tupper Lake Free Press Print:* October 03, 2001

# TUPPER LAKE TIMBERLAND PURCHASES

IN THE SUMMER OF 1913, two principals of a company called The Oval Wood Dish Corporation, located at the time in Traverse City, MI, took a vacation trip through the Adirondacks. When they passed through Tupper Lake, they immediately noticed the large stands of hardwood and learned that little or no use was being made of it. At this time, there was little demand for hardwood in this area, and the price for Adirondack timberlands was very attractive. Consequently, as an investment and with no thought of relocating in Tupper Lake, the O.W.D. management purchased in November of 1914 its first timberlands in the Adirondacks.

Timber supply in the Lower Peninsula of Michigan, where the Traverse City plant was located, was beginning to be depleted, and the company was considering building a new plant in the Upper Peninsula of Michigan, where they owned substantial acreage.

The late Gerald (Gerry) Hull, who was closely identified with the Tupper Lake plant from the outset and headed the firms as president for many years, describes the purchases this way (Simmons 1965, p. 151):

"From the Santa Clara Lumber Co., we acquired the Follensby Tract, with the exception of Follensby Pond itself and its shoreline, together with a portion of the Mt. Morris Tract and lands in Township 22 adjoining the Follensby Pond Tract.

"The news of this tract soon became generally known and we were immediately solicited to purchase other timberlands in the

*Getting to O.W.D. lands along the Racquette River was easier when this bridge, located at the end of Dugal Rd., was in place (Underhill Rapids). Public lands are a necessity for increasing recreational demands. Unwarranted restrictions and flawed regulations make more acquisitions controversial. (Bill Frenette photo)*

area. We sent cruisers from Michigan to the Tupper Lake area to take a hasty look at the timber, and some time in the spring or summer of 1915, we secured an option on lands owned by the A. Sherman Lumber Co. and the Racquette River Paper Co.—both of which were owned by the same individuals—and also for the timber on Township 19 which was owned by Charles Turner of Malone. The Santa Clara purchase, plus the later options, rounded out a total of 75,000 acres."

History will record that the O.W.D. was a financially successful firm, particularly during the 1940s when the war in Europe resulted in a great demand for wood products, and the popularity of its new "Ritespoon" line produced increased sales and production.

However, during the Depression years in the 1930s, with a choked economy, competition to their woodenware from paper plates and poor initial estimates of its hardwood supply (which proved inadequate from wood rot), the company was experiencing financial difficulties.

This situation caused the O.W.D. management to rethink its

policy of allowing its lands to be open to hunters and fishermen. Increased taxes, which had steadily grown, made it necessary to lease those lands for the revenues that would be realized. This would be a major change for a traditional way of life in this community. Suddenly, if you had no access (through membership) to the recently leased lands, your only recourse was to hunt and fish state land, which in this area was sharply limited. The land affected compromised more than 40,000 acres lying in St. Lawrence County, chiefly in Townships 8, 9, and 12, and upwards of 6,000 acres in Franklin County, largely in the vicinity of Mt. Morris, Big Simonds Pond and along the Racquette River.

Approximately 1,200 acres in the vicinity of the Oxbow section of the Racquette, between the Barbour road (Follensby) and the state holdings near this village were held open (recently offered for sale by O.W.D. real estate division and presently under lease to the Spring Hill Club).

In the immediate vicinity of the village, two leases were consummated, covering approximately 3,600 acres on the slopes of Mt. Morris and around Big Simonds Pond. A group of local men—Percy Alexander, George Delair, Aime Martin, Emile Themens, A.J. Deshaw and Karl King, leased 1,300 acres extending to the Litchfield line on Mt. Morris (Waukasha Club, now largely Sugar Loaf Club). A tract of some 2,400 acres, which completely encircled Big Simond on three sides, was leased by Dr. R.L. Cook of Sunmount and associates, who owned camps on the pond. This lease was to be called "Big Simonds Fish and Game Club," and it stretched between the Read and Strange and the Barbour (Follensby) park lines. It was noted that it produced some of the best deer hunting in the area (now Simonds Pond Club aka Teachers Club).

An additional 1,400-acre section lying behind the Tupper Lake Country Club golf course and including Sugar Loaf Mountain was leased to John Wood of Rochester. Some other leases were: The Luke Usher tract (Jo-Indian Club), 2,400 acres; former Congressman Bert Snell (Kildare Pond), 1,600 acres; the Inlet Club, 5,500 acres; the Hollywood Club, 5,000 acres; Potter Brook

Club (north of Kildare), 7,000 acres; F.R. Bates and I.H. Hollenbeck of Fort Jackson, NY, 7,000 acres (in Parishville, including two miles of the West Branch of the St. Regis River). The leases were to be for 10 years with option to cancel on one year's notice on the part of either party.

Thus, practically all of the extensive O.W.D. holding in the north one-third of Township 25, which for years was noted for excellent deer hunting, was at once thrown into private hunting clubs. Fifty thousand acres, which for 20 years since being acquired by the O.W.D. was always open to hunters and fishermen without hindrance. It is to be noted that the company had received requests for leases for many years, which were refused so that the area could remain open to local hunters, and it was with great reluctance that leases were negotiated.

Note: Sixty-three years have elapsed since leased land and posted signs became a way of life here. Today, we are undergoing a swing in exactly the opposite direction. Once again, what has become a traditional way of life is suddenly changing. Only this time it is not the granting of a lease that presents the problem, but rather the loss of a lease and its attendant hunting camps—some having been occupied by several successive generations, which, regrettably, will be no more as New York State acquires private lands and sets a time limit on structure removal. Another factor is that as the available private land diminishes, lease fees rise that generate higher dues for members, which makes belonging to a private club increasingly expensive.

Thus, history proves that it is seldom stable. The dynamics of change are its framework, and who knows where the pendulum will next swing in this fast-paced society?

*Tupper Lake Free Press Print:* October 31, 2001

## DEER HUNTING LONG AGO

DEER HUNTING IN THE ADIRONDACKS was much different around the turn of the last century than it is today.

In the 1880s, for example, this area was largely untracked wilderness. There were only nine families living here, most of them in rough log shelters along the river below what is today called LeBeouf's Bridge, which leads to Follensby Pond. It was common and even necessary for sportsmen to hire locals familiar with the surroundings, such as members of the Moody family, as guides, and to expect that the best thing a guide could do for a "sport" was to get him in range of something to shoot.

The guides, for their part, generally employed two methods of hunting to guarantee that expectation. One was "night hunting" or "jacklighting" in which a light was placed on the bow of a guideboat and the hunters would stealthily approach deer feeding in the marshes and along the shore of the waterways. The deer would be fascinated by the light, and once transfixed by curiosity, its eyes reflected like two laser beams. Then the guide would gently rock the boat—a signal for his client to shoot.

There is a story that on one occasion, upon such a signal, the sportsman, excited and confused, jumped out of the boat instead of firing and was promptly returned to camp in disgust by his guide. Still to be seen locally are several vintage boats with a circular hole cut into the bow deck that were used to hold the large reflector that surrounded the torchlight. Also still in existence are

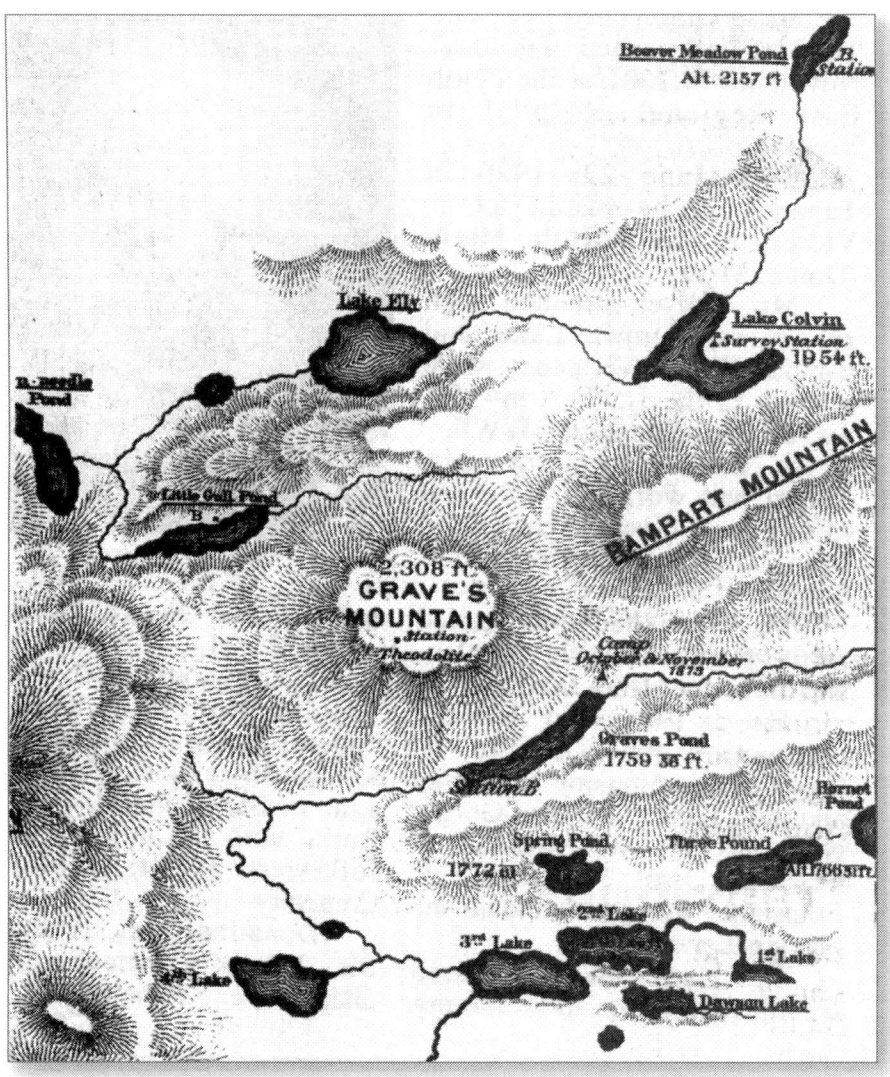

*The names of some of the ponds have changed, and lakes 1 through 4 are now one large lake (Lows). However, Graves and Rampart mountains remain as stalwart landmarks.*

the long-bladed guideboat paddles with their extra thin, knife-sharp edge that allowed the guide to more easily return the paddle for another stroke by feathering the paddle and soundlessly bringing it forward, edge first, parallel to the gunwale without lifting it from the water, which would alert unsuspecting prey.

*Permanent station marks were left only at the corners of the more important primary triangles. Pictured is bolt (station mark) #15 placed on Graves Mountain.*

A second method of hunting was the use of dogs to drive the deer to standers, or watchers, a technique called "hounding." Both methods were highly effective, so effective that concerns arose that with the advantages of numerous railroads now penetrating the Adirondacks and the many people becoming interested in hunting, the deer of the state would surely become exterminated.

In 1899, a law was passed that for a term of years, hounding would be prohibited. In two years time, the deer increased over 50 percent, and the legislature of 1901 enacted a law that would forbid for all time the hounding of deer.

Unfortunately, the law arrived too late to save the life of a local hotelier named William Graves, who drowned while hunting deer with his dog, who turned out to be anything but man's best friend.

Mr. Graves' lodge, which he called "Sportsman's Lodge," stood on the site of the former women's infirmary of the American Legion Mountain Camp, which is now a handsome summer home. A rough little wilderness inn was first erected there by a man named Blanchard back around 1860, and it was enlarged by a subsequent owner, Sid Jenkens. Under the ownership of Mr. Graves, it developed into quite a resort, the goal of most of the sportsmen who navigated the Saranac-Racquette-Tupper route, and a jumping-off place for the hardier adventurers who pushed on through to Mud Lake, where as my friend Paul Jamieson once put it, "the last moose was killed many times" (now Lows Lake, much greater in size since A.A. Low built his two dams). Successive owners included, "Tish" McClure and Alembert Corey, son of Jesse Corey, founder of one of the earliest hotels in the region—Rustic Lodge on Upper Saranac.

In 1894, when the Graves place was being operated by John Hatch as the Tupper Lake House, it was destroyed by fire.

The details of Mr. Graves' death, as reported by the Plattsburgh Republican and reprinted in the *Tupper Lake Free Press* are as follows:

"Mr. William W. Graves, proprietor of the Sportsman's Lodge, was at Horseshoe Pond with his son, watching for decr. A large buck being driven in, Mr. Graves attempted to drive it near the shore so that his son might shoot it.

"Mr. Graves had the deer by the tail, and was pounding him on the head with an oar when suddenly the deer turned and swam under the boat, capsizing it. The boat, being old and leaky, he could not right it, but thought he could get ashore by taking hold of the dog's tail and being towed, but the dog, instead of swimming, would turn and get on Mr. G's shoulders. He then tried to swim ashore, but could not reach it. The water was very cold and he was quite worn out from his tussle with the deer.

"When near the shore he told his little son he could swim no further, and bade him good-bye, telling him to bid his mother and little sisters the same, and sank to the bottom. The water where he sank is not over 10 or 12 feet deep, and very clear. His little son could see his face when he was sinking until near the bottom. Mr. Graves will be sadly missed by the sporting fraternity."

Afterward

Two years later in October, Verplank Calvin, superintendent of the state-authorized topographical survey of the Adirondacks would row down the outlet of Horseshoe Lake, enter the Bog River and row up that river to Lows Lake, then called Mud Lake (no dams at that time). He would then carry to and row across Graves Pond to the foot of the already named Graves Mountain. Unlike today, this was true wilderness by every definition of the time, untamed and unmoderated." In August of that year an assistant had placed a reflective signaling device Calvin called a stanhelio. These were reflective sheets of tin that caught the sun. On a clear day, they could be seen as far as 60 miles away and helped in triangulation and barometric altitude computations.

Once on the summit, Calvin then drilled holes in the rock to hold the legs of his surveying instrument (called a transit theodolite) and cemented in a copper bolt below the plumb line of the transit. This was done on only the most important summit stations and would serve to aid future surveyors in centering their instruments. Graves Mountain was the 15th station thus established, and the drilled holes and bolt number 15 can still be found today on the southwest corner of its rocky summit.

Note: Graves Mountain is today the property of Bishop Paul Moore, who has a summer home on Lake Marion on what is known as the Otterbrook Tract, Doug Crary caretaker. The title to 7,573 acres of this tract was acquired by New York State in 1991 with certain rights reserved to Otterbrook, some of which will expire in December of 2005.

*Tupper Lake Free Press Print:* November 14, 2001

# OF LUMBERJACK SPRING

THE PAVED ROAD had yet to come to this area. Indeed, it was a novelty to most of the United States. Wilbur and Orville Wright had only recently proven with their 59-second flight that man could fly. The "Age of Invention" was only beginning to establish the technological foundation on which our present-day society depends (the light bulb, the automobile, the telephone, etc.).

The year was 1910 and Louis Oshier, one of this community's early settlers, stood at the south end of Tupper Lake, about 10 miles from the village and very near where he no doubt had landed his guideboat after rowing the length of the lake. Mr. Oshier was near the tri-county corner of Franklin, St. Lawrence and Hamilton counties and the historic line of the Totten and Crossfield Purchase, and this was at the time a remote and isolated place. Consider: It would be another eight years (1918) before voters would approve Route 30 from Tupper Lake to Long Lake.

A log bridge built in 1894 crossed the Racquette River at Moody, but the road crossing the Moody Flow was a rough, corduroy (log) route covered with earth and was under water for a part of every year. Until Edward Litchfield extended the road for five and one half miles, linking his park with the hamlet of Moody, the road ended approximately where Charland Road begins today.

The Tupper Lake House at the head of the lake was no longer, having been destroyed by fire 16 years earlier in 1898. Camp Welcome sat on the rocky ledge overlooking Bog River Falls and for a time provided lodging and food to river drivers running logs from the Little Tupper area until it was abandoned by Raphael Cameron's (Hinkson) family two years earlier in 1908.

I would like to imagine that on that day Mr. Oshier was fishing Cold Brook, which empties into South Bay, stealthily wading that fine stream, careful of vibration and shadow as he attempted to lure a fat, speckled beauty from its hiding place beneath an overhanging bank. No matter what he was doing, he made a monumental

*Pictured is the Spring House at Lumberjack Spring. (Bill Frenette photo)*

discovery that day when he happened upon a wonderful spring, which today we know as Lumberjack Spring, that still runs clear, cold and pure. That spring, which continues to bubble up through a sparkling sand bottom at a temperature hovering around 48 degrees, has been welcomed by countless travelers and lumberjacks since Mr. Oshier discovered it 91 years ago.

Note: A recent and reliable testing of seven north-country roadside springs, conducted by staff of *Adirondack Life*, noted, "The Lumberjack Spring Waters were unassailable when tests came back." The springhouse located at this site is supported by a concrete wall sunken into the ground with a height three feet above water level. This structure was built by three local residents and their employer, Mr. Charles Goodman, former owner of the Sheltered Cove Camp on Tupper Lake. Some background on its construction and the philosophy that prompted it may be of historical interest.

Mr. Goodman headed the Grow Construction Company, one of

the most prominent engineering firms in New York City, his firm having built many of New York's subway tubes and arterials as well as sewer tunnels in Queens and Manhattan. Other major projects included construction and engineering work on the New Jersey and Connecticut turnpikes, the New York State Thruway and the George Washington Bridge. He and Mrs. Goodman were frequent visitors to Tupper Lake during the late 1920s, attracted by the area's scenic splendor, its lovely lakes, the beneficial fresh air and its friendly people. Mrs. Goodman had become seriously ill and always found that her health improved on the Tupper Lake visits. As a result, Mr. Goodman decided to build a seasonal home that would provide longer and more comfortable visits. After much deliberation, he chose a location on the spine of the Esker, a ridge that rises abruptly from Tupper Lake's south bay, where Cold Brook enters the lake on one side and where Bog River runs parallel to the Esker on the other equally abrupt side. He then situated Shelter Cove Camp, as it came to be called, where it commanded a wonderful view of the lake and surrounding hills. At the same time, in the early 1930s, there was construction on the road to Long Lake and Mr. Goodman was able to obtain fractured cyclopean blocks of Adirondack anorthosite, a highly durable, erosion-resistant rock, greatly valued for construction. Near the top of the magnificent chimney that faces the entrance, a skillful stonemason chiseled out the numerals "1933," the date the house was completed.

On a recent day, I stood on the massive stone deck overlooking the lake, and with the sun at just the right angle, the crystals of feldspar, the main mineral in anorthosite, reflected the light as though ignited by some internal fire. The "camp" remains today a tribute to the local artisans who built it and to Mr. Goodman who envisioned it—as enduring and impressive as the true "rock of ages" from which it was built.

Mr. Goodman, of course, knew of Mr. Oshier's spring. Impressed with the beauty of the spring's natural setting and the quality of its waters, he undertook to protect it permanently at his own expense. After some discussion with Earnest Reandeau of the State Highway Department, he put his men to work building a concrete wall about the spring and a sturdy springhouse to protect it (see photo). A one and one-half inch pipe set in the well wall carried a flow of six and one-half gallons per minute from the spring. The 10-inch thick concrete sidewalls support an inverted "V" roof, also of concrete. Embedded in the roof is a steel framing of 28 angles supported on four corner steel posts set in the sidewalls. Steel plates touch steel framing and project three feet above the roof and, acting as lightning rods, hold the sign "Lumberjack Spring." A bronze tablet on the side of the springhouse, its inscription still clearly legible, reads, "Lumberjack Spring: Cool Drinking Water; 1582 Feet Above Sea Level Discovered by Louis Oshier in 1910/ Structure Erected in 1937 by Sheltered Cove Lumberjacks, Ed Sabourin, Emil Sabourin and Pat Arsenault."

In addition to protecting the integrity of this wonderful spring, Mr. Goodman had in mind that his project would "provide a lasting memento to the lumbering industry, so famous in this region, and to the hardy French Canadian lumberjacks of the Tupper Lake community."

## The Scorecard

| Source | Location | Nitrates | Coliform | E-Coli |
|---|---|---|---|---|
| McConley | Moriah | 0.84 | absent | — |
| Lumberjack | Tupper Lake | 0.46 | absent | — |
| Watering Tub | Brant Lake | 0.38 | present | absent |
| Cold Spring | Piercefield | 0.20 | absent | — |
| Mystery Spot | Ausable River | 0.18 | present | absent |
| Page Street | Speculator | 0.10 | present | absent |
| Giant Mountain | Keene | 0.10 | present | absent |
| King Phillips | North Hudson | 0.10 | present | absent |

Admittedly an inexact science, the above test results for potability conducted by Alchemy Laboratories in Plattsburgh for *Adirondack Life Magazine* are considered reliable, and both local springs scored high.

*Tupper Lake Free Press Print:* December 05, 2001

## SKIING EDITOR LOUIS SIMMONS

IN THE *FREE PRESS* OFFICE, there is a greatly enlarged circa 1930 picture of former editor Louis Simmons sitting at his editorial desk.

It is a compelling photograph. Louis looks so content, so confident, so very, very young, so thin and fit. His wire-rimmed glasses give him a scholarly look that hints to the powerful intellect of this newly minted magna cum laude Syracuse University School of Journalism student.

I have seen that picture many times since it has been hung over his old desk. Louis is sitting on a high stool that was necessary to reach the massive desk, but it was only recently that I noticed he was wearing ski boots! Not the buckled hi-tech boot of today, of course, but the ankle-high, soft leather lace boot with a box toe and a groove cut into the heel. I was momentarily puzzled about that strange, somewhat inappropriate footwear in the newspaper office until I remembered that Louis would often ski to work. Here is the story as I remember it:

Louis had started working in 1931 for L.P. Quinn, his former high school principal. Mr. Quinn had just converted what had been a throwaway handbill called, *Tip Top Topics*, into a weekly newspaper. These were Depression years and Louie had no car, and at a salary of $15 per week, he had slim prospects of getting one for awhile. This meant walking nearly two miles to and from the shop, which was then located on Mill Street.

*In the 1930s, clothing specifically designed for skiing was just beginning to appear as shown in photo above. Baggy (for movement) and woolen (for warmth) was the style. Tapered, non-baggy cut and hard-finish material to prevent snow from sticking would appear much later.*

In the winter, I remember him telling me he found it easier to ski back and forth, laying out "a short-cut trail" from behind the new home his father had built in 1923 at Demars Boulevard in the Junction (next to the beautiful stone Presbyterian Church built three years earlier). By skiing across Racquette Pond, he could reach the shop in about 15 minutes.

Those skis served Louie well for many years. They were long by today's standards with a narrow, graceful cut made from a single straight-grained piece of ash noted for its flexibility and lightness. The bottom of the ski was a deep brown color from repeated coats of pine tar heated into the wood over the kitchen stove. The pine tar provided waterproofing and a surface that more easily accepted canning paraffin, which was then applied for glide.

In his use of skis in 1930, Louie was slightly ahead of the curve in terms of skiing popularity. It wasn't until after the 1932 Winter Olympics, held in nearby Lake Placid, that skiing held any interest locally, and then only in the most rudimentary way in terms of know-how, facilities, and, indeed, equipment. For example, the first ski bindings, or ski harnesses (as we called them,) the youth of my day used were oversized rubber bands or loops cut from inner tubes. The rubber loop went over the rubber boot all kids wore, one end placed behind the heel and the other end stretched over the toe to hold the foot into the simple leather toe strap fastened to the ski with screws or through a mortise in the ski itself.

Up until the 1936 Olympics held in Germany, when Alpine events (downhill or slalom) were introduced for the first time (Lake Placid had only jumping and cross-country events), skiing was pretty much limited here to gliding along modest terrain or going straight down (easy ski down, climb back up) inclines like Bloody Nose Hill, located near the Racquette River on Stetson Road.

Gradually, however, downhill skiing, as opposed to cross-country skiing, became the dominant branch of the sport and the almost exclusive department of it for almost a generation after

*Rope tows had their own set of hazards. The rope would often twist ever so slowly and snag scarves, long hair and loose clothing that locked the skier to the rope that then fed into a returning pulley with the skier attached if the safety release failed.*

WWII. That change began here in the late 1930s, sparked by the energetic local group, the Pioneer Sno Club. The Rod and Gun Club, headed by Dr. Glen Delisser (beloved family doctor here for many years) also pushed the effort.

An uphill lift was constructed that consisted of a continuous rope around pulleys, powered by the rear wheel of a propped-up Ford truck. It was called, of course, a rope tow. It was located on what was known as Manning's Hill, or simply the Reservoir, at the rear of present-day Veterinary Clinic just beyond Moody Bridge.

The touring, or cross-country ski, for the part, languished in the attic until the fitness boom and other considerations (expense of Alpine skiing, love of nature, etc.) caused a revival in the late 1970s. It continues today with increasing popularity, many skiers enjoying both aspects of the sport. As a youngster, as that change was occurring, I would often join Louie (my mother, Anne, was his sister) on long ski trips on the many nearby wooded roads that offered gentle contours laid out for logging with horses—perfect for skiing.

It was on some of those excursions that I learned more about those Depression years and the struggle to keep the *Free Press* a viable concern. It meant, for example, a 12-hour day, six days a week and no vacation up until the 1940s, then only one week a year thereafter.

Cash money was scarce for everyone in the community, and hard work was the key to survival. Yet, as Louie would relate: "The work was enjoyable, even while demanding, because of the primitive second-hand equipment. Some years, the total revenue from advertising was $28 and, along with the weekly paycheck, a warning that 'we'll keep going as long as we can.' Mr. Quinn was easy to get along with (unless you were called to his office at school for discipline, as I often was) and gave me a free hand in editing the paper. The work was interesting and the shop crew all friends, and I never regretted casting our lot with the hometown paper."

Note: Louie had many offers from larger metropolitan papers but never considered them seriously. I think that in reading

*Mostly Spruce and Hemlock*, the highly regarded definitive history of this community written by Louie during a long winter when he was rendered immobile by a broken leg, you can get a hint of why he declined those offers. The book is truly a labor of love and, excellent resource aside, it reflects in its pages a love for his hometown. You can see that affection also in his talented skill as an artist who produced a vast number of oil paintings, based on Adirondack landscapes, and studies in other media such as watercolor and pen and pencil. These works represent in their artistry and subject matter a deep love and respect for the woods and waters where he grew up. And, as previously noted, he never regretted not leaving his hometown.

This Tip Top Town was a huge beneficiary of that decision.

*Tupper Lake Free Press Print:* January 09, 2002

# What You Lose On The Banan' You Make Up On The Peanut

GUESS WHAT? THIS YEAR, 2002, marks a time period of 100 years—a full century since our great little village was given its official status and incorporated. It is a wonderful and major milestone.

Remember, we are one of the youngest in the family of north-country villages. Malone became incorporated in 1863 and Saranac Lake became the first village to be incorporated in the Adirondacks in 1892.

So Happy Birthday, youngster! You are a little spoiled, a little headstrong and often too independent and temperamental. No matter! You can celebrate your birthday with well-earned pride. We love you!

With the editor's blessing, this column in the coming months will draw on the *Free Press* files and other sources to present some reminiscences from this village's history. A modest, anecdotal look at some interesting personalities, some events and other happenings that contributed to sustaining our development and continued settlement and our extraordinary heritage.

In today's column, we print in its entirety the *Old Timer's Column* from the January 1933 edition of this paper. The column was written by "Rufus" (the late Almon Taylor Clark, Jr.), one-time local postmaster and reporter. It was a popular feature of the *Free Press* during the 1930s. His column follows:

"Do you remember, one year ago, 1932, when they played golf on the Big Wolf links on January 14-15-16?" Note: The nine-hole Big Wolf Golf Course was located between the Pitchfork Pond Road and the north shore of Little Wolf Pond, largely the Haymeadow Development today. The Tupper course was not completed until August of 1933.

"At that time there was no frost in the ground and the grass was bright and fresh on the greens. The players were in their shirtsleeves and said they were too warm for comfort, after they had gone over the nine-hole course once or twice.

"Ice harvesters in this section were frightened over the outlook for a crop, and it was not until late in February and early March, 1932, that ice formed of sufficient thickness to warrant activities by the 'Ice Man,' and the old jokes about that personage became so pointed that they began to hurt.

"But the crop developed just the same—late, of course—and

*The circa 1930s models shown here are a collector's dream. Only the stone wall remains of what was the A.A. Low Hitchins Pond garage where this photo was taken. Photo courtesy of Ricky Vaillancourt.*

the ice was of the finest quality in many years."

Note: Harvesting and selling ice was a huge business here before the introduction of electric and gas refrigerators to preserve perishables. Two operations that come to mind among others were the Trudeau Bros. on Vachereau Street and the Forkey Bros. concern on downtown's Cedar Street. Normally the ice was cut when it was 12 to 14 inches thick, and each block would weigh about 300 pounds. It would take two men with ice tongs to lift and load these blocks onto the sleigh or, later, the truck bed. The blocks were stored in icehouses—large double-walled frame buildings—and insulated with sawdust. Softwood sawdust was preferred over hardwood because it has air cells, which is why it floats and hardwood does not.

One icehouse I distinctly remember was the former Altamont Milk Co. Icehouse, located to the rear of what is today Dick Rule's Marina storage on High Street. It could hold up to 400 or more such blocks. The ice would keep all summer and was a great play spot for the kids of my day.

Another icehouse, but of smaller capacity, was located to the rear of what was the Robert Brown, Sr. home next to the fire station. Both of these icehouses utilized the Tallman Hill rock ledges that parallel High Street as their back wall. Whether this was by design or necessity or both, I don't know. Most of the large lake "camps" had their own icehouses, usually holding 30 cakes or so and partitioned so that the front section could act as a cooler—meats on one side, vegetables on the other. Filling these icehouses each winter is one more chore present-day caretakers don't miss.

Residential homes had their own miniature icehouses in the form of a cabinet or box. You can still hear older people refer to the modern refrigerator as the "ice box." A "flip top" insulated lid opened to a tin-lined compartment with a drain that held a block of ice. A lock-lid insulated door below the ice container opened to a compartment where perishables were stored and kept cool from the ice above. A card placed in the homes' windows reading "ICE" would indicate to the iceman on his daily rounds that ice was needed. Using an ice pick, the vendor would chip a suitable piece of ice, depending on the size of the ice box, weigh it (you paid by the pound) on a set of spring scales hung from the rear of his truck or wagon and, using ice tongs, would carry the ice and place it in the ice box. We continue *Old Timer's Column:*

"And then came the reaction and the famous old slogan was fully verified, 'What you lose on the banan' you make up on the peanut.'

"To accentuate that fact, it is recorded that during the first week in June 1932, after the Big Wolf links were in full swing, that players on a certain day were compelled to don their sweaters and Mackinaws and then shivered in a snowstorm that lasted for over a half hour.

"The winter of 1933, insofar as January is concerned, is similar to that of a year ago.

"With the month nearly gone we have no snow to speak of and what few lumbermen are struggling to 'get in' moderate sized jobs are sweating 'drops of blood' for fear they will not be able to complete their jobs.

"In December of this present winter (1933), unusually low mercury records were made. There were several days when the marks of 25 to 30 degrees below zero were registered in the Tupper Lake sector, while at Sabatis, Upper Saranac Lake, Piercefield and surrounding points, 31 to 41 degrees below zero were recorded.

"The intense cold broke late in December, however, and the Adirondacks saw a 'Green Christmas' with plenty of rain and bad weather and much illness due to flu and pneumonia.

"Luckily the flu did not attain alarming propensities and few deaths occurred, unlike the flu scourge of 1918, when more than 60 deaths were recorded in the town and all in a few weeks.

"On January 14, 1932, the mercury stood at 56 degrees above zero and the air was real balmy and summer-like.

"On January 14 of this year (1933) 47 degrees above zero was recorded, the ground was bare and the only great difference from that of last year was the fact that the extreme cold in December had frozen over all the lakes and ponds in this section of the mountains and the ice is apparently here to stay—a joyous outlook for ice harvesters as the crop is clear as crystal, free from snow and of best quality.

"John D'Avignon, hardwood lumberman for the O.W.D Corp., and William Smith, who has a 2,000 cord pulp contract, both on the Meacham Lake area, are suffering from the lack of snow. The O.W.D. plant has been obliged to curb operations to some extent although a fairly good supply of hardwood logs is being brought to the mills by powerful motor trucks over the Malone-Tupper Lake highway from Meacham Lake.

"'There is no great loss without some gain,' is an old and trite saying and the mild weather is materially aiding the large force of laborers now employed in clearing old stumps, sunken logs and other debris from Racket Pond. This work was made possible through the activities of Supervisor John H. Black and Franklin County Relief Committeeman Frank R. Seigel.

"It has proved a boon to scores of unemployed and will eventually create one of the largest inland bodies of water for navigation for large motor craft, when Big Tupper Lake, Big Simond Pond and Racket Pond are united in one continuous body of water with over 50 miles of shore line."

*Tupper Lake Free Press Print:* January 30, 2002

# ALL ARE WELCOME AT THE LAKE

WHEN THE AUTHOR S.H. HAMMOND boated across Tupper Lake in 1850, he noted his impressions in a book entitled *Rambles of a Journalist*, published in 1855. He waxed downright poetic in describing the beauty of Big Tupper Lake, walled in by primeval forest, with quiet bays stealing back behind craggy promontories and islands, some of which he likened to domed cathedrals and some to rocky and ruined battlements soaring straight up 60 feet from the dark waters of the lake.

That view has changed little. Norway Island and Bluff Island (with its Devil's Pulpit and sheer walls of granite), Grindstone and Bridge Brook bays remain, for example, absolute and protected gems in the necklaces of islands and many bays that make Tupper Lake so special and so increasingly rare in the present-day hunger for a "place on the lake" that is invading the Adirondacks.

There were only two settlers on the lake when Hammond wrote of that 1850 visit, "The one is at the outlet and the other at the head of the lake." The first, he wrote was "a fisherman and a hunter, who has some two or three acres cleared raising simply vegetables for his family. Taking the world easy, seldom sweating from hard labor or tired from real work."

"The other settler is a lumberman, energetic and industrious, who has small taste for hunting or fishing. He has some forty acres cleared, a good log house for his family. This family is eight miles from the nearest neighbor, fifty miles from a doctor, the same distance from a school house or church."

Note: This was probably S.S. Jenkins, for whom the bay beyond Rock Island Bay on the Tupper—Long Lake highway was named. He later moved up the lake near the former American Legion Mountain Camp. His place became a favorite boarding and sleeping quarters for the many lumbermen and river drivers during early logging operations on the Big Bog, Little Tupper, etc. areas.

Hammond would have been startled beyond belief had he been on the lake this past weekend during the Rod and Gun Club Fishing Derby. With good ice conditions measuring from 18 to 24 inches and a cloudless, sun-filled day, the lake was a beehive of activity. One seasonal camp owner here for the weekend was fascinated by the scene, remarking: "It looked like I-90 out there. More people zipped up the lake on Saturday afternoon than I will observe in an entire summer."

One camp on the lake that traditionally plays host during the ice derby had, in an admittedly hasty count, at least 40 snow machines, pickup trucks and 4-wheelers parked on the ice in front of the camp on Saturday afternoon. There was an "all are welcome" ambience, the quintessential Adirondack spirit of "the latch is open," which is, unfortunately, in the time of needed security, fast becoming an anachronism.

As one of the fishermen enjoying the day said to me, "Is this a great place to live, or what? This is a winter wonderland—we are so lucky to live here!"

That handsome log camp recently constructed by the owners is located on the west shore between Grindstone and Bridge Brook bays. It is very near what was formerly one of the earliest camps built on the lake in the 1890s before it was destroyed by fire in 1936.

Perhaps that story will be of interest to readers. What follows is excerpted from the *Old Timer's Column* in December 3, 1936, issue of the *Tupper Lake Free Press*, written by the late Almon Clarke. Note that the property described is still owned by Warren Slater III, a grandson. Warren grew up here on Racquette River Drive (John Quinn home) and presently has a summer home (formerly W.D. Wilson/DeSilva property) at Moody.

*A unique view looking southeast from outcropping Station Mountain near Piercefield.*

The column follows:

"Do you remember forty years ago when a fine group of camps was erected for Mr. and Mrs. John Sprague on the west shore of Big Tupper Lake, between Grindstone and Bridge Brook bays?

"The fire that occurred last Thursday (Thanksgiving Day) and destroyed three of the large main buildings and a 16 x 20 tent cabin structure on the 90-acre tract preserve, formerly occupied for many years by Mr. and Mrs. John Sprague of New York City, has recalled to old timers some of the details in connection with the camps that date back for forty or more years. The site is located on the west shore of Big Tupper Lake midway between Grindstone and Bridge Brook bays.

"It was originally part of the 1,100-acre park purchased from the International Paper Company by the late Colonel William Barbour who established and made famous the Paradise Point estate.

"The Colonel John Sprague camps—nine in all—were erected on the 90-acre tract of virgin forest, in early history days known as the Moores Camp Grounds. The main building was a 30 x 60 structure with a 16-foot ceiling and was connected with the other main buildings by ample covered walks. There was also a boat house, a guide house for men's quarters, a building for the maids, an ice house and cooler and all the camps were luxuriously furnished and contained all modern conveniences.

"Electricity had never been installed, but there were eighty lamps in the several camps. The cuisine was equipped with every modern device for preparing meals for the many summer guests and the lakefront is protected by a 120-foot solid concrete seawall. On the property there was also a private camp for Colonel Barbour's mother, known as the 'Leaning Maple,' so-called for a large maple tree that tilted at an apparently dangerous angle yet provided shade for the camp."

Note: Mrs. Barbour, whose mother once had a camp in the 1880s on what is now Litchfield's Lake Madeleine, was a strong, independent lady. She had her own guides headed by Charles Simons and was an excellent woodswoman who loved to hunt and fish.

"After the demise of Colonel Barbour and Colonel Sprague, the property lagged in interest to the survivors—including Mrs. William Barbour and her four sons, Thomas, Robert, Warren and Frederick Barbour, all of whom were ardent summer and fall visitors yearly to the beauty spot, well named Paradise Point Park by Colonel Barbour.

"During the settlement of the estates, the late Warren J. Slater and his son, Francis H. Slater, acquired title of the Sprague 90-acre tract, now the property of F.H. Slater.

"The transfer was made of the Sprague property in 1920, one year before the death of Warren J. Slater, who was a pioneer guide and boat builder in Saranac Lake and Tupper Lake and the first secretary of the Adirondack Guides Association, nearly half a century ago."

Note: Slater founded one of the early partnerships to build guideboats—Slater and Ack Moody Inc. Other builders at that time were Alex Murchison of Moody, Lute Owen and, later (1936), Leonard Anderson and Daniel Hinkson. These early local builders have not gained the recognition they deserve. This is due partly to the praise of writers who have created their own culture heroes. New studies and a renaissance in guideboat building may correct this shortcoming.

"Last summer (1935) while a party of local people were in the camp during a terrific electrical storm Miss Priscilla Martin of this village was struck by lightning as she was unlocking the front door to the camp.

"The door was torn loose, and much damage was caused by the bolt, but no fire resulted.

"Miss Martin was picked up with life apparently extinct. A New Jersey life guard, a member of the party, used artificial respiration methods and in 30 minutes Miss Martin regained consciousness.

"She was hospitalized for several days but has since recovered her usual health.

"Last week on Thanksgiving Day occurred the burning of the three main buildings with all furnishings, at a loss of $18,000, partly insured.

"Mr. Slater was in camp to see that everything was secure for the winter. Unable to cross the lake by boat due to ice, he had driven his car to the Legion camp and started through the woods around the head of Bridge Brook Pond, a difficult trail even in good weather. The snow was deep, and it took him two and a half hours to reach his camps where he arrived in a semi-exhausted condition with limbs torn and bleeding and chilled through and through.

"He built fires in two stoves and the main fireplace and planned to stay overnight. He had no food except two doughnuts, as he expected to return home as soon as camp inspection was over.

"His suffering was intense, and then came the fire which he believes was caused by flying sparks. His description of the frantic efforts to stop the flames makes a harrowing tale.

"He chopped a hole in the ice in the lake to obtain water, but all his efforts were futile, and he had to stand by and hysterically watch his valuable property go up in smoke.

"When Mr. Slater finally got back to Tupper Lake he was under the care of Dr. T.J. Collinson for several days."

*Tupper Lake Free Press Print*: February 20, 2002

# Town Feud Ends in Baxter Lake Murder

IN THE LATE 1940s, while I was a student in Canton, NY, a favorite break from studies was a visit to a palatial camp located at a place called Dexter Lake. It was about a 40-minute drive from the campus to the lake, which was near the village of St. Regis Falls. More than half a century has passed since those blissful undergraduate days, but those weekend "getaways" and the lasting friendships that developed remain as prevailing memories in an exciting time of life.

The camp was owned by the family of classmates, and Martha Thompson and her father generously allowed us use of the Dexter Lake enclave.

As I remember it, we were only dimly aware that the camp and property of 7,000 acres were once owned by a wealthy eccentric named Dexter, and that he had been mysteriously murdered.

In later years, Marty's father (Rex) gifted the property to the University (S.L.U.). Under this ownership it became a conference center and retreat for a number of years before it was eventually purchased by Shania Twain, well-known singer and recording artist.

Ms. Twain has abandoned extensive building plans that included a recording studio and other major projects. This was unfortunate and was greeted with dismay by residents of nearby Santa Clara and St. Regis villages. Not only was Ms. Twain welcomed as an important and talented personage to have as a neighbor, but she and her husband, Robert Lang, were also found to be warm,

*Orlando Dexter was driving his carriage, similar to the one pictured above, when he was ambushed and murdered by a single rifle shot to his back. (Stoddard photo)*

friendly folks who were well liked in both of those communities and the surrounding area. Needless to say, their significant contribution to the local economy was an important loss.

It turns out that the murder of the original owner was, in fact, a sensational event. I have even discovered, as we shall see, a Tupper Lake connection! The first part of this two-part column is from the chapter entitled *Santa Clara and Brandon in the Limelight* and is found in Alfred Donaldson's *History of the Adirondacks*.

"Santa Clara, as has been told, was a shantied creation of Hurd and his railroad. Besides his residence, he established his machine shops there and built two mills. For a while, therefore, it was a lively, bustling little place, but after Hurd's failure it relapsed toward the nothingness from which it sprang, the mills fell into disuse and were dismantled, and in 1915, fire destroyed the machine shops and other buildings that were never replaced.

"In 1903, the name of the little hamlet was suddenly thrust into headline notoriety through a sensational murder that occurred near it. Not far away, and in the town of the same name, lay a private park of 7,000 acres belonging to Orlando P. Dexter. Near the center of the estate was a body of water called Dexter Lake, and on its shores was a rather ornate and fantastical residence modeled after the Albrecht Durer house in Nuremberg. Here the eccentric owner spent much of his time.

"Orlando Dexter was a bachelor and 40 years of age at the time of his death. He was a graduate of Yale and a lawyer by profession. Having large means, however, he retired from active practice and devoted himself to the intellectual pursuits of history, genealogy and the higher mathematics. Absorbed in these studies, for which he had marked aptitude, he became more and more of a recluse in his habits and showed an increasing moroseness of disposition and irascibility of temper. His relations with his Adirondack neighbors developed a harvest of unusually bitter animosity. He bought his large estate by a process of gradual acquisition. When he had secured all the land he wanted, he fenced it in, 'posted' it, placed guards upon it and bid all men keep off it. These perfectly legal acts appear to have been the signal for a persistent campaign of lawlessness among his neighbors. They hunted and fished and even cut wood on his preserve with a reckless defiance of consequences that could have been prompted only by malice and hatred. He sought such relief and redress only as the law afforded, but then applied it, it is said, to the last limit of the letter and in a spirit of relentless retaliation. Under such conditions, however justified, it was bound to rouse resentment to the danger point. Personal violence was finally threatened in a series of anonymous letters, but Mr. Dexter was a fearless man and paid no attention to them.

"On the afternoon of September 19, 1903, he started to drive, as he often did, to the nearby post office at Santa Clara for his mail. He drove alone, but was followed by one of his employees. He had gone but a quarter of a mile on the lonely, winding road that led to the little village when someone fired a shot from ambush as he passed. He fell from his wagon and was found a few moments later lying dead in the road.

"His aged father, Henry Dexter, the millionaire founder of the American News Company, was at once notified of the murder.

After the first shock, he said he would devote his life and all of his wealth, if necessary, to ferreting out his son's assassin. But all his efforts and all his wealth failed to unearth the culprit. Besides hiring detectives, he had trained bloodhounds carried to the spot and offered rewards that would have made a poor man rich for life. But they unloosed no tongue, although it was said that even children knew the murderer's name. Be that as it may, it has remained sealed forever in a strangely impregnable conspiracy of silence."

Next week: The Tupper Lake Connection.

*Tupper Lake Free Press Print:* April 17, 2002

## PINKERTON DETECTIVE CLUELESS

WE CONTINUE THIS WEEK with part two of the Orlando Dexter murder. Today's column is a "behind the scenes" excerpt from the *Old Timer's Column* as it appeared in the April 20, 1933, edition of the *Tupper Lake Free Press*. I've labeled it *The Tupper Lake Connection*.

"In those early days, there were many old time guides, hunters and residents in the St. Regis Falls and Santa Clara sector, who had always been accustomed to freely roam over the vast woodlands, lakes and streams in that portion of the forest and they resented their exclusion from the old familiar haunts.

"Poaching was often attempted, and many arrests for trespass were made and fines imposed because the owner was determined to preserve the integrity of his rights and titles as landlord.

"Ill feelings were engendered, which developed into hatred in many instances where the older settlers could not accept the curtailing of their divine rights of freedom to the forests and streams.

"In the late 90s Warren Joseph Alfred, owner of the famous Waverly Hotel in St. Regis Falls when that village was at its apex of its financial and business importance, engaged in a large lumbering project near the Dexter Park property.

"At that time St. Regis Falls had a large tannery, a saw mill, a stave mill, an electric lighting plant, several hotels and the place was listed among the 'boom towns' of the Adirondacks.

"W. J. Alfred was always known to his intimate friends as 'Joe.'

*Shown here is the Hotel Altamont during the time a New York City Pinkerton detective registered there "under cover" in an attempt to solve the Dexter murder. The hotel had survived the 1899 fire that destroyed between 72 and 100 buildings in this community.*

When he undertook the lumbering project, he had no trouble in hiring a large force of lumberjacks and he 'put up a big job.'

"And then the trouble started to brew. Joe had negotiated a large loan from the Farmers National Bank at Malone, to carry on his extensive lumbering operations.

"When it came to hauling, it was found that in order to make the job a financial success, the logs had to be hauled over the shortest possible route, part of which had to cross a portion of the Dexter estate.

"Mr. Dexter was obdurate and refused permission to cross his land. Joe was desperate because his bank notes would soon be due and he didn't intend to repudiate an obligation as he had never done.

"He resumed the aggressive and hauled logs day and night over the forbidden route. Dexter built fences across the roads and detailed guards to watch, but Joe and his men tore down the obstructions as fast as they were erected, and the entire logging job was completed under semi-warfare conditions, but at a financial gain for the operator who met all obligations on time.

"Joe was arrested on damage and trespass charges and, after long litigation, was heavily fined, which he refused to pay. He was turned over to the sheriff at Malone for an extended period, but Joe didn't care so long as he was able to pay the bank notes.

"A man named Chambers who operated a mill on the St. Regis Falls River, also had similar trouble with Mr. Dexter regarding logging operations and his difficulties attracted much attention for a long period among lumbermen and saw mill owners along the river.

"Those troubles and the feeling of unrest among the old guides and hunters led people in those days to ask, 'how will it end?'

"In 1901, Joe Alfred came to Tupper Lake and bought the Hotel Altamont from Thomas L. Weir, still retaining ownership of the Waverly Hotel at St. Regis Falls, which was not sold till several years later.

"In 1903 came the tragic murder of Orlando P. Dexter on a beautiful summer day when he was driving over the five mile course to his camps.

"He was riding alone in a carriage at the time. The horse ran into camp, where members of the family and workers found the dead man in the bottom of the vehicle.

"Mr. Dexter had been shot through the back, evidently by a high powered rifle and the coroner and police officials declared that death must have been instantaneous.

"The course of the bullet through the body indicated that the shot must have come from an elevated position. The spot was located later by officers at a point in the road where the horse had apparently become frightened and started into a mad gallop.

"For months every possible clue was followed by a large number of officers and detectives. Scores of suspects were held and examined as 'material witnesses,' but no definite information was obtained.

"On the day that the murder was perpetrated, an excursion train ran over the New York and Ottawa line from Tupper Lake to the Ottawa fair and horse show. Crowds from Tupper Lake went on the trip. Among them were Mr. and Mrs. W.J. Alfred. Joe had planned to leave the train at St. Regis Falls to look after business interests, but Mrs. Alfred finally persuaded her husband to complete the trip with her.

"That afternoon Mr. Dexter was murdered while the excursionists were in Ottawa.

"Knowing the previous ill-feeling that had existed between Mr. Dexter and Mr. Alfred, scores of the latter's friends were firm in their belief that had he left the train that day and been unable to produce a perfect alibi as to his whereabouts that afternoon, he might have been charged with the deed.

"As it was, he was under suspicion with scores of others during the long investigation which followed.

"The murdered man's father offered a $30,000 reward which was later increased to $50,000, but no tangible results were ever obtained.

"A few months after the tragedy, a man from New York City arrived at Hotel Altamont and engaged board for an extended period, as he wished to stay in the mountains 'for his health.'

"He made frequent trips down the NY and O line and interviewed many people with reference to 'habits and doings' of old settlers and others who were well acquainted with the North Country.

"He kept this up for a month and a half, spent money lavishly, averaged $20 a day at the bar and plied everyone about him with questions in a subtle manner.

"He finally paid his bill and told Mr. Alfred that he was a Pinkerton detective from New York, one of several who had been hired by the elder Mr. Dexter in an effort to trace the murderer, or the leading spirit in the slaying of his son.

"The detective stated that his exhaustive search and questioning had produced no definite results and that he was personally satisfied that Mr. Alfred had nothing to do with the murder, either directly or indirectly.

"The elder Mr. Dexter left a clause in his will when he died, providing for a $50,000 reward for the conviction of his son's slayer.

"Mr. Alfred died early in December 1907, and many of the St. Regis Falls, Santa Clara and Nicholville suspects have also long since passed on."

*Tupper Lake Free Press Print:* April 24, 2002

# A New Village

IN 1890, PIONEER SETTLERS HERE, convinced that the new railroad and the untapped timber lands held enough potential to support a thriving community, petitioned for—and got—their own local government. Map lines were redrawn and reformed from the Waverly Township and the result was the Town of Altamont.

In 1899, a dramatic fire occurred which, according to newspaper accounts, left 169 buildings destroyed and the business section in total ruin.

Following initial indecisions of whether to rebuild or abandon the uptown site and move to Faust, the town fathers rolled up their sleeves and started rebuilding even before the ashes had cooled.

By 1902, what had been a rough frontier town emerged as a larger, more substantial, and far more attractive place. Thus, in twelve years' time since its birth as a lumbering hamlet of less than 300 inhabitants, in what was then almost all dense forest, Tupper Lake had grown to have a population of more than 2,000 people.

Personal note: Part of that population growth included my maternal grandparents and their seven children. My grandfather, William Simmons, an engineer on the New York Central Railroad and who was based in Syracuse, found his work taking him on runs over the Adirondack Division, which had only been in operation a few years.

*Tupper Lake Station (not Tupper Lake Junction) of Hurd's New York and Ottawa Station was located at the end of Cliff Avenue and was retired in 1933. Stage coach and steamboat connections to various hotels could be made here between 1896 and 1909. (photo courtesy of Dick Wettereau collection)*

He apparently liked what he saw here—a new village being born with excited and industrious people and a small town in which to raise a family, surrounded by mountains not unlike those of his ancestral home in Dusseldorf, Germany.

My grandmother, Mary Jane Flanagan, was born in Westport, County Mayo, Ireland, and she came to America at age 14 with her mother, brother and sisters after her father had preceded the family and got a toe-hold in this country. This week, as you read this column, I should be tent-camping on the site of the former Flanagan homestead.

Matt O'Malley, an aged but ebullient gentleman who is a direct descendent of the former Flanagan neighbors, now owns the property and has promised a rousing Irish welcome for his American "cousins."

Let's return to the subject at hand. With the rapid growth came a great debate: "Should Tupper Lake become incorporated as a village under the laws governing the state of New York?" Many people were against it, saying that it would "increase taxes," that it "was unnecessary," that "no benefits could be gained," and besides, "the place was going to go down as soon as lumbering was finished in the immediate vicinity and the town could never succeed as a summer resort or tourist center."

Fortunately, there were others who held a stronger vision of the settlement's future. Their enthusiasm and their confident and forceful convictions won the debate, and the petition to the state went forward. Thus in 1902 Tupper Lake became an incorporated village, organized under the laws of the State of New York. The coming of the railroad had brought with it a new era, a revolution in transportation, and the tiny sawmill settlement located at the "junction" of two railroad lines would grow and thrive, justifying the confidence of those "strong men" who pushed for incorporation. Those early settlers must have been tough, and we can only imagine how difficult clearing and hewing out homes for themselves with nothing more than a broadax must have been.

If the majority of them were unlettered and unlearned, yet certainly they were also resourceful. "One thing is peculiar on this wilderness," writes an early missionary to Northern New York. "Every countenance indicates pleasure and satisfaction. The equality of circumstances cuts off a great proportion of the evils which render men unhappy in improved societies, and the influence of hope is very apparent."

Once the village was incorporated, residents then elected themselves a mayor or village president, as mayors were then known. The first mayor to head the village board was Charles Sisson, whose family members were prominent in the paper-manufacturing industry and were owners of the Racquette River Paper Co., one of the best-known paper mills in Northern New York.

Mr. Sisson came to Tupper as general manager of the A. Sherman Lumber Co. Mill. Older readers will remember "Sissonville," the cluster of homes located midway between uptown and downtown Tupper Lake along Demars Boulevard, which was named after the Sisson family.

One of Mayor Sisson's first responsibilities was laying out and mapping the dividing lines that would become the corporate limits. He was aided in this by Dr. Eugene Austin, who was at the time the town supervisor. Those original lines remained until 1928 when the village corporate limits were extended as found today.

One-hundred years ago, the streets in this community, as in other villages, were of dirt and for the most part just paths. Improving those paths with crushed stone, which was often sunk deep in the mud and rain washout and lacked lights, became the next item for Mayor Sisson and his board of trustees.

Sears Hill, for example, was almost solid woodland, and a good-sized brook came down the hill and crossed the road near the present site of Day Wholesale and then ran into a gully that paralleled today's Hill Street. The hill was much steeper than it is today and the top needed to be cut down and the bottom filled in to ease the grade. Before that it often required four horses to haul a heavy load over the top. In the winter, if the brook overflowed the steep grade, it became a solid mass of ice.

As this work progressed, Tupper Village built its own generating plant (1903) for an electric system, one of the first Adirondack communities to do so. It was steam-powered and fueled by waste wood from the Brooklyn Cooperage stave mill plant located east of LeBoeuf Street. Profits from this village-owned electric system helped pay for the street and road work and there was no bond indebtedness needed.

Tupper Lake Station (not Tupper Lake Junction) of Hurd's New York and Ottawa Station was located at the end of Cliff Avenue and was retired in 1933. Stage coach and steamboat connections to various hotels could be made here between 1896 and 1909.

*Tupper Lake Free Press Print:* May 22, 2002

# OF RAQUETTE POND

IN TODAY'S COLUMN WE continue our look at some aspects of the village's past history as it celebrates 100 years of incorporation under state charter.

Following what seems to be an Adirondack custom, Tupper Lake Village is a mile away from the lake whose name it bears, and not only that but there is another lake called Racquette Pond. (Saranac Lake is on Lake Flower and Lake Placid is on Mirror Lake as other examples of this strange place-name custom.)

In his definitive *History of the Adirondacks*, Alfred Donaldson notes that "Racquette Pond is an artificial body of water." Indeed, another historian, Seaver, in his *History of Franklin County*, also erroneously describes it as "simply an expansion of the Racquette River, caused by the reservoir dam."

The truth is, a beautiful little lake existed there before Setting Pole or any other dam was built and was mentioned by many early writers as early as 1849.

I have in my files a yellowed monograph on Racquette Pond written by Louis Simmons, editor and historian. What follows is from that paper:

"Racquette Pond is the northernmost of the three lakes fringing the Tupper area, all of which lie at an altitude of about 1,542 feet above sea level, held at that level by the Setting Pole Rapids dam on the Raquette River, a mile or so below the railroad bridge which spans the outlet.

"Raquette Pond has borne at least three other names over the years, including Whitney Pond, after an early surveyor, Cyrus P. Whitney, who helped survey the area; the Lothrop Stretch, after a member of the Lothrop family of Saranac Lake who lived for awhile on its shores; and Lough Neagh, after a beautiful lake in Ireland, a name given it in nostalgic memory of the Ould Sod by one of the early Irish landowners of the nearly four million acre Macomb Purchase. 'Lough Neagh' was promptly corrupted into 'Long Neck' by area Adirondackers, who finally settled for Raquette Pond instead.

"The earliest logging operations in the Tupper area centered around the east shore of Raquette Pond, where the clearing that was left after the virgin pine was cut off in the 1850s by the Pomeroy Lumber Co. became the site some 40 years later for Tupper Lake village.

"Probably no other body of water in the Adirondacks was the setting for more intensive or extensive lumbering operations.

*Before the roads came, the guide's boat was the chief means of transportation. The many waterways surrounding this village were a necessary and popular conduit for travel by visiting sportsmen and locals alike. (photo by Seneca Ray Stoddard from* Early Days in the Adirondacks *by Jeanne Winston Adler)*

Starting around Civil War times and continuing down through the 1920s, spring river drives brought logs cut throughout the Raquette River watershed, Cold River, Bog River and numerous smaller tributary streams down to the sawmills clustered around Raquette Pond shores. A good idea of the size of the annual timber cut is offered in the annual report of the New York State Forest, Fish and Game Commission for 1900, which shows that the A. Sherman Lumber Co. sawed more than 17 million board feet of softwood lumber that year, while the Norwood Manufacturing Co., then operating the 'Big Mill' on Raquette Pond, had a total cut of nearly 22,000,000 feet.

"Lesser cuts were handled at other mills then operating around Raquette Pond, including the pulp mill operated by Champlain Realty near the outlet, where a little separate village, Underwood, complete with district school, flourished from 1899 until the mill shut down in 1910. The foundations of the homes and roofless brick walls of the plant, largely concealed by second growths, are all that remain to mark the site. Gone also is almost all trace of a pulp mill operated by the Santa Clara Lumber Co. near where Little Wolf Creek empties into the pond.

"Raquette Pond was a headache for boaters in the heyday of logging, the network of log booms, anchored by rock cribs and piles driven deep into the bottom, making navigation a hazardous business. At the point where the Raquette River swinging north after crossing the foot of both Lake Simond and Big Tupper begins it roundabout course through Raquette Pond, the 'Sorting Gap' was a key link in the logging operations of the past.

"Here logs in the thousands converged after the long river drive. Over the years, many major lumbering firms harvested timber along the Raquette River watershed, and to distinguish their own cut, stamped the end of each log with a marking hammer, which imprinted the owner's mark in the wood. Log marks, registered with the state, included many familiar to Tupper old timers, among them the marks of G.W. Sisson, Augustus Sherman, Burnham, Leveless Co., Norwood Mfg. Co., Export Lumber Co. and others. Keen-eyed lumberjacks manned the floating catwalks of the Sorting Gap around the clock during the closing days of the spring drive, spotting company marks and shunting the logs into the owner's holding booms, from which they were herded, in an Adirondack version of the western roundup, to the firm's mill on the pond shore, or on down the 70 or so miles of river to the mills at Potsdam. International Paper Company's 'Sorting Gap' lean-to, open to public use, stands on the shore nearby today as a memorial to a colorful operation of an earlier era. A couple of generations of Tupper Lake boys rated 'running logs' on the pond one of the major sports of their growing-up years, and although many of them paid for their fun with a chilly bath when a log bobbed out from under them, there's no record of one of these small fry log runners ever losing his life as a result.

"Two stories about the Raquette Pond area . . . deserve telling here: One deals with massive rocks rising out of the river just below the present Underwood railroad bridge at the foot of the pond. They were known to the earliest white visitors to the region as 'Captain Peter's Rock,' and were so marked by the early mapmakers. Captain Peter Sabattis, whose military title was in recognition of his services as guide during the Revolutionary War, including Benedict Arnold's 1776 wilderness journey up the Kennereck River to assault Quebec, made the Tupper-Long Lake area his base for trapping and hunting expeditions, and he used to cache his traps and gear in recesses and crevices which now bear his name.

"The other tale, recounted by Alfred Donaldson in his History of the Adirondacks, tells how Raquette Pond got its earlier name of Lough Neagh. The story goes that an Irish nobleman, who lived on the shores of Lough Neagh in the old country, had occasion to fight a duel and wounded his antagonist, as he supposed, mortally. He fled the country and sailed for Montreal. From there, for greater safety, he penetrated into the Adirondack wilderness and settled on the stretch of water which he named Lough Neagh, in memory of the beautiful lake in his native county of Antrim, Ireland. After living there in seclusion for several years, he was discovered by friends an informed that the duel had not resulted in fatality after all. On learning this, he returned home. The name lingered after him, and the site of the Irish nobleman's wilderness home, where the little village of Underwood flourished briefly more than a century later, was dubbed 'Irish Clearing' or 'Paddy's Choppin' by old settlers here."

Indian Park

"Indians made the Tupper campground on the river between the foot of Big Tupper and Raquette Pond, as 'Indian Park.' Meritt's 1858 map of this area shows the Indian encampment, where arrowheads and bits of pottery were picked up by early settlers and sportsmen visiting the area. The Indians had something in common with present-day tourists departing for sunnier climes with the first fall frost, and there was never a year-round Indian settlement in the Tupper sector.

"The first hotel at the north end of Big Tupper Lake, the Mt. Morris House, was built in 1865 by 'Uncle Mart' Moody, whose fame as guide and teller of tall tales helped lure early sportsmen here. Mr. Moody sold it in 1888 to Pliny Robbins, who enlarged the place and renamed it the Prince Albert, under which name it operated until 1956. It was torn down in 1968 after standing empty a dozen years.

"Martin Moody moved up the lake a mile or so and built 'Camp Redside' beside the brook of that name, which provided shelter and food to some notable visitors, among them President Grover Cleveland, President Chester A. Arthur and Governor Horatio Seymour. Renamed Waukesha after its 1893 sale to Jabez Alexander, it flourished under that name until 1960."

*Tupper Lake Free Press Print:* July 31, 2002

# Tupper's Lake and The Lake Simond Trio

WE CONTINUE TODAY a few aspects of this community's history as it celebrates 100 years as an incorporated village.

Following the Revolutionary War, the lands we now call the Adirondacks, which had formerly belonged to the British Crown, were appropriated by the State of New York. They accomplished this by a bill in the legislature in 1779, which declared that the lands belonging to the crown before 1776 were "forever after to be vested in the people of this state."

As historian Frank Graham has noted, "forever" turned out to be a very brief time, indeed, for five years later, the legislature, in desperate need of money, passed another measure calling for "the settlement of the waste and unappropriated lands within the state," and providing for their "speedy sale." While lands in other parts of the state went quickly, those in the Adirondacks were generally ignored, despite the promise that all taxes on them would be waived for seven years.

Finally, a group headed by a speculator named Alexander Macomb purchased one enormous bundle of four million acres (at eight pence an acre). That purchase included this area, and thus it was that a surveyor named Tupper, while working on the original survey in 1796 of the Macomb Purchase, discovered the lake and named it after himself. The lake subsequently bore several names, including a number of Indian names. One of those was Paskungameh, meaning "going out from the river." The

*Hard to believe, but shown above is the "short cut" to Simond Pond from the Racquette River. Known today as the "cut off," it is twice this size and the water level much higher due to the dam at Setting Pole Rapids. It was dug out by hand by a man named Will Read in 1882. (Stoddard photo, 1888)*

name Tupper's Lake has prevailed, of course, with the "s" later being dropped to simply Tupper Lake.

The lake is slightly over seven miles in length and, with a surface of 3,200 acres, is second only to Cranberry Lake in this section of the park.

According to Frank Morrison, the energetic and knowledgeable former president of the Tupper Lake Rod and Gun Club, the lake has a unique range of depths that support a two-tiered fishery.

Deep spots, Frank notes, that approach 100 feet, support lake trout, salmon and whitefish. It also has shallows that are warm enough to support walleye, northern pike and small-mouth bass. It has many indented bays and rocky cliffs harboring peregrine and raven nests and its many beautiful wooded islands clothed with towering pines hundreds of years old. One of those pines was chosen by a pair of bald eagles (for the first time in many years) and resulted in the successful fledgling of two eaglets early this August.

Nor can we discount the glorious sunsets and the breathtaking change of lights and colors, all of which make the lake such a special place.

Five years ago on a July 4th day, my son, sitting on the summit of Mt. Morris with the full expanse of the lake below, counted not a single boat passing his field of view in an hour's time. With the new boat launch and the popularity of "party boats," which has allowed to many people to enjoy the lake (many for the first time), and the new camp properties, this isolation is changing—but in a nice "slow growth" way that is, so far, easily absorbed by the size of the lake. Indeed, on many afternoons I'll not observe another boat, a rare thing not found on neighboring lakes that have sadly become overwhelmed.

## Lake Simon Trio

No account of the Tupper area waters would be complete without a note about Lake Simon, one of the trio of lakes linked by the Raquette River, in close proximity and sharing a common water level. Old timers remember it better as Big Simon Pond. It was named for Elijah "Life" Simon, reputed to have been the first white man to establish a year-round home on its shores. Along about 1840, he cleared a patch of land at the foot of the lake near the present Moody Bridge and built a log cabin, which he occupied for several years before selling his "betterments" in 1850 to Cortez Moody.

The lake, a handsome body of water encompassing some 537 acres, was the setting for the usual tall tales. One was reported by Albert B. Street, New York historian, after an 1858 hunting and fishing trip to this area. It was related to him by Harvey Moody, his guide, and concerned another hermit named Kelsey, who "shantied" in the area 20 or so years earlier and was described by Moody as "about the worst-looking man I ever saw." Hunters found him dead near a wolf trap he had set near Little Simon Pond, and on searching his cabin, they found a cutlass, sailor's jacket and an old New Orleans newspaper account of the breaking up of a "nest of pirates," some of whom were hanged while others escaped. The newspaper description of "the fieriest and bloodiest one of the lot" convinced Harvey Moody that Kelsey was, indeed, the missing buccaneer. Who knows?

*Tupper Lake Free Press Print:* August 21, 2002

# LOGGERS LEARN MR. BYRAM'S VISION

THE SUN WAS JUST BEGINNING to appear above Round Top Mountain east of my bedroom window. It was the time of day early lumbermen referred to as "daylight in the swamp," and in most camps work would have already started in the "cutting" despite the early hour—what a work ethic. It should be noted that the ethic continues today in most well-run logging operations, even if they don't arrive to the work site by means of a torch with wicking in the neck of a catsup bottle.

I wasn't too surprised, then, to suddenly hear the high-pitched, ear-splitting sound of a powerful chain saw coming from across the street. Now, here's the thing from a frequent chain saw user, who is, admittedly, a rank amateur (I once almost killed a retriever when I misjudged the lean of a tree and it fell the wrong way), I try to observe an expert at every opportunity.

Before you could say "Paul Bunyan," I was across the street to a neighbor's property on Byram Road. Here, I found Glen Gignac and Scott Martin, both first-class loggers, busily engaged in work. Quick as light, Gignac, moving as sure-footed as a mountain goat along the trunk of a fallen pine, was skillfully lopping the tree's branches. As I watched, my thoughts wandered to an earlier age when most certainly he would have been a river driver, pike pole in hand, adroitly riding the sawed logs along the sweep and rush of a raging current as the logs headed for the screeching saws of the mill downstream.

*Guests staying at Byram's summer tourist home, called "The Crow's Nest," could be assured of good fishing. (photo courtesy of SLCHA)*

Scott was operating a Caterpillar 207 front-end loader. As quickly as Gignac would finish the lopping, he would move in and cradle the log with the front tongs and hurry it to join a neat pile of other logs. They would become boards milled by a portable mill owned by Christmas & Associates.

On one occasion, as I stood well out of the way watching, a problem arose. A large Tamarack, aged and twisted, had a complicated lean, and when cut, it threatened to fall on a young maple the owner wished to save.

After studying the tree for a time to determine its lie, Gignac made a felling hinge-cut and quickly stepped aside as Scott somehow maneuvered his machine into position at just the right angle, and with a push of the extended bucket and a groan from the tree, it fell precisely alongside the valuable maple just where they wanted it.

As Gignac was refueling his saw, Scott explained that the owner had carefully marked the trees that were to be removed, trees that were diseased or weakened or, in some cases, crowding out valuable species.

In addition to being a prudent preventative measure, the "thinning" would allow more open space and sunlight. The result would be an improved and healthier piece of property.

As Scott hoisted himself up to the machine's cab to return to work, he turned to me and said, "Hey Bill, I've got a question for you—who was this guy, Byram?"

Fortunately, having earlier talked to neighbors like the Johnsons, Gen Sutter and Dick and Shirley Meisenberg, long-time residents on Racquette River Drive, I could offer an answer. Perhaps you will find it of interest:

Byram Road, which is today a privately owned no-exit road, was named after David Byram, who came to the community in its earlier pioneer days from Vermont. If you proceed along Racquette River Drive from the village, the road will make a sharp turn at what, for many years, has been called "bend of the road." The road now parallels the Racquette River before it joins Route 30.

Notice that the land rises sharply from the river's shoreline, allowing just enough room for the road and homes located there. Indeed, the landform is one with a fair sized hill of exposed bedrock from glacial sediment that has allowed some forest growth. Mr. Byram owned most of that extended hill (200 acres).

There was no bridge across the river at Moody at that time, and the town in 1896 built a log bridge where the present-day Moody Bridge is located. Two years later, they agreed to pay Byram $100 for a right of way and $125 for the timber that would have to be moved to open a road across his property to Moody—the present-day Racquette River Drive.

Mr. Byram would then build a summer tourist home on the crest of the before-mentioned hill where Byram Road ends today. He called it the "Crow's Nest," and it commanded an extraordinary view that overlooked Lake Simond, Big Tupper and Racquette Pond (it remains today an outstanding view of lake marsh and mountain but only to the south and east. Forest growth now obscures the north and west views so prominent in earlier times).

As the years progressed, Mr. Byram sold off parcels for summer homes or permanent residences.

Byram Road cuts along a contour below the top of the hill and bisects what is known as a bench land or flat. Here Byram cleared the land, and, on sandy soil, he established a sizable truck or market garden that became well known for its excellent produce, berries and apples.

After Mr. Byram's death, the property reverted to his sister, Mrs. Margaret Slasson, who came here from Vermont to take possession of the estate and carry on the work of market gardening established so many years before by her brother. She added poultry raising and became an acknowledged expert in that activity.

The Byram property extended to the Moody Marsh, and she sold portions of it to New York State when they constructed today's Route 30.

Mr. Byram certainly had a vision when he acquired that property so long ago, and it is today, 100 years later, still a special place with attractive, well-built homes. And the river below still rolls along on its way to the sea.

*Tupper Lake Free Press Print:* September 04, 2002

# A Place of Sanctuary

AS MENTIONED IN an earlier column, Moody resident Scott Chartier faithfully sits at his spotting scope each morning before heading on to work at the Adirondack Museum, where he is employed as master carpenter and exhibit specialist.

Scott's scope is located at a window in the den of his attractive home, which is located on a slight rise of ground among elegant pine trees between MacDonald's Boat Livery and the Moody boat launch site. This location provides him with an extended view of Big Tupper Lake and the Moody Marsh, or "Flow," as it is known locally.

Scott keeps a log, and its daily entries reveal a great many noteworthy and interesting sightings among the wildlife that are drawn to the lush environment of the lake and the marsh that exists in Scott's uninhibited view. No observation was more startling, however, than one early morning in late February this past spring.

Focused in the lens of his scope was a mature bald eagle, its 7.5-ft. wings beating powerfully as it crossed the ice-locked lake carrying a large limb the size of a man's wrist in its talons.

As he watched, Scott was even more surprised to see a second eagle, also with a large limb, flying on the same course. Both birds headed to a location on the lake's outlet called the "Bluffs." (These bluffs should not be confused with Page's Bluff, which is further to the south and on the lake itself. This spot was the location of one of the earliest camps on the lake owned by Robert Page, local businessman and one-time proprietor of the former Prince Albert Hotel at Moody. Mr. Page also ran the first general store in this village in partnership with Clarence King. This store was located on the corner of Cliff and Lake streets and would become the starting point of the disastrous fire of 1899, which destroyed the business section along Park Street.) Scott continued to log and monitor the frenetic stick-carrying activity of the eagles until it suddenly ended in early March.

Had the eagles constructed a nest? Were they now sitting on eggs? Scott would have to wait until ice-out in mid April to answer these questions.

Chunks of ice were still floating on the lake when Scott and wife Mary launched their kayaks and paddled to the white pine stand where the eagles had each time disappeared with the sticks in their talons.

It would require careful scrutiny before Mary spotted the massive collection of sticks that made up the nest. It was near the top of a pine tree, later measuring 97 feet high, hidden by the canopy of neighboring pines and barely visible except at that precise angle from the water.

Scott had discovered, identified, monitored and, later, reported the first documented bald eagle nest on Tupper Lake in at least half a century!

Note: In case you are wondering, osprey nests, which closely resemble that of the eagle, have historically occurred on County Line Island (vacated after forest fires on the island), at a point of land near Grindstone Bay and also in Black Pond swamp off Black Bay—perhaps because of competition from the more aggressive eagle osprey, which now seem to prefer the Racquette River corridor.

It is important to realize that with the banning of D.D.T., which had rendered the eagles' eggs fragile and unproductive, and with the very successful New York State Bald Eagle Restoration Project in 1976, the eagle has made a dramatic comeback. Significant obstacles still remain, however, such as continued loss of habitat and the West Nile virus—which poses a new threat. Protective management such as prey analyses, predator control (human as well as animal) and data from the banding of eaglets remains necessary.

That is why information such as Scott provided is important and welcome by the Fish, Wildlife, Marine Resources in Albany (Ph: 518-478-3053). As Pete Nye, head of the D.E.C.'s Endangered Species unit, has noted: "In 1976, New York had only a single pair of nesting eagles. New Yorkers were literally a feather away from losing our national symbol as a resident breeding species. We cannot ever again allow that to happen."

In a summary then of today's column, it can be pointed out that from the earliest effort to reestablish the bald eagle in the Adirondacks, Tupper Lake observers, because of their cooperation and the reliability of their reports, have had a good rapport with the Albany Endangered Species Unit. This relationship probably accounted for the prompt reaction to Scott's report and the assignment of Mary Beth Warburton, regional research assistant, to evaluate the site.

In the next *Transitions*, we will follow the initial field check, the helicopter flyovers to determine hatching success or failure, the banding procedure (which required scaling the 90-ft. pine) and, finally, the eaglets' adventure as they gained the ability to fly. Scores of residents and non-residents alike have been thrilled by the sight of eagles over Tupper Lake this summer.

We can be pleased and proud that our clean waters and pristine environment have provided a place of sanctuary and have contributed to this majestic bird's well being. It's a privilege many people have worked hard to restore.

*Tupper Lake Free Press Print:* September 29, 2002

## Transitions

Bill and brother Jim sitting on the porch of their home with their father, Charlie. Charlie was the proprietor of Frenette Bros. beer distributors and Tupper Lake Coca-Cola Bottling. Bill, Jim, their sister Sue and her husband Bob LaBarge all worked in the family business.

Bill joined the U.S. Marine Corps before attending University.

*The Collection of William C. Frenette*

Bill was fascinated by raptors and spent a lot of time studying them. He is releasing "Herman" on the summit of Mt. Morris. A local logger found this injured hawk in a felled tree and Bill nourished him back to health.

Transitions

Bill spends spring break from St. Lawrence on Mt. Morris well before the trails of Big Tupper ski areas were envisioned and created here.

*Coureur de bois*
A skiing enthusiast, Bill competed in ski events with his family in New England and Canada. A favorite event was the Canadian ski marathon—160 miles over two days from Montreal to Ottawa.

*The Collection of William C. Frenette*

Always checking on local bottlers. A Coca-Cola man through and through, Bill is seen here giving a thumbs-up in southern France.

Bill was passionate about saving the fire towers on peaks in the Adirondacks. In this picture Bill and son Charlie sit on the steps of the St. Regis tower.

*Transitions*

Bill with his wife, Ginny, on the top of Haleakala Crater, Maui, Hawaii 1992, while visiting with daughter Ellen and her family.

Bill was an early Adirondack 46'er, climbing all 46 peaks in both summer and winter.

Most paddles included a carry. This was a trip on a fall day, most likely into a favorite hunting spot.

*The Collection of William C. Frenette*

Skiing with daughter Pam at Big Tupper. Hundreds of young people developed their passion and skills for skiing on this true family oriented mountain. Bill was a founder and first director of the ski patrol.

Bill was always engaged in a story. His love of rivers provided a good source for stories and brought him to remote and beautiful places around the country. No matter how great the adventure, he loved returning to his home in the Adirondacks.

Bill "On Watch" (or more likely enjoying a pristine fall day on Lake Lila).

*Transitions*

Bill competed for many years in the C1, and with Ginny and his daughter Mimi in his C2 (two man canoe) in both down river and slalom races.

One of Bill's favorite hunting places was on a ridge overlooking Lake Lila. Here he is making the five-mile trek on a bicycle with sled to either take out his camp or bring out the elusive buck hanging in a tree… or both.

*The Collection of William C. Frenette*

Always exploring—on this day Bill carrying his mountain bike over a beaver dam.

One of the many benefits of his job was listening to tales from outdoorsman who knew of an amazing fishing hole or two. Bill returning on his bike with a nice hover of trout, most likely based on a tip from someone he met on his sales route.

*Transitions*

Bill had scores of boats. His favorite was this century old McCaffrey guideboat. He rowed nearly every day, mostly on the rivers near his home, and loved the local competitions. (photo by Mark Bowie, 2004)

*The Collection of William C. Frenette*

Bill and Ginny on the bridge that connects to their home to the Racquette River.

What he would say was his greatest accomplishment—eight children and their offspring.

# From Near Disaster to Eaglets in Flight

IN TODAY'S COLUMN, we continue a previous account of a pair of bald eagles constructing a nest on Tupper Lake. (Do you think it should be called Lake Tupper so the lake isn't confused with the village?)

Anyway, you will recall that Scott Chartier had observed and reported the occurrence of nest-building activity near the International Paper Co. lean-to, built as a public relations courtesy by that company, open to the public and known variously as the Sorting Gap or Indian Point lean-to.

Note: Many Indian artifacts have been discovered in the past at this point. It was a camping and fishing spot used by traveling Indian parties. Of course, it was also near here that river-driven logs were sorted according to brand marks of the various lumber companies, which were stamped out on the log's end. The name choice is yours, but recent maps now label it Sorting Gap.

Scott's report received immediate follow-up from the Endangered Species Unit. Peter Nye, who heads the unit with headquarters in Albany, assigned Mary Beth Warburton, his regional assistant, to field check Scott's discovery. Mary Beth confirmed that the eagles had built a nest and that, in her opinion, were in breeding mode.

The next step at the proper time interval, when the eggs should have hatched, was to authorize a helicopter flyover to determine if the breeding was successful. That flight revealed that two very active eaglets had been produced! Finally, almost a month later in late July, just prior to the time when it was expected that the birds would attempt the defying feat of flying from their lofty perch or fledge, as it was called, Peter Nye came to Tupper Lake from his Albany office. He scaled the 90-ft. pine and placed identifying aluminum leg bands on each eaglet. This technique is called banding and is an important management-oriented procedure that is invaluable to eagle study and restoration efforts.

As you might expect, climbing a giant pine tree and sitting in the nest with two eaglets requires great skill and is not a task for the faint hearted.

Pete turned out to be more than equal to the task. He has been associated with the Eagle Restoration Project for 26 years, and his field activities searching out nest locations in remote areas, scaling cliffs and climbing trees, has kept him strong and exceptionally fit. For instance, one of the first steps in reestablishing the eagle to New York State was the importation of young eagles from Alaska. In collecting those nestling eagles, Pete and crew climbed 18 100-ft. plus Sitka spruce trees and collected 21 eaglets. Here was an expert, clearly loving his work, happy to be free of his Albany office for a few days.

I asked Pete about those early restoration days and he replied with obvious pride that the program was successful beyond anyone's wildest dreams. The idea, he said, "was to rear those nestlings obtained from Alaska, release them when they could fly and hope they would survive and set up nesting territories of their own and increase the eagle population in the Adirondacks. Falconers from early times called this 'hacking,' but it had never been done, at least on a large scale, with bald eagles." He noted further, "that the hacking tower locations were critical. It had to be in a remote location, free from human interruption."

The best way to describe these towers is that they resemble fancy tree houses in the form of an apartment complex. Water and food were delivered by a pulley system up to the eagles in the tree house complex, which had remote-controlled doors on a noiseless sliding track. All of the sophistication was to prevent the nestlings from

*In his first year, the immature eagle will have mainly black plumage. This Tupper Lake eaglet remains curious as a data band is about to be placed on his leg. (Pete Nye photo)*

"imprinting," which occurs when a human provides the water and food directly and becomes a parent figure—something to avoid.

One of the most successful locations was provided through the interest and generosity of Mr. and Mrs. John McCormick, who allowed large mega-hatching towers to be built in a remote corner of Follensby Pond, which is on their private property near here.

Pete rappelled rapidly from the Tupper Lake nest, looking like a U.S. Army Ranger coming out of a Chinook helicopter. As he struggled out of his descending harness, the parent birds glided in circles a respectful distance overhead, making a click-clacking sound to show their displeasure at this intrusion into the lives of their offspring. (Quite unlike the goshawk or the great horned owl, for example, which are fiercely aggressive in any perceived danger to their young. The eagles, if not happy, are more tolerant. A zoologist friend once suggested to me that this may be due to a higher order of intellect that allows them to see humans as superior predators and that their own survival becomes paramount to continuing their species.)

Pete's concern at this time, however, was that the nest was not overly stable. He explained, "Eagles who have reached sexual maturity at five years quite often lack the skill to select and secure a strong nest on their first nesting attempt." He added, "Trial and error eventually leads to the eagle's building a proper site but sometimes human intercession is necessary to prevent the useless loss of young or a whole year's breeding attempt." Readers may be familiar with the nest off Route 30 near Duane, where the D.E.C. erected a support base to strengthen that weakened nest.

Two weeks after Pete returned to Albany, his worst-case scenario became a reality. It has been called Murphy's Law, a rule originated by engineers stating, "If something can go wrong, it will." The nest had blown out of the tree! Massawepie Boy Scouts camping on the bluffs had reporting finding the nest on the ground and two eaglets running around like chickens in a farmyard. A hurried boat trip to the nest location confirmed the Boy Scouts' discovery. Fortunately, the nest waited to fail only days within the eaglets' ability to fly.

Mary Beth theorized that after a couple of frightening days of being on the ground, the birds gained flight, possibly becoming airborne by launching from the heights of the bluff. Her theory was given credibility when suddenly we heard the continuous high-pitched call made by an eaglet informing his parents that he was hungry. Jumping into our boat, we rowed offshore and glassed the area surrounding the plaintive call. High in a pine and tight to its darkened trunk, which offered perfect camouflage to black plumage, were the eaglets. Fantastic!

With any luck, these juvenile birds will return to the location of their birth. The privilege of watching these magnificent birds soar over Tupper Lake waters will continue to be ours and, hopefully, future generations.

*Tupper Lake Free Press Print:* October 09, 2002

## TENT CAMPS—TOO GOOD TO LAST

IT MAY BE HARD TO BELIEVE, considering today's restrictive rules and regulations that are part of any recreational use of the Adirondack Park, that prior to the mid-1970s it was possible to have a permanent state permit camp. They were known as tent camps or platform camps and many local people had permits that allowed them to build such a camp on state land. The idea got its start during the administration of Conservation Commissioner George Pratt, 1915-1921.

Commissioner Pratt wanted to open the woods for recreational use of all people. He introduced the first recreational circulars (trail description maps, etc.), built the first lean-tos with state funds and labor, erected the first fireplaces on lake shores that developed into the public campgrounds of today, and started a system of trail marking.

Anxious to get people to camp and enjoy the woods, he started the system of allowing a standardized platform with a standardized roof of canvas over a support frame that also had to follow dimension standards, and which allowed three feet of boarded sides.

It was an idea that was probably too good. Soon hundreds of these tent camps were springing up on almost every lake, especially on Lower Saranac Lake and the Regis Chain of lakes. The shores of Long Pond in the St. Regis Chain, for example, in 1970 had 16 tent camps that virtually monopolized all the best camping sites, almost to the exclusion of anyone else wishing to camp. Follensby

Clear Pond, in one bay alone, had over 18 raised tent platforms, all furnished and padlocked. Many of the nice, flat clearings you can spot as you travel the Raquette River between the "Crusher" (Route 30 boat launch) and Raquette Falls were once occupied for the exclusive use of tent platform permit holders. One of the best maintained and most pleasant of these sites on the river was the Chet Johnson camp, just below Raquette Falls, where Palmer Brook enters. Chet and his two sons, Bill and Stan, hauled scores of dead heads from the river to help navigation, and they maintained buoys on the many obstructions. That lovely location, so full of fond memories, is today a prime D.E.C. designated camping spot.

The privilege of owning a permanent tent camp was, as one old timer told me, "too good to last." The winds of change were blowing. Those winds carried an expression of the belief that the Adirondacks were in danger from pressures of increased recreational use and large developments by well-heeled corporate developers.

What became known as the Park Agency Bill then went before the legislature with the governor's support, and on June 2, 1970, the Assembly voted 123 to 24 in favor. The next day the Senate approved it 22 to 14.

This highly controversial agency then designed a state master plan. Among the many recommendations in the plan was one that involved all non-conforming uses in the classification categories they labeled as Wilderness. Primitive and Wild Forest would be phased out by 1975. Those non-conforming uses included roads, power lines, snowmobile trails and tent platforms. It was the beginning of a major change.

I didn't own a tent platform, but I know many folks who did. It was like having a tank pull into your front yard, lower its cannon and having the tank commander holler, "Out! Get out! Take what's yours but get out!" After the initial shock wave came disbelief, dismay and finally anger. Strong protests were made but to no avail. The legislature had just restructured the Conservation Dept., creating a super agency called the Department of Environmental Conservation that absorbed the old department and several other state agencies. This new D.E.C., as it became

*In 1916, platform tents, such as shown, were authorized by state permit. In 1971, the state rescinded the process since the sites were not temporary. (photo courtesy of Women's Civic Chamber of Saranac Lake)*

known, gave its approval to the master plan. The plan, with some modifications that were decided on during three public hearings, became state policy in July 1972.

The battle to save the tent platform is practically forgotten today and even unknown to many younger residents. Nevertheless, it is an important historic milestone in what the late William Verner termed the "park making progress" in the 1970s.

It would be one of the signature changes that would determine how the Adirondacks would be managed. Many of the permit holders simply walked away from their sites as the phase-out of the tent platforms commenced, and it became a formidable task to clean up the former sites. It would take until 1978 before D.E.C. work crews razed all of the structures and cleaned the clearings of stoves, sinks, beds, propane tanks, etc.

To take a dispassionate look back, we could probably agree today that permanent tent platforms were, in fact, inequitable. As the outdoor boom with camping and hiking increased at unheard levels of a nature-hungry public, complaints began to inundate the Governor's Office. As I remember it, the local residents had little objection. After all, they had grown up with tent camps as a fact of life and were, for the most part, on the friendly side of neutral in the ensuing debate.

Prior to the 1970s, backpacking was still an alien concept to most Americans, but the new wave of tourists and campers found prime camping sites pre-empted by the tent camps. The biggest complaint, however, was that the permit was a special and exclusive privilege that constituted a "holding" on state land and was a violation of the park's "wilderness character."

Admittedly, there were also many abuses of the permit system. Some permit holders actually rented out their camps, to name just one abuse among many—a perfect example of a few individuals ruining it for the majority who did follow the rules and regulations of their permit. That having been said, there remains little doubt that Commissioner Pratt's idea had outgrown its original intent and was in need of being rescinded.

Today it is still possible to obtain a "temporary" permit that allows the camps on state land (usually for a specified limit of time). As the private land continues to shrink under state acquisition with the subsequent loss of lease arrangements for hunting camps, such permits will become increasingly popular, even necessary, if the wonderful tradition of the hunting camp experience is to survive for many people.

We can only hope that this temporary permit system, which reflects the original philosophy of former Commissioner Pratt to encourage primitive camping and the wise use of great woods and waters for all people to enjoy, is allowed to remain and is recognized as an essential part of the Adirondack way of life.

*Tupper Lake Free Press Print:* October 23, 2002

# OUR BELOVED MT. MORRIS

YOU WILL NEED A SPARKLING CLEAR DAY with lots of sunshine. A day toward the end of March is best. Winter snows have usually consolidated by that time, making optimum conditions for travel by ski or snowshoe. In addition, the days are longer at that time of year, but the angle of the sun is still lower, an important ingredient for the observation that you will be seeking.

The goal is the summit of Mt. Morris, a modest, pleasant climb with special views that extend unobstructed for up to 25 miles on all points of the compass; a panorama of high country and lake-studded forest as well as this community's very own mountain, loved by generations of Tupper Lakers who have discovered its many charms.

The summit of our friendly mountain was once totally wooded, but is today denuded—a bold dome of exposed anorthosite, the trees having long ago been cut to establish sight lines to other signal towers by an early surveyor.

A note of trivia: In 1890, when early settlers here demanded—and got—their own townships (they were originally under the Town of Waverly), they needed a name. Mt. Morris, at 3,163 feet, dominated the landscape and thus Altamont, from the Latin "alta," meaning high, and "mont," meaning mountain, was chosen.

You will pass a cluster of small buildings, each humming its own signal to enhance today's high-tech communication network. You will also pass what is the first steel fire tower to be built in the Adirondacks (July 1909).

Aerial surveillance has made the tower's original function obsolete, but it remains structurally strong as ever—a tribute to its designers, the Aeromotor Windmill Company (note that the state no longer maintains the tower and the mountain's summit, and its access requires permission from various private owners).

Go to the south, facing part of the mountain where the earth seems to have fallen away, leaving a steep cliff face. Looking almost due south, you will spot a beautiful sheet of water called Lake Madeleine surrounded by what appears to be miles of unbroken forest.

If you have timed it right, as the sun begins its descent to the west, you will observe an ethereal glow of color, a mix of orange and rose, that is as startling and beautiful as it is mysterious. The source of this reflection? The legendary Litchfield Chateau and the more than 50 windows that face Lake Madeleine, one of the Adirondack's most fascinating structures. The chateau sits back from the lake, situated by its builder, Edward Litchfield, so that it is in perfect harmony with its pristine surroundings. If that appears to be a paradox, so be it.

You will need binoculars from your vantage point to pick out the two great towers rising so impressively above the tree line — "a bit of Bavaria in the North Country woods," as one writer describes it, who noted further that the grandson of the builder affectionately called it an anachronism of the first order as well as a magnificent Edwardian dream.

Many readers will be familiar with this storied place, but readers who have not had that opportunity or are unaware of its existence may find the following excerpt, from a newspaper column found in a 1932 *Free Press* edition, of some general interest. The column was written by Rufus, the pen name of A. Clark, Jr. Mr. Clark was an energetic newspaper columnist as well as the local postmaster during the construction of the castle/chateau, which was completed in 1913. Excerpts from his column follows:

"Edward Litchfield first came to the Adirondacks in the summer of 1893. He is a noted attorney and realtor of New York City and a multi-millionaire.

"His first purchase was the south third of township 25, known as the Gilchrist tract. Later he bought the middle third of the same township called the King tract. Both tracts having been previously lumbered over nearly a half century ago by the Norword Manufacturing Company.

"A few years later he sold the east half of the King tract to Read & Strange, wealthy New York bankers, which included the beautiful body of water then called Simond Pond but changed to Lake Wilbert by the owners of Read & Strange Park (now Little Simond Pond).

"After selling the large tract of land to the above firm, Mr. Litchfield still retained about 13,000 acres for his park, in which are located Lake Madeleine (formerly Jenkins Pond), Heaven Lake, Duck Lake and Lake St. Hubert.

"After Mr. Litchfield acquired the property, he erected a camp for his family to live in when visiting the preserve. Then a force of workmen enclosed 8,000 acres with an eight-foot wire fence, with heavy posts set quite close together, to insure greater strength. This enclosure was intended as a wild game sanctuary to preserve the large numbers of deer frequenting that section.

"In 1894, a large force of men began clearing a 40-acre tract on which the spacious farm buildings were erected and still stand.

"The land proved to be fertile and large quantities of hay, grain and farm produce have been annually raised for consumption by the stock and employees on the estate.

"Several other buildings were erected in the park and many miles of stone roads formed an outlet from all parts of the property, converging at the main entrance.

"Eight miles from Tupper Lake on the Long Lake road, the fence skirted the highway (Note: This was the old highway) and at a point near the crest of the famous 'Litchfield Hill' was located at the main entrance.

"The entrance was guarded by an attendant who was on duty

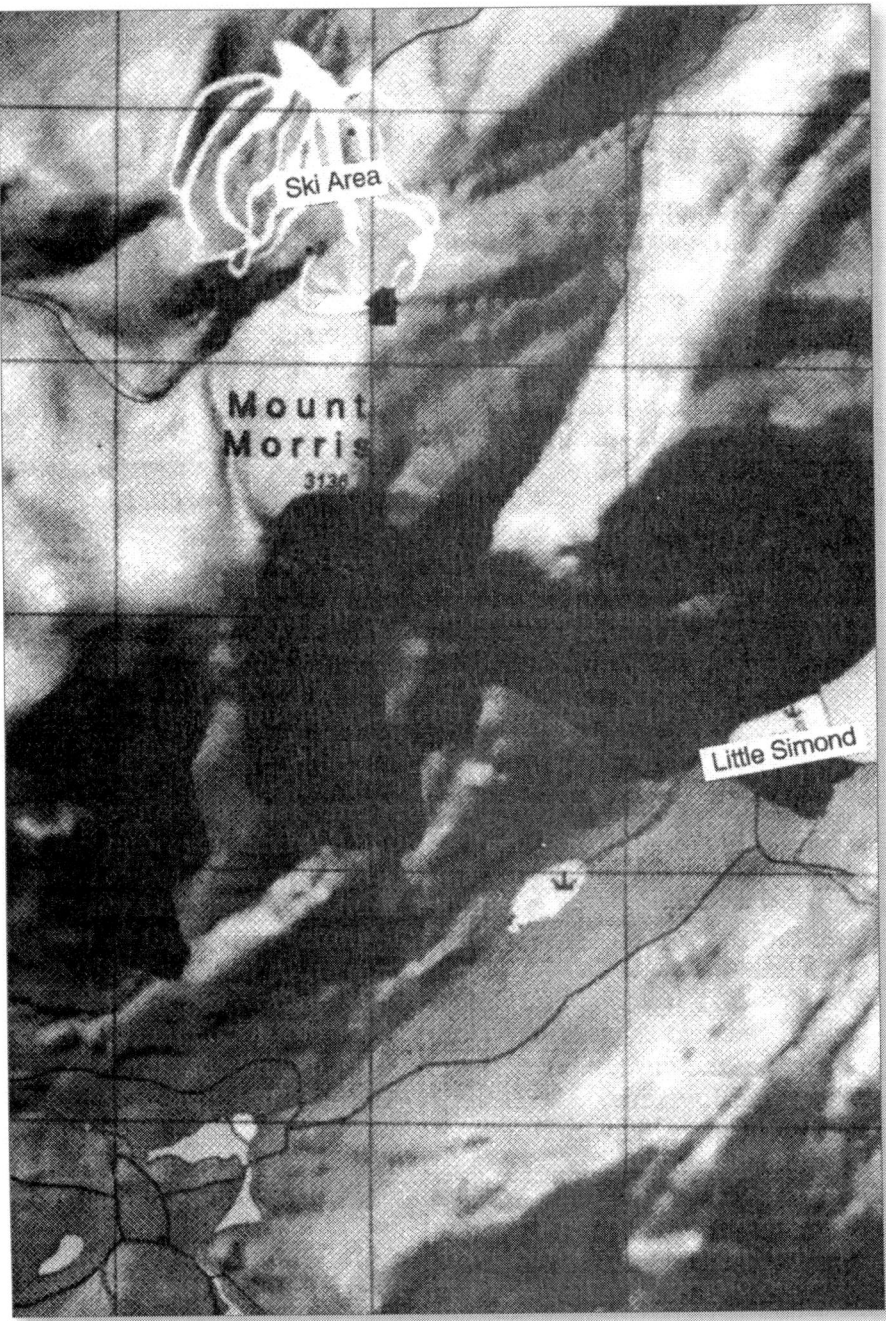

*Litchfield Castle, one of the most fascinating structures in the Adirondacks, lies protected on the shore of Lake Madeleine by the imposing rampart of the Mt. Morris cliff face, facing south.*

year round, living in a stone gate house erected just inside the fence (now leased as a hunting camp).

"For 38 years the position of watchman was faithfully filled by Antoine J. Robitaille, who had been in Mr. Litchfield's employ for 41 years at the time of his death. During the last few years of Mr. Robitaille's advancing age, Xavier Mareil of Tupper Lake was engaged as his assistant and companion.

"In 1911-1912 Mr. Litchfield built the 'Chateau,' intended to stand through the ages to come as a perpetual monument to his name.

"It is a stately structure, built in the style of ancient feudal castles, such as was visited by the owner during his trips to European and other foreign countries.

"It was built from solid granite blocks, quarried nearby, hewn and shaped by expert stone cutters skilled in the art. There are two great towers at either corner in front, built rampart style, like those of centuries ago, when lords and princes erected castles for defense.

"Every window on the lower floors is protected by heavy iron bars set in solid rock and concrete. In the basement is a dungeon, protected by stone doors which may be opened only by touching certain concealed and secret devices.

"The dungeon is used for storing valuable and its existence would not be noticeable to the casual visitor, if it were not pointed out to him."

*Tupper Lake Free Press Print:* November 27, 2002

# LITCHFIELD PARK

IN TODAY'S *TRANSITIONS* COLUMN, we continue excerpts from an *Old Timer's* column in a 1932 edition of this newspaper, written by Rufus, the pen name of A. Clark Jr. Mr. Clark's focus was the interior of Litchfield Chateau as follows:

"The decorations of the spacious interior are lavish beyond description. In many of the rooms are fireplaces, designed and carved in Italy and other foreign lands, which add greatly to the decorative beauty of the different floors and parts of the building.

"In the 'great hall' there is a fireplace of wonderful design, which formerly adorned the palatial drawing room in the Madison Square apartments in New York City, owned by the late Stanford White who was shot in 1906 by Harry K. Thaw during an alleged quarrel over the famed actress, Evelyn Nesbit, wife of Thaw.

"When the White estate was settled and his princely belongings sold at auction, Mr. Litchfield bid on the fireplace and rated it as being one of his most valuable possessions.

"In the large hall there are 174 heads and animals, trophies of the hunt, shot by Mr. Litchfield, his son, Hubert, and members of his party on hunting expeditions to Africa, Scotland, Europe and other lands.

"The vast collection is said to be one of the largest and most varied groups extant, privately owned.

"In the art gallery is a collection of oil paintings, priceless in value, comprising many historical Biblical works, one being a painting of the Head of John the Baptist. Another is a work of art executed in oil centuries ago by an early master, which was purchased in Vienna 125 years ago by Mr. Litchfield's father while on a continental tour.

"For nearly 20 years the owner set apart Thursdays of each week as 'visitors' day. Attendants were provided and hundreds of eager sightseers visited the grounds and castle and enjoyed the hospitality of the beautifully ordained place.

"When the owner was present with guests, he always took special pains to call their attention to the long lines of heads and hunting trophies, nearly all of which were bagged by himself and his son, Hubert.

"He would also recount with well deserved pride, of one of his late trips to a friend's hunting lodge in Scotland, during which he brought down five stags out of six shots.

"Mr. Litchfield would remark facetiously, 'Pretty good for a 76 year old hunter, isn't it?'

"The first superintendent at the park was Orlin Puffer of Lowville, appointed 38 years ago. Among those who have since held the position, we recall the following: A. Shuhardt, Thomas Scott, John Johnson, M. Mayhew, James Minogue, Andrew Chase, John J. McCoy, Oscar McNeil, William Rice and Joseph Greene, the present incumbent.

"Their duties were to supervise the work by park employees, see to it that repairs were made when needed and everything about the large preserve kept up according to orders from the owner."

Note: these duties and many others are today under the competent supervision of Kevin Littlefield, the current superintendent of the park.

"Eight years ago (1924) it was decided to begin lumbering on a scientific scale to clear the forest of all over grown and fully ripened timber.

"Mr. Litchfield appointed as woods engineer to take charge of the operations Floyd A. Hutchins of Tupper Lake, a son of the late Almanzo Hutchins of Brandon, well known timber cruiser

*This massive bronze of an English stag atop of 12-foot granite tower protects the entrance gate of Litchfield Park. (photo courtesy of Lou and Frank Morrison)*

and surveyor throughout Northern New York.

"William W. and John B. McCarthy, comprising the firm of McCarthy Brothers of Tupper Lake, were awarded the contract for lumbering which has been continued for seven years by sub-jobbing firms of this place. All trees permissible of being felled were so marked by Mr. Hutchins and every effort was made to preserve the young and growing timber."

Note: Mr. Hutchins' management approach was to cut half the mature trees over a certain diameter. The idea being to provide a factor of permanence to the lands of his employer. Mr. Hutchins retired in 1959 and was succeeded by the late John Stock, formerly forester for the Emporium Lumber Co. of Conifer and an independent forestry consultant. Scientific management continues today under the guidance of a well-known lumbering firm. It is estimated that between 75,000 and 100,000 cords of pulp wood have been cut that were sold to the St. Regis Paper Co., and the International Paper Co. Upwards of 15,000,000 feet of hardwood logs have also been cut and sold to C.H. Elliott and Son for their Tupper Lake mill to be converted into hardwood lumber and mangle rollers for export to England and foreign countries.

"Edward H. Litchfield, the founder of this large estate, died in March 1930, leaving the property by will to his son, Major Hubert Litchfield, officer in the World War, who is carrying on the great projects his father began nearly 40 years ago."

Note: Major Litchfield died in 1951. He was succeeded by Edward S. Litchfield. Today the park is under the direction of Pieter Litchfield, a fourth-generation, great grandson of the builder. Innovation, creativity and an ethic of resource management have allowed the perpetuation of the original "magnificent Edwardian dream" of its founder, Edward Litchfield.

Litchfield Park remains a welcome and valued neighbor—a major influence and a significant contributor to the history of this community.

*Tupper Lake Free Press Print:* December 04, 2002

# LITCHFIELD WILD GAME SANCTUARY

FRANK MORRISON called me last week. He had a comment on a recent *Transitions* article in which some of the origins of Litchfield Park were detailed. Those who know Frank will recognize that he wasted no time in getting to the point: "Hey Bill," he said. "How come you didn't mention anything about the wild boar that Mr. Litchfield imported to stock his Adirondack holdings?"

Even before I had an opportunity to reply, Frank fired another question: "By the way, do you know why they had those iron bars on the windows?"

"For security?" I weakly replied.

"Nah," said Frank. "It was to keep the boar from entering the Chateau. Of course, after the boar disappeared from the park, someone recognized that if there was a fire, the iron bars might prevent an escape, so they removed them."

Frank insists that his source for that story is reliable, and that readers would be interested to know that at one time not only moose and elk but other exotic species were imported by Mr. Litchfield with an idea toward developing "a game preserve equal to the finest Europe can provide."

If Frank is right, perhaps a brief sketch of that noble experiment to create a wild game sanctuary on the outskirts of this community will be of interest.

The story begins around the middle 1890s, when Mr. Litchfield enclosed 8,000 acres of his property with a woven wire fence eight feet high. He then stocked that enclosure (at great expense) with elk, moose, wild boar, European grouse, quail, jackrabbits and fallow deer.

Louis Simmons, in his seminal local history entitled, *Mostly Spruce and Hemlock*, noted that the "elk were transported from Wyoming (Moosehead Ranch in Jackson Hole) and the moose from Minnesota, Maine and Canada. Red deer and fallow deer were imported from England. The wild boar were natives of the Black Forest in Germany and were supplied by the Hagenbach of Hamburg."

Unfortunately, despite the great expense, a colorful part of Adirondack history, to which early Tupper residents had a grandstand seat, did not survive.

An early observer summed it this way: "Within a few years, Mr. Litchfield's hope for a sanctuary were blasted due to the constantly

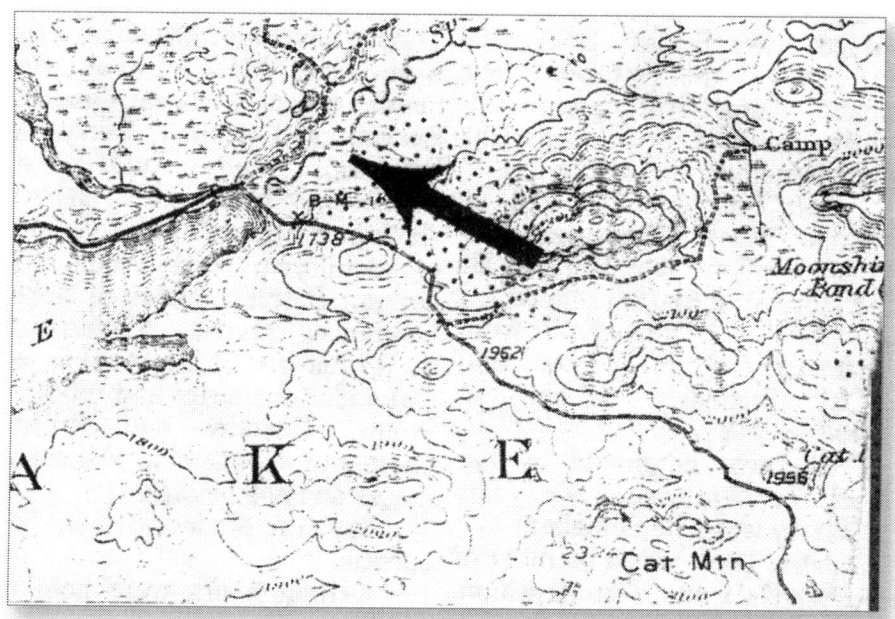

*In 1919 a European wild boar, weighing more than 200 pounds and a fugitive from the Litchfield lands, was killed in the large swamp near the outlet of Little Tupper Lake on the Whitney Estate as shown on the map above (now lands of the Adirondack Nature Conservancy).*

breaking down of sections of the high and strong fence. Practically all the herds of moose and elk escaped. Vandal hunters would occasionally shoot an elk for the valuable and highly prized teeth used for lodge charms" (Elks Club).

Note: Some elks were still frequently seen in later years. One female became semi-domesticated and was a common sight as she foraged with the cows near the foot of Little Tupper Lake (1920s). Joe Haile, one of this area's preeminent woodsmen, once told me that an elk hung around his trapping cabin near Handsome Pond as late as the middle 1940s.

The wild boar also escaped, but multiplied and turned out to be one of the most exciting additions of the wildlife imported by Mr. Litchfield.

I grew up with Floyd Hutchins, Jr., whose father was park superintendent for 35 years, and I heard many thrilling stories about this ferocious, swift-footed species of wild swine. They were considered very dangerous because of their great speed and strength, their long lethal tusks, their lack of fear and their willingness to charge a hunter.

Note: Hunters and many lumberjacks reported many encounters with wild boar in this area. They had long and heavy dewclaws and, when running through the snow, their feet spread and a made a track much like that of caribou. They would also leave large areas uprooted in their search for edible roots and other forage. The last one reported killed was in the 1920s just across from the Sorting Gap on Racquette Pond.

I will conclude this week's column with an excerpt from an account of a great boar hunt that occurred in Whitney Park in March of 1919. The article was made available by the late John Stock and appeared in a publication called *State Service* in May of 1919 under the title, *First Wild Boar Hunt* in the United States, with a sub caption which read, "It took place only a few weeks ago in the wildest part of the Adirondacks."

The article was written by James Whipple, a former New York State Forest, Fish and Game commissioner. I will quote only the section of the article in which the author lets one of the hunters,

Ernest Johnson, well-known in this area at the time as the general manager of the Whitney Preserve, tell "in his own words," the story of the hunt:

"There is no doubt about this being one of the wild boars that escaped from Litchfield's park about ten years ago, and finally worked its way across onto the Whitney preserve. These fierce animals have wintered on Moose mountain near the outlet of Little Tupper Lake, north side. As they are very keen and wary, much more so than deer or bear, we have never been able to get sight of one until this winter. For years I have seen workings where they have fed, but have never been able to locate one. Having an idea about where they were wintering, I had been thinking that when conditions were right I would indulge in a little kingly sport now that nearly all kings have abdicated and one man is as good as another and go wild boar hunting as did the kings and nobles of olden days. Therefore, a few days ago a guide, William Sibley, my two sons, Alfred and Dyenley, accompanying me, we started out before daylight on snow shoes. After traveling about six miles, we saw some old signs of their workings where they had dug through the snow for roots. Alfred and Dyenley then traveled long on one side and the other on the opposite side of Moose pond, while Sibley and I made a circle and came in from the east.

"After traveling about half an hour, I heard Sibley shoot and in a few minutes I saw a large black animal running by on the hillside. Under the snow conditions it ran very fast. I knew instantly it must be a wild boar, and fired one shot at quite a long range. The boar was running quarterly toward me, and when I fired the animal swerved in its course and came on directly at me, and when within about forty feet I fired again. The second bullet from my 25 Savage apparently struck the animal pretty well back and through the intestines. The boar let out one loud squeal and plunged into a thick copse of brush and out of my sight.

"I have done much hunting of moose, deer and bear, and am unusually cool, but am obliged to admit that this first wild boar hunt had me going a little. In about a minute I heard a shot up near where my son, Dyenley, was on the high ground, and in about two minutes I heard a shot in the direction further on, where Alfred was supposed to be. I followed the trail as fast as I could on snow shoes, finding blood all the way, and in arriving over near the foot of the pond I heard the boys yell, 'We got him,' and on coming up to them found they had the boar dead.

"To show the wonderful vitality of the animal, I will tell you more particularly about the affair. Sibley had jumped three of the boars and hit the one that came toward him a glancing shot, not fatal. My shots went clean through a little back, as I said before. Dyenley shot one hind leg off and Alfred finished him. His first shot went through the lungs of the animal, and at that the boar made for him, and when within about twelve feet he fired again, striking him in the top of the shoulder and ranging back; it sort of paralyzed the boar but he did not fall. He simply stopped and stood with his feet well apart, a real fighter, game to the last. In that condition before he finally succumbed, Alfred took several pictures of him. Of all the game animals I have seen and killed during forty years in the woods, I have never seen any gamier animal, and doubt if any, even the lion or the tiger of Africa, have more stamina. Sibley jumped the three boars from a nest made of green spruce branches and dead grass."

Note: The boar was later turned over to Joseph Sabattis, taxidermist of Long Lake, to be mounted full life size.

*Tupper Lake Free Press Print: December* 18, 2002

# DR. THISSELL AND THE HOLY TREE

THE TELEPHONE CALL was from the Chamber of Commerce office. The caller indicated that a study for the revitalization of the village's Main Street was in progress, and an element of that plan, with historical overtures, would involve what the chamber spokesperson described as the "Holy Tree," located on Park Street near the Tupper Lake National Bank drive-in window exit.

"Did I know the whereabouts of the commemorative nameplate hat had been attached to the tree?" Also, "What kind of tree was it?" etc., etc.

Intriguing questions! The folks at the chamber deserve good grades for not allowing it to get lost from the chronicles of this community, this prominent feature on our Main Street that was transported from its home on the eastern shore of the Mediterranean Sea and endured, indeed thrived, through countless seasons of unfamiliar and often hostile Adirondack weather.

Having grown up in this community, I was somewhat familiar with the tree in question, although I don't remember it being referred to as the "Holy Tree." I knew, for instance, that it was a gift of Dr. Thissell, Tupper Lake's beloved dean of physicians, from the earliest pioneering days of this community. I could remember it as a spindly sapling at a time when Francher's diner was located next to where the NY Telephone Dialing Center (now Verizon) is currently located.

Because that property has a connection with this account of the tree, I'll interject some background on what was known in the late 1930s as the "Post Office" lot. This lot, fronting 65 feet on Park Street, was purchased by the government from A.J. Deshaw in 1941 as a site for a proposed post office. WWII and other considerations held up the project, and the government subsequently decided the lot was too small. It offered it to the village at a 95 percent discount from its $13,500 cost to the government ($675) with the provision that construction of a library be started there within 18 months. The village, however,

*Shown here is Dr. J.A. Thissell, beloved dean of physicians, who served this community tirelessly for 52 years.*

withdrew it purchase application to permit the property sale to the Telephone Co. The sale price? $14,000!

The point is that the property was originally owned by Dr. Thissell, who also owned the "Opera House," today remodeled as our village office, police station, etc. It, along with the former Hotel Altamont, had miraculously escaped the fire of 1899 that leveled most of the Park Street business section. It was all saved largely through the efforts of a women's bucket brigade that kept the fire from spreading. The property extended to the corner of Cliff Avenue, which was known at the time as "Thissell Block."

To carry the connection with the tree a bit further, note that in 1915, this block was purchased by the Tupper Lake National Bank, which had outgrown its location in the Maid block (now Littlefield Insurance) and built the beautiful building we know today. Dr. Thissell was an organizer of the original bank in 1906 and a continuing long-time director, so we might easily speculate why the tree was planted in its present location.

You must admit that this towering tree that dominates our Main Street is remarkable and special. For something like 100 years, it has been able to overcome the stress of drought and penetrating cold, and it has resisted attacks from virulent pathogens.

Perhaps only the majestic 70-ft. elm tree (which boldly thrives when large American elms have now died from Dutch elm disease) located near the Demars Boulevard entrance of Day Wholesale offers a challenge to it for the wonder of survival against overwhelming odds. No matter the challenge, both of those century-old denizens represent an exceptionalism, which, if you think about it, mirrors this community. Tupper Lake has also defied the odds and has lived on when similar places that were also based on a sawmill economy have become ghost towns today.

My boyhood memory of Dr. Thissell planting this tree was largely anecdotal, and I needed assurance that it was valid. I placed a call to Lois Brosseau, who not only is a history buff but also has a sharp memory. In addition, she had grown up here and had worked at the bank. Lois confirmed what I knew.

Dr. Thissell always strongly opposed any effort to remove the tree. Lois carried my inquiry a step further, and in a quest to locate the commemorative nameplate once fastened to the tree, called Frank Morrison, who had worked with her at the bank.

Frank in turn called the bank and a quick search revealed that some time ago the plaque, having fallen from the tree, was placed in a file drawer and forgotten. Frank and his wife, Lou, recognizing the historical significance, recently polished and restored it. They will replace the plaque on this community's "Holy Tree" so that the memory of the beloved physician who transplanted it will live on.

In the next *Transitions*, we will offer a sketch of Dr. Thissell, who came to this undeveloped logging community in 1887, fresh from Harvard Medical School as a young doctor, and remained for 52 years of tireless labor both as a businessman and a caring physician.

*Tupper Lake Free Press Print:* January 15, 2003

# DR. THISSELL AND THE WATER COMPANY

THE CURTAIN RAISED in a strange way on the career of the newly minted doctor, who was to become this community's grand old man of medicine.

Dr. Thissell was living in Boston, near his home of Berkely, M.A., and he had recently joined the Massachusetts Medical Society. One day he walked into the society's headquarters where he was introduced to a tall, attractive lady, elegantly dressed in the finery of that period, the daughter of one of Boston's wealthiest residents. It seemed she had received a telegram from her brother, Addison Child, telling her that he was ill and that she was to come to his estate located in the hamlet of upper New York State (called Childwold, which he named after himself) and to bring a doctor.

Fifty years later, Dr. Thissell, in an interview given to the Malone Telegram while he was a patient at the Alice Hyde Hospital under the care of Dr. F. H. Dalphin, his friend of 46 years, had this to say of that fateful meeting:

"The society's director had recommended me to Ms. Child. I didn't want to go. I wanted to go to Europe, France and Germany to study. I told them so.

"'What did you study medicine for?' they asked me.

"'To relieve human suffering and maybe save lives,' I said.

"'Well, here's your chance!' they told me. I went."

The brother, of course, was the scholarly, wealthy Bostonian who, in 1868, along with two partners named Kin and Bigelow,

*The stagecoach was the important connecting link from water or rail. Much depended on it for mail, for passage to remote hotels, for parcels and the news. The high-sided carriage shown here was called a "tally-ho." Up to six horses carried 12 to 15 passengers. (SLCHA photo)*

purchased 36 square miles of Adirondack timberland. This tract was later divided, and Mr. Child acquired the north third of 12 square miles.

It was on this acreage that he established, in 1878, the farm settlement he named Childwold, and later in 1889, he built the famed Childwold Park Hotel with accommodations for over 300 guests on the shore of beautiful Lake Massawepie. An original hotel brochure boasts of a "qualified young doctor in attendance," which, of course, was our own Dr. Abbot Thissell, who was to figure prominently in Tupper Lake history.

In 1887, when Dr. Thissell first came to Massawepie, it meant a 50-mile buckboard ride on a dirt road from Potsdam, a long and tedious trip up the Raquette River valley, emerging at Gale on Catamount Pond, a short distance from the Park hotel.

Three years later, in 1890, when John Hurd had pushed his railroad to Tupper Lake from Moira (the New York and Ottawa, also called the Northern Adirondack Railroad), a stagecoach road was completed from the hotel through the woods to a station on the shore of Pitchfork Pond, four miles north of Tupper Lake Junction, which Hurd called the Childwold Park Station.

Always an entrepreneur, Hurd ran the stagecoach that took passengers and guests up the shoulder of Mt. Matumbia, over a wooden bridge across the Raquette River and came out at Gale. Hurd's stagecoach was a high-bodied carriage of a type called a "tally-ho" pulled by six horses, and it could hold 12 to 15 people (steamer trunks and other luggage were transported in a separate wagon). Hurd had it painted a bright red with the letters, N.A.R.C. on the sides in bold relief.

It was a lucrative business (in those years, the hotel was usually filled to its 300-person capacity), but it suffered a setback two years later when Dr. Webb completed his railroad (the New York and Montreal or Mohawk and Malone, as it was originally called) and established a station on his line also called Childwold.

It was a more accessible route to the hotel, and guests could take a stagecoach here along a route called the bridle or carriage road, which continues as a woods road today. Note: this station was just beyond where the Mt. Arab road from Route 3 crossed the track today at milepost 106. Snowmobilers and others using the tracks might wonder at the large letter H preceding each numbered mile on the signposts along the railroad line. A year after completion, in 1893, Dr. Webb, in a profitable move and a laugh of his critics, sold the M&M to the New York Central, and the southern terminus became Utica, no longer Herkimer. Mileposts along the grade, however, always tied into Herkimer, hence the H.

Tupper Junction station was a milepost 113.68. Beaver River to the south on the line is at 77.69 miles, and Horseshoe is at 99.91 miles.

The hotel ran into lean times in the 1900s, and it closed permanently in 1909 with all its fittings intact (including Brusell carpeting). It would remain this way in ghostly splendor for 36 years.

By this time, Dr. Thissell had relocated, first at the south end of Tupper Lake, later at Moody, and finally at Tupper village.

Medical facilities didn't exist here at the time, and the village was fortunate to have Dr. Thissell and, later, Dr. Austin, also a hard working and dedicated practitioner. Still, it was a grim outlook for anyone seriously injured in the sawmill or woods operations, which was so common in those hazardous occupations. It would be quarter century before this community would have a hospital (not until 1916, when four rooms were set aside in the Morgan home on the corner of Cliff and High streets, across from today's fire hall).

It is reported that Dr. Thissell before that time traveled over 10,000 miles on horseback to reach patients. Lumbermen also came for miles to see him, even to have teeth extracted.

"Sometimes," he once related, "they would stop me on the road. 'Well,' I'd say, 'you sit down on that log over there. Now, which one is it?' And I'd pull it out. No ether or gas or anything like that in those days. One fellow came 84 miles to get a tooth pulled."

The doctor was a great believer in the health benefits that could be obtained by eating blueberries. In fact, he wrote a paper to the medical association detailing what he felt were the scientific reasons for that conviction. He also felt that the aroma given off by spruce, hemlock and other coniferous trees influenced the ozone layer of the atmosphere and was a positive contributor to the balms of health. It was his opinion that the purity of our forests was an extra reason to live in the exciting frontier land we now call the North Country.

Dr. Thissell was a wonderfully kind person who did not bill patients who lacked the money to afford his services, and in many other ways, he helped many people.

In our next *Transitions*, we will relate more about this remarkable physician and his medical and civic contributions to the community, including his ill-fated reservoir dam above Dr. Scranton's veterinary clinic at Moody.

*Tupper Lake Free Press Print:* January 29, 2003

# Historical Wanderings

YOU WILL UNDOUBTEDLY DETECT a certain circumlocution in today's column. I plead guilty, and in my defense, I hope "writing around" the main topic, which is Dr. Thissell and his tireless career of physician and businessman in this community, will be excused as I attempt to include historical items of interest.

When Dr. Thissell first arrived in Tupper Lake in 1875, a Maine outfit, the Pomeroy Lumber Co., had already logged off the virgin pine (1850). Sears Hill and the French village (Broad Street section) remained totally wooded, but the clear-cut area overlooking Racquette Pond and along its shores would become the site where the village was to spring up some forty-odd years later. Dr. Thissell would have a front-row seat and become a major player in the growth of the Tip Top Town that expanded with the rapidity of magic.

The clearing would prove to be an ideal location. Racquette Pond, according to geologist Jim Carl, retired professor at SUNY Potsdam, was once a huge lake (which was completely separate from Tupper Lake). In post-glacial time as the lake receded, it left behind a flat, sandy floor that was perfect for industrial operations to locate. Here, logs could be floated from long distances on navigable rivers (the dam at Setting Pole, having been built as early as 1870, raised the level of the pond, making it contiguous to Tupper Lake).

It would no longer be necessary to ship all logs downstream to

*Once the sandy floor of a much larger lake, the old lake land along Raquette Pond was ideal for industrial plants such as the sprawling O.W.D. plant. At the upper right of Demars Blvd. is Sissonville village. Shown at center right of the boulevard is stacked firewood for sale (peeled veneer), and at left, N.Y.O. tracks, chemical plant and stack. (photo provided by Jon Kopp/Swiss Kitchen)*

Potsdam, and the huge sawmills erected here as well as the arrival of railroads would provide immense employment opportunities, resulting in a mushrooming population as people located here. Not only was this flat floor of the old lake ideal for building, but is also provided plenty of room for storing and stacking logs and lumber before they were shipped out by train, whose rails reached into and through the terminus next to the present-day Coca-Cola plant on lower Wawbeek Ave.

Professor Carl, who was from the Illinois plains, where "there was no shortage of flat land, unlike the Adirondacks," noted that the "vast acreage of flat and sandy land at Tupper Lake and Racquette Pond was a Godsend for railroad surveyors." What better place to build freight sheds, yard facilities, row houses for workmen (Webb Row) water towers, coal chutes and round houses.

The high mound that rose above the pond further embellished this ideal industrial location. This was a glacial hill that professor Carl described as "having its highest point, a bedrock knob (Tallman Hill), but that most of the hill consisted of glacial depositional material," perfect for building homes and the business section that would be needed to service the residents who would occupy those homes.

In 1877, as the embryonic village began its feverish building boom of hotels, stores and homes, G.W. Smith, a surveyor from Potsdam, arrived in Tupper Lake one April morning in 1895 onboard "Hurd's Railroad" from Santa Clara and wrote the following in a letter to his wife:

"If beauty of location could ensure a city, this would be one, for the ground is gradually rising from the shores of the pond back quite a distance with then an abrupt rise of twenty or thirty feet and then a gradual rise giving every part of the fine view of Racket Pond and when the woods are cut away of the lower end of Tupper Lake."

Readers who enjoy walking might consider a short detour from their usual route and walk up Tallman Ave. and pause at that pinnacle of bedrock now known as Tallman Hill. For a tiny extra effort, the view is quite rewarding.

Look down at the village and its wide main street—a tribute to the foresight of those early village planners. Note how the village is built on the high ground and how the streets are laid out north, east, south, west, parallel to the side of the hill so that houses can face the lake and its view, and how further west on more level ground the streets are planned to be aligned north/south, east/west. Look out to the Sorting Gap, Moody Flow and across the pond to the ghost town called Underwood and the bridge Dr. Webb found necessary to build so his rail line could cross the Racquette River.

In the distance, Arab Mountain, Station Mountain, Matumbia Mountain, Iron Mountain, Floodwood Mountain and Long Pond Mountain, all modest in height but impressive nonetheless, rise as sentinels overlooking the pond and our special village.

As the community expanded, the need for water, both for drinking and for fire protection, became a priority. Only a two inch pipe, laid on the top of the ground from the Big Mill along

Lake St. and Wawbeek Ave. to the Park St. corner, was in place, which, of course, was totally inadequate. Providing that need launched Dr. Thissell on a dual career as both a physician and businessman. He established, with others, a private company incorporated as the Tupper Lake Water Co. This company quickly completed negotiations with the A. Sherman Co. to buy a marshland body of water called Cranberry Pond (currently owned by Big Tupper and located near the seventh tee at the Tupper Lake Country Club). Pipe was then laid from the pond to be fed by gravity to a pumping station on Simond Pond. The water company then installed hydrants to serve the new fire district, established after the disastrous 1899 fire, with a charge to the town of $25 for each hookup.

The need for a backup supply soon became advisable, and Dr. Thissell, who was now the sole proprietor of the company, hired a contractor to erect a dam that would contain the waters of a brook located below Cranberry Pond on top of the hill above Moody Bridge. The reservoir thus formed was 150 feet by 160 feet, with a depth of eight to ten feet.

In our next column, we will relate how, upon the first filling, the reservoir wall failed, and tons of water bore down the hill. The wall barely missed the McBride home (today's veterinary clinic) and tore a huge hole in Route 30, just beyond Moody Bridge.

*Tupper Lake Free Press Print:* February 12, 2003

# DR. THISSELL AND EARLY PIONEER LIFE

WE CONTINUE TODAY the series of articles about the early physician, Dr. Thissell. As mentioned in an earlier column, Dr. Thissell arrived in this area in 1875 as the personal physician for Addison Child and later as the "in-house" doctor for the guests of Child's new Childwold Park House and the farm community that Child named Childwold. Dr. Thissell would be witness to the ultimate fate of that great hotel—a wonder in its day—that flourished for only a short time, its register carrying the names of U.S. presidents, visiting European royalty and the greats of the 1890s.

He would also be at the scene of the disastrous fire of 1899 that destroyed up to 72 buildings in this village.

From the organized settlement of the village following that fire, Dr. Thissell would serve the medical needs of this community until his death in 1945. Among other contributions, he would help organize the Tupper Lake Water Co., the Cliff Ave. Sewer Co. and the Tupper Lake National Bank.

This was a period of overwhelming growth and feverish building activity. You could go directly to one of the mills and buy lumber for $10–$12 a thousand. This village became a boomtown in a frontier land, as real as any in the legendary West. The settlers who came here in their search for "something better" needed, as Frederick Remington once noted, "to have their bark on." The growth of science and industrialism was just beginning

*This photo shows the failed wall of Dr. Thissell's ill-fated reservoir (located on Manning's Hill). Moody flow, Racquette Pond and Chalmer's (Quarry) Point can be faintly seen in the distance. (Crane photo)*

to emerge (the light bulb, the telephone, the airplane and the automobile), and Tupper Lake was a place of stark simplicity. The streets were only dirt paths that turned into a mire of mud after every rain. In the winter months, the snow would simply be packed down by heavy rollers pulled by a team of horses.

Homes were heated by wood stoves (as many as three in some homes), and obtaining and cutting firewood was a constant chore in an already long, work-filled day. Water was obtained from nearby brooks, wells and the many springs found in the valley. Not even the gas light had yet appeared, and homes were lighted by candlelight and smelly kerosene lamps. Nor were there any streetlights, and if you ventured out at night, you carried a kerosene lantern to find your way. Nature's call, as it was known, was accomplished first by chamber pots in each room and later by holes in the ground over which was placed a bench with openings cut into it. This arrangement was enclosed by a rude shelter for privacy and protection from the elements. Such structures were placed downwind away from houses and came to be known as "outhouses" or "privies." Toilet tissue consisted of dried moss, corncobs and pages from any available newspaper, etc.

As you might expect, the odor from these outhouses could be overwhelming. Our pioneer families would use fresh dirt, lime or wood ashes from their stoves added to the ditch in an attempt to mitigate this problem.

Sidelight: This fall a local hunting club, whose camp in a remote location, required such an outhouse. They employed the same technique of using wood ashes to temper the odor. It worked fine until the day an overzealous club member used ashes that, unbeknown to him, contained live embers. You guessed it! The outhouse caught on fire. It has been reported that following the initial excitement, the members treated the episode with great humor.

As the town's population continued to explode, two needs quickly became evident. The first, spurred by the lack of sanitation and fear of disease, was the need for sewer connections to carry off wastewater, etc. The other, with the devastating 1899 fire still fresh in memory, was the need for water for fire protection, for general use and for a potable drinking source. The problem was quickly solved when five local businessmen, including Dr. Thissell, formed a private stock-holding company, incorporated as the Tupper Lake Water Co. The first order of business was to hire local civil surveyors, William LaFountain and James McBride, to survey the Mt. Morris sector for a suitable water supply. Two locations were discovered: "Little Simon," a deep glacial pond of cold pure water nestled in the col between Buck Mountain and Mt. Morris, at an elevation of 1,789 feet. This location allowed a 223-ft. descent for gravity to feed the pond's water to a pumping station to be built on Big Simon Pond.

The other source was a small marshland pond called Cranberry, less than a mile above Big Simon Pond, also with proper elevation for gravity feed. Despite a strong recommendation for utilizing Little Simon Pond by the surveyors, who feared Cranberry Pond would not prove adequate for an expanding community, the Water Co. elected to go with Cranberry Pond. The added expense of the longer connection to Little Simon was of considerable financial concern and the deciding factor in their decision.

The pond and surroundings were purchased by the Walter Company from the A. Sherman Lumber Company, and pipe was laid to the pumping station on Big Simon Pond. Several years later, Dr. Thissell became the sole proprietor of the stock company. About this time, the need for a backup source became apparent, and Dr. Thissell contracted for a dam reservoir to be built. This would have been in 1905, and the reservoir was located on Mike Manning's hill above the Moody Bridge. (Note: In the late 1930s, an early ski slope and rope tow were located on this gentle slope, the bull wheel or terminus of the towline being a short distance below the earthen walls of the reservoir. As kids skiing on that hill, we often explored that site and wondered about the gaping hole in its wall.)

In a September 24, 1964, edition of the *Free Press*, the editor ran a photo of the reservoir taken by a well-known local photographer by the name of Crane. In the photo caption, the editor wrote that he had not found any reference to the reservoir in his files and asked any "old settler subscribers to fill him in on this picture." The following excerpt is from a letter he received on October 8, 1964, in reply to his inquiry. The letter is from David Balch of Monticello, NY, a boyhood resident in the 1900s and a summer resident:

"The picture of the damaged reservoir on the front page of your September 24th issue brings back a lot of memories. It was built in 1905 and was located on the top of the hill directly up from the old red bridge over the Racquette River. It served as an impounding area for village water which drained down out of Cranberry Pond, a region resembling a swamp that lay back on a plateau about a quarter of a mile away.

"The pond area was Tupper's first water supply. Then, finding the supply inadequate, the reservoir was built by a contractor named Nims, at the direction of Dr. J.A. Thissell, who was president and principal owner of Tupper's first water company. The reservoir was about 150 feet long and 100 feet wide, with a depth of eight to ten feet. It was an auxiliary supply, supplementing the direct flow and feed from Cranberry Pond.

"The break occurred in the spring of 1906, as I remember, and the subsequent litigation in Malone in the fall of that year. It so happened I was a boarder at LaFountain's at the same time the contractor, Nims, was. He was sued by the Tupper Lake Water Co. for improper construction. The west side of the reservoir, facing the village in the distance, lacked sufficient supporting girders, and in addition had an inadequate sheath of solid concrete. It seemed that the water company had a clear case for damages.

"But as events proved, it didn't. The testimony of the principal witness for the water company, the good doctor, became confused, it appeared, and so many conflicting statements were made of his oral contract with Nims that the jury was forced to find a verdict for the defendant. Dr. Thissell afterward arranged with Colonel Barbour to take over his interest in the water works, and thereafter, under Colonel Barbour's direction, all proceeded in a regulation manner, with a pumping station installed down on the edge of the Racquette River, by which the water was pumped into a standpipe that was constructed on Sears Hill on the outskirts of the village at its north end.

"It might be added that the night the reservoir broke and swept in a torrent down the steep hillside, Mr. McBride, who lived in a log house at the foot of the hill, said he was awakened by something that sounded to him like rain. As his log house was directly in the path of the torrent, only a slight twist in the terrain saved the occupants of the McBride cabin from being swept into the river... It was a narrow escape from a real tragedy."

*Tupper Lake Free Press Print:* March 05, 2003

# WHY SO HEALTHY

"MANY PEOPLE ASK what makes Tupper Lake such a healthy place. Here is the answer."

That statement was the title of an essay written in the 1930s by Tupper Lake physician, Dr. Thissell. The good doctor was convinced that Tupper was just about the healthiest spot on the globe. He put together a little story and had the *Free Press* print 500 copies so he could spread the word. Over the years, those copies pretty much disappeared and, in fact, became rare. Some years ago, a copy that survived came across the desk of this paper's editor, who noted, "Probably no Chamber of Commerce publication every commanded more reader interest than this little leaflet." That copy came from Marge LaRouque of Long Lake and was passed along by Roland Richer. It is offered in today's column for reader interest:

"Years and years ago—not too many—there lived at Tupper Lake an old-fashioned family consisting of father, mother, five sons and five daughters. Besides, there was a grandfather, making a baker's dozen in all. Grandpa was of the 'Old School'—fine in every way. They lived happily together in those days. As time went on, the boys and girls grew up and were married. All continued to live here except one son, who bought a dairy farm not far from Utica, NY.

"Grandpa, always an early riser, took turns living with the married grandchildren. As sometimes happens, the in-laws, both men and women, did not get along at all with the old gentleman.

Gradually that got on his nerves, so to speak, and as we are all what our nerves make us, this whole family was in deep trouble. Grandpa was getting older and older—going on a hundred at this period and decidedly set in his ways, making it still harder to get along with him. Among other things, he was extremely garrulous, although his brains were tracking well, both sides. (To understand this otherwise queer expression we must add grandpa was born left-handed and being a worker from childhood, he soon became ambidextrous. Our brains, having two sides, are developed more thoroughly when we use one hand as well and cleverly as the other.)

"A family council was held, and in desperation it was finally concluded to pack grandpa off to the farm where he had never been. So he was put on the train, and the other son agreed to meet him at the station near Utica.

"Several weeks passed, and news came back that grandpa was growing feeble. The home folks were surprised at this because he had always been so spry and husky here. A few weeks more and a telegram came saying the poor old gentleman had died in his sleep.

"One of the grandsons, who had a softer spot in his heart than the others, was detailed to go down and bring the body home. They left on the night train that arrives at Tupper Lake at 5:25 next morning. The casket was put in the baggage car, and the grandson, feeling sorry, decided to sit up with grandpa. A few miles north of Big Moose, the highest point on the New York Central Railroad (2034 feet above sea level), he heard a little noise in the opposite corner. He had been dozing off and on and did not pay much attention to it at first. Finally, wide awake, he went over to look. There was grandpa getting up in is coffin, crying gently and talking to himself—a habit he had acquired during the past twenty or thirty years. Bending over him he heard him say between sobs, Too bad, I am sorry; pity me. I died down there on the farm. Now they are bringing me back up in the mountains and the air has brought me to, and I have got to go all through it again.

*Winter snows slowly lose their grip on the lush berry grounds of the Spring Pond Bog near Derrick, 11.5 miles from this village. Until 1936, Tupper residents would board the New York and Ottawa railroad on one of two scheduled morning runs and return on an afternoon train with pack baskets filled to overflowing with blueberries. (photo by Bill Frenette)*

"Naturally this broke the grandson all up. By the time he had quieted grandpa by telling him he should live with him and not others, the train pulled in at Tupper Lake, and they both rode home in Dan Hayes' bus. This favorite grandson took good care of him, and the whole occurrence was so unusual that grandpa had everything going, especially his buttermilk, without ever having heard that was the very thing that kept the Bulgarians alive longer than any other people in all Europe—105 to 125 years old—the lactic acid in it destroying the unfriendly germs and allowing the friendly ones to grow and propagate. Also being fond of blueberries and having nothing else to do, he picked and ate them every day during season, and his granddaughter put up so many that the whole family flourished on them summer and winter. They never knew that the peculiar acid blueberries contained worked on the liver and that the pulp skin and seeds acting as roughage, altogether formed the most scientific laxative known up to date. (Use at least 1 quart a day—more would be better—without sugar or cream.) But they did know enough to stick to their blueberries and so kept right on living, including grandpa.

"The amount of water around Tupper Lake contributes a large share towards its healthfulness. One can step into a motor boat at Owens Wharf and travel over 150 miles by following the shorelines of Raquette Pond, Big Tupper Lake, Big Simond Pond and up the river to Raquette Falls, and down as far as our new dam without getting out. This is one of the very few mountain towns known where such a thing can be accomplished, and yet the drainage is so perfect, and the air containing an excessive amount of oxygen and ozone is so drying that a short time after a shower the surface of the ground is dry as a chip.

"It is easy for us to understand why, with all the above in his favor and contributing to a long and healthy life, grandpa continued to live. (Having practiced medicine here for over 48 years, the writer is an undisputed authority.)

"However true the above is, the writer wishes to be conscientious and will not vouch for the ending of this remarkable story of the life-giving properties of the air of Tupper Lake. Tradition and legend, however, back each other up in this case, and they both say that when near a hundred and twenty—the age of Moses, who led the Children of Israel out of bondage in Egypt over 3,500 years ago—he was taken out and shot on the far side of Mt. Morris."

—*Dr. Thissell*

*Tupper Lake Free Press Print:* April 02, 2003

## Enough is Enough

MARTIN MOODY WAS ANGRY. He was so angry that he clamped down hard on the pipe in his mouth and broke the stem. It was his favorite pipe and he had just loaded it with his best tobacco, a hard-to-get brand called Climax, and that didn't help his disposition.

Muttering something that sounded like, "enough is enough, I'm going over to Johnson's," he sloshed through ankle-deep water that had reached above lake level to the veranda of his modest hotel located on the shore of Tupper Lake.

Jumping into his guideboat, Mart rowed furiously to his neighbor's cabin, the ash oars that he had handcrafted yielding in a subtle arc under the skillful rowing of strong arms accustomed to pulling such a craft across miles of Adirondack waterways. This was the same boat that he had used to arrive at remote and isolated Tupper Lake ten years before in 1861. Despite his present upset mood, Mart chuckled as he remembered that trip. He and 16-year-old Minerva Reid from Bloomingdale had recently married in Saranac Lake. Mart recalled how she had insisted on adding a fancy oak parlor table that had been a wedding gift to their already overburdened boat as they started their long trip across the Saranacs to their new homestead on the isolated and largely unsettled shores of Tupper Lake.

Note: Some years ago, I remember seeing this table in Aunt Helen's, a combination boat livery and store that is now the

*Martin Moody and his wife, "Aunt Minerva" Moody, are shown here on the porch of their first hotel called the Mt. Morris House. Friend of presidents Chester Arthur and Grover Cleveland, "Uncle Mart" became the first postmaster in the Tupper Lake region. He died in 1910, making this picture close to 100 years old.*

Garrelts' summer camp at Moody. "Aunt Helen" was Helen Minogue Cutting, a grand niece of Aunt Minerva. She had lovingly restored this family heirloom.

We'll have to turn to the Chronicles, as they say in the *Prince Valiant* comic strip, to understand why Mart, this gentle Adirondacker, was so angry.

Up until 1850, only the lower part of the river had been used to drive logs to the mills located at Potsdam, Norwood and South Colton. As the need for a greater supply of timber that was close to the river became recognized, the industry began to eye the vast timber resources largely untouched in the upper watershed.

Potsdam, some 50 river miles downstream from this community and the first permanent settlement founded in 1803 on the river, had ambitions to become a great manufacturing center and became one of the first to seek that resource.

Mill owners there, led by influential resident Dr. Henry Hewitt, began intensive lobbying with the New York State legislature to pass a law making the Racquette a public highway. Dr. Hewitt's legislation was passed in April 1850, together with authority, to spend $10,000 on improving the river channel (a huge sum of money when you consider that the average hourly wage was between 50 and 75 cents, and a dozen eggs cost 10 cents).

Almost immediately, lumbermen swarmed further up the Racquette, now protected by law from riverfront property owners' objections to the log running that prevented local navigation and often caused flooding damage. Charles Bryant Jr., in *The Raquette: River of the Forest* (1964), notes that "at the peak of operations on the river from 1880 to 1910, groups from some fifty odd camps were cutting in the area tributary to Tupper Lake and the neighboring Raquette waters." The ink was hardly dry on the legislative paperwork before a dam was built to ensure an ample reservoir of water needed to sluice the spring log drives downriver. The first dam was located above a section of fast water known as Setting Pole rapids, two miles below Racquette Pond. This was a low dam, temporary in nature, that proved inadequate to the task of flushing logs through the rapids and falls that marked the 1,000-foot drop to Potsdam.

My great-grandfather, Ezra Frenette, who lived in South Colton during the late 1800s and was a boatman on the river drives, notes in his memoirs that the section of the river below Colton, known today as Stone Dam, and Jamestown Falls below Sevey's Corner, were the most troublesome and dangerous.

Low water also often hampered operations, and in 1870, a number of prominent Potsdam lumbermen formed the Racquette River Reservoir Company to build a new and larger dam at the

*A Tupper Lake guide sits in a muddy wasteland surrounded by the bleached stumps of a ruined forest—the result of flooded lands caused by Setting Pole Dam. (Stoddard photo)*

same Setting Pole rapids site.

Seaver, the Franklin County historian, records that with no mill in the vicinity, all of the timbers that went into the dam had to be hand-hewed: "These were mostly 12 by 14 inches, and 200 acres were stripped of all the trees that would square to that size. Including the wings, the dam was 300 feet long and had ten gates. Its height was ten feet above still water, and 38,000 cubic feet of stone went into it."

The result was a flooding of lands for nearly 30 miles upriver, the land where Faust sits was totally under water, as was most of uptown. Trees on the flooded land died, leaving a ruined forest and desolate-looking slime and mud-covered flats. The river corridor to Racquette Falls became completely despoiled, and the docks and boathouses along the lakeshore were either washed away or at other times left high and dry when the dam gates were opened to flush logs downstream.

When the dam was built in 1871, only ten families were settled here. Four families were located along the river next to what are now the Gontowich farmlands below LeBoeuf's bridge. They were Reuben Stetson, William McLaughlin, Simeon Moody and Mose LaFountain. Further downstream, along what would later be known as Moody, were the pioneer families of Geo. McBride, William Johnson, Fred Moody, Judge P.M. (Pop) Freeman, Ernest Johnson and Martin Moody. All of these families had arrived here by boat, and the Racquette River was their prime artery of transportation. In addition, most of them were guides, depending on the river's charm and scenery to make a living.

This village and Faust had yet to be settled, so there was no objection raised to the dam's destructive potential in that quarter. However, the pioneer settlers at Moody became seriously impacted by the dam. After 15 years of protests that fell on deaf ears, a secret "vigilante" meeting was held. (Now you know where Mart was headed, muttering "enough is enough" that day in 1885.)

In the next *Transitions*, we will relate how the men from Moody—all tough, independent pioneers—took matters into their own hands with a "vigilante committee."

*Tupper Lake Free Press Print:* April 23, 2003

## DUALITY RESOLVED

WHEN WE CONCLUDED LAST week's *Transitions* column, pioneer settlers from Moody were engaged in a secret "vigilante" committee meeting. Frustrated after 15 years of unsuccessfully protesting the serious consequences and hardships of the uncontrolled dam level, these hardy pioneers were about to take matters into their own hands.

Before we review that dramatic activity, however, it should be noted that the dam was of substantial size—300 feet long by 10 feet above still water high, with 14-inch timbers and 38,000 cubic feet of stone. It was built in 1870. Despite its massive construction in May of 1871, a heavy spring runoff caused the dam to give way. John Snell, a prominent lumberman, killed a team of horses by driving them to death in order to get ahead of the flood and warn people in Potsdam. Note: It took 36 hours for the flood to reach that village.

The *Potsdam Herald Recorder* carried in its files an account of the incident. John Snell, uncle of long-time Congressman Bertrand H. Snell, was logging this region at the time. He started with is team of blacks for Potsdam from South Colton, "running his horses all the way," the newspaper reported. He reached Potsdam before dark. The townspeople turned out and worked to strengthen the booms at the head of Oak Island. About noon on Saturday, the river began to show the effects of the freshet, the wreckage of a sawmill near Hannawa being the first evidence. The

*Setting Pole Dam in 1870 was a type lumbermen called a "driving dam." It had a superstructure with timbers squared by a broad axe that held a plank gate that could be raised vertically to allow logs to be driven through or sluiced. (photo courtesy of Scott Paper Co.)*

water flowed over Raymond Street, people moved out of their houses and machinery was taken out of the factories. Bridges and streets were crowded with sightseers.

About noon, a bulkhead guarding the water wall east of Fall Island gave way and the flood rushed through. The Wathins, Leete and Co. foundry was inundated, Gatchelders Mill torn from its foundations and the Sparrow and Swan machine shop crushed. Booms were carried out with a heavy loss of logs. Thanks to Snell's dramatic ride, there was no loss of life and damage was held to a minimum.

Within a year, the Raquette River Reservoir Co. had fully repaired the dam, and millions upon millions of logs continued to be sluiced through its gates to downstream mills.

As mentioned in an earlier column, the Reservoir Co. was composed of influential Potsdam lumbermen. In reviewing the names of the members of that company, I was struck by the remarkable fact that all of them would later become not only residents of the community but also powerful and noteworthy contributors to our history and subsequent growth. Those principals were: Henry Day, John Snell, Luke Usher, Albert Hosley and George Sisson.

Henry Day was a founder of the Norwood Manufacturing Co. Later, when that firm purchased John Hurd's "Big Mill" on Racquette Pond, he became its president. He was an original director and founder of the Tupper Lake National Bank and later became president of that institution.

John Snell and his brother, Hollis, owned much land here. Betrand Snell, Hollis' son, would become a U.S. Congressman, whose power and prestige in the nation's capital would be a major influence in Tupper Lake being chosen as the location for Federal Hospital #96, later called Sunmount.

Luke Usher was a former Potsdam banker (First National). He established the mill that would bring Piercefield into existence. Financial problems resulted in the Roswell Flower interests acquiring the Piercefield property that was then sold to International Paper Co. He also owned several farms here, including what was known as the Hayes Farm, where Sunmount is now located, and Usher Farm, located on what today is a pine plantation on lands leased to the No-Mis Hunting Club by the John Hancock Trust Co., and which are currently up for sale.

George Sisson was a member of the prominent Sisson family that had extensive land holdings here. Charles Sisson, sent here to manage the family firm, the A. Sherman Lumber Co., was the first mayor of this village (1900).

Albert Hosley was an officer of the Norwood Manufacturing Co., located on the shore of Racquette Pond. When that firm sold to the Santa Clara Co., Mr. Hosley retired and purchased the 160-acre farm once owned by associate Usher. He later sold that farm to this village for $20,000, and it was later offered to the U.S. Government for $1 as a site for the Veteran's Hospital. Mr. Hosely was a vice-president of the Tupper Lake National Bank, and he was one of the founders of the highly successful Altamont Milk Co.

Readers may detect a certain duality in the above profiles. Here we have respected, vigorous, highly successful individuals on the one hand, yet whose methods of moving product to their mills was suspect and caused such wanton environmental destruction and harm to others' properties. But I'll let readers smarter than I resolve that conundrum.

The Moody pioneers didn't wait for any "ethical awakening" from those mill owners. In 1885, armed with iron bars, cant hooks and pick axes, a vigilante committee, in what must have been a Herculean task, tore the dam apart. This afforded temporary relief, but two years later, in 1887, the huge central pier that had been left intact had gathered logs, flood wood and debris, and it held a great amount of water in check (not unlike the current situation most spring seasons when the LeBoeuf Bridge piers collect such debris. Just don't be downstream when the caretaker employs a crane to clear the mess and release everything to continue elsewhere).

The vigilantes made a second visit to demolish the pier. Unfortunately, this time a large section of the log-bound rock formation (crib) gave way suddenly, and Fred Freeman, one of the workers and 21-year-old son of Judge Freeman, was carried down the falling mass. He was still alive when taken from the river but died before his father and comrades could get him home across the three miles of water to the Moody landing.

With the dam no longer in place, the water level reduced the flooding of certain lands and made it possible for industry to locate along the Racquette Pond and present-day Demars Blvd. It also allowed the junction point for two railroads and the building of Faust.

There were, however, some new problems that surfaced. With no dam in place, there was no way to control area water levels. It was quickly realized that a dam was necessary if the water levels were to be kept to a "moderate fluctuation between high and low limits." It would not be rebuilt, however, until 1933, when a new stone and concrete reinforced dam would be built on the site of the original dam at Setting Pole Rapids.

The dam, over the years, would prove to be a major headache to this community. Costly repair and maintenance items, lawsuits and controversy have plagued its existence. In addition, the dam stilled a free-flowing river, a section that had become famous as early travelers and writers extolled its extraordinary trout fishing and pristine surroundings. It had been a place where Indians, since the retreat of the ice sheet, had used setting poles to ascend and descend its shallow stretch of rapids on their way to summer hunting and fishing grounds. One of their favorite destinations was a place they called "A-rey-una," or "green rocks," now called Tupper Lake.

*Tupper Lake Free Press Print:* April 23, 2003

# THE LONG JOURNEY TO THE ST. LAWRENCE

THE MOHAWK INDIANS called it "To-War-Loon-Dah," or Hill of Storms. It has also been called Clinch, Emmons and Tallow. Today we know it as the more aptly named Blue Mountain. You can spot its imposing, recognizable profile that dominates the landscape as you travel south to Long Lake on Route 3 from this village. Tiny rivulets are born in the hidden springs and spongy mosses of its steep flanks, adding their ice-cold waters to the St. Lawrence Watershed, one of the five major drainage basins in the Adirondack Park.

The Racquette River, one of the rivers in that watershed and a powerful force in the history of this community, rises in the shadow of Blue Mountain in a series of lakes knows as the Eckford Chain, named after Henry Eckford, a noted shipbuilder and early surveyor of its waters. The three lakes that make up the chain were originally named after Eckford's daughters, but regretfully like so many Adirondacks place names, they have been lost to change.

Janet Lake, augmented by underground seepage and springs, its clear waters reaching depths of over 100 feet, is now called Blue Mountain Lake. Catherine Lake is now called Utowana, and Marion Lake is now Eagle Lake. Marion's name has survived in a fashion because the 11-mile water connection between Blue Mountain Lake and Raquette Lake (Utowana and Eagle lakes are simply a widening of this water connection) is called locally the Marion River.

*Shown above is the interior ranger station at Racquette Falls, one of only four left remaining in the Adirondacks. The clearing was once the supply depot for lumbering operations in Cold River and, later, the site of the Racquette Falls Lodge. (Bill Frenette photo)*

The Racquette will flow 170 miles from this source before it joins the mighty St. Lawrence, the widest, longest, deepest river in the northwest Adirondacks. No river within the Blue Line can match it for its boating mileage. To be sure, in the river's lower sections, dams and power demands often dry up the river for short distances, and penstocks and turbines divert its flow in places.

July and August certainly are busy times on the river corridor, enjoyed by scores of recreationists of all stripes. In early spring and late fall, however, when the river is at its most appealing, there are many days when you can have most river routes entirely to yourself.

The river has been a main artery of travel for at least two centuries, and many of the early settlers who located on its watershed reached these places by its water route. Some came up the river from the St. Lawrence, others crossed Lake Champlain and accessed the river via the Saranac chain of lakes, perhaps by trail to Long Lake from the road that, in 1862, went as far as the Henderson Iron Works (Tahawus). Or they came from the Mohawk Valley via the Fulton Chain to Racquette Lake.

*Zachary Frenette pauses briefly on his way across the mile-long Racquette Falls carry.*

Thus a trip along the river is a trip through Adirondack history. Sir John Johnson used it as a route to escape into Loyalist Canada. He was met (where the river joins the St. Lawrence) by Caughnawaga Indians, who escorted him safely to Montreal. It also includes the terrible clashes between the Mohawk tribe of the Iroquois confederacy, whose domain included the upper river watershed, and who resented and resisted intrusion from the Algonquin Indians of eastern Canada, who would claim the area as their hunting ground.

Among many other such gems of history is one that occurs just five river miles below where the river emerges as the outlet of

*(Raquette River map courtesy of G. Glyndon Cole)*

Blue Mountain Lake. Here in 1878, a dam, which still exists as a low concrete wall, was built to deepen the water upstream for navigational purposes.

Below the dam is a shallow stretch of rapids that requires a carry or portage on a wide pleasant treadway. You can walk on what once was the roadbed of the shortest standard-gauge railroad in the United States—.87 mile. It was built in 1900 and called the

Marion Carry Railroad. The carry today ends on state land at the site of a former trestle that crossed the river. The lower half of the railroad grade is across the river and is on private land, but the river here (the trestle long gone) is navigable for small craft and continues for five miles to Racquette Lake. (Note: Some writers have incorrectly described the railroad trackage as narrow gauge, 3.5 feet wide. However, in the files is a public service inspection report that indicates the track's width was 4 feet, 8.5 inches—standard gauge.)

Why, you may be wondering, even in the so-called Gilded Age of the rich and powerful, would anyone build at great expense a railroad less than a mile long and equip it with its own 0-4-0 locomotive and three passenger cars with a capacity of 125 per trip, which took only a matter of five minutes or so of travel? We will attempt to shed some light on that intriguing question in the next *Transitions*.

*Tupper Lake Free Press Print:* May 21, 2003

## A Place of Refreshment

IN THE EARLY 1950s, my summer vacation job was that of working for my father delivering soda produced in his bottling plant here in Tupper Lake. One of those deliveries was a grocery store in Long Lake. Some of the store's inventory, including beverages, was stored in the cellar that was accessed by a set of steep, narrow stairs. The cellar was a dimly lit place with just enough headroom to avoid the massive timbers supporting what must have been a very old building.

On one of my deliveries to the store, I discovered a large auger alongside one of the log beams resting on the cellar's stone wall foundation. The store's manager told me that it had been there as long as he could remember, and knowing that I collected lumbering items like branding irons, peavey's, etc., told me that if the auger was of interest to me, it was of no value to him and that I could take it.

The auger was of an unusually large size, and when I removed the accumulated dust and grime, I discovered a handsome wooden handle with the initials W.W.D. professionally branded on the flat face where the bit was embedded in the T-shaped handle.

To be honest, I remember thinking that the D was probably for Duane, a prominent name in Long Lake at the time. It wasn't until some years later when reading Harold Hochschild's *Township 34* that I realized that the W.W.D. was probably William West Durant. In building his many architectural masterpieces, he often employed over 200 workers, mostly moonlighting lumberjacks and guides, many no doubt from Long Lake, and thus it is not surprising the splendid auger found its way to that community.

The point of all this is that in the *Transitions* column mention was made of the Marion River Carry Railroad that, at .85 mile, was the shortest standard-gauge railroad in the U.S.

That railroad was built by W.W.D.! Its main purpose was to transport passengers and freight across the short carry necessary because of shallow rapids in the river connection between the Blue Mountains Lake and Raquette Lake where his steamboats could not go.

Still the question remains: why would anyone build a railroad grade and trackage equipped with three passenger cars and an H.K. Porter engine to go only slightly less than a mile?

Part of the answer to that question lies in the fact that in the early 1800s, the section we know today as the "Adirondacks" was labeled on the maps as unexplored, unpeopled terrain called the "Great Northern Wilderness."

In 1837, Gov. William Learned Marcy recommended to the legislature a natural history survey of that state's northern wilderness. That challenge and assignment was taken on by a William's College professor named Ebenezer Emmons.

In his survey, Emmons climbed what proved to be the highest summit in the state (it was previously thought the highest peak was in the Catskills). Later in his report he named not only this mountain ("Marcy" in honor of his boss, the Governor) but also gave the name "Adirondack Group" to the entire mountainous region. A name, he wrote, "by which a well-known tribe of Indians, who once hunted here, may be commemorated."

The region now had a name, and the public was surprised such a wilderness remained in the Northeast United States that contained such scenic wonders and unbelievable fishing and hunting opportunities. They soon began to explore and visit not only the fringes but also the interior lakes and mountains.

Writers and artists at the same time began to publicize the region as "a place of refreshment for the body as well as the spirit," and the rush to the Adirondacks was on.

**1881. ADIRONDACK COMPANY'S RAILROAD. 1881.**

—THE—

## ADIRONDACK WILDERNESS,

—VIA—

*Adirondack Company's Railroad,*

CONCORD STAGES AND STEAMBOATS.

**BLUE MOUNTAIN LAKE,**
      **RAQUETTE LAKE,**
            **FORKED LAKE,**
                  **LONG LAKE,**

And all of the principal Lakes and **CAMPING GROUNDS**, are best reached by taking the

**ADIRONDACK COMPANY'S RAILROAD**

At Saratoga for North Creek, thence by Six-Horse Concord Coaches through to BLUE MOUNTAIN LAKE without change, connecting with the

### New Line of Steamboats

Through BLUE MOUNTAIN LAKE, EAGLE LAKE, UTOWANA LAKE and MARION RIVER to principal camps on RAQUETTE LAKE.

Stages Leaving North Creek on arrival of morning train from the south, reach Blue Mountain Lake early same evening.

**The Only Route to SCHROON LAKE and LAKE LUZERNE.**

**Stages Leave Riverside on arrival of all Trains from the South, connecting at Pottersville with Steamboats for Schroon Lake.**

**THROUGH TICKETS** to Schroon Lake, Blue Mountain Lake, Raquette Lake, Cedar River, North River, and principal points on Adirondack Company's Railroad, can be procured at Ticket Offices in New York, Troy, Albany and Saratoga.

BAGGAGE CHECKED THROUGH.

**C. E. DURKEE, Superintendent.**

*This advertisement for the Adirondack Company Railroad appeared in the Adirondack Illustrated 1881 edition by S.R. Stoddard.*

The journey to get here, however, was a tough one. In truth, you had to be vigorous with what I would call a high tolerance for hardship and even pain. Consider getting to Raquette Lake from New York City in the middle of the 1800s. First you took a train to Albany, then changed to one bound for Saratoga and then still another on Durant's Adirondack Railway to its terminus at North Creek. You would then have to board a stagecoach for a 30-mile bone-jarring, tiring ride (that took an entire day) to Blue Mountain Lake. From there, a fleet of 22 rowboats were available that you either rowed yourself or hired a guide for the 12-mile water route to Raquette Lake.

Despite those arduous difficulties, escaping the turmoil of the city and its oppressive heat, crowded and noisy conditions, and dirt and disease was reward enough to make the trip to the lakes.

It soon became fashionable to build a camp in the Adirondacks, and super-rich industrial and financial giants such as the Webbs, J.P. Morgan, Litchfield, the Vanderbilts. etc. built luxury camps not only on Raquette Lake, but also on Upper St. Regis, Upper Saranac Lake, etc.

W.W.D. built many of the finest camps on Raquette Lake, and his architectural genius set the style for many of the lavish camps that followed.

In 1921, Alfred Donaldson, regional historian from Saranac Lake, wrote, "In planning his camps, he had the happy inspiration to combine the Adirondack features of the crude log cabin with the long, low lines of the graceful Swiss Chalet.

"From this pleasing blend there sprang a distinctive school of Adirondack architecture. Before it was built, there was nothing like it; since then, despite infinite variations, there has been nothing essentially different from it."

Today, many local contractors are involved in building and creating homes and camps based on Durant's designs. They may question some of those "architectural inspirations" as they contend with such things as bark infestation from wood borers, premature peeling of the bark on the requited cedar logs (they need to be cut only on the coldest of winter days), the inherent varying diameter of the logs (that requires painstaking measurements) and the high cost of a shrinking supply of proper cedar and pine logs, etc.

Thus said, Tupper Lake craftsmen have gained the reputation of being among the best builders in the North Country, and many of the recently constructed, multi-million dollar "camps" stand as tribute to those skills.

In our next *Transitions*, we will explore how the rigors of travel to the Adirondacks were greatly reduced as Dr. Seward Webb completed the first railroad to cross the heart of the mountains, running from Herkimer to Malone. We will also look at the ultimatum given to her husband by Mrs. Cornelius Vanderbilt and how that demand created another new railroad line that included the tiny Marion River Carry Railroad.

*Tupper Lake Free Press Print:* June 04, 2003

# THE RACKET POND HOUSE

THE 1911 PHOTOGRAPH accompanying this week's column shows a much different Lake Street than today's busy boulevard.

A beautiful grove of trees, almost park-like in the shade of their leaf cover, stands where today is a carwash operation. Gone is the hotel originally called the Racket Pond House, an appropriate name since it overlooked Racket Pond (or Raquette or Racquette). The handsome homes that stood adjacent west of the former hotel, however (other than the William McCarthy home that was recently razed), have survived and are still today well kept and attractive.

Mr. Bujold, who ran the hotel for 21 years, sold it in 1945 to George Donaldson. Mr. Donaldson and his wife, the former Madeline Panye of this village, operated it for two years.

Lawrence Rafferty then bought the property, held it only a few months, and sold it to Mr. and Mrs. Albert Richer in 1947. It was recently razed in the late 1980s to facilitate the Day Wholesale operation. What follows is from an *Old Timer's Column* that appeared in the *Tupper Lake Free Press* on December 26, 1935:

"In the fall of 1889—46 years ago—the 'first hotel' was erected in Tupper Lake. It was named the 'Racket Pond House' and was a somewhat primitive structure intended as a boarding house for railroad men and employees on the Northern Adirondack Railway (now the New York and Ottawa division of the New York Central), then under construction from Moira on the old Ogdensburg and

Lake Champlain R.R. through the woods to Tupper Lake.

"The line terminated at a point near what is now the site of the O.W.D. plant. In 1890 the station was erected at Tupper Lake and the line extended to that terminal.

"At that point of early history, here, John Hurd, promoter and pioneer lumberman, had a large force of men erecting the 'Big Mill.' Employees from the mill and the railroad kept the hotel well filled with boarders and transients and the place was taxed to capacity to take care of all.

"Nelson Parks of Dickinson Center, who had been conducting for Mr. Hurd a boarding house at Santa Clara, was appointed manager of the Racket Pond House, which position he held for several years until the property was acquired by the Export Lumber Company of Albany, which firm operated the large saw mill and erected a row of houses extending from the hotel property along Lake Street to the corner of Mill Street.

"The row of houses is today—after rebuilding and modern improvements—one of the most desirable residential sections of the village and includes the following property owners: William W. McCarthy, Thomas Creighton, Charles O'Hara, Isaac Boudage, John Timmons and Supervisor Paul E. Martin.

"It is a matter of history that the first time the dining room tables were set up in the Racket Pond House, Mrs. Nelson Parks was assisted by Mrs. Henry Bruce, a school-girl companion of the early days.

"Thirty-five years ago—in 1900—Mr. and Mrs. Henry Bruce (both since deceased) bought the hotel and the name was changed to the 'American House' by which it is still known throughout the North Country.

"From 1907 until 1925 the deed and mortgage right remained in the hands of the Bruce estate and subsequent heirs until it was purchased by George Bushey, well known lumberman from the Harrisville—Cranberry Lake region, now a prominent business man of Tupper Lake in company with Charles Fletcher.

"During the 18-year interval above mentioned, the hotel was successively tentatively owned or leased by the following men:

*Shown is the former American House in the 1911 photo. One of the earliest hotels to open in Tupper Lake.*

"William Shells; Joseph Corneau (since deceased); Frank J. Wood, who later founded the Wood Laundry plant in High Street, John Cowett, former proprietor of the "Corn-Eta" Lunch in the Holland House and now a restaurant owner in New England.

"After Mr. Bushey bought the hotel he operated it for one year and then leased it to Alex Bujold for two years, who bought the property outright in 1927.

"Since the sale of the hotel to Mr. Bujold, the continued improvements, enlarging and modern features have changed the old time structure to such an extent that it is worthy of more than passing comment.

"For the past month a force of men under Harry Villnave has been erecting an addition to the dining hall, planned to have a seating capacity of 200 persons.

"Fronting the dining hall there will be a large lounging room with a bay-window facing the street.

"The cuisine and storage rooms will be moved back and greatly enlarged.

"The house is being remodeled from top to cellar and there will be 37 rooms with baths and showers on two floors.

"Mr. Bujold came to the U.S. in 1902 from St. Charles de Chalon, Canada, as a mere lad. In the World War he served with the A.E.F. and became a citizen of the United States when the war ended.

"His brother, Edmond Bujold, paid the 'supreme sacrifice' in action in France, and Edmond Bujold Post 3120 Veterans of Foreign Wars is named in his honor.

"Mrs. Rose Bujold, who has been a valuable aid to her husband in hotel management, is a Canadian by birth but is a naturalized citizen of the U.S.A.

"She came to the States as a child of seven years with her parents, Mr. and Mrs. Edward Santerre, who were among the early settlers in this section."

*Tupper Lake Free Press Print:* June 25, 2003

# MAKING THE ADIRONDACKS ACCESSIBLE

IN A RECENT *TRANSITIONS* COLUMN, the rigors of getting to the Adirondacks in the early 1800s were described. It included an arduous, several-day, tiresome journey of cramped guide-boat rides and jolting stagecoach rides on rough roads that were little more than trails through the woods, but the rewards of getting here proved to be worth the hardship.

Here is what a writer, who was known as "Our George," wrote in 1884 in a series of letters to the *Republican Journal* in Belfast, Maine.

"It is no wonder that city people, and a great many are from New York City, Brooklyn and Philadelphia, should like to get away from the noise and bustle and the bills that are overdue to come here where the air is so pure and dry and there is not even any dew on the grass, and to get into some old clothes and a flannel shirt and lie around, smoke, hunt and fish. It is these blessed vacations that take the kinks out of a man's mind and body and knock some of the years off his head and set him back a few points in the game of life."

Tourism, as we know it today, began in the Adirondack region in the 1830s, but at that time, you had to be venturesome, vigorous and rich. Slowly, from 1845 to 1875, as more hotels were built so people had a place to stay and the profession of guiding arose to aid the city-bred "sport," the wilderness became more available to many.

*Shown in this photo taken at his Forest Lodge on Lake Lila is Dr. Seward Webb. He was known as a wonderful individual who inspired a degree of loyalty among his railroad workers that is seldom seen. It was said, "There was not a man on the line who would not stand on his head for the doctor." (Photo: Frontpiece Conquering the Wilderness by Burnett)*

The difficulties of getting here remained, however, until a remarkable individual named Dr. Seward Webb entered the scene. Surgeon, Wall Street broker, president of the Wagner Palace Car Company (in two year's time he increased that company's sale of railroad cars five-fold), he was a hard-driving executive of great ability and a talent for organization.

Dr. Webb had married Lila Vanderbilt, granddaughter of railroad magnet Cornelius Vanderbilt. Both were from socially and historically prominent dynasties, and both fell in love with the Adirondacks for the same reasons urbanites still do.

Lila loved the outdoors, as did her handsome and talented husband. As an early member of the Kildare Club (originally the Vanderbilt Club), Dr. Webb knew this area as early as 1882, and it was while buying land near here to create his own preserve centered around Smith's Lake (renamed Lila after Mrs. Webb) that Dr. Webb became "impressed with the need and the possibilities of a railway running north and south through the heart of the Adirondacks."

Building this railroad would be the most ambitious and difficult undertaking in Dr. Webb's career. Others had tried, but many plans never got off the drawing board. All had failed. Most historians agree only someone like Dr. Webb could have achieved what most considered to be an impossible undertaking.

In 18 months time, against all odds, he succeeded in building a railroad 191 miles long, and the sound of a locomotive whistle joined the call of the loon and the howl of the wolf in the Adirondack wilderness.

Dr. Webb spent a lot of time here, solving problems and offering encouragement during the construction of his railroad, and he was well known by many local residents.

It should be pointed out that Tupper was an important receiving point for supplies needed for construction. These were brought in on Hurd's Northern Adirondack Railroad Line that predated Webb's Mohawk–Malone Line and, in fact, its trackage crossed Webb's projected route (hence the place name "Junction") at a point 100 yards northeast of today's Main Street at Faust.

Dr. Webb wanted to buy Hurd's railroad but a breakdown in

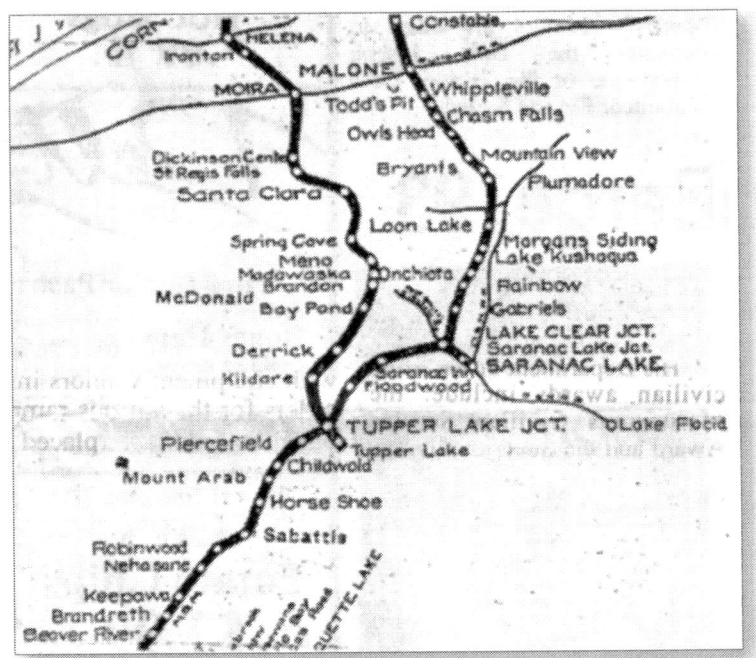

*Note where Webb's railroad coming from Horseshoe had to cross Hurd's line coming from Derrick, which predated it.*

negotiations resulted in Hurd closing off his crossing and posting guards day and night. No problem for the resourceful Dr. Webb; he purchased a heavy steel crossover plate that enabled trains to pass at points where lines intersect. After waiting several weeks, on a stormy night when vigilance was relaxed, his crew worked all night and effected the installation of the crossover. Possession being nine points of the law, according to old tradition, the work was permitted to stay, and "trains from each road were allowed to pass without hindrance" (Rufus, 1/30/30 *Tupper Lake Free Press*).

Another problem at Tupper was that he was stopped cold in laying four miles of track north of here that was on state land and protected by the constitution (no trees could be cut). This was a section in Township 20, roughly from Rollins Pond to Lake Clear.

That serious problem was solved when it was proven that the state had acquired it illegally through a tax sale without having notified nonresident taxpayers, and the property was reverted to private owners.

The charismatic Dr. Webb was able to convince those owners (Upper Saranac Association) to allow him access, to which they agreed as long as the line was placed so the train whistle could not be heard at their seasonal camps on the lake!

Scores of Tupper Lake residents onboard train and, more lately, onboard snowmobiles, have traveled across the 42-foot high bridge that spans Twitchell Creek on Webb's railroad line six miles from the settlement of Beaver River. The bridge is located at milepost 71.5, and .5 miles south at milepost 72 is the spot where the final spike on the Mohawk–Malone Railroad Line was driven on October 12, 1872.

The railroad, which was to become the Adirondack Division of the New York Central, had a profound influence on the entire Adirondack area; not only did it set the stage for the settlement of this village and others along its route, but it also opened new recreational opportunities now easy to get to, and the Adirondacks became one of America's most popular resorts.

After 73 years of colorful and important service, economic forces closed the railroad. The last passenger train #167, with longtime local railroader Louis Malerba as fireman in the diesel cab, passed through here in 1965, with freight service ending in 1972.

Today the former Adirondack Division of the New York Central is called the Adirondack Scenic Railroad, and it is operated by the Adirondack Preservation Society. Hope remains bright for a complete restoration of the line as funding becomes available.

*Tupper Lake Free Press Print:* July 09, 2003

## Tahawus—He Splits the Sky

THE VOICE ON THE OTHER END of the telephone line was straightforward and businesslike, "Is this the beer distributing firm in Tupper Lake?"

I remember replying, "Yes, it is."

"Good," the voice continued and then declared, "I'm the manager of the company store in Tahawus, NY, at the iron ore mine. Look, I've finally received an okay from the company that will allow me to sell beer at the store. I'm new at this, not having sold beer up to now. Can you put together a variety of brands and packages – whatever you think best, maybe 400 cases to start and get it here today?"

Could we ever! A full truckload at one stop? A salesperson's dream order (I'm thinking to myself), but I replied something like, "Yes sir. Glad to oblige. We'll be there this morning." I'll never forget that delivery. I'd never been to Tahawus, and that first visit was right out of a John Wayne western movie location.

It was a remote, almost intimidating spot: A dead-end plunk in the middle of wild forest. A genuine, bona-fide rough and ready mining town—no doubt about it! The aboriginal name Tahawus was given to the town from a similar Seneca-Iroquois word meaning, "He splits the sky." It was highly appropriate.

The town was surrounded on all sides by spectacular towering peaks rising directly from the main street. It was that day, a busy, energetic place of machines and throbbing equipment, noise and dust, intense—almost frenetic activity.

*In 1971, National Lead owned eight of the "Lectra-Hauls" shown above. Powered with 1,000 horsepower GMC 12-cylinder turbo-charged engines and standing 17.5 feet high with 8-feet high tires, each truck could haul a 100-ton payload.*

Located across from a large earth-moving equipment maintenance shop was the company store. The scene that ensued as I began to unload the cases of beer from my truck is also indelibly etched in my memory. It seemed that the entire town had turned out as the news spread that "the beer has arrived!"

As soon as I brought in eight cases on my hand truck and deposited them on the store's main aisle they would disappear. It was a total frenzy, with long lines waiting to make a purchase. I have never experienced anything like it before or since. Yes, those were the days!

The village had risen like a Phoenix from the ashes of what had been called the Lower Works of the Adirondack Iron Works. It was established in 1840 to mine rich ore deposits discovered in that area. In all, 105,000 acres had been purchased from the state by that venturesome company at a cost of 10 cents per acre. (Note: The Open Space Institute that recently purchased 9,600 acres of that land for $8.5 million will eventually sell 6,200 acres back to the state for inclusion to the forest preserve, probably with federal Forest Legacy funding.) Here at Lower Works, a sawmill and boarding house and several other operational buildings were constructed. In addition, a monstrous dam was created that flooded the valley back to the outlet of adjacent Lake Sanford to aid in the navigation of the ore-laden barges that came from the mining operation located approximately eight miles to the north, where a forge was located and was known as the Upper Works.

A settlement near the Upper Works was also established that consisted of a large boarding house, 16 cottages and homes, school and bank. The owners originally gave it the name MacIntyre but then changed it to Adirondack. (Note: Today that once proud settlement is a ghost town—a ruined village of boarded windows, crumbling foundations and caved-in roofs. One hundred to 400 acres associated with the ruins will be held privately by the Open Space Institute to be managed as a historical site.)

In 1843, in what could be considered one of their best years, the Upper Works was turning out from 12 to 14 tons of iron a day that was commanding the highest price paid because of the quality of the ore. Between 300 and 400 men were employed there at the time.

A series of deadly blows that included high transportation costs, floods, financial problems and the death of two of the original owners, Mr. Roberson and Mr. MacIntyre (both men of great stature, highly motivated and possessed of great entrepreneurial skills) culminated in the collapse of this great venture whose ore produced the best steel in this country.

It would seem that the words of surveyors Rueben Sanford and John Richards in their 1827 report to the mine's founders rang true. It said in part: "The winters are unforgiving, there are no roads. Once mined, the ore will lie in your hands. It is our advice, though not asked for, to abandon this scheme and seek your fortune elsewhere. Leave this pathless waste to the panther and the bear."

Yet in terms of history, the founders, men of vision who dared to take great risks and pursue a dream, set the stage for what was to follow—namely, that what was considered a century before only a troublesome impurity in the iron ore, a titanium-bearing mineral called ilemite, suddenly came into great demand.

In 1941, with the world locked in war, the chief source of this important mineral was India, and the sinking of ore-laden ships in the Red Sea prompted the need for a new supply to keep the manufacture of titanium pigment going. When the mine at Tahawus was confirmed to be rich in titanium, its new owner, the National Lead Company with full support of the federal government, reopened it.

In late winter, 1941, construction was started. Roads were built, houses constructed, new bridges installed and, wonder of wonders, a railroad line was laid across constitutionally protected lands from North Creek. During the peak of these construction efforts, required manpower ran to 1,600 employees. Tahawus was born again!

Few people standing alongside the company store the day of my great beer delivery could have guessed that in a few short years the two-mile long crystal-clear waters of Sanford Lake, actually a widening of the Hudson River, would be drained and its waters diverted to a canal so that a new pit could be dug that would reach a depth of 300 feet by 1983. Nor could it have been imagined that in 1963, when a rich deposit was discovered where the village stood, that the entire village of 100 families, 93 buildings, church, school and the store were to be moved en masse 13 miles to a new town site on the outskirts of Newcomb and named Winebrook Hills.

*Tupper Lake Free Press Print:* August 13, 2003

# Fire Towers—A Symbol of the Adirondacks

"CLIMB THE MOUNTAINS and get their good tidings."

According to all reports, lots of people, visitor and resident alike, did just that this summer. Climbing mountains with fire towers remaining on their summits was especially popular as an outdoor activity. Perhaps the following brief fire tower historical overview will be of interest to readers.

Let's begin with the late 1960s when a decision was made in Albany that fire towers were obsolete, and starting in early 1970, the state began to close them. On the surface, it was a valid decision. Experiments with air surveillance, for example, had proven not only effective but also less costly. It was quickly determined that one flight pattern could cover an area that formerly required four or five towers to view the same area. In addition, the planes would need to be hired only on extreme hazard days, further reducing the cost of fire detection, a savings that was estimated by D.E.C. officials to approach $250,000.

Thus in 1971, the D.E.C. made out contracts for 22 flights that would cover the Adirondack region. Pilots like Herb Helms of Long Lake, Tom Duflo of New Bremen, Bud Bird of Sixth Lake and Jim Payne of Seventh Lake were hired to fly some of the routes using mostly Cessna seaplanes like the 206, 185 and 172 models. The same year that the air contracts were let, 61 fire towers were closed. Some of the towers of local interest and the

*Built in 1918, abandoned in 1970, the neglected fire tower on Adams Mountain is among those recently slated for removal due to its being located in an area classified as wilderness.*

*Two cables support this unsteady suspension bridge across the Opalescent River near Tahawus on the Hanging Spears Trail.*

year they were closed follow: Ampersand in 1970; Adams (Tahawus), Kempshall (Long Lake), Tooley Pond (Cranberry Lake) and Mount Morris in 1971; Azure (Santa Clara), Whiteface, Goodnow (Newcomb) in 1979; Arab Mountain in 1988. Two of the last to be closed were Blue Mountain and St. Regis in 1990 (list compiled by Marty Podskach, *Adirondack Fire Towers*, 2003).

Other towers that were not abandoned were removed. Some were reassembled and relocated on museum sites and D.E.C. demonstration areas. Others cited for removal were simply dynamited or cut down with chainsaws equipped with carbide blades.

Some of the latter, such as on Catamount, Moosehead and Electra, were left practically where they dropped. Today, years later, they are only slowly being obscured—their steel components surrendering to the succession of forest cover. Or, as in the case of the Ampersand tower, the remains are lying among the rocks of that mountain's north side. The helicopter assigned to remove it lost its sling load. I would hasten to point out that other towers, particularly those that were relocated, were treated more kindly (and legally). Various D.E.C. personnel spent long, hard and dangerous hours in taking down the towers, some 76 feet high, bolt by bolt.

Looking back at the history of the fire towers, it is clear that the early D.E.C. position was to close the fire towers, and in terms of cost effectiveness at least, it could be considered a prudent decision. In a 1989 study, only 4 percent, or 99, of the 2,383 fires statewide were reported by fire tower observers. That program cost $225,000 a year. Closing the towers became an easy determination – a slam-dunk, as today's youth would describe it. Except – hold on – what part of the equation was overlooked? Yep, you guessed it. Public indignation!

Few at the state level recognized that people had such a strong feeling for "their" fire tower. Here were childhood memories – a legacy of a romantic part of our history when the observer in his puttee-clad leggings and forest-green uniform would give you a card certifying "you have climbed xyz mountain." And the memory of peanut butter and jam sandwiches, comradeship, mountain spring water, stellar views, carefree youth and uncles, aunts, cousins and parents, now gone but not forgotten, who helped you climb that first mountain.

The plea to save some of the fire towers and not let them be lost as an important legacy of our past was loud and clear: STOP! That was the message and the D.E.C., sensitive to such concentrated and vocal objections, responded. They have been a valuable partner in the restoration efforts carried on by groups such as the Friends of Mt. Arab, the Azure Mountain Friends and current effort of people like these who want to save Owl's Head tower in Long Lake, etc.

Still remaining for inclusion in the history books is the chapter on which fire towers will remain. The access to Loon Lake's mountain near Onchiota is across private lands. Lyon Mountain is also private with little support to save the tower.

The fate of these towers is questionable. Hurricane, near Keene Valley, already has its lower stairs removed – it will most likely be taken down. St. Regis is on the list, but its removal is controversial, as many people want it saved. The tower on Mt. Adams seems almost certain to be removed. It is located on lands formerly owned by the National Lead Company. Purchased recently by the Open Space Institute with a potential transfer to ownership by New York State, it will become nonconforming under wilderness classification guidelines. I've looked at that mountain's severely steep profile many times over the years while driving along the old Tahawus Club road on the way to the various trailheads at the Upper Works. Yet, I had never climbed to its summit at near 4,000 feet elevation. With the tower's removal a certainty, I decided I'd better hit the trail.

As mentioned, the tower and the trail leading to it had been abandoned in 1971. Thirty-two years of neglect and poundings from windstorms had made this a trailess peak in the best definition of that term. It starts out easy on the trail to Hanging Spears Falls. It soon crosses the fast-flowing Opalescent River on a cabled suspension bridge and then quickly shifts to the swampy outlet of Lake Jimmy on a floating bridge of corduroy logs. What a challenge it must have been to log this place.

The point where my map showed the old Adams Trail bearing off to the NE was only a bulldozed log landing, the trail completely lost in an overgrowth of second-growth and berry bushes laden with ripe fruit.

Taking a bearing from the map, I plunged through the heavy cover, every so often discovering the imprints of an old skid road heading in the right direction until it turned on an old haul road that ran along a contour at right angles to my bearing. The route now went straight up 1,800 vertical feet in less than two miles' distance. Jumbled masses of fallen logs forced me onto the ledge drop-off of a steep mountain stream. Gone were the several ladders described in an early guidebook. The ascent became an unrelenting struggle that only ended when I came out on the narrow flat of dwarfed balsam that was steadily closing in on the summit, soon to engulf it completely.

There is no view from Adams unless you climb the tower. Therefore, I carefully ascended the stairs until finally, just before the trap door leading to the ruined tower camp, I discovered that the entire stair landing was missing, which halted my progress. The protective grids of wire along the stairs were also gone, which only added to my feeling of insecurity as the tower swayed in the wind. Holding tight to a steep support, I looked out at the view. It was pure magic—a wild, almost savage, scene of surrounding peaks rising straight to the sky like inverted ice cream cones.

Vaporous mist, not unlike the steam from a sugarhouse evaporator, rose from the forest basin below and was wisped away by the strong wind currents. It was as wild and memorable scene as could be imagined.

The tower on Adams has stood strong and noble since 1918. For almost 100 years, it has resisted gale-force winds, snow and ice, its structural integrity a tribute to its builder, the Aeromotor Windmill Company. However, it will soon disappear, the victim of both neglect and changing times. The mountain will continue to be seldom visited and will represent a true symbol, a sentinel of all that is really wild in the Adirondacks. A lonely place that will become once again a place "when silence was and not a word."

*Tupper Lake Free Press Print:* August 27, 2003

# Mining Across the Adirondacks

IN A RECENT *TRANSITIONS* COLUMN, it was noted that the Open Space Institute (O.S.I.) had reached an agreement to acquire 9,600 acres of land owned by the National Lead Company. The land located near Tahawus will be sold for $8.5 million.

The Tahawus operation was the largest open pit ilemite (titanium ore) mine in the world before certain market conditions forced its premature closing. At the height of its operations, few would have guessed that (along with Benson Mines near Star Lake) these important industrial giants, so vital to commerce and the daily lives of the many families involved, would ever become hauntingly abandoned and vacant, as is the case today.

The Sanford Pit at National Lead, 3,000 feet long, 1,599 feet wide and 300 feet deep, from which more than 80,000,000 tons of rock was mined, now lays idle, its very isolation and stark appearance not unlike photos of the moon's landscape. It is a sad ending to a once thriving place that employed many residents of this community and neighboring communities such as Long Lake.

It was a wonderful place to work—a happy family of engineers, electricians, millwrights, pipe fitters, mechanics and other skilled workers. It had vital, visionary, intelligent and caring management that fought hard to keep it operational, and it cared about the employees – their wellbeing and future.

If we look back into history, the discovery and production of iron in the Adirondacks has been a significant and important

Mining Across the Adirondacks / 447

*The huge stone furnace shown here was a part of the old Adirondack Iron Works. It was located at the head of Lake Sanford, near Tahawus. It stands 40 square feet at its base—as strong and firm as it was when made, nearly 160 years ago. (Bill Frenette photo)*

chapter. A brief look at some items of that chapter may be of interest to readers. We know, for instance, that the earliest settlers were aware of iron deposits. In fact, the Adirondacks were formerly named the Peruvian Mountains for Peru by the early French settlers in allusion to that country's mineral treasures. It was the same for the settlement, still known as Peru on the shores of Lake Champlain.

In my files is an 1858 map by Edwin Merritt of the Tupper Lake region. The map shows an Indian encampment of such permanency that it rated inclusion as a map feature. The encampment was located on what is today known as Indian Point, which is owned by the International Paper Company on Tupper Lake's west shore. As a youngster growing up on that lake, I was always told that, among other attributes, the Indians favored this location because a long reef (still there) allowed them to throw their fishing nets without the impediment of brush, etc., and they could more easily reach deeper water.

An account of a very early visit to this region by a writer for a sporting magazine tells how a family of Indians camped there took the writer and his companions to a bed of iron ore only a short distance from where today the Sorting Gap lean-to is located.

There were also iron deposits discovered on the aptly named Iron Mountain near Big Wolf Club property. Sometime before 1889 (and before Hurd's New York and Ottawa Railroad), Felix Trombley of Derrick made that discovery. Today the holes and pits of his short-lived operation can still be seen above the old railroad spur built by Brooklyn Cooperage to haul lumber from that area, now under lease to Township 19 hunting club.

The ridge northeast of Arab Mountain near Piercefield's Station Mountain has iron, and compass bearings can be influenced by its presence.

That same kind of magnetic influence led to the discovery of the Star Lake–Benson Mines ore body (Jones and Laughlin Steel Corporation). In 1810, engineers surveying for a highway between Albany and Ogdensburg found their instruments affected by magnetic ore, and those extensive deposits were thereby revealed. In its heyday, Jones and Laughlin Steel Corporation was to ship annually about one million tons of iron ore sinter from those deposits in Benson Mines to their plants in Pennsylvania and Ohio. They would employ over 500 people living in a 50-mile radius from the mines. In short, iron deposits became of paramount importance to the Adirondack economy.

The first forge was established near Plattsburgh in 1789. Many of the ventures were short-lived, but some of the present villages of the Adirondacks grew up around those early forges. In 1817, for example, a forge was unsuccessfully established near Brown's Tract in the central Adirondacks. The "old forge" became a landmark and, years later when a village grew up on its site, it became known as Old Forge.

Thirty miles from Tupper Lake a dam was built in 1811 on the Chubb River, very near what is today Lake Placid's beautifully restored railroad station. Here a substantial ironworks was erected on the present Power Pond. It was the creation of State Comptroller Archibald McIntyre and two partners, Malcom McMartin and David Henderson, and it was called the Elba Iron Works (the name Elba was derived from the Mediterranean island of Elba, noted for its rich source of minerals. That island would later become the place where Napoleon was exiled). The ore for the works was mined at Cascade Lakes, which motorists pass today on their way to Keene from Lake Placid.

That operation at North Elba lasted only six years—transportation and the quantity and quality of the ore were major obstacles to success. However, the principal owners never gave up their quest, no matter the financial risk and hardships involved. They would develop the McIntyre deposit that would lead to the giant National Lead operation many years later. We'll follow that adventure in the next *Transitions*.

*Tupper Lake Free Press Print:* September 07, 2003

# THE HISTORY OF IRON MOUNTAIN

IN A RECENT *TRANSITIONS* article, it was noted that the discovery and production of iron was an important and significant chapter in Adirondack history.

In the 1880s, mines in northern New York were turning out nearly one-fourth of the iron ore in the United States. By 1900, however, according to Floyd Hyde in *Adirondack Forest, Fields and Mines*, "activity in the Adirondack area entered a long decline and downgrade, and by the 1930s, it had become relatively unimportant in the nation's economy."

In a slender little volume entitled, *Camps and Tramps in the Adirondacks*, a rare booklet written in 1870 by Judd Northrup, a Syracuse newspaperman, the author offers an interesting note of explanation on why mining iron was so fraught with failure:

"This strange region is a vast bed of iron ore. Untold wealth is hidden in these mountains. Strong men have grappled with the problem of its removal; money and thought and skill and tremendous toil have been expended lavishly to that end, but all to no purpose. The wrecks are scattered here and there, monuments of ill directed energy and warnings against any future endeavor of the kind without the use of such modern appliances as shall absolutely conquer the stern resistance of this region to all attacks upon its treasures."

Good advice—but if you were Felix Trombley and you stumbled across deposits of iron ore on a nearby mountain, the compulsion to make your fortune had to be strong, no matter the obstacles. Indeed, so strong was the conviction that the mountain contained a rich lode that it was named Iron Mountain, located near a small settlement called Blue Pond (later Derrick), 12 miles from this village.

Trombley tried his best. A company was formed and excavation was started. However, insufficient transportation (Hurd's New York and Ottawa had not yet reached Derrick), primitive excavation tools and the remote location doomed the iron-mining project almost from the start, and it was short-lived.

About this time, Charles Turner of Potsdam-Malone arrived in Derrick and began lumber operations. The small village grew rapidly. A sawmill, shingle mill, lath mill and smaller structures were erected. Then followed the construction of churches, stores, hotels and homes. The U.S. Census of June 1905 reported 514 people living in Derrick that year. Such progress was not to last. Misfortune in the form of two severe forest fires, one in 1903 and another in 1908, devoured large amounts of valuable timber, and only rains that ended a 49-day drought saved the village. Mr. Turner closed his operations in 1910. Then followed another brief

*This gate near Floodwood provides access to the once ghost town of Derrick, which is now an oasis of recreation and clubs. It continues a rich tradition that serves to enhance the quality of life in this area.*

period in which iron mining reopened.

Mike LaPorte, a familiar figure in Derrick in those years, and Art LaPorte of this community, took out samples of ore, but to paraphrase Northrup: "All to no purpose. The region continued to sternly resist all attacks on its treasures."

In 1913, Charles Elliot started a mangle roller mill that shipped up to three carloads of hardwood rolls per week to markets abroad. Elliot only ran that mill for two years before he moved it to Tupper. In 1917, the Oval Wood Dish Company started another lumber boom at Derrick. A 19-mile railroad was built and logging operations flourished. But it died out after three years. In 1937, railroad service between Moira and Tupper was ended and Derrick began a steady decline, with many of its families moving to this community. Today, only one original building—a New York and Ottawa Railroad section house—remains, and Derrick became close to being on of the Adirondack's forgotten villages.

In 1980, however, a group known as the Township 10 Hunting Club leased property that included Derrick. (Note: The observations that follow are ones noted as I intermittently followed over the last two years the route of John Hurd's New York and Ottawa Railroad from Moira, near the Canadian border, to Tupper Lake – a vital part of our local history.) The club has a spacious clubhouse, neat and clean, with a well-appointed interior that includes a large fireplace and a gallery of related photographs. Comfortable seating arrangements sit on a height of ground overlooking Blue Pond, the centerpiece of the club's property. It is a communal place designed for members to meet and converse and to avail themselves, on weekends during the hunting season, of the offerings of the current chef de saison. Two roads intersect here: one from Floodwood was the original stagecoach road that brought guests from the station directly to the famous Saranac Inn, guest capacity 121. (In the late 1940s, when I caddied at that exciting place, it had grown to an 800-guest capacity.) The other road comes in from Tupper and follows exactly the former railroad grade. Both roads have gate attendants.

Small hunting camps are located randomly within the club's

boundaries and some can be found along the ponds, such as the Twin Willis Ponds, Mud Pond and Blue Pond, to name several. The club is managed by its members under enlightened guidelines. The surroundings are inviting and well maintained. Rules in place for deer hunting are based on Quality Deer Management techniques. The dues structure is modest (under $400 annually), and the club has a long waiting list for membership openings. Nearby is Spring Pond Bog, the second-largest open expanse of peatland (sphagnum) in New York. (The land where my grandmother was raised in Ireland was rich in similar peatland, and her family supported their farm by harvesting, drying and selling peat for fuel. It remains a valuable commodity there and in Scotland.) Efforts to harvest Spring Bog peatland for fuel and gardening purposes were sidetracked when the Adirondack Nature Conservancy purchased the site to "protect it in its natural, undisturbed condition for all to enjoy and study."

Gone today in Derrick is the high-pitched whine of the busy sawmills, some of which produced (in a 16-hour day) as much as 110,000 board-feet daily. Gone also is the rumbling clickety-clack, clickety-clack of four trains daily that coursed through the hamlet (early fare 5 cents a mile). Derrick is now a place of quiet, of recreation, a place to unwind and disconnect, and where – mirabile dictu – the natural beauty has remained. Blue Pond still reflects the color of the stately pines along is shorelines that, together with the unique mineral content of its water, produces the impossible cerulean blue that gave it is name. The sunsets over the great bog are as spectacular as Louis Grenier, a late Tupper Laker, who as a childhood resident of Derrick from 1899 to 1912, remembered them at age 90. In an oral interview, he said, "Derrick has the most beautiful sunsets that I ever saw in my life!"

*Tupper Lake Free Press Print:* October 08, 2003

## STILLWATER PLUNGE

IN A RECENT *TRANSITIONS* COLUMN there was a photo showing a train derailment that "reportedly" occurred on the NY & Ottawa railroad. Regretfully, this caption was in error. The date, April 12, 1925, was correct but the location on the derailment actually occurred on an embankment of the Stillwater Reservoir, which washed out near the Beaver River station of the New York-Montreal line. Today's railroad grade still hugs that embankment close to the dammed waters of the Beaver River. Many readers, especially those who are snowmobilers, will be familiar with the Beaver River/Stillwater location. The following account of that derailment, "The Montreal Express Goes Swimming," is from *The Fairy Tale Railroad* by Henry Harter. Hopefully, it will be of interest, and it is offered here to set the record straight:

"In 1924 there was a change made in the level of the Stillwater Reservoir. When the surveyors found that the new level of the reservoir would reach the tracks, officials of the Black River Regulating Board recommended that the tracks be re-routed around the end of the pond. This would also straighten out a curve in the road but the railroad questioned its right to go over the State Land. It was therefore decided to raise the tracks.

"At 12:24 a.m. on Sunday, April 12, 1925 southbound Montreal Express, train No. 43, was proceeding under a 'Slow order' across the newly raised fill when the embankment gave way and the locomotive slid off the embankment into Stillwater Reservoir in about

*The waters of the reservoir were lowered and in two days' time the locomotive, as shown here, was successfully raised and later rebuilt.*

15 feet of water. The mail and baggage cars followed the locomotive but were not totally submerged. About 200 feet of track was washed out. *The Utica Observer* dispatch said:

"During construction of the dam and the reservoir the New York Central was compelled to raise its tracks, so that the tracks would be many feet above the water level. Although no definite statement was given out it is thought by employees of the construction company that the materials used to bolster the tracks were not of sufficient strength."

The *Tupper Lake Herald* reported:

"The fill cut across a mere corner of the reservoir and it is subjected only to standing water. The banks when made first were covered with heavy granite riprap to prevent washing. The work was done in the winter which might have been the cause of its defective character.

"Engineer Elmer D. Kane and Fireman Charles Armstrong received minor injuries. They were pinned in the cab at first but worked their way free with Armstrong, a strong swimmer, practically rescuing Kane. They were assisted from the tank of the engine by a rope fashioned from Pullman sheets. Mail Clerk Daniel W. Bensley reached safety by the same method.

"Immediate steps were taken to pull the undamaged cars back to Tupper Lake where they would be rerouted over the Ottawa Division and sent down the Rome, Watertown and Ogdensburg to Utica. The train was composed of two New York Pullmans, two Buffalo Pullmans, a day coach, a combination coach and baggage car, a mail car and a baggage car. There were no reports of passenger injuries."

The *Tupper Lake Herald* described the repairs made and also the details on a second washout:

"A pile driver and a steam crane were run out to the middle of the fill to repair the damage and while working on it a second slide occurred leaving the heavy machinery marooned in the middle of the fill. The powerful vibrations of the pile driver no doubt contributed to the second slide.

"The work of repairing the damage proceeded night and day at the most rapid rate possible and regular passenger service was restored Thursday morning, April 16. This was at least 14 hours sooner than was thought possible. No further trouble is anticipated. The track will be gradually raised. The problem of salvaging the engine, embedded in mud and entirely submerged was postponed, until the fill had been repaired.

"Gates of the reservoir were opened to prevent further filling and slides and to permit work to proceed, thus temporarily delaying the complete filling of the great artificial pond built to store water for the industrial interests of the Black River into which Beaver River flows.

"The restoration of service in four days and ten hours was an extremely well done piece of work. Fill had to be brought in from a long distance. The total length of both washouts was approximately 800 feet.

"The locomotive was raised from its watery bed in the next few days and was sent to the shops for rebuilding. The fill was strengthened and brought up to the required height, service was restored to normal and once again the hazards of railroad life were a matter of history. The night that the Montreal Express went swimming at Beaver River was soon a nearly forgotten memory."

*Tupper Lake Free Press Print:* October 22, 2003

# LAYOUT OF THE NORTHERN ADIRONDACKS

THE YEAR WAS 1775. The revolt by Americans to win their independence from Britain had begun. Two years later, one of the major battles of that war took place in Northern New York. We know it today as the Battle of Saratoga.

Benedict Arnold, who had not yet turned traitor, was a leader of the American offensive that forced the surrender of the British troops. It became a turning point of the war because it increased the confidence of the French government in the American forces. They sent French ships and troops under the leadership of nobleman and soldier, the Marquis de La Fayette, which greatly aided the Americans' cause, and the war ended in 1783. The crown lands were now in American hands.

With the war over, the state decided to make an effort to dispose of the great tracts of unsurveyed and, to a large extent, unexplored lands in this area. There was a reason behind this. There was no certainty of continued peace with England. Feelings still remained intense. The British still hung on stubbornly, under one pretense or another, to many of their posts. The smallest spark could set the whole St. Lawrence border aflame once more.

According to historian Harry F. Landon, "It was probably with this in mind that State of New York decided to establish the first line of defense along the trails leading from Canada in the form of study settlers, who might be depended upon to fight at the drop of a hat when their homes were threatened." Consequently, Landon has noted, "The Board of Land Commissioners of the state directed the survey general to lay out 10 townships in the hope people would settle there—there were few prospects and practically all 10 townships were later sold to Alexander Macomb of New York, who had made a fortune in the fur trade with John Jacob Astor. Soon after this sale, the Indians ceded a large portion of their lands in this area to the state. The same Macomb, with two others (Constable and McCormack) purchased a large tract near here of nearly four million acres at a price of eight pence (cents) an acre. The purchase was divided into six great tracts: Tract #1, being in general, the present Franklin County; Tracts #2 and #3 being in St. Lawrence County."

The first order of business for these new landholders was to get their purchases surveyed so they could attract buyers. Thus, in 1791, Macomb hired two men, Medad Mitchell and a man named Tupper, to run the south line of Tract #2 of the Macomb Purchase. The two surveyed about 30 miles of that 50-mile line ending just short of the summit of what today is called Coney Mountain near Tupper Lake's south bay.

Their work completed, they set their course by the compass and started through trackless woods, hoping to reach Rome, NY (Note: you may ask, why Rome? The explanation is that one of the earliest routes by canoe and trail to the North Country, first used by the Algonquins, later by the Iroquois and, finally, by the white man – guided by the Indians—started on the Mohawk River near Rome. It went over the divide to the St. Lawrence and Canada. Later, surveyors used this route to the Raquette River, setting up supply camps as far up the river as Hanawa Falls as early as 1779.)

Instead of reaching Rome, they emerged at the High Falls on Black River—now Lyons Falls—and were forced to cross the river and proceed to the present Oswego County before they could locate themselves. These were excellent woodsmen, resourceful men accustomed to life in the woods—but what an ordeal that must have been. Yes, that surveyor named Tupper was allowed to name Tupper Lake after himself when they happened upon it near the place where they finished their survey. I bet most readers will agree that the christening was most fitting and deserving, and it gives our beautiful

lake a certain distinction of great historical importance.

That south boundary remains today (after four subsequent surveys) to establish its accuracy, as it was laid out 207 years ago.

Benjamin Wright, an engineer, later carried the line the remaining portion of 20-some miles to its corner at Preston Ponds. That line today crosses the road to Long Lake on Route 30 (there was no road there until 1918), where there is a parking space and snowplow turn-around (caution: this is a zoned tow-away from October to April). For an interesting short hike, you can follow this historical line east for a little over two miles distance. This easterly line is today part of the popular trail to Coney Mountain. Hikers using this trail will notice a steel girder embedded in the ground, splotched with yellow and red surveyor paint and an attached plate with the year 1903 inscribed on it. This survey marker, or monument, is #158 at 27.75 miles, one of almost 300 such girders, or I-beams, in the 50-mile distance of the original Macomb south property line.

*Shown above is the witness tree certifying the location of the boundary between Great Tract #1 and Great Tract #2 of the famous Macomb Purchase. Below is one of 300 such I-beams, or survey monuments, in the 50-mile distance of the south line of the 1791 Macomb Purchase.*

The designated trail to Coney's summit bears left a short distance above this marker, but if you continue east about 10 minutes to a saddle in the spiny ridge of Coney's painted blazes, you will find monument #159. Descend steeply here, still going east, and you will discover a double beam monument, #160. Before the county line was moved 7/10 mile west beyond Route 30 for funding purposes to build a new highway, this was the tri-country corner of St. Lawrence, Hamilton and Franklin counties and is the southwest corner of Mr. Litchfield's property.

Here, a large beech stub has the word "CORNER" spelled out along its length with surveyor paint. This is known as a witness tree in survey terms to mark the boundary between Macomb's Great Lots #1 and #2 and might be the original tree used in the early surveys, so it is of great historical significance. Webster's Collegiate Dictionary defines it as "something serving as evidence or proof: sign."

Beyond this point, it is private, but if you could follow it along successive girders, #161, #162, etc., you would arrive at the line's terminus (after crossing the Raquette River and going close to Noah John's old camp). You are now at Preston Ponds and the corner of Essex and Franklin counties. You won't find an original monument here, however, because the line ended in the pond. Preston Ponds are the source of the Cold River and have received much notice recently as part of the Open Space Institute's purchase of the so-called Newcomb Tract, with plans in place to make it part of the state's public land holdings.

This is Cold River country, where the Tupper Lake firm known as The Santa Clara Company once owned 400,000 acres. Here, for over 30 years, lumbermen from this community and associated with Santa Clara, timbered the steep mountain ranges and drove its rivers. It is a place rich in the history of Tupper Lake. Exciting, dramatic, phenomenal, even—it is an epic story of courage, skill and great dramas in the development of Tupper Lake, when lumbering was king.

More on Preston Ponds in the next *Transitions*.

*Tupper Lake Free Press Print:* November 05, 2003

# THE DAY THE WOODS BLEW DOWN
## A HUNTER'S PERSPECTIVE

IN THE LAST *TRANSITIONS*, mention was made of the south boundary of the Macomb Purchase. That line ended at Preston Ponds, recently purchased from the National Lead Company by the Open Space Institute, with plans in place to make it part of the state's public land holdings.

In early times, the ponds were referred to as the Upper, Middle and Lower Prestons. Lower Preston became known as the Duck Hole, and today's reference to Preston Ponds generally means Lower (formerly Middle) and Upper. All three are still connected by water with the outlet of Duck Hole spilling over a dam and becoming the Cold River, which flows 18 miles before it joins the Raquette River just downstream of Long Lake's outlet.

Many readers of this column know the Preston Ponds—Cold River area well. Indeed, a number of local nimrods, this writer among them, were hunting in that section the last day of the open whitetail season on November 25, 1950. Most of us will not soon forget it. That was the day of the Great Storm, the Big Blow or simply the Blowdown, as it was variously called. The winds picked up about midmorning that day, and when limbs and then entire trees started falling everywhere with terrifying crashes, day hunters like myself hit for home on the double. (Winds up to 100 miles per hour were recorded that night.)

Others, hunting further from the trailhead out of tent camps,

*Located quietly in a bay on Preston Ponds, this cabin, formerly owned by the National Lead Company, may be subject to removal under the new state ownership.*

were not so fortunate. Those hunters were marooned, locked in by a complete blockade of fallen trees. Amazingly, no hunter in the Cold River section was injured. It took one group, who traditionally used mules to bring in supplies to their Ward Brook site, three days using chainsaws and the mules' drawing power to clear their way and meet up with Tupper Lake forest ranger Delbert McNeil and crew coming in from Coreys direction.

The wind had come from the east and northeast, and the mature trees had grown wind-firm in the direction of the normal prevailing west winds. The soft woods, especially a lot of virgin spruce with their shallow root systems, suffered severe destruction from nature's sucker punch.

The Cold River-Preston Ponds area would never again be the same place. Thirteen thousand, seven hundred acres—100 percent down, another 10,000 acres, half of which were down

(Conservation Dept. Survey). The woods were an almost impenetrable jungle of twisted, toppled, jack-strawed piles of timber, so dangerous and so vulnerable to fire that almost all of the area was closed for five years. No hunting, fishing, hiking or travel of any kind. (You can imagine how anxious everyone was to get to some of the remote ponds when that authority against trespass was finally lifted.)

The next major change to our Cold River country came in the form of an amendment to the "forever wild" provision in the state constitution that decreed, "The timber on lands constituting the Forest Preserve cannot be sold, removed or destroyed." The Attorney General, with the approval of the legislature, gave the green light and the authority to the Conservation Dept. (today's D.E.C.) to proceed with salvage work "given the extreme fire hazard and the foolish waste of a valuable resource." Lumbering would once again take place in Cold River.

Contracts for lumbering were let on a bid process, the bids depending on estimates of pulpwood and the board feet of saw timber, hard or soft, that might be salvaged. A number of local loggers won contracts. Wilfred Madore would have a crew in the Raquette Falls section (today's Calkins Brook Horse Trail was one of his haul roads). Also bidding was the U.S. Bobbin and Shuttle, whose plant was then located, interestingly enough, near LeBoeuf

*The traditional water route to Preston Ponds, closed for many years, in now open to the public. Jim Frenette (left) and Peter Hornbeck pause on Henderson Lake to view Wallface Mountain and the famed Indian Pass.*

Street. Alfred LeBoeuf was a famed woods superintendent for the Santa Clara Lumber Company, which once owned most of Cold River (sold to the state in 1919).

In 1952, the Bobbin Company salvaged 120,000 cords in the Cold River and National Lead tracts (Barbara McMartin). They would close their Tupper Lake plant in 1953 after only four years here, during which time they employed as many as 100 people in addition to the 125 in their logging operations. Ed Bohin and his father had a sawmill above Coreys known as The Thick and Thin Lumber Company (not exactly a state-of-the-art mill). Roy Parent and crew would later push a road through from Coreys (Ampersand to Shatuck Clearing), a part of which is today's Cold River Horse Trail system.

Those are only a few of the local people involved in the salvage operation where, in earlier times, their fathers and grandfathers had earned the reputation of being unsurpassed with an axe or a team of horses and had "let the light in." The days when you stayed in a log camp all winter and each day, long before first light, woke up to the call of "Star Leve" (Get Up). A contraction of the French "C'est l'heure à lever"—it is the hour to rise.

The primary reason for allowing the lumbering operation was, of course, the fear of fire. The recent disastrous fires this fall in California provide proof that this was a genuine concern, and that the downed timber was tinder ready to ignite if there was a lightning strike in that remote country that would smolder and then burst into flame uncontrolled.

Next article—that nightmare becomes a reality.

*Tupper Lake Free Press Print:* November 19, 2003

## THE BIG BLOW OF 1950

IN THE LAST *TRANSITIONS*, it was noted that a number of hunters were in the Cold River interior when the land hurricane of 1950 hit the area and hit it hard. One of those hunters, blocked by fallen timbers in that "Big Blow," was the mayor of Cold River City, population one (Town of Newcomb, Essex County), the honorable Noah John Rondeau.

Noah had pretty much retired from being a hermit at this time of his life. In fact, he had spent part of that summer of 1950 at the Corey-Saranac Lake road intersection, where he had an exhibit. Later in August, he worked as a substitute Santa Claus at the North Pole in Wilmington.

That November, however, he returned to his old camp to do some hunting. His journal, left with his nephew, Chester Rondeau, as part of his estate, tells us that on the 14th, he shot a 200-pound, 12-point buck (he had seen the sun glint from the buck's antlers as it sneaked through the forest cover across the marsh):

*November 14, 1950*

"At Cold River—mild and cloudy, 9 a.m. I shoot from Town Hall door and kill a 12 point Adirondack buck. I knew nine of his beds —today two bullets took him almost instantly."

Eleven days later, Noah had an almost ominous feeling about the winds. Could it have been because he had lived so close to nature most of his life that he had a special sense, much like the creatures around his camp? At any rate, Noah decided to get out

*Louis Simmons, left, and Dave LaVoie smile for the camera in this March 1959 photo taken at Noah Rondeau's hermitage. Note that Dave is taller than the roof of Noah's main cabin. (Bill Frenette photo)*

of the woods and headed for the Avery Rockefeller in-holding on Ampersand Pond.

The Rockefeller family knew Noah. The caretakers, Frank Blanchard and this community's Lucien Martin were his friends. Lucien once told me that they had helped Noah many times over the years – giving him a ride on occasion, shuttling supplies where

Noah could pack them into his camp, providing him quite often with food, allowing him to stay overnight in a guide's cottage to break up his 17-mile walk to Coreys, and, in general, keeping an eye out for him, particularly as he got older. Noah's journal entry tells us about that day:

*November 25, 1950*

"Cold River—cloudy and fierce wind. Snow all gone. I re-canvas Town Hall. I find 1 gallon glass jug full of sugar hid since 1934.

"I walk eight miles to Donkey Lodge 4-7 p.m. Stop with Marcellus Hunters 7 p.m. to Ampersand Pond with Frank Blanchard... hunting season close."

A few notes in this entry might be of interest. Before the blow down, Noah could use a shortcut through a pass between Seymour and Seward mountains. An old haul road located there, built by the Santa Clara Company, was at that time still in good shape. It was known as Ouluska Pass (an Indian name for "a place of shadows"). Today, that pass is still complicated by the blow down and is seldom used.

Donkey Lodge, which Noah mentions in his journal entry, was the tent camp located on Ward Brook near the Ampersand Pond private gate. It was a traditional location used for years by a Syracuse group (Marcellus) that used mules to bring in supplies and to get their deer out.

Noah stayed over at Ampersand that night of the storm and the next day and, with the Ampersand caretakers and the Syracuse group, spent the next three days cutting a way out to Coreys.

As noted previously, the woods, following the 1950 storm, would become closed to the public. Lumbering and salvage would take place near Noah's old camp until March of 1956, when the state ended all contracts. As Maitland DeSormeau tells us in his book, *Adirondack Hermit*, "That edict (which closed the woods) plus the realization that he was then, at 67, too old to ever seriously consider the resumption of the uncertain ways of the wilderness, ended forever that phase of Rondeau's life." Note: Noah would never return to his old hermitage. In March of 1957, Louis Simmons, in com-

*His Honor, the Mayor of Cold River, sits in his favorite rocking chair. Noah made the chair from an old river driving boat that once belonged to the Santa Clara Lumber Company. (E.A. Harmes photo)*

pany with Dave LaVoie and this writer, visited his abandoned camp high on the bluff below Cold River Flow.

We didn't realize it at the time, of course, but the three of us would be almost the last people to see Noah's hermitage as it had been when he lived there. The very next week, just days before the spring breakup, when the log roads softened and became a morass of axle-high mud, lumberman Paul Crofut used his bulldozer to load Noah's main camp ("The Town Hall of Records," as Noah called it) for transportation on a log truck via Huntington

Forest on the Newcomb-Long Lake Road to the Adirondack Museum at Blue Mountain Lake, where it is currently on display in the Woods and Waters building.

It is just as well that Noah did not return to Cold River. Two years after the blow down, a tall pine near Noah's old site, which somehow survived the wind's onslaught and remained the highest thing around, served as a lightning rod that attracted a bolt from the sky.

Forest Ranger Earl Blanchard was standing on the porch of the ranger station at Shattuck Clearing, six miles below Noah's old place. He saw the lightning strike. First came wisps of smoke and then, suddenly, a monstrous cloud of more intense smoke that billowed into the sky, followed by a roaring inferno of fire. At a point four miles up the Cold River from Shattuck's, a fire started in the blow down. Earl immediately got on the phone and called George Youngs, the district ranger at Saranac Lake. Pieter Fosburgh summed up that disaster best when, in his book, *The Natural Thing*, he wrote: "And so at last it had happened. The nightmare that had been troubling our sleep for more than two years was now a reality; there was now a real fire in the blow down and where and when it would stop was anybody's guess. We've been expecting it. Now, let's give it the works."

Next *Transitions*: The state's master plan design to "give it the works."

*Tupper Lake Free Press Print:* November 26, 2003

# 1908 ADIRONDACK FOREST FIRES

THE CONTROL OF FOREST fires has long been the chief responsibility of the Dept. of Environmental Conservation (D.E.C.).

Over the years, trial and error and improved budgets corrected deficiencies and fine-tuned what is today pretty much acknowledged nationwide as a first-class fire suppression system.

It wasn't always that way. At the turn of the century, huge fires erupted in the Adirondacks. In 1903, following a long drought, the tinder-dry forests became unchecked, and roaring infernos of fire and smoke prevailed until rains finally came to the rescue and put out the fires. Over 428,180 acres of land were burned that year.

Five years later, in 1908, another disastrous fire year occurred that devastated more than 368,000 acres. Fires that were so hot that the very soil was so badly burned in some areas that no new forests would ever grow. The bare rock summits of nearby Coney Mountain, Hitchens, Graves and Grass Pond Mountains on the A.A. Low property, to name a few, are good examples.

The late Louis Simmons, former editor and historian, in his autobiography, tells of that 1908 fire:

"1908, the year of my birth, was also the year of some of the worst forest fires in the Adirondack history. They started during a long summer drought and continued until doused by autumn snow, burning over more than 368,000 acres. My mother often recalled how terrified she was that first summer here, when a pall of smoke from forest fires encircled Tupper Lake for weeks on end.

*The fire tower on Mt. Morris, located on private land, serves a different purpose today, but it is still as structurally solid as when it was erected in 1919.*

Sawmills were repeatedly shut down and the crews set to fighting the fires, which encroached on lumber yards and burned outlying buildings. Prayers for rain were offered in the local churches, and some residents had rafts and boats ready against the danger of fire destroying the village. Uptown Tupper Lake had been totally destroyed by fire less than ten years earlier and the memory was still painfully fresh. The neighboring village of Long Lake West, about 14 miles south of Tupper by rail, was wiped out by a raging forest fire that fall. My father was engineer of a rescue train which brought the residents out to safety. Old photos show the rails twisted by the intense heat, and the ties burned in the roadbed."

Long Lake West that Louie refers to was the railroad station for Long Lake. Stage lines connected it with Little Tupper, four miles away and Long Lake 18 miles away. The name was changed to Sabattis, a common Indian corruption of Jean Baptiste, in 1923. Sabattis was a famous guide and hunter, and the name change was in his honor.

Virginia Jennings of Long Lake has written a fascinating account of that 1908 fire entitled "The Day The Town Died", published in the

November 17, 1991, Sunday edition of the *Glens Falls Post Star*. Her father-in-law, Arthur Jennings, was just a baby when fire destroyed the town, and "his mother was so afraid that he would smother that she didn't save a thing except the baby." The next day, Virginia noted in her article, "The only living thing found was a horse burned to a blister—moaning in pain."

*Students of the New York State Ranger School at Wanakena relocated the obsolete fire tower on Tooley Mountain to Cathedral Rock on the school's campus at Wanakena and renamed it the Ranger Tower. It is open to the public.*

Destroyed in that fire was the village containing a dozen dwellings, railroad station, large hotel, store and storehouses belonging to lumber dealers, new electric plant, livery with accommodations for 200 horses, schoolhouse and large lumber yard.

Every structure was consumed. The horses in the livery had been turned loose before the flames reached the village, and they found safety in flight. Soon after the flight of the villagers, the 1,300 pounds of dynamite used in blasting out tree stumps exploded with a deafening roar that was distinctly heard at Nehasane, eight miles to the south.

These Great Fires, as they were called, of 1903 and 1908 became the catalyst for sweeping changes that became mandated improvements in fire suppression.

The job title, Fire Warden, now became listed as Patrolman—Ranger, and John Timmons in 1909 became the first in Tupper Lake to bear that title. Mr. Timmons was paid $75 per month. His job was to patrol the woods to stop fires before they started, or at least before they got out of control. He would also enforce new fire law regulations such as the requirement that branches be cut from all evergreen trees down to a three-inch diameter

(Top Lopping Law).

The next change was the adoption of a technique successfully used in Maine—observation towers. These towers located on mountain summits would be manned by an observer who would report any sign of fire. Map tables with a locator device called an alidade and an improved telephone system made this a major breakthrough in early detection, an important ingredient in fire control.

Most towers gave the observer a 15-mile radius of coverage. Eventually, 102 towers would be built. Today, only 28 towers remain standing as more effective detection methods eventually evolved.

The 16th Annual Commission Report of 1910 notes that the first of these towers or stations was built here in Tupper Lake at a cost of $928.84, and that six miles of telephone line was laid on Mt. Morris in July of 1909. This was a wooden structure and was replaced by a steel tower in 1919. Richard Giles of Moody was hired as the first observer ($60 a month, $12 extra for provisions if he lived on the mountain instead of going home each night).

Moosehead, near Childwold, had a 20-foot wooden tower built on its summit in 1910 with J.W. Hinkson as its observer. A steel tower was erected in 1916.

In 1911, a station and a telephone line that connected with the Bell Telephone Co. at the Childwold railroad station was established on Mt. Arab. A steel tower was erected there in 1918, and it remains as one of only two left of the seven originally built in St. Lawrence County. Note: Mt. Arab remains today one of the last stations that still has its standard design (look-alike) observer cabin intact (12x16 feet with asphalt strip shingles).

The cabin has been restored to its original construction, placed on the historic registry and maintained. This cabin is unique among observer stations that remain in the Adirondacks. Mt. Arab also boasts a full-time summer season summit steward, whose salary is met by contributions to the treasury of the energetic, spirited group known as the "Friends of Mt. Arab," chaired by Tony Gensel.

The next big change, according to Louis Curth in his seminal book, *The Forest Rangers*, was to abolish the position of patrolman and that of ranger to be created. The salary was to be $750 a month (the name came from Roger's Rangers of His Majesty's Corps, whose famous wood lore and courage helped the British turn the tide in the 1775 war against the French). In 1915, Earl Owen (later famous as a boat builder) of Wawbeek Ave., would be become Tupper Lake's second forest ranger, followed the next year by John Black, Sr. Other rangers that readers may remember are Ed Harvey (1919-1921), Del McNeil (1922-1950), Ed Reed (1967-1972), Clyde Black (1973-2001) and Scott Murphy (2001-present).

*Tupper Lake Free Press Print:* December 10, 2003

## THE ORIGIN OF TUPPER LAKE

IT WAS NOTED IN THE DECEMBER 31, 2003 issue of this newspaper that consideration is being given to bring a name change from Town of Altamont to Town of Tupper Lake. The following historical background may be of interest to readers.

Donaldson, in the *History of the Adirondacks*, explains for us the term "Town" by noting, "Towns are the political subdivisions of a county. Within their boundaries, the inhabitants have minor administrative powers—the care of roads, the schools, and the poor and like matters of community interest. They are always designated by a name as: the Town of Newcomb; also as one word, Harrietstown, Elizabethtown, etc. 'Townships' are purely geographical subdivisions of land and are designated by a number" (Township 19, Township 20, etc.).

Note: The Town of Altamont became a political entity in 1890, and its name reputedly came from the prominence of Mt. Morris within its boundaries (alta—high, mont—mountain).

Louis Simmons, in his definitive history of this community, *Mostly Spruce and Hemlock*, tells best how the formation of the town occurred:

"In 1808 Franklin County was set off from Clinton, its area substantially the same as today with the exception of a five-square-mile tract in Altamont, taken from St. Lawrence County in 1913 and annexed to Franklin so that a highway, in which St. Lawrence was not particularly interested, connecting Tupper

*The town minute books, fortunately still available for the years following the first meeting in 1890, reveal many problems facing the new Town Board. One deliberation concerned building a road and bridge to Moody, then accessible only by boat. In 1894, a log bridge was constructed, followed in 1898 by the iron bridge shown in the photo above. It was financed by a bond issue of $6,000.*

Lake with roads leading to Utica and Albany, could be completed. During 1808 four towns were formed comprising all of Franklin County—Chateaugay, Malone, Constable and Dickinson.

"Dickinson was, literally, the grandsire of Altamont, and the more patriotic and politically aware pioneers of this region who wanted to cast a vote, particularly in heated presidential campaigns, had to do it the hard way. The polls were at Dickinson Center, and they had their choice of a hundred miles or so if they went by way of Potsdam and Moira, or 35 or 40 miles on foot if they tramped through the woods. Isolation had its advantages, too. The early teachers who acquainted Tupper's few children with the mysteries of the three Rs didn't have to worry much about supervision.

"Seaver, county historian, notes that the school commissioner resided at Moira around 1880 and visited this district 'but once in six years.'

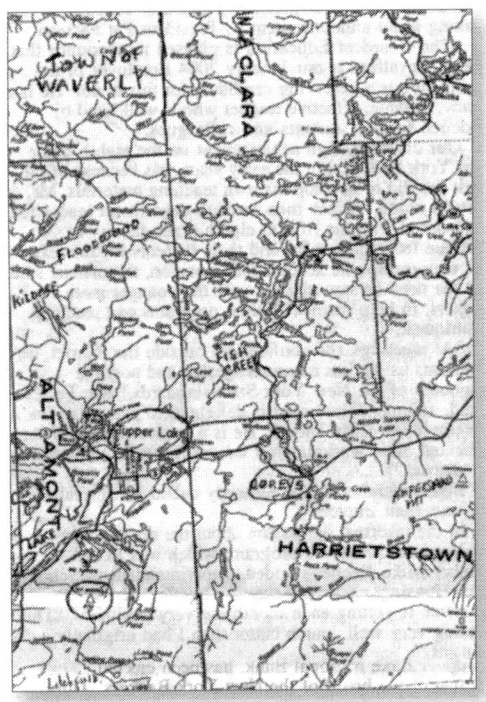

*The Town of Altamont boundaries are shown here. It is 15 miles on its N/S line, with an average width of five to six miles. It comprises an area of 76,168 acres with Mt. Morris, with an elevation of 3,163 feet at its highest point.*

"The pioneer settlers who swarmed in and cobbled together a village on the shores of Raquette Pond almost simultaneously with the arrival of Hurd's Railroad demanded—and got—their own local government. In 1890, the Town of Altamont was formed from the Town of Waverly, which had itself been set up only 10 years earlier, from Dickinson. Altamont then comprised three townships, or 76,168 assessed acres, to which was added a strip a mile wide and five miles long, taken from St. Lawrence County in 1913 for further road construction, as noted earlier in the account. Altamont was the last of Franklin County's 19 towns to come into being, and it proved to be a lusty baby. It had a newspaper by the time it was five years old, but unfortunately only a few scattered copies of the *Tupper Lake Herald* still exist dating back prior to 1911. They would have constituted an irreplaceable record of Tupper's growing pains."

*Tupper Lake Free Press Print:* January 07, 2004

## TUPPER LAKE WILDLIFE

I WAS HAVING COFFEE with Sonny Zurowski this week, and he mentioned how the wildlife had changed here over the years.

"We never had wild turkeys, and the ravens are more plentiful even in winter, and I don't ever remember turkey vultures this far north until the last couple of years," he said. He added, "There seems to be more deer on the outskirts of the village and in people's yards than I can remember seeing as a kid growing up here."

Sonny lives on the Racquette River, upstream from the Oxbow, a travel corridor for eagles, which is an occurrence that is also a wildlife change from just a few years ago. Indeed, 26 years ago, in 1975, the bald eagle was listed as "threatened and endangered." In 1961, there was only a single nest in New York State. This past year, 2003, a record total of 75 breeding pairs raised 87 eagles.

As a note of local interest, a nest in this area that successfully raised two young before the nest was blown out of its lofty perch 40 feet above the ground was not rebuilt this year. It is the opinion of the wildlife biologist involved that the birds simply chose to not nest last year. Or, if it was rebuilt, the new nest remained undisclosed, despite aerial surveys and field checks.

Some noteworthy items contained in the New York State Bald Eagle Report for 2003 may be of interest to readers of the column. It states as follows:

"During a visit to a new nest in territory #65 (Franklin County), upon climbing to the nest, we discovered not only two dead

*This is how a soaring eagle views the local landscape. The open water inlets and outlets of the many waters are prime feeding opportunities. Shown bottom right: McBride Pond with Lake Simond and Raquette River, center right. Tupper Lake center overlooked by Mt. Matumbia. (Bill Frenette photo)*

eaglets (approximately two weeks old), but one year-old immature male lying dead on top of the nest."

The pathologist reported injuries to the immature consistent with an attack by another eagle (talon puncture wounds). It would appear that this immature may have invaded the nest and killed the two young nestlings, then in turn, was killed by the resident adults.

We have witnessed immatures trying to access nests before, and it has been reported that they occasionally kill nestlings if not well guarded by the adults.

At another Franklin County site (NY #33), we had an interesting encounter with military jets during our annual banding visit.

While halfway up the 132-foot tree on June 10, three jets (believed to be A10s) doing low-level training runs "screamed" by. Of course, in response to the banding team, the resident adults were off the nest, soaring around it and vocalizing. During this brief episode, one of the jets passed directly over the nest tree and between the soaring female (lower, abut 100 feet above the nest) and male (soaring higher directly over the nest), bringing into stark focus the distinct possibility of such jets colliding with soaring eagles in their territories.

Perhaps also of local interest is that 21 bald eagles were recovered in 2003. Some of these were dead, others rehabilitated and released. Among the causes of injury and death were electrocution (3) (Note: landing on high-power lines) and also nestlings that succumbed to fishing tackle (3) (Note: parent birds would bring

*While the eagle has made a dynamic comeback from possible extinction, the Spruce Grouse, or partridge (often mistaken for the Ruffled Grouse) shown here is in peril, and its extinction is threatened. (Bill Frenette photo)*

in fish that had broken a fish line with attached lure still embedded in its mouth, and the young would get entangled in the monofilament—fall out of the nest or starve because their bills were locked or they were strangled). Two eagles fell from their nest, two were lead poisoned and two others were killed by another eagle.

This year a number of local residents have joined the over 100 other participants in New York's annual mid-winter Bald Eagle survey.

The purpose of the survey is to estimate the wintering population and to identify previously unrecognized areas of important winter habitat such as this area, which has been overlooked and underestimated by wildlife personnel. Local observers include Jim and Carol Richer, Lake Simond; Scott Chartier, Big Tupper Lake; Charlcie Delehanty, at large; Jim Frenette, Racquette River; and Jake Chartier, Middle Saranac.

Snowmobilers have also been a big help in the survey. One group directed this observer to a Bald Eagle feeding on a deer carcass on the former Draper lands along the South Branch of the Grasse River. Ice fishermen, especially along Lake Simond, have been more than cooperative by recording their sightings (eagles feed on the discarded minnow bait).

On a personal note, visiting with both the snowmobilers and the ice fishermen was one of the most pleasurable parts of the survey.

Here were people completely attuned to their environment. Each in his own way, albeit, different, enjoying to the fullest the benefits of living in the North Country during winter.

Buzz Dumas of Childwold and Scott McWhauf of the New York State D.O.T., based in Cranberry Lake, have also been of great assistance. Scott keeps detailed and knowledgeable entries, which lend great credibility to our state report.

Despite the severe low temperatures, several areas of open water have allowed observers to watch our local eagles rob otter of their fish catch. One observer's report read this way: "There was open water on the river, about the size of a pickup truck. An otter popped to the surface and flipped a good-sized fish onto the ice surface. Suddenly this beautiful bird with a white crown of feathers on its head and an immense wingspread of at least seven feet across, glided down, seemingly out of nowhere, snatched the fish and soared away. Time: 10:30. Date: January 10. Location: River below Underwood. Temp: 18 degrees F."

Yes, a tiny piece of wild animals' lives that, because we live in this special place, we are blessed to see! Tupper Lake lies in a unique area, conducive to wintering eagles. The many open water locations, like the Sorting Gap, Bog River Falls, Setting Pole Dam and the rapid water sections below Piercefield and Racquette Falls (to name just a few) allow the eagles to winter over here.

In addition, it would appear that there is increased deer kill on the highways and, of course, those unpolluted open water locations just mentioned have ample fish supply, a mainstay of the eagle's diet. All in all, this area provides favorable habitat to the eagle, which is not found everywhere, and we are richer for it.

*Tupper Lake Free Press Print:* January 21, 2004

# THE CHAIRLIFT—REVOLUTIONARY PEOPLE MOVER

IT WAS JUST ABOUT THIS time last year that I received a phone call from my daughter, Aimee, who lives and works in Idaho's Sun Valley.

"Hey, Pops," said the voice over the wireless that all young people seem to be using these days. "Stop whatever you are doing and get out here – the powder is up to my waist, the backcountry slopes have stabilized and the sun has been shining forever!"

Three days later, I found myself lathered in SP 45 and dressed only in windpants and a T-shirt, standing on the loading platform at Sun Valley's Baldy Mountain, a wonderful, hardcore skier's paradise, waiting to be whisked straight up one mile to the 10,000-foot level for a gain of 3,200 vertical feet. (Note: Averell Harriman, who founded Sun Valley, later became governor of New York State in 1954. His influence and driving support resulted in the construction of Whiteface Mountain Ski Area, which has gradually become a first-class ski area and successful destination resort.)

The ski lift was a new one of a type skiers call a "quad," so named because it carries four skiers at one time in padded seat comfort up the mountain at a speed not thought possible only a few years ago. There is also a lift called a "six pack," which allows six skiers to be carried up the mountain at one time for even greater efficiency and cost effectiveness in transporting skiers and reducing lift lines.

*Sophisticated technology has resulted in operational units that resemble a space ship. Shown above is a "quad" chairlift. Aimee Frenette and her mom, right, wait patiently for the photographer before descending the mountain. (Bill Frenette photo)*

Corrals with narrow wands, not unlike subway turnstiles, keep skiers four or six abreast, depending on the lift. The wands automatically lift, allowing each skier to move forward as the chair in front departs, and your chair bolts around the turntable only by some technological magic from remarkably slow to a creep as it gently touches you at the back of your knees—a signal to sit back as the chair regains acceleration at a dizzying speed to take you, tout de suite, up the mountain.

The chairlift design has improved greatly since a single chair (hence the name) was hung from a moving cable, and it was here at Sun Valley that the very first device was installed. If you are a long-time skier who grew up skiing down a hill and having to laboriously walk or ski back up, or have experienced the primitive arm-tugging, muscle-straining rope tows, such as the early one at Manning's Hill here, you can appreciate how innovative, how amazing and how important the chairlift was to skiing, and how it propelled the sport into the modern age.

Sometimes we forget the pioneering efforts of those before us, or perhaps tend to ignore the historical and chronological events involved, or simply are not aware if we happen to be new to the sport.

What follows is an excerpt from an article, "Going Up", which appeared in the February 2004 issue of *Ski Magazine*, and which best illustrates how skiing was transformed by the brilliant development of the chairlift. It was written by long-time ski racer, photographer and one of the world's best-known ski movie producers, Warren Miller—a legend in the world of skiing. The excerpt follows:

"A pickup truck, a clever railroad engineer and a pair of roller skates transformed skiing one dusty day in Omaha. Skiing forever

*Needing to know the speed at which a chair could scoop up a skier, engineers attached a boom to the back of a pickup truck and a chair was suspended from it, as shown in the photo above. (Bill Frenette collection)*

changed in 1936 when a Union Pacific Railroad engineer invented the chairlift to move skiers uphill at Sun Valley, Idaho. Not coincidentally, Averell Harriman, owner of the Union Pacific, also founded Sun Valley to help fill his passenger trains.

"Finally, you could ski downhill all day long and never have to climb back up. You could just sit down in a moving chair and be hauled back for as many rides as your strength, skill and money allowed. And all of this for only a couple of dollars a day.

"When it was decided to build Sun Valley, one of Harriman's first memos called for mechanical devices to take people to the tops of the slides. Engineers in Omaha, Neb., home base of the railroad, immediately went to work on variations of the ropetow and J-bar, invented in 1934 and 1935 respectively.

"A young railroad engineer named Jim Curran, who had helped build equipment for loading bananas onto fruit boats in the tropics, was a member of the railroad team assigned to the task. To him, transporting skiers or bunches of bananas without bruising them presented the same problem. All Curran did was replace the banana hooks that hung from a moving cable with chairs for people to sit on.

"By July, a mock-up of the chair was built in the bed of a pickup truck in a railroad yard in Omaha. Timbers were hung out over the side of the truck. Attached to the boards was a free-swinging pipe. The chair seat was welded to the pipe and was the same distance off the ground as a normal chair with legs. Curran's team thought they could drive the pickup with the chair facing forward and scoop up a waiting skier. Driving the truck at various speeds, they could eventually decide which speed was the best to collect skiers without injuring them.

"They had less than five months to design, build and test the chair before Christmas, when they were to begin hauling paying passengers. A decision on the design had to be made quickly, so expert skier John Morgan was summoned. He arrived with skis, boots, poles and woolen ski clothes. He had to feel silly sweating amid the steam engines and a handful of railroad engineers. At first, Morgan stood on a pile of straw as the truck drove up slowly and tried to scoop him up. Straw proved not to be slippery enough, and Morgan picked himself up a few dozen times. At lunch, someone suggested, "Why not add some oil to the straw?"

"They did, and now John had oily straw stuck to the bottom of his skis. Then a junior engineer suggested, 'Let's try roller skates. There's concrete out by the roundhouse that we can drive on.'

"A couple of hours later the maximum speed for loading live bodies on a chairlift was decided—a speed that is still used in chairlift designs today. In the railroad machine shop, fabrication of the various parts began as soon as they were designed.

"While this new device was under construction, Sun Valley's publicity genius, Steve Hannigan, gave the remote Idaho tramway a name that is as famous today as the sport it serves. Looking to project a favorable image, Hannigan called the new people-mover a 'chairlift.'

"Not bad for a new revolutionary means of winter transportation invented in Omaha by railroad engineers who had never skied a day in their lives."

*Tupper Lake Free Press Print:* February 11, 2004

# A Town of Descriptive Names

IF YOU LOOK CLOSELY at the area between the fire department building and the United Community Church, located on High Street, you will notice a set of crumbling cement stairs. Those stairs once provided an easy and direct way—a shortcut, if you will—to access Tallman Hill, Arden Street and a section of the community known as French Village. It should be pointed out to more recent residents that French Village was not a separate village as the name would imply, but was a descriptive term. It described a section of the community that roughly encompassed Arden Street south to Stetson Road and was bounded by Church Street and Chaney Avenue. I'm not sure why it was labeled French. People living in that section were no more or less French than those living in other sections of the community, whose population consisted of many residents of French descent. The French language was commonly heard throughout the village. Sermons at the Catholic Church, for example, were given in French as well as English, and most storeowners found it convenient to be bilingual in the early days of this village.

Other sections of the community, also with descriptive names, now mostly fallen into disuse, are easier to explain. Sears Hill, for example, meant the section of town roughly from above the present Day Wholesale building on Park Street to the water tank above Shaheen's Market. It was called Sears Hill after an early settler, Richard Cyr (later anglicized to Sear). Mr. Sear owned a large

*Tupper's Town Hall was fully engulfed when this photo was taken in March 1942. In the center, water is being directed though the window in the library. Note the bars on the window next to the library where the jail was located. The beautiful building was totally destroyed.*

boarding house at the brow of the hill leading up Park Street, and the name Sear's Hill was applied to that district. As years passed, the possessive case was dropped and it became simply Sears Hill. That boarding house was destroyed in the great 1899 fire, and A.F. Carbary built a large home on the site. Many descendants of the Sear family still reside as prominent citizens here.

Another section that described a certain area in earlier days was known as Sissonville, site of the A. Sherman Lumber Company, located midway between uptown and the Junction, and it is presently an open field bordered by tag alders and Racquette Pond shoreline. It was named after the Sisson family, who owned the A. Sherman Lumber Company and the Racquette River Paper Company. Charles Sisson, who managed the Tupper operations, was elected Tupper's first mayor in 1902. The local A. Sherman Lumber Company site was acquired by the Oval Wood Dish Company (O.W.D.) that took over some of the former A. Sherman Lumber Company buildings in 1916 for much-needed employee housing. Many were remodeled. Additional houses were built and two residential streets, Ohio and Michigan, were laid out.

Note: The O.W.D. firm was organized in Delta, OH, and started manufacturing in Mancenola, MI, in 1883, accounting for the otherwise puzzling reason for these street names. Most of those houses, except the girls' dormitory, had been removed by 1964, when Adirondack Plywood purchased the mill site and plant of the O.W.D. Corp.

The United Community Church, previously mentioned, still today borders that stairway, but in the 1940s it was known as Grace Methodist Church. Later, in 1971, the congregation of the Tupper Lake Methodist Church and the Tupper Lake Presbyterian Church united to form one congregation and the name was changed. The original church located there, which had been built in 1891, was destroyed by that August 1891 fire that consumed the village. It must be remembered that following the disaster most of the church members had themselves become homeless. The original church lay in ashes, and it must have been a discouraging, trying time. Yet, by February of the next year (six months' time), a new church of brick veneer and slate roof stood on its present site. Insurance coverage of $2,600 and monetary subscriptions helped cover the $5,000 cost with only a $200 indebtedness on the church property. This was soon retired, allowing the church to be totally free of debt for the first time in its history.

Adjacent to the church, where the fire hall is located today, was the town hall. This had been the headquarters for the fire department since 1901. That great building, so rich in the memories and history of this village for over 40 years, was totally destroyed by fire on March 14, 1942. As you might imagine, Tupper Lake firemen took a lot of good-natured kidding from neighboring fire fighters on that one—a little humor mixed in with dismay and sadness of that loss.

I grew up practically next door to that town hall and knew it well. It was the center of all sorts of activity in the village. Built shortly after the 1899 fire by a contractor named Howard Wert, who was a prominent local builder, it was a stately, beautifully designed building. In later years, when Dr. E.M. Austin was the

*Shown is one of the A. Sherman buildings that, once remodeled, became part of the 1916 O.W.D. employee housing at a location known as Sissonville. The gent on the left is Jerry Hull, who started as timekeeper and bookkeeper on the construction project, and who would later head the O.W.D. operations here for many years.*

town supervisor (1904-1910), 30 feet of extra space was added by cleverly extending the rear of the building over the rock wall of Tallman Hill. That four-foot high foundation of large stone construction was so well built that it remains today, almost 100 years later, as sound as the day it was built. Located to the rear of today's fire hall, it is worth viewing for its historical value and its masterful workmanship.

That extension (not utilized as part of today's fire hall footprint) doubled the size of the stage and dressing room space and increased the seating capacity of the main floor for viewing the many theater productions and other events held there. It also provided a first-class basketball court when the many folding seats were placed along the wall—a chore, incidentally, that neighboring kids never objected to undertake so they could use the court. Many of those kids, thanks to those Saturday morning basketball games, became outstanding players in their later high school days. Former Mayor Bill Delair, for example, developed a deadly reverse shot from the keyhole in those days that always bewildered the opposition in later years when he was a standout varsity player.

The lower floor housed the fire department trucks and hoses. Above was the town clerk's office with its 15-ton safe, filled with valuable papers and records of vital importance (still in use today— it was rescued from the 1942 fire, all papers intact). There also was the town welfare office, fireman's room, meeting place and voting space for three districts of the uptown sector of the community. If that wasn't enough, the building also contained a jail, under Chief Timmons, and the library, under the guidance of that wonderful lady, Mrs. Jennie Bruce. It was Mrs. Bruce who first succeeded in having the library registered under the New York State Education Department, after which all books were accessioned and cataloged under the Dewey Decimal System. We can only imagine the horror Mrs. Bruce must have felt that March day, exactly 62 years ago, when all 6,000 of those painfully acquired books owned by the library lay in a sodden mess among the ruins of a burned-out town hall building.

*Tupper Lake Free Press Print:* March 10, 2004

# FRENCH VILLAGE

IN A RECENT *TRANSITIONS*, the question was raised as to why a certain section of our community became known as "French Village."

Former Town Clerk Lou Marconi called me this week with an idea: "Is it possible," Lou asked, "that the name came about because of the Canadian Hotel located in that section?"

Now, it so happens that the origins of place names can be an elusive pursuit, especially those names that have been around for many years, so I listened carefully to Lou's theory.

Note: Few people know our local history as well as Lou Marconi. Her keen eye, sharp memory and love of history have often aided this amateur, your local historian.

Now retired, Lou is currently working on a book (leisurely, she told me) that is a recollection overflowing with wonderful memories of when, as a young girl, she and her friend, Rena, spent the entire summer at her father's lumber camp near remote Brandeth Lake country.

The book, which is a work in progress, also simmers with hands-on knowledge of draft horses, tote roads, work ethics, train rides and much more.

Lou's father, Albert Brooks, was a prominent early lumberman here, and he graduated from being one of the best river drivers of his day to running many large, successful wood operations, fulfilling his wish to one day "be his own boss."

Here is a portion of Lou's introduction in the first draft of her book, which gives us some insight of why she is recording those memories: "The days of the lumber camp will never return.... I wish that my children could have experienced life in a lumber camp as I did as a child. I would like to share my memories of a bygone era with young people who will never experience and perhaps never heard of a lumber camp."

So let us return to exploring the Canadian Hotel idea as the reason behind the name "French Village."

Readers will note that Canadian was spelled in French with an "e" rather than an "a." We can begin by noting that in the early days of that hotel, Tupper Lake was the acknowledged "lumbering capital of New York State."

There were many different ethnic groups working in the woods at that time, especially during the beginning of the European war (1914-1918): Lithuanians, Poles, Russians, etc., many sent here by labor-recruiting agencies. However, French Canadians dominated the work force.

In these periods between jobs, such as the spring mud season, when lumber roads were unfit for travel, or waiting for the sap to begin running so the peeling of the hemlock bark (used to tan leather) was easier, or simply waiting for "ice out" so the river drives could start, many of those French Canadian "Jacks" almost exclusively crowded the Canadian Hotel to capacity.

The Brooks family home was next door to that hotel. Lou has told me that she remembers hearing that the reason for the hotel's great popularity was because, though modest in size, it was large in hospitality.

Mr. Gauthier had himself been a lumberjack and spoke fluent French, and he was well liked and respected. Mrs. Gauthier, the former Mary Provost of Redford, NY, was an excellent cook, set a bountiful table and maintained a clean and orderly premise.

It would seem quite natural that this section of the village would be referred to as the French Village, and it gives strong support to Lou's theory of how the name became established. Place names are changed often, and trying to trace their origin can be interesting.

There's room left in this column, so let's expand on that fact as a further piece of history.

In the formative years around 1900, village fathers listed four descriptive sections. One section was called Faust, which was the name given to downtown Tupper Lake. That name came about because the postal department objected to the name Junction when a post office was to be established there. Goethe's Faust was the operatic hit of the day, and that name was selected for the new post office. It was never a popular name and, except for governmental matters, most people used the original name of Junction, thus named because Dr. Webb's Adirondack and St. Lawrence Railroad (later, New York Central Adirondack Division) and Hurd's Northern New York Railroad (later, New York and Ottawa) intersected, or "junctured," at that section of town.

The second section was called Sissonville. This was a cluster of homes and buildings on the site of the A. Sherman Lumber Company, which was owned and operated by the Sisson family. It was midway between uptown and downtown Tupper Lake, along what was known as the "Junction Road." This road was later renamed Demars Boulevard in honor of Leon Demars. Mr. Demars was an officer of the Santa Clara Company. He was also town supervisor (1918-1932) and a highly respected and influential member of the New York State Assembly.

A third section was named Lake View because it offered, in those days, a full view of Racquette Pond. That name soon changed to Sears Hill after Richard Sear (Cyr), who owned a large rooming house on a height of land across from the present Day Wholesale warehouse.

The fourth section described by village officials was called Mt. Morris View. That name was short-lived and, as we have seen, soon became French Village, located roughly between Arden Street and Stetson Road and bounded by Church Street and Cheney Avenue.

In 1926, fire totally destroyed the Canadian Hotel. Fire records placed the loss at $35,000, a devastating blow since the owner carried only $2,500 insurance, which was nearly all used up in clearing the mass of debris from the basement and repairing the foundation. Undaunted, Mr. Gauthier, with help of his two sons, ages 14 and 16, spent the next two years rebuilding. They did most of the work themselves, aided by a $15,000 inheritance left to Mrs. Gauthier. That 14-year-old boy was the late Hubert Gauthier, the father of Theresa Gauthier and Chalice Gauthier Dechene. The result was an imposing three-story structure of concrete and brick construction containing 24 rooms that they named The Northland. In 1935, Charles Abdallah, businessman from the Sears Hill sector, purchased the hotel for a reported $32,000.

Mr. and Mrs. Abdallah made many improvements, including an upscale dining room that earned the hard-won prestigious Duncan Hines endorsement, and with Charlie running the bar and Mary reigning over the kitchen and dining room, the hotel under the new owners remained popular and successful. In 1963, the hotel was sold to Mr. and Mrs. Alex Kulpecsha. Successive owners/operators were Lance Galvin and Ed Magedson, who ran it as a rooming house. On February 2, 1990, it was bid on at a foreclosure auction by Mrs. Albert (Clara Kulpecsha) LaLonde. Later owners also included the R and G Realty Company, and a sale is currently pending.

*Tupper Lake Free Press Print:* April 07, 2004

# GUNK HOLING LITTLE WOLF LAKE

CANOEISTS HAVE A STRANGE expression called "gunk holing." I have no idea where it originated, but it means canoeing on out-of-the-way set backs, flows, beaver impoundments and the like.

Places like this abound on the Racquette River below Axton. Set back from the normal canoe route are hidden coves and backwaters, some with names like Four Corners, Oxbow, Follensby Marsh, Trombley's Slough, Long Draw and Short Draw, to name a few. These are often transitional zones, called eco-zones in biological language, where one habitat meets another and both are rich in species.

"Gunk holing" also includes out-of-the-way streams and creeks, some of which appear at first glance to be unnavigable, only to discover to your surprise that after a few turns down the crooked course of the stream, the canopy of twisted alders opens up, the water deepens and beaver dams downstream have flooded a marsh that still allows passage.

Here is the perfect, tucked-away sanctuary that is a magnet for species ranging from herons to otter to osprey, all seeking vulnerable fish in the shallow waters.

Another bonus with "gunk holing" is that often these obscure places are close by, and it becomes easy to drop your canoe in the water and spend a pleasurable hour or so without the demand of extra time and travel. Add to that the fact that many of the creeks are fast-flowing and narrow, and they are the first to become ice-free. And while the lakes and ponds are still frozen, you can put your ski poles away, put your Skidoo on blocks, pick up your paddle and go canoeing—something your downstate friends have been doing for weeks.

One interesting paddle, which is nearby when early spring conditions prevail, is to go down the outlet of Little Wolf Lake to where it empties into Racquette Pond, which will most years still remain ice-locked until the middle of April. Put your boat in the

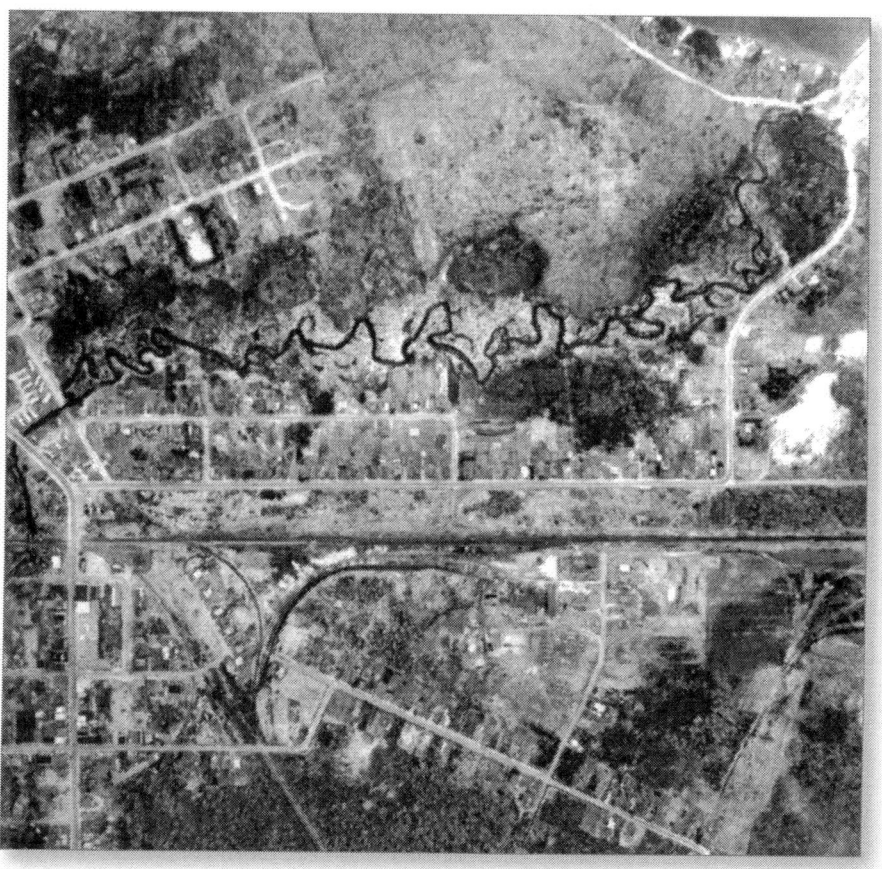

*A corner of Little Wolf Lake is shown at the top right in the picture above. The outlet winds its curvy way across the photo until it leaves the camera's view under the railroad bridge near the Junction's Main Street railroad crossing, shown at lower left. Prospect and Murray Streets are pictured at top with Pine and Cedar streets located at bottom.*

water just below the dam that controls the water level in Little Wolf Lake at the intersection of Coney Beach Road and South Little Wolf Road. The water level below the bridge at that location should be even or no more than slightly below the abutments under the bridge for best boating conditions (or it may be too shallow). Paddle under that bridge just below the dam, duck under a few alders, pick up the added flow from the entry of Lead Pond's outlet and you are soon spirited along on a nice current. Don't let the stream's many curves discourage you—they will improve your boat-handling skills.

On a recent trip, I noticed almost at once, many peeled sticks or cuttings left by beaver after they had peeled the bark to get at the more nutritious inner layer. Most of these were along the shore, where the beaver had dragged them from inland to the water's edge for greater safety and escape. Here they would roll the sticks with "fingers," chewing off the bark, just as we eat corn on the cob. Thus I wasn't too surprised to exit a curve in the outlet's flow and enter a large flooded area—a sign that the beaver had built a dam downstream. All things being equal, that dam could drastically change this stream into a pond, which eventually would become a meadow and create a whole new ecosystem.

As we sorted out the maze of water channels, seeking the main one in this flooded area, a great blue heron with its lumbering wing beat rose from a mound of marsh grass and landed in a tree. Three goldeneyes, our earliest spring visitors in the duck family, beat the water with a noisy take-off splash. If I mentioned that an osprey at this same moment soared over, you'd no doubt call me a liar, but that's what happened.

The first of what turned out to be three beaver dams was soon encountered. That dam and the next were built to a height only slightly above water level, which allowed the canoe to slide easily over the mass of sticks and mud.

The third dam had been built up to a height some two feet above water level, the butt end of the branches facing downstream and the wide ends acting as a snag to catch debris, which the beaver had arranged across the stream. This dam required stepping out of the canoe, standing on the dam and pulling the canoe over.

Not far downstream from this dam, you will pass under the second bridge of the five bridges on this short canoe trip. Along with two others of the five, this bridge has historical significance, even though its original structure has been modified with steel girders and a county plate identification number.

The bridge is significant because the village of Tupper Lake was almost non-existent until a gospel-preaching, hardheaded, daring businessman named John Hurd reached that site with his railroad construction crews in late 1889 and set the stage for the settlement of this village with his Northern New York Railroad (later, the New York and Ottawa).

That rail line needed to cross Little Wolf outlet, and that bridge today serves auto traffic on what is called Wolf Avenue. An extension of that avenue, called (appropriately enough) Hurd Avenue, follows the original rail line that came via the Kildare Road from Moiria, 53 miles away, and ended 1.7 miles further at a handsome passenger station at the end of Cliff Avenue, near Flanders Park.

Stagecoach timetables from 1896 to 1909 show connections between Hotel Wawbeek (now the Stiles residence) on Upper Saranac. The steamer Altamont, run by the Tupper Lake Navigation Company, connected with the train to serve resorts on Big and Little Tupper lakes, including the Tupper Lake House, Moodys and Camp Welcome on the ledges above Bog River Falls.

One of the first houses to be built in the Junction at the time was Murray's boarding house near Washington Street and close to where the tracks crossed that street. Here, most of the construction workers found board and room, and it was only a short walk to one of the other early buildings, a rough and ready saloon called "The Burning Stump."

These were rough and tumble frontier town days, as real as any in the storied West.

Seaver, the historian, gave us a graphic description that bears reprinting: "At once with the completion of the railroad, settlers began to arrive in considerable numbers and founded industries, established stores and opened hotels. The growth was marvelously rapid for a wilderness town, but raw and tough at first."

John Hurd was probably more responsible than any other individual for the founding of this village, and he rates a big "thank you" when you pass under or over his former railroad bridge on Wolf Avenue.

*Tupper Lake Free Press Print:* April 21, 2004

# 1934 BRIDGE TO NOWHERE

IN A RECENT *TRANSITIONS*, a boat trip down Little Wolf Creek as far as the former New York Ottawa Railroad bridge on Wolf Avenue in the Junction was described. We continue that boat trip in today's column. The creek continues under yet another bridge, one that allows traffic to cross on Route 3 near Vern Friend's Auto Repair.

Stay center in the river under the bridge and then river right as the passage narrows and the current accelerates you along for a short distance to bridge #4 of the five bridges on that route, the New York Central Railroad crossing that bears the date 1927 on its underpinnings. The original bridge was built in 1891 by Dr. Seward Webb's railroad crews as they were laying rails north and south from Utica and from Malone.

Older residents will remember the pump house along the tracks above the bridge that pumped water from Little Wolf Creek into twin towers adjacent to the Main Street crossing (now under repair), where locomotives could take on water. Those tall towers were familiar landmarks until they were taken down in the late 1950s.

Mr. St. Onge was, for many years, the operator and custodian in the pump house building there, and veteran railroader John Amoriell has told me that on his lengthy walks inspecting the track on foot, he would sometimes seek refuge here to chat with St. Onge and get warm on the many below zero days in winter.

Dr. Webb's crew laid 3,000 ties to the mile here, 400 more per mile that the standard. That was a wise decision because Tupper Lake engineer Willie Roumonado, in later years, freight-hauled a record 100 cars with his UMI Diesel across this rail bed (Willie was fire chief of Tupper Lake in 1938-39 and retired from the railroad in 1952 after 37 years on the job).

The creek now flows alongside the well-tended grounds of the Savard property and goes under bridge #5, located on what is called Pine Street extension. From this point, at some earlier time, the former winding creek underwent a major "face lift." In what must have been a work-intensive effort, it now becomes a straightened, almost canal-like, stream – wider and deeper, hugged by a lush marsh on both sides until it empties almost unannounced and hidden as it braids unobtrusively through the grasses to become part of the Racquette River.

Here, dear readers, is a puzzle. Who straightened this crooked stream? And how? And why? One more question: etched into the concrete wall of that Pine Street bridge is the date 1934. Huh? How is that correct? And if it is, why was it built?

The bridge serves only two structures: one a handsome home on a road that soon dead ends in a twisted mass of alders, and the other, today's town garage building – an orderly, neat-appearing complex that is a credit to the town crew that maintains it. That building didn't exist until it was constructed in 1960, 26 years after the bridge was built. You may remember that the building was financed by a successful funding effort conducted by the Greater Tupper Lake Industrial Development Corporation. An item in the November 10, 1960, *Tupper Lake Free Press* tells us that it then became the new factory to house the expanded operations of the North Country Manufacturing Company, which was expected to employ up to 200 people, mostly women, to make dresses for the parent firm, the Helen Whiting Company. Rod Beaulieu won the bid at $92,593 for the construction of the 70-ft. x 183-ft. building, with an interior that stretched 180 feet of clear span without a pier or post. The dress factory operated until 1972, and then it was sold to the McDonald Steward Textiles of Montreal.

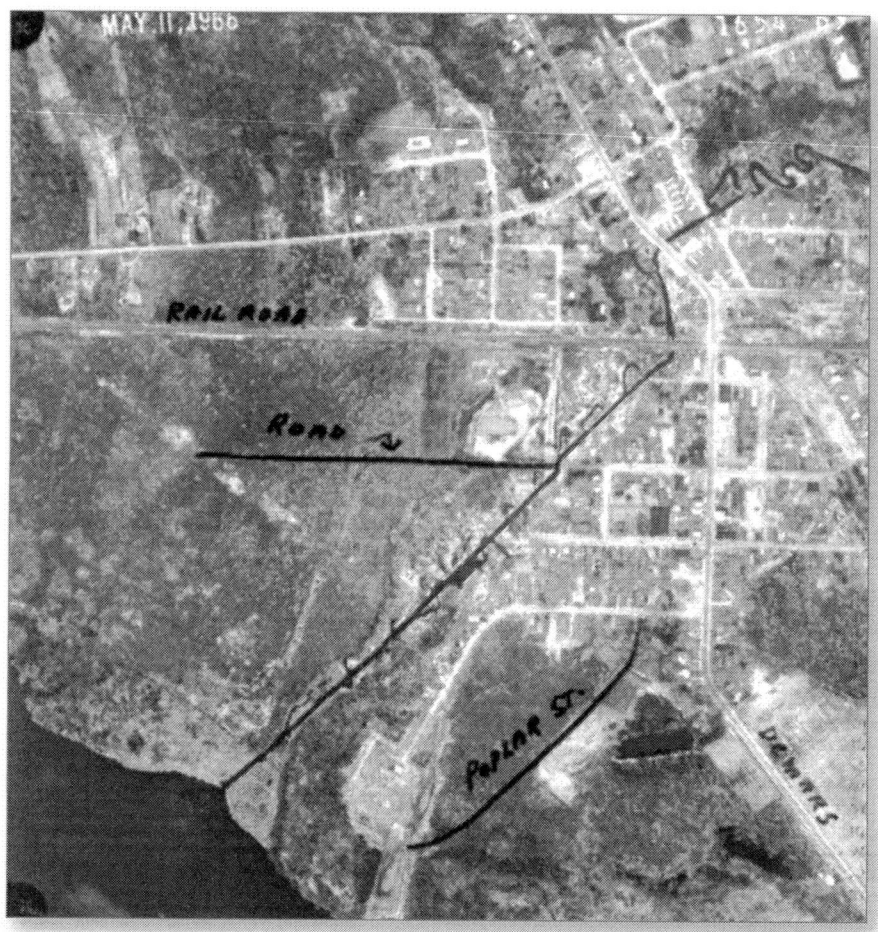

*The Pine Street bridge, at center, is just below the railroad grade, and the faint road, still visible, is part of a failed Depression era project. At bottom right is Gull Pond with discarded Poplar Street leading off Water Street to the former site of the Santa Clara Rossing Mill on Racquette Pond.*

So what is the story behind this 1934 bridge that accessed a road that went no where and serviced nothing, other than a small planning mill, until 1960? The clue lies in the date 1934, and the newspaper files of that year provide an answer. First, we have to remember this was the time of the Great Depression, a slowdown in the economy that became the worst in the country's history with the many failed businesses and huge unemployment. Tupper Lake probably weathered those "threadbare thirties" better than most communities. McDonald in 1934 had a large lumbering job going on at Whitney Park. The first river drive in years was ready to bring millions of logs down the Racquette River to the Jack Works at Underwood. Sunmount was well established, but at the same time, as the economy became further throttled by the Depression, local firms like the huge O.W.D. plant were experiencing financial difficulties as sales dropped sharply, causing job layoffs. Many people simply could not find work.

But Adirondack people are survivors! A friend now living in Maine wrote to me recently, commenting of those days: "I learned years later that my father, who was a caretaker of a prominent camp on Upper Saranac Lake, received no salary for two years during the Depression. (The wealthy owner had lost everything in the stock market crash.) He continued to clothe and feed a family of eight. I was too young to realize that white fish, trout and venison, along with my mother's vegetable garden, met the needs of that growing family. I have such great respect for our parents who endured with faith and fortitude."

Help came under Franklin Roosevelt when billions of dollars were poured into work and home relief programs. Workers (anyone unemployed was eligible) were paid 40 cents an hour for a 40-hour week, enough to get by on Depression prices.

The result in Tupper Lake was more civic progress than at any other time in our history. The golf course was expanded from nine holes to 18, and a beautiful log clubhouse was erected. The Municipal Park was developed, which was a $137,000 project. A new junior/senior high school was built at a cost of $300,000. The Rod and Gun Clubhouse was built with a crew of 32 men using selected spruce and hemlock logs. The process to gain these federal and state funds under what was called the Civil Works Administration was for the town to submit any project under consideration to the Federal Relief Administration for approval, all work to go to the unemployed listed on the relief rolls. The first projects our town fathers recommended in 1934 were:

1. The rebuilding of the Setting Pole Dam to employ 25 men at a cost of $30,000.

2. The extension of Murray Street to Little Wolf Creek and the construction of two 20-ft. bridges with a dam across the outlet at a cost of $3,656.50.
3. The construction (called the Big Simond Project) of a road along the south shore of that lake leading off the Moody Road, making possible building sites, which was certainly a prophetic recommendation.
4. The laying of a road (aha!) beyond Pine Street to Underwood and then along the shore of Big Tupper Lake to the American Legion Camp. Also the construction of a bridge across Little Wolf Creek off Pine Street to access that road.

Of these four applications, all of which were approved, three succeeded wonderfully, but for reasons I haven't discovered, the Big Tupper shoreline project, except for the bridge, failed completion.

*Tupper Lake Free Press Print:* May 05, 2004

## THE REST OF THE STORY

IN LAST WEEK'S *TRANSITIONS* column, a question was raised concerning the outlet of Little Wolf Lake. "Who," we asked, and "why" and "when" was the crooked stream straightened out from the Pine Street bridge to the creek's confluence with Racquette Pond?

An item in the January 23, 1936, issue of the *Tupper Lake Herald* provided an answer, which may be of great interest:

"A great change, improvement and betterment of conditions of residents in certain sections of Faust will be a thing of the past if W.P.A. approval of a project to straighten out many of the tortuous kinks in Little Wolf Creek and thereby prevent the accumulation of refuse against the banks at the numerous bends is obtained.

"Low water in past years along the creek (frequently dubbed Dead Creek) has brought with it unpleasant exhalations from decaying refuse and consequent unhealthful conditions. It is proposed to straighten the channel, widening and deepening it where necessary, between Main Street bridge, just beyond Washington Street, and the outlet at Raquette Pond. Engineers point out that cutting across many of the twists and "S" bends of the creek would result in a faster flow of current and obviate the backwater areas where refuse tends to accumulate.

"If approved the project would provide about three month's work for 60 men. The job would extend over about 3,770 feet of channel. Some 9,000 cubic yards of soft ground would have to be excavated and 5,000 cubic yards of fill would have to be placed to affect the changes in the direction of the creek's flow. About 1,850 feet of sewer and drainage lines would be laid to extend to present lines. It is proposed to make the straightened channel average three feet in depth and ten feet in width at the bottom."

And as Paul Harvey would say, "Now we know the rest of the story!"

Note that in the above news item, sewer lines were to be extended to Little Wolf Creek. Local kids in my day had another less flattering name for that creek: SH-- Creek. In fairness, it should be remembered that the village at the time was only 36 years old. It was still undergoing "growing pains," and as former historian Louis Simmons has noted, "In justice to the community, there wasn't much of any other solution for sewage disposal in those days."

*Little Wolf Creek, shown lower right, flows under the New York Central railroad bridge. Follow the trackage across the Junction Main Street crossing to the railroad station removed in 1975. The four-story Faust hotel is at left center—gone by 1958. Note tree-lined Demars Boulevard at top of photo. Circa 1950.*

Yet, while it may be hard to believe in this day and age, as late as 1960, 17 public sanitation sewer outlets, in addition to the V.A. line from Sunmount and numerous individual lines, were polluting area waters, pumping sewage directly into our ponds, lakes and streams.

This was, of course, highly unacceptable to most residents and, in particular, to the V.A. hospital, which threatened to build its own system if the situation was not improved. Fortunately, as the community struggled for a solution, Public Law 660, passed by the 84th Congress, authorized grants of federal aid that amounted to $250,000. The Veterans' Administration agreed to a $127,000 contribution as a connecting charge. This left a balance of $253,000 toward the estimated maximum cost of $630,000 to be raised locally.

Community taxpayers quickly approved that amount by a 3-1 margin in a special March 1960 election. One year later, in 1961, Tupper Lake had a water pollution control system.

Disgusting, indiscriminate pollution that had been, in the words of one official, "a reproach to the citizens of Tupper Lake," was now history (almost).

Today, a modern, well-managed state-of-the-art pollution control system sits proudly on a former Santa Clara Company mill site. Here, its unappetizing, pea-green exterior—painted to presumably meet A.P.A. visual guidelines—overlooks a recovered Racquette Pond, whose waters are once again as clean as the days when members of the Indian nations camped on its shores. The days when, in early times, it was called "Lough Neah," after a beautiful lake in Ireland.

*Tupper Lake Free Press Print:* May 12, 2004

## SPOTLIGHT ON O.W.D.

IT STARTED AS A RUMOR, one that had escalated before in the community, namely, "The Big Tupper Ski Area has been sold."

This time, the rumor had panache, for it was further rumored that the forest property owned by family members of the former O.W.D. Corporation that surrounded the ski area was also to be sold. Yes, Moody Pond, Cranberry Pond, Sugar Loaf Mountain, river and lake frontage and, even more intriguing as rumors go, the buyers were representing Robert Redford, owner of the fabulous Sun Dance Ski Area in Utah.

Aside from that latter embellishment, which turned out to be false and created good-natured amusement and wonder for the actual negotiators (one principal had, at a time, owned a home at Sun Dance), this later rumor was more sustainable.

Successive press releases confirmed that, yes indeed, great plans were in place to create a well-planned, seasonal home complex that included the reestablishment of the Big Tupper Ski Area.

Those lands have been owned by the O.W.D. for almost a hundred years (1914). While older residents will easily identify or connect with that firm, its owners and possibly the property involved, perhaps readers new to the community or of a younger generation will be interested in a brief look that puts the spotlight on that venerable firm.

Established here in 1915, it was the largest lumbering firm ever to operate in this village as well as the largest industrial plant ever

*The distinguished gentleman shown above is William C. Hull, founder of the O.W.D. Corporation, which, in 1916, erected the largest industrial plant in Franklin County.*

erected in Franklin County.

The company's first land purchase here was encouraged by Ferris Meigs of the Santa Clara Lumber Company. It was, at the time, an investment with no plans to build a plant here. The land, some of which was owned by the Santa Clara Company, was called the Follensby Tract, "with the exception of Follensby Pond itself and its shoreline, together with a portion of the Mt. Morris tract and lands in Township 22 adjoining 'the Follensby Pond tract.'" The company would eventually buy stumpage and land on tracts that would add up to 80,000 acres, much of it in Macomb Township 19, according to Barbara McMartin in her comprehensive history on the Adirondack lumber industry, *The Great Forest of the Adirondacks*. Ms. McMartin further noted that "the exhaustion of the timber supply and changing times caught up with the company in 1961 when it closed its Potsdam and Quebec plants and sold 20,000 acres of Adirondack timberland in 1964."

That year, the company also sold its Tupper Lake plant to the Adirondack Plywood Corporation, which quickly sold to U.S. Plywood. Note: That company invested $2,000,000 to modernize its operation here. Unfortunately, fire destroyed the large warehouses in 1967, and caused U.S. Plywood to curtail operations here.

Although smaller companies later occupied the site, large-scale manufacturing from hardwoods essentially ended.

With the sale of the O.W.D. 40 years ago, a lasting influence and impetus to our cultural and economic vitality became an important page in the history of this town. Regional historian, the late Harry Landon, in his 1932 *History of the North Country*, offers us a profile of the founder, William Cary Hull. An excerpt from that account follows:

"Among the principal industries of Franklin County and indeed in the front ranks with the chief wood-working plants in this section of the state is the Oval Wood Dish Corporation, Tupper Lake Junction, of which William Cary Hull is president, Gerald P. Hull, vice-president and Henry C. Hull II, lumber sales manager.

"William C. Hull, Sr. was the son of Henry S. Hull and Kathleen (Pfeiffer) Hull who was engaged in the mercantile business in Wauseon, OH. In 1833 he became interested in the manufacture of an oval wood dish that could be used by retail merchants as a receptacle in the sale of lard, butter and other similar items of merchandise and then discarded like a paper bag.

"In 1887, he moved the manufacturing plant to Mancelona, MI, and subsequently in 1992 to Traverse City, MI, near the hardwood lumber supply, so necessary in the manufacture of his project.

"The company, which had been a partnership, was incorporated under the name of the Oval Wood Dish Corporation. The Michigan company was also active in the hardwood lumber business and owned vast tracts of timber in the state. When plans were made to build a plant in Tupper Lake, Henry S. sent his son William C. to be in charge. William, a military school graduate who had played professional baseball for one year with the Jamestown Club, moved here in 1916, and in 1919 succeeded to the presidency of the company."

Note: William then built a strikingly handsome home on Water Street in the Junction. The present owners are the Cubby LaFrance family. It was, in my youth, a showplace unmatched by any other home in the community. The entry, which faced Water Street, was served by a porte-cochére, through which ran a circular drive. A group of white pines dominated a spacious lawn, always carefully maintained.

To the rear of the house, a large glass-enclosed sunroom looked out upon a vast flower garden. Paths led through flowers of every color and variety, lovingly tended by Mrs. Hull (the former Katherine Lola Peckman of Mancelona, MI) and her team of gardeners. A long hedgerow of rose bushes led to a pond where Mrs. Hull had workers build stone benches placed in secluded nooks and crannies among the white pines surrounding the pond, a place of seclusion, rest and meditation. Note: The pond was formed when a large knoll was leveled for the fill it contained to prepare the low-level site for the plant under construction along Demars Boulevard. The resulting excavation filled with water from natural springs and seepage from nearby Racquette Pond.

Historian Langley listed Mr. and Mrs. Hull as parents of the following family:
1. Henry C., who later became sales manager for the lumber department of the O.W.D.
2. Gerald P., who became vice president and later succeeded his father as president after the latter's death in 1941.
3. Richard, who later owned a sign manufacturing company in West Winfield, NY.

4. William (Bill) C., Jr., who attended Cornell and graduated from the Massachusetts Institute of Technology, and who later was in the employ of F.L. Carlisle Company, bankers in New York City, and who eventually became vice president of the O.W.D.
5. Jane J., a graduate of Smith College, who later was engaged in secretarial work in New York City.

Note: The Hull family played a prominent role in the founding of the Tupper Lake Country Club. It may be worth noting that the first golf tournament held upon its official opening was won by Jane, also a star tennis player—beating all male opponents.

Mr. Langley concluded his profile of William Cary Hull, Sr., by pointing out that "Mr. Hull has always been a Republican. He is a past master of Traverse City Lodge F and A.M., a Knight Templar and is also a 32-degree Mason, a member of the Masonic Club of Tupper Lake. In 1907, Mr. Hull organized and was president of the North Branch Flooring Co. of Chicago. He is also an officer in two other lumber companies in Michigan. Mr. Hull's recreation is golf and baseball."

*Tupper Lake Free Press Print:* June 30, 2004

# THE PEOPLE AND CAMPS OF SIMONDS POND

DURING THE DEPRESSION YEARS of the 1930s, this village took advantage of federal aid to put through a number of worthwhile projects. One such project was the construction of a road along the south shore of Lake Simond. Before that road became a reality, there were only a few camps on Simonds Pond, as it was then known. Note: On petition of the Tupper Lake Chamber of Commerce, the New York State Committee on Geographic Names in 1957 officially approved the renaming of Simonds Pond to Lake Simond. That new name has only met lukewarm acceptance – most residents and even recent maps apparently preferring the traditional Simonds Pond.

Indeed, as Louis Simmons has pointed out in his comprehensive history, *Mostly Spruce and Hemlock*, "that beautiful body of water did not attract its first permanent camp until 1912."

That first camp, still remaining sheltered by tall pines, was built by Warren G. Hubert of Yonkers. Mr. Hubert and his bride spent their honeymoon in this area in 1911. Intrigued with the scenic beauty and fabulous fishing, they purchased 20 acres on the north side of the lake from the A. Sherman Lumber Company, which had built in 1888 one of the first mills here. A. Sherman was owned by the Sisson family of this community and Potsdam. Their total holdings encompassed 90,000 acres, much of it along the Racquette River.

Mr. and Mrs. Hubert spent 50 consecutive summers there. For

many years, the Huberts were a common sight as they would head up the lake to their camp that has remained in the memory of this writer. They kept their beautiful chris-craft on a slip at Bill Shea's family camp. Dr. Hubert never failed to start out in low power until they were beyond the shoreline camps. Only then, when he had reached the broader expanse of the lake, would he accelerate, the engine making an impressive roar of power as the boat's bow pointed home to Hubert Point.

Homer Folks, a neighbor of the Huberts at Yonkers, erected the second camp on the lake in 1914. The third camp on Lake Simond was erected in 1916 by William Adams of Lawrence, Long Island. He was the father of Lewis Adams, a New York City architect, who drew up the plans for the Adirondack Museum at Blue Mountain Lake. The camp still exists under the careful stewardship of family members. It is located in a sheltered bay where the outlet of Little Simond Pond (then called Lake Wilbert) tumbles off a shoulder of Mt. Morris and quietly enters the lake.

I grew up spending most of my youthful summers at one of those camps that was erected when the south shore road was extended. Simonds Pond by this time had quickly become a busy summer colony. It was a mix of year-round residences and seasonal camps. There were many youngsters of my own age whose parents had built camps or rented camps for extended periods.

A close-knit group of friends soon developed, and each succeeding summer during those youthful years (until well up into the middle 1940s and the war years) Simonds Pond was an exciting place for youngsters.

Next door to my parents' camp was the Flower City Camp (now the year-round home of Mike and Mary Chartier), owned by an energetic, resourceful, wonderful gentleman by the name of Jacob Hauser from Rochester, NY. Almost every morning, just as the sun rose over Roundtop Mountain up the lake, Mr. Hauser would boat three miles to neighboring Tupper Lake. Here, located just off County Line Island, he had a whitefish buoy that he kept baited with a mixture of rice and perch chunks. This buoy was located in over 80 feet of water, and Mr. Hauser had developed a method of lowering a weighted can full of bait to the very bottom of the lake to insure the large fish laying there received it. Once the can was lowered to the bottom, he would trigger the cover, thus releasing the bait, or chum. Mr. Hauser used a stout rubber band to attach his baited hook (baited with a minnow) to his leader so he wouldn't tear the tender mouth or miss the sensitive strike so deep down in the water.

He was usually back from fishing as our family was finishing breakfast. He rarely took more than three or four fish, mostly seven and eight pound beauties, often shared with his neighbors. I might mention that in those days, whitefish were considered the ultimate, best-tasting, most delicious fish in the lake.

Among other fine neighbors were Mary and Joe Mercurio, who rented cottages and called their place Peace Haven. The people who rented there came back year after year. Joe was originally from Boston, a personable, soft-spoken host whose voice reminded me of Bing Crosby. Today, when on occasion I can't remember my own telephone number, I can distinctly remember a sign tacked to the wall of the Mercurio's boathouse: "Allah does not deduct from one's allotted time those hours spent fishing."

A list of some of the camps, starting at the head of the lake, is as follows:
- William Adams, Lawrence, Long Island
- Mrs. Charles Hathaway
- Franklin Sidway of Syracuse
- Howard Smith of Potsdam

On the Island:
- Mrs. Helen Skinner, New York City
- Warren Hubert, Yonkers

On the Mainland:
- "Teacher's Camp," Beaver Burton, New York City
- Clinton D. Fuller, Conifer
- Emporium Forestry Company
- Mrs. Bhina Burton, New York City

- Dr. R.L. Cook, former chief of staff at Sunmount
- Al Brockman, commander of the Benjamin Churco Post (1935)
- Fred Clark, Faust, owner of Clark Lumber Company (later C.E.L.)
- Harold Bentz, Saranac Lake
- Dr. R.J. Patten, Sunmount
- George Lewis, Potsdam
- Archie Baril, Superintendent of Highways here for many years
- M. Herd, New York City
- Eugene Germain, New York City
- Tom Somers, owner of Ford Distributorship
- Mrs. Mayme Greene, owner of Greene's Dress Shop
- Frank Dinet, whose confectionary company was later purchased by Major Day Sr.
- J. Howard Brown, trustee of the bank and owner of Brown Brothers store, located in the former Sabin's Building on Park Street
- Mr. and Mrs. Ed Hervieux, owners of New Brunswick Hotel
- Miss Stella Kiebel, Rochester
- Jacob Hauser, Rochester
- The Frenette Camp
- George Harrington, famous pioneer guide
- William Shay, marina
- Arthur Huntington, early settler
- Joe Mercurio
- Allen Flanders
- Peter La Montagne, Superintendent of Tupper Lake Power and Light Company and partner in the Sabin Electric firm
- Harold Emmons, Rochester

Next we come to the "pump house," built by Colonel Barbour to push the water of Little Simond to the village. After that was the home of Michael Manning, located on the site of the George McBride homestead (late 1850s). And we must mention Gaustaf Sonnleitner, music composer, whose Camp Lure lay adjacent to the Manning home.

This collection of the 1935 Lake Simond camp colony, where once a lone hunter named Elijah Simond was the only person on the lake, brings us to "Hill Crest Farm," owned by Charles Hathaway, who was famed for his strawberry crop and maple syrup grove where the Moody village line begins.

*Tupper Lake Free Press Print:* August 04, 2004

## Mt. Morris

IT STANDS AS A PROMINENT LANDFORM of this community. Rising 1,621 feet above the level of Tupper Lake, its familiar profile has been a welcoming beacon to generations of residents and visitors alike. The very earliest maps indicated it and listed its name as Mt. Morris.

Our most friendly mountain is located in what is known as Great Tract One of Alexander Macomb's 6-tract purchase. Great Tract One consisted of nearly four million acres, for which he paid the giveaway price of eight pence an acre. It lies wholly within Franklin County and was originally owned by Daniel McCormick, a silent partner of Macomb who was simply the front man. It was purchased with the intent of selling parcels at a profit. To encourage settlement (and sale), McCormick divided the tract into 27 townships of about 32,000 acres each.

The townships were given names as well as numbers to identify them. Most of the names were Irish, accounted for by the nationality of the namers. Macomb and his two silent partners, McCormick and Constable, were all from Ireland.

Some examples include Township 4, named *Moria*, "a place in Ireland," or Township 22, named *Lough Neah*, also a lake in Ireland. An exception was Township 25, named *Morris* for "a mountain in that township." (In 1892, Township 25 became one of three townships that would comprise the Town of Altamont, now legally known as the Town of Tupper Lake.)

Incidentally, only a few of those original names became perpetuated in the designation of later formed towns, as Township 21 —still Harrietstown—Harriet being a daughter of Constable. Bangor, Moria and Malone are also names of the few remaining from the original list of 27 townships marked for sale.

So who was Morris, and why was our mountain named for him? I have no written authority or factual information, only a strong suspicion that the mountain was named to commemorate a man named Gouverneur Morris (note that his first name is spelled correctly; he was not a governor).

Gouverneur Morris was a staunch member of the Federalist Party, as were his friends, William Constable, John Jay, Daniel McCormick and Samuel Ogden (Ogdensburg). All of these friends believed in the rules of the rich, the wellborn and the able, and they enjoyed gambling in "wild lands," which had become a pastime of the wealthy in those days.

Morris owned wide tracts of land in the North Country and first visited his St. Lawrence County holdings in 1809 (with his French chef) at a place called Morris Mills, but now known as Natural Dam.

He also owned land that was a settlement called Cambray. He changed that name in 1810 to Gouverneur—after himself—and, of course, that name remains today.

Morristown, outside of Ogdensburg on the St. Lawrence River, was also named after Mr. Morris.

*This extremely rare photograph, taken in 1900 on the summit of Mt. Morris, shows a signal tower erected in the 1870s by state surveyor Verplank Colvin. A sun-reflecting signal placed on top of the wooden tower allowed other summits to mark Mt. Morris for mapping purposes.*

*When this photograph was taken in 1900, it was a six-hour, nine-mile trip to Mt. Morris via Little Simond Pond access. Note the shirt and tie.*

Mountains were often given names to honor individuals (Marcy, Colden, Seward, McIntyre, etc.), and would you agree that McCormick, who owned the land, named one of the mountains located there after his good friend Morris, probably in the early 1800s?

It was the era of settlement, but it would not be until 1840 before anyone settled near Mt. Morris, and even then the nearest neighbor was 20 miles away through trackless forest.

There have been many title changes in Township 25 since the McCormick ownership – too many to detail here, but several may be of interest to readers of this column.

In 1893, Edward H. Litchfield purchased from the Robert Gilchrist estate the southern third of Township 25 in order to create a private park of some 9,000 acres. Initially, he had a slight problem – some deeds to parts of his purchase were questionable tax titles. Mr. Litchfield spent considerable time making sure they were unchallenged. And, in fact, the miles of eight foot tall fence that later enclosed the park were placed there as much to provide legal status as they were to protect the many species of game, such as elk, caribou and wild boar, that he imported to stock his game preserve.

If you were to view Litchfield Park in its forest setting today from the summit of Mt. Morris, you would spot a clearing with a cluster of white buildings. This clearing was originally a summer pasture of some 100 acres, cleared for the logging horses of the Sisson operation that was lumbering the tract under contract with Gilchrist. This pasture was later operated as a farm for many years by the Litchfields before it was discontinued in 1956. It is today still referred to as "The Farm," and in my youth the Ed Fletcher family lived on the premises. I believe Mr. Fletcher managed the farm along with his other duties as foreman.

The focal point of the property, called Jenkins Pond (now Lake Madeleine), also presented a problem to Mr. Litchfield's purchase. It was owned by Thomas Barbour's wife, Sarah, who had a camp on the lake called The Crow's Nest. Thomas Barbour, who owned 20,000 acres, including 15 miles of shoreline on Tupper Lake, and Mr. Litchfield were acquainted and a trade was made. Mr. Litchfield obtained the property on Jenkins in exchange for Lot 42, which was the only lot Barbour didn't own in his surrounding property on Tupper Lake.

Mrs. Aurore Alexander, whose family ran the Waukesha Hotel and who was a friend of the Barbours, once told me that Mrs. Barbour then built a camp on Tupper Lake that she called The Leaning Maple, or sometimes The Crow's Nest. It was located a quarter mile toward Bog River Falls from what was then known as the Sprague Camp on Tupper Lake's southwest shore (now the Slater property adjacent to the Martin family camp).

Next *Transitions*: More on Sarah Barbour and other Township 25 owners. Also Read Preserve, O.W.D., Liquid Properties and Preserve Associates, L.T.D.

*Tupper Lake Free Press Print:* August 24, 2004

# READ PARK—STEWARDS AND NEIGHBORS

WE CONTINUE IN THIS WEEK'S *Transitions* the second part of a three-part series on Mt. Morris. As was previously noted, that mountain lies in Township 25 (originally called Morris) of Macomb's Great Tract One, which is one of the three townships that comprise the newly named Town of Tupper Lake (formerly Altamont).

That township remains today almost entirely in the private sector (no public lands). The southern third of some 9,000 acres was acquired in 1893 by E.M. Litchfield, and some aspects of that ownership were outlined in the first part of this series.

In 1899, six years after Mr. Litchfield established his private park, William Read and his cousin, Albert B. Strange, purchased 7,365 acres that represented another third of Township 25, north of the Litchfield property. They also established a private preserve. It should be noted that eventually Mr. Strange's interests gravitated toward the West (he had a lodge near Jackson Hole, WO. which later became the well-known Jenny Lake Ranch, familiar to readers who ski, boat or hike in that area of the Tetons). In 1924, Mr. Read acquired his cousin's half interest in their park. Interestingly, despite the fact that members of the Read family have been the single proprietors for 80 years, the preserve is still referred to here as the Read and Strange Park.

It wasn't an easy task to get to the Read Park in 1899. Dr. Webb's Adirondack and St. Lawrence Railroad had arrived seven years earlier, but it was still a long day's travel from New York. By the time the Reads would have traveled on the railroad in 1988, it had become known as the New York Central and Hudson Railroad.

Arriving at the Tupper Lake station, they would probably have hired a buckboard or carriage from D.J. Hayes. Mr. Hayes, who became mayor and a bank board member, also kept boat wagons (for the various canoe carries or portages) and saddle horses, and he "provided private conveyances" to and from Tupper Lake and Wawbeek Lodge, where he also kept a livery and boarding stable. The Wawbeek, at that time, was owned by J. Ben Hart. D.J.'s local stable and livery was located at the corner of High Street and Wawbeek Avenue, where the K&C building is today undergoing a handsome "facelift." His home, the second one to have been built here, was across the street. It was razed in 1941 to make room for the St. Alphonsus Church.

From the railroad station, the Read family would cross the carriage road across Moody Flow, most often under water to the height of the plank seats. They would then cross the Racquette River to Moody hamlet on the new steel bridge erected in 1894 to replace the older log bridge. Their route would follow along the lake's east shore for five rough wagon miles to the Litchfield Park entrance, located off what is today Route 3. Under agreement with their neighbor, Mr. Litchfield, their trip would continue across that preserve and around the base of Mt. Morris to Little Simond Pond and to their camp, many times a longer trip than the train ride from New York.

In 1922-1923, Mr. Read resolved his access problem by constructing a six-mile road that enters Route 3 across from McDonald's boat livery and follows the east flank of Mt. Morris to Little Simond Pond and his camp.

In later years, after 1901, the Reads could have been met at the station with their own "conveyance." One of the best-known early guides here, Fred Moody, had become the overseer of the Read Park and stables, which were a part of the camp's complex.

Fred was the son of Simeon Moody, pioneer settler who first cleared the site for a farm around 1857 on Stetson Road, later

*Mt. Morris rises boldly in the background as it shelters the deep glacial waters of Little Simond Pond, a prime source for this community's domestic and fire-protection needs. (Etman photo)*

called the Pioneer Place (Barry Farm). Simeon also opened the very first store in this area, catering to guides and travelers coming down the river and to the few residents living mostly along the river below today's LeBoeuf's Bridge, which was close to the farm. Fred Moody was without peer as a woodsman and hunter (he had to be to survive). Certainly Mr. Read, a New York City investment banker and wilderness lover, must have been thrilled to hunt and fish and learn woodcraft from this pioneer who came down the river from the Saranacs as an infant in 1857 in the bottom of a guideboat that served as his bassinet.

In 1905, Mr. Read commissioned a New York architectural firm to build a camp on his Township 25 land. That camp still remains today as the Three Star Camp and is considered by current architectural experts as a masterpiece. The camp has been featured in early architectural magazines and in several books on Great

Camps. A second camp, somewhat more modest but equally handsome, is known as The Birchery.

Mr. Read was a careful and conscientious steward of his land. An article in the *House and Garden Magazine*, dated December 1907, related his desire not to disturb the natural setting and how he required that: "The logs for the various buildings (10-inch-diameter spruce) were cut from the surrounding forests, each one selected with great care as to size, and more particularly to location, not more than one tree being taken from any one spot so that its loss would not be noticed from the lake. The stone for the foundations, chimneys, etc., was all quarried from the mountainside in out-of-the-way places."

Volumes could be written, both storied and factual, about the close connection over the past 105 years between the residents of this community and Read Park and its succession of family owners. They have been what former town historian Louis Simmons has labeled "our neighbors," whose outstanding Adirondack retreat has been their "home away from home." It has been a connection that is warm, friendly, supportive, interesting and caring. We can all hope that such a tradition continues as the challenges of maintaining and owning a Great Camp and its surrounding lands become more and more difficult and complex.

*Tupper Lake Free Press Print:* September 15, 2004

## Lumber is King

MT. MORRIS HAS TAKEN ON A NEW and increased prominence in recent weeks with the announcement of a planned resort and seasonal home complex on its forested shoulders.

In recent *Transition* articles, we have taken a cursory glimpse at the Litchfield and Read preserves that include substantial portions of Township 25, in which the geographical boundaries of Mt. Morris are located. In today's column, we will take yet another "cursory glimpse" at a current Township 25 land owner, the Oval Wood Dish Liquid Properties, Inc.

That look starts by noting that in the late 1800s, a firm owned by the Sisson family of Potsdam, known as the Racquette River Paper Company, had logged the lands of Mt. Morris heavily for its softwood. The Sissons had acquired the "Big Mill," located on what is today's Municipal Park near Racquette Pond. That mill was one of the largest of its day and held for many years the world's record for lumber cut in a single day.

In 1913-1914, the Santa Clara Lumber Company purchased the mill and some of its land holdings from the Racquette River Paper Company. In need of funds, Santa Clara resold, in 1914, 11,805 acres in Townships 22, 25 and 26 to the Oval Wood Dish Corporation (the Follensby Tract, with the exception of the Follensby Pond and its shoreline, a portion of the Mt. Morris Tract and lands in Township 22 that adjoined the Follensby Tract). The price of that transaction was $225,000.

That sale came about, in part, when two years before (1912), two principals of the Michigan-based Oval Wood Dish firm, while on vacation in the Adirondacks, were amazed at the rich source of hardwoods—so necessary in the company's production of wooden articles such as spoons, dishes, clothespins, flooring, etc. Not only were there large amounts of beech, white and yellow birch and maple, it was also available at low prices. At that time, except for a rare logging railroad, water was the only means of transportation for logs, and the lumberjacks didn't touch hardwoods. Not only was there no market, it had not yet been discovered that it could be used to make pulp paper. More importantly, it didn't float and there was no way to get the logs out.

That problem didn't faze O.W.D. They were highly successful, resourceful lumbermen who had operated for 30 years in Michigan, and they would know how to get the logs out. As so often happens in ventures that turn out successfully, timing is important, and the Oval Dish was in the right place at the right time. A fellow named Lombard had designed a machine powered by a steam engine that, in place of wheels, had a broad band of lugs that furnished traction and could haul up to 20 sleds.

World War I had ended, and the O.W.D. also made use of surplus military tanks and gasoline tractors. Such a machine was the Linn, made in Morris, NY. Mechanization had arrived! In addition, while they didn't use railroads on Mt. Morris, they did utilize them heavily in other sections, especially in Township 19 around Kildare. Indeed, at one time they owned two locomotives and 65 rail cars, and they laid many miles of railroad trackage. One line, designed by Floyd Hutchins Sr., used three switchbacks that climbed 500 vertical feet to the 2,060-ft. level of Mt. Matumbia, a feat rare in logging railroads, according to railroad historian Michael Kurdish of Paul Smith's College.

However, in the years before trucks and tractors largely replaced horses, the O.W.D. relied greatly on them, especially on the slopes of Mt. Morris.

My father loved to relate how, as a young man, he walked his cherished horse from the family farm, located alongside the

Lumberjacks of Old
*Shown is the typical layout of early lumber camps. Note the number of horses and also the wooden barrels, right center, which were the main way supplies were "toted" to the camps. Millions of these barrels were produced here by the Brooklyn Cooperage Company located off Washington Street in the Junction, now the Wayne LaPierre property. (photo courtesy of the Adirondack Museum)*

Racquette River near Norwood, up through Colton and the South Woods 80 miles to Tupper Lake, where his horse was used to log the slopes on Mt. Morris. This was, at the time, before big western horses became common, and lumbermen depended on the surrounding farms to supply horses during the winter months when they were not being used on the farm. Hundreds of horses were supplied this way, a win-win for both farmer and lumberman alike.

As the O.W.D. began its harvest of hardwoods, Mt. Morris became a scene of renewed and frenzied activity. If you look carefully, you can still today find traces of the many camp bottoms where camps were established to house the lumbermen. The camps were usually built near a spring or brook and consisted of a cook shack and dining room, a men's bunk room, a small office, a filer shack for men to sharpen saws, a blacksmith shop and, downstream from the spring, a horse stable and multi-seated outhouse.

Also discernable today on Mt. Morris is a clearing that the 3-mile water supply line from Little Simon Pond crosses on its way to Lake Simond Road. The clearing is on O.W.D. land, currently under lease to the Teacher's Camp hunting club and is still called Donahue Clearing. It was named for Jack Donahue of Potsdam, well-known lumberman who ran lumbering operations until 1913 on Mt. Morris as superintendent for the Norwood Manufacturing Company. Donahue Brook, which is born from a spring close to the Mt. Morris summit on Read lands, was also named for Mr. Donahue. The course of this beautiful brook takes it close to the Sugar Loaf Hunting Camp, also currently under lease from O.W.D. Liquid Properties, before it empties into Adams Bay on Lake Simond.

There is an interesting story that concerns Mr. Donahue and the discovery of coal on Mt. Morris. Moody resident and famed guide Chester Gile was digging in the ground on Mt. Morris searching for ginseng roots when he discovered coal. He excitedly brought samples to town and sent them to the State Department in Albany, who informed him it was high-grade bituminous (soft) coal. This created quite a furor here with dreams of fortunes being made, not unlike the gold strikes of Alaska. Unfortunately, it was learned from Mr. Donahue that a load of blacksmith's coal, being hauled up the mountain to a camp's shop, had overturned on a steep bank the previous winter and only a part of the load had been salvaged from the snow.

This was a time of great human energy—hundreds of men working in the woods, booming hotels, busy stores, river drives, mills operating 24 hours a day—lumber was king! Tupper Lake, then only 12 years old, was on the move, and the O.W.D. became a powerful economic engine.

*Tupper Lake Free Press Print:* September 29, 2004

# FOLLENSBY

MOST READERS OF THIS COLUMN are today no doubt aware of Follensby Pond, which can be viewed so prominently from the summit of Mt. Morris, the focus of a series of *Transitions* articles.

As late as the middle 1800s, the lake was in a remote area, known only to a few guides and the solitary hermit of mysterious origin and demise, who left behind a romantic legend—his name originally spelled "Follensbee."

As Paul Jamieson tells us in *Adirondack Pilgrimage*, it became better known when a group of intellectuals from Boston in 1858 enjoyed a camping adventure on its shores.

Camp Maple, named after the maple grove that canopied their shelter, was soon dubbed the "Philosopher' Camp" by their guides. And so it has been known ever since in popular tradition—a title befitting the slightly bizarre aspect of these sophisticates turned primitive for a fortnight.

Older residents like this writer knew Follensby as Barbour Park. It was a private place, remote and virtually unknown. Its caretaker, Mr. Clyde Campe, brooked no nonsense, and his owners' wishes regarding privacy were followed closely. Barbour Park, for all purposes in those days, was little known. Only a few locals had been beyond the gated entrance off Stetson Road.

As an amateur historian, I was curious about the transformation that took place between the carte blanche of the early guides that allowed them to row up the outlet from Racquette River and reveal its presence to amazed clients (who had never heard of it) to its privileged status today. Here is what I discovered: When William West Durant sold his father's Adirondack Railroad in 1889 to the Delaware and Hudson, that company allowed him to retain lands that were not needed for the railroad operation.

In 1890, Ferris Meigs of the Santa Clara Company and others formed a stock company they called Adirondack Timber and Mineral Company, and they purchased 400,000 acres from Durant. It was, according to Mr. Meigs in his unpublished autobiography, "purchased mostly for taxes paid and unpaid, and amounted to a total of $600,000, all cash."

Santa Clara, who held one-fourth interest in the stock company, then acquired 35,000 acres of that purchase, mostly in Townships 25, 26 and 27 (Follensby Tract, Cold River, Ampersand Pond, Axton, etc.) for $4.50 per acre.

It was, in Mr. Meigs' words: "a very good purchase – by 1900 we had cut most of the softwood timber on the west half of Township 26 leaving the hardwoods standing. This beech, birch and maple were then used for cooperage (barrels). A sale was made to the Tupper Lake plant of the Brooklyn Cooperage firm of 10,000 acres for $6 per acre!"

Some three years later, in 1905, Brooklyn Cooperage discovered that the only cost-effective method to transport the hardwood was to build a railroad as they had done successfully in other operations such as Cross Clearing.

Railroads were smelly, noisy affairs, and their wood-burning, ember-throwing engines were notorious for starting fires. This was unacceptable to Mr. Meigs and family, who had retained ownership of Follensby Pond, some surrounding lands and a camp they called Stag Head. In 1905, in a friendly negotiation with Lowell Palmer, president of the Cooperage firm, Santa Clara repurchased the 10,000 acres at cost, plus an additional 5,000 acres. Camp Stag Head and the lovely seclusion of Follensby were saved!

In 1914, some of the Follensby Tract, with the exception of the lake and shoreline, was sold to the O.W.D. Shortly thereafter, parts of this sale, mostly in Township 26, were repurchased, and

*Follensby Pond in 1950, viewed from the deck of J.E. Barbour's main camp, White Birches. Today, Follensby Park, with 15,000 acres, ranks 15th among the 30 largest Adirondack landholders. International Paper Company heads that list with 327,000 acres.*

Santa Clara again became the sole proprietor of Follensby.

If those numerous transactions wouldn't confuse even a real estate lawyer, hold on. A wealthy gentleman by the name of John E. Barbour was searching for a special Adirondack retreat. Follensby was exactly what he wanted and, according to Ferris Meig's autobiography, 4,000 acres were purchased at a cost of $75,000, which included the lake and camp.

Mr. Barbour was the nephew of Colonel William Barbour, millionaire manufacturer of linen thread in Patterson, NJ.

Colonel Barbour's land holdings around Big Tupper Lake consisted of about 20,000 acres, a portion of which later became the American Legion Mountain Camp. The Barbour family had been coming to this area as recreationists since the late 1800s.

The ink was barely dry on the Follensby purchase contract when John Barbour ordered the removal of Camp Stag Head and built his own camp a fourth-mile distant. The construction was completed in 1917 and named White Birches.

A brief description of that camp, as contained in a preview listing by Previews Incorporated when the property came up for sale in 1951, may be of reader interest. The property by that time consisted of approximately 14,310 acres and included a ten—room lodge (caretaker's home), five—room gatehouse, boathouse, icehouse and chauffeur's cottage as well as White Birches Camp. Asking price: $148,500, furnished. The main camp was described as follows: "21 rooms, cedar-shingled roof. Built in 1917. In excellent condition. Hardwood floors, cypress finish woodwork. Included in sale price—all furnishings. Living room 20' x 25', 24' ceiling, balcony three sides, bay window, hand hewn beams, huge cutstone fireplace, large kitchen, maid's dining room, two wings, three bedrooms and bath in each."

*Tupper Lake Free Press Print:* October 20, 2004

# THE TOWN OF AXE AND SURROUNDINGS

THE YEAR WAS 1854. Harvey Moody, together with his younger brothers, Cort and Mart, were rowing their guideboats, each with gear and a single passenger, down the Racquette River. The Moody boys, all well-known Adirondack guides, were leading Alfred B. Street, the New York State Librarian, and several of his friends on a leisurely hunting/fishing trip that would take them across the Saranacs, up the Racquette to Long Lake and then back down the river to Tupper Lake.

After several side trips to picturesque smaller ponds such as Dawson, Palmer and Follensby, they would return to their starting point on Lower Saranac and take the long, rigorous stagecoach ride to the steam boat on Lake Champlain.

As they passed the canoe carry that leads to Upper Saranac, Harvey announced that it was only another 3.5 miles to the outlet of Follensby Pond. That area near the carry's end was years later called Axton. The name was derived from the "town of Axe" of a Santa Clara Lumber Company camp and referred to, in the 1800s, a large area with many buildings that included Coreys and extended along the east side of the three Stony Creek ponds.

Today, Axton means only the sandy beach at the southern end of that same Indian-carrying place, and it still provides access to the river from Upper Saranac.

Let's leave the librarian's party as they continue down river and take a closer look at the three guides.

*Shooting matches were a favorite pastime for guides and sporting clients alike in the late 1880s. This photo was taken at Mart Moody's relocated hotel called Moody's, later, Redside Camp. It became the Waukesha when purchased by Jabez Alexander.*

Harvey, the chief guide on this trip, was the oldest son of Jacob Moody, the first permanent settler of the Saranac Lake region, having arrived there in 1819. Harvey had four brothers: Cort, Mart, Smith and Daniel, all of whom became famous hunters, trappers and guides, and their names appear frequently in early travelogs by various authors, journalists and historians.

The Moody's had early on discovered the richness of game around Tupper Lake. They had marveled at its scenic surroundings and its many hidden ponds full of speckled and lake trout, which Harvey described as "some of 'em full grown, too."

"Yes," he once said, "that Tupper's Lake, it's all sorts of a nice place. As for huntin', the deers about those slews, it's real inkstand with them. There's Stetson Slew and Simons Slew. If there ain't the places for night huntin', then there ain't none."

Cort would become the second or third settler in Tupper Lake, arriving here in 1850. It should be mentioned that Cort, born in 1822, was the first recorded birth within the present-day village limits of Saranac Lake.

Maitland DeSormeau in his book, *The Heydays of the Adirondacks*, relates "the Saranacs were once Cort's favorite stomping grounds." His main bailiwick was on Deer Island, opposite the original Wawbeek Hotel (now Stiles' residence) on the Upper Lake. Of further local interest, Deer Island was once owned by the Tupper Lake Santa Clara Company, of which Ferris Meigs was president.

Having a large camp on Big Wolf, the Ferris Meigs family didn't build on Deer Island. However, the Ferris family, who were related to the Meigs, owned half of the island, a part of which was later bought by Dr. Craig Potter. Alfred White bought the other half of the island from Meigs and built a camp named Rest-a-While (now Bircholm, and six generations later it is currently owned by members of the Lyons family—*A History of Sekon and*

*A section of the traditional Indian Carry to Stony Creek ponds from Upper Saranac Lake has been relocated to avoid vehicular traffic on Route 3 and Coreys Road. Its south end is now ¾ mile further east/northeast on Upper Stony Pond. Cort would have disliked that "No Camping" sign.*

*Its Surroundings*, private printing, Longacker).

In 1850, Cort decided to move even further into the wilderness, so he bought the cabin and "improvements" at the foot of Lake Simond (Simmons Pond) near the Moody bridge from the legendary Elijah (Lige) Simond, himself a pioneer settler, hunter and trapper who roamed over the entire northern and central Adirondacks before making the Tupper area his headquarters in the early 1840s. Later on, Cort sold his place to George McBride. George appeared listed in our 1860 census as age 25. His son, Jim, would become a well-known Tupper Lake engineer and surveyor, and Jim's name appears on many property maps yet today. After selling his property to McBride, Cort then moved up river to the vicinity of today's LeBoeuf's Bridge.

A small settlement called Racquet, consisting of six families, grew up there along the river, some foundations still discernable today.

As the children of these families reached school age, a school of log construction was erected in 1862, probably the first school here, and it was located on Stetson Road near the present-day Dennis Dechene home.

Cort's four sons would cut across what is today the fields of the Gontowich farm to attend school.

Simeon Moody, Harvey's son, had built a house on Stetson, and his four sons also attended that school. Until the hamlet of Moody built its own school (near Pine Terrace, torn down in 1946), the McBrides on Simond Pond would also attend the Stetson school. Those children were Sarah (Johnson); Jim the engineer; Allie, who never married; Dell (Huntington) and Millie (Manning). Manning Hill, the first rope tow here, was located to the rear of Dr. Scranton's Veterinary Clinic.

Those children would go by boat to the turn called Bend O' the Road on Racquette River Drive. They would then walk from there to Stetson Road and down to the school. When the river was frozen and they could not use a boat, they walked the entire distance from Moody.

Cort died in Saranac Lake in 1902, leaving five sons, several of whom became well-known guides and woodsrunners.

In the files of the *Tupper Lake Free Press* for January 2-9, 1914, there is a story, probably about the oldest son, also named Cort (Cortez), that may be worth repeating:

"In response to a newspaper ad placed by C.M. Daniels, who wanted live otters to stock his fur farm at Sabattis (now the Boy Scouts of America property on Bear Pond), Cort got busy and caught one only to find that he had tangled with a buzz saw. He managed to cram the formidable animal into his packbasket—and then put his coat over it and sat on it while the angry otter clawed frantically at the obstruction. He finally was able to put sticks and bits of board across the mouth of the basket and bound them on with his trapchains. The otter earned him $100 delivered but Moody's coat, pants and packbasket were just about ruined."

*Tupper Lake Free Press Print:* November 10, 2004

## THE MOODY BOYS

THIS WEEK'S *TRANSITIONS* column continues to look at the "Moody Boys," as they were known. Members of the Moody family from Saranac Lake, who came to this village, were our pioneer settlers, and they had early gained reputations for being outstanding guides, hunters and woodsmen.

These Tupper Lake Moodys, as I will call them, arrived here each in his own time, rowing a guideboat built by his own hands. They crossed the Saranacs, carried boat and gear over the divide to the Racquette River and continued downstream to the unsettled area, where "one would meet more Indians than white men," near Tupper's Lake, the wild heart of the wild northern forest.

The river was the only truly accessible route to this place, and their only possessions were items that could be stowed in the narrow confines of their boat. They would, no doubt, have had blankets, some cooking utensils such as pots and pans, a few items of homespun clothing, a few dishes, candles, perhaps a lantern or two fed by bear grease or deer tallow and, above all, an axe to build a rude shelter and a rifle so necessary to provide food.

What giants those early settlers-turned-guides must have been! Here is how one early writer described them: "A fine, quaint lot of fellows, they were usually splendid physical specimens, intelligent and witty, thorough woodsmen, good cooks and tireless workers."

It only makes sense that if you weren't a good hunter, trapper, woodsman, cook and builder of shelters in those primitive days,

*The "Moody Boys," like so many of the guides in the 1800s, built their own guideboats. Alric Moody and Warren Slater, as partners, started an early commercial venture to produce boats in this community. Other early builders were Lute Owens, Alex Murchison and, later, Leonard Anderson, whose boat shop at Moody is today the Dick Garrelt property. (photo courtesy of E.H. Lindsay)*

you wouldn't survive. The Moody Boys were survivors and their reputations made them famous and frequently sought after as guides. During their lifetimes here, they would guide many distinguished visitors to this region. That list would include two presidents of the United States, Chester Arthur and Grover Cleveland. They would be guides for the Emerson party at the Philosopher's Camp on Follensby Pond and they would guide Verplank Colvin when he surveyed this section as part of his topographical survey of the Adirondack wilderness, to name a few of their guiding accomplishments.

The Moody Boys didn't just sit on the dock or on their front porches waiting to guide visitors. Two of the Moodys also established the first farms here. Cort, who had arrived in 1850, cleared land along the river and Stetson Road, which later became the Fred LeBoeuf farm. Only a few years later, Simeon, Harvey's son, established a farm also off Stetson Road, which later became Mark Barry's "Pioneer Place" (now the Richer farm).

Mart, who became one of the original settlers further downstream on Tupper Lake in 1886 and the third Moody to settle here, would become a famous and successful hotelier and this community's first postmaster (originally Tupper Lake Post Office when this village got its own post office). Mart was also a justice of the peace, an assessor and a highway commissioner.

If you were to look at the current tri-lakes area telephone directory, you would discover a listing of 34 Moody names. I am going to hazard a guess that most of those Moodys are direct descendants of Jacob Moody, who became Saranac Lake's first settler in 1819. A friend of mine recently observed that one reason there are so many Moody names is the fact that "Jake" had seven children, and five of them were boys. Harvey had eight children, seven of whom were boys, and Cort had five children, all of whom were boys. This, of course, helped perpetuate the Moody name.

It is beyond the scope of this article to pursue a genealogical study of the Moody clan. Perhaps of some interest, however, is a brief look at some of the Moodys who were so prominent here.

Let's start with Simeon, Harvey's son, who, as previously mentioned, established a farm on Stetson Road as early as 1857, and who also had the first store here that catered to the guides and "sports" trickling into this area downriver near "Sims' Place." Sims had four sons: William, Fred, Charles and John. John was only one week old when his mother died, and he was adopted by Mr. and Mrs. Henry Johnson of Lewis, NY, and given the name of his adopted parents, which he legally used throughout his lifetime. Strangely enough, some 20 years later, he met and married Sarah McBride, who was working as a nanny for a family in the same town of Lewis. Sarah was the daughter of George McBride, early settler, who had bought Cort Moody's "betterments" near today's Moody Bridge before the Civil War.

In 1892, John and Sarah returned here, where each had been born. For 14 years, John was employed as superintendent of Litchfield Park under Edward Litchfield. For 11 years, he was then employed as a guide in Canada by Ernest Ryle of New York City, who was a brother-in-law of Bert Strange, one of the founders of the Read and Strange Preserve. He also worked for a time as superintendent at Whitney Park, where, as noted in an earlier *Transitions* column, he was in the exciting "Last Wild Boar Hunt," killing several wild boar that had escaped from confinement at Litchfield's game preserve. Like the earlier Moodys, he was considered an outstanding woodsman and a prominent resident. Following retirement, Mr. and Mrs. Johnson, who at the time had been happily married for half a century, lived with their daughter, Mrs. Charles Hathaway at Hillcrest Farm in Moody, across from today's MacDonald Boat Livery.

*Tupper Lake Free Press Print:* November 24, 2004

# COLONEL BAKER—BALLAD OF GLENCOE

IN THE FIRST SERIES of articles about the "Moody Boys," it was noted that they had been hired in the 1850s as guides by New York State Librarian Alfred Street. Mr. Street and three of his friends had planned on an adventuresome trip through the untouched woods and waters of the region.

At the time of which we are writing, the Moodys still lived in Saranac Lake, which was then a settlement of fewer than a dozen families and where the Moodys were the first settlers on record. It was essential in those days to have guide for wilderness travel. This part of the Adirondacks was largely unsettled. Maps, if available, were often inaccurate and sketchy at best, and even trained surveyors like Benjamin Tupper and Verplank Colvin got "turned around."

After the 1890s, when railroads brought in thousands of people, settlements grew into population centers, lumber roads crisscrossed the woods, mapping improved and the need for guides diminished, a situation that pretty much continues today.

Mr. Street had arranged to meet Harvey Moody, who would be the chief guide, at a hotel called Bakers, also known as The Lake House. This small hotel was located on what is today Saranac Lake's Pine Street, alongside the Saranac River.

The hotel was quite famous in its time and was visited over the years by many famous people. The owner, Colonel Baker, has been described by one observer as "a man of commanding presence with a tinge of aristocrat in his manner and bearing." It has been further related: "He always met his guests on the footing of assured equality. They were his guests rather than his boarders."

Colonel Baker was a rabid Democrat, as the following story found in Donaldson's *History of the Adirondacks* reveals: "One night the stage brought a New York gentleman to the hotel, who carried with him a brand-new and very expensive fishing outfit. He carefully laid these things on a chair on the piazza and then addressed the proprietor. 'Colonel' he said, 'this stuff if worth several hundred dollars. I want you to put it in a safe place for the night.'"

The next morning on stepping out on the piazza, the guest found his treasures just where he had left them the night before. He sought out the proprietor and remonstrated with some heat.

"By Godfrey, sir!" exclaimed the Colonel, using his favorite obsecration, "By Godfrey, sir, your things are as safe there as in the Bank of England. There's not a Republican within 10 miles of here!"

Mr. Baker would become one of Saranac Lake's (then known as Bakers of Harristown) earliest, if not its first, postmaster, and he opened the first store in that sparsely settled hamlet. Today, the bridge that spans the river near the former hotel is called Bakers Bridge (aka Pine Street Bridge). The prominent, beautiful mountain seen upon entering Saranac Lake from Tupper Lake on the LaPan Highway is still called Baker Mountain.

Most of the important hotels, such as Baker's, had at that time their own staff of guides. As a general matter, there were several classes of guides. (Not unlike the local golf course classification when this writer was a young golf caddy. There were "Honor Caddies," then "A Caddies" and, low on the totem pole, "B Caddies." You were "sent out" by the caddy master accordingly.) Thus, there were "hotel guides," the lowest category of all (errands down the lake, row older ladies on scenic trips). The next step up were the "house guides," usually employed by an estate and subject to the owner's needs. The top category, the aristocrats of the class like the "Moody Boys," were called the "private guides," who were reserved in advance and paid and tipped well, and who were eagerly sought after for their expertise and dependability.

Upon arriving at Baker's Hotel after a long, tiring ride by stagecoach from Port Kent on Lake Champlain, Street and his friends went for a quick and frigid swim in the modest rapids alongside the hotel. (Note: if you see Paul O'Leary, ask him about his unintentional swim in those very same rapids during the annual Ice Breaker canoe race one recent and early spring day.)

Refreshed in body and spirit, "their blood tingling in every invigorating vein," the Street party retired to the hotel's small bar to await the dinner bell. As planned, they met Harvey. They also met Harvey's son, Will, who was known to Mr. Street from one of his earlier visits to the region. Following a friendly greeting and having ordered "punch for all hands," Street asked Will, who had a reputation for having a fine voice, to sing them a song.

"Sing us Glencoe, Will," Street said, and Will somewhat bashfully obliged, his voice strong and clear. The words from that song were written down by librarian Street and translated from what he called the Saranac vernacular. There is a lot of meaning in that ballad Will rendered, especially in view of today's global conflicts, where loved ones are being separated for long periods. I've reprinted it here, and I do hope you enjoy reading it:

"The young leaves of May had just feathered the trees,
And the heatherbell's fragrance was filling the breeze;
I went as of old, to see the dipping low,
On the wild, gloomy grandeur of rocky Glencoe.
The bank of a burnie beside me that run,
Displayed a bright lassie, as bright as the sun;
All flowing in tartans, a lass long ago
That loved young Macdonald, the Pride of Glencoe.
With heart beating wildly, I slowly drew nigh,
The lily and rose in her cheek seemed to vie;
I asked in soft tones where her thought was to go,
And she answered, I'm straying to gaze at Glencoe!
Said I, lovely lassie, thy look and thy smile,
My pathway forever with joy can beguile!
If thou thy affections on me will bestow,
I'll bless the glad hour we met at Glencoe.
Said she, My affections no more can I claim;
I once had a true love, Macdonald his name;
He went to the wars, alas long years ago,
And I live but to see him once more at Glencoe.
It may be Macdonald thou'll never more see,
That he loves some far lassie more fondly than thee,
That he thinks not of tartans so simple in flow,
But of jewels that shine in disdain of Glencoe.
False man my Macdonald truehearted will prove;

The valiant in battle are faithful in love!
And soon will the Spaniards in dust be laid low,
And in joy will my true love return to Glencoe.
So loyal I found her, I pulled out a glove.
She gave me a parting, her token of love;
She hung on my bosom her tears all aflow,
Oh, art thou Macdonald returned to Glencoe!
Yes, Nannie, dear Nannie, thy sorrows are o'er!
I come from the battles to wander no more!
The rude winds of war at a distance may blow,
And fond and contended, we'll dwell at Glencoe."

*Tupper Lake Free Press Print:* December 08, 2004

# RACKET—RACQUETTE—RAQUETTE FALLS

IT WAS A PLACE KNOWN to the earliest travelers. Long before the dissection of this area by roads and railroads in the 19th century, it was a necessary part of a transportation route first used by the Native Americans in their spruce bark and birch canoes, and later it was used by trappers and our pioneer settlers. It was called the Falls of the Racket. We know that place today as Racquette Falls.

There are actually two falls, upper and lower, on this section of the river. The first, or upper, falls is located six miles downstream from where the river exits the basin, which has allowed the river to widen and is known as Long Lake. According to geologist Jerome Wyckoff, this lake is a perfect example of a large valley having eroded from the weaker rock in a fault zone millions of years ago and subsequently filling with water. The end result became a beautiful lake 14 miles in length with unsuspected vistas of the Seward Range as well as a combination of long, sandy beaches and lovely islands. A composition of rock, wood and water—a mix of public and private ownership loved by all who know it.

After having been rejoined by two major tributaries, Cold River and Moose Creek, the river cascades 15 feet over a rock outcropping that the ancient glacier's relentless action failed to wear away. A large foam-flecked pool of recirculating water has been formed below that drop that canoeists call a hydraulic jump. Momentarily

*Racquette Falls has flowed free since ancient geological times. It looks much the same today as it appeared in this 1917 photo by early Byram Road resident Reverend LeRoy Griggs. (photo courtesy of Meg Sheldon)*

stalled, the river quickly regains its energy and drops 80 feet in the next vertical mile of distance, creating a stretch of rapids of slightly over half a mile. Millions of logs were driven down this corridor, and if you paddle this stretch, you can still see the bolts and their hand-forged eyelets and rings that were drilled into some of the midstream boulders by early river drivers to contain their booms. The river then plunges over the second, or lower, falls through a volcanic dike and a worn passage that lets the river drop with a roar through clouds of spray into a short, rocky gorge. It then quiets down and forms a pool cluttered with large rocks, where a canoe "carry" at a strip of sand beach is located. Note: This lower falls is a complicated section best left to only the most competent paddlers, and then only at optimum water levels. It is important that you determine your exit eddy if you plan to take out above the falls and run the section above.

On a personal level, I hang a large bandanna from an overhanging shoreline tree because the horizon line that drops away at the falls is hard to see before it's too late. A 1.3-mile carry, or portage, allows the hiker or canoeist to avoid the stretch of rapids. Once just a narrow footpath, it was gradually widened to allow wagon travel. In fact, at one time during the late 1880s, a former lumberjack named Fournier (Anglicized to Funia?) would use his team of oxen to cart you and your boat across the carry. It has been reported that he often ferried as many as 20 boats a day. Cost: $1.25 for boat and gear on his wagon equipped with boat rack, or $1.50 for three passengers on his buckboard. Although the river is out of sight for the most part of the carry, the sound of the falls is distinctly heard.

The noise made by the many rapids on this river is heard frequently along its 170-mile course. Hedgehog and Moosehead rapids below Childwold, for example, can be heard a significant distance form the river. It is not surprising then to find that the St. Regis Indians (a branch of the Mohawk tribe), who knew the river as no one else, called it Ta-na-wa-deh, which, when translated to English, means "roughly swift" or "noisy water." This soon became corrupted to Racket on account of the noise it made. That name and spelling was the one used by the earliest surveyors in their reports and appeared labeled as such on maps as early as

*No partisanship allowed in the naming of Racquette River Drive. Shown are the entrance and exit street signs.*

1802. Several other theories of the name's baptism and its spelling exist, some of it necessarily folk etymology. Others take us into the territory of invented tradition or myth.

One interesting account comes from notes left by John Constable, a member of one of America's first families, whose father, William, was a major player in the Macomb Purchase – the acquisition of the huge land tract in northern New York. Today that area constitutes all of St. Lawrence, Lewis and Jefferson counties as well as parts of Oswego and Herkimer counties.

John was one of the earliest gentleman sportsmen to explore the Adirondacks at a time when they were still unmapped and largely unknown. Annotated in the margins of his personal 1860 map of "Racket River Waters" by Merrit is this: "The Raquette River derives its name from a large quantity of snowshoes found on an island near Potsdam during the Revolution."

According to historian and author Edith Pilcher in her 1992 narrative, *The Constables, First Family of the Adirondacks*:

"The note is of considerable interest, if true, because John Constable's information does not appear to be generally known and is contrary to accepted accounts. It suggests that Raquette Lake is named after the Raquette River, rather than vice-versa.

"The opposing version of this story asserts that the snowshoes (called Raquettes in French) were found at the lake, rather than the river, as recounted by historian Alfred Donaldson. He related that the snowshoes were abandoned on the southern shore of Raquette Lake by Sir John Johnson and his Tory followers when they were overtaken by spring thaws while fleeing from the Mohawk Valley to Montreal in May (some say March) of 1776. The same story is told by historians Hochschild and Trimm.

"It is impossible at this late date to determine who is correct, but it seems probable that John, who recorded his note nearly a century before Donaldson's book, was apt to have been in personal contact with original sources of information."

Another theory insists that the name was derived from the resemblance to a snowshoe (Fr. Raquette) at the river's mouth before it enters the St. Lawrence. The spelling Racquette with a "c" appeared about 1870 and was jointly used along with the spelling Racket. Later, the spelling Raquette with no "c" appeared. Today, all three spellings can be found, and all have their strong supporters. That makes it easy—take your choice!

Maybe the local highway department has the answer—the entrance to Racquette River Drive from the village off Route 30 has a street sign that reads "Racquette River Drive." A mile further, where that street exits near Trail's End to rejoin Route 30, the street sign reads "Raquette River Drive." Now that's diplomacy!

*Tupper Lake Free Press Print:* January 05, 2005

# A (True) Fish Tale

ONE OF ONLY SEVERAL remaining interior ranger stations in the Adirondack Park is located at Racquette Falls. The station located there is a handsome log and stone structure with polished wooden floors and handcrafted furniture. A striking stone fireplace helps lend a Great Camp arts and crafts look to the main room, which is kept faultlessly neat by its bachelor seasonal ranger. A small office and efficient kitchen share the rear of the building with a small bedroom and a larger bunkroom designed to house personnel in the event of a fire or other emergency.

I would add to this description of the cabin a point of historical interest and recognition. This is done because certain occurrences need to be recorded, and deserved recognition is often overlooked. For example, that fireplace was built by my former classmate and longtime friend, Howard Reandeau, who at the time of construction was the D.E.C. caretaker at the "Falls."

Howard (Wigs) was a skilled stone mason and his masterful work graces many of the pretentious homes and residences in this area, not to mention his exceptional work (along with other local artisans such as Washington Street resident Tony Rovito) that is so highly admired throughout the grounds and buildings of the Adirondack Museum at Blue Mountain Lake. It should be noted that the stone used for the fireplace and chimney at the ranger station was not, as might be expected, of native origin. Rather, it originated in Tennessee, arrived here on a freight train, offloaded at a siding off Mill Street and trucked to Blue Mountain Lake. It was originally acquired because of its outstanding color and form and was a specific requirement in the architectural plans for various exhibits and buildings at the present monumental and world-famous museum, which was then undergoing construction.

When there was no longer any need for the stone at the museum, the surplus was made available to the D.E.C. through the generosity of the museum and Chet Johnson of this village, whose firm, W.C. Johnson and Sons, began the original museum construction in 1955. The stone for the station was then transported to Coreys by truck and then, over the winter, sledged into the clearing on what is today's foot trail.

Chet Johnson had a special affection for the clearing and river. He was a friend to several of the previous owners and for many years had a platform tent camp a short distance downstream where Palmer Brook enters the river. Chet will also be remembered for the countless hours he toiled for others over the years, removing hundreds of partially submerged river drive logs to improve navigation on the river's twisting course. Can you imagine his indignation today over the proposal to ban motors on his beloved river? (Even as he would severely condemn the yahoos whose reckless and inconsiderate behavior with their motorboats threaten that traditional privilege.)

Some sort of dwelling has existed in the clearing since about 1800. It was once much larger than it is today and at one early time around 1860 was the headquarters and supply depot for goods brought up from this village and destined for use there and in the many remote lumber camps in the Calkins Brook and Cold River areas. After the lumber operations ended, successive owners maintained a lodge and cabins, offering boarding and transport services. More on those owners in a later column, but let me tell you about meeting the last private owner before it was acquired by New York State.

A number of years ago, Dave LaVoy and I, not having any luck fishing, decided to try the upper falls of the river. Here, we experienced incredible luck catching our limit of large speckled trout.

*The original Racquette Falls Lodge is shown above in this photograph by Seneca Ray Stoddard. By the time Charles DeLancett of Tupper Lake took over the property in 1900, little remained of the original structure. He erected a frame lodge in 1910, which went the way of so many old Adirondack hostelries in 1934—destruction by fire. It was replaced by a log lodge, shown in the below snapshot, built by Ross Freeman of Coreys. That too met a fiery end, burning to the ground on September 8, 1973.*

There weren't supposed to be trout in the river, but we didn't know that! The pool below the falls was thick with white foam, not unlike the head on a fine glass of Guinness Stout. Almost each cast of our lures into that foam produced a fat trout, strong and wild. Landing those fighting beauties, our reels screaming in protest as the trout made long runs and sought the fast current below the pool, was an experience Dave and I will always remember as one of the best days in a lifetime of fishing.

Having finished fishing, we headed back to the clearing and on the trail we met an older gentleman. As wood travelers often do, we fell into conversation. I remember that he was skeptical about our fabulous catch. Only when we opened our creels did he acknowledge ours was no fish tale. He told us that he had known the river for almost 40 years and, to the best of his knowledge, an invasion of pike had long ago cleaned out any trout. He wondered out loud if the recent high water had flushed trout into the river from its Cold River tributary, a known trout fishery.

Earlier that day, while returning from Dawson on the old supply haul road, I had found a large, handsome leather portfolio, or wallet, laced with protected multiple sleeves of beautiful trout flies. I took the case from my pack and asked the older gent if it could belong to him. If I had returned a gold Rolex watch, he could not have been more overjoyed, nor, I suspect, more surprised. We were, after all, a couple of smelly, rough-looking customers. That gentleman turned out to be Charles Byran, Jr., of Chicago, former president of the Pullman Standard Car Manufacturing Company and a distinguished engineer. At the time of our meeting, he was the owner of the Racquette Falls clearing, the lodge and cabins there and, along with Mrs. Byran, had been a summer visitor to the area since the early 1920s. Mr. Byran died in 1966 in Chicago. In 1970, Mrs. Byran sold the 89.2-acre parcel to New York State. Two years later, the Racquette Falls Lodge, built by Ross Freeman of Coreys, was destroyed in a spectacular night fire that broke out in the generator room of the two-story log structure. The D.E.C. interior ranger residence is near the footprint of that former lodge.

Racquette Falls is a unique, charming and magnetic place. From the early Tupper Lake lumbermen 145 years ago, it has commanded a special niche in our local history. We are so lucky to have this cherished legacy in our back yard! As Peter, Paul and Mary have chorused, "This land is my land—this land is your land!"

*Tupper Lake Free Press Print:* January 26, 2005

# MOTHER JOHNSON

WE CONTINUE IN TODAY'S *TRANSITIONS* the four-part series concerning Racquette Falls. It will be recalled that some sort of dwelling has existed in the clearing at the falls since about 1860. Also that it was headquarters for a large distribution point for supplies brought up from this village and destined for use at the clearing and remote camps on the Seward Mountains. It is 20.25 river miles to the Moody Bridge, 10 miles to the outlet of Follensby Pond and 17.75 miles to the Oxbow and the Natural History Museum observer platforms from that location.

Old maps between 1860 and 1890 indicate the clearing as Johnson's. This name was in reference to Lucy Johnson—a cook at the lumber camp there. When lumbering operations halted, Mother Johnson, as she was known, stayed on there with her husband, who had the wonderful first name of Philander. The Johnsons then ran an inn and stopping place for travelers.

The late Tupper Lake historian and editor, Louis Simmons, reported in an article printed in the *Tupper Lake Free Press and Herald* (January 19, 1961) that a Newcomb census in 1860 recorded a Lucy Johnson and her husband, Philander Johnson, as living on the Old Chester to Canton Military Road in that community. (Another settler at that time was named Valorous Hall. How about that for poetic first names?) The Johnsons evidently came to the Falls shortly after that 1860 date.

Do you wonder which way the Johnsons would have traveled to

arrive at the Racquette Falls Lumber Camp from Newcomb? The stagecoach road to Long Lake wasn't built until 1876, so that left two possibilities, the first one being 16 miles on the Chester to Canton Military Road that went by their Newcomb home and then crossed the outlet of Long Lake, which was at that point seven miles further downriver to the falls. The second possibility was the waterway route that led across a series of lakes and ponds to the Racquette River in roughly the same distance as the overland route. A description of both routes may be of reader interest, and you can form your own opinion which route the Johnsons might have used (in the absence of any documented account that I could locate).

Donaldson, in his *History of the Adirondacks*, tells us that the Chester to Canton road was one of the earliest of three so-called Military Roads opened through the Adirondacks. It was authorized by an "act of 1807 to lay out and open a road from the town of Chester to the town of Canton." Chester is in the part of Warren County just south of Schroon Lake. The exact course of the road is as follows: Starting at Chester, it ran northwest into and through Essex County, following approximately the north branch of the Hudson River. The road then swung, according to an 1851 map of Hamilton County, "around the foot of Long Lake, crossing the Cold River and the Racquette River in its course." Thence it passed into the extreme southwest corner of Franklin County, skirting the southern end of Big Tupper, crossing a brook near there on a bridge (Bridgebrook Outlet). After that, it approached the Grasse River (near Mt. Arab Lake and Massawepie) and followed that river to Canton. Incidentally, if you have visited the Interpretive Center at Newcomb near Rich Lake, you may have walked along trails there that were once part of the Newcomb section of this long-ago road. The road also passed by the "Catlin Clearing," named after Cromwell Catlin, an early settler. A woods road leading to Cold River through Huntington Forest Preserve off 28N passes by this clearing today, which is overgrown but still discernable—as members of Tupper Lake's hiking group on its annual guided Huntington Forestry tour will confirm.

Further evidence of that road comes from Tom Bissell of Long Lake, a fourth-generation Adirondack native. Tom's great grandfather arrived in Newcomb in 1822 from Shoreham, VT and knew and used that road. In a letter to the *Elizabethtown Post and Gazette*, dated around 1900, Tom's grandfather, Charles Bissell, noted that the Bissells "traversed the country there (Newcomb) far and near, often accompanied by Indians, and knew well the location and outlets of the Military Road visible at that time." It seems, he noted, "that it was not known by any other name."

Since the Johnsons were known to own oxen, this may have been the route of choice. On the other hand, a boat builder by the name of Caleb Chase was turning out boats in Newcomb as early as 1850 – "such as one a man can carry on his head through the woods from river to river and lake to lake." A boat built by Chase that, along with contributions from other builders found in Saranac Lake and Tupper Lake, evolved into the guideboat as we know it today. A Chase boat in the woods ranked with a "Brewster buggy" in the city. Thus, like Mart Moody and others, whose chief transport were their boats, the Johnsons may have elected to use the water route, a description of which follows:

*Shown is Mother Johnson's, located at Racquette Falls. Its humble appearance was offset by excellent food and hospitality.*

"By boat through Belden Pond, carry of 12 rods; Rich Lake, three miles; west branch of river, one mile; Catlin Lake stream to Lilly Pad Pond, one mile; Catlin Lake, three miles; Round Pond, one mile; one mile carry to Long Lake. A little over 13 miles in all. Note: Much of this route is now on Huntington Wildlife Forestry (Syracuse University) property and is off-limits to the public."

"Mother Johnson's" as the modest halfway house or inn was called, became a popular stopping place. That this was successful probably comes to no surprise, given Mother's extended reputation as hostess and cook. Consider that a cook employed at a well-run lumber camp didn't last long unless they were a hard worker and could provide excellent meals for calorie-consuming, vigorous lumberjacks. It was not unusual for one lumberjack at his 3 a.m. breakfast to consume 10 pancakes, four eggs, bacon, six doughnuts, fried potatoes and many slices of heavily buttered toast in addition to black tea, coffee and juice. It was a fact that the best lumberjacks went to work at only the camps that had good food. Camp bosses and owners stepped softly around a prized cook. Rules such as "no talking during meals" were a direct result of the cook's demand for silence – talking would slow the meal time and delay cleaning tables and doing dishes. Mother Johnson, as lumber camp cook, was noted for her pancakes, beans and molasses and, especially, her prune pies. Prunes were also a camp staple, both as stewed and in pies. As one French Canadian cook, probably at a Santa Clara Lumber Company camp once remarked, "For me, I'll take the prune. It makes even better apple pie than the peach."

On a bitterly cold February night in 1987, Mother Johnson quietly passed away, those in the adjoining room not knowing she had left them. The *Tupper Lake Free Press* of January 19, 1961, quotes an account of her burial as follows:

"Larmie (Fournier), the Frenchman who had driven the oxen on the Racquette Falls Carry for the past two years, immediately started down the Racquette. He was joined at Calkins place by Mr. Wood.

"They came through to William Dukett's on the Indian Carry on snowshoes. Mr. Dukett brought them here (Bartletts), and they got the boards for the coffin, which Mr. Dukett made. They will bury her at the foot of Racquette Falls until the river opens up, when she will be buried at Long Lake."

Dukett owned the Hiawatha House on Stony Pond, now the residence of Anne Disotelle Whittum and her husband, Stan.

Note: Today a marker in the Long Lake cemetery bears her name and stands among other stones dated back to her era. However, it is generally believed that her body was never moved.

*Tupper Lake Free Press Print:* February 16, 2005

## GENERATIONS OF STURDY STOCK

MOST OBSERVERS WILL AGREE that the coming of the railroads in the late 1800s contributed more than any other factor to the rapid growth of this community. Indeed, when John Hurd completed his railroad from Moira to Tupper Lake in 1890, it triggered the construction of over one hundred buildings in one year. The population, which consisted of 17 families in 1889, exploded to an amazing 1,051 residents just two years later, and by 1900 the number had reached 3,045 residents.

Of course, the sawmill Hurd erected on the shores of Racquette Pond also became a huge incentive for people to establish here. It was arguably the largest sawmill built in New York State. Over two hundred feet wide and four hundred feet long, it was a two-story structure with a capacity of 300,000 feet of lumber per day.

Its seven huge boilers were fired with sawdust and shavings blown through a system of pipes. A large percentage of the slabs and edgings that were a by-product of the sawing operation was transferred over a high tramway that crossed above Demars Boulevard near today's White Birch Restaurant. It then continued above ground along what is now Pleasant Avenue (Railroad Street in my youth) and served several kilns that turned the waste product into charcoal.

Thousands of cords went to "floor" the marsh along the pond, which helped create today's Municipal Park, and the rest of the waste was burned in a huge burner that towered 100 feet into the air.

*One of the early pioneers in this village was graduate pharmacist L.C. Maid, who arrived here in 1897. He had been advised by a hospital supply salesman to try Tupper Lake, which was in the early stages of a boomtown, as a place to establish a drugstore. Shown is his early store, located where the present Gachowski building stands today (remember Maid's Corner?), which soon developed into one of the leading North Country Rexall stores. Mr. Maid would become a prominent and influential resident for the next 63 years.*

Readers may be interested in what was termed a world record for sawn lumber at this mill. According to the *Pittsburgh Gazette and Times* of July 1919, Tupper Lake workers converted 2,303 spruce logs into lumber in nine hours and 20 minutes. The newspaper further stated: "Two saws making the cut on an 8-ft. band saw running 1,500 revolutions a minute. All spruce was 12 to 16 feet in length. No cut was made over 10 inches in width and all were cut to 1¼-inch lumber.

"The mill was set up to do 60,000 feet a day but rarely fell below

*To make charcoal, kilns that had the appearance of huge beehives were used. They were loaded from the top with slash, set on fire and kept smoldering. After a time, water was poured on the wood and charcoal resulted. Dozens of such kilns lined the length of Pleasant Avenue.*

100,000 feet, which meant an average of 2,000 logs each day."

Is it any wonder, I ask you, that historians such as Floy Hyde, in her book, *Adirondack Forests, Fields and Mines*, declared that "many of today's residents are descendants of long lines of sturdy, enterprising, hard workers who did not come and go with the change of seasons. They were not summer 'guests.' They stayed put." The mountains became their homeland, wherein they found or developed their own way of making a living.

Year by year, other persons joined them, perhaps enamored with the lakes and mountains, possibly seeking to regain their health in the Adirondack air or, in rare cases, sensing an opportunity to develop a promising business enterprise from the mountain resources.

From the days of the pioneer, the road has been "uphill" all the way. Yet somehow, according to Mrs. Hyde, "despite the forbidden circumstances of isolation, poor soil and a short growing season when only 10 to 12 weeks can be counted on to be free of frost, many people made their homes here accepting as part of their way of life not only the beauty and allure of Adirondack summer, but the biting cold and severe hardships of the long, cold winter."

Those sturdy people who set that world record sawmill cut and other pioneers who established themselves here have many descendants in this community. Like their ancestors, those descendants have also, "surmounted the odds and have adapted and prospered and would not choose to live anywhere else." Tupper Lake remains a wonderful place to live and raise a family. Let's hope we can keep it that way!

When that rush of settlers arrived here in 1891, they found an ideal location for building. An early lumber company had cut all the virgin white pine along Racquette Pond and up to what is today's Main Street as far as Tallman Hill above Vachereau Street. This left a clearing that was being used as a pasture by a man named Bill McLaughlin.

McLaughlin had been a foreman for the Pomeroy Lumber Company, the firm that had made that early clear cut of pine. He had stayed behind when Pomeroy moved out and owned most of the land upon which the village was built.

Geologist Jim Carl has noted, "The combination of high ground for living below Tallman Hill (the highest point of which is a bedrock knob, but the hill itself is mostly glacial depositional material) and the low ground next to the lake for industry (perfect for stacking and storing logs prior to sawing) was utilized for the full extent."

In 1880, G.W.F. Smith, a surveyor from Potsdam, came through Tupper on his way to Tahawus to meet Verplank Colvin, the state surveyor. He wrote the following observations (in part) to his wife: "The people here have all gone crazy. They seem to think they are going to have a city immediately. There is a large clearing here and this clearing and all surrounding woodland is all run out (surveyed) and laid into streets and lots. This embryo city now has a genuine western boom. If beauty of location could ensure a city, however, this would be one, for the ground rises gradually from the shore of the pond back quite a distance, with then an abrupt rise of 20 or 30 feet and then a gradual rise again, giving every part a fine view of Racket Pond for miles and when the woods are cut away a view of the lower end of Big Tupper Lake."

Next *Transitions*: Growing pains in a new community.

*Tupper Lake Free Press Print:* March 23, 2005

# GROWING PAINS IN A NEW COMMUNITY

THE YEAR WAS 1899. The surveyor named Tupper, who long ago had named Tupper's lake after himself, could never in his wildest dreams have imagined the frenetic activity that was taking place in the settlement near that lake he had stumbled across in 1795.

A rush of settlers touched off by the completion of railroad access and the potential of employment opportunities by the start of mill operations had transformed a wilderness into a frontier town as real as any in the famed Wild West. It was build now – civilize later. Sewage: Dig a hole in the ground. Water: Tap one of the many springs or dig a well. It was as though the town had come in on the wind. No thoughts of infrastructure and only the beginnings of any sort of administrative organization.

Yes, one accomplishment did occur: a demand by those pioneers to have their own local government. Ten years before, in 1890, they had formed the Town of Altamont, setting itself off from the Town of Waverly. That division included three townships and a geographic area to be governed of some 15 miles in length along its north/south line and about six miles wide along the southern baseline, or about 70,000 assessed acres.

We became the last of Franklin County's 19 towns to be established. "One thing is certain: our town fathers were literally starting from scratch to create a clearing in the wilderness to an outpost of civilization." In the words of former historian Louis

*Shown are the smoldering fire ruins of the village business section on the morning of July 30, 1899. This view was taken from the corner of Wawbeek Avenue and Park Street. The buildings remaining on the left are the Hotel Altamont and the Opera House (now the village office). Note Tallman Hill, upper right.*

Simmons, "It proved to be a lusty baby."

Unfortunately, only a few scattered copies of the early newspaper, the *Tupper Lake Herald*, still exist dating back to 1911 and, as Louie lamented, "they would have constituted an irreplaceable record of Tupper's growing pains."

Descriptions by others of that period were not always complimentary. Donaldson, in his *History of the Adirondacks*, noted: "(Tupper Lake) grew with surprising rapidity, but as a lumbering center only. Its structures were crude and ugly and its inhabitants were tough and lawless."

Donaldson was a well-to-do former banker who came to Saranac Lake for his health. He only devoted a very short paragraph about this village in his basic history. I've often wondered (uncomfortably because of his ability) if this was due to a certain snobbishness that existed for many years among some Saranac Lake residents toward Tupper Lake's lumber town image. A feeling, perhaps, encouraged by that community's more cosmopolitan status. It was, of course, a world-famous center in advanced research for the cause and cure of pulmonary disease, and it attracted artists, writers and the wealthy and famous, all seeking the fresh air cure that before the advent of wonder drugs was the last hope for a fatal disease.

Today that feeling about our sawdust town has largely evaporated, as well is should, and I hear only admiration from Saranac Lake friends about the progress and many exciting happenings occurring here.

The point is, my suspicions not withstanding, Mr. Donaldson's two-volume history is a valuable contribution to Adirondack history, and Tupper Lake was a major part of that history. At the time it was published in 1921, this community, after all, had just (against great odds) successfully convinced the federal government to build a huge cure facility here. The Oval Wood Dish Company was at its peak in sales, production and employment. We were the lumbering capital of New York State. The American Legion Mountain Camp had been established. It was also a significant economic and cultural engine, and its presence was due, in part, to an enlightened citizenry that contributed influence and substantial financial support—all monumental achievements that were totally ignored by Mr. Donaldson.

Donaldson did mention (and concede) that the town improved after purification in our big fire of 1899, which he termed "a blessing in disguise, for on the site of the old village, there soon rose a far more slightly, more cleanly, more orderly, and more prosperous one."

It is pretty well agreed that the so-called "Big Fire" of 1899 was a "blessing" in some respects, but it was also a paralyzing blow to our embryo town. Imagine the distress, the anguish, the absolute horror that those Tupper Lakers must have experienced as the sun rose that July day and revealed an entire business section as well as areas around Lake and High streets laying in the smoldering ashes of fire ruins. Close to one hundred buildings were destroyed within three or four hours, and 700 people became homeless with a loss of all their possessions that ill-fated night.

Next *Transitions*: More on the Great Fire.

*Tupper Lake Free Press Print:* April 06, 2005

# THE GREAT FIRE

IN 1890, CLARENCE KING, Edwin Page and Robert Page, partners in a hardware store in Moira, made a corporate decision. They would build a store in Tupper Lake.

Their friend, a go-getter named John Hurd, who had started building his Northern Adirondack Railroad from Moira seven years earlier in 1883, had pushed his trackage 54 miles into Tupper, and the place was booming. Hurd had also begun surveying and grading an extension of his railroad southeast from Tupper, up the Racquette River to Racquette Falls and Long Lake. Note: The plan was to connect with the Delaware and Hudson at North Creek. However, newly enacted legislation prevented laying tracks on Forest Preserve Land that the route would have crossed. Part of this grade remains, now under several feet of water in Racquette Pond, and can be readily seen from Rockridge or the south end of Lake Street.

Meanwhile, three trains each way were running daily between Tupper and Moira. By 1900, Hurd's line, now known as the New York and Ottawa, was connecting at the Canadian border with the Canadian National Railroad at Helena. Travel to Ottawa, 128 miles away, could now be accomplished in four hours if all went as planned. Travel to the Canadian capital city became a popular excursion for Tupper Lake residents. It also allowed cordwood from here to be shipped to Montreal for use as fuel, hemlock bark and charcoal (Seaver, 1918, p. 535). It also opened vast new areas for lumber cutting, transportation and, consequently, employment opportunities.

Robert Page stayed in Moira temporarily that year of 1890 to close out that store's inventory, and Clarence and Ed built a large general store here on the corner of Lake and Cliff streets, across from today's post office. It was a case of "right place at the right time," and by 1899, the venture was an established success.

Let us go now to what was a beautiful summer weekend in July 1899. Robert Page is at his camp on Tupper Lake at a place still referred to as Page's Bluff and which has remained one of the most beautiful and outstanding locations on our lake. Patriarchs of an earlier generation of pine can be found towering 100 feet in height here today, many with an impressive diameter breast height (DBH) of 40 inches or more. Page's Bluff has been under the careful stewardship of the Gibson family for many years and has remained as pristine as Mr. Page would have found it over one hundred years ago.

Mr. Page didn't hear the St. Alphonsus Church bell that was the signal for a fire (there was no fire department at the time). However, his partner, Mr. King, who lived on the cliff above High Street, did hear the bell and along with other able-bodied men ran to answer the alarm only to discover that it was his store that was ablaze. The time was 11:45 p.m., July 29, 1899. The fire had started in a small building located to the rear of the King/Page store. It was a place where the owners kept their kerosene supply, an important commodity in those days of no electricity. The cause of the fire would remain unexplained, although arson was suspected but never proven.

In less than five hours, almost one hundred buildings would be destroyed and 700 people would be homeless with the loss of all their possessions.

How, you might ask, could this have been allowed to happen? Find the answer in the next *Transitions*.

*Tupper Lake Free Press Print:* April 20, 2005

# A Frantic Bucket Brigade

MANY READERS OF THIS COLUMN may remember Joe Potvin, who was a longtime resident and early settler in this community. In 1899, Mr. Potvin was living on High Street. His home was right next door to the McCloskey's Bottling Works, which was then located on the corner of Vachereau and High streets.

At a few minutes before midnight, July 29, 1899, the continuous ringing of the St. Alphonsus Church bell woke Joe from a sound sleep. Fire! There was, as yet, no organized fire department, and such fire protection as the town had in the early 1890s was provided by the lumber companies that organized the firefighting units among their employees.

Joe was one of those employees working for the Export Lumber Company, which owned the Big Mill located near today's Municipal Park. Tupper also had no water system at that time, and the only source of water pressure was a single pipe laid on top of tile ground from the Big Mill. Joe had been assigned, in the case of fire, to go directly to the mill and start the pump that forced water through the line.

There were no streetlights and, with only a smoky lantern to light his way through complete darkness, Joe found his way down Mill Street to the planning mill where he and fellow employee Joe Martin started the pump. Screams of "No water! No water!" resonated down the street from the corner of Cliff and Lake

*One of the first buildings to be rebuilt after the Great Fire of 1899 was the Propp building shown above. Barnat Propp had built his original clothing and jewelry store on the corner of Park and High streets (now Stewart's) in 1889.*

streets, where the King and Page General Store had become an uncontrolled inferno that rapidly engulfed surrounding buildings. A distraught Joe Potvin soon found that drainage valves had unknowingly been left open, but before that discovery was corrected, the town was doomed.

A.J. Clarke, former postmaster here and well-known newspaper correspondent, recounted his personal memories of that fire in an article dated July 30, 1935, which appeared in the *Tupper Lake Free Press*. Parts of the following description were excerpted from

Mr. Clarke's account. With the failure of the water supply, volunteers formed a bucket brigade to Racquette Pond in a vain attempt to stem the fire that had quickly spread to the large Hotel Windsor (today's Old Northern Pub). As the flames spread, air currents set up by the heat of such a large fire carried embers across the street, igniting a building owned by Harry Cohn (next to today's Tip Top Electric). This building housed the post office, where only two weeks before Clarence King had been appointed our third postmaster.

The fire then raced beyond all hope of control up Park Street, destroying everything in its path as far as Sears Hill. This included the Commercial Hotel (later rebuilt as the Iroquois Hotel, now the Stewart's Store location). The fire consumed the John Sears boarding house and the home of Medie Sears and Patrick Edwards, finally stopping at the Cheney Avenue corner.

Moving down Park Street, the flames turned everything there into a raging inferno, destroying in its path the Thissell building near the present Tupper Lake National Bank location. The Thissell building, owned by beloved physician Dr. Thissell, housed the L.C. Maid drug store, the John Goff jewelry store and, on the upper floor, the offices of the Santa Clara Lumber Company as well as the offices of Attorney J.L. Tallman, justice of the peace. It then raced up Wawbeek Avenue, totaling everything, including the Hayes Livery, where the Knight of Columbus Hall stands today.

In an ironic twist, Mr. Hayes was using the horses and wagons from his livery to bring buckets of water from the pond to wet down blankets that were being placed on the roof of the Hotel Altamont (corner of Park and Wawbeek), a method that, together with a providential shift in the wind, saved that building, even as fire destroyed Mr. Hayes' livery. Meanwhile, across the street from the hotel, dynamite was being detonated in a vain attempt to stop the flames spreading by blowing up three buildings.

It didn't succeed in stopping the fire beast that then torched and destroyed the small Bernier Hotel on High Street (located near today's Stewart's Store dumpster). The fire then jumped

Vachereau Street (then just a lane leading to Cheney Avenue) and engulfed the McCloskey Bottling Works (today's Frenette building). Next to go was Joe Potvin's house along with a bakery owned by Archie LeBoeuf, a machine shop, three residential homes and finally the Grace Episcopal Church before the fire stopped just short of reaching the P.H. McCarthy home, where Ed LeBlanc lives today.

What a chaotic, frightening bedlam our Main Street must have been on that ill-fated night. Imagine wagon teams of exhausted horses bolting trip after trip in the darkened night. Imagine an army of frantic residents, many of them women, wetting down blankets and forming a relay to successively smother the roof fire on the two-story Hotel Altamont.

Imagine the scene across the street from the hotel, where dynamite charges were exploding in an attempt to blow up three buildings, and imagine the entire business block as a mass of roaring flames. Imagine watching in horrified disbelief as building after building is consumed by fire so intense and hot that it deformed and melted iron. As resident John Timmons was later to exclaim, if Hell were any hotter, then he was certainly going to try to keep away from it.

*Tupper Lake Free Press Print:* April 27, 2005

## DRUGSTORES AND DINERS

*TRANSITIONS* THIS WEEK offers a delightful essay written by former Tupper Lake resident Joan (Propp) Potter, who has graciously given permission for it to be reprinted in this column.

The essay first appeared in 1999 in *Adirondack Life*. It was later selected for inclusion in an anthology of best Adirondack authors, *Rooted in Rock: New Adirondack Writers, 1975 – 2000*, edited by Jim Gould. The essay follows:

<u>Diners, Drugstores and Dives</u>

"In my teenage scrapbook, which I have carefully carried from place to place over the forty-nine years since I graduated from Tupper Lake High School, I find a booklet with a yellowed paper cover embossed in gold: *Senior Class Memories.* I riffle through the pages, reading snippets of sentiments from my long-ago buddies: 'Remember Willie's dock and the good times we had!' 'Good luck to the walky-talky of the third period gym class.' And an old saw, 'Remember Grant, remember Lee, to hell with them, remember me.'

"One inscription, in neat adult handwriting, stands out from the youthful scribbles. 'You are to be congratulated on your graduation,' it reads. 'I hope you never graduate from your friends at Maid's Pharmacy.' It's signed by John Maid, owner of the drugstore in whose red leather booths my friends and I spent many after-school hours, sipping chocolate Cokes and gossiping about our teachers, boyfriends, and female rivals.

"I remember Maid's as a sunny, cheerful spot with a soda fountain; booths along a wall; shelves of ointments; powders, pills and cosmetics; and a counter for prescriptions. Our other teenage meeting place, the Miss Tupper Diner, was in retrospect more grown-up. Instead of chocolate and cologne, the diner smelled like fried eggs and Lucky Strikes. Working men ate there, settled on stools at the counter so they could banter with the cook as he tossed burgers on the grill.

"My friends and I sat in booths for hours and always ordered the diner special—toasted sweet rolls dripping with melted butter. I don't remember if we drank coffee and smoked cigarettes. Maybe we did, taking a chance that no relatives or friends of our mothers would push open the door, bringing in a blast of cold, icy air, and catch us in forbidden pursuits.

"My most vivid Miss Tupper memory is of the evening my girlfriends and I decided to bleach our bangs. The six of us were on the cheering squad—later kicked off for drinking Tom Collinses in a Potsdam restaurant before a basketball game—and were among the most daring eleventh-grade girls. We each had hair of a different color and style, but we all had bangs, and somewhere we got the idea to bleach a streak into them.

"At Maid's drugstore we bought the fixings—peroxide and some kind of white powder. Then we headed for the diner. Two by two, while the others waited in a booth, we locked ourselves in the tiny women's bathroom, spread the mixture on our hair, and waited for the magic transformation. It worked—more or less—and each of us emerged with bangs in various shades of blond and orange. But what I wonder is, why did those incredibly tolerant diner owners let six giddy teenage girls hold their bathroom hostage for what must have been an entire evening?

"The drugstore and the diner were our weekday hangouts. On Saturday nights my girlfriends and I got dressed up in our twirly calf-length skirts, short-sleeved sweaters and black flats and headed for the Hotel Altamont. There we sat around a table in the dimly lighted Mountain Room tapping our fingers to the music and waiting for someone to ask us to dance.

"Although I clearly remember drinking rum-and-Cokes at the Altamont, none of us had yet reached the legal drinking age. In fact, pasted in the back cover of my high-school scrapbook is a cardboard sign I lifted from the wall of the dance hall the month before I left for college. In thick red letters the notice reads 'No Minors Permitted in Bar or Mountain Room at any Time.' Below the message, some jokester had printed 'John L. Lewis.'

"One Saturday evening after I'd left the house, the police chief telephoned my father to warn him that his officers were going to 'raid the Altamont' that night and catch all the underage drinkers. 'Just in case your daughter's there, Jess,' he stated, 'I thought you'd like to know.'

"With that news, my mother leapt into action and headed for the hotel. I can still hear the astonished voice of my friend across the table in the dark, smoky Mountain Room. 'Joan, your mother just walked in.' Unthinkable. My proper mother in this raffish place. But I looked toward the door and there she was, huddled in her woolen coat and motioning to me. We all hid our cigarettes under the table and I rushed over to her. 'Chief Timmons called and said there's going to be a raid tonight,' she whispered. 'You'd better come with me.' She gave me just enough time to warn the other kids, and by the time the cops arrived, everybody under eighteen was safe at home.

"A police raid was an unusual event; we teenagers always felt quite comfortable at the Altamont. But our ultimate Saturday night destination was the Waukesha, a rambling log roadhouse a few miles south of the village. We headed there whenever we could find someone with a car to give us a ride.

"Inside the Waukesha, neon beer sings hung over the bar near the entrance, and lamps on each table in the long main room illuminated the woodland paintings hanging on the walls. At the far end of the room was a space for dancing and a bandstand where Corky Arsenault and his combo played tunes like 'Tangerine' and 'A Cottage for Sale.' I distinctly remember the piano player as a skinny old woman who always kept a mug of beer within reach. Probably, though, she was a lot younger than I am now.

"It was at the Waukesha that I slow-danced with my boyfriends and then rushed into the women's bathroom to gossip with the girls about my current love object. It was in that very bathroom that someone described to me just exactly what was meant by a French kiss. And it was at the Waukesha, not long after I graduated from high school, where my friend Arthur celebrated his safe return from the Korean War.

"Everybody at the bar wanted to buy Arthur a drink, and he couldn't refuse. Finally he clambered up on the bandstand and announced that he was going to sing 'The Marine Corps Hymn.' I can still see him up there, singing his heart out and swaying to the music until he fell over backwards, crashing into Corky Arsenault's drum set.

"I don't know where Arthur is today, and the wonderful Waukesha is gone, destroyed by fire in 1975. The Miss Tupper Diner was transformed into a more upscale restaurant called The Rose in the mid-eighties, but that has closed too. Maid's sold to Monakey & Meader, then overwhelmed by national chain pharmacies, it is today an optometrist's office. And after the Grand Union Company bought the old Hotel Altamont, a wrecking company came to demolish it, tearing away—according to a newspaper report—eighty-five doors, including the one my mother had nervously pulled open when she came to rescue her underage daughter."

Joan Potter was born and raised in Tupper Lake and returned to the Adirondacks in 1990 when she and her husband moved to a log cabin near Elizabethtown. There, they founded Pinto Press, a small publishing company that specialized in Adirondack books. Joan co-authored the press's first book, *The Book of Adirondack Firsts*, and edited several others. A regular contributor to *Adirondack Life*, she wrote the book *African-American Firsts*, published in 1994, and co-authored the children's book *African Americans Who Were First* (1997). The selections reprinted here first appeared in *Adirondack Life* in 1999.

*Tupper Lake Free Press Print:* May 04, 2005

# SUSTAINABLE WATER SUPPLY

IN THE DAYS FOLLOWING the Great Fire of 1899, the residents of this community considered, for a short time, abandoning the destroyed uptown site and building downtown.

Louis Simmons, in his local history, *Mostly Spruce and Hemlock*, tells us: "With few exceptions, Tupper residential property had survived as had the Racket Pond House (later the American House, now the vacant lot on Lake Street to the rear of the Day Wholesale building) and also the Hotel Altamont had survived so shelter was not too pressing a problem. Lumber was plentiful and cheap at the local sawmills, business was brisk and the despair of the 'morning after' was quickly replaced by optimism. Rebuilding started almost at once, led by the crude and temporary little one-room, unpainted board shack put up by Paul Prespare on the Holland House site (next to today's movie theater), labeled 'The Klondike Saloon,' whose beverages may have helped contribute to the return of optimism and confidence in the future. In any event, photos taken only a couple years after the big fire show Park Street pretty much restored and back in business as usual."

As has been related previously in this column, the lack of water pressure and the fact that there was no fire department, other than that of a loosely organized group of lumber company employees, contributed in large part to the total destruction that occurred in that 1899 fire.

Our first settlers were well aware of these shortcomings. The

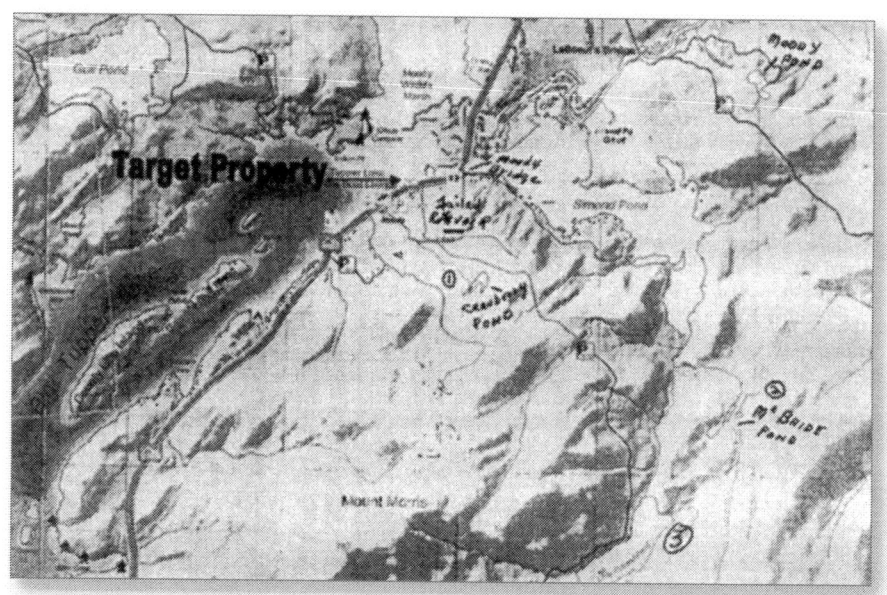

*Shown on a current map above are the potential water supply sources on Mt. Morris, located in an 1895 survey for that purpose. It was, at that time, a raw and undeveloped area.*

minutes of town board meetings show that in 1895, and again in 1896, local businessmen petitioned the town board to organize a fire company and purchase fire-fighting apparatus.

It took the 1899 fire to get effective action, however. The next month in August, following the fire, the board voted to establish a fire district comprising the entire town, and on October 7, 1899, it contracted the Tupper Lake Water Company (more on that company later) to supply water for fire protection. On December 28, 1899, the board voted to spend $600 on fire apparatus and christened the infant fire department the Tupper Lake Fire Hose Company of the Town of Altamont. Hose Company 1 was organized January 20, 1900, and Hose Company 2 followed soon afterward.

The Tupper Lake Fire Department would grow to become one of the best volunteer departments in the state. Hose Company 3 downtown unit was organized October 31, 1902 with 59 members (of whom 23 were "dropped" the first year, apparently for inactivity). The October 19, 1902 fire destruction of the Junction House, a pioneer hotel opposite the railroad station, had apparently jolted the downtown men into forming their own fire-fighting unit.

The need for a water supply was also realized even before the fire. In fact, in 1897 Jim McBride and Will LaFountain, local surveyors, were hired by several prominent local men to survey the Mt. Morris area with the idea to locate a suitable water supply. That project languished, however, until the fire kick-started the idea into action, and a month after that conflagration, the Tupper Lake Water Company was organized.

This was a private stock company, and they decided to go with Cranberry Pond, which they purchased from the A. Sherman Lumber Company (east of hole seven on the golf course) as their water source. (Note: Other sources on Mt. Morris had been located. The surveyors' recommendation was to "tap" Little Simon Pond, prophetically pointing out, as the town's population expanded, that Cranberry Pond would be inadequate. However, the cost of laying a line to Little Simon was considered financially out of reach for the stock company.)

The stockholders of that first water company consisted of David Hayes, P.H. McCarthy, Barney Seigal, James Jacobs and local physician Dr. Thissell. Shortly after the forming of that company, Dr. Thissell bought out his partners and became sole proprietor. He then hired a private contractor to build a reservoir located on Manning's Hill as an auxiliary supply, supplementing the direct flow and feed from Cranberry Pond. As noted in an earlier column, the reservoir had been excavated back into the ridge, thus forming the back (the side furthest from the river below) and parts of two sides: the side nearest the river consisted of nearly all fill material, and then a concrete lining was placed inside. The fill and lining were too thin, and at the first filling of water, the side facing Moody Bridge failed, sending a torrent down the hill that barely missed the McBride home (located near today's veterinary clinic) and tore up a large section of the highway beyond Moody Bridge.

After an unsuccessful lawsuit for damages against the contractor,

Dr. Thissell then arranged with seasonal resident Colonel Barbour to acquire the water company. Colonel Barbour's association with this village extended back to the 1880s when the Barbours had a camp on Jenkins Pond (now Lake Madeleine on Litchfield Park), and he gradually expanded the system, installing a pumping station by which water was pumped into a standpipe that was constructed in 1908 on Sear's Hill, improving water pressure for domestic and fire-fighting use.

Colonel Barbour died in March 1917, and his extensive holdings (20,000 acres around the head of the lake alone) were liquidated. In 1918, New York State purchased 13,900 acres, and in 1928 the American Legion Department of New York acquired 1,260 acres of waterfront that included 18 buildings. Colonel Barbour's camp on Fox Hill Point, built in 1895, became the site of the women's infirmary, and a camp owned by his son, Senator Warren Barbour on Warren Point, became the men's infirmary for veterans of WWI and, later, WWII. This estate sale was a golden opportunity for the village to acquire title to the water system that for 20 years had been under private ownership, and they jumped on it.

In 1920, the village purchased the system for $100,000. A bond issue at 6 percent was floated, and the village retired it 21 years later in 1941. The resulting local water department has been a well-managed asset over the years. Reasonable service charges (village average rate is $15.40 per month) have prevented it from being a tax burden. Major investments, additions and improvements have kept pace with the needs of our growing community. Water quality standards are closely monitored by well-trained employees and include "treatment through diatomaceous earth filters and additional chlorine contact provided on the Little Simond source."

Tupper Lake has water quality that is the envy of many of our neighboring communities.

Next *Transitions:* We build a pipeline.

*Tupper Lake Free Press Print:* May 18, 2005

# WE BUILD A PIPELINE

SHORTLY AFTER THE VILLAGE purchased the private water company that had served this community for over 20 years, it became evident that an additional source of water was needed other than that of Cranberry Pond. The surveyors' original recommendation in 1895 to use Little Simond Pond proved to have been well founded.

Little Simond Pond lays in a basin between Buck Mountain and Mt. Morris in Township 25 in the Town of Tupper Lake. It is a secluded, deep pond that has been privately owned by members of the Read family since being acquired in 1895 by William Read and his cousin, Albert Strange.

Most Adirondack lakes were born with the arrival of the Continental Ice Age, when tons upon tons of glacial ice finally ceased to move and lay melting away, the melt water filling the depression formed by the glacier's massive weight. Someone with more knowledge of geology than this writer would need to confirm this, but it would seem, when viewed from a neighboring height like Buck Mountain or more dramatically from River Road off Old Wawbeek Road, that the Little Simond Pond was formed differently. It is probable that it was "gouged" out by valley glaciers. This cycle of erosion would have occurred even before the arrival of the ice sheet and the melting glaciers, which would make that extraordinary pond even more unique among Adirondack waters.

At any rate, the size of the pond and its extreme depth that

*Teamsters and their horses played an important role in laying the water pipeline through tough terrain to Little Simond Pond from Lake Simond.*

approached 100 feet of crystal clear water made it an unrivaled source for this community. Thus it was that in 1931, the people of the village took a bold step. They would lay a 12 inch pipe, 20,000 feet in length to Little Simond Pond. If, by chance, you have observed the difficulties contractors with modern earth-moving equipment encountered while recently laying a sewage line along Racquette River Drive, it becomes easier to appreciate the challenge facing our early residents with only the rudimentary equipment, which consisted mostly of pick and shovel, available to them at that time. The pipeline would cross a portion of O.W.D. lands, which that firm had acquired in 1915 from Norwood Manufacturing Company (Sisson) for its hardwood that had been left behind by that paper company. The line would then continue beyond the O.W.D.–Read boundary to Little Simond Pond. Here, it would extend 150 feet into the pond, with the intake approximately 30 feet below the water's surface. In charge of the project was village engineer Floyd Hutchins Sr., assisted by Peter La Montagne, who was the superintendent of water works. A $65,000 water bond provided the financing, and construction started in

November, continuing through the next January. Over 150 men were employed on this welcome work project in those Depression days. The weekly payroll approached $2,500, which figures out roughly to about $16 per week for what was probably a 10-hour, six-day week. But in those dark days of economic despair and unemployment, it was probably a welcome compensation.

As a youngster in the late 1930s, spending summers at the family camp on Lake Simond, the "pipeline," as it was known, became the "secret trail" to the fire tower on the summit of Mt. Morris. There were a half dozen lively youngsters of the same preteen age, whose parents either owned or rented summer camps on the lake in those days. That fire tower trip was the highlight of a summer spent exploring, canoeing, swimming and picnicking on the quiet lake. Without the aid of compass or map, or the ability to use either, we would follow the pipeline, often walking on the top of the pipe where it lay above ground for purposes of elevation. We first crossed O.W.D. lands where there was, as yet, no restricted access (Dr. R.L. Cook of Sunmount and associates would not lease 2,400 acres of this land until 1938, and even then, hikers were welcome in the summer season). We would soon arrive at a former lumber camp clearing known as Donahue's (named after Jack Donahue, a prominent Potsdam lumber jobber who cut timber on Mt. Morris under contract with the Sisson family).

Here, the pipeline continued across to the Read property, and we would turn and leave the pipeline, following Donahue Creek up the mountain to the recently abandoned Conservation Department observer cabin next to a wonderful spring near the Read property line. Note: The cabin had become obsolete when a crew of 25 CCCs from Camp 15 of S-63 Cross Clearing Station had completed in 1934 a shorter, more accessible trail to Mt. Morris from Route 3, starting near the Waukesha Hotel at Moody. A new observer cabin was built on what became the official state trail. From the old cabin, we would follow the original trail used by long-time observer Andrew Gebo to the fire tower. Note: The steep waterfall on Donahue Creek that cascades hundreds of feet over ancient moss-covered granite is little known, but it is one of the more outstanding scenic falls in the Adirondacks.

We were too young in those carefree days to appreciate the rigors and hardships that must have prevailed in laying that pipeline; nor were we even slightly aware of the give-and-take that would have allowed the village to cross two private parcels and siphon water from a pristine private lake.

In retrospect, and this is just speculation on my part, it is likely that Mr. Hutchins played a large role in the success of the project. As a case in point, Mr. Hutchins had, at one time, worked for—and was highly respected by—both owners. He had first arrived in Tupper Lake in 1916 as a construction engineer for the O.W.D. Corporation, laying out and surveying the building of their logging railroads in the Kildare section. He had also worked for Read & Strange for two years and, in fact, had laid out their access road from Route 30. Those connections and his acknowledged skill as an engineer and surveyor must have enhanced the negotiations between the village and the owners, even as both owners had always been generous and cooperative in matters where this community was involved.

Afterward

With the need for even more water in the still growing community, in 1950 a new water pumping station was built on the shore of Big Tupper Lake to supplement the Little Simond source. A strip of fill 120 feet long and 60 feet wide, extending 70 feet in the lake and rip-rapped with stone, was laid, on which a brick and stone station was erected in 1951 by Johnson Construction on today's Maddox Lane. A 14-inch intake was laid 800 feet into the lake at a depth of 43 feet, and a new 12-inch line connected with the Little Simond line near Moody Bridge (Simmons, *Mostly Spruce and Hemlock*). During 2004, 200,000,000 gallons were drawn from Little Simond and 182,000,000 gallons from Tupper Lake. (See the Annual Water Quality Report from 2004, Tupper Lake Village Water Department.)

*Tupper Lake Free Press Print:* June 01, 2005

# 1856 Saranac Racquette Journey

IN THE LATE 1850S, Alfred B. Street, the New York State Librarian, and a group of his friends rowed up Tupper Lake on a leisurely trip from the Saranac via Bog River to Mud Lake (Low's Lake) and back. There was only one settler at the head of the lake, Sid Jenkins, whose name is perpetuated in Jenkin's Brook, which enters the lake from Litchfield Park at Jenkin's Bay on the lake's east side. Note: Lake Madeleine on Litchfield was once known as Jenkin's Pond. A drive dam on that pond's outlet (Jenkin's Brook) allowed lumbermen like Albert Hosely (1984) and, later, John D'Avignon (late 1920s) to drive or float their logs down this outlet to the lake and then to be rafted (towed) to the mills located either on Racquette Pond or others downstream on the river. They could also be taken out of the river near the Underwood Railroad Bridge by conveyor belt (Jack Works) and loaded on railroad cars for shipment to St. Regis Paper Company at Deferiet, NY, etc.

As Street's party passed Long Island (today's Country Line Island), Street's guide, Harvey Moody, exclaimed, "Bog River Falls," pointing, as Street related in his book, to "what appeared to be a sloping plate of pearl amid the rounded shores of the lake, three miles distant. About a mile further you'll hear the roar. In the spring when there's high water, the falls gets up considerable young thunder, the foam splashes over ugly. I've seen mighty big trees dashin' and squirlin' and crashin' over the rocks as though

*Fourteen years after Street's visit, high water, the result of an unregulated dam at Setting Pole rapids, created a graveyard of drowned trees and a visual nightmare. The photo shown was taken from Marlow's or Indian Point on the outlet of Big Tupper Lake. Note the few buildings at Moody.*

lightin' had sent them; and then a deer come rollin' and strugglin' and be pitched down 'ords like a duck's feather in a ripple. The deer 'ud be dead enough though when it got to the bottom."

Street's party continued up the lake, passing what he described as: "Two Norway Islands (later named Norway and Pine, now Norway and Green) and cast successfully at the mouths of three trout brooks that crept into coves upon the east side. We then crossed the lake, passing a small island with a leafy dome (later named Pearly Island) and entered a beautiful bay at the head of which was a small clearing (later the women's infirmary). On the left a wild mountain frowned against the sunset sky (Twin Mountain).

"'Jenkins who has a choppin' up there, is the only one who lives on the lake,' Harvey said

"'It isn't that rather solitary for him, Harvey?' Street asked.

"'Why bless ye, no!' Harvey replied. 'In his boat with any kind of rowing, twill take him only about two hours to go the Racket – there's some five or six families there.'"

That would have been the families of Sim Moody, Phineas

Moody, Rerben Stetson, William McLaughlin, George McBride and S.E. Clark, who lived along the river below today's LeBoeuf's Bridge.

Street's party landed in the bay on a dry, small knoll near a spring in a little hollow, which Street described as "about six feet in diameter, boiling clear as dew and cold as snow from a deep floor of pearly sand."

The party made camp at this spot, and Street tells us, "It was now just after sunsetting. A blush was painted on the lake below a streak of golden purple with a white star trembling at its edge. Merry was our meal in the eye of the star and we fell asleep with the camp fire drenching our camp in pleasant light."

That 1856 Saranac/Racquette journey made by Street and his friends was the vanguard of what was to become a popular destination for adventurers and tourists seeking to explore the virtually unknown Adirondacks. The south end of Tupper Lake became the "jumping off" spot for the land and lake trips via either the Bog River or Little Tupper outlet. The Little Tupper route, which still today follows an early portage or carry trail along that beautiful stream to Round Pond and Little Tupper Lake, has been closed to the public for over a century but is currently scheduled to become transferred as a result of a recent Nature Conservancy purchase (from I.P. Company) to New York State sometime this summer. It will then be reopened to the public. Fishermen will be pleased to learn that, unlike neighboring Little Tupper, a limited harvest of brook trout will be allowed on Round Pond, with a minimum size of 12 inches and limit of three per day caught with artificial lures. Hopefully, a proposed snowmobile trail utilizing an existing log road will be allowed under the new guidelines.

Most travelers in that early period would cross from the Saranacs using the Sweeney Carry to the Racquette River, where Tupper Lake resident Oliver Tromblee kept a small house that could accommodate six or eight people and provide acceptable meals (a state lean-to is located near that location today, which is still referred to as Tromblee's).

Thus it was that the head of the lake became a strategic place to build a hotel for "city sports" to gain shelter and meals before continuing their journey upstream. A man named Blanchard was the first to recognize such a need, and he built in 1860 a crude shelter on the present site of the former women's infirmary of the American Legion Mountain Camp.

Blanchard subsequently sold out to Sid Jenkins, who later sold to William Graves (Graves Pond and Graves Mountain on Otter Brook Preserve were probably named after Mr. Graves, who drowned in Horseshoe Lake when a wounded deer tipped over his boat).

In the 1890 edition of Stoddard's popular Adirondack guide book, he had this to say: "Tupper Lake House is on the west shore of the lake, near its south end. It is about 35 miles by water from Saranac Lake, making a pleasant day's journey by rowboat. The opening of this section by John Hurd's Northern Adirondack Railroad this year makes it possible to leave New York in the evening at 6:25 and reach the Tupper Lake House in time for dinner the next day. The fare from New York to Tupper is $12.40."

According to Marian Corey of Bridgewater, CT in a letter to the NY Conservationists some years ago, at one time around 1886, the Tupper Lake House was operated by her father, Alembert Corey, who founded one of the earliest resort inns of the area, Rustic Lodge on Upper Saranac Lake, and who gave his name to the Corey's area. It was a welcome haven for some of the great men of America in its day. Among them President Grover Cleveland, who, according to Miss Corey, spent his honeymoon there. She said, "And when his daughter, Marian, was born the following the year, all the babies for miles around were named Marian—including me!"

The original Tupper Lake House was destroyed by fire in 1894 and later acquired by Colonel William Barbour as part of his 20,000-acre timberland holdings. Today, an energetic family has transformed that Tupper Lake House location into a splendid seasonal home.

*Tupper Lake Free Press Print:* June 22, 2005

# RACQUETTE RIVER WATERSHED

IN 1933, THIS VILLAGE WAS MADE the headquarters for a biological survey of the Racquette River Watershed, conducted by the State Conservation Department (D.E.C.). Offices and laboratory facilities were made available at the Tupper Lake High School.

A staff of 34 scientists and fish experts had been recruited, mainly from the educational institutions of the state. Many were professors from Cornell, Syracuse, Buffalo and St. Lawrence universities. Specialists in the field of fisheries science from R.P.I., Wesleyan and Johns Hopkins universities were also drawn upon. Following a three-month investigation and study of the entire watershed, a detailed report, which I have in my files, was published. It includes maps of the entire stream system and other maps that carried the boundaries of privately owned and posted properties as well as other useful data. Included also is a group of 12 colored plates of fishes native to New York State and inventories and recommendations of the study area.

Originally, it was feared that if access were denied to lakes under private ownership, the study would suffer from not securing a satisfactory picture of the system as a whole. However, this did not occur and the team of scientists found only the best of cooperation from private owners as the caliber of the scientists involved manifested itself. In many instances, access to several of the private properties afforded means of studying waters typifying primitive fish associations with authentic records carrying back to a period before the introduction of nonnative species to the Adirondack waters!

One of those private lakes was Ampersand near Coreys. It had never been stocked nor intensively fished, thus it had not been disturbed by introductions, and it represented a natural Adirondack association. Both lake trout and brook trout were present in considerable numbers.

Another of those private waters was Follensby Pond near this community, and perhaps the fishery report of that pond may be of some interest to readers of this column. At the time of this biological survey in 1933, Follensby Park was owned by J.E. Barbour, the nephew of Colonel William Barbour, prominent Tupper Lake landowner. Mr. Barbour had acquired Follensby Pond and 4,000 surrounding acres in 1916 for $75,000. He later increased his holdings to over 15,000 acres, paying $450,000 for 11,805 acres to the Santa Clara Lumber Company.

Note: The Santa Clara Lumber Company had purchased the land from Dr. Thomas Durant and his son, W.W. Durant, for $1.50 per acre in 1890. Dr. Durant, a principal of the Union Pacific Railroad, had hoped to extend the Adirondack Railroad Company's line from Saratoga, which ended at North Creek, to Canada, following, in part, the Racquette River Corridor, a dream that did not materialize.

Other owners of the Follensby Tract, which space doesn't allow detailing, included over the years the Brooklyn Cooperage, which wanted to put in a railroad and was discouraged by Ferris Meigs of Santa Clara and the O.W.D., which harvested its hardwood before being repurchased by Santa Clara and Elliot Hardwood.

Today, the Follensby Tract is owned by John McCormick of Manchester Depot, VT, who purchased it in 1952. The pond itself and its buffer zone remain protected and beautiful and are in the careful and loving stewardship of its owner. At least four hunting clubs lease land on the property: River Ridge, Adirondack Hunting Club, Gatehouse Club and the Inlet Club. Hopefully, if any transfer of title should take place in the future, these clubs can be allowed to retain privileges, at least during big game season. Such arrangements are more and more crafted into purchase agreements to ensure a long-standing tradition is not lost.

The tract has been extensively lumbered and is laced with miles of roads, some of which are "all-season roads," as they are called. Many of the roads were constructed by local lumberman, Paul Mitchell, whose skill at road building is considered without equal by his peers. Unfortunately, one road crosses an unsightly, huge metal culvert, placed to provide a crossing over the famed outlet spitting the pond's pristine waters in a profane manner into the outlet stream, which follows a circuitous but navigable course through a magical marsh and enters forest preserve land before joining the Racquette River.

In his poem, *The Adirondacks*, Emerson describes it much the way it is today:

> *... a small tortuous pass.*
> *Winding through grassy shallows in and out.*
> *Two creeping miles of rushes, pads and sponge.*

### Follensby Pond

Follensby Pond is an L-shaped lake with an area of 908.8 acres and a maximum depth of 100 feet when at normal level. It lies at an elevation of 1,548 feet and drains by way of a short outlet directly into the Racquette River.

During the past 17 or 18 years, the lake has not been stocked, but excellent fishing has been maintained throughout this period. Early introductions included the small-mouthed bass, yellow perch, northern pike and whitefish, and following the establishment of these species, brook trout became extinct as a lake fish.

Lake trout are abundant, however, and grow to a large size, a 31-pound specimen having been taken a few years ago by trolling. The introduced whitefish is exceedingly abundant but averages rather small. Yellow perch, so often a menace in ponds and lakes, are present, but apparently due to the character of the lake, they have not gained ascendancy over other species. The common sunfish is infrequently taken. Bullheads, now rare, were reported

*One of the oldest buildings on Follensby Park is this well-built log cabin, located just outside the state boundary near the outlet. Once occupied by an early trapper named Vosburgh, it is now a leassee camp. The porch and stovepipe are recent additions. (photo by Bill Frenette)*

to have been plentiful until recent years. Small-mouthed bass and northern pike are both abundant and grow to a large size.

In attempting to determine what elements have had a part in maintaining the fish population at such a high level over many years, consideration has been given to the fact that the lake is privately owned and not open to public fishing. It is obvious that this factor alone is not responsible, for many privately owned waters are so restricted but provide indifferent fishing. A partial explanation is to be found in the character of the water itself, for it is clear and white and contains more dissolved oxygen at the bottom than many lakes at the surface. The contour of the lake basin and the almost total absence of weed beds may account in part for the relative scarceness of the yellow perch, for the lake has few real shallows, and bass and pike can forage to the shoreline.

Examination of stomach contents indicates that perch and whitefish contribute to the diet of the lake trout. The whitefish in turn rely mostly on bottom foods, and perch on crayfish and insects.

Reference is frequently made to weed beds and plants in general as the ultimate source of food for fishes. The absence of any extensive beds in Follensby Pond would seem to indicate a dependence on the microscopic forms, almost to the exclusion of other types.

*Tupper Lake Free Press Print:* September 07, 2005

# This Community's First Murder

TUPPER LAKE'S FIRST MURDER
    Dramatis Personae
Will McLaughlin—Farmer, Landowner
John Smith—McLaughlin's Son-In-Law
Zeba Westcott—McLaughlin's Stepson
Name Not Known—Boarder at the Farm

SCENE
    McLaughlin farmhouse on McLaughlin Hill.
    The year is 1889.

The sun had just set. The sky a blazing red, its color fired by the setting sun as it dramatically lowered itself behind the shoulder of Mt. Arab, west of Will McLaughlin's farm, located on the crest of the hill on what would later be known as Racquette River Drive. The chores were done, supper was finished—a hearty meal, the bounty of the farm's fertile richness, prepared by Mrs. McLaughlin, the former Sally Cole Westcott, daughter of Michael Cole (Charbonneau), this community's first settler.

As was the usual custom following the evening meal, a deck of playing cards was produced and a card game would take place. However, on this particular Sunday evening, February 24, 1889, what was always a friendly game suddenly turned ugly when one of the players was dealt a "hand" that held not a playing card but a razor-sharp knife that would cut his windpipe and cause almost immediate death in a flow of blood that would stain the wall for all time.

History will show that what occurred was this community's first murder, and here is the background:

Zeba Westcott, one of the players, accused one of the other players, John Smith, of having cheated. Fredrick Seaver, Franklin County's historian, said of the incident: "Westcott was slight, sightless in one eye, and Smith, a physical giant with muscles like tempered steel, the most powerful man in the locality and said to have been of vicious disposition.

There had been previous bad blood between the two, and Smith was said to have threatened to "get" Westcott. Instantly following the accusation, Smith struck Westcott a smashing blow over the eye, cutting a gash from which blood flowed into the one good eye, blinding him completely.

Westcott drew a knife, and in the striking and parrying which

*It may be hard to imagine, but you are viewing the hill up today's Racquette River Drive in this early 1900s photo taken from the intersection of Stetson Road and Wawbeek Avenue. The farmhouse and barn at the crest of the hill, left of center, belonged to William (Uncle Mac) McLaughlin with part of his extensive farm fields in the foreground.*

followed, Smith's throat was cut to the windpipe and he expired within a few minutes . . . Westcott was indicted for manslaughter in the first degree. His defense was that, having been blinded by blood, he used the knife only to stand Smith off and did not even know that the affair was over and he was told of its fatal issue. The jury returned a verdict of "not guilty."

Afterward

Interestingly, three years later in 1898, Zeba would become this newly created town's first constable. Historian Louis Simmons told us, "Before a suitable building for detaining prisoners was built, Constable Westcott had solved the problem of what to do with law breakers by "detaining" them in his home on Wawbeek Avenue until justice could be meted out. His solution was simple but effective. A chain, secured by a hasp on the outside, was passed through a hole drilled in the wall. It ended in a leg iron that clasped around the prisoner's leg and proved an escape-proof "detainer."

Perhaps of further interest is the fact that Zeba was Mrs. McLaughlin's son by a previous marriage, which took place in 1850 to Theodore Westcott, one of our earliest settlers. Sally, also known as Sarah, would become Tupper Lake's first bride at 23 years of age. There was no clergy here at that time, and when a passing timber cruiser was found to be also a justice of the peace in St. Lawrence County, the couple grasped the opportunity, rowing out to a little island in Big Tupper Lake near Grindstone Bay, just over the Franklin County line in St. Lawrence County and which is still referred to today as Sally's Rock. Mr. Westcott would die only five years after that marriage and Sally would marry McLaughlin two years later.

Will McLaughlin continued to operate the farm where the tragic murder occurred—a farm known for its fertile soil, well-tilled fields and large apple orchard. He also catered to tourists, guides and hunters until his death in 1902 at the age of 95. The farm was then operated by his son, Wallace, for several years. Upon his death, the farm went into the McLaughlin estate.

Sometime around 1918, in an estate settlement, P.H. McCarthy, newly minted Realtor (who operated a grocery store until 1918 where the Sorting Gap store is presently located and who was village mayor from 1921 to 1924) purchased about 320 acres of McLaughlin's property. McCarthy's purchase extended from the former Mercy General Hospital along both sides of today's Racquette River Drive to what was known as the Crow's Nest property (today's Byram Road).

Soon after acquiring that property, McCarthy started selling lots, with prominent citizens like attorney Francis Slater, auto dealer Art Cronin, O.W.D. official Roy LaVoy and boat builder A.B. Moody buying parcels and building attractive homes.

*Tupper Lake Free Press Print:* September 21, 2005

# Storied Lumbermen and River Drivers

THE EARLIEST LOGGERS IN THIS AREA were from Maine, employees of a Maine-based company called the Pomeroy Lumbering Company. Their initial operation consisted of a small sawmill located on the outlet of today's Big Wolf Pond, which they called Kitteridge Lake.

As was custom in those early lumbering days, when transportation was largely undeveloped, they cut in a circle rarely more than a three-mile circumference surrounding the sawmill. When that source was depleted, they moved the sawmill to another stand. Pomeroy moved from Big Wolf to the virgin pine along Racquette Pond, then called Lake Whitney, and later, Lough Neagh, after a lake in Ireland. The clearing they left behind would become, some 40 years later, the site of our present village.

Maine Lumbermen and, later, those from the Maritime Provinces, who were called P.I.s (Prince Edward Island), were considered without equal as lumbermen. They were famous throughout the United States for their ability and the knowledge of their peculiar tools and methods. They were also considered reliable workmen who knew how to handle an axe or a team of horses. Note: Many were hard-working farmers, and in the slack season, they would leave the womenfolk to milk the cows and do the necessary chores, and they would take to the woods to earn a few welcome dollars.

As a matter of interest, many readers will be familiar with one of those peculiar Maine tools—a tool they called a Peavey, named after its inventor, a blacksmith from Stillwater, Maine. According to Robert Pike, in his anecdotal lumbering history, *Tall Trees, Tough Men*, it was originally called a cant dog or cant hook and was used for lifting and prying logs, both in loading sleds and on river drives.

Pike tells us: "It originally consisted of a straight, heavy handle set into an iron socket that might or might not be pointed and fitted with a swivel hook that had nothing to hold it in position and was as likely to miss catching a log when a logger made a pass at it as it was to grab hold. In 1868, Joseph Peavey, a blacksmith at Stillwater, Maine, was watching through the cracks of a wooden bridge, the river men working beneath him and swearing at their refractory hooks. Right then and there Joseph had an idea that revolutionized the logging industry. Returning to his blacksmith shop, he made a rigid clasp to encircle the cant dog handle, with lips on one side. These lips were drilled to take a bolt that would hold the hook, or dog, in place, allowing it to move up or down but not sideways. It was a marvelous invention and it rolled billions of feet of logs into American rivers, but Joe got drunk on his way to get the thing patented and a friend stole the patent from him. It is good to know, however, that regardless of patent ownership, he manufactured his brainchild and did right well with it. The Peavey gravestone in the Bangor cemetery bears a large letter P crossed by two beautifully carved peavies."

Note: A peavey in excellent condition, which was used in area river drives, part of the late Greg Smith collection, has been gifted to the Tupper Lake Museum Gallery by Greg's brother, John.

The "Yankees" from Maine stayed in the Tupper sector for only a short time. Maine, after all, was then the leader in the logging business, and while later many of the Maine men would follow the receding pines westward to Pennsylvania, Michigan and even Wisconsin and Minnesota, there was plenty of opportunity in their home state. Thus, when the arrival of the railroads here and the attendant opening of the sawmills, which catapulted Tupper Lake to the leading lumbering capital in New York State, the

*A good river man could stick his pike pole into a log, lean on it for support and ride turbulent waters for miles. Note the "stagged" pants and his Croghan calked (spiked) boots.*

labor force in the lumbering business was locally made up of largely French Canadians. For example, the Santa Clara Lumber crews here for many years were at least three-fourths French Canadian, according to Ferris Meigs in his autobiography, *The Santa Clara Company.*

In writing about French Canadians, Pike says, "They often had more than a score of children in a family." As a result, they sometimes ran out of names and resorted to numbers instead. He recalled a Vingt-Six (French for 26) Gagnon from Three Rivers, Quebec.

Frequently a camp would not have a single English-speaking

lumberjack in it and in the mornings, long before sunrise, the cry "Se Levez! Se Levez!" would echo throughout the bunkroom. (C'est l'heure à lever, as I think my former and wonderful French teacher, Mrs. Austin, would have explained.)

By and large, the Canucks, according to Pike, were "small, trim, quick men, fond of gay sashes and toques and unsurpassed with an axe." Note to local readers: Have you ever called your woolen ski hat a "toque" and had a nonresident wonder to what you were referring? The axe was the French Canadians' natural weapon, and they handled and practiced with it until they acquired unbelievable dexterity. They could throw an axe at a running rat and spit it in two, or they could hurl is at a mark 15 yards away and hit it three time out of three.

Many observers have claimed that the French Canadians were the best river drivers, a dangerous and very difficult skill, and it has been said that good river men were "born, not made." Many had developed their skills as youngsters on the rivers in Canada, learning early how to handle a pike pole and a peavey on the still waters of the mill booms so common in this area until better transportation methods and the emerging market for hardwood, which didn't float, rendered such drives obsolete.

The last river drive occurred here in 1935 when jobbers like Gasper LaPorte, George MacDonald and quick-footed river men like young Alex Reandeau, among others, drove logs from Whitney Realty lands down the Little Tupper outlet and I.P. lands along Bear Brook and the Bog River and over the falls to Tupper Lake, where they were towed down the lake to the mills on Racquette Pond. Or driven further down the Racquette River to other mills such as Piercefield and Colton.

As a youngster, I remember always being able to recognize a lumberjack who was a river driver when they would hit town after the completion of the spring drive. His wool Malone, or Ballard, pants were always stagged—or cut off above his boot tops. He walked with a sort of swagger, a river man's walk. Note: Probably because river drivers, whose feet were immersed in cold water for hours on end, would often paint their feet with white lead, and most camps would have a barrel of lard near the door, which the river driver could use to put inside his socks before putting them on. For many years, many of the floors in the hotels of my youth were pockmarked from the spikes in their boots, known as Croghans, which was where the best boots were made—a town now famous for its bologna. These boots were his badge. The spikes were core-hardened and resembled yesterday's golf shoes, and they were called calks (pronounced "corks").

River drivers lived in danger most of the time on the drives, especially when the dams were opened to flush the logs downstream, and mild rapids became wild, raging torrents. Perhaps that was why river men were known to be a feisty bunch with a confident, devil-may-care attitude.

One anecdote tells of a river driver going into Larry Rafferty's Hotel Altamont in this village, where longtime employee, Jim Sullivan, was tending bar. Jim knew his customers and had a good sense of humor. As the story goes, one day a fierce lumberjack strode into the bar and bellowed to Jim, "They tell me you're the man who sells the stuff. All right, give me some!"

Jim just looked him over and made no haste to answer. The man went on, "I'm a son of a bitch from Black River, and I want service."

Jim, still polishing his bar, said, "I knew you were a son of a bitch the minute you opened your mouth, but I didn't know you were from Black River."

To be continued in the next *Transitions*.

*Tupper Lake Free Press Print:* October 19, 2005

# REMINISCENCES OF EARLY LUMBERING DAYS

IN THE LAST *TRANSITIONS* COLUMN, it was noted that French Canadians made up a heavy percentage of the crews that worked in the woods and ran the record-setting sawmills of our local lumbering industry at the turn of the century and beyond up to 1920.

Tupper Lake was the leading lumbering capital of the state during those years, and there was a high demand for lumbermen experienced in the use of the axe, horse teams and, later, the saw.

With our close proximity to Canada and with four to six trains running daily to Ottawa and Montreal, it is not surprising that many Canadians were attracted to this fast-growing community and its employment opportunities.

Those lumbermen came by their skills naturally because long before lumbering began here, the French (as servants of the king) had been cutting and rafting masts and ship timbers, procured from the monstrous virgin pines, along the St. Lawrence and Ottawa rivers for use in His Majesty's navy.

They became excellent woodsmen from the beginning of this activity, according to Charles Bryan Jr. in *The Racquette River of the Forest*, and they exhibited outstanding aptitude and skill.

In his autobiography, Ferris Meigs, president of the Santa Clara Company here, recounts one crew of Canadians who escaped the inclination to celebrate and "blow" their wages, as was sometimes the case when the lumberjacks left the woods after the cutting was finished. This crew was made up entirely of Canadians of Scottish descent. "The foreman, Jim Wiley, was five feet, 11 inches tall and the shortest man in the crew. These Scotchmen rarely ever visited the 'van' in camp."

Note: The "van" was also called a wangan or wannigan, a word of Indian origin, and it referred to the company store where lumbermen could purchase tobacco, clothes, soap, matches, etc. Maine canoeists still refer to their food box carried in the canoe on river trips as a wannigan.

"Those particular Canadians," Mr. Meigs explained, "would bring from Canada all the home-grown and home-cured tobacco they would need for the season. Their socks, mittens and extra pants were made by their sisters and mothers. They were young men and spent not a cent of their wages. The payoff nearly broke the bank when camp broke up. The boys saved all, and in a few years, by their thrift, were able to buy farms, marry and be lost to the 'bush' and become an asset of value to their Canadian communities."

*Local lumberman, George Bushey, built the log slide, or trough, shown above in 1915. Logs would hurl down the slide off Indian Mountain and drop into Cranberry Lake's South Flow and then were rafted down the lake. It was moderately successful and was later dynamited in 1920, and the logs used in its construction were cut up for firewood.*

What follows are some reminiscences and nuggets of early lumbering days by the late Beatrice LaVigne of Parishville, who grew up in a lumber camp in the 1900s, where both parents were employed. Mrs. LaVigne went on to earn a master's degree in education at Columbia and taught at the campus school in Potsdam. She had this to say in an interview on logging, conducted by Kate Klien:

"I loved my life as a child in the logging camps. My mother was a camp cook in the Colton woods called 35 Pond Note: Town of Hopkinton, northwest of Little Jordan Lake, later O.W.D. lands, where my father, Ed LaVigne, was a lumberjack. She earned $1.50 per day and he earned $1. Camp cooks were the highest-paid jobs in the camp. The best lumberjacks went where the best food was found. I remember how hard they all worked. Mother prepared meals for 100 or more every day. She made 200 loaves of bread every other day—mixed them in huge, galvanized tubs, and oh, how wonderful the camp smelled when the bread was baking. Everything the men ate, my mother cooked. They had huge appetites and required many calories, for the work was hard, and they worked from long before daylight to well after dark, often by the light of torches and lanterns. They went out no matter how cold. Cold weather is good logging weather, and frozen feet were a big problem. The food came in by train to Potsdam, where it was carted to 35 Pond. Flour was in barrels; coffee came in a big chest weighing more than a hundred pounds. I still have one of the tea chests. Pie filling came in large pails. My favorite was apricot pie, but she made a raisin pie that was something to remember. The Sissons owned the lumber business my father worked for. It was a hard life but a good one."

Ms. LaVigne doesn't mention it, but the humble prune, according to lumber historian Robert Pike, deserves a special mention. In later days of the camps, it was very common, both stewed and in pies. As a French Canadian cook (I think it was Joe Buckshot) once remarked: "For me, I'll take the prune. It makes better apple pie than the peach."

In 1916, the Oval Wood Dish Corporation set up logging

headquarters at Kildare near the main line of the New York and Ottawa railroad and its Kildare passenger station not far from Pitchfork Pond.

From here, O.W.D. ran railroad spur lines that reached as far as 35 Pond, O.W.D. camps run by jobbers like DuMoulin, a prominent family name here. Sullivan from South Colton and Buckley were served by this rail line, an occurrence that would have astounded Mrs. LaVigne.

The O.W.D. owned two locomotives and 65 flat cars that were used to haul hardwood logs cut on their extensive land holdings in this area. In 1926, Sisson and White took over the logging railroad and moved the tracks a year later.

*Tupper Lake Free Press Print:* October 26, 2005

# THE BIRTH OF OUR FIRST REAL HOSPITAL

IN 1890, A PIONEER FAMILY by the name of LaFountain built a handsome home on the outskirts of what was to later become the busy village of Tupper Lake. It was of a famous farmhouse design, pretentious by the local standards of the day, and one of the first homes built here. The location of the home is where the present Mercy Health Care Center is today. There was no Route 3 then, and the house was sited on the north edge of the extensive McLaughlin farmlands. LaFountain, who was an assistant surveyor under Meekham of St. Regis on Hurd's NY & Ottawa Railroad, had married Rebecca, McLaughlin's daughter. After a prominent career here as surveyor, LaFountain moved his family to Cass Lake, MN.

This was at a time that Dr. Livingston Trudeau, who was to become the father of modern tubercular therapy, had come to Saranac Lake prepared to die, wracked with pulmonary consumption that was considered an absolutely fatal disease. The mountain air was so beneficial that Dr. Trudeau regained his health and vigor and lived for another 40 years.

During his stay in Saranac Lake, Dr. Trudeau chanced upon the theories of the German physician, Brecher, who was advocating the outdoor and institutional treatment of tuberculosis. Based on his own successful experience of fresh air and rest, and noting the similarity with the German physician's theory of regulated fresh-air cure, Dr. Trudeau became convinced that what was then a fatal

*The Will LaFountain home, which was converted into the Tupper Lake Sanatorium in 1911 and was taken over by the Sisters of Mercy in 1918 as Mercy General Hospital, is shown above. The barn at left rear still stands at the rear of the hospital property.*

disease could be prevented in its early stages and eventually cured.

"From that moment on," historian Alfred Donaldson tells us, "the doctor's life suffered a radical change. The quest of his own health became secondary to the saving of others." Note: He even cut back on his hunting and fishing, activities he so loved. He did continue to visit his favorite hunting camp, called Little Rapids on the Beaver River, provided for him and kept exclusively by his friend Dr. Seward Webb (Nehasane). Indeed, he shot his last buck there while confined to a special chair that could be carried, constructed for him by his guide and placed at his favorite watch (he was a crack shot). Donaldson further explains, "He exemplified to full the maxim of a great French physician, which he was fond of quoting: 'Guerir quelquefois, soulager souvent, consoler toujours.'" (Meaning "to heal sometimes, to relieve often, to console always.")

The Adirondacks, with their natural endowments of climate and quality of dry, pure air, fulfilled that philosophy. Many were healed, many were relieved, if only for a time, and always was the loving care—rich or poor—given by this remarkable physician, himself suffering with the disease.

Saranac Lake soon became known as "The Town of Second Chance," and a large private sanatorium developed there. William Chapman White, in his regional study, *Adirondack Country*, notes, "When the infectious quality of the disease became known, tourist hotels refused to take invalids. The result was the appearance of many boarding cottages in Saranac Lake after 1890, run exclusively for the sick and served by those doctors who had remained as private physicians."

As Saranac Lake's reputation grew, the number of cottages increased. By 1920, more than 150 of them cared for the 2,000 patients who were in the village. The big, screened-in porch, a part of the cure, became a feature of Saranac Lake architecture. Saranac Lake became world famous.

You may wonder what the foregoing had to do with the LaFountain home. The connection is this: that home began the groundwork for our first hospital here. The background that follows, which I hope you find of interest, especially in view of its recent purchase by the Adirondack Medical Center, is the Genesis of a desperately needed facility.

The birth of our first real hospital in this community began as a result of some prominent local businessmen who observed the success of the cure cottages just a few miles away. They quickly realized that the Tupper Lake climate and elevation also had the same virtues for the sick as their neighboring community of Saranac Lake, that the surrounding forests contained just as much ozone and had lots of conifers that produced the resinous odor considered beneficial as part of the tubercular fresh-air cure then in vogue. Yes, you guessed it—they decided to build similar sanatorium facilities here.

Those businessmen were L.C. Maid, pioneer pharmacist and astute investor; Barney Seigel, owner of the large and successful Seigel Hardware Company here; and H.H. Day, bank officer and president of the Norwood Manufacturing Company, which was then operating the Big Mill on Racquette Pond. These gentlemen, in 1910, purchased the Will LaFountain home and, according to Louis Simmons in *Mostly Spruce and Hemlock*, "remodeled the building, adding sun porches and heating system." In 1911, it opened as the Tupper Lake Sanatorium. These three entrepreneurs were what today we would call heavy hitters: successful, well to do, venturesome—all had many irons in the fire with a proven track record.

Tupper Lake's first and only "San" would be an immediate success and enjoyed great patronage from the outset, many of its patients coming from New York City. The first doctors were Dr. Charles Rytennberg and Dr. A. MacDonald Bell, New York physicians who had been practicing at Saranac Lake. Other doctors who practiced there included Dr. P.J. Barrett, who later served as a much-loved physician at Faust for many years.

As Louis Simmons states in his local history: "More serious than the need for sanatorium facilities here was the pressing need for a hospital equipped to administer properly to the seriously ill or injured for whom the long trip to a downstate or Canadian hospital was a grim form of 'Russian Roulette.'"

Tupper Lake was entering a period of great activity at this time: hundreds of lumber camps nearby, five sawmills on the shores of Racquette Pond, cranking out millions of feet of pine and spruce. We were the undisputed lumbering capital of New York State. Gang saws, shingles and lath machines, axes and falling trees made this occupation a frightfully dangerous one in which to work. Life-threatening injuries were common, as might be expected, and, as Louis notes, the only recourse was to wait for a train and send the injured to an Ottawa, Ontario or Utica hospital and hope they survived until they arrived there—frightening!

Next *Transitions:* The challenge of a hospital was met head on.

*Tupper Lake Free Press Print:* January 18, 2006

# The Challenge of a Hospital

IN THE LAST *TRANSITIONS*, it was noted that the sudden meteoric growth of the town in the early 1900s was almost overwhelming in terms of providing services for the exploding population. Water supply, sewage, schools, fire protection, police department, jail, and library—all were practically nonexistent as the town recovered from the disastrous fire of 1899.

It was a monstrous problem for our town fathers. The requirement for a hospital was especially pressing. Sending seriously ill people and those with injuries requiring life-saving care by train to Canada or Utica was simply unacceptable by any humanitarian standard.

A temporary solution that occurred in 1917 was to rent space from Mrs. Evelyn Morgan, a registered nurse and widow of one of Tupper's early physicians, Dr. Robert L. Morgan. Four rooms were set aside in the spacious Morgan home, located still today across from the fire station on the corner of Cliff and High Street. (In later years, as I was growing up on High Street, it was the home of classmate Al Vom Scheidt, whose father was a justice of the peace here for many years.)

*Dr. Seward Webb*

*Cure cottages for tuberculosis fresh-air therapy had porches, as shown above. Here, patients sit reclined in special "cure chairs," even in the coldest weather. Heated soapstones placed in breadboxes warmed the feet, and fur coats and heavy shawls provided extra warmth.*

This measure was, of course, only a temporary solution, a "finger in the dike," so to speak. Adding urgency to the medical care problem was the reality that alongside Junction Road (Demars Boulevard) the Oval Wood Dish Corporation was constructing the largest industrial plant in Franklin County, with the completion date only months away—a plant that would employ up to 600 people, most of whom would have family members.

I pose a question to readers, especially those acquainted with the O.W.D. over the years: Would you agree with the following scenario given the absence of any record I can find? William Cary Hull, general manager and vice president of the O.W.D., summons his young son, Gerald, to the company's temporary office in his beautiful home on Water Street and issues a three-word order: "Fix this problem." I think we can agree this was highly probable. W.C. was a highly successful industrialist, a hard-hitting executive with factories in Chicago, Michigan, etc. He would have had great concern over the morale and welfare of his work force.

As my grandson and his young friends would say in today's

language, "he was all crankshaft—no horn."

Not having a hospital for his employees would have been unacceptable to Mr. Hull, and I believe we can add the creation of our hospital, in part at least, to the O.W.D. civic legacy that would include the golf course, the Sugar Loaf and Mt. Morris ski areas, etc.

Would young Gerald, fresh from Olivet College studies and fully involved with his company duties as time clerk and payroll officer (later in 1941, its president), dutifully delegate his father's order to his friend, Riley Swears of the O.W.D. sales staff, who had time on his hands while waiting for production to start?

Speculation aside, we do know from the records that Swears was the individual who approached the late Monsignor Edmund Hervieux and convinced that influential young priest to accompany him to nearby Gabriels Sanatorium so he could petition the Sisters of Mercy to establish and staff a hospital at Tupper Lake.

The Sisters of Mercy, it should be noted, had at this time acquired the Tupper Lake Sanatorium mentioned in last week's column. Fortunately, they recognized the need for a medical care hospital. That, of course, was their mission, and the young sales manager's overture to them was successful and ingenious.

On September 14, 1918, three members of the order came to Tupper Lake. A modern hospital was about to be born!

Let's depart briefly at this time from the central thread of this article and say hello to the Sisters of Mercy, whose successors still today operate the Uihlein Mercy Nursing Home in Lake Placid and the Mercy Healthcare Center in this community. Most of the material that follows comes from *Forest Leaves*, a quarterly publication of the Gabriels Sanatorium, 1903-1934, and *The Brighton Story*, a delightful history of the Town of Brighton, compiled by the late Geraldine Collins, former historian and longtime librarian at Paul Smith's College.

As early as 1890, the Sisters had wanted to establish a nursing institution in this area. Near the end of 1894, the Bishop of Ogdensburg Diocese, the Right Reverend Henry Gabriels, urged the Sisters to attempt the establishment of a much-needed sanatorium for the cure of tuberculosis. With this encouragement, the

Sisters began to consider where to locate such an institution, but attempts to purchase land in Saranac Lake, Lake Placid and Tupper Lake failed because of excessive costs. This was a major obstacle, of course, but before they were ready to give up their idea, they traveled to New York City in an attempt to secure funds and/or land for their project. Somehow, they knew Dr. Seward Webb, who had just completed the fist railroad (the Mohawk and Malone) to traverse the Adirondacks.

Aware of their good works, Dr. Webb arranged for a land gift from himself and Paul Smith. It turned out to be a beautiful piece of land in the wilderness of lot 78 in the Town of Brighton. Their plot was situated close to Dr. Webb's railroad on a rolling piece of land that gradually rose to a good-sized hill that they called "Sunrise Mount." History tells us that the first year of their new institution started with very little. All the Motherhouse could give them was $15, yet that $15 was increased through their efforts to many times that amount and went into the building of Gabriels Sanatorium, named in honor of their bishop.

It was a nonsectarian endeavor and no distinction of creed or color was made. One of their early publications stated that 15 percent of the patients were treated free, only a few paid the entire cost, and the greatest number less than the per capita cost.

Note: In rapid order in 1897, Rest-A-While was completed, and then St. Joseph's the next year. Slumberland consisted of 10 street cars placed in an oval, with plenty of space between. This was the first Knights of Columbus unit at Gabriels. The sanatorium continued to grow quickly.

More on the Sisters of Mercy in the next *Transitions*.

*Tupper Lake Free Press Print:* February 01, 2006

## DIVINE INTERVENTION

IN THE LAST *TRANSITIONS* COLUMN, it was noted that in 1917, a petition to the Sisters of Mercy to establish a modern hospital here proved successful. The Sisters were, at that time, operating an institution they called Gabriels Sanatorium, which was dedicated to the care and cure of pulmonary tuberculosis.

The Sanatorium had grown steadily from humble beginnings in 1895 and enjoyed recognition for its humanitarian work and financial support from wealthy benefactors. A small hamlet grew up around the "San," and, by 1910, it had a population of several hundred residents, a railroad station and a post office, which was granted to the Sisters by none other than Theodore Roosevelt, who had summered at Paul Smith's as a 10-year-old boy and later while a student at Yale.

One of the earliest stores in the embryo village of Gabriels was run by Larry Rafferty, and it must have been successful. Senior readers will fondly remember Mr. Rafferty as the genial Irishman who lost his hair (he had an ill-fitting red wig) but never his Irish brogue. He bought the Hotel Altamont here in 1924 for $40,000 and made many improvements, and the hotel became the center for social and fraternal dinners with a first-class dining room and a lively bar under fellow Irishman Jim Sullivan.

Mr. Rafferty sold the hotel in 1946, and it continued to prosper under Hugh Beaton, who added the large Mountain Room and other renovations until he sold it in 1951 to Bill Snider, who only

*The Rafferty Store in Gabriels. (photo courtesy of Alice Warner)*

ran it for a few years until it was sold to the Grand Union Company at a mortgage foreclosure. That company razed the building and erected a supermarket the same year. It is now the site of the physical therapy center on Park Street.

Improvements at Gabriels came rapidly. The water supply came from springs on Sunrise Mount, as the Sisters named their rolling piece of ground given to them by Dr. Webb and Paul Smith. Eighteen wells were pumped into a reservoir and were of the purest, natural water.

The Sisters had their own electric light plant and eventually acquired a 200-acre farm that supplied them with all the milk and cream required, most of the eggs needed, chickens and turkeys so they could serve fowl often and veal and pork in moderate quantity. All of the bread used was baked there. Some of the Sisters themselves supervised the farm work and lived there (the farm is still known locally as the Sisters Farm).

In the *Brighton Story*, by Geraldine Collins, from which much of the Gabriel history has been excerpted for this account, Ms. Collins tells us of a fire that was caused by a defective flue in the attic of the administration building:

"A call went out over the telephone wire to Paul Smith's Hotel and every man was gathered from the shops, mills, stores, ice cutters and so on. All were sent to help fight the fire. When the call for help went to the Saranac Lake Fire Department, a special train was dispatched with about 50 men, hoses and ladders. It left Saranac Lake at 8:55 and arrived at Gabriels at 9:30. Not until they had laboriously carried all their equipment up to the fire from the railroad did they discover that their hose, which was standard size, would not fit the San hydrants. When the smoke cleared, all that was left was the foundation."

The "winds of change" ultimately reached the Gabriels San. A declining patient census and the successful drug therapy that made fresh-air therapy obsolete presented almost insurmountable obstacles in addition to the financial deficit in operations. During the 70 years of operation, over five and a half thousand patients had been treated.

The focus of care changed from tuberculosis to the care of the frail and elderly, and the mission for the Sisters embraced the need for skilled long-term care. In 1963, a decision was reached to sell the Gabriels property to Paul Smiths College and to investigate alternate sites for a nursing home (Paul Smiths College would utilize the property for student and faculty housing as well as for some classes in forestry before selling the property to the State of New York, which operates it today as a minimum-security prison called Camp Gabriels). Unable to buy existing buildings, land was donated by Henry Uihlein, longtime Lake Placid seasonal resident.

Substantial support came from many other Lake Placid benefactors, including: the Uihleins, Mrs. Alton Jones, Kate Smith and the Reiss family. On a beautiful tract of land with views of the High Peaks in the distance just outside Lake Placid, Uihlein Mercy Center opened its doors in 1968. It quickly became noted for its excellent facilities, its caring staff and its strong financial position. A new page had been entered to the history of the Sisters of Mercy in the Adirondacks.

That chronicle continues today with the announcement recently that the Adirondack Medical Center's Board of Trustees voted to purchase both the Uihlein Center and Mercy Healthcare

Center in this community. The Tri-Lakes would see a new era of healthcare come into place. If purchase price negotiations and applications for a Certificate of Need to the New York Department of Health are successful, elder residents will be assured of a "continuum of care" that is so vital and important to so many people (over 1,600 people signed a petition urging the acquisition).

As Chandler Ralph, C.E.O. of Adirondack Medical, so eloquently stated in the January issue of the hospital's newsletter, *Well Aware*: "This purchase was a significant strategic decision and was not made lightly. I think the board made absolutely the right decision for the home's residents, their families and the communities."

Mr. Ralph also explained, "The joining together of two very strong mission-based organizations can only create something that is greater than the sum of its parts individually."

Most members of this community will whole-heartedly agree with that sentiment. We can thank the many people who helped the complicated process that saved our desperately needed care center. We can especially thank Sen. Elizabeth Little, who was instrumental in guiding the process through the Department of Health, and who continues her untiring encouragement in all matters that benefit the Tri-Lakes. The senator is simply outstanding—there is no other word to describe her dedication and energy.

Also, don't you agree that Sister Mary Perpetual Help Kiernan and Sister Mary MacCauley Connelly, those indomitable Sisters of Mercy whose human idealism and endeavor originally created those institutions of health and ministry and spirituality, are smiling from the heavens above, assured that their dream will continue strongly forward and will remain to fulfill a vital community need under the competent leadership of the Adirondack Medical Center?

Next *Transitions*: An influenza epidemic strikes this village and paralyzes the new hospital.

*Tupper Lake Free Press Print:* February 08, 2006

## Skenandowa's Kick-Start

A DESPERATE NEED FOR A HOSPITAL here, as noted in a previous column, gained momentum when, in 1918, the Sisters of Mercy of the Gabriels Sanatorium agreed to send three members of their order to Tupper Lake.

The initial plan was to convert the Tupper Lake Sanitarium on Wawbeek Avenue into a medical care facility. A good plan, far better than the kitchen table at the former Dr. Morgan's home, which had been serving the community as a temporary medical facility. However, almost before the doors of the new facility were opened, the Sisters were faced with an epochal dilemma: an influenza epidemic that swept the nation "filled every bed and overflowed with patients on mattresses hastily brought in to the sun porches."

Former town clerk Lou Marconi has told me the records kept in the huge town hall safe showed page after page of deaths during that period, often several members of the same family dying within hours of each other.

It had become painfully obvious that the former sanitarium facilities were not going to be adequate. The Sisters struggled on for 10 years doing the best they could under difficult circumstances. Then, in 1924, Sister Mary Victoria, one of the original three Sisters of Mercy who had come to Tupper Lake in 1918, took over as director. Her first official action was to instigate a move to build a modern, fireproof hospital. That initiative was, of course, met with great skepticism. "Where are you going to get the money?" "Never happen." "Dream on, Sister, dream on."

That determined goal, however, was suddenly made possible by a set of circumstances that require noting here, if only for its historical value and, hopefully, for the readers' interest. It begins this way: Marshall Sheppy, affluent businessman from Toledo, OH, commissioned in the early 1900s the construction of a camp on Tupper Lake's undeveloped west shore—one of the earliest camps on that beautiful lake.

Mr. Sheppy named his camp Skenandowa, a delightful Indian name that means Big Horn. He had a disdain for pretension. The main camp sits discreetly and quietly, perfectly integrated with the land on which it rests and hidden from shoreline view. One also has to look closely from the lake to spot the several cottages on the grounds. "Hillside," traditional and lovely in its rusticity, sits back high on a ledge overlooking the lake and beyond to views of Mt. Morris and the spectacular Seward Range. Access to the Skenandowa compound was only by water or across the ice in

*President William Howard Taft tries his luck at angling from a launch on Big Tupper Lake during his 1910 visit to the Marshall Sheppy camp. The guide at center is the late Henry Smith of this village, and at right, the late Del Delosh, who has either hooked a big one or, as friends here suspected, is putting a little action in the photograph for the benefit of the Pictorial News Company photographers of New York, who took the photograph.*

winter from a boathouse off what is today Charland Road.

This was the way Mr. Sheppy wanted it. He simply refused to build a road from, let's say, Piercefield or Gull Pond direction. He wanted—no, demanded—his isolation and untamed remoteness. Yet, Mr. Sheppy loved to entertain. No less than three presidents of the United States were his guests as Skenandowa. He had a special cottage called "Springside" built for his friend, Bishop Carney. Famous poets and authors were invited guests among many other important and notable personages of the day.

Enter now the interesting coincidence so meaningful in the construction of our first modern hospital. Mr. Sheppy, the wealthy Ohio businessman, whose enterprises included a large grocery supply business and a canning factory, among others, was originally from Ogdensburg, a member of a poor family there, and yes, also from Ogdensburg was Sister Mary Victoria, who has been known by the Sheppy family. Small world, indeed!

Mr. Sheppy always displayed affection and generous interest in the Tupper Lake community, so whether that hometown connection was of any influence remains unknown (at least to this writer). We do know, according to historian Louis Simmons, that Mr. Sheppy "recognized the excellent work the Sisters were doing under trying circumstances and limited equipment," and in 1928, he offered to contribute $25,000 toward a modern hospital, provided the Tupper Lake community would raise $50,000. How is that for challenge? It was, of course, a great kick-start to the funding campaign, and in characteristic fashion, this community not only met that challenge but also quickly pushed the total goal of $100,000 needed to build and equip the modern hospital to completion. (Remember that the average wage in 1929 was $1 to $1.68 per hour and the Great Depression was just around the corner when 40 cents per hour for a 40-hour week was the standard for government work relief programs.)

Today the modest sign reading "Skenandowa," that has been nailed over a boat slip's opening in the boathouse since I was a youngster on the lake, is missing—a victim, no doubt, of its long existence. What is not missing is the legacy of care and love for the camp. Family members have maintained a careful stewardship that mirrors that of its original owner. They cherish this beguiling and special place—an important part of Tupper Lake's early history. I should also note that some of the information concerning Skenandowa came from Sister Barbara Whittemore, now of the Spiritual Center known as Cenacle in Chicago.

I was a high school classmate of Sister Barbara in this community, where her parents, Mr. and Mrs. Charles Whittemore, were the longtime caretakers for the Sheppy family. The Whittemores stayed year round at camp, often isolated for many weeks at a time, especially during winter, subject to conditions that prevented or allowed travel across the often-treacherous lake. During those periods, Sister Barbara stayed at various homes in the community so she could attend school here, where she was an outstanding student. The many people who remember Sister Barbara will not be surprised to learn that today she is a published author and an important chief administrator at Cenacle. This year, she will celebrate 50 years of spiritual dedication to her chosen mission in life.

*Tupper Lake Free Press Print:* March 08, 2006

# AN OASIS OF HEALTHCARE

THE YEAR WAS 1928. Ten years had elapsed since the former Tupper Lake Sanatorium had been converted into a hospital here and staffed by the Sisters of Mercy of Gabriels Sanatorium. Almost from the very beginning, these facilities had been found to be inadequate, despite the heroic efforts under trying conditions by the good Sisters of Mercy.

An effort to erect a modern, fireproof hospital was started under a committee composed of Peter Propp, chairman, W.W. McCarthy, Floyd Hutchins and Sister Mary Victoria. The financial drive, with a goal of $100,000, was rapidly pushed to success.

Former historian Louis Simmons tells us: "The new hospital was built on 13 acres of land, excellently located near the intersection of Stetson Road, Moody Road and Racquette River Drive, and with ample room for expansion. It was opened on February 14, 1929, with a capacity of 23 beds and 10 bassinets. The first addition was made in 1932 when the old frame hospital was razed and a convent for the Sisters was erected directly connected to the hospital."

That new, modern hospital was a wonderful, reassuring addition to the community, especially to residents with young children or those with serious ailments. The community supported the hospital at every turn with efforts like the Mercy General Auxiliary, which was formed with the direct purpose of providing a community link with the hospital. Grace Grabenstein, local teacher, and Mose Ginsberg were the original officers of that

*The first brick Mercy General Hospital, completed and opened in 1929 was the pride of the community in its day. A brick convent for the Sisters was added in 1932.*

group along with Mary Quinn.

For more than fifty years, Mercy General Hospital would continue as an oasis of healthcare. A quick overview of three rather distinctive periods during that time frame may be of interest to readers:

1) <u>Industrial Revolution, 1920s.</u>

We can begin with the 1920s when the first modern hospital was established and saw an advance of technology not dreamed of in earlier years. Automobiles and good roads were first coming into common use. An instrument called the radio became more than the unsatisfactory crystal ear set then is use. Radio stations that provided clearer sound were springing up everywhere. A young Tupper Lake electrician, Gordon Bisson (Bee-saw) installed equipment and towers at the Hotel Iroquois, and a very early radio station, WDHL, was established here, providing exceptional reception. Another dramatic change in this time period was in the lives of women here. Electric irons became available. Gone was the flat iron heated on a wood stove. Electric washing machines did away with washing by hand (even though, as a youngster, I remember my mother setting aside an entire Saturday—she taught school during the week—as a wash day). The refrigerator replaced iceboxes and indoor plumbing replaced the outhouse.

2) <u>Great Depression, 1930s</u>
Then came a period during the 1930s called the Great Depression, which paralyzed the nation's economy. A grim time here, yet in some ways, through relief and work projects, allowed greater progress than any other time in the community's history (the expansion of the golf course and the erection of Rod & Gun Clubhouse, municipal park, Setting Pole Dam, etc.).

3) <u>World War II</u>
The 1940s brought with it the global nightmare known as World War II, one of the most terrible periods of modern times. A fight to prevent the destruction of the world as people knew it, and bringing with it an unyielding sea of blood. Nearly a thousand Tupper Lake men and women served with the armed services during the four-year participation of the United States in that war. Ten percent of that number were killed, wounded (61), missing in action and prisoners of war.

That brings us to 1946 and the war's end. The original medical staff was then organized, and eight years later in 1954, Mercy General was finally fully accredited by the Joint Commission on Accreditation of Hospitals. Unfortunately, at about that time, Tupper Lake, as in many other rural communities, was suffering from a steadily increasing shortage of doctors. With that trend, as historian Louis Simmons has noted, came a decline in patient load, and the Sisters of Mercy warned that unless things improved, it would appear advisable to utilize the time and efforts of the nuns elsewhere, where there was greater need for them.

Next *Transitions:* Crisis looms.

*Tupper Lake Free Press Print:* March 29, 2006

# NOSTALGIA FOR TWO GENERATIONS OF CARE

THE MAY 16, 1957, ISSUE of the *Tupper Lake Free Press* carried grim news for this community under bold headlines: "MAY CLOSE MERCY GENERAL HOSPITAL."

The simple fact behind that heading was that the hospital was only operating at 40 percent of capacity. That figure was not acceptable to the Sisters of Mercy, who reluctantly explained to the local hospital advisory board that unless the facility operated at or near 75 percent of capacity, it could not break even financially, and it would appear advisable to utilize the time and efforts of the nuns where there was greater need for them.

The community struggled with this announcement for several years, with the situation steadily deteriorating.

Historian Louis Simmons tells us in his local history book, *Mostly Spruce and Hemlock*, "It assumed crisis proportions in 1962 when the Joint Commission on Accreditation advised the hospital that it could no longer be accredited unless a huge rebuilding or replacement program was undertaken."

Loss of accreditation would have made the hospital ineligible to receive payment for hospitalization for patients with Blue Cross or Blue Shield insurance coverage. It could also not care for welfare, workmen's compensation patients or others covered by any group insurance carrier.

There was only one answer and it was not an easy one—build a new hospital at an estimated cost of $750,000! Federal grants of

$375,000 were available to ease this financial burden but only if matching funds were raised by this community.

Many readers will remember the huge fundraising campaign that followed the decision to build. A professional fundraising firm from Texas was quickly hired. Then came a series of kickoff dinners, and a huge campaign thermometer was set up to focus public attention on "pushing the temperature over $300,000" by December 20, 1962.

As I remember it, the entire community got behind the drive, and committees were formed that left no stone unturned when soliciting pledges and contributions. Summer residents contributed some $75,000, and additional cash and pledges soared to $475,000 by the goal date, ensuring the erection of the new hospital.

Part of the plans for the new hospital involved tearing down the Sisters' convent, and the former L.C. Maid home was purchased at this time, remodeled slightly to serve as a new convent for the Sisters of Mercy staffing the hospital (now the residence and office of attorney John Ellis).

The winning bid went to construct the new hospital went the A.J. Beaudette Construction Company of Syracuse, with a low bid on the general contract at $711,200. That firm was headed by a Tupper Lake native, Arthur (Art) Beaudette, who was well known here.

Construction started in January 1964. The new Mercy General Hospital, a 36-bed facility with provisions for caring for 50 patients comfortably as well as having the option for future expansion, was dedicated two years later on May 9, 1966, with hundreds of area residents participating, despite a snowstorm.

The community had once again reacted with solidarity and spirit, and it assured the area of continued hospital protection. The old hospital had been a blessing to Tupper Lake. It had served two generations faithfully, and its obsolescence was bittersweet.

There was a powerful nostalgia not easily dismissed. Many in the dedication ceremony that snowy May day were thankful for the care it had provided. Many had been born there; many had their tonsils and appendixes removed there; others had their

*Mercy General Hospital, completed and dedicated in 1966, is shown in this architect's rendition. The original section is at right center.*

wounds sutured and even their lives saved in that place.

What follows are three personal reminiscences that I trust many readers will share with this writer:

1. It is after hospital hours. I enter the Mercy General's front entrance. Low lights, almost to the point of darkness, point the way down the long, cathedral-like hallway. It is quiet, silent, celestial, like an empty church. At the far end of the corridor, a single desk in the center. A young, attractive nurse works on her charts, her work lighted by a single lamp. Blonde curls spill from her traditional peaked nurse's cap, its colors those of her nursing alma mater; the two stripes indicate her rank of staff nurse. Her cap resembles, in the dimness, a halo over her head not unexpected because when your are in pain, a nurse can be like a saint to you. You feel reassured, thankful—this is a place of mercy and of care, and you can sense that and thank the Sisters of Mercy and the community for building this hospital.

2. Dr. Roy Bury, the quintessential family doctor, is kind, gentle and caring. Few knew that he had come here expecting to die from the shrapnel that laced his body. Saved from death in the trenches of war-torn France during the First World War—saved to do his considerable good works for mankind. You meet him in the corridor of the hospital's second floor OB unit. He is dressed in green surgical scrubs, surgical mask covering his face, his hands

stretched out like wings to dry their sanitation bath before entering sterile gloves. A frightening scene—he looks like someone you would imagine from space, and he is about to deliver your firstborn. You thank God for saving this man and his consummate skills that helped so many in this community by giving them hope, strength and wellness.

3. The year, 1962, a late March afternoon. Hundreds of skiers on the newly opened slopes of Big Tupper Ski Area. For the sixth time in an hour and a half, the area's red town-owned station wagon has backed up to the hospital's side door. Six trips, six leg fractures—a result of what ski patrollers know as the "last-day-last run syndrome," when skiers are tired, the light is flat and deteriorating conditions often become troublesome. The nun at the inadequate receiving door is shocked. Raised on a farm in southern France, she is mystified by the strange footwear consisting of multiple layers of leather and laces and the form-fitting ski trousers, whose seams often had to be cut away to access a limb. What madness is this, she must have thought, that people spend such money and risk such injuries and still term it fun? Who are these people handling the litter, rust-colored jackets with large yellow crosses emblazoned on the back? Competent, professional, helpful in removing the strange padded plywood box splints used to immobilize the broken leg so it can be x-rayed. "Mon Dieu!" she exclaims. "More fractures in a single day than the hospital ordinarily sees in a year—and on a Sunday!"

*Tupper Lake Free Press Print*: April 05, 2006

## IMPORTANT MAN THINGS

ONE DAY LAST SUMMER, my son-in-law, Randy Sapp, excitedly told me that while sitting on his boat dock, he had observed an eagle do a power dive into the lake: "It was an amazing sight. The eagle folded his wings and plunged straight into the water and disappeared. Then he suddenly reappeared, flapping his wings and becoming airborne again with a good-size fish between his feet."

I hated to "bust Randy's bubble," as today's younger generation would term it, but I suggested that rather than an eagle, Randy had probably witnessed an osprey, which is often mistaken for an eagle. Randy's reaction to this comment was a half smile that I have come to recognize as a polite disagreement—you know—such as when we debate whether a worm is more effective when trailed behind a Lake Clear Wabbler than a streamer fly. Or what type of wax to use on a given winter-day ski tour. You get the picture—important man things. We will worry about the world situation, etc., some other time. There are priorities, after all.

I decided to go to a neutral corner and quickly explained that a prominent biologist friend of mine once told me that he was careful in scientific queries in using the words *never* or *always*. In other words, it could have been an eagle, even though they do not ordinarily submerge in obtaining fish. Do they *never* exhibit this behavior? Do they always just pick up injured or dead fish or fish close to the surface? In other words, Randy could be correct.

*The osprey nest shown was relocated by the utility company to prevent the occupants from being electrocuted. (Bill Frenette photo)*

Perhaps it was an eagle despite the odds that the behavior he witnessed would suggest, in all probability, it was an osprey. After all, even seasoned birders sometimes confuse the two birds, especially when they soar overhead and are observed in flight.

But hey, what the heck? It was a thrilling sight, something not observed every day. So what if it wasn't an eagle? Ospreys, like eagles, are majestic birds—a sign when we see them here that we live in a very special place, a place where the waters thus far have remained pure, and creatures like the osprey and eagle can find proper habitat and raise their young to the continued enjoyment of us homo sapiens and our future generations.

There have been many literary tributes to both of these majestic birds. Tennyson's two stanzas below refer presumably to the sea eagle, but they might well have been addressed to our native birds:

> *He clasps the crag with*
> *crooked hands;*
> *Close to the sun*
> *in lonely lands*
> *Ring'd with the azure*
> *world he stands*
> *The wrinkled sea*
> *beneath him crawls;*
> *He watches from*
> *his mountain walls,*
> *and like a thunder-bolt*
> *he falls.*

As most readers are aware, the osprey is fairly common here, readily seen hunting along the Racquette River corridor. A number of their nests can be seen near ponds in the Massawepie area and, of course, practically every pond in the St. Regis chain of lakes has a conspicuous, bulky nest of sticks and grass usually on the top of a tall pine and generally so situated that a wide view of the surrounding country can be seen.

In the recent April issue of *Audubon* magazine is a short article concerning the osprey, a portion of which I have taken the liberty to reproduce in today's column with the hope it will be of interest to *Transition* readers:

"When northern lakes and estuaries are still rimmed with ice, the osprey—a.k.a. the fish hawk—welcomes spring with a shrill, ascending kyew, kyew, kyew. On every continent, save Antarctica, you'll see these white-crowned, black-masked raptors hovering over water or perched on stick nests that can weight 1,000 pounds. Note the slightly crooked wings that can span six feet, the long legs and the aerial acrobatics of courting males. Ospreys will take the odd mink, muskrat or snake, but their diet is almost exclusively fish. Spines on footpads and a front claw that swivels to the back assist in gripping their slippery prey. Oil in the feathers repels water. Ospreys hit the surface in an explosive spray, closing their nostrils (unlike bald eagle who can submerge completely); then they rise laboriously, shaking like a dog. If they've been successful, they'll immediately turn the fish so the head points forward. Sometimes an osprey will strike a fish that's too big for it and, unable to release its talons, will down."

*Tupper Lake Free Press Print:* April 19, 2006

# 1927 Grand Jury Court Case

I RECEIVED A FILE RECENTLY from the Franklin County chief assistant district attorney, Jack Delehanty, that he had discovered in his county office. Documents in the file contained the extensive paperwork and numerous photos of evidence that pertained to a court case involving area residents and local geographic points of interest.

Attorney Delehanty explained that he felt not only did the case contain interesting material of local import and judicial procedures, but it also was of some historical significance, and I think readers will agree wholeheartedly with Mr. Delehanty. The file will be protected with acid-proof envelopes and placed in the town's archival records. Here, they will be available for future generations to research and gain insight into some aspects of those early pioneer days.

The photos depicting the logging equipment of that time period are especially valuable historically, and this column is indebted to A.D.A. Delehanty for his insight and courtesy in making the file available.

Much of the paperwork in the file is written in longhand with stick pen and ink, as was the custom in those days before the invention of the fountain pen or ballpoint pen. The penmanship is exceptional in the style then known as "Palmer Method," and it is of particular interest as educators worry that today's wired generation in this cyber age may be losing their penmanship as they depend more and more on the computer and its keyboard.

Before we review the court case charges, here is a brief background to set the location and introduce the "culprit." As you will note, the incident took place approximately six miles south of this village. That would place it near today's Rock Island Bay but on the original Tupper-Long Lake Road that lay east of today's Route 30 and the Rock Island rest area.

The charges were against Clayton Elliot, age 47, head of the Elliot Hardwood Company, which at that time (1927) was operating a mangle roller plant on the former site of Hurd's Big Mill on Demars Boulevard. The Elliot firm had a seven-year contract with Litchfield Park for blocks taken from trees over 16 inches in diameter, a condition that was a part of the Litchfield forestry plan under Floyd Hutchins Sr., the park's superintendent (i.e. cut half of the mature trees plus half of the younger trees over a certain size). We will expand on both the location and the Elliot firm later, which will provide a glimpse of the historical interest involved.

*Transporting logs from the Litchfield lands to the Elliot Hardwood mill in Tupper was easier using the public highway as a "landing" area. Motorists and the Highway Bureau of N.Y.S. didn't agree, and the outrage resulted in an arrest of Clayton Elliot, owner.*

## The Situation

Elliot had placed his log loader on the highway from which he offloaded logs brought in by horse and sleigh from the cutting operation on Litchfield lands. The loader then transferred the logs to a truck (also on the highway) for transport to the Tupper mill. This, of course, blocked the entire highway for periods often up to an hour, enraging motorists traveling to or from Long Lake.

What follows is a timeline as the complaints went forward and the various agencies became involved:

January 27: Local attorney Francis Slater writes a letter to Bureau of Highways commissioner A.W. Brondt. In his letter, Mr. Slater asks, "Has a permit to place a log loader on highway been issued to Elliot?" Mr. Slater doesn't indicate if he represents a client, and there is no further correspondence from him in the file.

February 04: The commissioner fires back the terse reply, "No such permit was issued." He directs Major John Warner, state police superintendent, Albany, to remove the Elliot operation within the highway limits at once.

February 10: Lt. Gorenflo of Troop B has a conversation with Clayton Elliot in Tupper Lake that evening. Elliot states that he is owner of the machine, and he placed or directed said machine to be placed in the highway.

February 12: Lt. Gorenflo returns to Tupper-Long Lake highway with state police photographer G.W. Bouchard. Numerous photos are taken (later to become "People's Exhibit A, B, C, D, E, F, G" to show correctly the location of the loader and the manner in which the highway is blocked by the operation).

February 16: Lt. Gorenflo appears before local Justice of the Peace John Chalmers and requests a warrant for the arrest of Elliot.

## Questions

1. Why wasn't Elliot simply told by the New Yok State Police to remove the loader, given the fact that it constituted a public nuisance and was illegal? No indication is found in the files that such an order was issued to, or ignored by, Elliott.

2. Why was the bail set so incredibly high? The going wage of $.38 per hour tells us that $1,000 was a huge sum at that time, and the risk of flight was minimal.
3. Why did Elliot waive examination and risk the action and expense of a grand jury hearing for such a low-level violation?

Next: The Chamber of Commerce drafts a letter signed by prominent citizens asking Judge Main for clemency. Witnesses are found, a jury selected and a date set for grand jury proceedings.

*Tupper Lake Free Press Print:* May 17, 2006

# THE ELLIOT FILE

WE CONTINUE IN THIS WEEK'S column the March 1927 Franklin County Grand Jury case of the People of New York State vs. Clayton Elliot. Mr. Elliot had been arrested on February 16, 1927, for the crime of public nuisance under section 1530, paragraph 2, of the penal code (closing a public highway with his log loader).

Appearing before local justice John N. Chalmers, Elliot waived immunity and was held for the March term of the Grand Jury and released on $1,000 bail, a vast sum of money that remains a tantalizing mystery of why it was so high. The bail money was provided by William McCarthy, who listed his total assets at $2,000.

William McCarthy's name in the files provides this column an opportunity to detail some local history. Even though I was very young, I remember Mr. McCarthy. He was a large man, impressive in stature, almost intimidating in his bearing. He had a decided limp, a result of a childhood injury, but this didn't in the least slow him down. For over 39 years, he was the leader of the local Democratic Party and influential at the county and state levels. Part of that tenure was when that party ruled mightily with Franklin Roosevelt as governor of New York State and his four White House victories unmatched in American history.

Imagine the patronage that existed in assigning employment politically in those job-related programs as the nation sought to recover from the Depression that paralyzed the country and this area.

*This photo shows the McCarthy—Deneshaw building and the west side of Park Street, probably before 1910 because the Goldberg—Ginsberg store is shown, which was destroyed by fire in December 1911. Note the cement crossing and the dirt road. Our Main Street was arising anew from the ashes of the 1899 fire.*

Mr. McCarthy came to Tupper Lake in the late 1800s, and together with his brother, Patrick, ran a successful wholesale grocery store that supplied most of the many, many lumber camps in this area. That store was destroyed in the 1899 fire. Almost before the ashes cooled in that disaster, the McCarthy brothers, along with Dave Deneshaw, built one of the community's first modern brick buildings on the corner of Park and Mill streets as the town struggled to rebuild its business section. Today that building houses the Sorting Gap store and the offices of the Woodmen of the World firm, and it has apartments on the second floor. It is owned by Don and Jean Ann Donah.

In addition to the store, the McCarthys also acted as important lumber brokers for the St. Regis Paper Company in Deferiet. If that didn't keep them busy enough, they also erected a massive 100 x 38 foot barn on High Street with stalls for over 50 horses.

Lou Simmons in *Mostly Spruce and Hemlock* tells us that over 1,500 to 2,000 horses were traded there yearly. An indication, he noted, of how important a role horses played in the lumbering business at that time.

That horse sale operation ceased in the middle 1930s, probably due to the mechanized logging techniques and the introduction of high-powered trucks. The vacant barn became the favorite playground for us neighboring kids on High Street. Here we would scramble, climb and swing among the many rafters in the high-ceilinged, cavernous, two-story building. No one was more agile, daring and acrobatic than the late Eddie Martin, who could easily have been hired as a double for, or played the part of, Tarzan, the movie hero of that day.

Later, the floor was covered with cement, and an enterprising fellow from Norwood opened a popular, well-attended roller-skating rink with dance music and a drink bar. The place, as I remember, only rocked for a few years before it closed, a victim,

*Dave Deneshaw's original restaurant on Park and Mill was destroyed by the 1899 fire. Dave and the McCarthy brothers built a modern fireproof building called the Union Building (because it was jointly owned) in 1900, and Dave reopened his restaurant, now the office of Woodmen of the World.*

perhaps, of the Depression.

Incidentally, the rink floor can still be seen behind a row of cedar trees on the vacant lot between the former Potvin residence (now Frenette) and Mrs. King's Tea Room (now Eisler) on High Street. The barn was torn down in 1938.

Let's return to the Elliot file. Following the arrest of Mr. Elliot, Lt. Garenflo of the New York State Police then sought out witnesses to the charges that the highway was obstructed in violation of the law. As might be expected, because there were frequent users of Route 3, many of those witnesses were residents from the Long Lake area.

Readers familiar with Long Lake will recognize many of the names still prominent in that neighboring village, so I will list them here: Oakam Helms, Edward Shappe, Charles Hammer, William Helms, John Fry, Harrison Jennings, Howe Stanton and George Stanton. From Tupper Lake: John Trainer, Albert Deshaw and Alaide Belair.

Thirty-six jurors were then selected from throughout the county. Local residents drawn to serve were Albert Hosley, George Bristol and John Villeneuve. The file contains only four items that pertain to witness testimony.

Charles Hammer stated that "he was held up for 20 minutes in a funeral procession." Other times, often accompanied by his wife, he was held up for 15 minutes. O.H. Helms testified that often "he was held up for seven minutes and other times a shorter period." Lt. Garenflo noted that the loading operation lasted from early morning to 5 p.m., and that between those hours, the road was completely blocked to travel for up to 15 minutes and did "interfere with, block and render dangerous for public travel without authority."

John Frye, in his testimony, stated that he was employed as a mechanic at T.K. Somers Garage in Tupper Lake, and that at least six times in traveling to Long Lake West (Sabbatis) and returning, he was held up. Also on one occasion, as he was passing the loader, it turned. Then he said, "If deponent had not been on the alert and applied the brakes, said loading machine would have hit deponent's car and caused serious damage and possibly killed deponent."

Meanwhile, the local chamber of commerce, under the signature of John Twohey, secretary, sent a letter to Harold Main, district attorney: "We are not asking you to do what is impossible but do ask that you do what you legally can so that Mr. Elliot may be as little inconvenienced as possible."

Enclosed with the letter was a petition, written on impressive legal stationary, with plenty of "whereas" and "wherefores." The petition noted that Elliot was a highly respected citizen who employed over a hundred men, with a early payroll of over $100,000, and the withdrawal of that business would do "irreparable harm and injury to the town."

The petition further noted that "the loading operation had ceased and was innocent and unintentional." It ended with a "respectful request and urgent recommendation that the D.A. use his influence and the power at his command to dismiss the charge against C.H. Elliot."

Next *Transitions*: Prominent local citizens who signed the petition to the district attorney. Will Elliot be found innocent or guilty?

*Tupper Lake Free Press Print:* May 31, 2006

# PEOPLE VS. CLAYTON ELLIOT

WE CONTINUE OUR SERIES on the 1927 Grand Jury criminal case identified as The People vs. Clayton Elliot.

Following the arrest of Mr. Elliot by the New York State Police for blocking the state highway with his log loader, a jury was selected, witnesses subpoenaed and a trial date set. In the meantime, the local chamber of commerce penned a passionate letter of support, including an impressive petition to "go easy," which was directed to District Attorney Harold Main. The petition was signed by many of this community's leading citizens, which lack of space in our last column prevented listing.

Those names represent the "movers" and "shakers" in our pioneer days here, and they are listed because they are historically important personages. The occupations following the signatures was listed on the petition:

J.H. Black, supervisor Town of Altamont; Paul Martin, acting president (mayor) of village; A.J. Deshaw, village trustee; Ralph Hasting, chamber president; A.J. Grenier, village trustee; George Charland, village trustee; J.H. Littlefield, merchant; Archie Baril, highway commissioner; Charles E. Kassus, cashier T.L. National Bank; Albert Woods, Woods Garage; People's Pharmacy Druggist; J.E. Bruce, T.L. Transportation Co.; A.M. Bissell, Hotel Iroquois; J.J. Collison, physician; E.H. Harve, druggist; F.E. Smith, merchant; Donavan and Bedard, merchants; Martin Bros. Grocery; Propps, Inc., merchant; McCarthy Bros., retired grocers

*Hotel Faust was the skyscraper of downtown Tupper Lake in the early 1900s—the lone four-story structure. It did a lively business through the boom logging years, entered on lean times in the Depression decade and was razed in 1958.*

and lumbermen; N.F. Foote, dentist; M. Ginsberg, merchant; George Delair, town clerk; W.H. LaRocque, dry goods merchant; Brown Bros., grocers; and Thomas and Camelo, merchants.

Many of those people signing that petition arrived in Tupper Lake when it was a frontier village. They took great risks and grew and prospered as the village grew and prospered. They raised families here and built homes. They would outlast the Depression that destroyed so many others. They would struggle through the shortages and despair of WWII. They were tough, resourceful, energetic and visionary.

Tupper today is still a vibrant community, thanks, in large part, to those early settlers and their exceptional business acumen, faith, optimism and love for this wonderful place we call Tupper Lake. Those signatures were a veritable "Who's Who" in this community during the 1920s.

There are no court proceedings in the file. However, we do find a notice from the county judge, The Honorable E.C. Lawrence, to a lawyer named George Moore, informing him that he is to represent Clayton Elliot for the March term. There are 10 names with charges on the list that Attorney Moore is directed to represent. As I read the various charges against the other defendants, I can only wonder what Elliot, with his seemingly low-level offense, is doing on that list which included burglary, forgery, assault, manslaughter, etc. Oh yes, also on that list one other Tupper resident was charged with the offense of "common gambler." It would seem that crime was alive and well in Franklin County in 1927.

Also of interest in the file is a single piece of hotel stationary. The letterhead reads "The Faust Hotel—Charles and Bill Girard Prop." History note: The Faust Hotel was probably the most familiar landmark in downtown Tupper Lake, situated near what is now Rebel's Video. It was a large, four-story hostelry, built as early as 1895. I remember it being operated by Dick Hosford and Art Bates in the late 1940s. Later it was sold to Naja Ellis as an apartment building. It was torn down in 1958.

The Girards, Bill and Charlie, who ran the hotel in 1927, need little introduction. Bill, of course, later became the popular Franklin County sheriff. He was a large, personable man well known here. Generations will remember Charlie as the successful, wonderful host at his Waukesha Grill, along with his wife, Philema Skiff Girard, as well as with daughter Dorothy and son Charles Jr. How that dance floor would rock on Saturday nights. It's amazing the log walls stayed intact. Who could forget Ray Bourdage and his sweet saxophone playing the sentimental "Good Night Sweetheart" that announced closing time?

Written on that Faust Hotel stationary was what appears to be arguments Attorney Moore apparently planned to use in his defense of his client Clayton Elliot. These arguments are in strong handwriting in what appears to be random thoughts. Perhaps, given the primitive roads and automobiles of the day, the lawyer, who was from Malone, had taken the southbound train from that village and needed stay overnight in order to catch the northbound coach the next day. We can imagine him sitting in his hotel room, with a boisterous bar below, jotting down several arguments he would use in defending Elliot. Here is what he wrote:

"Highway under construction . . . farmer with hayrack . . . railroad track and train . . . all authorized by law . . . reasonable interruption . . . operating on own land . . . claims to a good landing."

That's it, folks! No information can be found in the county file concerning the actual trial except the following legal document, "Record of Conviction," which reads as follows:

"At the trial term of the County Court, held at the courthouse in Malone, June 13, 1927—the District Attorney moves that the defendant be sentenced—defendant being interrogated by the court says his name is Clayton Elliot, age 47 years, occupation is lumberman, one child, age 28, and that he received religious instruction in Baptist church and that he has never before been convicted of a crime. Defendant being asked by the clerk if he has any legal cause to show why sentence should not be pronounced, shows none. Whereupon it is adjudged by the Court that the defendant be confined at hard labor in the _____ at _____ for the term of _____ years and _____ months. FINED $200."

*Tupper Lake Free Press Print:* June 14, 2006

## Moody Flow—Contrast of Old Clashing With New

RECENTLY THE COMMUNITY received the good news that, after three years in the planning stage, approximately 2.8 miles of the Moody Road proposed for reconstruction has met with APA approval.

Almost .75 mile of that reconstruction will involve what is locally referred to as "Moody Flow" but is labeled as "the causeway" by the D.O.T. The flow skirts the shallow delta waters of the Racquette River and is an emergent wetland rich in it diversity, renowned for its numerous variety of birds of passage and other wildlife.

Some power/telephone poles will be removed and the lines they carried will be buried, enhancing the exceptional view. Several overlooks will also be established, including a wonderful proposal that would place one overlook on the rise of ground south of the bowling alley. This will provide an unsurpassed view encompassing the marsh, lake and surrounding mountains. Interpretive signage would accompany parking space at the overview location.

In 1849, the flow was described by S.H. Hammond, editor of the Albany State Register, and an early visitor to the region as "a beautiful prairie stretching away, skirted by tall trees. As you look upon it, you can hardly believe that it is not a pleasant meadow and you wonder where the farmhouses and all the cattle are."

Louis Simmons in *Mostly Spruce and Hemlock* expands on

*A saddened guide sites among drowned wastelands of a once beautiful forest, the result of man's reckless disregard for the land. Shown in the left background is Crow Hill, located above the Lois Rockcastle Noble summer home on Racquette River Drive.*

Hammond's visit when he notes that Hammond's description of the area between the foot of the lake (Tupper Lake) and Racquette Pond or Long Neak, as Hammond called it, is interesting.

Simmons tells us that Seaver's history of Franklin County erroneously describes it simply as an expansion of the Racquette River caused by the dam. Granted, Louis concedes, the lake or pond was considerably expanded as the dam flooded lowland areas, but a beautiful little lake existed there before the first reservoir dam was built and was mentioned by many of the early writers. When Hammond visited the Tupper area in 1849, no dam had yet been built, either at Setting Pole rapids or anywhere else in this area.

Long Neak is a garbled, mispronounced name for the original name of Racquette Pond, which was Lough Neagh (Lock Nay), a beautiful lake in Ireland. It was labeled such by a nobleman who lived on the banks of a lake in Ireland. In a duel over the affections of a fair lady, our expatriate Tupper nobleman feared he had killed his opponent and fled to America via Montreal and the St. Lawrence River to St. Regis. There he found Captain Peter

Sabattis, chief of the tribe.

Captain Peter took pity on him and, for a fee, carried him and his effects up the Racquette River to his old hunting ground and built him a snug, warm log house on the banks of Racquette Pond, near the place where the river and the pond merge. For many years, this clearing was referred to by early guides as Paddy's Choppin or Irish Clearing. The Irish nobleman lived there for many years, clearing a piece of land and raising a few potatoes, but he mainly lived on game and trout, then abundant here. Finally, his friends in Ireland in some way learned of his whereabouts and sent for him, notifying him that he had not, after all, killed his adversary. He returned to Ireland, leaving only his name for the pond—a name that sadly was short lived.

So, what happened to those once pastoral lands that existed in the 1800s along what is today's causeway? Shortly after the close of the Civil War, Potsdam lumbermen found it difficult to drive their logs down the Racquette River below Tupper, especially in low water when rapids and waterfalls obstructed the passage of the logs. So they built a dam in 1870 at Setting Pole rapids (a mile or so beyond the Underwood Bridge on the New York Central Railroad). This dam was huge, over 300 feet long and 10 feet above still water, and it had 10 gates. The result was the flooding of lands for a distance of nearly 30 miles upstream. The location of today's Junction (Faust) was completely under water. Of course, all of the fine timber lining the shores was killed, transforming a beautiful section into a dead forest.

The dam, despite its massive construction, gave way in May 1871. It took 36 hours for the wall of water that was released to reach Potsdam, where it caused great damage. The dam was repaired in 1872, but Moody residents, with flooded boathouses and the hope that meadows could be restored if the dam were removed, tore the dam apart in 1885. (Note: The dam would not be rebuilt until the 1930s.)

## Some Personal Thoughts

After a recent visit to our impressive Wild Center, I was struck by the thought that the Adirondacks are a land of emerging contrasts—the old clashing with the new. And in between, nature tries to keep a balance. The Moody Flow is a classic example that if man steps back a little, nature will respond and heal and renew. What was an ugly land of drowned and dead trees is now a beautiful marsh, a rich biome, a diverse sanctuary for all manner of wildlife, and it is a great sponge filtering out assaults (like acid rain) that drift into this place where we live. A new understanding and relationship is happening here as we respect and harmonize with Mother Earth that will make all the difference in the future of the Adirondacks, a fragile gem that deserves our protection.

*Tupper Lake Free Press Print:* August 02, 2006

## SETTING POLE DAM

IN THE LAST *TRANSITIONS* ARTICLE, there appeared an 1888 photo, "The Drowned Lands of the Lower Racquette River," taken by famous Adirondack photographer Seneca Ray Stoddard. The photo, generously provided by the Adirondack Museum at Blue Mountain Lake, shows a guide sitting in the midst of drowned trees, and in the apt words of the photographer, was "a scene of malodorous desolation in what had been a most beautiful place."

Stoddard showed that picture, among 225 others, at a meeting held in 1892 at the Assembly Chamber of the State Legislature in Albany. The real purpose of the meeting was to obtain favorable action on pending legislation that would create the Adirondack Park. That legislation was later passed, and history tells us that the Stoddard photos and lecture played an important part in laying the groundwork toward the preservation of the Adirondacks.

Long before the floodwaters were put under control (the water level was to be maintained at 1,544 feet above sea level, or nearly four feet below the high watermark), the downed timber remained lifeless, ugly and hazardous to boat travel. There was one slight redeeming feature, however. Bill Johnson, my neighbor on Racquette River Drive, recalls that when he was a youngster the residents would obtain excellent firewood in winter by simply walking out across the ice and cutting the standing derelicts. It was an easy and effective way to obtain necessary fuel, and the surface made for easy transport of the firewood to the homeowner's woodshed.

For many years, the local officials had tried in vain to control the area's water level, which fluctuated from flood stage—entirely drowning the road to the Junction—to extreme low levels that prevented boat traffic, isolated docks and prevented access to shoreline, etc.

In the Depression year of 1933, several simultaneous situations, when knitted together, helped drive an opportunity for finally achieving water level control.

The first situation was the fact that with no dam in place and an exceptionally dry summer, the lake and river levels reached an unusual low. Ugly, foul-smelling flats appeared. Boathouses and water lines on the lake were left in a sea of muck, and to add to this desolate scene, millions of fish spawn were lost.

This deplorable situation prompted the second driving force: the approval by the government for a W.P.A. project to reconstruct the dam. It also helped that a state biologist said Racquette Pond and surroundings were "an eyesore to everyone and a reproach to the Village of Tupper Lake."

With the approval to give the green light to the dam's reconstruction, Frank McCarthy, the mayor, and Frank Seigel, the chamber president, continued pressing the I.P. Company for land and flowage rights, making repeated trips to Boston and New York, often at their own expense, to branch offices of that company, then known as Systems Properties, Inc. Those negotiations finally succeeded and the necessary deeds obtained.

In October 1933, the *Free Press* carried the announcement that "a new stone and concrete dam would be built immediately on the site of the old Setting Pole dam at a cost of $30,000."

Relief labor and state reimbursement lowered the cost to local taxpayers to the $12,000—$14,000 range, a few cents per annum to smaller taxpayers and a few dollars to larger taxpayers, which, according to one report, "would be a lasting benefit of incalculable value."

With the announcement that water levels would be controlled,

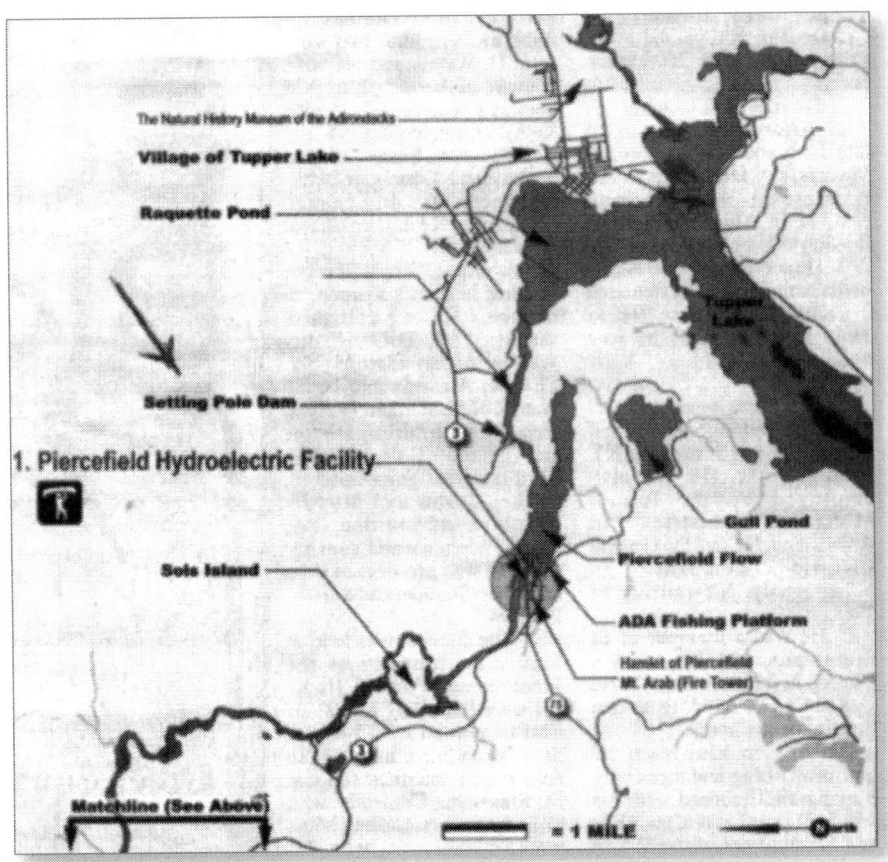

*Shown is the location of Setting Pole dam. From this point, the river tumbles 94 miles northward to the St. Lawrence River. (Map courtesy of Brookfield Power)*

owners on the lake took advantage of that 1933 low water. Big Tupper Lake owners such as Amberman, Ferguson brothers, Townshend, Levy, Downing, Baker, Sheppy, Slater, Wheeler, Ketchum, Goodman, LaRocque, McGill, Hutchins and Alexander built new boat houses, constructed retaining walls, cleared debris and extended water supply lines in anticipation of the New Deal dam project.

In addition, the dam project, with its promise of stable water levels, prompted the Civilian Conservation Corps (C.C.C.), another work-relief agency that had a camp at Cross Clearing called S-15, to employ many of the enlistees at that camp to work many weeks clearing rocks, stumps and debris for miles up the Racquette River, allowing that once magnificent waterway to again become navigable to boat traffic.

Afterward

The builders of the 1933 Setting Pole dam would no doubt be amazed that today there are no less than seven dams in the next 38 miles of river below Piercefield, making it the largest hydro-electric installation on New York State's inland waters. The new owners, Brookfield Power Company, have continued the enhancement of recreational opportunities afforded by the resulting reservoirs.

To visit the location and remaining evidence of the historical, once-thriving C.C.C. camp, park at the Deer Pond trailhead below Wawbeek corners. Walk across Routes 3 & 30 to where there are two separate spans of guardrails. Go east to the beginning of the second span and locate a well-defined path that will lead to the former S-15 encampment clearings in a little over a hundred yards.

Here, wooden barracks housed hundreds of men who found gainful employment during the troubled years of the Great Depression.

Many years ago, before the federal government controlled the Allagash waterway in Main, a patrolman at the I.P. Realty Company gate would not allow Mrs. Frenette and I entry to the river until we obtained what was known as a setting pole used by all Maine guides and watermen at that time and considered essential to running the shallow and rocky section of rapids in that great river. Typically, 12-14 feet long and two inches at the butt (preferably of spruce or tamarack), such setting poles were also used by early Adirondack guides and Indian parties in the rapids of the Racquette—such as found at the present Setting Pole dam location. Hence the name given to the dam.

*Tupper Lake Free Press Print:* August 23, 2006

# Sunmount—Federal Hospital No. 96

THERE IS LITTLE DOUBT the year 2006 will go down in the annals of this community as the year of the Wild Center.

As thousands of visitors arrived here to visit the Natural History Museum (over 52,000 at this writing), a frequent question directed to museum staff and volunteers is in reference to the large, sprawling complex of white buildings off Routes 3 and 30 we call Sunmount. It may be worthwhile to provide some historical background to those questions in today's column. After all, it has been 82 years since the formal opening of that institution.

At a cost of $4 million (1920), the facility was built as a federal hospital for ailing WWI veterans, may of them suffering from tuberculosis or mustard gas poisoning. In government-speak, it was referred to as U.S. Veterans Bureau No. 96, and in my youth, simply the Federal Hospital.

It has been 41 years since that hospital became a victim of governmental phase-out as new drugs reduced the need for institutionalized care for tuberculosis—an announcement that sent shockwaves throughout the community—resulting in a valiant effort for "Save Sunmount," and an eventual transfer to New York State to be operated as the Sunmount Development Center. The point is, many younger and/or recent residents may not realize some of the history of this very important place.

The background can begin with the knowledge that there wasn't always a clearing there. Until 1850, it was a primitive forest

*There have been many changes, especially on Hosley Avenue, since this photo was taken. The former Hosley Farm was a perfect location for Federal Hospital No. 96, which opened its doors in August 1924 for the care of patients with pulmonary tuberculosis.*

of stately virgin white pine—monarchs of the wild, towering over 200 feet or more, certainly one of the more noble sights to greet our early settlers as they came down the Racquette River.

The first lumbering of those pines was done in 1870 by Sisson and Greenbar. Sisson later became associated with the A. Sherman Lumber Company of Potsdam and the Racquette River Paper Company, a prominent firm with many logging and sawmill projects here. Many of the homes and cottages along Lake Simond today are on land originally purchased from A. Sherman Company, whose holdings at one time encompassed 90,000 acres—all of it adjacent to the Racquette River.

After the land now occupied by Sunmount was partially cleared, Simeon Moody, an early pioneer, lived there for a short time before he moved to the land on Stetson Road, later to become gentleman farmer Mark Barry's Pioneer Place—today the Richer farm.

The next tenant was Samuel Moriarity and his sons, William and George, who occupied the tract for several years. Sam Moriarity drowned in 1883 at Bartlett's Carry near Upper Saranac Lake.

Many years ago, his name was immortalized by the naming of

a small glacial pond, known as Murati, a corruption of Moriarity. It is located just off the Deer Pond Trail one mile from that trail's beginning, which starts from Old Wawbeek Road below Sunmount near the John Mann property. Unfortunately, a recent guide to Adirondack Trails (Northern Edition) incorrectly called that pond Mosquito, confusing it with another pond nearby which correctly bears that name. As town historian, I have requested that it be corrected in deference to one of our early and notable pioneers, whose name deserves historical permanence.

Clearing of the property continued under Luke Usher and John Snell, who had a headquarters on what later became the LeBoeuf Farm on Stetson Road. Around 1892, Daniel Hayes purchased the land, and for many years, the property was referred to as the "Hayes Farm." At this time, a portion of the land was cleared of stumps and boulders. Large quantities of hay, grain and vegetables were raised and many horses and cows grazed the fertile fields. It became a wonderful farm. After the fall harvest, Lacrosse matches, often with noted teams from Canada, were held. Wild West shows and circuses sought the level acreage fronting Wawbeek Road as an ideal location.

Mr. Hayes sold his farm to the Norwood Manufacturing Company, which was operating the "Big Mill" on Racquette Pond and doing extensive lumbering in the area. It provided an ideal place in the summer off-season for grazing the many horses used in their lumbering operations. The barns were used to shelter the horses and store the hay that would later be distributed to the many lumbering camps once wintering operations were resumed. Norwood Manufacturing sold out its local interests to the Santa Clara Lumbering Company in 1913, and Albert Hosley, a member of the Norwood firm, purchased the farm. For years, Mr. Hosley operated one of the finest dairy farms in this section.

On July 4, 1919, a large celebration to welcome the returning veterans of WWI was held at the Hosley Farm. The big event of the day was the first landing of a plane in the Tupper area. The U.S. Army cooperated in the welcome-home celebration by sending a Handley Paige plane, which Lt. Melville flew up from

Hazelhurst field on Long Island.

Mr. Hosley became a moving force in the organization of the Altamont Milk Company, a venture by local farmers to market their milk production. This company became a highly successful business with milk and ice cream plants at Dickinson Center, Carthage (which supplied Camp Drum), Potsdam and Plattsburgh. Mr. Hosley called his farm Ossco, an Indian name meaning "beautiful view."

In the next *Transitions*, we will follow how that 160-acre farm became the site of Hospital No. 96 and was the biggest single construction project in Franklin County history.

*Tupper Lake Free Press Print:* September 06, 2006

# WWI Creates Need for Veterans Hospital

WE CONTINUE IN TODAY'S column this community's success in being chosen in 1924 as the location for a federal hospital to treat and care for veterans with pulmonary disease. The need for such an institution was a direct result of the global conflict we know as World War I. A brief look at that war might be of interest.

In 1914, Europe was engaged in one of the bloodiest conflicts the world had known. Some historians have called it a war so brutal and unnecessary it gave new meaning to the word "absurd." Over 10 million died and 20 million were wounded on battlefields across three continents in this war "to end all wars."

The United States had endeavored to remain neutral in this European conflict and for two and one-half years succeeded in doing so, even under stress caused by such lawless acts as the sinking of the British liner *Lusitania* on May 7, 1915, in which 128 American vacationers lost their lives.

That neutrality did not last, however, and on January 1917, Germany ignored her pledge to the U.S. and began a ruthless submarine war "against all vessels neutral and enemy alike that should be found in a war zone." American merchant ships and even pleasure liners all became targets without any warning—absolute acts of war against the U.S. and a violation of international law in sea warfare, which Germany had agreed to observe.

Germany knew that it risked drawing the U.S. into the

*Shown here is U.S. President Calvin Coolidge during a 1926 visit to Sunmount shortly after its opening. The man at left is a Secret Service agent. Partly obscured by the agent is Joseph Burns. Next are Frank Frenette with the bow tie and Albert Deshaw. Just to the right are President J. Howard Brown looking at Mr. Coolidge, Dr. Foote, L.C. Maid, another Secret Service operative and Edward Frenette.*

conflict by its actions but decided it was worth the gamble. It wasn't. After enduring several months of submarine attacks, the U.S. declared war on Germany. Its hope of a diplomatic role, not a military role, was doomed by the German treachery. It was a controversial decision.

Americans, history tells us, had little enthusiasm for going "over there." Nevertheless, by the middle of June 1917, the first transports carrying American fresh-faced, confident soldiers arrived in war-torn France.

History relates that American soldiers, derided by the Germans as a mongrelized army (not a pure race like themselves), became in a short time an impressive fighting force, and their eagerness for battle proved infectious, inspiring the British and French armies to find new sources of energy. Still, it remained a brutal war, and care of the many wounded left much to be desired. It's no wonder that so many American soldiers returned stateside needing hospitalization, many of them with weakened lungs from various infections that became susceptible to the tuberculosis bacilli that were spread on the battlefield.

Here is an excerpt of what WWI nurse Laura Smith has recounted in her memoirs of serving in France with the U.S. Nurse Corps:

"The horrible thing about dressing the wounds was this technique that we used, which I think was started in the Spanish American War. When the soldiers lay wounded out in the battlefield, the flies would lay their eggs and leave behind these worms in the wound. Someone figured out that these worms worked around in the wound and cleaned it. This was a terrible thing to look at, but that was what they did to keep the wounds clean—certainly not something you would do today."

Three of my uncles, Frank, Ed and Marshall Frenette (my father was too young), were part of that impressive four-million fighting force. All three won battlefield commissions, and although I knew all three of those men quite well, other than talking about a German field phone given to me by my Uncle Ed (who had carried it back from France as a souvenir) I never heard them discuss that war. I do know from my late Aunt Dorothy Gaffney, who kept their letters, that they all saw action on the front lines in what she described as "No Man's Land." She told me of horrific trench warfare, intense hand-to-hand combat, fixed bayonet attacks, days of standing in ankle-deep mud, rats the size of alley cats and days of intense boredom followed by gripping fear.

Ed and Marshall were lucky—somehow they escaped the war unscathed and came home to lead highly constructive and successful lives. Frank, on the other hand, was not so fortunate. In the last days of the war, German tanks, taking advantage of winds blowing toward the American lines, unleashed clouds of mustard gas. That attack destroyed U.S. Army First Lt. Frenette's lungs and shortened his life. In an ironic twist, after being a patient in several other veterans hospitals, he landed in the Tupper Lake V.A. hospital.

The war ended for America a year and a half after its entry on the 11th day of the 11th month at the 11th hour: November 11,

1918—the date that was originally honored as Armistice Day, we now call Veterans Day. A total of 230 men and women from Tupper Lake served in that war and six died: Edmund Bujold, Benjamin Churco, Leon Duane, Lawrence Hays, Henry Mosher and Leon Savard.

Fast forward now to sometime in the year 1922. The government, overwhelmed by ailing veterans, many suffering from tuberculosis, begins a search for a satisfactory site for a much needed hospital. As you might expect, the competition among communities anxious to be selected as the location was fierce. Over the years, friends in Saranac Lake would often remind me—some wistfully, others not—that the Veterans Administration had proposed building the 500-bed hospital just outside their village, but they rejected the offer.

Note: This community would know other such competitions:
1. The proposal to get state support to build a major ski area here, which instead went to Wilmington.
2. The proposal to be selected as a location for Interpretive Center, which went to Newcomb and Paul Smiths.
3. The proposal to build a prison, which went to Malone.

Next *Transitions*: We examine Saranac Lake's refusal and Tupper Lake's successful bid.

*Tupper Lake Free Press Print:* September 20, 2006

# The Fight for the Veterans Hospital

THE VETERANS HOSPITAL Medical science labeled it tuberculosis but it was also known as the White Plague. For many years, it was considered an incurable, unpreventable, inherited disease. Its victims were doomed to die, the sooner the better. Some hope for treating and surviving the disease occurred when Dr. Edward Trudeau, who himself had gone to the Adirondacks expecting to die from tuberculosis, found that a cure regime of rest, fresh air and exercise could, in many cases, arrest the dreaded disease.

Dr. Trudeau later found that the climate was not as important as how he lived —under careful regulation of air, food, rest and exercise. In other words, while Dr. Trudeau felt that the Adirondacks had some special virtue for the sick with its large amounts of ozone in the air (produced by the woods) and the resinous odors from the evergreens, a strict regime had to be followed. The best way for that to happen was a sanitarium where the fresh-air therapy, as it came to be known, could be supervised.

Many of Dr. Trudeau's patients were doctors who stayed on in Saranac Lake and opened boarding houses exclusively for pulmonary patients, and the community developed a large sanatoria industry.

By 1920, more than 150 such facilities, with room for four to 50 patients each, housed 2,000 patients in the village. The big-screened porch became a feature of Saranac Lake architecture and can readily be seen today, especially along Park Avenue.

*Shown above is Federal Hospital No. 96 as it appeared shortly after its formal opening on August 15, 1924. The giant complex for veterans covered more than 700,000 square feet and included a golf course and a baseball field on its 130 acres. It has its own P.O. box (Sunmount) and fire department.*

I provide this background so readers can better understand why Saranac Lake reportedly rejected the offer of building a veterans hospital, as noted in the last *Transitions* column.

Here is what William Chapman White had to say on page 176 of his regional study, *Adirondack Country*: "A fateful decision for the future of Saranac Lake was made in the village. The Veterans Administration proposed building a five hundred-bed hospital just outside the village. For various reasons, some logical and some fearful, the influential doctors prevailed on the Veterans Administration to build that sanatorium elsewhere. It was built eighteen miles down the road at Tupper Lake, where Sunmount Hospital, with a payroll of four hundred and ninety, has been an important factor in the economic life of that town. For that decision many of the townspeople never forgave the doctors, no matter how well reasoned their arguments."

With Saranac Lake out of the running, Tupper's chances to be approved as the site for the veterans hospital improved tremendously. We should be mindful, however, that 114 northern New York counties were eligible. This included four congressional districts. The synergism of at least three other factors may have been more important to this community's efforts:

1. An enlightened and visionary electorate here overwhelmingly approved a referendum that allowed a purchase of the 160-

acre Hosley farm. The price was $20,000, a considerable sum in 1920 money, probably approaching $180,000 in today's dollar. That location was then offered to the federal government for the legal consideration of $1. This spacious, cultivated area, with its outstanding peaks, was a highly desirable location. One magazine article described the area as "God's specifically created country to nurse back to health those unfortunate enough to be overtaken by pulmonary afflictions" (*Adirondack Life*, September/October 2006, page 18). It was a gutsy, effective move on the 1920s generation's part.

2. Bertrand Snell of Potsdam, an influential congressman in Washington, was especially helpful. His father, Hollis Snell, was an early lumberman here, who at one time owned extensive landholdings in Tupper Lake. Congressman Snell had many local friends and a special interest in this area.

3. Jay Howard Brown and Joe Gokey, delegated to present our bid to Washington officials, were well chosen. Jay was a highly regarded grocery store owner and a Tupper Lake National Bank director from 1916 to 1943 (Brown Brothers store was located in a building recently razed on Park Street next to the Trillium). Joe was the superintendent of the Santa Clara Mill—the largest such operation in New York State. He was also twice mayor, county Republican chairman, school trustee and, later, sheriff.

In my files are notes of the town's history compiled by Mrs. Aurore Alexander, longtime resident. Here's what she says about Joe, including a little-known story about how he lured government officials to view the site: "Joe was a big, handsome man, physically, with no formal education. He could barely write his name, however, he was a mental giant. He had keen perception, great vision and unbounded enthusiasm." Mrs. Alexander insists that "without our unschooled Joe Gokey, we would not have our V.A. hospital at Sunmount."

Joe had many political connections in Washington, including President Warren G. Harding (Joe is credited with starting the boom for Harding at the Republican National Convention). However, no one knew anything about Tupper Lake in Washington. At a meeting attended by General Frank Hines, administrator of Veteran Affairs, Joe saw his opportunity and engaged the general in conversation.

"General," Joe said, "do you like to fish?"

"Yes, very much," answered the general.

"Well," Joe continued, "my boss has a beautiful camp on a private lake, away from everything, with a guide to take you fishing and people to take care of you. If you'd like to go there for a week or two, I know Mr. Meigs would be very happy to have you."

The general did come to fish, and then Joe, Howard Brown and others from the chamber of commerce took him to see the site they had. It immediately caught the general's eye. The rest is history. That was Joe—nothing too big to tackle. Note: the camp was a summer home on Ampersand Lake, arguably one of the most beautiful, pure, deep-water glacial lakes anywhere, belonging to Ferris J. Meigs, longtime president of the Santa Clara Company and Joe's boss.

Located in the shadow of Ampersand Mountain and surrounded by the Sawtooth and Seward ranges, it was purchased in 1938 from Mr. Meigs by Avery Rockefeller and remains today under the Rockefeller family stewardship.

In 1922, Tupper Lake was designated as the site for the veterans hospital. On August 15, 1924, the hospital was formally opened, accompanied by one of the most impressive ceremonies in the Tip Top Town.

### Conclusion

An undated, anonymous paper in my files proved to be very prophetic: Under the heading, *The Institutionalized Economy of This Village*, it states that the hospital was an economic enterprise that can be regarded as indispensable, citing a relatively constant employment level of 475 people, a payroll in the millions and hundreds of thousands of dollars of purchases made in local businesses. Approximately 95 percent of the employees resided in the immediate area and had above average earnings (and therefore a higher purchasing power), constituting a very important asset to the local economy.

The report went on to say that a highly placed government official declared: "There are no plans in the foreseeable future for a change in the mission of this [Sunmount] hospital. While this is a comforting assurance, the realization of which is to be earnestly hoped for, a certain degree of vulnerability always attaches to a situation such as this, where so much of a locality's wellbeing is directly dependent on a singe enterprise. No effort should be spared by the locality to maintain whatever climate is required to retain this hospital and to ensure the continuance of its present scale of operations."

### Afterward

In 1965, after spending millions in upgrading the facilities, the federal government stunned this community with a terse January 1965 statement: "Sunmount will be closed—be prepared to vacate within 60 days."

In what has been described as Tupper Lake's finest hour, an immediate response took place as the community rallied with a vigorous but unsuccessful "Save Sunmount" effort. That disappointment was softened when on September 23, 1965, after much hard work, an agreement was reached to transfer the federal institution to the New York State Department of Mental Hygiene. The transition was surprisingly smooth, and Sunmount has remained by far the single most important factor in the economy of the village.

*Tupper Lake Free Press Print:* October 04, 2006

# OTTERBROOK—A HISTORICAL GEM

TEN MILES SOUTH of this village on Route 3 is the intersection of Route 421. Take this road west along Horseshoe Lake, cross the New York Central Railroad tracks and, at the track, 6.2 miles from Route 3, you'll note a gated, private road on your left. This road leads in three miles to an isolated preserve known as Otterbrook, also sometimes called Lake Marion, or simply Bishop Moore's. It is a special place in the cultural and architectural legacies of our area.

Over the years, I have been extended courtesies from various caretakers who have allowed me to pursue raptor studies on the property. Many other Tupper Lake residents as well have come to know Otterbrook as caretakers (Vailancourt, Zande, Crary, etc.), employees or guests. They care deeply about this place. The owners have been salutary neighbors whose loving stewardship has maintained what is truly a precious heritage, even as other such preserves, one after the other, are being lost in the war of increasing costs and hungry developers.

History tells us, sadly over the years, another reason for the loss of some of these historical gems has been destruction by fire. Many such isolated camps have burned to the ground, sometimes through carelessness, more often through natural catastrophic events. The fact was not lost on the owners and staff at Otterbrook, and routine fire drills and every possible precaution has been put into place and strictly adhered to. Despite such careful

*One of at least nine charming alpine ponds on the Otterbrook tract is shown above. Long Tom Mountain and Rampart Mountain are in the background. Two ponds named Iron and Otter are connected by Iron Pond's outlet, which flows downgrade as the shallow 50-yard water slides over a rock outcropping, smoothed by years of nature's wear. This has allowed several generations of the owner's children to slide in an adventurous, uncontrolled flight using a square canvas to sit upon as a vehicle from one pond to another. (photo provided by Rick Vailancourt)*

diligence, that fear, after 116 years, came to reality at Otterbrook this past Thursday, October 12, when four original cottages situated in a cluster of other buildings burned to the ground.

### The Beast is Tamed

In what can only be described as providence, caretaker Doug Crary, making an unscheduled visit to the camp, discovered the buildings already fully engulfed in flames. After a quick call to the Tupper Lake Volunteer Fire Department, Doug managed to start up a water pump and lay hose that enabled him to successfully save the enjoining building that housed the library, even as the flames were consuming the walls.

The T.L.F.D., in an immediate response, covered the 20 miles in less than 40 minutes across very rough roads. This prompt action helped prevent the fire from spreading, and the fiery beast that is so feared was tamed.

The Lake Marion property, consisting of some 16,000 acres, was purchased by Paul Moore Sr. in 1918 from the Low estate. Mr. Moore always called his purchase Otterbrook.

The main camp, built in the late 1800s and still standing, was the summer home of A.A. Low. It was sited on mile-long Lake Marian, which Mr. Low named after his wife. It is one of nine lakes on the property, and at the time of Mr. Moore's purchase, the surrounding forest was a mess of burnt-over land from the disastrous 1903 fire that destroyed thousands of acres in the near vicinity.

Mountains surrounding Lake Marian, like Mt. Rampart and Mt. Graves, still today have bare rock summits from the intense heat that destroyed ground cover and vegetation. Somehow, the original Lake Marian buildings escaped destruction, probably because they were in a clearing and some, now 116 years old, have remained essentially as they were when Mr. Moore made his purchase.

Otterbrook is now owned by the third generation of the Moore family—a dozen descendants of the original owner. The Adirondack Nature Conservancy has protected 4,756 acres from development under conservation easement (no public access).

*Tupper Lake Free Press Print:* October 18, 2006

# SURVIVORS, NEIGHBORS AND CHARLIE'S FRENCH VANILLA

IN THE 1860S, DEEP-SEATED DIFFERENCES between the social structure and economy of north and south sections of the U.S., most notably over slavery, led to the South forming a Confederacy. The purpose was the seceding of the southern states, in which the Confederacy sought to establish itself as a separate nation. This attempt was resisted by the northern states (Union), which didn't want to see our nation divided. From 1861 to 1865, a civil war occurred, also known as the "War Between the States." It would become the most serious test yet of the ability of the U.S. to remain one nation.

Most of the battles were fought in the South, with the exception of the Battle of Gettysburg, and the war ended in the South in 1865 with Robert E. Lee's surrender to General Ulysses S. Grant. According to records, most Franklin County men belonged to the 16th NY Volunteer Infantry – 2,042 men served in the Civil War and 461 of these lost their lives defending the Union.

Among the first enlistees here were four brothers, members of the Charbonneau aka Cole family, who were the first settlers here in the 1840s. That they survived four years of that ugly war can possibly be attributed to the fact that living alone as the only settlers, the Charbonneau family were survivors. Living off the land as hunters and gatherers, they would have developed marksmanship skills and the ability and fortitude to weather the great hardships and rigors of pioneer life that would have made them excellent soldiers.

Still, we can only imagine the cultural shock and amazement of someone who was raised in a bark shanty along the Racquette River finding themselves thousands of miles from the Adirondack wilds and among the plantations and grand homes of the deep South.

In 1864, shortly before the Civil War ended, two young men from Moody, George McBride and Hiram Averill, enlisted in the Union army. They went by boat up the Racquette River to the Upper Saranac Lake/Lower Saranac Lake carry route to Saranac Village. From there, they went by stagecoach to Ticonderoga and ultimately to training camps in Albany. The war ended some months later in 1865, before either boy was called to the front, and they were soon discharged from the service. When McBride returned to Moody, he bought a piece of land near the foot of Big Tupper Lake from Cort Moody, one of the earliest pioneers in this section. George McBride came to Tupper Lake in 1856 and is listed among the first five settlers. He died in 1915 at age 80. McBride Pond between Lake Simond and Little Simond was named for George. His son, Jim, was born in Tupper Lake in 1863 and became a prominent surveyor who surveyed most of the village of Tupper Lake.

When I was growing up in this community in the late 1930s, only two veterans of the Civil War remained in residence here: Charles Dwight and Charles Cote Sr. I have been told that Mr. Cote had enlisted under the name of Side, which is the French meaning for Cote, when his father would not give him consent to enlist. Originally from Potsdam, Mr. Cote lived all of his late years in Tupper Lake and still has descendants here. In a cruel twist of fate, Mr. Dwight, who had lived through the bitter horrors of that war, was killed here by an automobile on Sears Hills. Note: Many older residents will remember the beautiful Dwight home that sits up on the ledge at the corner of Cheney and Vachereau.

The Dwight family consisted of Dorothy, Warren and Roland.

We were neighbors. I was raised in the large apartment over my father's ice cream and beverage bottling plant located on the corner of Vachereau and High Street. One of the chores delegated by my mother was to take turns with my brother drying the dishes before rushing off to school (sweeping the front stairs and emptying the garbage were the alternate chores). The second-story kitchen window looked out to the sidewalk on Vachereau, and on a regular basis each morning, I would observe an attractive Dorothy Dwight hurrying to meet the O.W.D. wooden-sided Ford station wagon on the Park Street corner (remember those Woodies?) that would transport the office staff to the O.W.D. administrative building on Demars Boulevard, today the town hall. If I remember correctly, Kenny Brunette's father, Gene, was the longtime chauffeur, and Dorothy was the personal secretary to Gerald Hull, the president of the O.W.D. firm. She would later marry "the boss."

Living over the ice cream plant had its advantages. My father was an excellent ice cream maker. Following what was known as the Agriculture Short Course at Cornell, he was employed by the General Ice Cream Company in Rutland, VT, before locating in Tupper Lake. He knew his craft and took great pride in Frenette's Ice Cream. He also distributed a popular brand called Fro-Joy and a delicious silver-wrapped chocolate ice cream bar called the Eskimo Pie. Most drug stores in those days had a soda fountain where you could buy ice cream sodas, sundaes, milkshakes or ice cream placed in a wafer cone. Frenette's Ice Cream was distributed in steel tubs that fit exactly in several refrigerated compartments at the fountain, two tubs high, conveniently placed for access by the "soda jerk." A well of circulating water served to keep the ice cream scoop clean. A moveable bar controlled by a thumb lever moved the bar along to the inside of the scoop, freeing the ice cream. A special detachable handle would grip a raised rig on the steel tub for carrying, replacing and removing the tubs from the refrigerated compartments. Most of the drug store fountain sections would have high stools along the front of the fountain. Usually booths, tables and chairs could be found within the vicinity. These were popular meeting places for young and old alike and a primary outlet for Frenette's Ice Cream. In my day, local customers would have been Cohn's Pharmacy in the Junction and, uptown along Park Street, Harvey's Pharmacy, Monakey's Pharmacy (People's Pharmacy) and Maid's Pharmacy.

I recently ran across a file with my father's ice cream recipes. Here are the ingredients listed for "Charlie's French Vanilla":

2 dozen egg yolks
5 gallons of 25 percent cream
1 ounce gelatin
1 ounce salt

Heat egg in one gallon of cream to 160 degrees F. Cool. Add balance of mix. Freeze and sell for $1 per quart.

*Tupper Lake Free Press Print:* November 08, 2006

# THE GREAT OXBOW

IN A RECENT COLUMN, it was noted that when Charles McBride returned from the Civil War in 1865, he purchased a piece of land and cabin from pioneer settler Cort Moody at the foot of Tupper Lake. Cort (Cortez) was a well-known guide, six feet, six inches in stature. My photos show him to be as lean as a fence post, a characteristic, it would seem, of the Moody family even today.

Cort's father, Jacob, was the first settler in Saranac Lake (1819), when the nearest neighbor, a man named Mose Hamilton, was five miles away toward Lake Placid. Of historical interest is the fact that Cort was the first white baby born in this region (1822). Jacob Moody had seven children. Eliza, the only girl, died young, and Franklin, one of the six boys, also died young. The remaining five Moody boys all lived to become famous hunters, guides and trappers.

Donaldson, the historian, notes, "They were known far and wide in the early days, and their names are of constant occurrence in all Adirondack books."

Cort did most of his guiding from Deer Island on Upper Saranac Lake across from the original Wawbeek Club. However, like his brothers, he soon discovered Tupper Lake, Piercefield Falls and the Bog River. If you had a client and wanted to ensure him success, the undiscovered Tupper Lake area was a sure bet.

The Moody boys felt that the finest place for night hunting

deer (jacking with a light was then legal) was the large marsh near the east bay in Lake Simond—they called it Simon's Slew—where today a cutoff leads through that marsh to the Racquette River. They had found a hunting and fishing paradise and they knew it. This discovery enhanced their reputations as guides. They could be counted on to produce game, and they made the most of it.

In the 1850s, the Moody boys guided Alfred A. Street, the New York State Librarian, and some of his friends on a leisurely hunting and fishing trip through the Saranacs and the Racquette River to Long Lake, with a return downstream to Tupper Lake.

Here is how Mr. Street, in his book that followed that trip, *Woods and Waters*, described the Oxbow as they approached Tupper Lake on the Racquette River: "Down the river we went, checking our course at the mouth of two or three spring brooks for the speckled prey. Passing a shingle weaver's camp and threading the rapids were a dozen rocks of differing sizes in the channel [that] caused various currents and eddies, we came to the Great Oxbow." Note: Those rapids later became known as the Underhill Rapids, a name now seldom used.

Today those rapids may be recognized by the many navigation buoys as the river parallels River Road beyond its intersection with Dugal Road. Supporting cribwork for a much later bridge, which crossed the river at the upper end of the rapids to transport lumber, can still be seen as you descend the river.

Street continues: "This Oxbow is a two-mile sweep of the river around a long point. Across its base, however, if you know where to look, is a portage, scarcely more than a score of paces." Note: Shortly after Street's visit, the New York State Legislature passed a law making the Racquette River a public highway for the use of Potsdam lumbermen and their mills downstream from Tupper. Authority was given to spend $10,000 on improving the river channel to make it easier to float large quantities of logs down the river to Potsdam. Many twists and turns of the river were straightened out, and that short portage known to the Moodys to save rowing the two-mile loop, or bow of the Oxbow, was dynamited to make a straight run.

*By the time renowned Adirondack photographer Seneca Ray Stoddard came down the Racquette River in the 1890s, the two-mile row around the Great Oxbow had been eliminated, a passageway having been opened by dynamite across a narrow strip of land to facilitate the log driving. Two guideboats shown on the right head downstream to Tupper Lake.*

This spot is located just below the Wild Center observation deck in front of the Klueck summer cottage, the former Dechene camp. This, of course, made the Oxbow an island.

Walt Zurawski has told me that the McCarthy brothers at one time had a slaughterhouse above the Oxbow and used the island to house a large number of pigs, which were thus contained because of their intense dislike for water.

Street notes, "Having tugged their guideboats and gear across the narrow strip of land before launching, crushing the lush wood plants into an emerald paste, we regaled ourselves on the whortle berries, whose misty eyes glanced at us in every direction."

Harvey Moody, oldest brother and chief guide for the Street trip, seated himself at the foot of a birch, a position Street followed, and listened as Harvey recounted: "But about old Ramrod, as I was tellin' on ye, he made a good deal o' this place; he camped here for some years, and in his young days, he had lived here in a sort o' cave, or rather a holler, in a big pine tree, the biggest, 'cordin' to his tell, I ever seen in these woods. You switched a thick cedar bush a one side, and crawled inter a shelvin' place 'twixt the roots like a woodchuck's hole, and there was a place in the body of the tree big enough to stand up in and walk a leetle about and lay down too, curled up, though, as a hound sleeps. Old Ramrod made two or three knot holes in the tree bigger to give 'im air and light. They made good places to shoot from too; and the St. Regis Injuns, bein' about the Racket in them days, these 'ere loopholes, as 'twere, stood him a good turn sometimes.

"He was a great Injun fighter, was Ramrod, for he had an idea the Injuns had no business comin' on the Racket to hunt and fish, as they had their own waters all around the Upper S'nac. 'Twas treadin' on his toes, so he was done on 'em, and got up a fight whenever he could, 'tickelly when there wasn't more 'n two or three agin 'im. He popped over all he could, and finally at last the Injuns didn't never go on the Racket without expectin' a row with Old Ramrod, or the Quick Wind, as they nicknamed 'im, 'caze he'd pounce so dreffle sudden on 'em with his rifle.

"Old Ramrod had been up to Folin'sby's Pond and had fell agin a rock, so as to break the lock of his rifle. Well, he started torts hum, and just as he rounded the lefthand p'int o' the brook [outlet] down inter the Racket, what did he see but an Injun canoe hauled up on the bank. He got at the same time a squint o' two Injuns crouched up like a couple o' mud turtles, or like a couple o' black squirrels, we'll say, crackin' hickory nuts. The Injuns, though, was a smokin' through them queer kind o' things o' theirn—hatchets hollered out in the handle with a bowl in the head.

"There they was, with their backs torts him. Well, he'd got fairly inter the Racket, and he was in hopes they wouldn't see 'im 't all, as two to one with rifles was too much odds for the old feller, farse as he was, when he hadn't got no rifle, or what was next to 't, one that was broke. But jest as he was turnin' a bush, didn't they screech! Did you ever hear a war whoop, Mr. Smith? It's so (clapping his mouth and playing it with a rapid motion): Hoo-oo-oooooee, hoo! And as they sung out, they started for their canoe in sich a hurry that they didn't never think o' their rifles. Old

Ramrod see the whull consarn, and he put to 't. Didn't he make his dugout spin! I tell you! But he unly got clear by the skin of his teeth, that is, by rushin' his canoe up and dashin' crost with it to t' other side here, for the Injuns didn't know this place and kept straight on, an lickety splittin' it down'ards to Simon's Slew, where he hid a whull day in the bushes."

Afterward

The Racquette River has remained a priceless resource. My friend, Mark Bowie, says it best: "It is a river that is in places wild, places recreational, yet a working river . . . . It is at once tamed and civilized, pristine and remote, tranquil and tumultuous."

*Tupper Lake Free Press Print:* November 22, 2006

# Trouble in Paradise

EACH YEAR, THE ENDANGERED Species Unit of the Department of Environmental Conservation (D.E.C.) issues a report on the status of nesting bald eagles in New York State.

This year's report runs to over thirty pages and includes many beautiful eagle photographs and data on eagle management research, satellite tracking and productivity information.

The report notes that in the 2006 midwinter bald eagle survey (in which a number of local people participated), the coverage, both ground and aerial, was the most complete ever, thanks to perfect weather conditions during the January 4-18 survey dates.

Statewide, a total of 442 bald eagles were tallied, 252 adults and 190 immature birds, and it is suspected that many of these wintering birds are resident eagles as opposed to transient birds that make their way south from locations such as Canada.

Northern New York

The northern New York winter count of the state survey tallied 42 eagles this year (up from 31 in 2005), 26 adults and 16 youngsters. These observations, according to the report, continued to confirm the importance of these wintering areas, not only to resident state eagles, but also to numerous eagles from eastern Canada. Note: The Tupper Lake, Racquette River and St. Lawrence localities, with their open water, Setting Pole Dam and Racquette Falls are a crucial part of that area.

*Naturalists at the Wild Center have recently erected the tower and nest platform shown here. Overlooking the museum's Blue Pond, the platform, hopefully, will encourage an osprey to adopt the manmade structure and build a nest. Osprey nests are often preempted by Great Horned Owls, who nest much earlier. The experiment should be interesting. (Bill Frenette photo)*

## Reproductive Success

So what was the breeding success (egg laying and hatching) for the state's bald eagles? April 2006, the primary egg-hatching month for New York State, was the warmest April on record for the United States. This ideal weather provided a high hatch rate. Of the 110 nesting pairs, 172 young fledglings successfully flew from the nest—a whopping 54 percent increase over 2005, and a figure the report terms as "short of remarkable." Interesting, though, was the fact that "an amazing and never-before-seen 30 percent of all successful pairs fledged three young." Normally, the long-term average is five percent.

## Trouble in Paradise

Unfortunately, the high hatch rate was not the case in our area. Only three of seven pairs were successful (43 percent), and then these three nests only fledged one young each—likely because the Adirondack pairs were just far enough behind the rest of the state to be negatively affected by the later cold, wet weather.

I had hooked up my outdoor shower water pipes during this critical period, and then the weather turned bitter cold and busted a pipe, so it is no surprise that the eagle's vulnerable eggs could have been chilled, interfering with incubation.

If cold weather didn't provide a big enough handicap for our local eagles, a well-constructed, productive nest located in a lofty pine on a private lake near here was blown over and the nest destroyed. It occurred this summer during a violent localized storm called a derecho, which cut a swath through many of the significant pines on that property.

The good news is that the eagles have been observed building a new nest, an encouraging sign that they intend to resume production.

We can only hope that the research specialists are correct in their assumption that chilled eggs were the chief cause for the failure of eggs to incubate. Hopefully, there are not other causes at work repressing nesting and reproduction here in the Adirondacks—things like high levels of mercury or lead poisoning factors that have increasingly threatened our beloved loons, causing them to exhibit bizarre behavior, such as chicks not riding on their parents' backs, abandoned nests and reproductive failure.

## Jeopardy

The report listed 21 birds found dead or injured:
Trains—2
Vehicles—6
Shot—1
Killed by another eagle—3

Disease—2
Fishing tackle—1
Lead poisoning—1
Weak and starving—1
Fell from nest—1

Despite the wonderful success of the bald eagle that was in danger of being extirpated, the research by the D.E.C. Endangered Species Unit remains vitally important. Such studies that highlight problems in the animal world are somewhat like the canary in the coalmine in the sense that those studies can reveal environmental problems, and for us humans, act as a warning signal for our health conditions.

## Sobering Thoughts

Who would have imagined six years ago that serious mercury problems existed in our deep and beautiful Tupper Lake? A warning to not eat more than a meal a month of fish from those waters was, to me, outrageous, incredible and very, very sad and troubling.

Unfortunately, the warning was valid and of serious concern to all of us who love that lake. Sadly, the loons, eagles and otters don't have an opinion—their survival depends on these fish for food.

The mercury is concentrated in these predators because they are the top of the food chain, and such concentrations are among the most toxic substances known to nature. Most of the mercury pollution that reaches our lakes is spewed into the atmosphere by large coal-burning power plants and municipal waste incinerators in the Midwest and central Canada. Fortunately, this problem has been recognized, and efforts are being made through litigation to curb some of the violations.

*Tupper Lake Free Press Print*: December 13, 2006

# NUGGETS FROM A 1938 BANK BULLETIN

A FRIEND OF MINE WHO LOVES Adirondack history and is a collector of all things early Tupper Lake, telephoned me recently, asking if I knew of Southworth's Mountain View House. It seems that after some spirited bidding, he had acquired a postcard on eBay. The postcard, dated 1899, had a one-cent stamp and a color photo labeled Southworth's Mountain View House, Tupper Lake, NY. The card was postmarked Tupper Lake and the sender had written, in a strong legible handwriting a short message to his brother in the Midwest that all was well, and he expected to be in Tupper Lake only a few more days.

My friend went on to say, "You know, Bill, a bigger mystery than where that hotel was located was how a postcard mailed to a destination thousands of miles away ended up on eBay in perfect condition 108 years later." Good question, n'est pas?

I had never heard of Southworth's but it was located on the corner of Park Street and Wawbeek Avenue (today Tom LaMere's convenience store). I found the answer in a souvenir booklet prepared by then town historian and bank president James Jacobs. The booklet was in observance of the Tupper Lake Bank's silver birthday anniversary, which occurred on June 18, 1931. In the booklet, historian Jacobs describes the first stirrings of both the bank and the town in its dual march toward growth and prosperity.

## The Odd Order Changeth

This past August 2006, the bank produced another anniversary booklet, this one celebrating 100 years of service to this community, chronicling challenges, growth and prosperity. I like one quote that Muriel Ginsberg (her father, Mose, was bank director for 15 years) offered: "A bank that gets to be 100 years old must be doing well." I am compelled, for history's sake, to quote one other statement in the booklet: "The banking business can be unpredictable, but the board in 2006 is committed to maintaining T.L.N.B. status as an independently local-owned bank."

Thus it was that the announcement this month that Community Bank Systems Incorporated has entered into an agreement to acquire T.LN.B. Financial Corporation, parent company of T.L.N.B., came as a shock and saddened many in this community.

Local bank officials have made a difficult decision and assure us that "it's an excellent relationship and perfect partnership for us." Yes, nostalgia has no place in the world of hard business decisions,

*The steam yacht "Altamont," which operated daily between Sweeny Carry and Tupper Lake House in the late 1800s, was cruising along in Racquette Pond when this picture was taken. The boat made daily trips from Owen's dock at the foot of Wawbeek Avenue and Bog River Falls in the early 1900s.*

but 100 years of success and service is a long time. It's a piece of local history that is one of its highlights in importance, and it is like losing an old friend, even as you know that friend has gone on to better things.

Back to the Postcard

Let's get back to our postcard. Mr. Jacobs wrote in that fascinating 1931 booklet that the first hotel to open for guests was the Mountain View Hotel, built in the 1890s by W.P. Southworth, on the corner of Wawbeek Avenue and Park Street. He goes on to say, "Several hotels then under construction were built soon after, among them the Altamont Hotel, built by J.H. and T.L. Weir, Racquette Pond House (later the American House on Lake Street) and a hotel run by J.D. Alexander (on the site which later became the Iroquois Hotel, now Stewart's convenience store).

The Mountain View House must have commanded a sweeping, unobstructed view across Racquette Pond to the mountains beyond such as Arab, Matumbia, Floodwood and Iron. It was a good location as well. Wawbeek Road was then the only road in and out of this village. It ran directly from Racquette Pond, where steamboat service (costing $1.25) was available to transport tourists to hotels located on Tupper Lake to the Wawbeek Hotel (a portion of that road was later renamed Stetson). The hotel had a large livery that provided stagecoach travel between Upper Saranac Lake and Tupper Lake.

Historian Jacobs, a graduate of the U.S. Naval Academy at Annapolis, came to Tupper Lake as a youth, taking over as manager the Dodge Meigs Company in 1891 (later, the Santa Clara Company).

He was one of the founders of the T.L.N.B., and he also helped to organize the Tupper Lake Water Company in 1899. This was a highly important venture. Not having adequate fire protection (no water system was available) provided such a hazard that insurance rates were prohibitive, and there was the grave question if the village would rebuild after the 1899 fire, which destroyed the central part of the village. Mr. Jacobs and his partners in the water company gave assurance that protection would be available. Confidence was restored and village plans to rebuild went forward.

### Cranberry Pond Purchased

A further word about the water company: True to their promise to provide a water supply, the company hired local surveyors Will LaFountain and James McBride to locate a suitable source of water. They investigated McBride, Little Simond and Cranberry ponds. Their recommendation was to use Little Simond Pond, pointing out its purity, size and depth, which would guarantee a continued source as Tupper's population grew. However, the cost of a pipeline to transport the water was prohibitive, and the water company investors elected to go with Cranberry Pond.

Mr. Jacobs, one of those investors, notes, "Land on the slopes of Mt. Morris, embracing Little Cranberry Pond and the fine springs that embrace it, was purchased from the A. Sherman Lumber Company. A modern gravity water system was installed under a 200-foot head, which provides ample pressure for fire protection."

Eventually, the water company passed into the hands of Colonel William Barbour, who substantially upgraded the system and later sold it to the village on November 23, 1920. Mr. Jacobs died in Middlebury, VT, on June 27, 1962.

I've mined a few other nuggets from that 1931 bank booklet, which I hope you will find interesting, and I will share them with you in a future *Transitions*.

*Tupper Lake Free Press Print:* January 24, 2007